The
outrageously
BIG
ACTIVITY, PLAY
and
PROJECT BOOK

The outrageously BIG ACTIVITY, PLAY *and* PROJECT BOOK

HH HERMES HOUSE

This edition published by Hermes House in 2001

Hermes House is an imprint of Anness Publishing Limited
Hermes House, 88–89 Blackfriars Road, London SE1 8HA

Published in the USA by Hermes House, Anness Publishing Inc
27 West 20th Street, New York, NY10011

A CIP catalogue record for this book is available from the British Library

The activities and projects in this book were created by:
Nick Huckleberry Beak, *Clowning Around, Magic Fun and Cheeky, Sneaky Tricks.*
Petra Boase – *Painting Fun, Friendship Bracelets, T-shirt Painting and Modelling Fun.*
Stephanie Donaldson – *Growing Things*
Hugh Nightingale – *A Magic Show*
Steve and Jane Parker – *Stunning Science*
Michael Purton – *Making Music*
Thomasina Smith – *Party Fun, Magical Masks, Face and Body Painting and Modelling Fun.*
Jacki Wadeson – *Fabulous Hairstyles*
Sally Walton – *Making Things and Growing Things.*

Previously published in two seperate volumes, *The Ultimate Show-Me-How Activity Book* and *The Really Big Book of Amazing Things to Make and Do*

Publisher: Joanna Lorenz
Managing Editor, Children's Books: Sue Grabham
Editor: Joanne Hanks
Photography: John Freeman, Tim Ridley
Design: Siân Keogh, Axis Design
Design Assistant: Christos Chrysanthou, Axis Design

Printed and bound in China

10 9 8 7 6 5 4 3 2 1

Foreword

If you feel like being creative but are low on inspiration, look no further! In here you'll find a mind-boggling selection of ideas to get your teeth, eyes, ears, hands, tummies and toes stuck into. Excite an audience with a vibrant musical jamboree or astonish them with cheeky magic tricks – performances that are bound to rocket you to fame! If you dream of being an artist but lack the know-how, pull out your paintbrush, pencil or felt-tips and dash off a masterpiece on paper, fabric or clay. And there's more. If you dare, you could turn your kitchen into an experimental lab for scientific exploration, or your bedroom into a jungle with pots of flowers, fruit and plants. And there is still more, but not enough room here to tell you about it all. So delve in and let your imagination run wild…

Contents

Introduction 8

Making Things 16

Tasty Treats 48

Painting Fun 80

Stunning Science 110

Making Music 142

Party Fun 172

A Magic Show 198

Growing Things 230

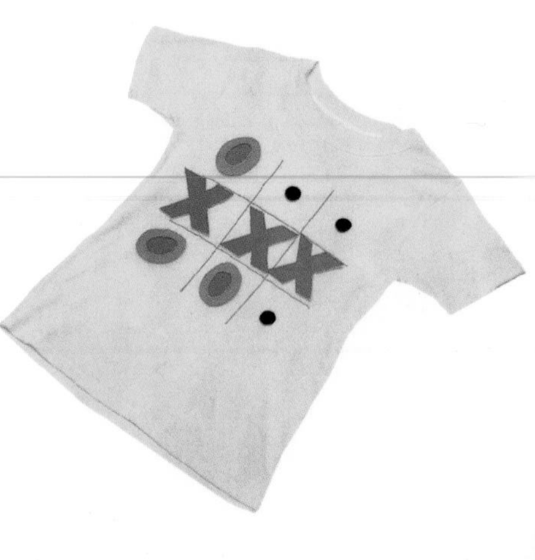

Modelling Fun 262

T-Shirt Painting 294

Friendship Bracelets 326

Fabulous Hairstyles 356

Magical Masks 386

Face and Body Painting 416

Clowning Around 446

Sneaky, Cheeky Tricks 476

Index 506

Introduction

All the projects in this book can be made easily at home. There are some basic pieces of equipment which you will need for many of the projects, such as scissors, glue and paints or felt-tipped pens. If you look after your basic equipment well it will last for a long time and you will be able to make lots and lots of the projects.

PVA glue This glue has many other names. You may know it as white glue, school glue, or woodworking glue. It is water-based, which means that your hands and brushes come clean under the tap. It is white, so that you can see where you have put it, but it becomes clear when it dries, so any mistakes are invisible. PVA glue sticks most things together – wood, cardboard, paper, cloth and plastic. It is great for applying glitter too – just mix it in and paint it on. You can apply the glue with either a paintbrush or a glue spreader.

You can make a good varnish by mixing three parts of PVA glue to one part water. To make a very strong papier-mâché, mix PVA glue and water with newspaper. Use the glue undiluted on parts that need extra strength.

Paints There are lots of different kinds of paint, and it is important to use the sort that is best for the job you are doing. Sometimes pale, watery colours are perfect and other times you need strong, bright colours that will cover up printing or pictures on a recycled package.

The paint recommended for painting most things is acrylic. It can be mixed with water, to make it runny, or used straight from the tube or pot to give a solid, bold colour. You can wash your brush out under the tap, but you must remember to do it straight away, because acrylic paint dries very quickly, and brushes will spoil if they are not cleaned before the paint dries. Stand your brushes in a jar of water until you wash them out.

You can buy acrylic paints from stationery shops and art and craft shops where they also sell acrylic gloss varnish, used in some of the projects. There are many other kinds of paints available and you can find out more about them in the introduction to the painting chapter.

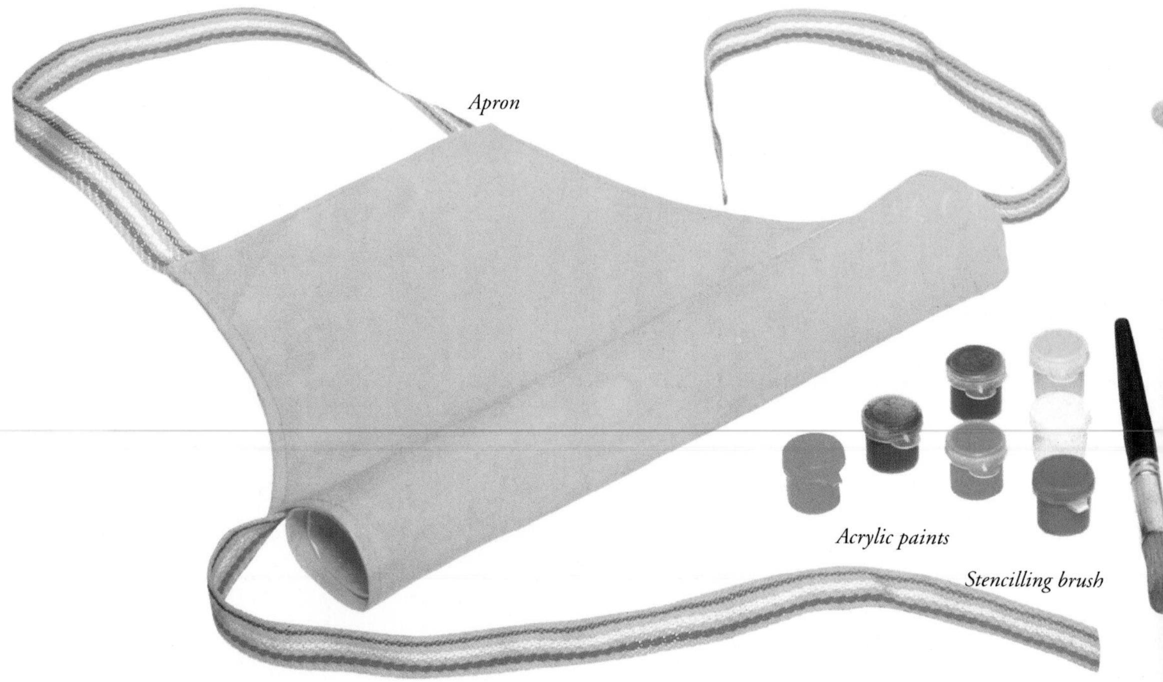
Apron

Acrylic paints

Stencilling brush

Paint pots There are special paint pots with lids to stop you spilling the paint. They are very useful if you need to mix up a large amount of paint or to dilute paint with water. They come with lots of different coloured lids so you can match the colour of the paint to the lid. Always wash out the pots thoroughly before putting a different colour in them. If you are using undiluted paints in small amounts you can put them in a paint palette.

Paintbrushes Paintbrushes come in many different shapes and sizes. Use thin, pointed brushes for painting fine lines and thick or flat-ended brushes for large areas. For stencilling you will need a short, fat brush with stiff hairs.Take care of your paintbrushes, and try not to damage them by being rough. If you move them in one direction this will keep them smooth and make them last longer.

Apron To prevent your clothes from getting covered in paint, wear a smock or an apron, or ask an adult for an old shirt. That way you can make as much mess as you like.

Ruler Useful for measuring and drawing straight lines.

Scissors Scissors should not be too sharp and must be handled with safety in mind at all times. If you have to cut some thick cardboard and need sharper scissors, ask an adult to do the cutting for you.

Felt-tipped pens Felt-tipped pens are always good to use on paper. The colours can't be mixed like paint, so it's best to use them separately.

Sticky tapes Masking tape is very useful because it does not stick permanently, like other kinds of plastic tape. You can use it to hold things together while the glue dries, and then remove it easily. You can get lots of brightly coloured sticky tape – for decorating objects. Insulating tape, which electricians use, is ideal and comes in many widths.

Paper and card Brightly coloured paper and card are fun and quick to use. But you can use white card and paper instead and decorate them in bright colours using paints, coloured stickers or felt-tipped pens.

Look out for lots of useful materials around the home.

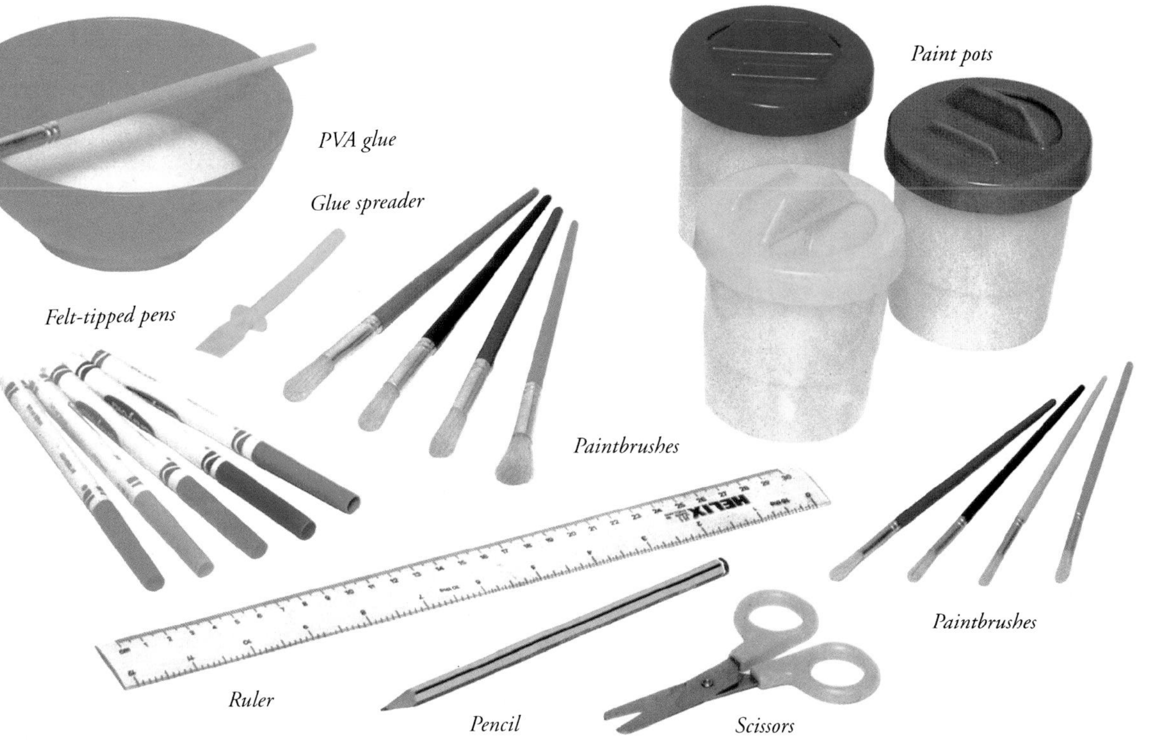

Paint pots

PVA glue

Glue spreader

Felt-tipped pens

Paintbrushes

Paintbrushes

Ruler

Pencil

Scissors

Recycling materials

Everyone's house is full of bits and pieces that can be recycled and used to make the projects in this book. Store your trove of recycled treasure in a large, empty box. Once you start making things, you will be watching out to see what can be saved from the dustbin and made into a gift. The sorts of things to look out for are:

- wrapping paper
- ribbon and string
- beads and buttons
- milk or juice cartons
- greetings cards
- empty tins with a smooth, rounded edge
- magazines and newspapers
- plastic drinks bottles
- remnants of fabric
- plastic bottle tops
- yoghurt pots
- lightweight card boxes used for food packaging
- boxes made of corrugated card
- cardboard tubes
- egg boxes
- lolly sticks
- foil pie cases
- corks
- shells
- cotton reels
- sweet wrappers

Always wash milk or juice containers and yoghurt pots in warm, soapy water before storing them away for later use.

If you have enough recycled packaging to fill your box, then stop collecting and start making things!

How to remove labels

Fill a washing-up bowl or basin with warm water and soak the bottle or container in the water for about 10 minutes. If the label is still not loose, soak again and use a scouring pad to help remove the label.

Flattening and cutting up boxes

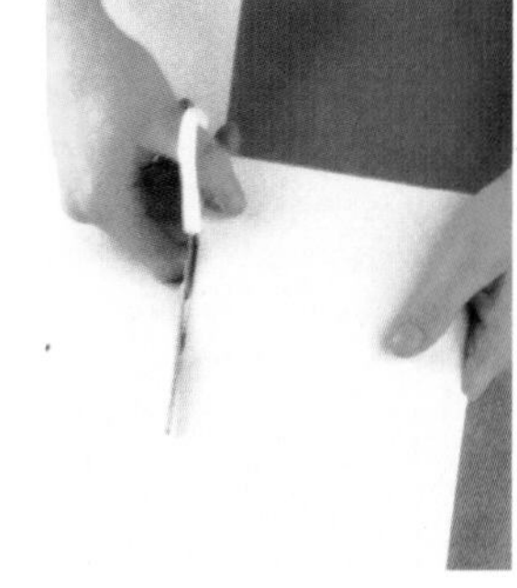

1 Remove any sticky tape that is holding the box together. Press the box flat.

2 Cut the box into sections following the fold lines and using a pair of scissors.

Recycle any scraps of paper or card left over from a project, they are bound to come in handy. Discard materials that are too damaged or creased to be of use. Store card flat.

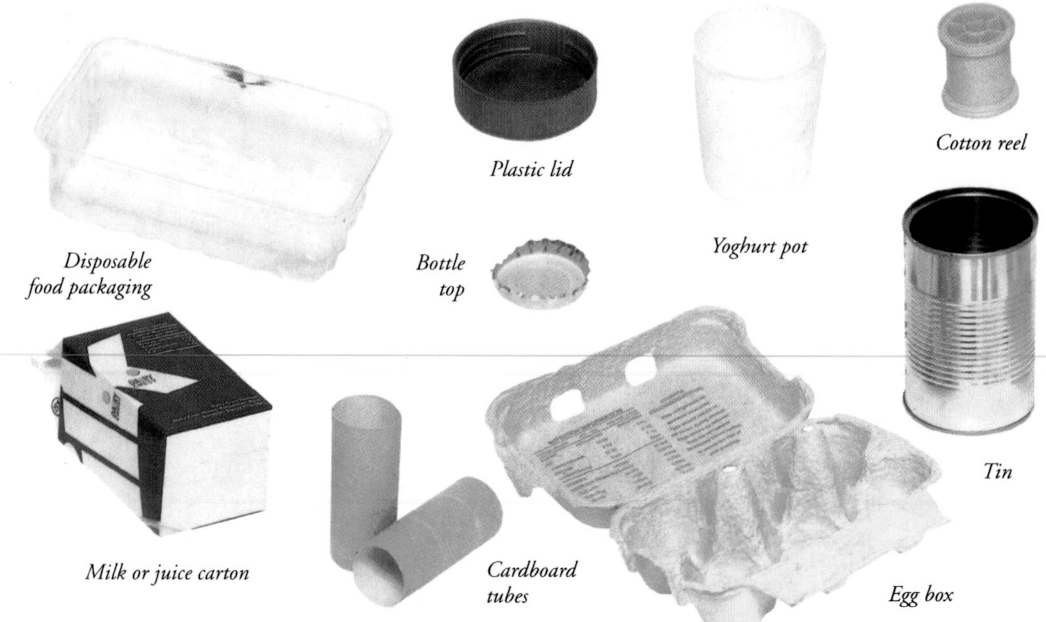

Disposable food packaging

Plastic lid

Bottle top

Yoghurt pot

Cotton reel

Tin

Milk or juice carton

Cardboard tubes

Egg box

Basic Techniques

Cutting out a circle

It is difficult to cut a circle out of thick card or cardboard. The best way to do it is to ask an adult to stab a small hole in the centre of the circle, using the point of a sharp pair of scissors. Make several small cuts outwards to the edge of the circle. You will now be able to cut around the edge of the circle quite easily.

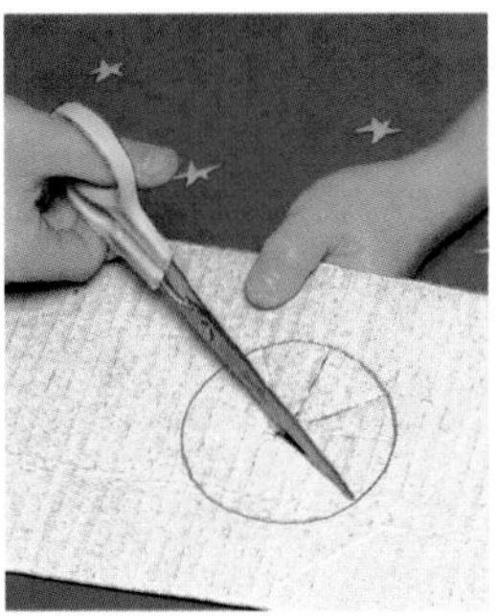

Cut out towards the edge of the circle.

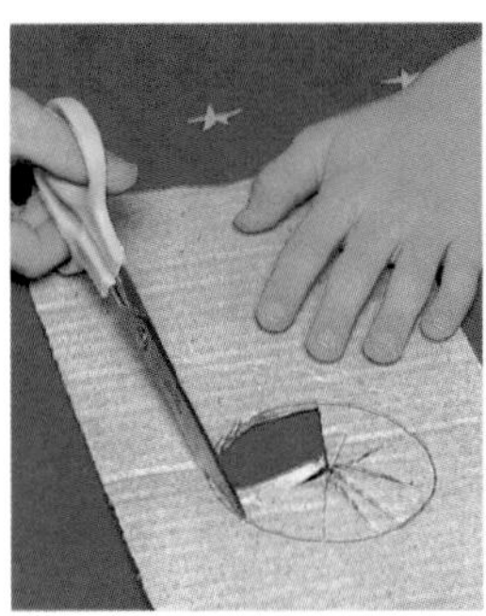

Then carefully cut around the circle itself.

Painting straight lines

Masking tape is very useful for this. Stick the tape along the line, then paint right up to it. You can paint a little over the edge. Wait for the paint to dry completely, then pull off the tape and you will have a perfectly straight line. This is a good way to paint shapes like triangles and diamonds.

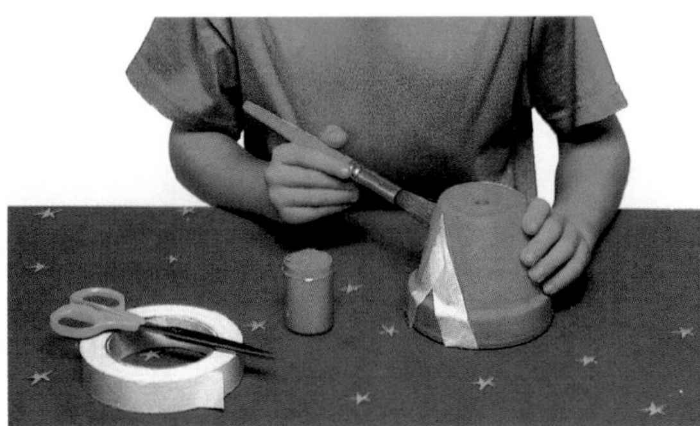

Use masking tape to help paint straight lines.

Painting plastic

To make paint stick to plastic surfaces, add the same amount of PVA glue as the amount of paint and stir well. If the mixture is too thick, add a little water.

Varnishing

PVA glue can also be used to make varnish, which will protect the surface of many of your projects. Mix the glue with one third the amount of water. The varnish is white when wet and clear when dry.

Mix PVA glue with water to make a varnish.

Painting round objects

It helps when painting an object, especially when it's curved, like an egg or a ball, to rest it in a holder. That way it won't roll around when it is drying. Plastic pots, mugs and egg boxes make excellent holders.

Tracing a Template

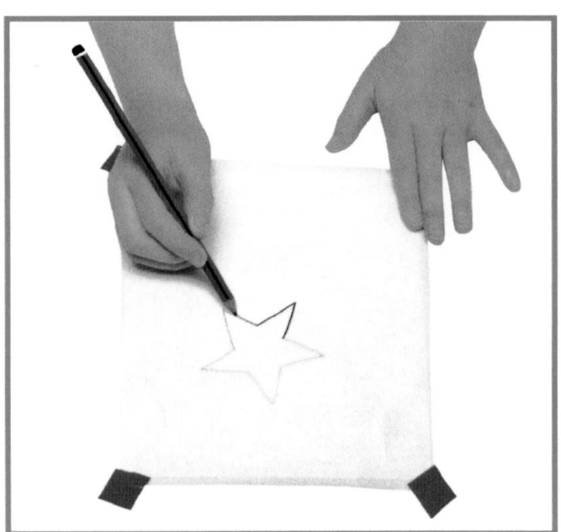

1 Place a piece of tracing paper over the template and secure it at the corners with tape. Carefully draw around the shape using a soft lead pencil.

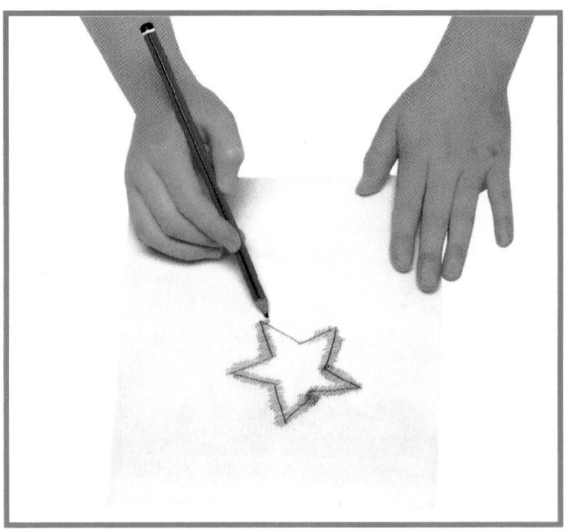

2 Take the tracing paper off the template and turn the paper over. Rub over the traced image with the pencil on the reverse side of the tracing paper.

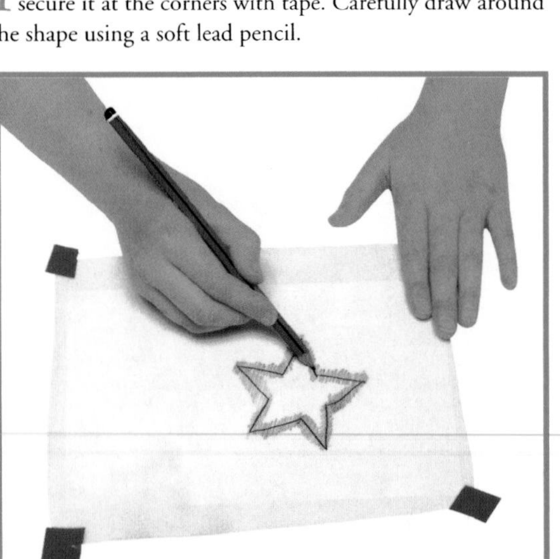

3 Place the tracing paper on a piece of card, with the traced outline face up. Draw firmly over the outline to transfer the template on to the card.

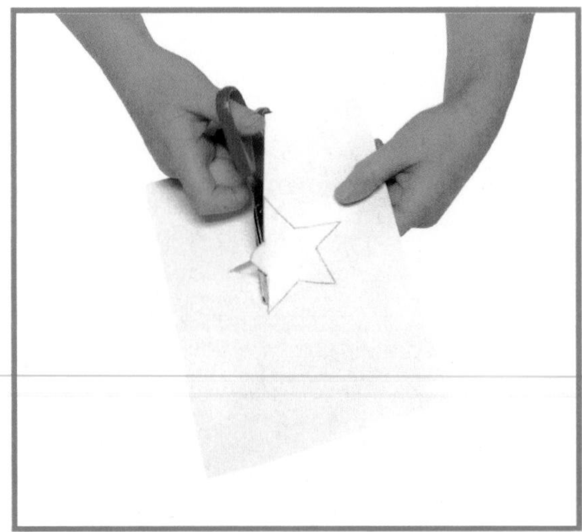

4 Cut out your template. To use a template on paper, card or fabric, simply draw around the shape with a pencil, felt-tip pen or fabric marker pen.

Safety First!

❖ Be careful with small items, sharp tools, glues and modelling materials. Keep these and all other dangerous items out of reach of young children.

❖ Ask an adult to supervise when you are using an oven or stove. Wear oven gloves when handling hot items. Wait until baked items are cold before you touch them.

❖ Always ask permission to use an electrical appliance.

❖ Check with an adult before using any type of make-up remover, cream or cleanser on your face or body. Face paint can be washed off with mild soap and water.

❖ Never use acrylic or poster paints, felt-tip pens, crayons, craft glues or other stationery items on your face. If using glue, paint or glitter try not to touch your face or rub your eyes. They may cause irritation so wash your hands after using these materials.

❖ Point the tip of scissor blades away from you. Never put your hand under an item while making a hole in it.

❖ When cutting any material that might fly up into your eyes, wear some protection over your eyes.

❖ Read the instructions on any packaging.

You will need to use these templates for some of the projects in this book.

Template for Palm Trees

Template for the mouth of the Monster Sock Puppet

Template for the Stencilled Cork Place-mat

Christmas Crackers
Flowery Glass

Spotty Dog-bone Picture Frame

Dinosaur Cake

Flick-painted Starscape

Star and Moon Stencilled Gift Wrap

Making Things

Introduction

Making things is great fun and very rewarding. It takes time and you have to concentrate to understand how things are put together. But all the hard work is worth it, because when you have made a rattlesnake or painted a flowerpot, it has some of your own very special magic in it. You will feel so proud, and everyone will admire your work. Once you understand how to make a mobile or cut flowers from felt, you will always know how it is done. Then you will be able to make up new designs of your own.

Look at the photographs of the children making up each project. They show you each stage and the words explain what they are doing. You can do it too, just follow what the children do.

Remember to ask a grown-up for permission before you begin making things. There are some projects that need a grown-up's help. Leave all the dangerous cutting-out to a grown-up, and never use a craft knife on your own as they are very dangerous. You may have to remind grown-ups that you are the one making things, because once they get started on the projects, they may not want to stop!

Be a crafty collector

We all like to recycle as much as possible. Once you start making things, you will be watching out to see what can be saved from the dustbin and made into a toy or a gift. You will need a good strong box for your collection and somewhere to store it. If you save milk cartons and yogurt pots, give them a good wash in soapy water and dry them well, otherwise they may get smelly. Old tins and bottles are often covered with labels which you will want to take off. The easiest way to do this is to fill a washing-up bowl with some warm water and soak the bottle in the water for approximately ten minutes. The label should peel off very easily. Collect small cardboard boxes and tubes, lollipop sticks, safe-edged tins, straws, corks, string, shells, bottle tops and cotton reels.

It is important to know when to stop collecting. If you have enough recycled packaging to fill your box, then start making things!

Colourful materials

For some projects you may have to use materials which you don't have at home, such as coloured card, felt, tissue paper, beads, pipe cleaners and wrapping paper. If you buy something special for a project then always keep any left-over scraps as they are bound to come in handy for any other project in the future.

Keeping clean

When you make things you can also make a lot of mess! It is most important to start off by protecting your work surface with old newspapers. Or putting down a tablecloth that will wipe clean. Do this first, because once you get involved with a project, it is easy not to notice the mess that you are making.

Wear an overall, apron or a big, old shirt to protect your clothes when you are painting. Before you start, roll up your sleeves as high as possible as they have a habit of dangling in paint pots and glue!

Getting started

When you have decided which projects you are going to make, collect together all the materials and equipment you will need and lay them out on your work surface. You will then find it much easier to work.

Clearing up

When you have finished, always clear up and put away all your things. Ask a grown-up to help you if you need to, but don't just leave a mess behind. Keep your equipment in good order and you will be ready to make something else another day.

Giant Sunflower Card

Sunflowers are among the tallest plants that we grow in our gardens, and this card takes its unusual shape from them. A sunflower has bright yellow petals and a big, rounded brown centre packed with seeds. This is the special part of the card that Kirsty is making.

This card would make a lovely present for Mother's Day, or a special gift for your teacher. Envelopes this shape may be difficult to find, so wrap up your card as a present. That is, if you can bear to part with it!

Tricky and sticky

The seed centre is the trickiest part of the sunflower to make, but once you understand how it is done, you will be making them all the time. The most important thing to remember is that too much glue will spread through the fine tissue paper and stick the next layer as well, and then the pop-up won't work. So use a tiny dot of glue, carefully pinching the two pieces of tissue paper between your finger and thumb to stick them together.

If you want to have leaves with jagged edges ask an adult to cut them out with pinking shears.

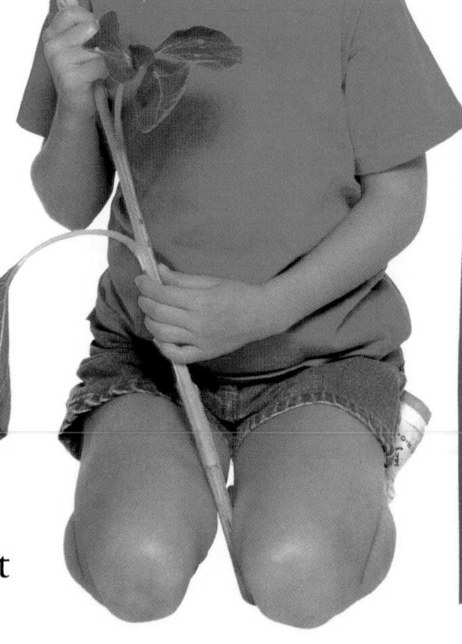

YOU WILL NEED THESE MATERIALS AND TOOLS

Large piece of blue card plus yellow, brown and green tissue paper

Needle and thread

Also a ruler, pencil, scissors, table knife, PVA glue, matchstick and a glue spreader

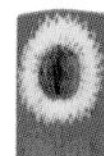

1 Cut out the card to 22 x 56 cm (8½ x 22 in). Find the middle, and score the card using a blunt table knife against a ruler. Just press firmly, so that the knife dents the card.

2 Fold the brown tissue paper over so that you have 10 layers. Cut out a circle that measures about 10 cm (4 in) across. Use a needle and thread to sew a running stitch down the centre line.

3 Cut out the petals, leaves and stems. You will need a lot of petals, about 30 to start with, two stems and five leaves.

4 To make the centre, think of a clockface. Imagine that the stitches go from 9 to 3. Using the matchstick, put a dot of glue at 12 o'clock.

5 Fold over the first layer of tissue and pinch it together where the dot of glue is.

6 Then, make two dots on the next layer of tissue. These go at where the 10 and 2 would be on the clock. Pinch together to stick. The next dot goes on the 12 spot and after that the 10 and the 2 again. Keep going like this until you reach the last layer. Let it dry.

7 Draw a circle for the flower centre, and arrange the petals around it. Put a thin layer of glue on each one. Make two or three circles of petals.

8 Spread a stripe of glue down the centre line and stick the two stems on top of each other. Stick down the leaves and the flower centre in the circle.

Open up the card and there is your glorious sunflower.

Canal Boat

Canals are like roads made out of water. They were used to move all kinds of factory goods from one part of the country to another on long, low canal boats, called barges. A long time ago the canals were very busy, but now most factories use lorries or trains instead. People still use the canals and barges, but mostly as homes or for holidays. The barge people have always decorated their boats in the same way, using black, red, yellow and green paint. They would paint flowers and patterns on the barge itself and all their buckets, flower-pots, jugs and boxes. The skill of barge painting was passed down through families, and people took great pride in their painted boats.

YOU WILL NEED THESE MATERIALS AND TOOLS

Tall milk or juice carton, with a pointed end

Pegs

Cork

Bottle cap

Also scissors, ruler, pencil, black emulsion paint, white emulsion paint (optional), red acrylic paint, paintbrushes, PVA glue, strips of white paper 1 – 1.5 cm (about ½ in) wide, felt-tipped pens and acrylic varnish (optional)

Beautiful barges

Edward has decorated this barge in the traditional colours, but using felt-tipped pens to make the patterns. Every barge has a name, usually a pretty girl's name, like Jenny-Wren or Lindy-Lou. Choose a name for your canal boat.

1 Cut the carton in half lengthways. One half will be the boat. Cut off the ends of the other half, to leave a rectangle of card. This will be the roof of the barge.

2 To make the roof, measure 1.5 cm (about ½ in) either side of both the existing creases and score lines with a blunt pencil and ruler. The lines will make it easier to fold the card.

3 Paint the outside of the boat black and the inside too if you wish. The top can be painted white first. This will make the red much brighter. If not, just give the top two coats of red acrylic paint.

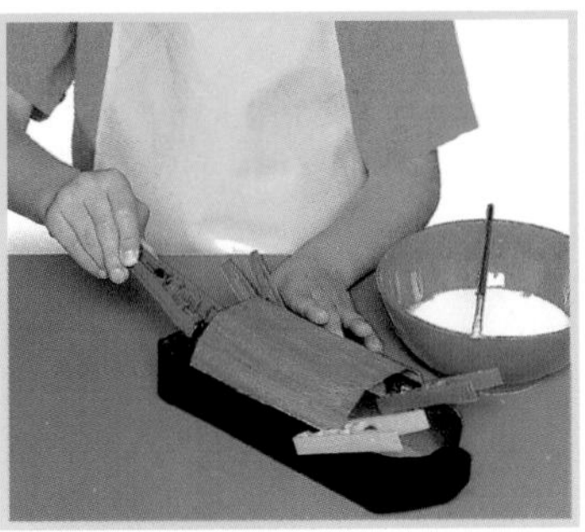

4 Fold the roof along the lines and glue the edges to the inner sides of the boat. Peg until the glue is dry.

5 Ask a grown-up to cut a cork in half lengthways. Paint the two halves black. When they are dry, glue one half across the back of the boat and one onto the back of the roof. Glue the bottle cap onto the front of the roof, as a funnel.

6 Decorate the paper strips with felt-tipped pens. Use red, yellow and green to make patterns, and write the name of your barge on the long strips if you wish. Draw windows and some flowers for the top, as bright and bold as you like.

7 Stick all the paper strip decorations to the boat with PVA glue. If you want to put the boat in water, give it a coat of acrylic varnish for protection.

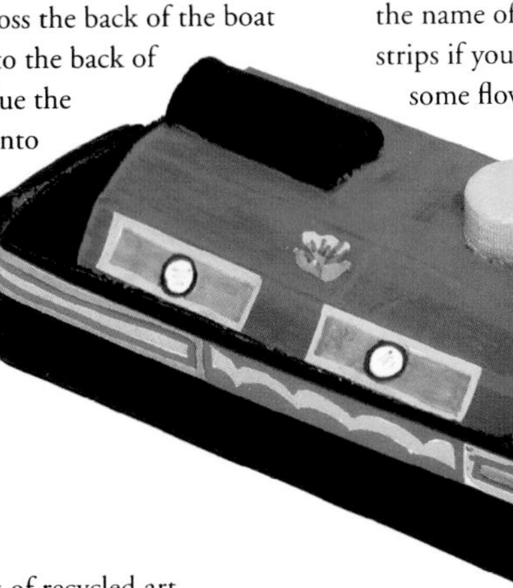

A real work of recycled art.

Stencilled Cork Place-mat

Make this place-mat, and brighten up the dinner table, even before the food arrives. It looks so good that the whole family will want one, and you will have to make a matching set. Start by making one for yourself. Ephram has used a carrot design for his mat. He could make a set using different vegetable stencils for each mat.

Stencilling technique

Stencilling is great fun and easy to do if you remember two simple rules. Always hold the stencil firmly in place with your spare hand and never use too much paint on your brush. The paint needs to be thick, so don't mix any water with it. Dip your brush in and then dab it on a piece of kitchen paper before you stencil on the cork tile. Use a different brush for each colour.

The felt backing will protect the table surface and also strengthen the thin cork and stop it breaking if you bend it. If you like a glossy surface, finish off your mat with a coat of acrylic gloss varnish, or PVA glue and water mixed three parts to one. This will add a tough, wipe-clean surface to the mat.

YOU WILL NEED THESE MATERIALS AND TOOLS

Unsealed cork floor tile and orange felt

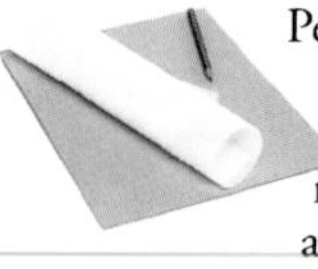

Pencil, tracing paper, card from a cereal box, to make your stencil and template

Also a ruler, craft knife, scissors, black marker pen (not water-colour), thick, soft stencil brush, acrylic paint – orange and green, kitchen paper towel, acrylic var-nish, PVA glue and a paintbrush

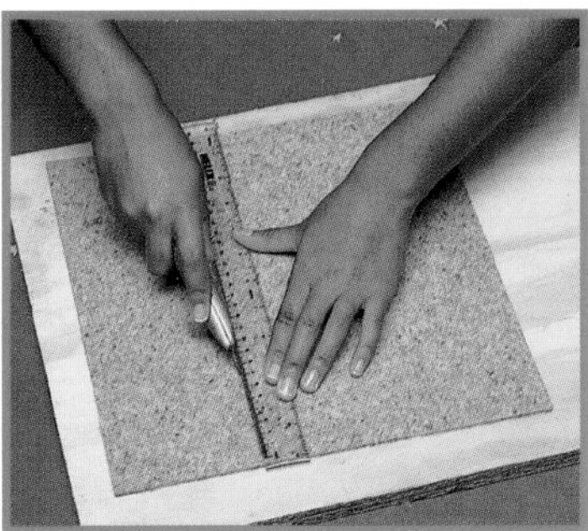

1 Using a pencil and ruler, measure and draw a line about 10 cm (4 in) in from the cork tile edge. Ask a grown-up to cut this strip off for you with a craft knife.

2 Find the carrot stencil pattern in the introduction, trace it onto the card and cut it out. Use the scissors to make a hole in the middle of the design, and then cut towards the outside edge. Move the card towards the scissors as you cut.

3 Make a template of the zig-zag border from the card. It should be the same length as the long side of the mat. Use the black marker pen to draw around it and colour the shape in. Fill in the corners to make triangles.

4 Stencil the carrots, starting with the one in the middle. Work from the stencil card inwards towards the centre, using a light dabbing movement. Always dab the paint from the pot onto a kitchen paper towel before using the brush on the cork. Use the paint very sparingly. You can always go over it again to add more colour, but too much at first will make blobs. Wipe the back of your stencil before painting the next carrot. The paint will dry quickly, but wait until it has done so or you may smudge the pattern.

5 To protect the design, either coat it with a glossy acrylic varnish or a coat of PVA glue mixed with water, three parts to one.

7 Spread the felt with PVA. Make sure that you reach right up to the edges. Stick this to the back of the cork.

6 Cut the orange felt so that it is the same size as the mat.

More Stencilling Ideas

If you are more likely to eat your dinner from a tray, then you could paint it in the same way. If you have an old tray at home, ask whether you may decorate it. A wooden tray will need rubbing down with sandpaper first, and a tin tray may need a coat of gloss paint before you stencil it. You could use fabric paints to stencil onto plain dinner napkins, or just stencil paper ones with acrylic paint.

Butterfly Mobile

The butterflies in this mobile are made from mussel shells. You may not live near a beach where mussel shells can be collected, or have a garden where butterflies flutter about, but you can make this mobile that has a little bit of seaside and countryside in it.

If you have never tasted mussels before, this may be a chance to try them. Most fishmongers sell mussels in their shells. When the mussels have been eaten, the shells are left, stuck together in the middle and already looking like butterflies. Scrub them well in warm soapy water.

YOU WILL NEED THESE MATERIALS AND TOOLS

7 mussel shells

Squeeze-on fabric paints, glitter, pearl or slick types

Gold paint and paintbrush

Pipe cleaners

Also 2 wooden boards, tin of paint for a weight, scissors, all-purpose clear adhesive, thin length of dowelling or garden cane, painted gold, and nylon thread

Fluttering in the breeze

Mobiles can be very relaxing to watch. Hang yours up above your bed and you will be able to drift off to sleep watching the butterflies gently turning in the air. Follow what Tania and Jade are doing and you will have a lovely mobile of fluttering butterflies.

1 Don't try to open out dry mussel shells, or they will come apart. Instead, soak the shells in warm water overnight. Open them out gently and place them face down on a board. Cover with another board and weigh it down with something heavy, such as a tin of paint.

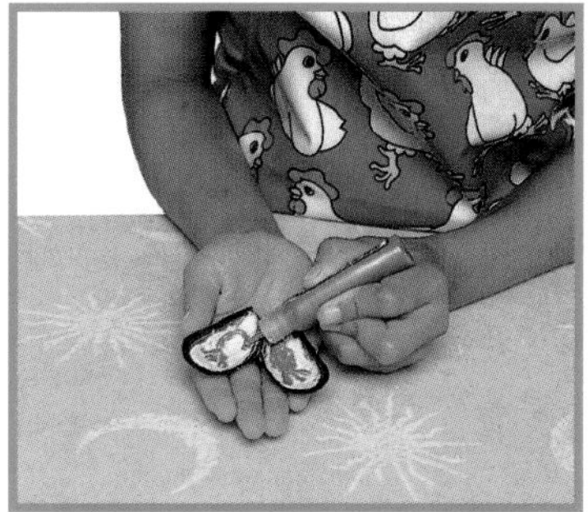

2 When the open shells have dried, decorate each one with a different pattern using the squeeze-on fabric paints. Practise on paper first to get the feel of squeezing the paint from the tubes. Look at pictures of butterflies – you will see how many different patterns you can use on your shell butterflies.

3 When the fabric paint is dry, turn the shells over and paint the dark side with gold paint.

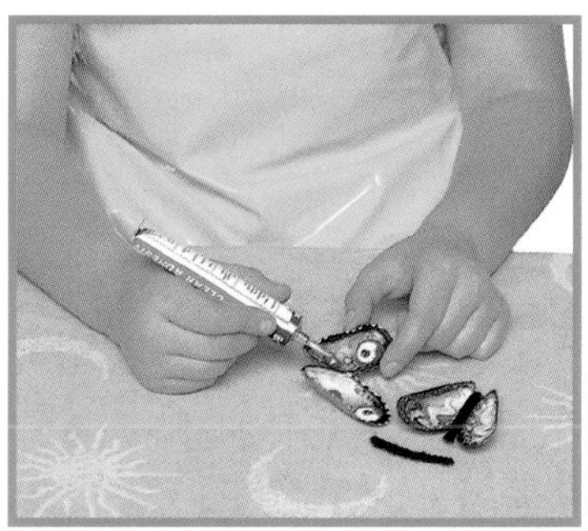

4 Cut up a pipe cleaner to make butterfly bodies about 4 cm (1½ in) long. Use glue to stick them in place.

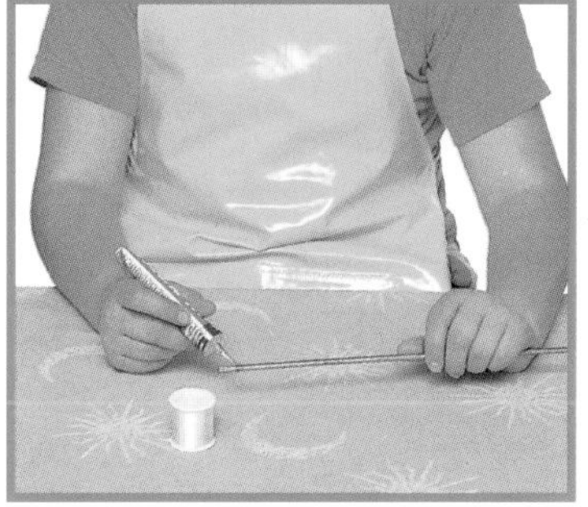

5 Put a drop of glue 1 cm (½ in) in from each end of the stick, then knot the nylon thread over one of the dots. The glue stops the thread from slipping, making the knot easier to tie. Measure roughly double the length of the stick and cut and knot the nylon onto the glue dot at the other end. This is what the mobile hangs from.

6 Put seven dots of glue along the stick, 6 cm (2½ in) apart, and tie lengths of nylon over each dot. Tie the other ends of the nylon around the pipe-cleaner heads of each butterfly. Arrange them at different heights. It is very easy to tangle up the nylon threads so take care to keep each butterfly and its thread separate.

7 Seven very rare butterflies.

Butterflies Everywhere

It would be most unusual to buy just seven mussels from the fishmonger, so you will probably have some left over. Decorate the shells with the paints and leave them to dry. Fix the bodies on as you did before and then glue them onto the corners of a picture frame or a mirror.

Feather Head-dress

The great Indian chiefs of North America wore head-dresses made from eagle feathers. They painted the feathers with patterns and each one had a special meaning, telling people how brave they were and how many battles they had won. Some chiefs wore head-dresses that reached all the way down their backs, from head to feet, called trailer war bonnets. When they held important gatherings or fought wars between the tribes, they would wear their feathers to show how brave and fierce they were. All the tribes understood the meaning of the feathers.

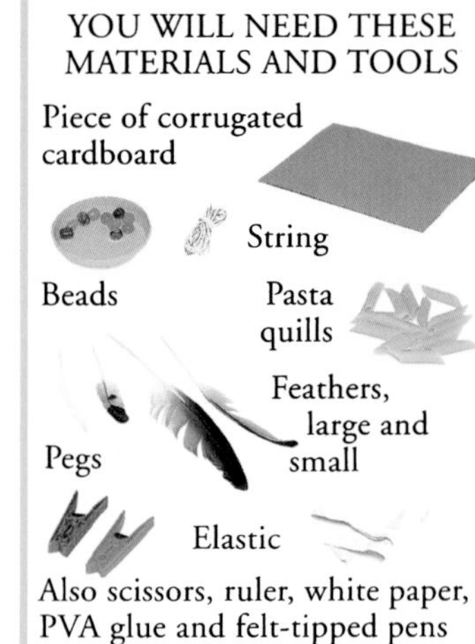

Magic feathers

Thomas and Edward are making this feather head-dress from seagull feathers, pasta quills, corrugated cardboard, beads and string. You can use any large feathers, so keep a look out when you go for a walk in the park or by the sea. If you live near a farm you can collect chicken or duck feathers.

Medicine men wore their feather head-dresses when they used their special powers, so perhaps you could wear yours and do a rain dance or, even better, a sunshine dance!

1 Cut the corrugated cardboard into a strip 4 cm x 25 cm (1½ x 10 in) and two discs 6 cm (2½ in) across. Cut white paper to match.

2 Glue the paper to the cardboard strip. Draw the beadwork pattern onto it with felt-tipped pens.

3 Glue the two paper discs to the cardboard discs. Decorate them with beadwork patterns.

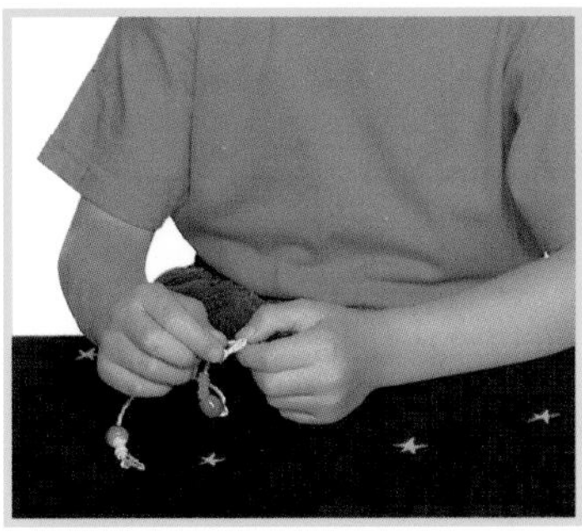

4 Cut two lengths of string 18 cm (7 in) long. Thread beads onto each end of the string and make a knot below them.

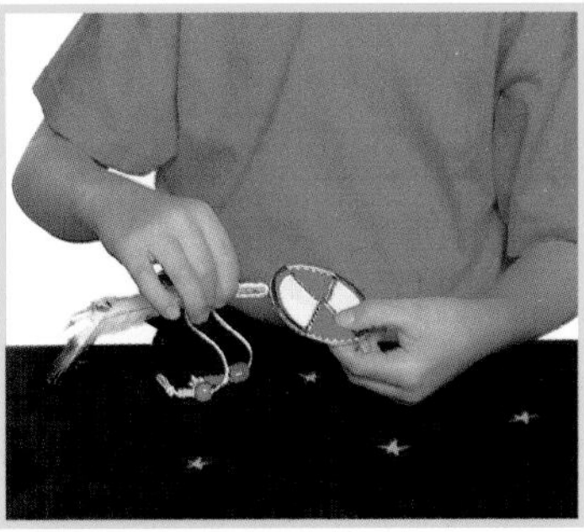

5 Dip the end of a small feather in the glue and use it to push the middle of the string up into a channel in the corrugated card disc. This is quite fiddly so ask a grown-up for help if you find it difficult.

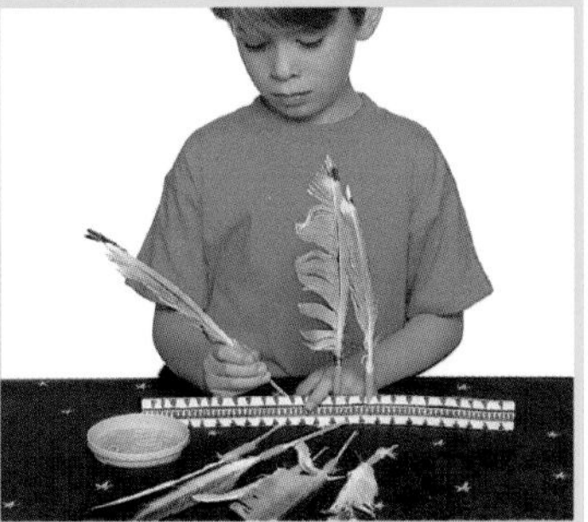

6 Place a pasta quill on each large feather and push the ends down into the channels in the decorated cardboard strip. Arrange the biggest ones in the centre, using smaller ones towards each side.

7 Glue on the discs about 2.5 cm (1 in) from each end. Peg the pieces together until the glue has dried. Make a hole at each end of the strip and thread elastic through to fasten at the back.

Beautiful Beadwork

The North American Indians made wonderful clothes and jewellery from beads, feathers and strips of leather. They believed that every living thing on Earth was precious and many of the patterns they used for beadwork or weaving told stories of nature and the lives of their ancestors. Ask at your library for a book about them, and copy the beadwork patterns to make pictures using felt-tipped pens or crayons. Try making jewellery from strips of chamois leather (we use it for car washing) threaded with beads and tubes of pasta, like macaroni. And don't forget to do that sunshine dance!

Jewellery Box

Some packaging is just too good to throw away. If you have a baby sister or brother, there may be some empty "wet wipes" boxes which have hinged lids and a clasp to keep them shut. You can decorate them with pieces of felt and make a very special box to keep your jewellery in. Felt is easy to cut, and craft shops sell squares 30 x 30 cm (12 x 12 in) as well as small bags of scraps in different colours.

The zig-zag edge is made by using special scissors called pinking shears. Dressmakers use them, so ask a grown-up who you know does a lot of sewing if they have a pair you can borrow. Felt is such fun to cut out anyway, so if you don't have pinking shears just cut your own fancy edges with scissors.

YOU WILL NEED THESE MATERIALS AND TOOLS

Plastic box with a hinged lid

Felt squares and scraps

Fabric paint and a paintbrush

Also thin paper, to make templates, pencil, pins, scissors, pinking shears (optional), PVA glue and a glue spreader

This box belongs to ...

Everyone has favourite colours, so choose the ones you like best when you cover the box. Fabric paints come in all colours and are either pearly, puffy or shiny when they dry. You will need to practise writing to avoid making blobs. Kirsty is making a box for her friend Maria. You could write your name instead. Try it out a few times on different pieces of felt, and choose your best effort to stick on the box.

1 Make paper templates by drawing around the top, long and short sides of the box. Cut them out, but make the patterns a bit smaller if your box has raised edges like this one.

2 Use pins to hold the patterns and felt pieces together. Choose different colours of felt for the top and sides of the box.

3 Cut out the felt pieces. Use pinking shears if you have them, or ordinary scissors if not. If you use pinking shears ask a grown-up to cut out the pieces of felt for you.

4 Stick the felt to the top and all the sides of the box.

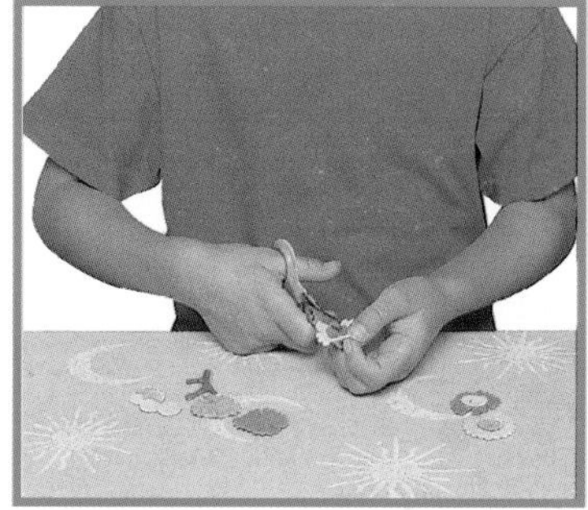

5 Cut out circles of felt, about 4 cm (1½ in) across for the flowers, and smaller ones for the flower centres. Stick the centres down and snip towards the centre to make petals. Cut out some flower stems too.

6 Glue the flowers to the top and sides of the box.

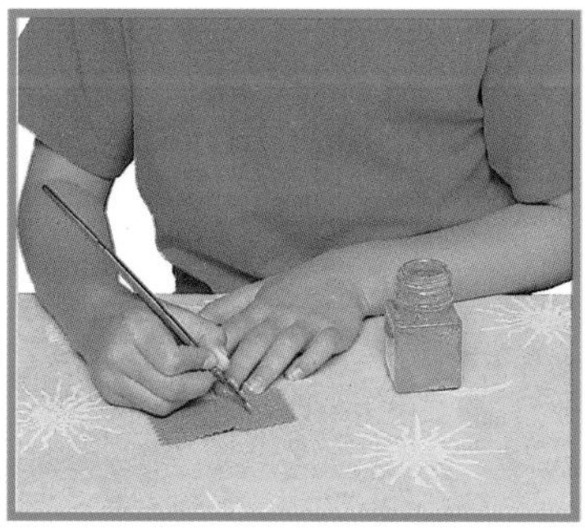

7 Using a paintbrush, write your name on a piece of felt with fabric paint. Try writing in small dots if lines seem too difficult.

Now that you have made it, you will probably need some new pieces of jewellery to go in your jewellery box!

Fun with Felt

If you enjoy snipping and gluing felt you could make a cover for your diary or a folder. Measure the shape and cut the background coloured felt to fit. Cut out shapes and patterns, letters and numbers, and glue them onto the background. Always make sure that the glue is spread evenly across the felt and right up to the edges.

Felt can be used on its own to make things too. A bookmark is useful. Just cut a long strip and snip 1 cm (½ in) into the ends to make a fringe.

Painted Flower-pot and Saucer

Everyone loves a gift that has been specially made for them. You may not be ready to make a flowerpot yet, but you could certainly decorate one as a special present.

Indoor plants can look dull in plain clay pots, especially the leafy ones without any flowers. This bright red and yellow pattern that Roxy is painting is very easy to do and is just the thing to brighten up a winter windowsill.

Preparing your pots

Clay pots need to be sealed before you can paint them, and PVA glue can be brushed on to give a good waterproof paint surface. When you paint stripes around a shape like a flowerpot, it is hard to keep the lines straight. A good trick is to put a rubber band around the pot wherever you need a guideline. It makes a slightly raised line to paint up to and can be slipped off when the paint is dry.

YOU WILL NEED THESE MATERIALS AND TOOLS

Houseplant

Clay flowerpot and saucer

Also PVA glue, to seal the surface of the pot, paintbrushes, acrylic paint – red and yellow, and a rubber band

1 Mix up three parts PVA glue with one part water and brush this all over the flowerpot and the saucer. Leave them to dry.

2 Paint the outside of the flowerpot and its inner rim and the outside of the saucer yellow. Mix acrylic paint with a little water, to make it thick and creamy. Leave it to dry and then paint on a second coat.

3 Stretch a rubber band around the flowerpot to mark the edge of the red section. Paint as shown in the picture. Leave the rubber band on until the paint is dry.

4 Make two red stripes with dots in-between them around the outer rim of the pot.

5 Paint the rim of the saucer red. Allow to dry. Then decorate the saucer with red spots on the yellow background and yellow spots on the red background.

6 Make yellow dots along the red stripes at the top of the pot. Paint yellow stripes down to the bottom edge, over the red. Paint big red dots in the middle and, when dry, put in smaller yellow dots. When all the paint has dried, seal the pot with the same PVA glue and water mixture that you started with in the first step.

A little bit of sunshine to put on the windowsill.

Go Potty Painting Pots!

Flowerpots come in all sizes and there are many different ways to paint them. Spots, stripes, wavy lines, diamonds, flowers – these are a few of the different shapes that you could use to make patterns. Stars look great too. Try making a stencil out of a piece of card. Cut out the shape with scissors and hold it firmly against the pot. Paint through the stencil, being careful to use only a tiny amount of paint on your brush.

Cork Rattlesnake

This cork and bead snake has a slithery feeling and will curl up or wriggle along, just like the real thing. Rattlesnakes get their name from the rattle at the end of their tail. They curl up and shake the rattle, holding their heads ready to strike when danger approaches. The rattling sound warns all creatures to beware as the rattlesnake is very dangerous.

YOU WILL NEED THESE MATERIALS AND TOOLS

10 winemaker's bored corks

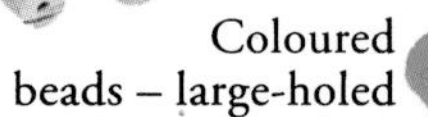
Coloured beads – large-holed

60 cm (24 in) of flat elastic 1–1.5 cm (about ½ in) wide

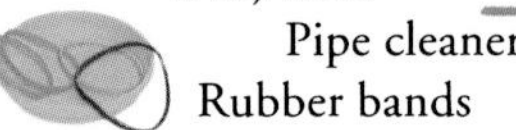
Pipe cleaner

Rubber bands

Also paintbrushes, acrylic paints – green, black, red and yellow, ordinary cork, cut in half lengthways, PVA glue, scissors and acrylic varnish (optional)

Colourful crazy patterns

The corks used in this project have holes through the middle and are usually used for making home-made wines. You can buy them from large chemists and shops that specialize in winemaking equipment. Ordinary corks could be used, but you would have to ask an adult to drill holes through the middle of them for you.

Snake colours are brilliant and their patterns are exciting. Zig-zags, diamonds, stripes, swirls and spots are all very snaky. Look at what Reece and George have done and then have fun with your patterns and make a really unusual rattlesnake.

1 Paint all the corks green. Leave them to dry completely.

2 Paint the black pattern first. Then paint the red and yellow patterns in-between the black ones. Don't forget to decorate the ordinary cork that has been cut in half. This will be made into the mouth.

3 When the paint is dry thread the main body of the snake onto the elastic, with a bead between each cork. The corks are thicker at one end than the other. Make sure the tail cork tapers to the thin end.

4 Thread five or six beads onto the end of the snake to make the rattle. Tie a knot at the end.

7 Cut the elastic into the shape of a forked tongue and paint red. The snake can be varnished with acrylic gloss or PVA glue diluted with water.

5 Pull the elastic up through the snake. Don't pull it too tight though, because the snake must be able to wriggle and roll up. Thread two beads onto the pipe cleaner to make the snake's eyes. Cut off the extra pipe cleaner leaving 1 cm (½ in) to twist and secure the beads in place. Flatten out the elastic so it runs along the flat side of the cork and sticks out at the end. Place the pipe cleaner across the elastic.

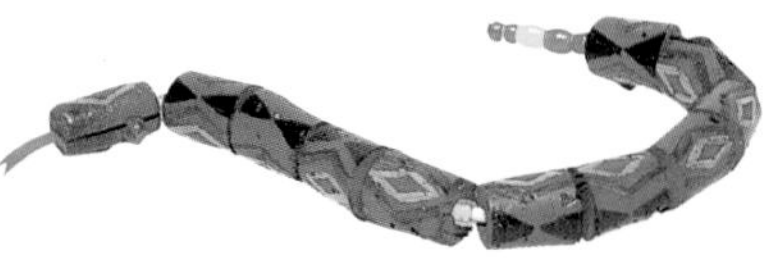

A slithery snake pet with no nasty nips.

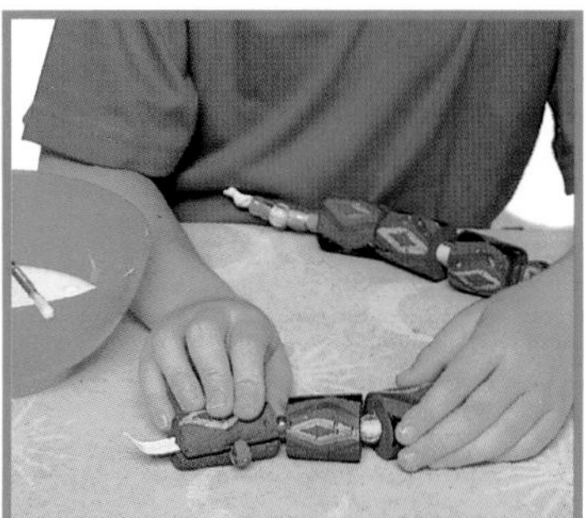

6 Paste with PVA glue and put the other half of the cork on top. Hold the two pieces together with a rubber band until the glue is dry.

Slithery Lizard

You could make a lizard out of corks. For the legs, ask a grown-up to make holes across two of the corks. Make the lizard up in the same way as the snake, then thread shorter pieces of elastic through the new holes. Thread three beads on each side and then a cork, with the wide end down. Add one more bead and tie a knot. Four corks added in this way will make four stubby lizard legs.

Peanut and Macaroni Jewellery

YOU WILL NEED THESE MATERIALS AND TOOLS

Peanuts in shells

Macaroni

Beads

Darning needle and shirring elastic

Also paintbrushes, acrylic paints – red, blue, black and yellow, a cup, acrylic gloss varnish (optional) and PVA glue

Who needs gold, silver and diamonds when you have macaroni and peanuts in the kitchen cupboard? You can make the bright and chunky necklace and bracelet very easily and all your friends will want to make them too.

The peanuts look great painted in very bright primary colours, and are light and comfortable to wear. The macaroni is perfect for threading and makes a good space between the peanuts. Use acrylic paints which dry in five minutes, and give the nuts a good glossy varnish to make them shine.

Miniature maracas

You will notice that when you wear the necklace you feel like dancing. That is because the nuts rattle in the shells as you move and it is like having lots of little maracas around your neck! You could make some ankle bracelets too and do a rattling, stamping dance. Ephram has made this necklace and bracelet for his friend Saadia.

1 Paint the peanuts different colours and leave to dry.

2 Mix some paint in a cup to colour the macaroni. Drop the macaroni in the cup and stir. Tip out and separate the pieces. Leave to dry.

3 When they are dry, varnish the nuts and macaroni with acrylic gloss varnish or PVA glue and water mixed three parts to one. Leave to dry.

4 Use a darning needle to make holes through the middle of the peanuts. There is a hollow space between the two nuts, where the shell goes in at the "waist". Push the needle through both sides.

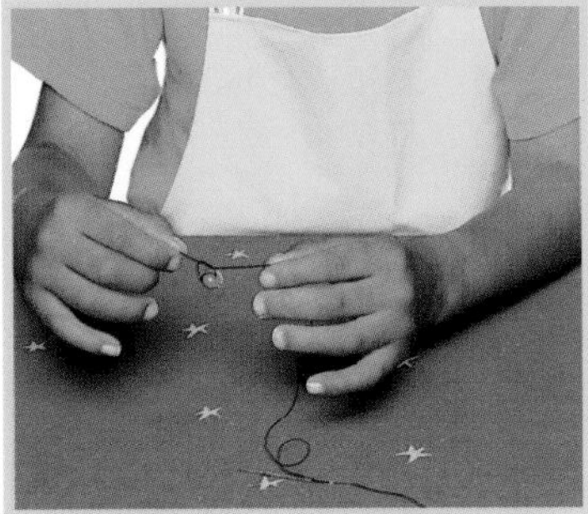

5 Measure around your neck and wrists and cut the shirring elastic just a bit longer. Thread the darning needle and tie a bead onto the end of the elastic.

6 Thread one piece of macaroni, then one nut and repeat the colours in the same order until you reach the end of the elastic.

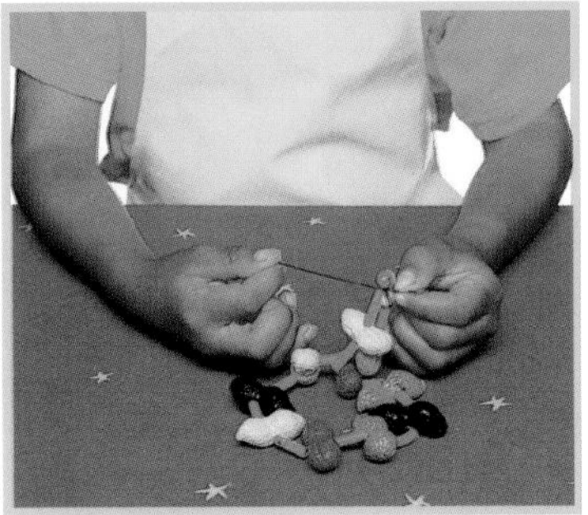

7 Finish with a piece of macaroni and then tie on a bead. Tie the two beaded ends together.

What Else Could You Thread?

Popcorn can also be threaded to make jewellery. You will need home-made popcorn that has no salt or sugar coating. You can paint and varnish it with acrylics, just as you did with the peanuts.

Thread the darning needle and push it through the middle of the popcorn, where the burst outer shell is, as this is the strongest part. When you have threaded enough for a necklace, cut the elastic and tie a knot. You could try combining the macaroni, monkey nuts and popcorn. There are also lots of pips and seeds that thread easily, so have a good look in the store cupboard. Ask a grown-up if it is all right and then get threading.

Doll's House

The next time you visit a supermarket, choose a good strong cardboard box from the check-out to use to pack the shopping. When the groceries are all put away, you can use the box to make this doll's house.

You will need a grown-up to help with the first stages. Never use a craft knife on your own as the blades are dangerously sharp. The step photographs show how the box is cut, and you can help with a ruler and pencil, measuring and drawing the cutting guidelines, just as Kirsty is doing here.

Paint the house and roof with a light-coloured emulsion paint, the sort that is used to paint walls at home. This will make a good base coat for felt-tipped pens.

YOU WILL NEED THESE MATERIALS AND TOOLS

Sturdy cardboard box

Corrugated cardboard

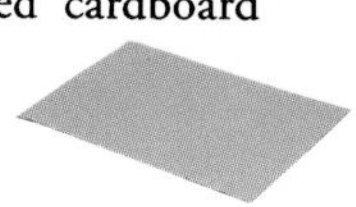

Also light-coloured emulsion paint, paintbrushes, pencil, ruler, scissors, craft knife, adhesive tape, table knife, PVA glue, acrylic paints – red, yellow, and blue, paper, and felt-tipped pens

Moving in

This house is empty, and will need furnishing. Look for little boxes and tins to cover with fabric or felt as they will make good chairs. A carpet sample could be cut to fit inside, or you could colour paper to make a patterned rug. And to make the house your very own, you could write your house number on the door.

1 Paint the box. On both sides measure 10cm (4in) from the top. Find the middle point along the top edge. Join the dots and draw a triangle.

2 Ask a grown-up to cut out the shape of the house for you using big scissors or a craft knife.

3 The back of the house should be cut away so you can reach inside. Ask a grown-up to do this with the craft knife.

4 Use the side flaps to create the roof peak. Score the lines where they fold but don't cut right through. Stick the flaps down with adhesive tape.

5 To make the roof, measure the top of the box. Cut the corrugated cardboard so it is 2.5 cm (1 in) wider each side and 5 cm (2 in) longer at each end. Score down the central line with a table knife. Ask a grown-up to help you if you need to.

6 Bend the roof along the scored line. Paint the inside with PVA glue and place it on top of the house. When the glue is dry, paint the roof with yellow acrylic paint.

7 To make the windows, cut out squares of paper and paint the edges with blue acrylic paint. Cut out a front door and paint it red.

A pretty country house complete with cat, ready to be moved into and furnished.

Budding Architect

You could make lots of different buildings out of cardboard boxes. Perhaps you would like a garage to go with your house. You could even make a whole street of different buildings, including shops and a church.

Look for different sized boxes, such as shoe boxes, and other things. What could you use to make a post box, for example?

Pencil-pot Découpage

Pencils, pens and brushes roll off tables or slip down between the cushions of a sofa when you are concentrating hard on making pictures. You can organize yourself by making this pencil pot from a food tin with a ring-pull lid. Tin openers leave dangerously sharp edges, so be sure to choose the safer type with a ring-pull for this project.

The word découpage means "cutting out" in French. You cut out pictures and glue them to the object you are making. Furniture is sometimes decorated in this way, and then given many coats of clear varnish. You can use clear acrylic varnish to give your pot a shine, or a mixture of PVA glue and water, mixed three parts to one.

YOU WILL NEED THESE MATERIALS AND TOOLS

Also blue paint, either acrylic or gloss, paintbrushes, scissors, PVA glue, soft cloth, acrylic gloss varnish (optional), small piece of corrugated cardboard and a pencil

Choosing your decorations

Jade has painted this tin blue and decorated it with cut-outs from a sheet of wrapping paper, but you could use the same method to make a pencil-pot to suit your own interests. Perhaps you have a comic-book character, pop star or sports person – someone whose picture you would like to see every day. Just cut out a combination of pictures that you like and glue them onto the painted tin. Take your time when cutting out, moving the paper to meet the scissors. It is a good idea to practise on a few spare sheets of paper before you cut out your most special pictures.

1 Paint the tin blue. Water-based paint is best, because you can wash your brushes under the tap. Acrylic will need two coats of undiluted paint.

2 Carefully cut out the motifs. The pattern looks best if you have two different sorts, such as butterflies and teddy bears.

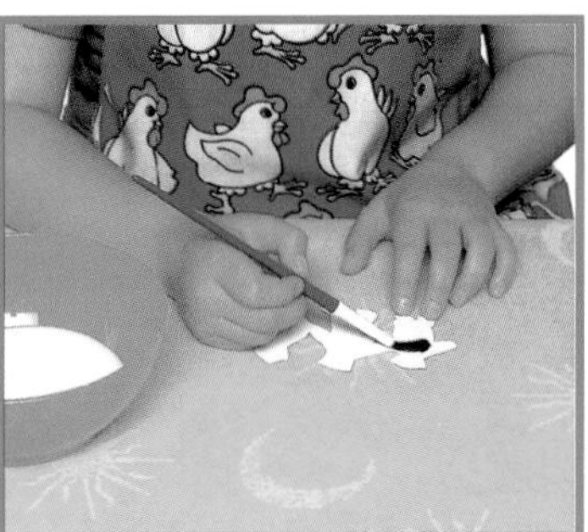

3 Spread PVA glue over the back of each motif, making sure you reach all the outer edges. Otherwise the sides will curl up.

4 Stick down the motifs, using a soft cloth to flatten out any air bubbles. Arrange them around the tin with the same amount of space between them.

5 When the glue is dry, paint on acrylic varnish or a mixture of three parts PVA glue to one part water. The varnish can be gloss or matt.

6 Stand the tin on a piece of corrugated cardboard and draw around it. Cut out a circle, just inside the line, to fit into the base.

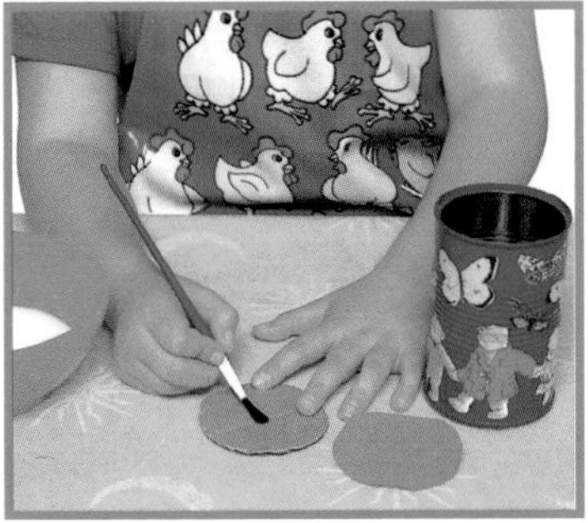

7 Draw a circle on the felt in the same way, but cut it out just outside the line. Stick the felt to the cardboard, then the cardboard to the pencil-pot with PVA glue.

Your very own, very organized decorated découpage pencil-pot!

What Else Deserves Découpage

You can cut out and stick all sorts of motifs onto all kinds of surfaces, not just tins. Wooden boxes, trays and bedroom furniture can all be brightened up with paper cut-outs, but always ask permission from a grown-up first. If you find a black and white picture or pattern that would make a good border, you can photocopy it as many times as you need. Cut out and colour your photocopies, and then glue them on.

Birdwatchers

If you have ever seen birdwatchers, you'll have noticed that they are very quiet and slow-moving. Any sharp movements or noises would frighten the birds and they would fly away.

These binoculars are green so they are camouflaged as you creep around the park or garden birdwatching. Stay very still and the birds will come quite close. If you have a bird-bath or table in your garden, the birds that use it will be quite tame, so they might not mind even if they do see you watching.

Sunny all the time

These binoculars have a very special feature. They brighten up dull days, making the world outside look sunny, even when it's grey. George has found some sweets with yellow cellophane wrappers – just the thing to cover the ends of his binoculars.

YOU WILL NEED THESE MATERIALS AND TOOLS

- Two toilet-roll tubes
- Green paper, ruler and pencil
- Piece of yellow cellophane
- Adhesive tape
- Black plastic tape
- Black cord

Also scissors, a wine cork, PVA glue, paintbrush, black acrylic paint and a rubber band

1 Cut out two squares of cellophane and tape them over one end of each cardboard tube. Ask a grown-up to help if you find this difficult.

2 Cut out two rectangles of green paper measuring 12 x 19 cm (4½ x 7½ in). Then cut a strip of paper to fit around the cork.

3 Ask a grown-up to trim the cork lengthways, so that one half has two flat sides. Paint the ends with black acrylic paint.

4 Take the strip of green paper and glue it around the cork. Paint on lines for the focusing winder.

5 Brush the pieces of green paper with glue. Line up with the tube ends without cellophane, then roll the tubes onto the paper.

6 Stick black plastic tape around the ends with the cellophane, then trim the paper and tape close to the cellophane ends.

7 Spread a stripe of glue along the side of one tube, and both flat sides of the cork. Assemble the binoculars, and hold them together with a rubber band until the glue is dry.

8 Push a hole through the sides of each tube, and thread the black cord through. Tie a knot on the inside.

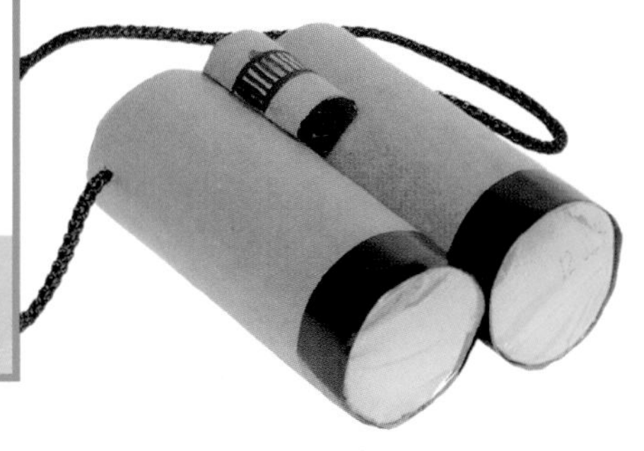

Now you are ready to go birdwatching – and the weather looks just fine!

Monster Sock Puppet

Everyone has an odd sock somewhere around the house, waiting to be brought to life as a monster sock puppet. Try to find one that is brightly coloured and use a contrasting colour felt for the mouth and fins. Kirsty has practised her monster noises, because she is going to need them!

Pins and needles

If you have never used a sewing needle before, be sure to ask a grown-up to help you. Sewing is quite easy, once you know how, and you will not need to use a very sharp needle to sew through felt and sock material. A darning needle will do the job.

If you use pins to hold the mouth lining in place as you sew it, be very careful, because they are sharp. Always position them so their points are facing in the same direction around the monster's mouth. When you start to sew, work towards the heads, not the points, of the pins. Each time you reach a pin, remove it and put it back in a pin cushion or tin, so that nobody gets a sharp surprise!

YOU WILL NEED THESE MATERIALS AND TOOLS

- Plain coloured sock
- Felt, different colour from the sock
- Darning wool and needle
- Two large buttons
- Also a pencil, tracing paper, paper, scissors, pins (optional), thread, PVA glue and a glue spreader

1 Trace the template for the mouth which you will find in the introduction. Cut it out to make a pattern. Put this on a folded piece of felt, so that the fold is along the straight edge of the pattern. Cut out the mouth and the other shapes. Just nip the felt to make zig-zags, spiky fins, and a tongue.

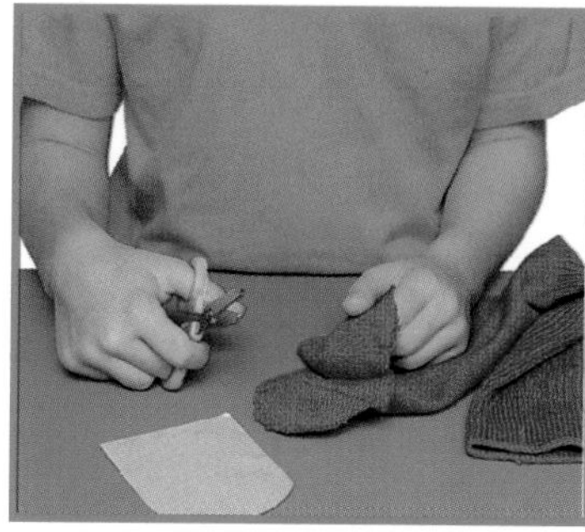

2 Turn the sock inside-out and cut along the toe seam and past it on both sides by about 5 cm (2 in). Measure the opening against the pattern for the mouth, to get the size right.

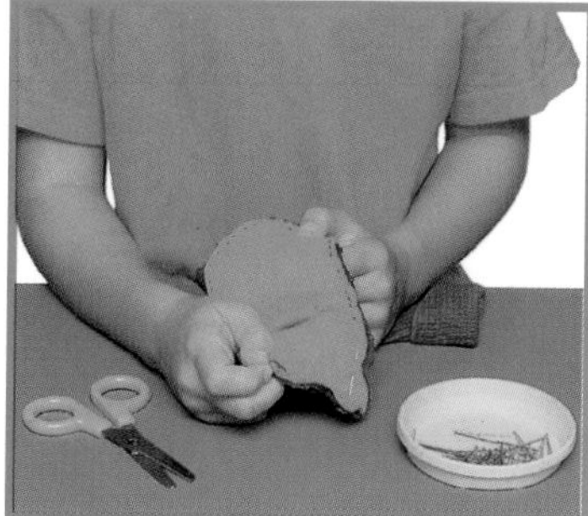

3 Pin the mouth lining into the toe end, flapping the top back, so that you can sew the lining in one flat piece. Sew along the seam using running stitches. Make a small cut along the fold of the mouth and poke the tongue through it, so that it sticks out on the other side. Sew the tongue in place.

4 Turn the sock right side out and sew on buttons for eyes. Use wool to do this, pushing the needle up from inside the sock, through the holes and back down again. Tie the ends of wool inside the sock.

5 Stick on the nostrils, spreading PVA glue across the back of the felt, right up to the edges. Stick on the triangles and zig-zags in the same way.

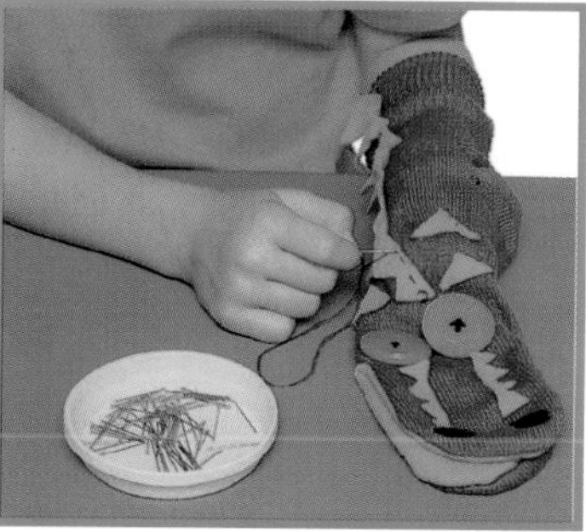

6 Sew the long back fin along the centre of the monster's back, using black thread or wool. Be careful not to prick your hand with the needle.

Now is the time to use those monster noises that you have been practising!

Shark Alert!

There are all kinds of creatures to be made from odd socks. If you have a grey sock you could try making a shark. You will need grey felt for the fins and red for the mouth lining. Nice white teeth are a very important feature, so cut them from felt and fit them into the mouth at the same time as the lining. Think carefully as they will need to stick up from the shark's gums. So cut triangles and sew the flat ends into the mouth seam, leaving the pointy teeth to stick up in the mouth. To make the big back fin, cut two triangles and put a bit of cotton wool stuffing in-between them. Sew around the edges and then sew the base of the fin into the middle of the back.

Magnetic Fishing

This game is almost as much fun to make as it is to play. You could make it at your birthday party with each guest having a fish to decorate. The fish shape is very simple, but your decoration can be wild or realistic. Roxy and Rupert like bright colours for their fish. Have a look at some fish in a shop or borrow a book about fish from your library – there are so many beautiful patterns and colours to choose from.

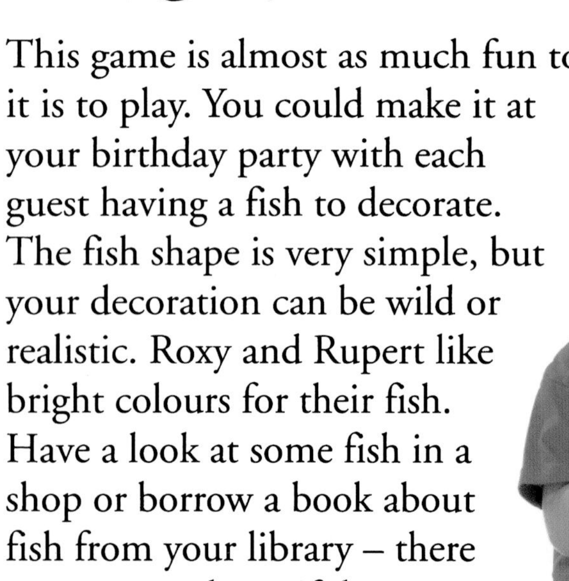

Playing the game

There are many different ways of playing this game. Dangle your rod over the fish until you connect with one, then lift it up. To make it harder, try this blindfolded or write points on to the fish and add up each player's score at the end.

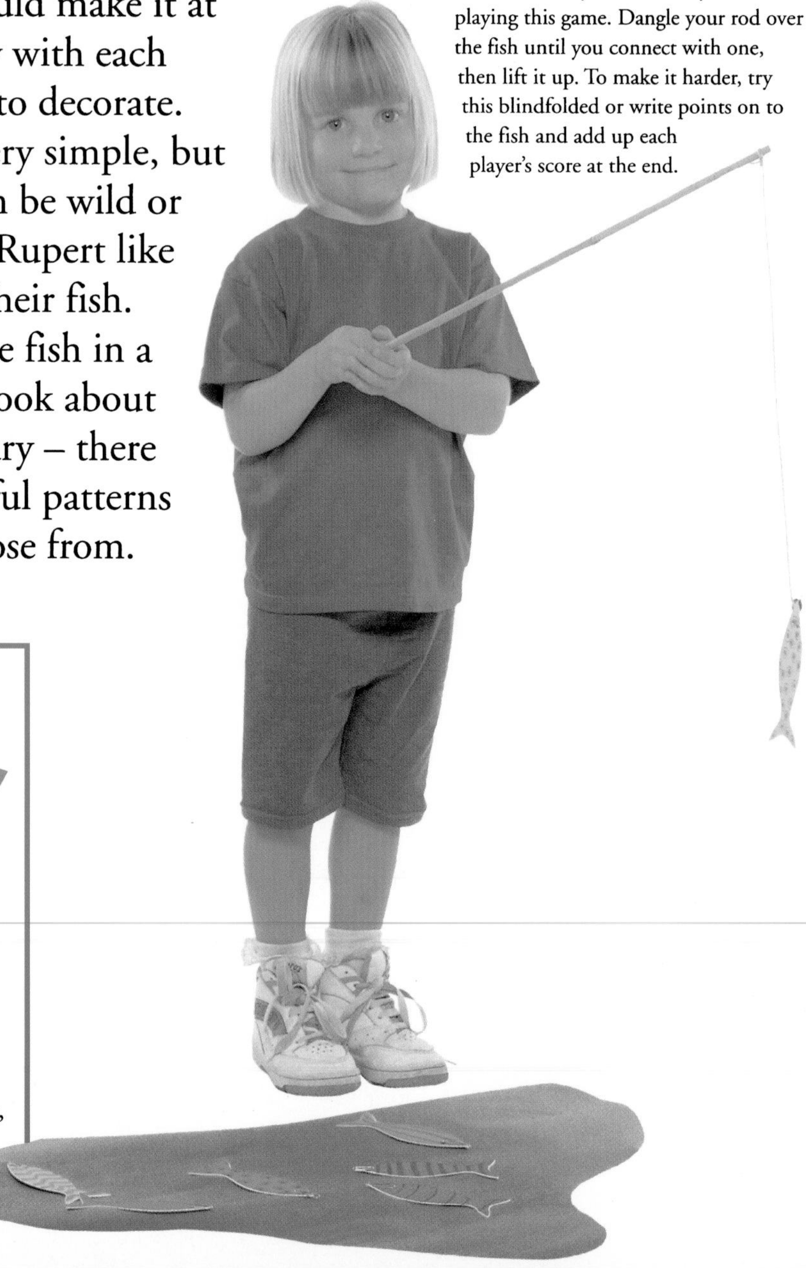

YOU WILL NEED THESE MATERIALS AND TOOLS

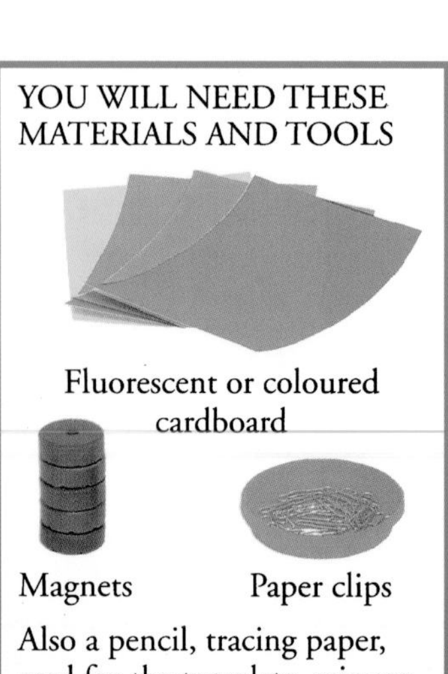

Fluorescent or coloured cardboard

Magnets

Paper clips

Also a pencil, tracing paper, card for the template, scissors, felt-tipped pens, string and bamboo poles

1 Find the fish template in the introduction and follow the instructions you will find there to trace and cut out your pattern.

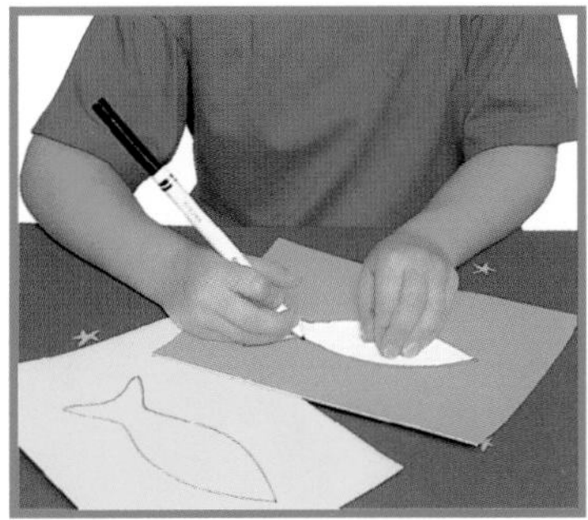

2 Use the template to draw fish on the different coloured card. Hold the template firmly so that it does not move while you are drawing.

3 Cut out all of your fish, taking care to do this as neatly as possible, by following the lines of the template.

4 Decorate the fish with different coloured felt-tipped pens. Try out different patterns on them as well.

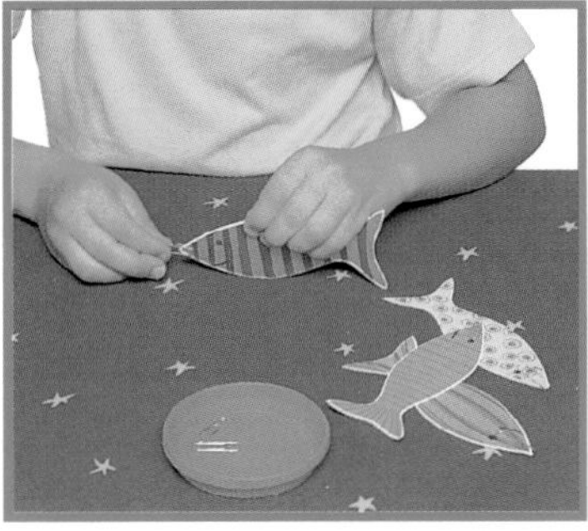

5 Attach the paper clips to the mouths of the fish. The magnets will attach themselves to these.

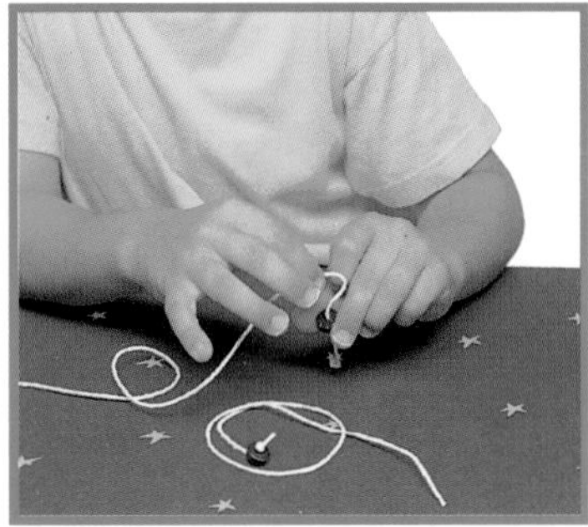

6 To make your fishing rods, tie a small magnet to a piece of long string.

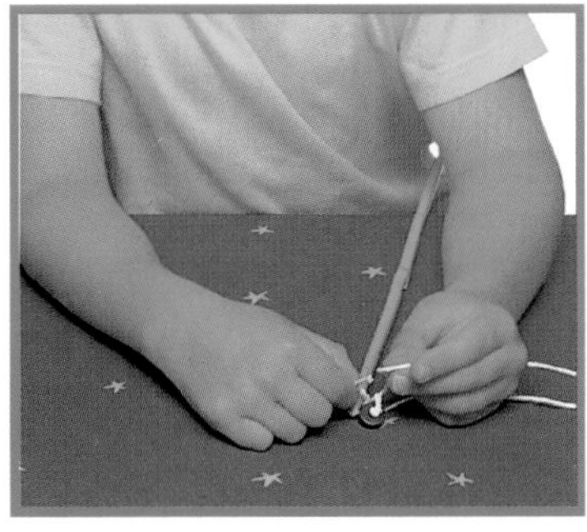

7 Then tie each piece of string on to the end of one of the bamboo poles. Knot it tightly!

Other Magnetic Games

Magnetic fishing does not have to involve fish. You could make sets of different parts of the body – head; bodies, legs and arms. Some can be girls and some boys and their clothes can be as silly as you like. Put them all in a box with paper clips attached and take turns to fish for them. It will be like a game of picture consequences when you have to fit your person together. Alternatively you could fish for letters to make words, or pictures of food to make up dinners.

Roxy and Rupert have made a pond where they can go fishing.

Tasty Treats

Introduction

This chapter is full of great ideas and recipes for you to create in your kitchen. Some of the recipes are quite simple to follow. Others will require a bit more concentration for you to get them absolutely right. A few allow you to really get your hands in and get as mucky as you like. There are recipes for starters and snacks, main meals and lots of ideas for special occasion treats that will really impress your friends. But remember, whether easy or difficult, all the ideas here have been specially designed for you to get lots of fun, pleasure and compliments from your cooking.

One thing is certain, by the time you have tried all the recipes here you will be an expert cook. Family and friends will be forever inviting themselves over to sample your famous cooking.

Whatever you are going to make, there are always a few very important rules to remember before you start. Be safe, be clean and be patient as recipes can easily turn into disasters if you try to rush things or cut corners to save time.

Peel potatoes with a vegetable peeler.

Always read through the recipe you are planning to make. Write out a list of what you need, but before you go shopping, check the cupboards to see if there are any ingredients you already have, so won't have to buy. It is also a good idea to make a note of how much of a particular ingredient you need, as this will stop you from buying too much and spending too much money. Ask a grown-up to have a quick look through your list before you set off, and always take a grown-up or big brother or sister with you when you go to the shops.

While you are cooking, there will be some stages when it will be useful to have a grown-up close by. More importantly, always ask a grown-up to help with potentially dangerous jobs like transferring food in and out of the oven and on and off the stove top. You will also need help from a grown-up with any stages in the recipe for which you need sharp knives, scissors or electrical equipment, and when anything hot is being handled. Make sure in advance that a grown-up is going to be available if you need them and always get

Always ask a grown-up to hold hot saucepans for you.

Garnish the finished dish to make it look more appetizing.

permission from a grown-up before you start creating your chosen dish in the kitchen.

The recipes in this chapter show you, in detailed stages, what you should be doing at each step of the cooking. Just look at the children in the pictures and follow what they are doing.

So, when you have read through the rest of the information in the introduction, off you go.

Good luck and have fun!

Biscuit cutters come in all different shapes and sizes and are great for making biscuits or cutting out fun sandwich shapes.

First Things First

You've chosen your recipe and bought your ingredients, but there are a few simple things to do before you actually start to cook. If there is anything you don't understand, ask a grown-up to explain it to you.

❖ Read through the recipe, from start to finish, very carefully so you have a clear idea of what you are about to be doing and in what order.

❖ Wash and dry your hands. If your hair is long, tie it back. Put on an apron to protect your clothes – plastic ones are best.

❖ Make sure the kitchen surfaces are clean and tidy and you have plenty of space in which to work.

❖ Get all the ingredients you will need sorted out and weighed.

Weighing and Measuring

The ingredients in the recipes are measured in grams (g) and millilitres (ml), known as metric measures, and also in ounces (oz) and pints (pt), known as imperial measures. You will also see tsp for teaspoon and tbsp for tablespoon (you might be able to get a set of special measuring spoons to help you weigh these small amounts).

It is very important that you choose *either* metric *or* imperial measures when you are weighing out your ingredients. Never mix the two units – use either grams or ounces, not a combination.

If you want to cook a particular recipe from this chapter, but you want to make it for more or less people, you can increase or reduce the quantities of ingredients to suit you. If you need help with the multiplication or division, ask a grown-up to help you out.

Why Things Go Wrong

If you find that things are not turning out as they should, then make sure you are following this list of handy tips.

❖ Don't rush.

❖ Do read the recipe through before you start, and follow the instructions and pictures closely.

❖ Do weigh and measure the ingredients carefully.

❖ Don't have any interruptions or distractions while you are in the kitchen, as this can cause you to forget where you are in the recipe, and leave bits out.

❖ If cooking in the oven, don't keep opening the oven door as this will cause the temperature to drop.

❖ Do make sure you cook things for the proper length of time.

A food processor makes mixing ingredients easy and quick. Always ask a grown-up to help you with this piece of equipment.

To cook successfully, you must always weigh your ingredients carefully.

Be Clean and Tidy

When you are cooking and handling food, you must be aware of the bacteria which are all around. Most bacteria are harmless, but it is important to keep the harmful ones away by following a few simple rules.

❖ Always wash your hands before you handle food and keep washing them every now and then while you are cooking, to keep them as clean as possible.

❖ Wear a clean apron and tie long hair back.

❖ Have a clean, damp cloth handy, so you can wipe the surfaces if you make a mess. Don't forget to rinse the cloth when you have used it.

Wash your hands before you start to cook and dry them on a clean dish towel.

Always wear an apron to protect your clothes when cooking.

❖ Try to tidy up and wash up as you go, so you won't have so much to do at the end.

❖ Wash your chopping board regularly and every time you use it for a new ingredient.

❖ Always wash fruit and vegetables before you use them and clear away any peelings.

❖ Have a rubbish bin near by, so you can keep putting things in it rather than letting the rubbish pile up as you cook.

Be Safe in the Kitchen

There are some things in the kitchen which can be very dangerous. Make sure you have a grown-up's permission before you start cooking and ask them to be around to help with the more dangerous stages of cooking. Always read through the recipe to see when and where you might need the help of a grown-up, then follow these basic rules:

❖ Always ask a grown-up to light the oven or stove top – never do it yourself.

❖ Go slowly and carefully in the kitchen – rushing around causes accidents.

❖ Always use oven gloves or a dish towel when handling hot things. Better still, ask a grown-up to do it for you.

❖ Never leave the kitchen when something is cooking – you don't know what might happen while you're gone!

Place hot bowls or saucepans on a trivet to protect the work surface, and use oven gloves or a dish towel to hold hot things.

❖ Make sure you turn saucepan or frying pan handles to the sides of the cooker when they're on the stove top. This will stop you knocking or catching yourself on them.
❖ Never touch electrical equipment, plugs, sockets or switches when your hands are wet. You might get an electric shock.
❖ Take great care when using sharp knives. Chop on a chopping board and point the knife downwards. Keep all your fingers well out of the way.
❖ Stand away from frying food or boiling water. Always ask a grown-up to do these stages for you.
❖ If you spill anything on the floor while you are cooking, wipe it up straight away, otherwise you might forget it's there and have a nasty accident later.
❖ It's a good idea to have a heatproof mat or trivet handy on the table to put hot pans straight on to.

Always use a chopping board when cutting things and keep your fingers away from the knife.

Preparing Vegetables

Most vegetables need washing and peeling before you can use them in your recipes. Some need chopping or slicing. It might be safer to get a grown-up to do this for you. If you can do it yourself, here are some common vegetables and ways to prepare them for use.

Slicing and chopping an onion To slice the onion in half, put the flat side on the chopping board and slice across the onion from side to side. If you want to chop it, try to keep the slices together and slice down from the top to the bottom.

Cut an onion in half, peel off the skin and then slice or chop it carefully with a sharp knife.

Shredding carrot Grate a carrot through the biggest holes on the grater. Or, with the help of a grown-up, you can do it in the food processor.

Shredding lettuce Use a crunchy lettuce such as an Iceberg. Remove the outer leaves and then cut the lettuce in half from the top to the bottom. Lay the flat side on your chopping board and cut across at about 12 mm ($^{1}/_{2}$ in) intervals. This will give you ribbon strips of varying lengths.

Cucumber slices and strips
Cut a length from the cucumber and peel it with a vegetable peeler if you like. Cut it in half lengthways. Put the flat side on your board. For slices, cut across the half as finely as you can. For strips, cut the cucumber half lengthways into three thick slices and then cut each slice from top to bottom into long strips.

Peel carrots with a vegetable peeler before you grate them.

Glossary

Here are some cookery words and their meanings that are used in the recipes. These will help to help make things clearer when you are following the instructions.

Beat Mix ingredients together very hard, stirring with a wooden spoon.
Boil Cook at a high heat on the stove top until the water or food bubbles fast.
Garnish Add a decoration to savoury food, to make it look more attractive.
Grease Cover baking tins or trays with a light layer of butter, margarine or oil to prevent food sticking to them when it is cooked.
Knead Squeeze, stretch and turn a mixture, usually bread dough, before baking.
Season Add just enough salt and pepper to a recipe to suit your own tastes.
Sift/sieve Shake, tap or press an ingredient through a sieve to remove any lumps and sometimes to add air.
Simmer Cook food over a low heat on the stove top, usually after it has boiled, so that it bubbles gently.
Whisk Beat very hard and fast to add air to a mixture, usually egg whites or cream, until the mixture is light, fluffy and sometimes stiff. This can be done with a hand whisk or an electric mixer.

Things to Have in the Kitchen

Kitchen shops and supermarkets are the best places to go if you want to buy cooking equipment. Here are some of the main things you will need in the kitchen to make the recipes on the following pages.

Knives for chopping and slicing should be sharp. Always have a grown-up nearby when using them. Other knives are useful for spreading or cutting soft things.
Wooden spoons for stirring, beating and mixing ingredients.
A rolling pin comes in handy for rolling pastry and dough.
Cutters and stamps made of metal or plastic are great fun for cutting out biscuits and sandwiches.
Mixing bowls for stirring, beating and mixing ingredients.
Saucepans and a frying pan for cooking on the stove top.
Weighing scales for weighing out ingredients.
A food processor or blender is handy for puréeing ingredients and mixing.

A grater is used for grating cheese and vegetables.
A can opener is used for taking the tops off cans.
A hand/balloon whisk is necessary for whisking air into things like eggs and cream.
A palette knife is ideal for spreading soft things, such as icing, and flipping pancakes.
A measuring jug is used for measuring liquid ingredients, such as milk and water.
A chopping board is needed for chopping and slicing things on. It is more hygienic than working directly on to the work surface or table top.
Measuring spoons are needed for measuring small amounts of ingredients, wet and dry. Most useful are 15 ml (1 tbsp) and 5 ml (1 tsp).
Sieves are used for getting the lumps out of ingredients.
Dish towels and oven gloves are for holding hot things, and putting dishes into and taking them out of the oven.
A trivet is used for putting hot pans on, as it protects the work surfaces.
A peeler is used for removing the outer layer from vegetables.
Salt and pepper are used to season (add flavour to) food.
Kitchen roll is handy for mopping up spillages, as well as absorbing excess grease from food.

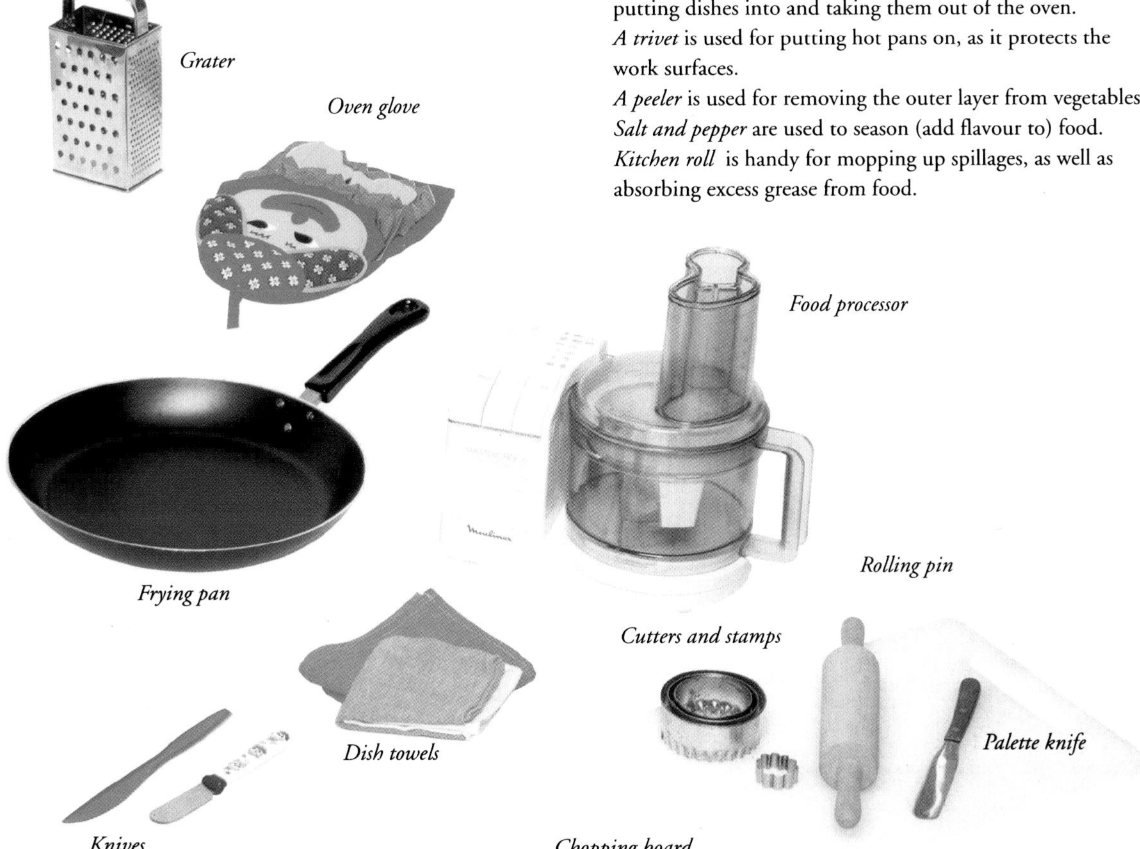

Egg Bugs and Toadstools

A good thing about this recipe is that you can make the egg bugs and toadstools up to two hours in advance and keep them in the fridge. But don't dot on the mayonnaise. This should be done at the last minute, just before you serve them. Follow what Alexandra is doing and then choose who gets an egg bug and who gets a toadstool.

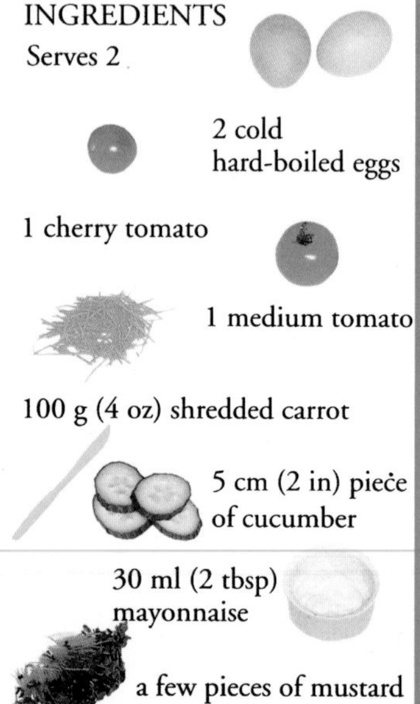

YOU WILL NEED THESE INGREDIENTS
Serves 2

- 2 cold hard-boiled eggs
- 1 cherry tomato
- 1 medium tomato
- 100 g (4 oz) shredded carrot
- 5 cm (2 in) piece of cucumber
- 30 ml (2 tbsp) mayonnaise
- a few pieces of mustard and cress, if you like

Special equipment:
cocktail stick

Handy hints:

❖ To hard boil the eggs, ask a grown-up to put them in a pan of cold water, bring to the boil and then simmer for about 10 minutes. To cool them down quickly after cooking, drain and return to the saucepan, then place them under cold running water for a few minutes.

❖ Don't bang the eggs too hard when you are trying to crack the shells to peel them. Just tap them gently on the work surface, turning them over as you tap, until the shell is cracked all over. Carefully peel away the shell, without damaging the egg white. It is easier to do this under cold running water.

1 Peel the eggs – see handy hints opposite. Cut a thin slice from the side of one of the eggs, and a slice from the pointed end of the other egg.

2 Cut the cherry tomato in half and then cut one half into four pieces to make the egg bug. Cut the big tomato in half for the toadstool.

3 To make a base on the serving dish, arrange the shredded carrot on a plate, spreading it out so that it is flat and even.

4 Peel away strips of cucumber skin and cut two slices to stand the eggs on. You can cut more for decoration.

5 Place the cucumber slices on top of the shredded carrot, then put an egg on top of each one. Don't forget that the egg bug lies down and the toadstool stands up!

6 To finish off the egg bug, use a cocktail stick to put some mayonnaise on the big end and top of the lying-down egg. Stick on half a cherry tomato for the face and two quarters on top for the spikes. Put a blob of mayonnaise on top of the toadstool egg and put a larger tomato half on top.

7 Use the cocktail stick to put tiny spots of mayonnaise all over the toadstool and to make the eyes, nose and mouth for the egg bug's face. Use mustard and cress for the egg bug's feet.

Cheese Dip with Dunks

This dish that George is making is great for a party and all your friends will love dunking their favourite crisps and vegetables into the rich and creamy dip. Watch out for dunkin' grown-ups, they are bound to want to join in all the fun! If you want to give the strips of vegetables for dunking a crinkled effect, use a crinkle-bladed knife to cut them.

YOU WILL NEED THESE INGREDIENTS

Serves 8–10

225 g (8 oz) carton of full-fat soft cheese

60 ml (4 tbsp) milk

small bunch of fresh chives

1 small carrot, peeled

For dunking: 7.5 cm (3 in) strips of cucumber, 1/2 of a red, orange and yellow pepper, seeded and cut into strips, 4 baby sweetcorn, tortilla chips

8–10 cherry tomatoes

Special equipment: scissors

Handy hints:

❖ If you prefer your dips to be less rich tasting, you could use a low-fat soft cheese instead of full-fat soft cheese.

❖ Chives are a fresh herb which look a little like grass and taste of onions. If you can't find any, you can snip the green tops off spring onions instead.

❖ You could also add celery, cauliflower florets, carrot sticks, slices of apple and radishes to your selection of dipping vegetables.

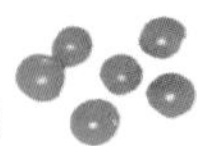

1 Spoon the full-fat soft cheese into a mixing bowl and beat it with a wooden spoon until soft and creamy.

2 Add the milk to the cheese, a little at a time. Beat the mixture well each time you pour more milk in.

3 Beat the mixture hard for about 2 minutes. If necessary, add more milk to make the dip runnier.

4 Cut the chives finely and add to the cheese mixture, saving some.

5 Grate the carrot on the smallest holes of the grater. Save some and stir the rest into the cheese mixture.

6 Spoon the mixture into a bowl and sprinkle on the remaining chives and grated carrot. Cut the cucumber, baby sweetcorn and peppers for dunking into thin strips.

7 Place the bowl of dip in the centre of a serving plate and arrange little groups of the strips for dunking around the edges. Add the tomatoes and crisps or tortilla chips and let your guests start dippin' and dunkin'.

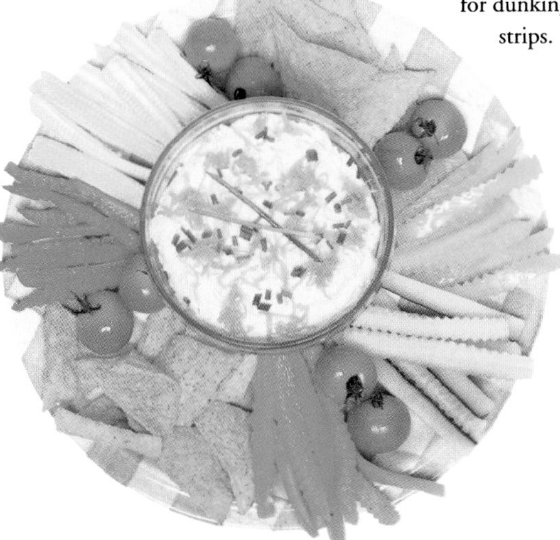

Pasta Shapes with Lentil Sauce

Tania is having great fun making this colourful and healthy dish. When you go shopping for the ingredients you need for this recipe, look out for fun pasta shapes, such as animals, vehicles or letters of the alphabet. If you can't find them, any small pasta shapes will do. This is a great recipe for your vegetarian friends because it contains no meat. Check whether the lentils need to be soaked before cooking. If so, follow the instructions on the packet.

Handy hints:

❖ Although the food processor or blender is safe to use once the lid is on properly, it is a good idea to ask a grown-up to help with the tricky stages of inserting and removing the sharp blade.

❖ Another way of serving this recipe is on a large serving platter. Put it in the centre of the table and let everyone help themselves.

YOU WILL NEED THESE INGREDIENTS

Serves 4–6

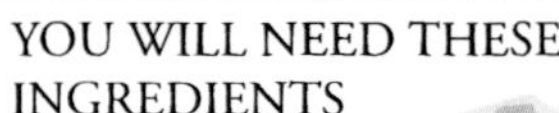

1 garlic clove, peeled,
1 vegetable stock cube

dash of olive oil

1 onion, peeled and chopped

175 g (6 oz) red lentils, washed and drained

10 ml (2 tsp) tomato purée

575 ml (1 pt) water

pepper

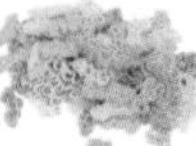

225 g (8 oz) pasta shapes

50 g (2 oz) grated Cheddar cheese

10 ml (2 tsp) chopped, fresh parsley

Special equipment:
garlic press, food processor

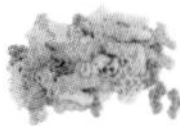

1 Place the garlic clove in the garlic press and squeeze really hard to crush it.

2 Put the crushed garlic in a saucepan. Add the olive oil, chopped onion, lentils and tomato purée. Stir well.

3 Add the water to the saucepan, pouring it over the lentils and other ingredients. Stir again to mix.

4 Crumble the stock cube into the saucepan. Season with pepper, then ask a grown-up to simmer the mixture on the stove top for about 15–20 minutes, until the lentils are cooked.

5 While the lentils are cooking, weigh the pasta shapes. Put the pasta in a saucepan and ask a grown-up to cover it in boiling water, simmer for about 8–10 minutes until tender and drain. Return the pasta to the saucepan, and replace the lid.

6 Ask a grown-up to sieve the hot lentil sauce to remove some of the liquid, leaving a thick, sloppy texture. Put this in a food processor or blender. With the lid of the food processor or blender on tight, press the button to purée the lentil mixture.

7 Ask the grown-up to remove the sharp blade from the food processor or blender. Serve the pasta on to plates and spoon the lentil sauce on top.

Garnish the finished dish with a sprinkling of grated cheese and a little chopped, fresh parsley. Delicious!

Funny Face Pizzas

Use your imagination to make your pizzas look happy or sad or just plain silly. Choose your ingredients to suit the expression you want. You can also make up your own hair styles for the pizza faces as Karina has done here, using as much or as little of the mustard and cress as you like. If you don't want a bow tie, then put the kiwi fruit in the hair as a ribbon.

Handy hints:

❖ If you prefer your pizzas slightly flatter, use small round pitta breads instead of burger buns.

❖ If you don't like or can't get mozzarella cheese, use Cheddar cheese instead. It is just as delicious but won't be so 'stringy' when you eat it.

YOU WILL NEED THESE INGREDIENTS

Serves 2

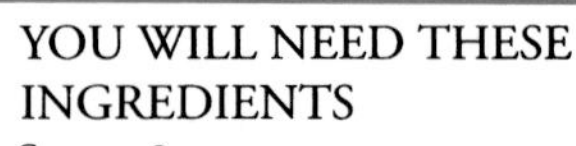

1 large burger bun, split into two halves

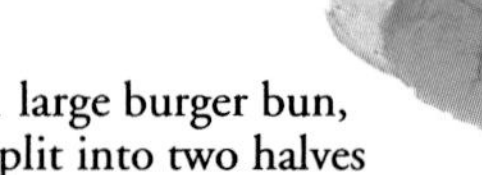

30 ml (2 tbsp) tomato and onion pizza topping from a jar

75 g (3 oz) piece mozzarella cheese

1 mushroom

1/4 green pepper, seeded and cut into thin slices

1 carton of mustard and cress

4 round slices of peeled kiwi fruit and a grape

Special equipment: rolling pin, small flower-shaped biscuit cutter

1 Put the bun halves on the work surface. Flatten them gently and evenly all over using the rolling pin.

2 Spread tomato and onion pizza topping over the top of each bun, making sure it goes close to the edges.

3 Cut the piece of mozzarella cheese into thin slices. You could ask a grown-up to do this with a sharp knife.

4 Using the flower-shaped cutter, stamp out four pieces of cheese for the pizzas' eyes. Put two in position on each of the pizza bases and set aside.

5 Wash the mushroom and slice it in half to make two noses. Position the noses on the pizza faces and press down lightly.

6 Use the green pepper slices to make mouths on the faces. Put the pizzas on the grill pan and ask a grown-up to cook them under a hot grill for about 5 minutes, until the cheese has melted a little and the buns are toasted around the edges.

7 Ask the grown-up to put the pizzas on to serving plates. Cut bunches of the cress with scissors or a knife and put them in neat piles around the top of the faces to look like hair.

Cut the kiwi rounds and grape in half and position them on the plates to make ears and bow ties.

Swimming Fish Cakes

There are lots of variations on this recipe that Joshua is making. You could serve the swimming fish on a sea of your favourite vegetable. Try a sea of peas or sweetcorn, or a mixture of both. If you particularly like modelling, make lots of tiny fish, and serve everyone with two or more. But remember to tell your grown-up helper that the small fish won't take as long to cook as the bigger ones.

Handy hints:

❖ Ask a grown-up to open the can of tuna with a can opener, as this can be dangerous and you might cut yourself.

❖ You could make the fish cake mixture and even shape the cakes up to several hours in advance, if you like. Keep them in the fridge until you are ready to cook and eat them.

YOU WILL NEED THESE INGREDIENTS

Serves 4

3 large potatoes

25 g (1 oz) butter

1 egg

dash of milk

200 g (7 oz) can tuna chunks in brine, drained

75 g (3 oz) fresh breadcrumbs

pepper

oil, for shallow frying

For the garnish:
4 peas

a few sprigs of fresh curly parsley

1/2 cucumber peeled, cut in half lengthways and very thinly sliced, 4 slices of lemon, 4 thin slices of tomato

Special equipment: vegetable peeler, potato masher, can opener

1 Peel the potatoes with the peeler, cut into small pieces and put in the saucepan. Cover with water. Ask a grown-up to boil the potatoes for about 15–20 minutes, until soft.

2 Ask a grown-up to drain the potatoes and return them to the saucepan. Place the saucepan on a trivet. Add the butter, milk and egg.

3 Put a dish towel between you and the saucepan to prevent you touching the hot saucepan. Mash the potatoes using the masher until they are smooth, with no lumps.

4 Spoon the mashed potato into a mixing bowl, making sure you scrape it all out of the saucepan. Use a wooden spoon to mix in the tuna, breadcrumbs and pepper. Place the bowl of potato mixture in the fridge to chill for about 30 minutes.

5 Take the bowl out of the fridge and wet your hands slightly. Divide the mixture into four equal portions and, working on a chopping board, mould them into fish shapes.

6 Ask a grown-up to shallow fry the fish cakes in hot oil for about 5 minutes on both sides. Drain the fish cakes on absorbent kitchen paper and transfer to the serving plate.

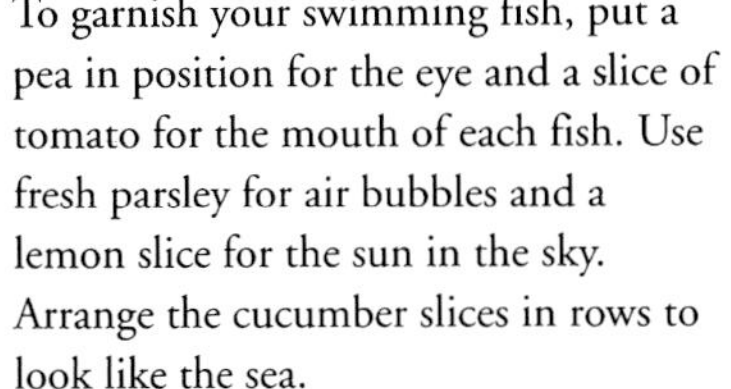

To garnish your swimming fish, put a pea in position for the eye and a slice of tomato for the mouth of each fish. Use fresh parsley for air bubbles and a lemon slice for the sun in the sky. Arrange the cucumber slices in rows to look like the sea.

Ham and Sweetcorn Roll-ups

With George's delicious recipe any day can be pancake day, so get flipping and tossing. Those with a big appetite can probably eat two roll-ups, otherwise serve one per person. If you and your grown-up helper manage to make them really thin, you might be able to make a few extra to serve sprinkled with sugar and lemon juice or with jam, for a totally pancake meal.

Handy hints:

❖ The frying pan should be very hot before cooking the pancakes, so ask a grown-up to help you.

❖ When you put the rolled pancakes on the baking sheet to heat through in the oven, make sure you space them a little apart. If you don't, they might stick together and break up when you transfer them to the serving plates.

❖ You can, if you prefer, sprinkle the pancakes with cheese and ask a grown-up to melt the cheese under the grill.

YOU WILL NEED THESE INGREDIENTS

Serves 3–6

100 g (4 oz) plain flour

small pinch of salt

1 egg

150 ml (1/4 pt) milk

olive oil, for greasing

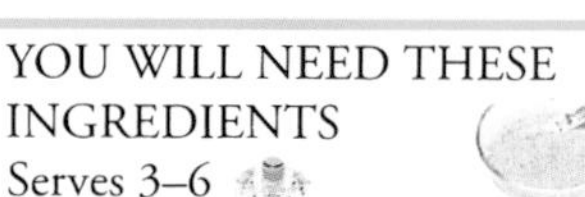

For the filling: 2 thick slices of lean(not fatty) ham

25 g (1 oz) frozen chopped spinach, thawed

50 g (2 oz) full-fat soft cheese

25 g (1 oz) canned sweetcorn, drained

pepper

100 g (4 oz) grated Cheddar cheese

Special equipment: can opener, balloon whisk, palette knife, baking sheet

1 Preheat the oven to 200°C/400°F/ Gas 6. Put the flour, salt, milk and egg into a mixing jug. Whisk together until runny and smooth.

2 Ask a grown-up to coat the bottom of a hot, oiled frying pan with the batter. Cook for 1 minute each side and flip with a palette knife.

3 Ask the grown-up to continue making the pancakes. Meanwhile cut the ham into strips and then into squares and put in a mixing bowl.

4 Add the spinach, full-fat soft cheese and sweetcorn to the mixing bowl with the ham. Season the filling mixture with a little pepper, if you like.

5 Stir the filling mixture well, until all the ingredients are mixed in. Lay the pancakes on the work surface.

6 Spoon some of the filling mixture on to each pancake, placing it along the edge nearest you. Roll the pancake around the filling and keep rolling until the filling is completely wrapped up in the pancake.

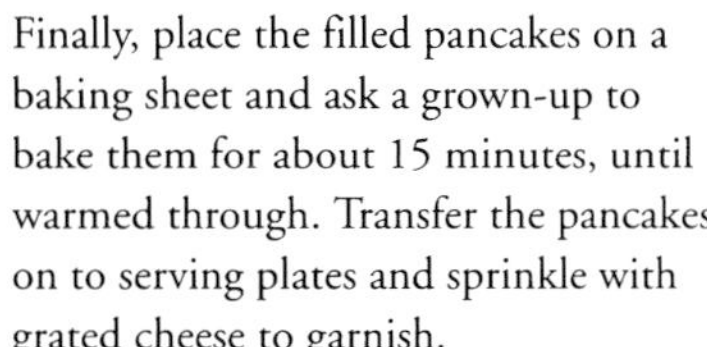

Finally, place the filled pancakes on a baking sheet and ask a grown-up to bake them for about 15 minutes, until warmed through. Transfer the pancakes on to serving plates and sprinkle with grated cheese to garnish.

Colourful Chicken Kebabs

You'll have a great time making your own kebabs and choosing what you put on them. They're brilliant to cook under the grill as Tania is doing here, or on the barbecue with the help of a grown-up. It is best to wash and prepare all the vegetables before you begin threading them on to the skewers. This will help you decide the order of ingredients and stop you getting in a muddle.

Handy hints:

❖ To make your own delicious salad dressing, mix 60 ml (4 tbsp) sunflower oil, 30 ml (2 tbsp) vinegar, 15 ml (1 tbsp) clear honey, and a dash of pepper together in a jar with a tight-fitting lid, then shake it well.

❖ Your grown-up helper may need to add a little more boiling water to the rice while it is cooking, if it looks as if it is drying out before it is cooked.

❖ The reason for soaking the skewers is to prevent them burning during grilling. If they have been soaked in water first, they will not burn so easily.

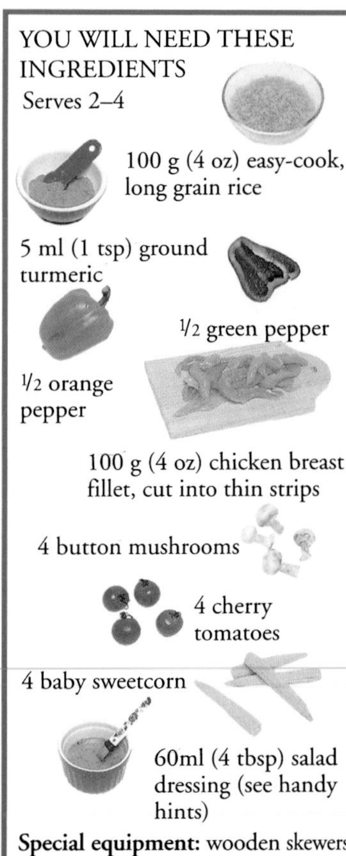

YOU WILL NEED THESE INGREDIENTS

Serves 2–4

100 g (4 oz) easy-cook, long grain rice

5 ml (1 tsp) ground turmeric

½ green pepper

½ orange pepper

100 g (4 oz) chicken breast fillet, cut into thin strips

4 button mushrooms

4 cherry tomatoes

4 baby sweetcorn

60ml (4 tbsp) salad dressing (see handy hints)

Special equipment: wooden skewers

1 Put the wooden skewers in a shallow dish of cold water. Leave them to soak in the water for about 30 minutes, then remove them and throw away the water.

2 Put the rice and turmeric in a saucepan. Ask a grown-up to cover it with boiling water, simmer for 15 minutes, then drain. Return the rice to the saucepan and cover with a lid.

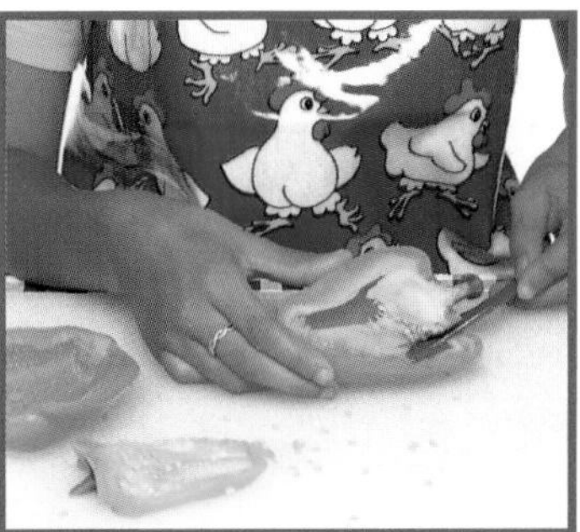

3 While the rice is cooking, put the peppers on a chopping board and cut out the white seeds and pith inside. Rinse the peppers under cold water and cut them into chunks.

4 Thread the chicken on to the skewers as shown. This will give a coiled effect when it cooks.

5 Thread the other ingredients on to the skewers in whatever order you like. Make sure you finish each one with a piece of baby sweet-corn, pushing the skewer only a little way in.

6 Put the kebabs on the grill pan and drizzle over some of the salad dressing. Ask a grown-up to put the kebabs under a hot grill for about 5 minutes, then to turn them over and continue grilling for another 5 minutes, until the chicken is cooked.

7 Just before the kebabs are cooked, put some rice on to the serving plates and spread it out.

Arrange the kebabs on the rice and they are ready to serve.

Crazy Popcorn

This multi-coloured cheesy mixture that Andreas is making will make your party the talk of the town. Have fun choosing your own colours for the popcorn and cheese. If you can't get or don't like Red Leicester or Sage Derby, use yellow Cheddar cheese instead. And if you haven't got a large enough container to hold all of the popcorn, or have a lot of guests who are going to want to eat at once, then fill two containers instead.

Handy hints:

❖ You must use powdered food colouring as liquid colouring will turn the popcorn soggy. You will find the powdered kind in specialist cake decorating shops.

❖ You can buy microwave popcorn which is especially for cooking in the microwave. Follow the instructions on the packet for cooking (ask a grown-up to operate the microwave) and colour it as directed in steps 4–6.

YOU WILL NEED THESE INGREDIENTS
Serves 10–15

- 15 ml (1 tbsp) vegetable oil
- 175 g (6 oz) popcorn kernels
- green, red and blue powdered food colourings
- 50 g (2 oz) grated Red Leicester cheese
- 50 g (2 oz) grated Sage Derby cheese

Special equipment: 3 large plastic bags

1 Put the vegetable oil in a large saucepan. Pour in the popcorn kernels and stir with a wooden spoon to coat them all in the oil.

2 Place the lid on the saucepan and ask a grown-up to heat the popcorn on the stove top, gently, for about 5 minutes, until you hear the popcorn starting to pop. Do not remove the lid.

3 When the popping noises have slowed down and you hardly hear any popping at all, ask the grown-up to put the saucepan on a trivet on the table. You can now remove the lid.

4 Put small amounts of popcorn in each plastic bag. The bags should be see-through so you can see the colour of the popcorn changing when you add the colour.

5 Use a tiny spoon to add a small amount of food colouring to each of the bags of popcorn. You can choose what colours you use and how much popcorn you want to make a particular colour.

6 Close the bag and hold it tightly in one hand. Shake the bag and tap it with the other hand, tossing the popcorn inside the bag to coat it evenly in the colouring. As you colour each batch, tip it into a large bowl.

7 When all the popcorn is coloured, add the grated cheese.

Wash your hands, then carefully toss the mixture together evenly. Try not to tip it over the sides of the container.

Frozen Banana Lollies

These lollies are great for a summer party. But if you haven't got any party plans, just make a batch of lollies and freeze them all for yourself. They will keep in the freezer, in sealed bags, for about a month. Sophie has coated her lollies with coconut, but if you don't like it, choose your own coating. Try toasted, chopped nuts or crumbled chocolate flake bars. They are all delicious!

Handy hints:

❖ You can buy lolly sticks in most hardware shops and supermarkets, but if you want to be crafty and environmentally friendly collect up your own and your friends' used ones. Wash and dry them and they'll be as good as new!

❖ Don't peel the bananas too early, otherwise they will start to go brown and mushy.

YOU WILL NEED THESE INGREDIENTS
Serves 8

red, blue and green food colourings (powdered or liquid)

100 g (4 oz) desiccated coconut

8 small bananas

a little maple syrup

Special equipment: 8 lolly sticks, pastry brush, baking sheet, clear film

1 Divide the coconut into three small bowls and add a small amount of food colouring to each. Stir well, until the coconut is evenly coloured.

2 Pour the red, blue and green coloured coconut on to separate plates and spread it out evenly.

3 Peel the bananas and cut a small piece off one end of each one, to make it straight. Carefully press a lolly stick into the straight end of each banana, taking care not to push the stick in too far, as it might break through the side.

4 Pour some maple syrup into a bowl. Holding the lolly stick and using a pastry brush, brush an even coating of maple syrup over each banana. Put on a plate when coated.

5 Still holding the lolly sticks, dip and roll the bananas in the coloured coconut until they are coated evenly.

6 Lay the bananas on a baking sheet covered with clear film. The bananas must not touch. Freeze for 4 hours.

Take the banana lollies off the baking sheet and arrange on a serving plate. Ideally you should wait about 15 minutes, to let the bananas soften a little before you eat them.

Cut-out Cookies

Any cutter, any shape and any size is good for this recipe. You can also use chocolate sugar strands or flaked chocolate, or even chopped, coloured glacé cherries as decoration. Whatever you choose, be sure to make lots as Alex is doing, because these yummy biscuits will certainly get eaten up very quickly. It's a good idea to have a second baking sheet and a second serving plate handy!

YOU WILL NEED THESE INGREDIENTS

Serves 10–12

100 g (4 oz) butter or margarine, softened, plus a little extra for greasing

100 g (4 oz) caster sugar

1 egg, beaten

few drops of vanilla essence

225 g (8 oz) plain flour, sifted, plus extra for sprinkling

For the topping: 100 g (4 oz) icing sugar

30–45 ml (2–3 tbsp) coloured sugar strands (hundreds and thousands)

Special equipment: rolling pin, scissors, greaseproof paper, baking tray, biscuit cutters in different shapes, wire cooling rack

Handy hints:

❖ To save your energy, ask a grown-up to help you use an electric hand mixer to make the dough, or you could make it in a food processor.

❖ When you have cut out the first lot of biscuits from the rolled out dough, gather up all the trimmings and roll them out again. Now you can cut out another lot of biscuits. Keep doing this until all the biscuit dough is used up.

❖ Before you start to drizzle the icing over the biscuits, put a big sheet of greaseproof paper under the wire rack. This will catch all the drips of icing and when you are finished, you just gather up the paper and throw it away.

1 Preheat the oven to 200°C/400°F/ Gas 6. Put the butter and sugar in a mixing bowl and beat with a wooden spoon, until light and fluffy.

2 Add the egg and a few drops of vanilla essence and keep beating until the mixture is smooth.

3 Carefully stir in the flour, mixing well, until a stiff dough starts to form in the bowl.

4 Flour the board and your hands and knead the dough until smooth. Sprinkle more flour and roll out the dough until quite thin. Keep your rolling pin well floured to stop it sticking to the dough.

5 Put a greased sheet of greaseproof paper on to a greased baking tray. Using the cutters, cut out the biscuit shapes and place them on the baking tray. Ask a grown-up to bake the biscuits for 10 minutes.

6 Ask a grown-up to put the biscuits on a wire rack to cool. Put the icing sugar in a bowl and stir in about 15 ml (1 tbsp) of cold water. Mix well.

7 Use a teaspoon to drizzle the icing over the biscuits.

Sprinkle the coloured sugar strands over the biscuits, to decorate. Put the finished biscuits on a plate. Do not pile them up or they will stick. Leave the biscuits for about 30 minutes to let the icing set, then serve.

Cake-cream Cones

These cones that Alex, Sophie and Otis are eating will fool everybody. If you put them on the table with lots of decorations around them, all your guests will think they're real ice-cream.

YOU WILL NEED THESE INGREDIENTS

Serves 3

- 100 g (4 oz) fondant moulding icing
- 175 g (6 oz) icing sugar
- 75 g (3 oz) butter or margarine, softened
- 30–45 ml (2–3 tbsp) milk
- green and pink food colourings, 10 ml (2 tsp) cocoa
- 3 small fairy cakes
- coloured sugar strands, chocolate sugar strands
- 3 ice-cream cones
- chocolate flake bars and wafers, to decorate

Special equipment: egg boxes (one large or two small), foil, pencil

Handy hints:

❖ Make sure you don't press the cakes too firmly into the cones, otherwise the cones might break.

❖ Use separate knives for the different icing colours, otherwise you'll mix the colours and they will look messy.

❖The cake-cream cones can be made up to 3 hours in advance and kept in the fridge.

1 To make holders for the cones, turn the egg boxes upside-down. Press the fondant icing into the hollows, shaping a hole to support the bottom of the cones.

2 Cover the boxes in foil, making sure the joins are underneath. Place on the work surface, with the filled hollows on top. Feel the hollows, then pierce the foil with a pencil.

3 To make butter icing, put the icing sugar in a mixing bowl with the butter or margarine and the milk. Use a wooden spoon to mix the icing until it is smooth and creamy.

4 Divide the butter icing into three bowls. Add a speck of food colouring to two bowls and the cocoa to the third. Mix until evenly coloured.

5 Remove any paper from the bottom of the fairy cakes. Gently press a cake into the top of a cone, twisting it slightly until it stays in. Repeat with the other cakes and cones.

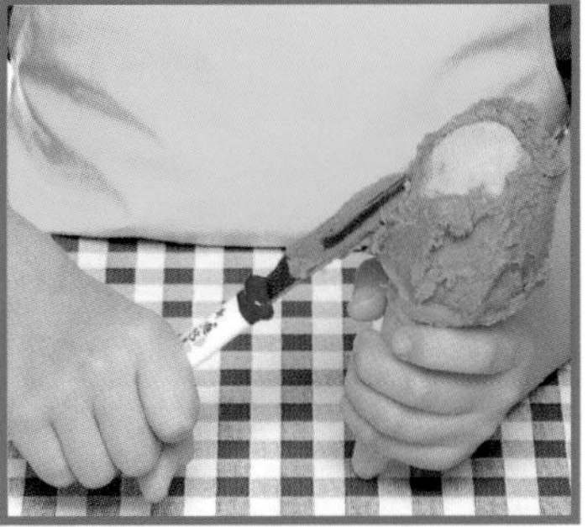

6 Spread the icing on to the cake, working from the top downwards. Put the cone in the stand to hold it safely while you coat the rest.

7 Sprinkle with sugar strands, and lightly press chocolate flake bars and wafers into the cakes.

Jelly Pond

By moulding fondant icing just like play-dough, you can be really creative with this recipe and make your own monsters for a lake or pond scene. Follow what Sophie is doing to see how. Try water snakes, ducks, waterlilies, fish and frogs. Your lake or pond will be even more realistic if you add a spot of green food colouring to the jelly while you are dissolving it.

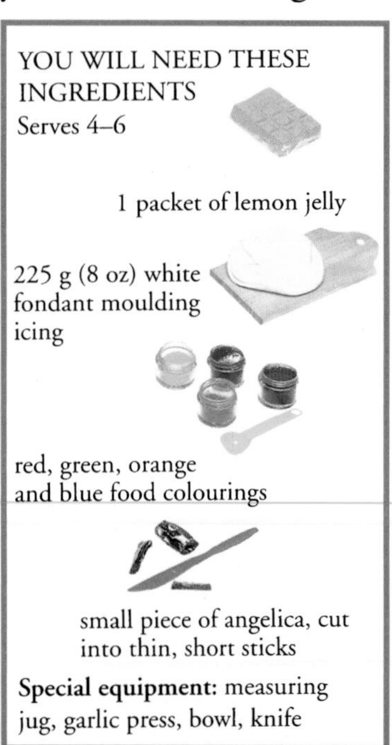

YOU WILL NEED THESE INGREDIENTS
Serves 4–6

1 packet of lemon jelly

225 g (8 oz) white fondant moulding icing

red, green, orange and blue food colourings

small piece of angelica, cut into thin, short sticks

Special equipment: measuring jug, garlic press, bowl, knife

Handy hints:

❖ It is a good idea to wear rubber gloves when you are colouring the fondant icing, otherwise your hands will get coloured too.

❖ The easiest way to get the colour of the icing even is to roll it out into a sausage shape. bring the two ends of the sausage together and start rolling out a new sausage. Carry on in this way until you are happy with the colour.

❖ Put the chopped jelly into the 'creature' bowl at the very last minute before serving, as the 'wet' jelly will make the fondant creatures start to leak some of their colour.

1 Break the jelly into small pieces and put it in the mixing jug.

2 With a grown-up, make the jelly according to the packet instructions. Put in the fridge to set.

3 Divide the fondant icing into four portions. Add a speck of food colouring to each, then roll and knead it in.

4 Shape your pond creatures and waterlilies, and press the angelica sticks into a blob of icing for the reeds. Put the shapes for the surface on a plate to dry.

5 To decorate the inside of the jelly bowl, press your underwater creatures to the glass on the inside. Brush a little water on to the creatures' fronts to help them stick better.

6 To make the pond grass, take a small piece of green fondant icing and put it inside a garlic press. Squeeze hard with two hands and watch the grass come out. Use a knife to cut off the grass and put it on a plate to dry and harden.

7 When the jelly is set, use a knife to stir and chop the jelly into tiny pieces. Spoon the jelly into the bowl, taking care not to knock the creatures.

Position all the shapes for the surface of the pond. Make a little scene with the ducks swimming in the pond with the waterlilies and grass all around. Serve immediately.

Painting Fun

Introduction

Before you begin, make sure you have everything you will need.

Painting is fun, but painting does not necessarily mean standing at an easel painting a picture of what you can see - although you can do that too if you want. The projects in this chapter show you how to have lots of fun with different sorts of paints on lots of different surfaces.

None of the projects in this section is difficult, although there are a few things you should do before you begin.

1 Carefully read through the list of materials you will need.

2 Read through the instructions and look at the photographs so that you have a clear idea of what you will be doing.

3 Assemble everything you need before you start on a project.

4 Some of the projects are messy and some aren't, but it is always a good idea to cover your work surface with newspaper, scrap paper or a piece of material. If you are working on a wipe-clean surface and doing one of the less messy projects, this is not essential, but it is a good idea to get into the habit.

5 Wear an old shirt or a painting overall and, when you have finished, always clear away everything you have used.

Wear an old shirt or painting overall

You may not want a grown-up around while you are being creative, but there are some things that you will need help with. Some of the projects call for sharp scissors and you may prefer a grown-up to do the cutting for you. Some types of card are easier to cut with a craft knife. These knives are very sharp and are quite tricky to use, so always get a grown-up to do any cutting with a craft knife. Always ask a grown-up to mix and thin oil paints for you as well. You can mix other kinds of paint such as water colour and poster paint yourself.

Colour mixing

You don't need a lot of different coloured paints to do the projects. It is easy to mix lots of colours as long as you have the three primary colours of red, blue and yellow.

Red + Blue = Purple
Red + Yellow = Orange
Blue + Yellow = Green

You can make different sorts of browns by mixing purple and orange, orange and green and purple and green.

If you start off with red, yellow and blue and, perhaps, white (with which you can make pink and pale shades of the other colours), you can easily add more colours as your pocket money allows.

You will also need black paint for some of the projects so check before you begin.

Be careful when you use scissors.

Types of paint

Each type of paint is different and takes different times to dry. Always read the instructions on the pot or tube before you start.

Acrylic paint This is rubber-based, flat and opaque so that it covers large areas easily but does not have the shine of oil paint or the texture of water-based paint.

Fabric paint Fabric paint is necessary for painting or printing on textiles. Each type is different so read the instructions carefully and clean your brushes accordingly.

Oil paints These are very greasy and must be handled with care. Ask a grown-up to mix white spirit or turpentine with oil colours to thin them. Ask an adult to clean your brushes with white spirit or turpentine.

Poster paint This is water-based and is available either as a powder to be mixed with water, or ready-mixed.

Coloured inks These are available in a wide variety of colours. If you can't find any, or can't get a colour you want, you can use food colourings instead. Always make sure they are washable.

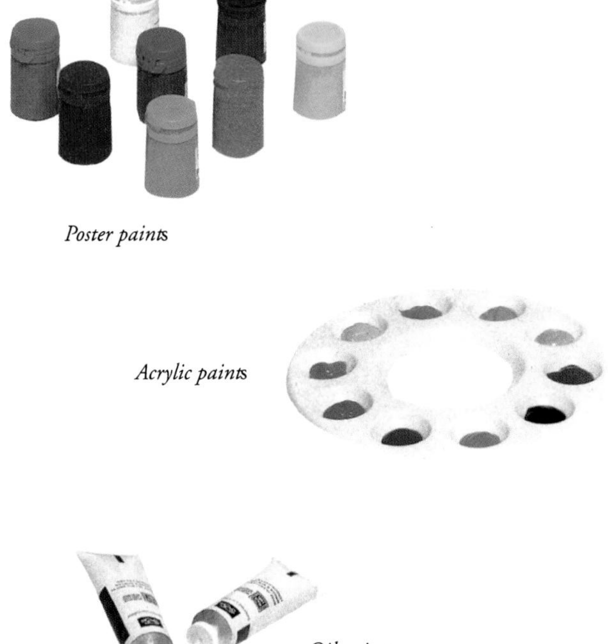

Poster paints

Acrylic paints

Oil paints

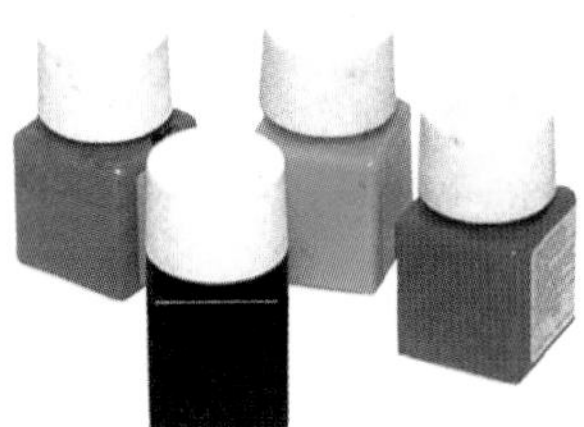

Fabric paints

Coloured inks

Star and Moon Stencilled Gift Wrap

If you have always wanted to make your own special gift wrap and matching greetings cards, now is your chance.

The moon and star shapes that Kirsty is stencilling are simple. She is only using gold paint, but you can use lots of different colours. If you want to stencil with lots of colours, use a different sponge for each colour and let each colour dry thoroughly before you add the next.

Stencilling technique

Stencilling is great fun and easy to do. For the best results, the paint needs to be thick, so don't mix any water with it. Do not use too much paint on the sponge, and apply it with a light dabbing movement. You can always go over it again to add more colour.

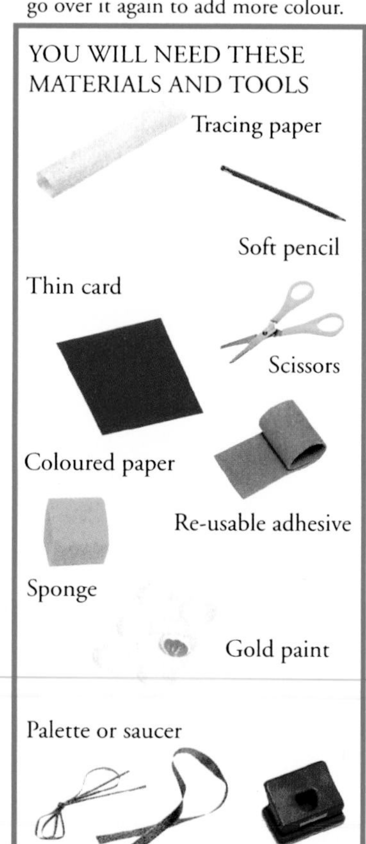

1 Using a soft pencil, trace the star and moon templates from the front of the book on to card.

2 Use the scissors to make a hole in the middle of the design, and then cut towards the shape. You should have three different stencils.

3 Place the stencils on the coloured paper. Secure them with re-usable adhesive. Dab the sponge in the gold paint and sponge over the stencils.

4 Let the paint dry, then move the stencils to another space on the paper and repeat. Continue until you have covered the whole sheet with gold moons and stars.

5 When the paint is completely dry, use the sheet of paper to wrap up a present. To make the gift extremely luxurious, add a gold ribbon and tie a bow.

6 Cut out a small piece of paper and stencil it in the same way to make a gift tag for the present. Using a hole puncher, make a hole in the corner and slip a piece of gold ribbon through.

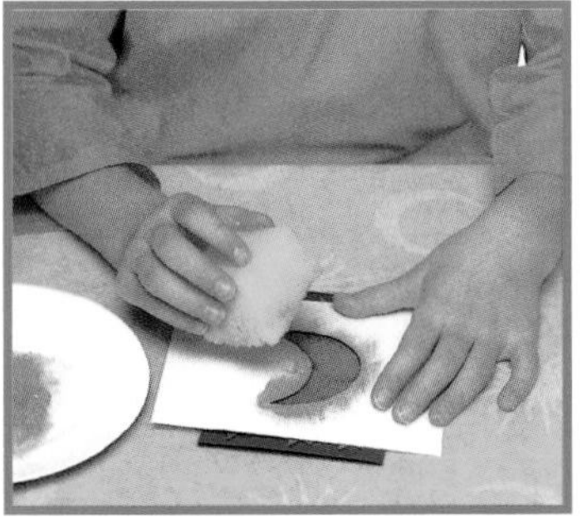

7 Here a moon is being stencilled on to a card for a different design.

A unique set of gift wrap for a very special present.

Christmas Crackers

Your family and friends will be delighted when you present them with these pretty crackers at the Christmas meal or at a party. You must plan this project in advance as you need a cardboard tube for each cracker.

Jessica is using traditional Christmas shapes and colours in her design, but you could choose your own instead.

Presents galore

If you are feeling generous you could also put a little gift inside each cracker, and perhaps write a joke to go inside as well. This should be done in step 7, when you have closed only one end of the cracker.

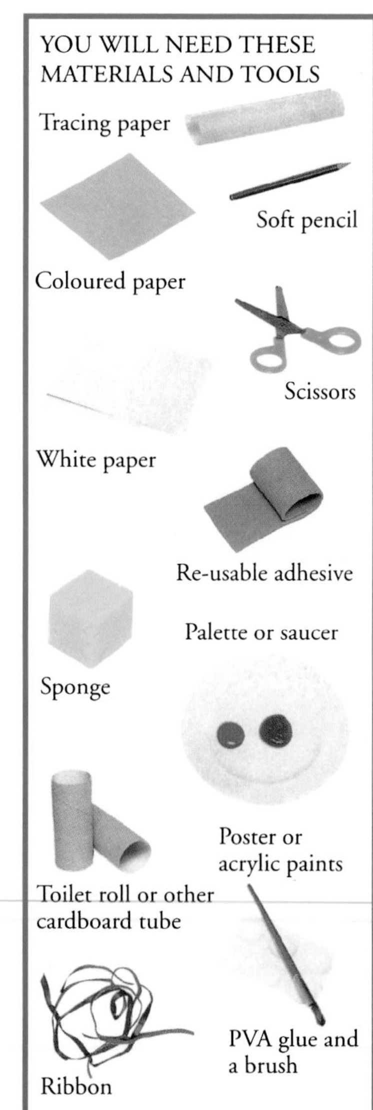

1 Trace the holly leaf and Christmas tree templates from the front of the book on to coloured paper and cut them out.

2 Scatter the shapes over the white paper, sticking them down with a piece of re-usable adhesive. Your pattern can be regular or random.

3 Dab the sponge into one of the paints. Wipe off any excess on the side of the palette. Sponge over all the shapes on the paper.

4 Rinse the sponge out under the tap, squeezing it as dry as you can. Dab it in the second paint colour and sponge over the shapes again.

5 When the sheet of paper is completely dry, gently peel the templates away to reveal a colourful Christmas design. Place it face down on your work surface.

6 Brush glue all over the cardboard tube. Place it halfway along one edge of the sheet of paper. Carefully roll the paper around the tube. Glue the edge down.

7 Feel where the ends of the tube are and pinch in the paper there. Finally, cut triangles from the ends of the paper and add ribbons.

The ideal table decoration for a Christmas party.

Painted Stones Caterpillar

If you are unable to get to the seaside to collect the pebbles, make some from self-hardening clay which can be bought in craft and hobby shops. When you have painted the pebbles with pictures or numbers, you will have hours of fun with them. Joshua is being clever with his pebbles by painting a caterpillar on one side and numbers and mathematical signs on the other, so that he can practise his sums and see how brainy he is.

Painting tips

You will find it easier to paint half of all the stones, then go back and finish them off. In this way, you won't be trying to hold an area of stone that is already wet.

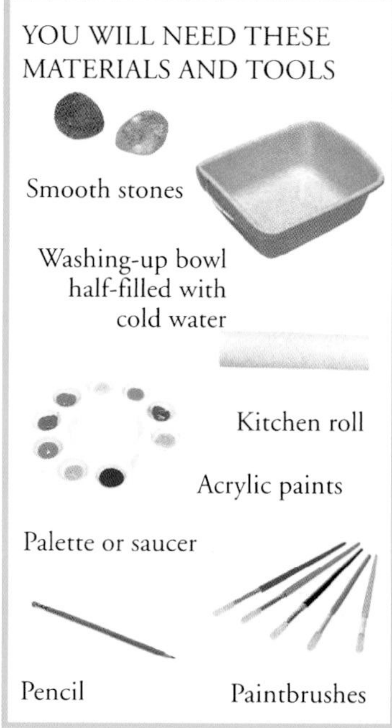

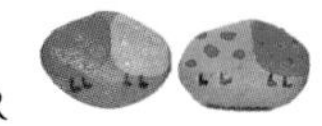

1 Wash the stones in the washing-up bowl and dry them well with kitchen roll. Use as many as you like.

2 Paint the stones. Try to make each one a different colour. Leave them on your work surface until they are completely dry.

3 Arrange the stones in a long line with the biggest at one end and the smallest at the other. Draw a caterpillar design on them.

4 Paint the caterpillar's body using different colours. Use black, brown or another dark colour for its feet.

5 Decorate each part of its body with different coloured spots. You can vary the size of the spots too.

6 Either use a new set of painted stones, or wait until the caterpillar is dry and turn the stones over. Paint in some figures and mathematical symbols.

7 Impress your family and friends by showing them how clever you are.

None of your papers will blow away when the caterpillar is weighing them down.

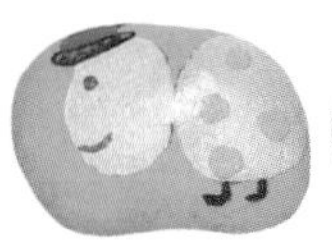
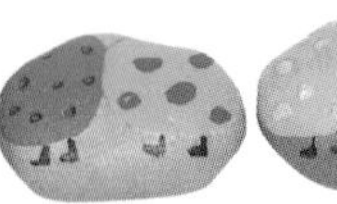
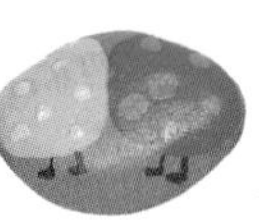
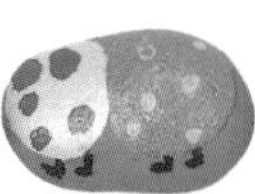

Butterfly Blottography Box

Blottography prints are easy to do and the results are always an exciting surprise. This technique is at least 100 years old. Alice is using her prints to brighten up a storage box, but you could also stick a blottography shape to a tray and varnish over it – ask a grown-up to help with this.

Blottography technique
Be sure to use a large piece of paper for your prints so that paint doesn't ooze out over everything and make a mess.

YOU WILL NEED THESE MATERIALS AND TOOLS

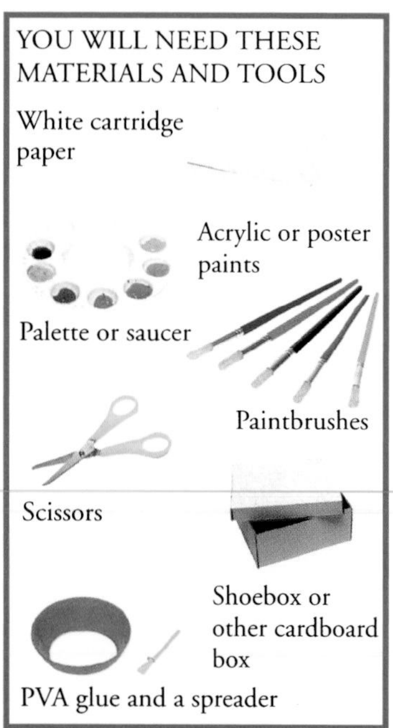

White cartridge paper
Acrylic or poster paints
Palette or saucer
Paintbrushes
Scissors
Shoebox or other cardboard box
PVA glue and a spreader

1 Make sure that your sheet of paper is longer than it is wide. Fold it in half lengthways.

2 Open up the paper and dab generous spots of paint on one side only. Use as many different colours as you like, but don't get it *too* runny.

3 Fold the paper in half once again, bringing the dry side over on to the wet side. Carefully smooth it down with your hand.

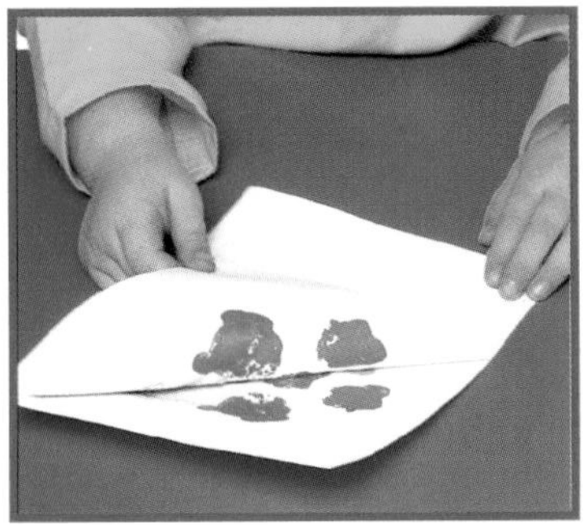

4 Open up the paper and admire the colourful, symmetrical pattern you have created on both sides of the paper. Leave it to dry thoroughly.

5 Make some more patterns of different sizes and using different colour combinations in the same way. Try using all pale colours or all dark. Cut them out when they are dry.

6 Paint the cardboard box inside and out. If you are using a shoe-box, or any other box that was coloured to start with, you will find it easier to cover the existing colour if you use acrylic paint. Poster paint is fine if your box is white to start with.

7 When the box is completely dry, glue your patterns to the box.

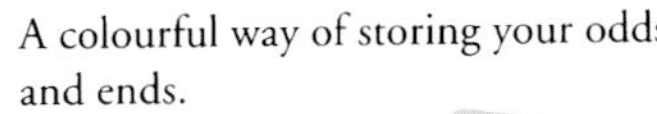

A colourful way of storing your odds and ends.

Vegetable-print T-shirts

Sasha is using different colours and all sorts of vegetables on a white T-shirt. If you don't want to make an all-over design, you could print just in the centre of the shirt. For a more intricate design, use smaller vegetables such as tiny onions cut in half, or a baby carrot. Use different sizes of mushroom too.

Design rules

If you are not sure about a design, print it on paper first to get a good idea of how it will look when it is on the T-shirt. Once it is on the T-shirt it will be difficult to remove or change.

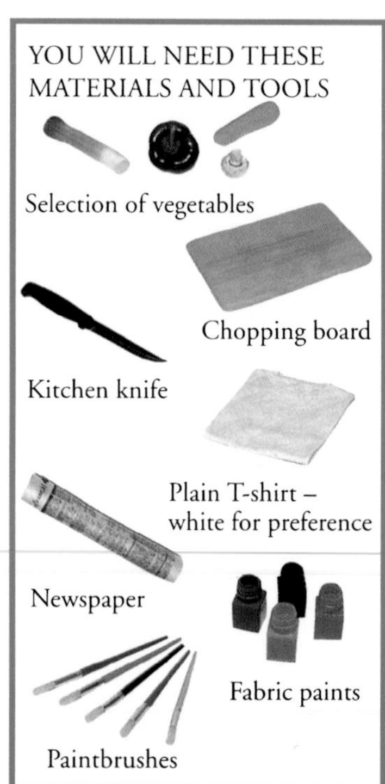

1 Choose vegetables that will make interesting prints of different sizes, such as a stick of celery (semi-circle), carrot (circle), pepper (crinkly circle), mushroom and leek.

2 Ask a grown-up to cut up the vegetables for you. Make sure that they cut round the pepper – you don't want a strip – and leave the stalk on the mushroom slice.

3 Lay the T-shirt flat and front side up on your work surface. Put some newspapers inside so that your design does not go through to the back of the T-shirt.

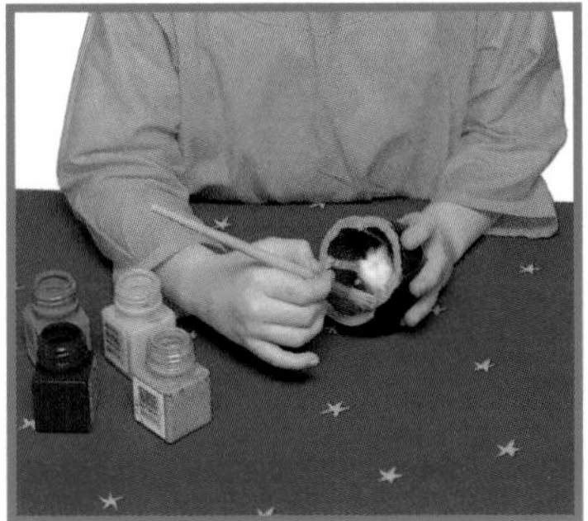

4 Paint the edge of the pepper with fabric paint. Make sure that the edge is covered with paint but don't get it too wet or it might smudge.

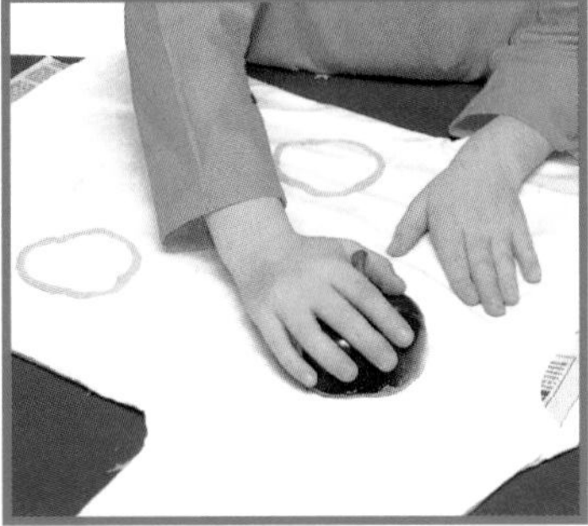

5 Print the pepper on to the T-shirt. Try to hold it still while it is in contact with the shirt so that the edges don't blur. You may need to repaint it between prints.

6 Paint the end of the carrot with fabric paint and use it to print in the centre of and all around the pepper prints. Try not to print over another print as the colours may run.

7 Use all the other vegetables in the same way, choosing different colours and building up an interesting design. Leave the T-shirt to dry.

Everyone will want to know where you got your designer T-shirt.

Spotty Dog-bone Picture Frame

Frame a picture of your pet with one of these fun frames. Nicholas is using a colourful photograph of his dog. Or you could frame your paintings and put on an exhibition of your works of art.

Framing

If you are making a frame for one of your favourite pictures then you will need to make sure that the hole in the middle of your frame is cut to the right size. Measure your picture before you begin and then make the hole slightly smaller than this. If the hole is too big the backing sheet will show through.

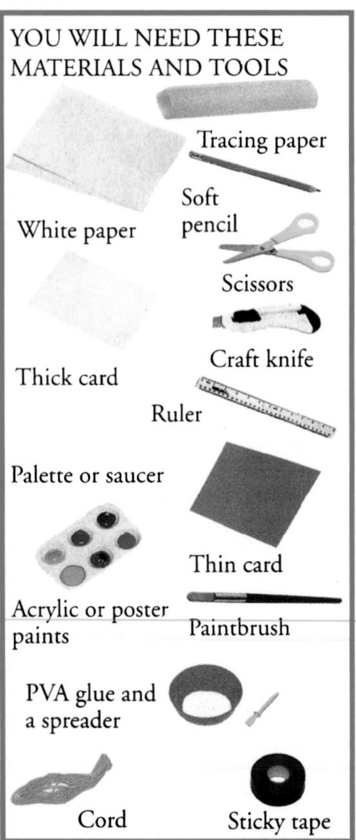

1 Using a soft pencil, trace the dog-bone template from the beginning of the book on to white paper six times.

2 Cut out the dog bone shapes using the scissors. Take care as you cut round the curves so that you get six even-looking bones.

3 Paint each bone. When the background colour has dried, paint on some spots. Don't choose very bright colours for either the bones or spots.

4 Ask a grown-up to cut the card for the frame, and to cut out the centre. Cut a piece of thin card slightly larger than the hole in the centre of the frame.

5 Paint the frame a plain colour that will look attractive with your bones and with the photograph you intend to display in the frame. Leave it to dry.

6 Glue the bones on to the frame. Push out any air bubbles with your fingers. If you have used too much glue, let it dry then peel it off.

7 Stick a loop of cord to the top of the back of the frame. Then attach the backing card with tape, leaving the top free so that you can slip your photograph inside.

A special frame for a special photograph.

Bubble-printed Notebook

Food colouring

If you can't find coloured inks you could use food colourings instead. You may find there are not as many different colours and most of them will be paler than some inks but you will still get good results.

It is a good idea to do bubble printing as close to the kitchen sink as you can since you need lots of water and washing-up liquid to make fluffy bubbles. Don't lift a full bowl of water yourself – ask a grown-up to do it.

The secret of bubble printing is not to pour in too many colours at once. Remember you can always add more if you don't like the first sheet.

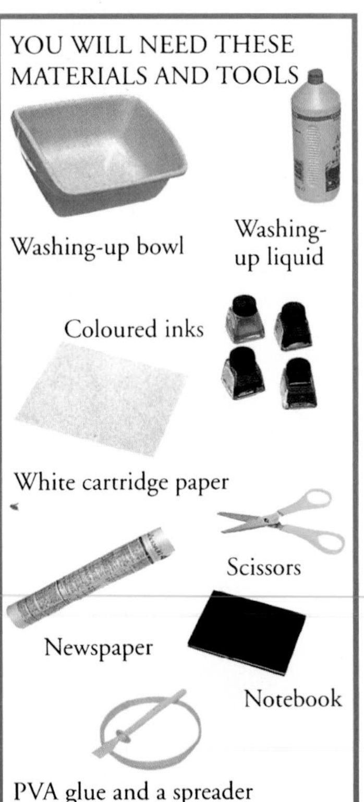

1 Squeeze a generous amount of washing-up liquid into the washing-up bowl.

2 Add cold water and swish it around so that there are plenty of bubbles in the bowl.

3 Gradually dribble different coloured inks on to the surface of the bubbles.

4 Cut a piece of cartridge paper about the same size as the bowl. Gently lay the paper on the surface of the coloured bubbles.

5 Carefully remove the paper from the bowl and place it face up on sheets of newspaper to dry.

6 If the paper dries crinkly, flatten it by placing it in between some heavy books and leaving it overnight.

7 Open the notebook and cut the paper, adding an extra 2.5 cm (1 in) all around. Cut across the corners and cut a V at the top and bottom of the spine. Glue the extra inside the cover.

Decorate your notebooks, diary and address book with your individual bubble-printed papers.

Finger-painted Flowers

These wild and colourful flowers brighten up any room and don't even need to be watered. The great thing about making your own flowers is that you can choose which colours you want them to be and if you paint the backs and fronts differently, you can turn them round when you get bored.

Flower arranging

To make a beautiful flower arrangement put a piece of florist's foam or crumpled newspaper in the bottom of the vase. This will help to keep the flowers upright.

YOU WILL NEED THESE MATERIALS AND TOOLS

- Tracing paper
- Soft pencil
- Thick coloured papers
- Scissors
- Palette or saucer
- Acrylic or poster paints
- PVA glue and a brush
- Thin paintbrush
- Sticky tape
- Garden sticks

1 Using a soft pencil, trace the flower, circle and leaf templates from the front of the book on to coloured paper.

2 Using the scissors, cut out the shapes. You will need two matching flower shapes, two circles and two leaf shapes for each flower.

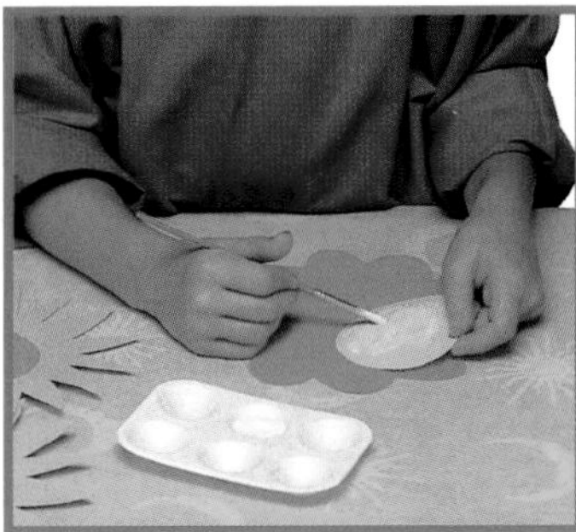

3 Glue a circle of coloured paper on to the centre of each flower. Make sure that the flowers and circles are different colours.

4 Dip your fingers one at a time into the paint and then press them on to your flowers. Use a different finger for each colour. Cover the flowers with finger prints.

5 Leave the flowers to dry thoroughly while you make the leaves. Finger paint the leaf shapes with different green paints and paint a fine line of colour down the centre of each one to make the vein. Leave them to dry.

6 Use a piece of sticky tape to attach a garden stick to the back of a flower. Glue a matching flower on to the back and gently press it down to make sure that it sticks.

7 Attach the back of one leaf to the garden stick with sticky tape and glue a matching leaf to the back of it.

Everlasting flowers brighten up the dullest day

Wooden-spoon Puppets

Tania and Joshua are having fun painting their puppets. Create your own theatre characters on wooden spoons then put on a show to impress the grown-ups. Hide behind the sofa and use its back as the stage. Try to give all the characters different voices too.

Drying tip

Stand the spoons in a jam jar while the wet heads dry. To dry the handles, stand the heads in a big lump of modelling clay.

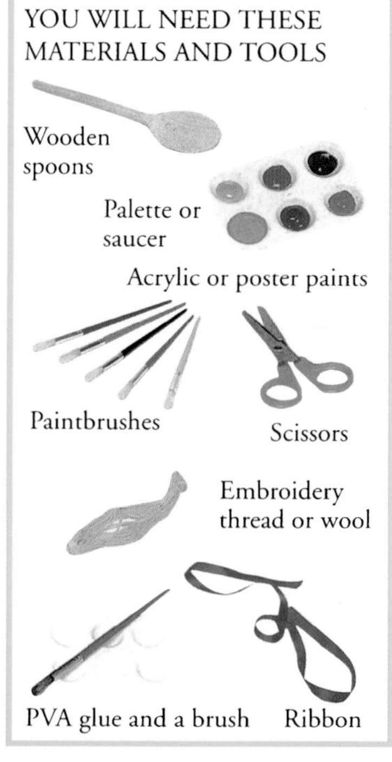

1 Paint the head of the spoon and leave it to dry.

2 Paint the handle of the spoon using a different colour and leave it to dry.

3 Decorate the handle with spots, stripes, collar, buttons or a bow tie.

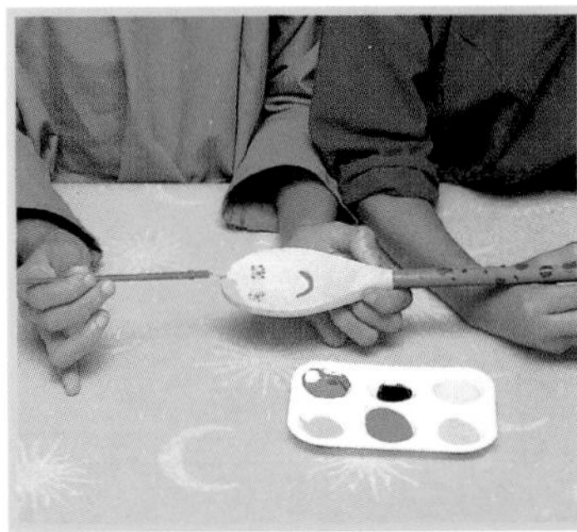

4 Paint a face on to the head of the spoon and leave to dry. If you are making a man puppet, paint on some hair or, if you prefer, leave him bald.

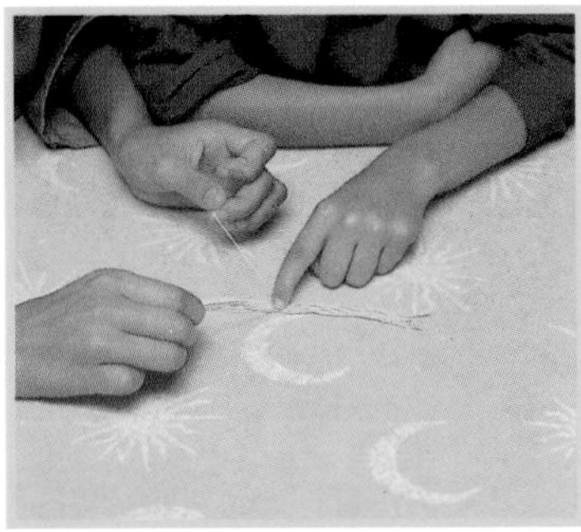

5 If you are making a lady, cut about 15 strands of embroidery thread all the same length. Tie a shorter piece around the middle of them to keep them together.

6 Glue the hair on to the top of the lady's head and leave it to dry. Try not to use too much glue. If you do, let it dry, then peel off the excess with your fingers.

7 Tie the ribbon into a bow and glue it on to the hair.

Make your own theatre and impress your friends with your own plays.

Wax-resist Badges

Add a personal touch to a favourite outfit with a badge made with the magical technique of wax resist. Alice is using wax crayons, which give a colourful result, but the technique also works in black and white if you use a candle to draw your design. Remember that as your badge is made out of card, you can't wear it outside in the rain.

Age badges

A variation on this idea is to make an age badge for you or a friend, or your little brother or sister. Vary the colours to suit the personality of the wearer.

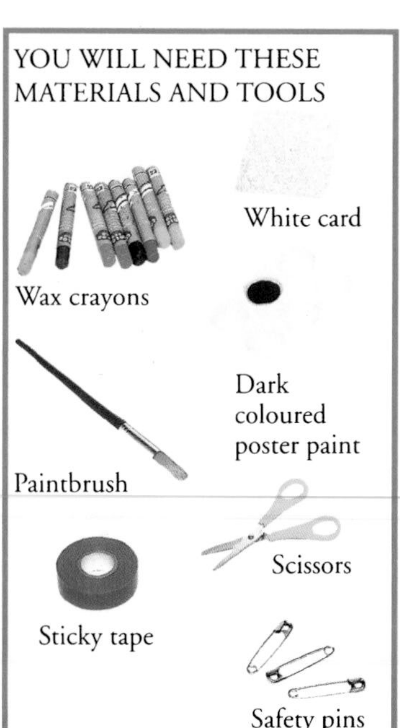

1 Collect together all the materials you will need for the project before you begin.

2 Draw a flowerpot shape on to the card with wax crayons. The brighter the colours, the more attractive the finished badge will be.

3 Add a cactus in a different colour, then decorate the pot and cactus using as many colours as you like.

4 Paint over your wax drawing with poster paint. Don't worry about the edges too much as you are going to cut out the picture later.

5 When the paint is completely dry, you should still be able to see your wax drawing. Cut around the edge of the cactus and flowerpot.

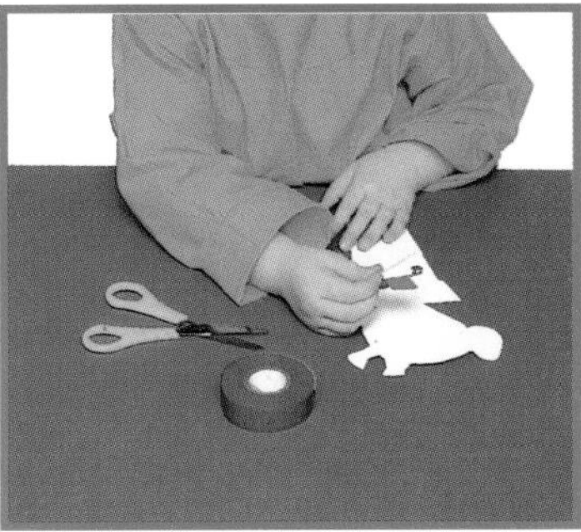

6 Turn the badge over. Cut a small piece of sticky tape and use it to attach the safety pin to the middle of the badge.

It's obvious who is on your team with these colourful badges.

Flowery Glass

These jolly flowers will liven up any glass frame. You could also use lots of smaller flower stickers to decorate a jam jar to use as a pencil pot or flower vase.

Aaron is decorating a frame but you can stick the flowers on the inside of a real window as in step 7.

Handy hints

Plastic film is quite difficult to smooth down without getting air bubbles trapped. The trick is to work slowly, peeling off a bit of backing and smoothing as you go.

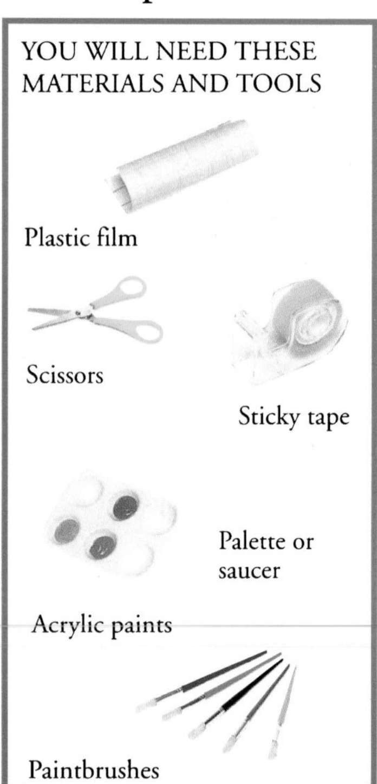

YOU WILL NEED THESE MATERIALS AND TOOLS

Plastic film

Scissors

Sticky tape

Palette or saucer

Acrylic paints

Paintbrushes

1 Cut two pieces of plastic film the same size. Stick the corners of one piece to your work surface with sticky tape. Do not remove the backing.

2 Paint the centre of a flower on to the centre of one piece of the film. Use a bright colour such as red, purple or yellow.

3 Using a different colour, paint five petals around the centre of the flower. Take care not to smudge the centre as you paint.

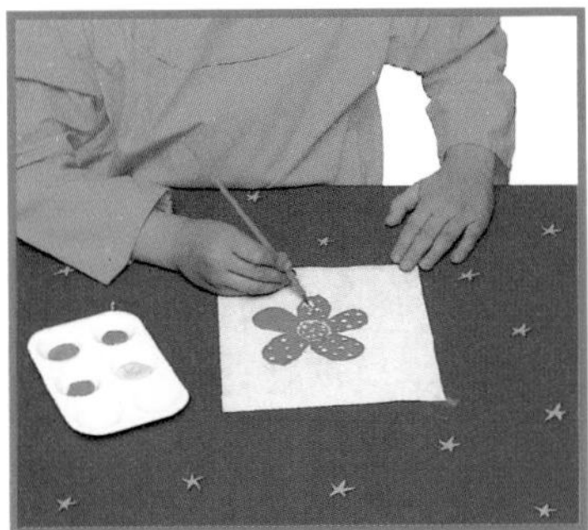

4 Decorate the flower with spots of a different, bright colour. Leave the flower to dry completely.

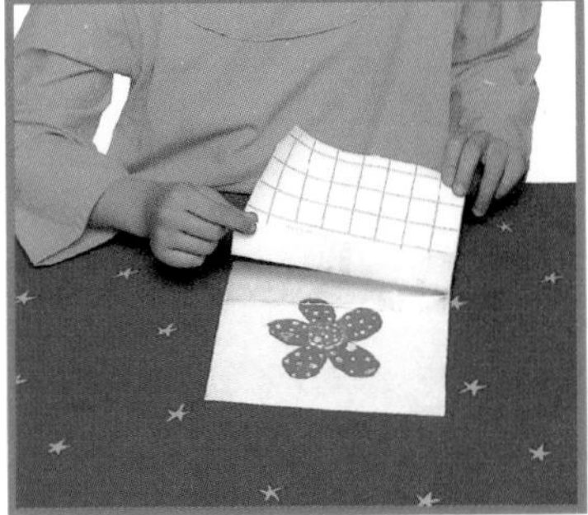

5 Take the second piece of film and carefully peel away the film's backing. Stick it over the flower. Work slowly, smoothing out any air bubbles with your fingers as you go.

6 If you get an air bubble, prick it with the point of a needle and smooth it out, then carefully cut around the flower.

7 Peel off the backing and stick the flower to the inside of your window.

Have year-round flowers on your bedroom window.

Flick-painted Starscape

This is a messy project so be sure to cover your work surface with lots of newspaper or scrap paper, or, if the weather is fine, do your flick painting outside. You can use any size of box for the planet story. The planet and rocket will move if you blow them or put the box by an open window.

If you want to make the inside of the box sparkle, add some glitter or cut out star shapes from kitchen foil and scatter them around the box.

Large-scale scene

A shoebox was used for this project but if you want to make a really big scene, get a box from the supermarket that had apples or oranges in it. Remember to make more than one of each mobile if you are using a big box.

YOU WILL NEED THESE MATERIALS AND TOOLS

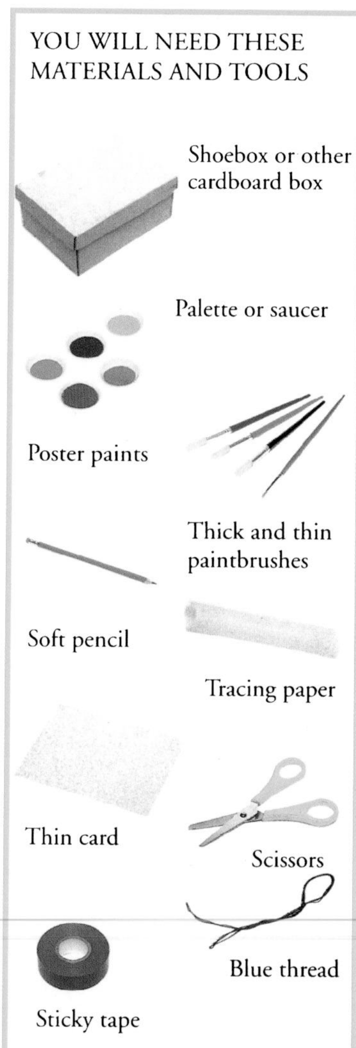

Shoebox or other cardboard box

Palette or saucer

Poster paints

Thick and thin paintbrushes

Soft pencil

Tracing paper

Thin card

Scissors

Blue thread

Sticky tape

1 Paint the shoebox inside and out using blue paint. You don't need the lid so don't bother with that. Leave the box to dry, then stand it on a wipe-clean surface, inside a cardboard box, or on a surface covered with newspaper.

2 Dip a medium-sized paintbrush in one of your pots of poster paint and flick the paint into the box. For fine splatters, tap the brush handle on the edge of the box. Repeat this with the different coloured paints.

3 Leave the box to dry thoroughly while you make the mobiles and decorations. Using a soft pencil, trace the star, planet and rocket templates from the beginning of the book on to pieces of card.

4 Cut out the shapes. If your box is large, you will need more than one of each. You will also need some stars for the outside of the box.

5 Cover your work surface with scrap paper, then paint each shape. Choose yellow, gold or silver for the stars and bright colours for the planet and rocket.

6 Use a piece of sticky tape to attach a length of blue thread to the shapes to hang inside the box. Glue some of the stars to the top and sides of the box.

7 Use sticky tape to attach the rocket and planet to the roof of the box.

Your own space scene will amaze your friends.

Marbled Pencils and Pencil Pot

The exciting thing about marbled papers is that each sheet is different and unique. Marbling is simple to do, but always ask a grown-up to mix the oil paint as you must not get turpentine near your eyes or mouth. You can buy ready-mixed marbling colours from craft or hobby shops.

Marbling technique

The secret of good marbling is not to pour too much paint into the water at once. You can always add more after you have made one sheet of paper if you think it is too pale.

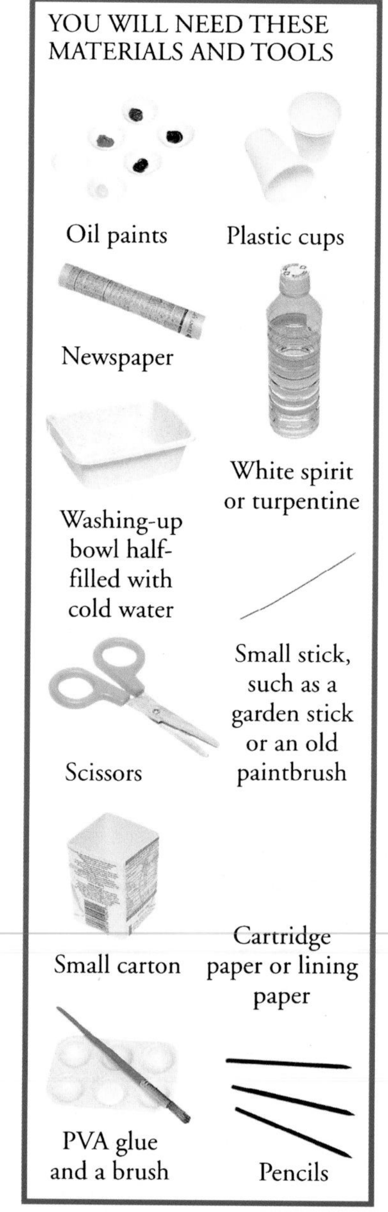

1 Squeeze a blob of about five different paints into separate plastic cups and ask a grown-up to add a small amount of turpentine. Mix well.

2 Cover your work surface with newspaper. Place the washing-up bowl on the work surface. Gradually pour the oil paints into the water.

3 Mix the paints around to make interesting patterns. Make sure that you haven't got a big blob of one colour completely unmixed.

4 Cut a piece of paper about the same size as the washing-up bowl and gently place it on the surface of the patterned water.

5 Remove the paper carefully and place it face up on a flat surface covered with newspaper. Try making different papers, experimenting with different colours and patterns.

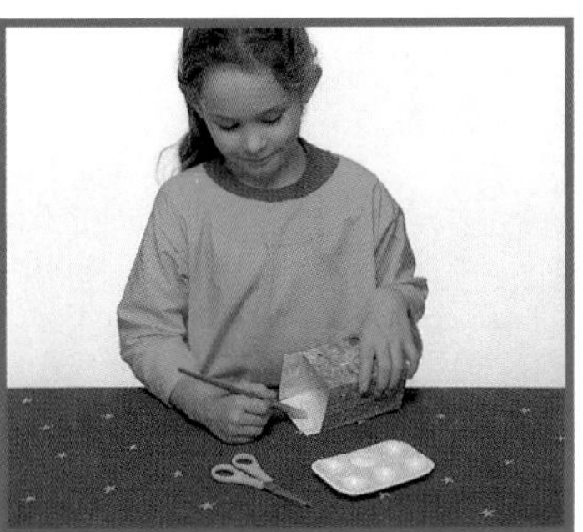

6 When your papers are completely dry, use one to cover the carton. Cut it to shape, then glue it down. Leave some paper at the top to glue down inside the box.

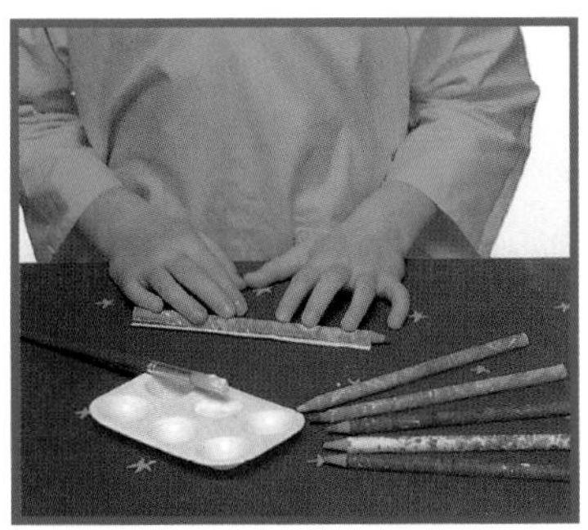

7 Cover some pencils with your marbled paper so they match your pencil holder.

Cheer up homework time with your unique pencils and pot.

MAX

Stunning Science

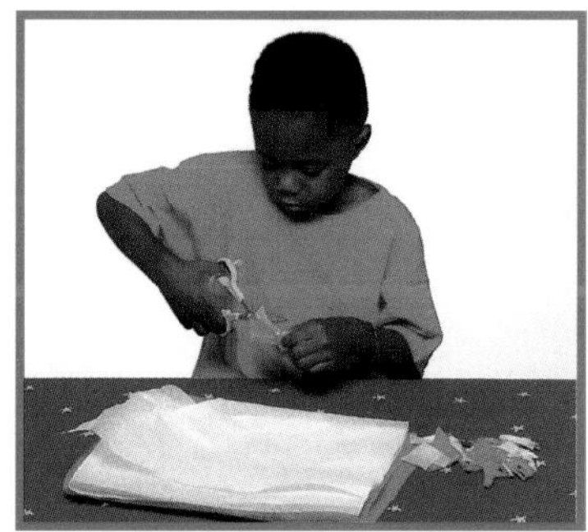

Introduction

Children are very curious people. So are scientists. Both ask questions about the world around them. How does this work? What does that do? Why do things happen? And can things be improved? You may already ask grown-ups how things happen. What, where, when and why? This means you are already a natural scientist. Scientists find the answers to their questions by doing experiments. You can do the same. This chapter shows you how to do tests and experiments for yourself. Then you can find out the answers to your questions, like a real scientist. You can also go on to invent more experiments and do more projects. Perhaps you will make a great discovery and become famous!

Find out why some things float and others sink.

Make a sound gun with a cardboard tube and discover how sound travels.

Young Scientists

You have already been doing experiments for years, probably without knowing it. When you were a tiny baby, you started to move your arms and legs about. You grabbed and kicked things, to see what would happen. When you were bigger, you probably did experiments when you played with your toys. Could you eat them? Did they make a noise when you dropped them? Could you pull them apart to see inside? Playing is experimenting, and playing is fun, so experimenting is fun, too.

Find out why things look back-to-front in a mirror.

As you do the experiments in this chapter, you will find out about light and electricity, how water and wind work, and how heat and cold affect things. Each project tells you what to do and then explains what happens. All these experiments are safe with the help of grown-ups. You can also make up your own experiments and find things out for yourself. In this way you will learn more about the world.

Different Kinds of Science

Science is so huge that no one can know everything about it.

So scientists usually specialize. This means they study just one or a few subjects. For example, medical scientists study why people become ill, and how to make them better. Biologists study animals and plants, where they live and how they grow. Chemists study chemicals and other substances, what they are made of, and how they can be changed and used. Physicists study how things move, what holds them together or pulls them apart, and how energy makes things happen. Astronomers study the planets, stars and the whole universe.

How to Do an Experiment

Whatever scientists study, they usually work in the same way. This is called the scientific method. They do not rush, and they always keep things clean and safe.

• First the scientist finds out as much as possible about the subject. This is called research. What is already known about the subject? What experiments have other scientists done, and what did they discover? Do people really know the facts, or are they just guessing?

• Then the scientist decides on a good question to ask. It should be a new question that no one has asked before. But it must not be too complicated. Most scientists find out more by working in small stages, bit by bit.

• The scientist may have an idea of the possible answer to the question. In other words, he or she may guess what will happen in the experiment. This possible answer is called a theory.

• Next, the scientist thinks of an experiment that will test the theory, to find the answer to the question. This is called planning or designing the experiment. In a good experiment, everything happens clearly and safely, and nothing can go wrong – hopefully!

• Now the scientist gathers all the bits and pieces to do the experiment. These are called the materials and equipment. Everything is set out neatly and cleanly, and labelled clearly, so that there are no mix-ups.

• At last, the scientist carries out the experiment, working carefully and safely. He or she finds out what happens by looking and listening, and perhaps by feeling or smelling. The things that happen are called the results. These are written down carefully in the Science Record Book. Everything is cleaned up and tidied away afterwards.

• Next, the scientist thinks about the results. Were they expected, or not? Is the theory right, or wrong? If the theory is right, the scientist has found something new. If the theory is wrong, the scientist can try to think of another theory, or perhaps the experiment did not work properly. Remember – no experiment is a failure. A good scientist can always learn from the results, whatever they are.

• After more experiments, the scientist will be able to gather the answers together. He or she must check everything, then check it again. Finally, the scientist may make a new discovery, and become famous.

Being a Good Scientist

Scientists are very careful people. They have to be. They often work with dangerous machines, equipment and chemicals. And science can be very costly. So scientists also need to be sure that their experiments are worthwhile, and that there will be no mistakes. So they make sure everything is thought out and prepared carefully.

When you do experiments, get the materials and equipment ready first. Have a clean, safe area to carry out your experiment in, as described over the page. And ask a grown-up to check that everything is safe.

Use a jug with a spout and a funnel when pouring liquids.

Never touch electric sockets, plugs or wires.

Wear a pair of rubber gloves when handling vinegar or lemon juice.

Always ask a grown-up to cut anything with sharp scissors or a craft knife.

Water is great fun to splash around, as long as you are working in a waterproof area.
Science tip For experiments with water or other liquids, see if you can do them in a large bowl, such as a washing-up bowl. This catches any splashes or spills.

Heat can be very dangerous. Hot water and steam can burn or scald your skin. And when very hot water is poured into cold jars, beakers or bowls, it can make them crack or melt. So *always* get a grown-up to help you with experiments that need hot water, and make sure your equipment can stand up to it. Cookers and kettles must only be used when a grown-up is present. Liquids can boil over suddenly, and things may catch fire without warning.

Put a metal teaspoon into a jar before pouring in hot water.

Science tip Put a metal teaspoon into a jar before pouring in hot water. This should stop the heat cracking the jar.

Ice can freeze skin just as badly as hot water can burn. Ice has the added danger that it sticks to dry skin. When you make ice in a freezer, get a grown-up to help you.
Science tip Use rubber or washing-up gloves when handling ice. Wet the ice and the gloves first, so they do not stick together.

Electricity from a small battery is usually safe, since there is not enough power to give a shock. Static electricity can sometimes be felt as a tingle that makes you jump, for example when it builds up on a car and you touch the handle. But the static that builds up on a balloon, as shown in one of the experiments, is too small to feel.
Science tip The electricity that is used in the home is very dangerous. It can kill! NEVER touch electric sockets, plugs or wires.

Chemicals used here are mostly substances used for cooking and they are harmless in normal quantities. But good scientists know that chemicals can be dangerous if they get into the wrong place. This includes near too much heat, or inside your body if you swallow them. Never taste or eat chemicals that you are using for experiments. Always ask a grown-up to get the things you need from the kitchen cupboard. NEVER touch cleaning chemicals, medicines or alcohol.

Science tip Use rubber gloves to handle large quantities of acids like vinegar or lemon juice.

Cutting and making holes can be quite difficult. Scissors and sharp points can be dangerous if they are not used properly. So ask a grown-up to help.

Science tip Draw a line where you are going to cut with scissors, before you start cutting. It is usually easier to follow a line.

Label everything – it is the sign of a good scientist. Your experiment might be ruined if you cannot remember what you put in each jar, or if you get your chemicals mixed up. Write labels on pieces of paper or use special sticky-backed labels. Stick these in the right place, or put them under jars or beakers.

Science tip Use a pencil for your labels. Some felt-tipped pens can blot and run if splashed with water.

Your Science Record Book

All scientists record their experiments and the results. You need to know exactly what you did during an experiment, so that you can repeat it to check the result, or change it to find out something else. Each time you do an experiment, record the following information in your book. If you find writing difficult ask a grown-up to help with some of the details and draw a picture of what happened instead.

- the day and date
- the experiment's name, and the idea behind it
- how you did your experiment, perhaps with a drawing or diagram
- the results, written in words, or perhaps as a chart with ticks and crosses

You can make a Science Record Book by covering a notebook or school-type exercise book with coloured paper. The paper needs to be about 3–4 cm (1¼–1½ in) larger all around than the book when it is opened flat.

Further Research

When scientists have finished their set of experiments, they often try to find out a bit more, perhaps by changing the experiment slightly. See if you can make changes to some of your experiments to find out more. Record what you do and your results in your Science Record Book.

Your Science Record Book

1 Place the book centrally on the coloured paper, with one cover open. Turn the edges of the paper over the cover and stick them down with glue. You can snip the corners of the paper to give a neater finish. Repeat with the other cover.

2 Decorate the cover with something scientific, perhaps numbers, bubbles and shapes, drawings of test-tubes and scientific equipment, or cut-out photographs of scientific gadgets.

3 Record all the information that you have learned from your experiments. If you like, you can stick some of the things you have made in the book, to keep.

Where to Do Experiments

Many scientists work in special rooms called laboratories. There they have all the equipment, materials, tools and machines they need to do their experiments. But not all science happens in laboratories. To do research, many scientists go to libraries to read books. They visit exhibitions and museums to find out more. They also meet other scientists and talk about their work.

The Home Laboratory

You can set up your own laboratory in your home or school. It might be in a kitchen, bathroom, shed or garage. You usually need somewhere with waterproof surfaces, where there is no danger of damaging furniture or carpets. Ask a grown-up to choose the best place.

The main thing you will need is a large work surface, like a table. The place should be brightly lit and not too hot or cold. For some experiments, you will need a freezer, or a refrigerator with a freezing compartment. You will sometimes need lots of water. Warm water can come from a hot tap or a kettle. You might also need somewhere to heat up a saucepan. Always ask a grown-up to help.

Science tip Cover your work surface with several layers of old newspaper. This stops paint and food colouring staining the work surface, and will also absorb spilt liquids and glue.

Materials and Equipment

You will find most of the materials, equipment and tools that you need for your experiments around the house. Always gather everything you need and check it before you start the experiment. If you do not, you may run out of something halfway through.

If necessary, you can buy extra supplies of pencils, pens, scissors, sticky tape, paper, card, blotting paper, glue, sticky labels and shapes, poster paints and similar things from a good stationery shop or office supplier.

You can find food colourings, bicarbonate of soda, vinegar, lemon juice, milk, cocktail sticks, skewers and similar things in the kitchen.

Batteries, wires and small torch bulbs are sold in electrical, DIY or model shops. You can buy small mirrors from the chemist, and sand or gravel from a builders' supplier or a timber merchant.

Be a Green Scientist

Good scientists know that they must look after our planet by saving resources, recycling things, and not damaging the environment or causing waste and pollution. This is called being "green" since it helps to save trees, plants, flowers, animals and natural places on our planet Earth.

You can be a "green scientist" by saving, reusing and recycling things. You will also save money!

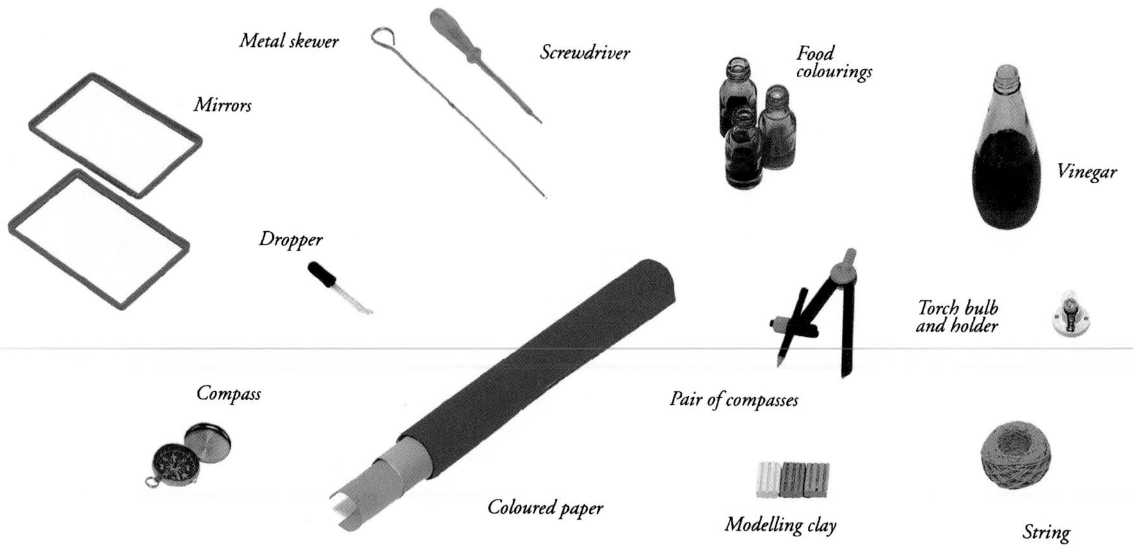

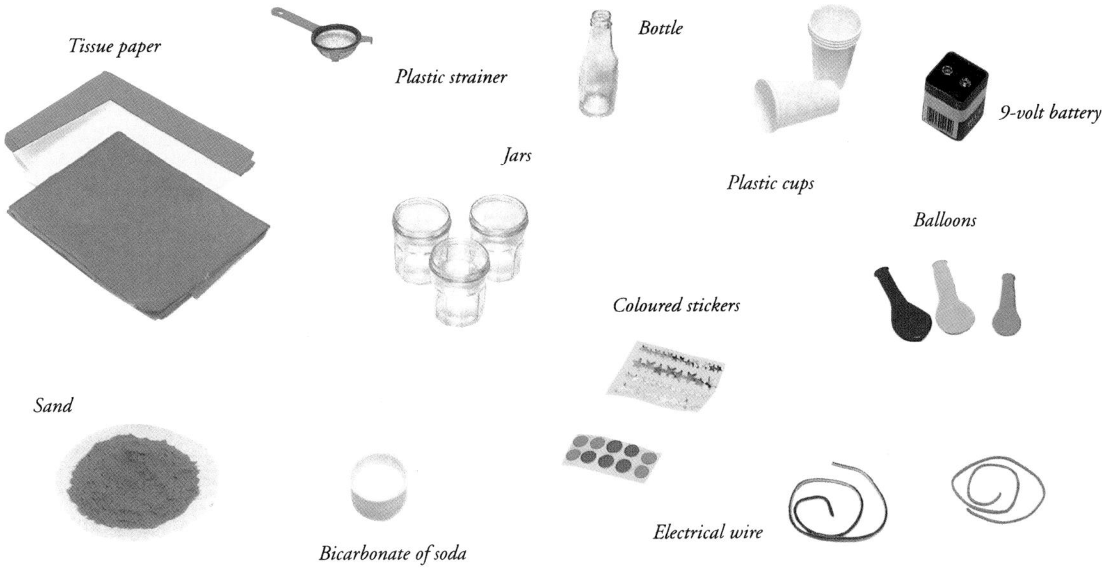

- Use old newspapers, and store your equipment in empty cartons or boxes.
- The card from cereal boxes is ideal for many experiments.
- Ask grown-ups for used paper that has been written on one side – you can use the blank side.
- After picnics and parties, wash the paper or plastic cups and plates. You can use them for your experiments.
- Save the cardboard tubes from the insides of toilet rolls and kitchen rolls.
- Wash and keep empty jars for your experiments. But remember that glass is easily broken and is then very dangerous to handle.
- Save plastic drinks bottles. Carefully cut off the tops and turn them upside-down to make funnels. The lower parts make plastic jars – safer than glass ones.
- When you have finished with your equipment, take it to your local recycling centre.

Have Fun

If you follow the safety rules in this book, and carry out your experiments slowly and sensibly, you will find that science is fun. You can make some amazing discoveries, and learn lots. Find out more by doing further research, by reading about science, and by watching science programmes. You can become an expert scientist and answer all your friends' questions. You might even make a discovery or invention that will change the world!

A Note for Grown-ups

Some of the experiments in this book can be followed by a child alone, but often adult help is needed. Always supervise your children closely whenever they are using home experiment materials. The places in the book where your assistance is vital, such as when sharp scissors or a craft knife are needed, are marked **!**.

Creatures of the Night

Light is bright, and when there is no light it is dark. A shadow is a patch of darkness. It is formed when something gets in the way of light beams, which can only travel in straight lines. In Alex's puppet show, some of the light from the torch shines on the wall. But the light that hits the ghostly black creatures cannot get through or round them. So the wall behind their shapes stays dark – as their shady, scary shadows.

You can make the shadows on the wall bigger or smaller. When the puppets are near the torch, they cover more of the light beam, and so the shadows on the wall are bigger, but their edges are fuzzy and blurred.

Light fantastic

Light is amazing. It comes and goes in a flash, weighs nothing, travels faster than anything else in the universe – and even scientists do not fully understand it. The light we turn on in our homes is produced by electricity. This passes through the very thin wire inside a light bulb and makes the wire glow brightly. The light beams then spread out in all directions, and always in straight lines. The light bulb in a torch has a mirror behind it to make all the light beams come out at the front only.

! Young children will need help cutting out card shapes with scissors and should not be allowed to handle craft knives. They might also need help in the "dark room", to hold the torch or just for company. Be sure they cannot get themselves locked in a dark room or cupboard.

YOU WILL NEED THESE MATERIALS AND TOOLS

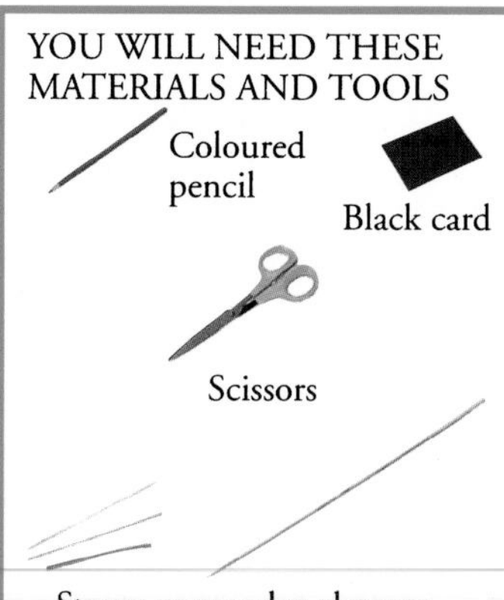

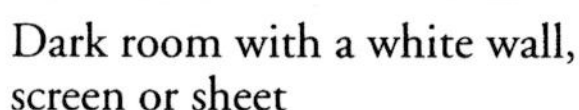

Dark room with a white wall, screen or sheet

1 Draw the outlines of some night-time creatures, like bats, owls and spiders, on the black card with the pencil. Make them big.

2 Draw some stars and a moon too. Cut out the shapes carefully with scissors. If the scissors are sharp, ask a grown-up to help you.

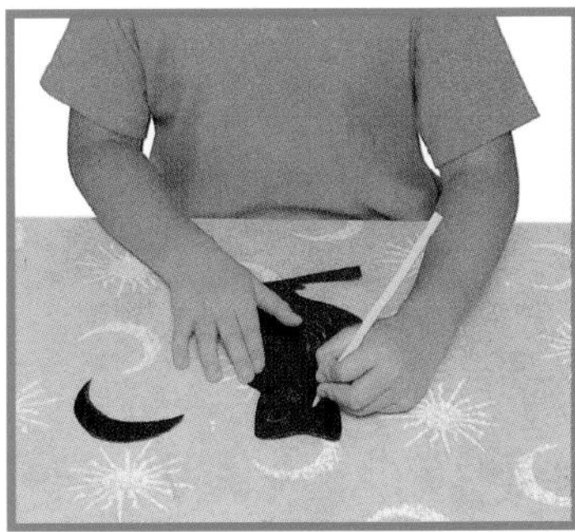

3 Draw features such as eyes and feathers or even bone patterns onto the night-time creatures. Keep these quite simple.

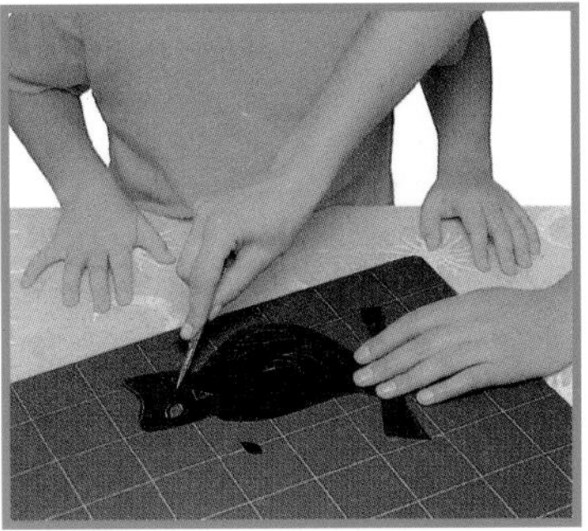

4 Ask a grown-up to cut out the eyes, feather patterns and any other details with a craft knife.

5 Stick the straws or skewers to the shapes with sticky tape to make handles.

6 In a darkened room, ask a friend to shine the torch on a light wall. Move the creatures and other shapes in the torch's light, to make their ghostly shadows dance on the wall.

Changing Shadows

Things that light can pass through easily, like air or glass, are called **transparent.** Solid things like your night creature cut-outs do not let any light pass through. They are **opaque**. A **translucent** substance is one that lets through some light but not all of it, like tracing paper or tissue paper. Cover one side of a cut-out animal with tissue paper. When you hold it up in front of the torch, less light will shine through the holes.

Mysterious Mirrors

Otis is discovering that what you see in a mirror is not an exact copy of the original thing. It is back-to-front – a mirror picture or mirror-image. His drawings and writing always look the other way round in the mirror. So does your face! The face that you see when you look in the mirror is a mirror-image. It is not the same as the face that your friends and family see when they look at you, or when you look at a photograph of yourself.

Reflections

Light beams travel in straight lines – unless they bounce off things. This bouncing is called **reflection**. Only a few things, like the Sun, light bulbs, candles and fires, give out their own light beams. These shine into our eyes and we see them. We see other things because they bounce or reflect light beams into our eyes. Very smooth, shiny surfaces like mirrors are very good at reflecting. When you look at your face in a mirror, you see light beams that have come from the Sun or an electric light to your face, bounced off it towards the mirror, and then bounced back again into your eyes!

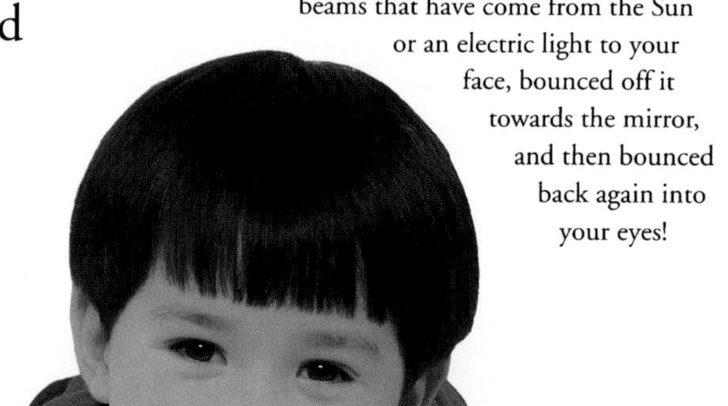

YOU WILL NEED THESE MATERIALS AND TOOLS

Otis is having fun making his drawings and writing turn around in a mirror. See if you can make a mirror-image come out the right way round.

1 Mirrors are made of glass or plastic. Some may have sharp edges. Ask a grown-up to put some sticky tape round them to make them safe.

2 Do a drawing and write the name of what you have drawn on a piece of paper. Be as neat as you can.

3 Hold the mirror up next to the paper. Can you read the writing in it? Does the drawing look exactly the same as it does on the paper?

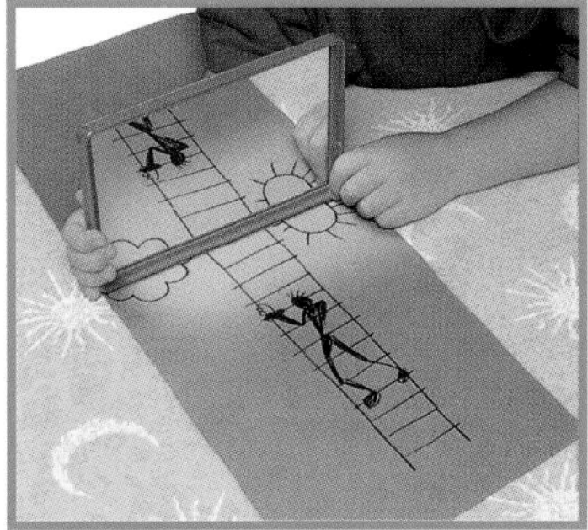

4 Write the name backwards or do the drawing back-to-front. What does it look like in the mirror now?

5 Think of a whole drawing. Draw half of it, using one half of the paper only.

6 Can you make up the rest of the drawing by holding the mirror alongside it? Is the result what you had expected?

See Back to the Future!

You can make an image bounce backwards and forwards between mirrors, almost for ever. Sit behind one mirror. Hold out another mirror facing you. Look into this mirror. Move both mirrors slightly until you can see the reflection of the mirror in the reflection of the mirror in the reflection of the mirror in the reflection of the mirror and on and on.

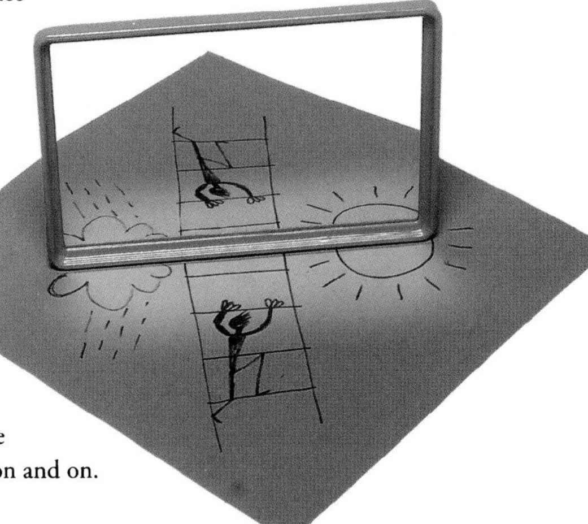

Tell the Time by the Sun

When the Sun rises in the morning, it is low in the sky. It shines on objects from the side to make long, thin shadows. As the Sun moves up and across the sky, the shadows get shorter and move around. At midday the Sun is at its highest point, and the shadows are at their shortest. As the Sun continues its journey across the sky in the afternoon, the shadows get longer again, but on the other side of the objects.

Gabriella has made a sundial so that she can watch the changing shadow of the dial pointer – and tell the time by it.

Light days and dark nights

Each day, it looks as if the Sun moves across the sky. But really, the Sun stays still, and it is the Earth that moves. The Earth is like a giant ball that spins round and round. We stay in one place on the surface of the ball, so it looks to us as though the Sun is moving. When the Sun disappears at night, we are on the shadowy side of the Earth. The Sun is still shining, but on the other side. For people there, it is daytime. For us, it is night-time.

! Young children may need to be shown how to draw a circle with a pair of compasses, and how to use a magnetic compass to find North and South. The sundial pointer should face North, since the Sun is in the South at midday, so it throws its shadows onto the dial.

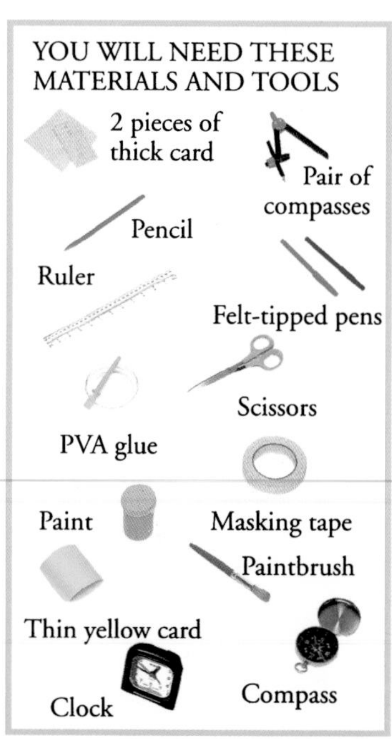

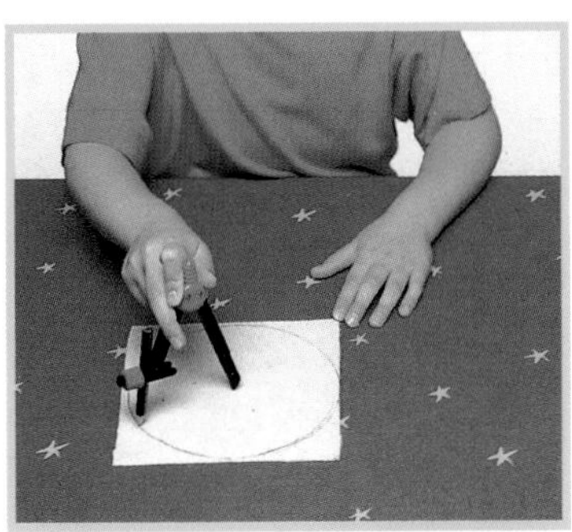

1 Open the pair of compasses so the point is about 8 cm (3 in) from the pencil. Push the point into the middle of the thick card and turn the compasses to draw a circle.

2 Draw a square on some thick card with a felt-tipped pen and a ruler. Each side of the square should be about 8 cm (3 in). Draw a diagonal line across the square to make two triangles.

3 Carefully cut out the circle and one triangle from the card. This will be the pointer of the sundial. (You can keep the other triangle as a spare.)

4 Draw a straight line from the centre of the circle, where the compass point stuck in to it, to the edge, using the ruler.

5 Stick the triangle to the circle along the line using PVA glue. Hold the triangle in place with masking tape until the glue dries.

6 If you like, paint your sundial bright yellow. Add a smiley face and some wavy sunbeams cut out of thin yellow card.

7 Put your sundial in a safe, sunny place. Find North with the compass. Turn the sundial until the long side of the pointer points towards North. Draw a straight line at the edge of the shadow.

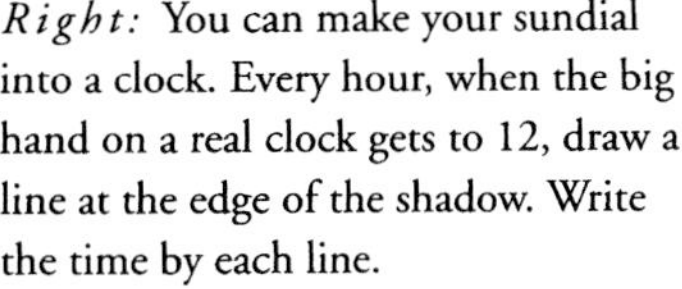

Right: You can make your sundial into a clock. Every hour, when the big hand on a real clock gets to 12, draw a line at the edge of the shadow. Write the time by each line.

Balloon Snowstorm

Electricity is strange stuff. It is invisible, which means we cannot see it. But it is also very powerful, and it can be very dangerous. We use electricity in our homes in lots of different ways, to make things work, such as light bulbs, heaters, vacuum-cleaners, washing machines, radios and music players. This electricity is very strong. NEVER mess about with this electricity. However, you can make your own electricity, which is safe and fun. It does not move along wires and it is not as powerful as mains electricity. It is called static electricity.

Lorenzo has charged his balloon with static electricity, by rubbing it. It sticks to his T-shirt and attracts the tissue paper "snow flakes".

YOU WILL NEED THESE MATERIALS AND TOOLS

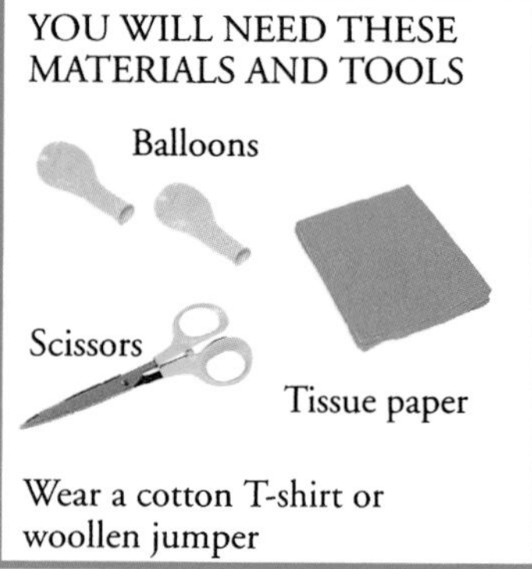

Wear a cotton T-shirt or woollen jumper

Charge your balloon

Static electricity is in tiny bits, called charges. These can be **positive** or **negative**, just like the two connections on a battery (see the experiment called Battery Light Show). An object such as a balloon has an equal number of positive and negative charges over its surface. They cancel each other out, so over a whole balloon there is no static electricity. But when a balloon is rubbed against a different material, such as a T-shirt, some of the positive charges go onto the T-shirt and stay there. This leaves extra negative charges on the balloon, which make it "sticky".

! Making static electricity is easier on cold, dry days. On warm, humid days, the air itself is full of static. Children might need help blowing up and tying balloons.

1 Blow up a balloon quite hard and tie the neck. Do not blow your balloon up so much that it bursts. But make sure it is fairly hard, since a soft, squashy balloon does not work so well.

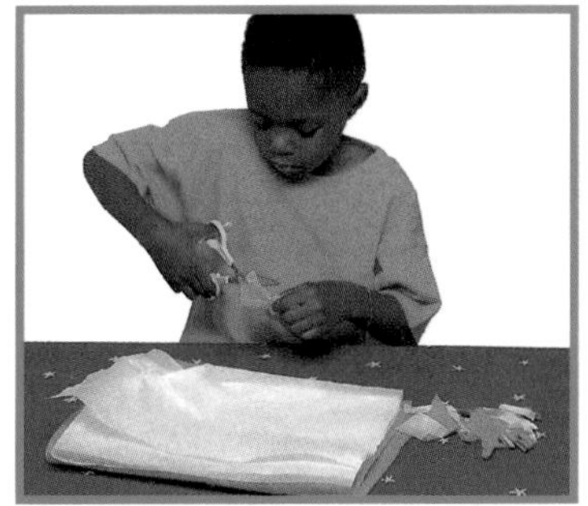

2 Make some "snow" by tearing or cutting tissue paper into little bits. If you have the time, you could make each "flake" a pointed star with six sides, like real snow flakes.

3 Rub the balloon several times on your T-shirt or woolly sweater. Rub it quite fast until the balloon tries to "stick" to the T-shirt or sweater. The balloon is now charged with static electricity.

4 Hold the balloon near the "snow". The flakes are lifted up by the static electricity on the balloon. After a little while, the electricity leaks away and the flakes fall softly.

5 Rub your balloon again to re-charge it, then hold it near a friend's hair and see what happens. For the best effect, choose someone with longish hair.

Push and Pull

There are two types of static electricity charge, positive and negative. Charges which are different attract, or pull each other together. So the balloon sticks to anything with the opposite charge, even water. Lorenzo is holding a charged balloon near a stream of water. It should attract the water and bend the stream towards it. Charges which are the same repel, or push each other away. So the balloon pushes away anything with the same charge as itself, such as another charged balloon. Write or draw what happens in your Science Record Book when you try out these experiments.

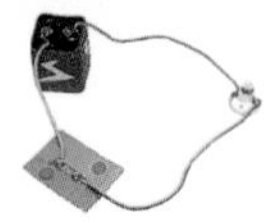

Battery Light Show

Kirsty has made a light show, to demonstrate how electricity works. Electricity is stored in the battery. It can only move, or flow, when it has a complete circle, or circuit, to go around. This circuit is made from wires, a switch and a bulb. When the switch is ON, the electricity goes from one end, or terminal, on the battery, along the wires, through the switch and light bulb, back to the battery's other terminal. As electricity goes through the bulb, it glows. When the switch is OFF, it makes a gap or break in the circuit. The electricity stops – and the light goes out.

Electric likes and dislikes

Electricity flows easily through some materials, like metals such as steel, iron and copper, and also water. These are called **conductors**. Electricity cannot flow through other things, like plastic, wood and pottery. These are called **insulators**. The wires in this experiment are made of metal on the inside, so the electricity can flow. The wire is covered with plastic to stop the electricity escaping.

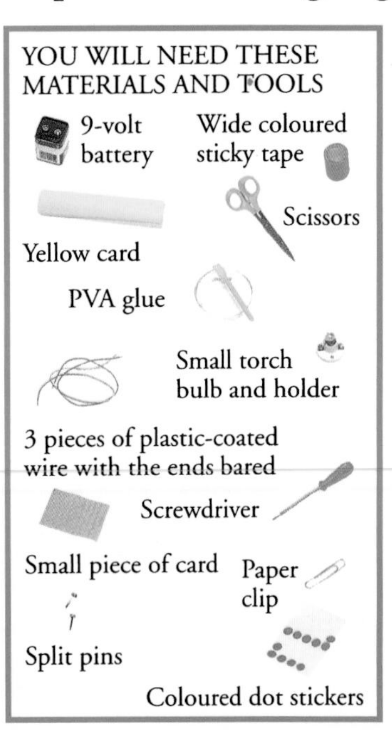

! A 9-volt battery is perfectly safe for doing experiments. A grown-up should strip about 1 cm ($^{1}/_{2}$ in) of plastic from both ends of each piece of wire. Be careful how you screw the light bulb into its holder, since too much force may break the glass. Young children might need help with screws and screwdrivers.

WARNING

NEVER TOUCH ELECTRICAL WIRES, SWITCHES, PLUGS OR SOCKETS WITHOUT HELP FROM A GROWN-UP.

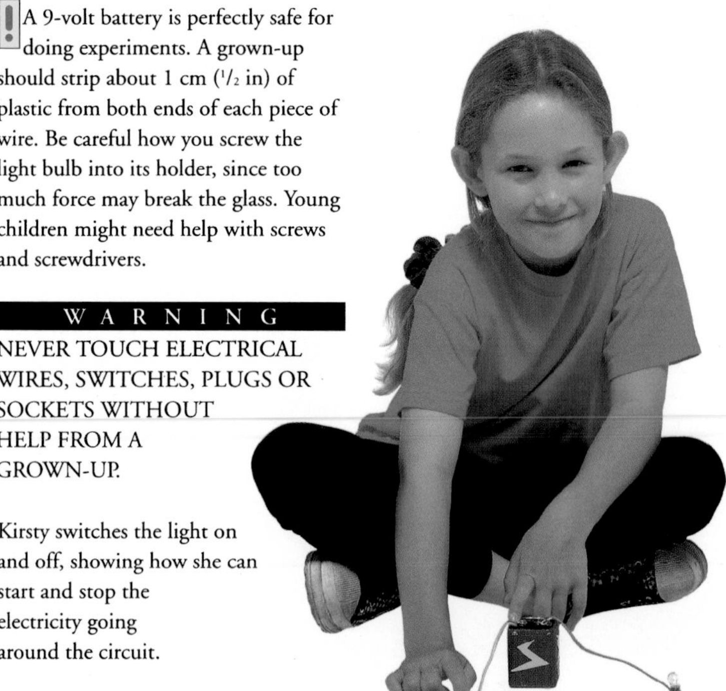

Kirsty switches the light on and off, showing how she can start and stop the electricity going around the circuit.

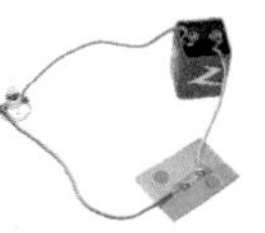

1 Decorate the battery to make it look powerful by winding a piece of wide coloured sticky tape right around it.

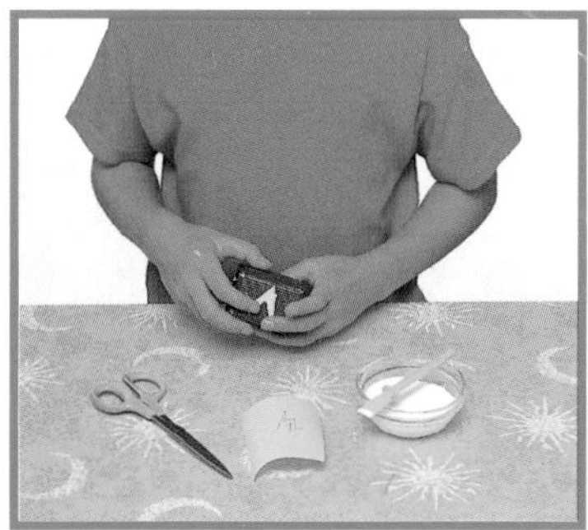

2 Cut out some zig-zag "lightning flashes" from the yellow card and stick them onto the sides of the battery with glue.

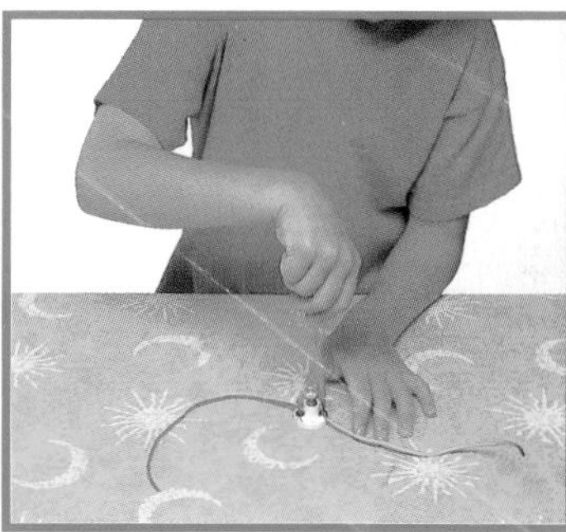

3 Screw the light bulb into the holder. Push the end of a piece of wire under one of the connecting screws. Screw it down. Repeat with another piece of wire under the other screw.

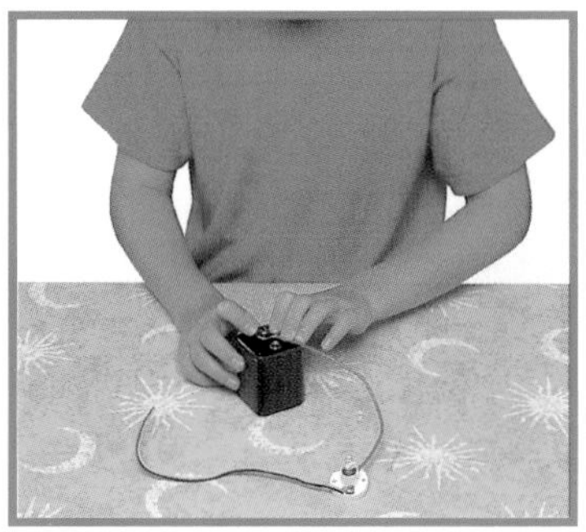

4 Take the end of one of these pieces of wire and twist it onto one of the battery terminals (the bits of metal on the top of the battery).

5 Twist the end of the third piece of wire onto the other battery terminal. Make sure that both these wires grip the terminals tightly.

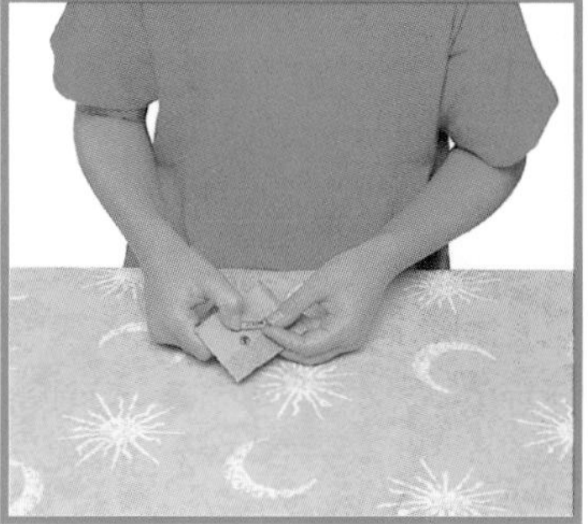

6 Push two holes in the piece of card, the length of the paper clip apart. Push a split pin through one hole. Push the other split pin through the paper clip and then through the other hole. Open the ends of the pins under the card. This is the switch.

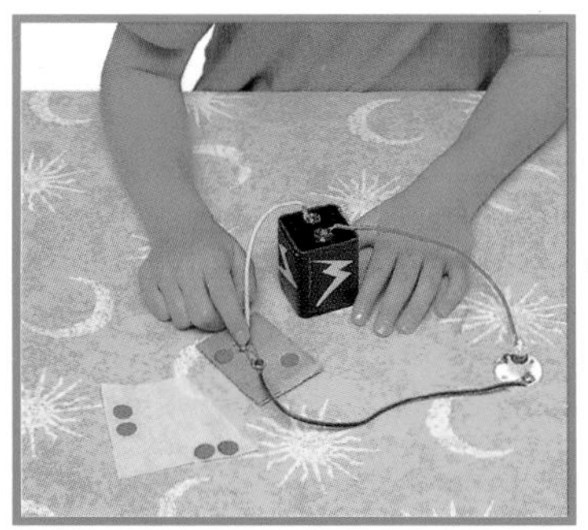

7 Twist one free wire end around one split pin and the other around the other split pin. When the paper clip touches both split pins, the switch is ON (green dot) and the light bulb shines. When the paper clip is moved away from the split pin, the switch is OFF (red dot).

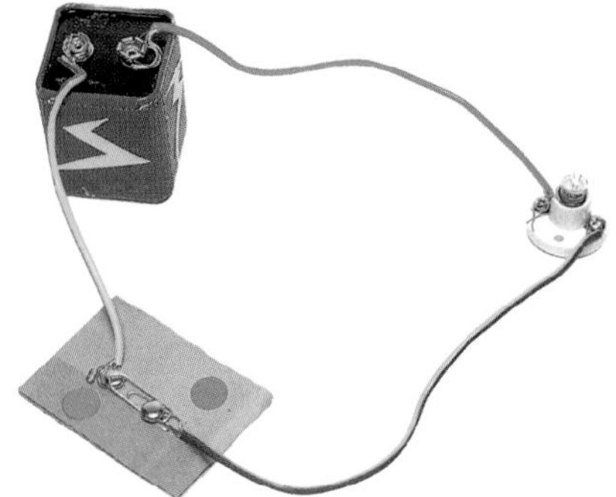

Tumbler Telephone

Can you talk to a friend quietly, when he or she is at the other end of a big room? Liam's telephone works by sending the sound waves of his voice along the string. They go along the string as very fast to-and-fro movements called vibrations. When Liam talks into the tumbler or cup, the sound waves hit the bottom of the tumbler and make it vibrate. The vibrations pass along the string to the tumbler at the other end. They shake the bottom of this tumbler, which makes sound waves that go into Lorenzo's ear.

With his own tumbler telephone, Liam never gets a wrong number, and the lines are never busy. Also, his calls are always free!

Travelling waves

Sound waves travel well through air. They go through lots of other things too, such as water, wood, metals and glass. In fact, sound travels much faster and farther as vibrations in water, metals and glass, than it does through air. This is why whales and dolphins can "talk" to each other across huge distances in the ocean.

YOU WILL NEED THESE MATERIALS AND TOOLS

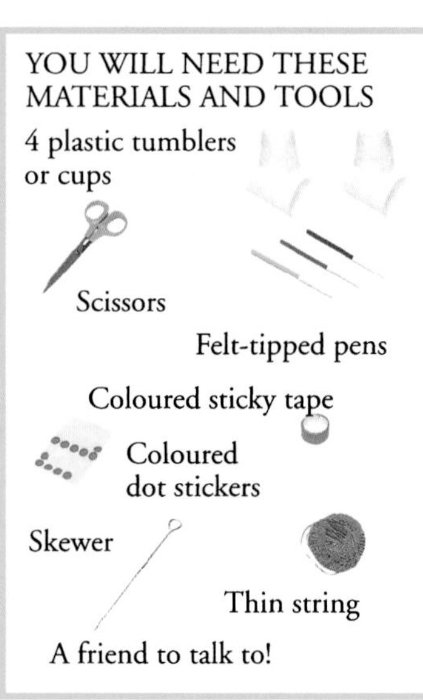

! The tumbler telephone works well if the string is stretched quite tight and straight, and nothing touches it. Otherwise the vibrations cannot travel along it properly. The tumblers should be held by their rims only, so the bottoms are free to vibrate. Children may need help with cutting the tumblers and making holes with a sharp point.

1 Carefully cut the bottoms off two of the tumblers about 2 cm (3/4 in) from the base. You may need to ask a grown-up to help you with this.

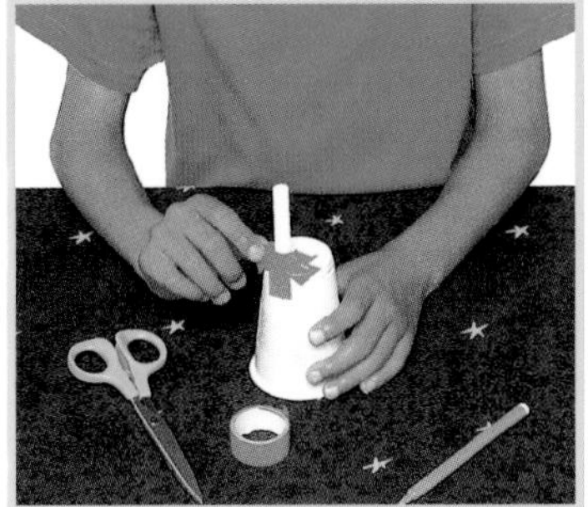

2 Stick a felt-tipped pen top to the bottom of each of the other two tumblers. These will be "aerials" – your telephones are like mobile ones!

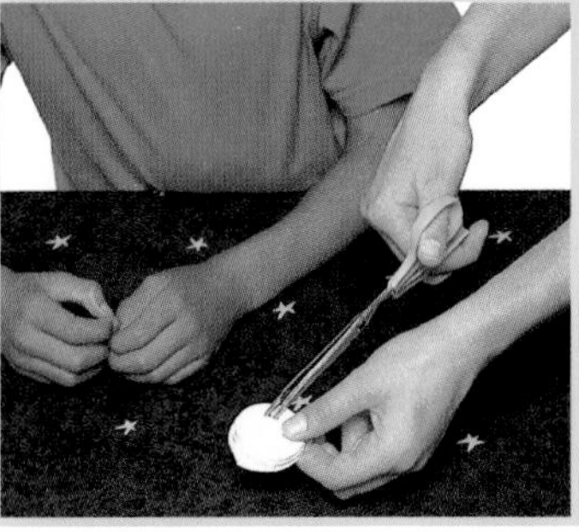

3 Ask a grown-up to cut out small holes in the cut-off tumbler bottoms. Slip them neatly over the "aerials" to hold them in place.

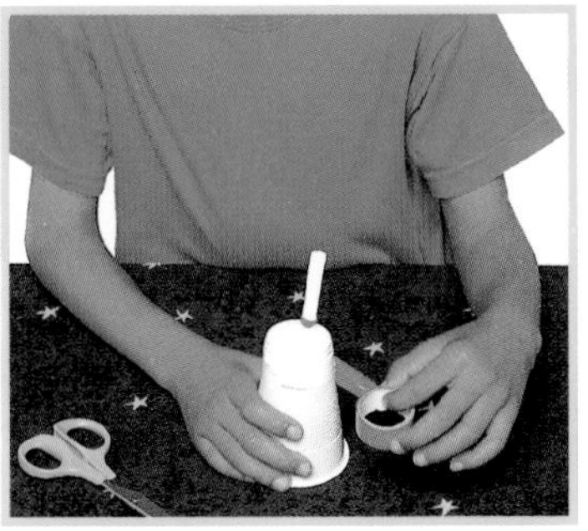

4 Sticky-tape the cut-off bottoms in place. Add more stripes of sticky tape for decoration.

5 Make a "key pad" on each telephone with coloured dot stickers. Write numbers on the dots.

6 Ask a grown-up to make a tiny hole in the bottoms of the tumblers, with a skewer.

7 Thread the ends of the string through the holes in the telephones. Tie a large knot in each end of the string.

Chatting on the Telephone

Your friend walks away with one of the tumbler telephones, until the string is stretched tight, and holds the telephone to his or her ear. You speak into the telephone, and your friend listens. When you have finished talking, say "Over" like a real walkie-talkie user. Hold the telephone to your ear, to hear your friend's reply. Try using longer string to see if the telephone still works. Measure the greatest length and write the results in your Science Record Book.

Marvellous Mobiles

Air is all around us. We can not see it or touch it. But when it moves, we can feel it. Moving air comes from your mouth when you blow, and from a fan. The wind is moving air. Stand outside on a windy day and sometimes the moving air nearly knocks you over. Antonino's marvellous mobile swirls and twirls when moving air pushes it. You can find moving air around the house, such as near a window, door, radiator or table lamp.

Rising air

Indoors, moving air is sometimes called a draught, especially when it is cold and unwanted. Draughts in houses are caused by the wind blowing through gaps around windows or doors. Draughts are also caused in other ways. Hot air from a radiator or table lamp rises up to the ceiling, and makes a warm draught. On a cold night, cold air near a window falls to the floor as a cold draught.

! Children may need help with cutting and balancing the mobile. Hanging the mobile near any heat source, such as a radiator or lamp, must be supervised.

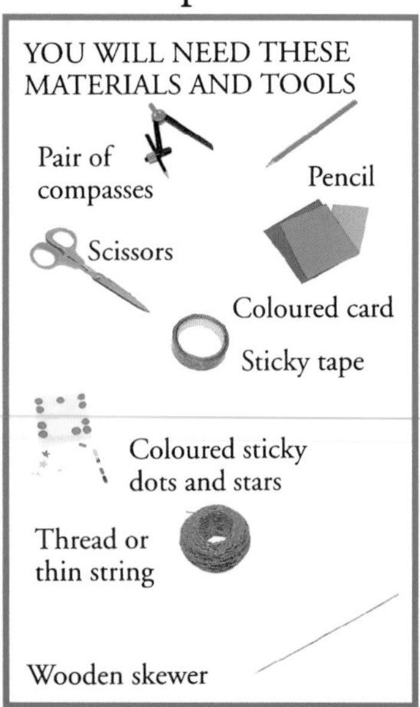

Antonino can use his marvellous mobile to detect wind, draughts and other moving air in his house.

1 Use the compasses to draw lots of circles on the coloured card. Make them any size but there must be two of each size.

2 Carefully cut out the circles using scissors. Arrange the discs in their equal-sized pairs.

3 Carefully cut a straight line or slit from the edge of each disc to its centre, where the compass point was.

4 Push the two discs of each pair together by their slits. Secure the joins with some sticky tape to make sure they hold together.

5 Decorate the discs with the coloured dots and stars.

6 Cut the string or thread into different lengths. Stick one end of a string to the centre of each pair of discs. Tie the other end to the skewer.

A Mobile Draught-detector

Balance the mobile by moving the strings along the skewer until it does not tip over. Now, find places around the house where you can hang the mobile. If it turns or wobbles, you know there is air moving past it. Make a list of the places you test in your Science Record Book. Can you think what might cause the draughts?

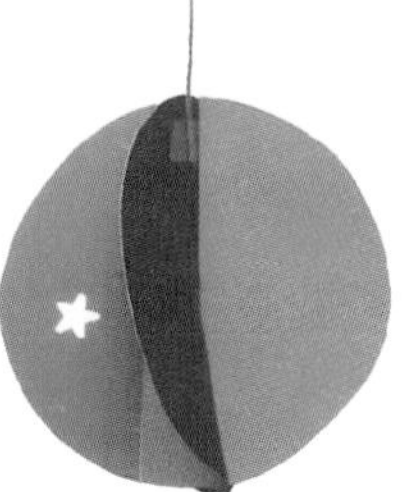

Above: Tie another length of string to the centre of the skewer so you can hang it up.

Hold Water Upside Down!

This famous trick looks impossible, or perhaps it is magic. Can you really hold water in an upside-down tumbler? Yes, Antonino shows that it truly does work. It depends on science. The force that pulls you, a cat, a chair and everything else in the world, down towards the ground, is called gravity. Gravity tries to make the water fall out of the upside-down tumbler towards the ground. But in this trick, air keeps the water in the tumbler.

Heavy air

Air has weight, although it does not weigh much. There is a lot of it pressing on us, since there is a huge amount of air high above. We do not notice this pressing force, because we are used to it. It is called **air pressure**, and it is this that keeps the water in the glass. The water is trapped inside the glass by the card. Air presses down, around and up underneath the card, holding it in place, and keeping the water inside the tumbler.

This experiment involves a lot of water and does not always work right first time. So it should be performed in a suitable waterproof area. Use a plastic tumbler and bowl rather than glass ones, for safety. We have used glass ones here so you can see how the experiment works. Clean, smooth, shiny, flat card is best. The experiment works less well if the card becomes soggy or bent. Children may need help cutting the card.

It looks like magic. But Antonino is using the science of air, water and gravity to stop his feet getting wet!

1 Add a little food colouring to the water in the bowl and stir it around. This is so you can see the water inside the tumbler.

2 Draw around the rim of the tumbler onto the card. Then draw a square around this circle, about 2 cm (3/4 in) larger than the circle all around.

3 Carefully cut out the square of card. It should fit easily over the top of the tumbler, with plenty of extra card around the rim.

4 Put the tumbler into the bowl of water. Hold it under, with the open end pointing up. Make sure that it fills up completely.

5 Make sure there are no bubbles of air inside the tumbler, by tapping it. The trick will not work if there is any air in the tumbler.

6 Turn the tumbler upside down. Lift it partly out, but keep the rim under the water. Slide the card into the water and under the rim.

7 Hold the card firmly against the rim of the beaker. Slowly lift the card and beaker, still upside down, out of the water.

8 Hold the tumbler upside down and level. Without sliding the card, take your other hand away from the card.

Air, Water and Weather

The layer of air all around the Earth is called the atmosphere. Air's weight changes when it gets hot or cold, and these changes cause our weather. When air is warmed by the sun, it rises higher. Cooler air moves along to take its place. This is wind. As air rises, the invisible moisture in it turns to tiny drops of water. These make clouds. As the drops get bigger, they fall as rain.

Sink or Swim

Water is very strong. It can push things. When it flows in rivers, or in sea currents, it pushes objects along. Water also pushes down all the time, because it is very heavy. But it also pushes up, too. This upward pushing is called upthrust, and it makes things float. Izabella is discovering that water's upthrust is strong enough to support some things and make them float, but that others are too heavy and sink.

Floating forces

An object floats if the upward push of the water, called **upthrust,** is more than the downward push of the object. The downward push of the object is called **displacement** because it moves aside (dis-places) some water. An object that is small for its weight, like a pebble, displaces only a small amount of water. So it sinks. If an object is large for its weight, like a sponge, it floats.

YOU WILL NEED THESE MATERIALS AND TOOLS

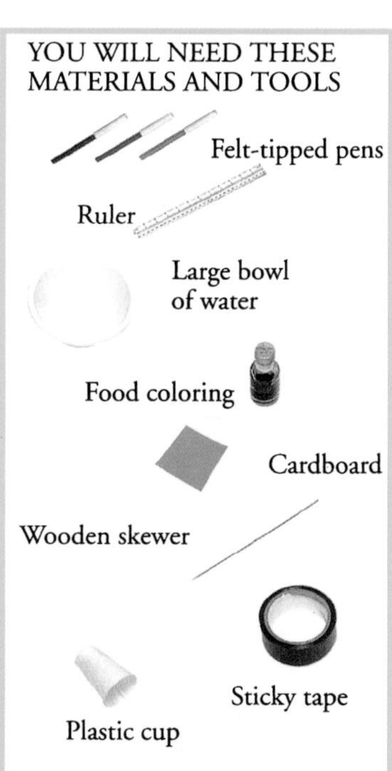

Household items or toys like a cork, pumice stone, pebble, small strainer, metal dish, clothespin, dry sponge, paper clip, wooden spoon, metal spoon, nail, piece of polystyrene, table-tennis ball

! Do not use glass or sharp objects in this experiment. A suitable waterproof area is essential.

Izabella tests some household things to see if they sink or float in water. You could try lots of other objects too.

1 Draw a chart in your Science Record Book with three columns. In the first column, write the names or draw the items you will test. The middle column is for those that SWIM. The last is for those that SINK.

2 Ask a grown-up to fill a large bowl of water. Stir in some food colouring – just for fun!

3 Make a float-marker by cutting out a sail shape from the piece of card. Tape it to a wooden skewer. Ask a grown up to push the skewer into the bottom of a plastic cup. Half-fill the cup with water and float it.

4 Put the cork, the pumice stone and the pebble on the surface of the water. Do they sink or swim?

5 Put a cross in the SINK or a tick in the SWIM column of your Science Record Book for each item.

6 Try to float the small sieve and the metal dish. Put the results in your Science Record Book.

7 Test a clothes peg and the sponge. Leave the sponge in the water for a long time. Does it still float as high?

Weight, Shape and Water

If something has air in it, like the dry sponge, it weighs less. So it is likely to float. The metal dish also has air "in" it when it is the right way up, so it floats too. This is how metal boats float. If the air is replaced by water, the object becomes heavier and it may sink. This is why the sponge gradually floats lower as it soaks up water. Tip over the dish and it fills with water and sinks. This is what happens when a boat capsizes. The float-marker is half full of water and half full of air, so it half floats. Pumice stone is bubbly rock full of air that is made by volcanoes.

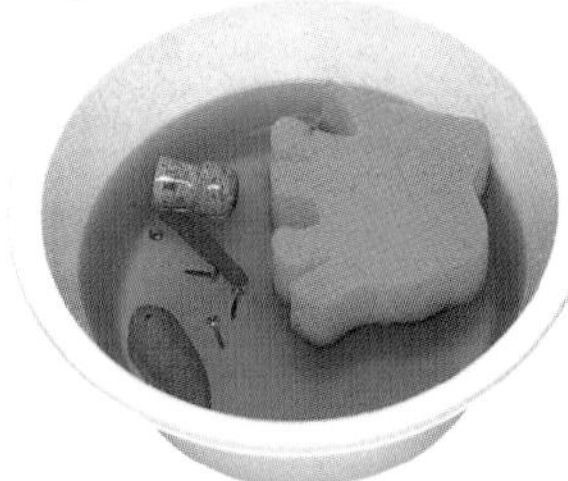

The Great Iceberg Puzzle

One of the great puzzles of nature is how icebergs float. Icebergs are huge lumps of ice that drift about in the cold seas near the North and South Poles. Some icebergs are bigger than cities. They weigh thousands of tonnes. As water gets colder, it gets heavier. So cold water sinks below warm water. Icebergs are frozen water and so are even colder. So why do they not sink to the bottom of the sea? Lorenzo finds out why in this experiment, by using tiny icebergs from a refrigerator or freezer. They will work the same as a real iceberg, but they are much smaller!

Lorenzo has made lots of coloured "icebergs". He is investigating how they float and then melt.

YOU WILL NEED THESE MATERIALS AND TOOLS

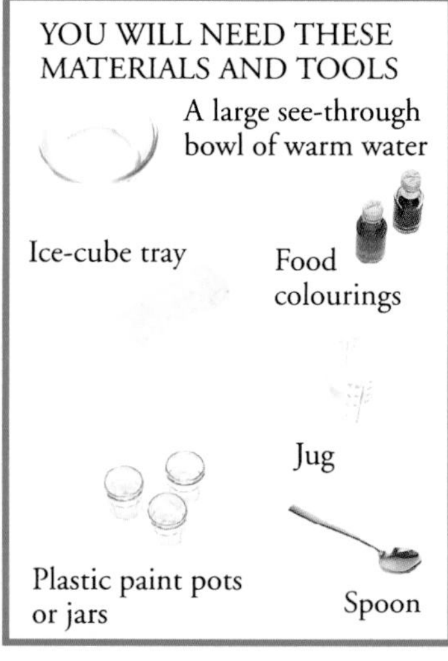

Light ice

As water gets colder, it becomes heavier. But this only happens down to the temperature of 4°C (40°F). If it gets colder than that, it begins to get lighter again and so rises towards the surface. When it cools to 0°C (32°F), liquid water freezes into solid ice. This cold ice is quite light and it floats on water. This means that animals and plants which live in water do not have to freeze solid themselves when the temperature drops to or below freezing. They can survive in the cold water below the ice that floats on ponds and lakes.

1 Make some mini-icebergs by putting food colouring into some water in paint pots or jars. You can make them in several different colours, but do not mix the colours together.

2 Spoon the coloured water carefully into the ice-cube tray or other containers, if you wish. Put this into a freezer or the freezing compartment of a refrigerator. Leave until frozen solid.

3 When the ice-cubes are frozen, fill the large bowl with warm water. Ask a grown-up to help you with this. Then remove the ice-cube tray from the freezer or refrigerator.

4 Drop coloured ice-cubes into the water. Watch what happens. Do they sink? Look at the bowl from the side. Can you see the ice melting? What does it do?

! This experiment needs a waterproof area. Young children will need help with warm water and with the bowl, especially if it is glass. Handle ice with care since it can stick to the skin and "burns" with intense cold. Dip the ice-cube tray in water to prevent this and to free the cubes. Also, use of the freezer must always be supervised.

Underwater Fountain

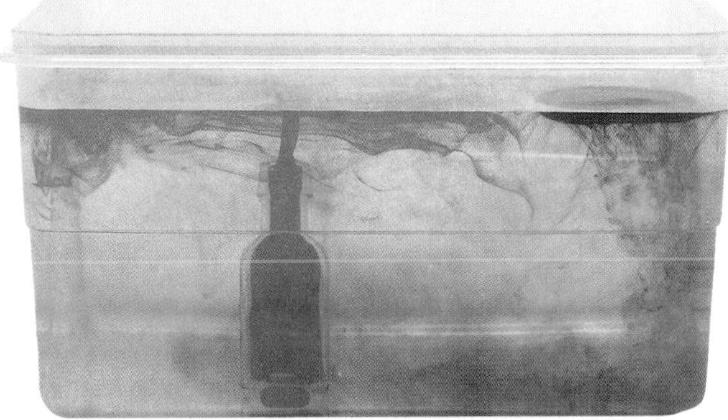

You can investigate how warm water floats and cold water sinks by making an underwater fountain. Fill a large bowl with cold water. Then fill a small plastic bottle with warm water. (The plastic bottle must be small enough to sink below the surface of the water in the bowl.) Add some food colouring to it. Carefully lower the bottle into the bowl and make it sit on the bottom. Does the warm coloured water stay in the bottle? Where does it go? Draw a picture of your fountain in your Science Research Book to show your results. You could also try dropping in some coloured ice-cubes, made with a different food colouring, into the water. The ice is lighter than the water around it, so it floats. The warmer water melts the coloured ice. But the coloured water that comes from the ice is colder and heavier than the water, so it sinks. Look very carefully to see the cold, coloured water trickling from the iceberg and sinking to the bottom.

Kitchen Chemistry

Everything in the world is made of chemicals. Some are artificial chemicals, like those made in factories. Others are natural chemicals, like those in your own body and in the rocks and soil. Even the food you eat is made of chemicals. Scientists who study chemicals are called chemists. You can be a kitchen chemist, like Dean, and study the chemicals in the cupboard. Cooking is a form of chemistry. You mix together the chemicals and make them join together, or react, to form a tasty snack.

The acid test

Some cooking substances, like vinegar or lemon juice, are sour. They are called **acidic**. Other kitchen substances, like bicarbonate of soda (bicarb), are slightly slimy and bitter. They are called **basic** or **alkali**. Bases are the opposite of acids. Chemists often need to know whether chemicals are acids or bases. If they do not know what the chemicals are, they should never taste them to find out, because many chemicals are poisonous. So chemists make special substances called **chemical indicators**, to test them. Red cabbage water is a good chemical indicator to tell the difference between acids and bases.

! Young children must be supervised in the kitchen, as some foods and liquids can cause sickness in large quantities. Chopping and boiling the cabbage should always be done by a grown-up.

Dean has put a strip of blotting paper into each of his test jars. The name of the test juice or liquid is marked on the paper in pencil. He can then let the strips dry and clip them into his Science Record Book.

YOU WILL NEED THESE MATERIALS AND TOOLS

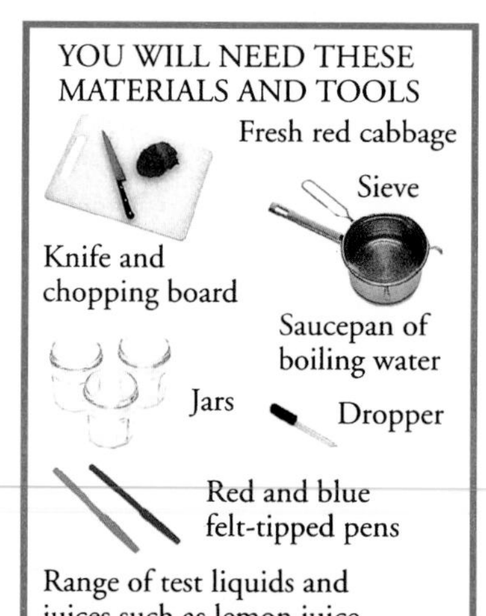

1 Ask a grown-up to chop the cabbage, put it into boiling water for about 15 minutes, then strain the water through a sieve.

2 While the chemical indicator (the red cabbage water) is cooling, put a little tap water into each jar. Get your Science Record Book ready.

3 Add about 15 drops of the chemical indicator to each jar, using the dropper. Look at the colour and note it in your Science Record Book.

4 Add one test liquid to a jar, such as a spoonful of juice squeezed from a lemon. Stir it in. Watch and note down any colour change.

5 Add another test liquid, such as a spoonful of milk, to the next jar. As before, mix it, and note down any colour change in your book.

6 Add the next test liquid, such as a few drops of vinegar, to the next jar. Note any change. Do this with the other test liquids and juices.

Recording Your Results

Colour in the result of each experiment in your Science Record Book. Draw three columns. In the first column, write the name or draw a picture of the test substance. In the second column put a mark for those that turned red or orange with a red felt-tipped pen. In the third column put a mark for those that turned purple or blue with a blue felt-tipped pen. Acids join or react with the red cabbage water to turn it red or orange. Bases do the same but turn it purple or blue. During the experiment, keep one jar that contains just the chemical indicator. Scientists call this a "control". You can compare the colour changes in the other jars with the original colour in the "control" jar.

Vinegar Volcano

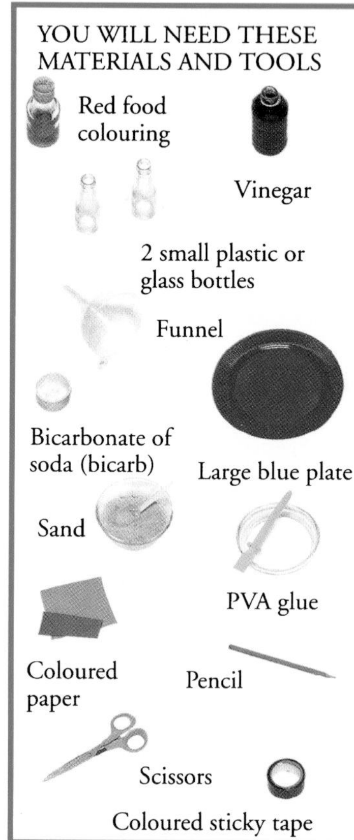

What happens when acids and bases, or alkalis, meet? Kirsty has made a peaceful-looking tropical island, but it is about to get shaken by a huge volcano. She can make the volcano explode or erupt using simple chemicals – the acid vinegar and the base bicarbonate of soda. The spectacular effect is caused by the reaction between the acid and the base. The food colouring makes it look like real, red-hot, runny rock.

Fizzy gas

Everything is made of chemicals. And all chemicals are made of tiny particles called **atoms**. During a chemical reaction, the groups of atoms are taken apart, mixed and shuffled, then joined together in different groups, to make new chemicals. When vinegar is mixed with bicarbonate of soda (bicarb), one of the new chemicals formed is a gas. The bubbles of this gas make the volcano fizz.

This chemical reaction is not dangerous. The gas produced is carbon dioxide, but with the recommended quantities of vinegar and bicarbonate of soda (bicarb), its amounts are very small and not harmful. However, the child should be supervised in case of spillage.

Kirsty's vinegar volcanic island is based on a simple chemical reaction. A real volcano is millions of times more powerful, and based on heat and pressure.

1 Add some red food colouring to some vinegar in a small bottle using the funnel.

2 Wash and dry the funnel. Use it to put 1 or 2 dessert spoons of bicarb into another small bottle.

3 Stand this bottle in the middle of the plate as the volcano. Pile the sand around it.

4 Paint the sides of the bottle with glue, to make it stick. Leave the bottle's mouth clear. This is the volcano's opening, or crater.

5 Make a palm tree. Draw some leaves on green paper and cut them out. Snip around their edges to make fronds. Roll up some coloured paper to make the tree trunk.

6 Tape round the top and bottom of the trunk and cut it off square, so it stands up. Tape the palm leaf shapes to the top of the trunk.

7 Using the funnel, carefully pour some of the coloured vinegar onto the bicarb in the bottle on the island, and quickly remove the funnel.

Lots of Eruptions

The red, bubbly "lava" fizzes out of the top of the volcano. The chemical reaction starts as soon as the vinegar mixes with the bicarb. When the volcano has finished erupting, stir inside the bottle with a skewer and pour in some more vinegar. You may get several eruptions in this way.

Making Music

Introduction

What is music? Very simply, music is made from sounds that are pleasing or interesting to hear. Birdsong can be described as music and so can the sounds of the wind or the sea. Many people who write music – composers – have copied the sounds of nature in their music.

Sound is caused by vibrations in the air. The stronger the vibrations, the louder the sound. Musical instruments help us to make music by producing many different sounds. Your own voice is a musical instrument. See how many sounds you can make by altering the shape of your mouth, by using your tongue in different ways, and by changing the pitch of your voice from high to low. We humans are a mixture of the different types of instruments described below: we are wind instruments because we use air to make sounds; stringed instruments because we speak or sing through our vocal cords, which are like strings low down in our throats; and percussion instruments because we can clap our hands and snap our fingers.

Gabriella's bottle xylophone is a percussion instrument.

Musicians divide musical instruments into different groups:

Percussion Instruments

These are all the instruments that you hit. They were probably the earliest instruments. People from long ago made music by hitting bones together, or hitting a hollow tree. Animal skins were stretched over pots or bits of tree trunks to make drums. It is not just drums that are percussion instruments. There are all kinds of fun shakers and rattles which are also used to give rhythm in music.

Claudius has made a bugle, which is a wind instrument.

Wind Instruments

These are the instruments that you blow. The air vibrates inside the hollow instrument and makes a sound. The first instruments of this kind were made out of hollow animal horns or bones. Wind instruments sometimes have a "reed" to help make a good sound, and a drinking straw works very well for this.

Stringed Instruments

These instruments can be plucked with your fingers or played with a bow. The strings were first made out of hair and silk. All stringed instruments need a hollow box of some kind over which the strings are attached. The box is full of air, which vibrates when you play the instrument.

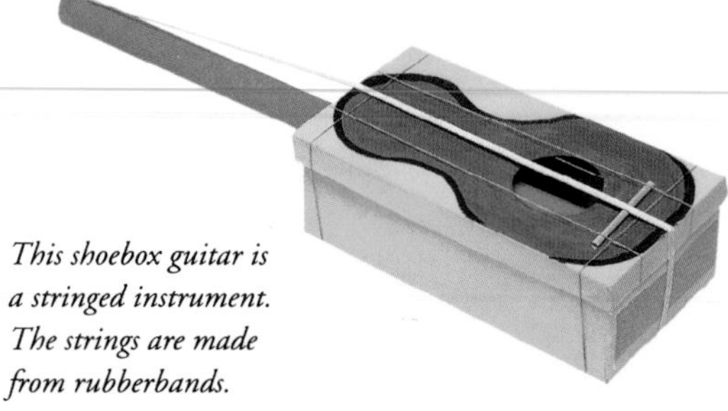

This shoebox guitar is a stringed instrument. The strings are made from rubberbands.

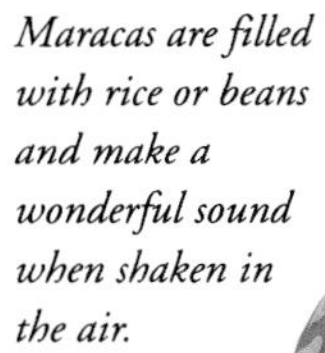

Jessica is making a drum from a mini plastic dustbin.

Musical Families

See how many instruments you can think of and try to place them in a family or group. Is the piano a stringed instrument? It has strings but they are not plucked or played with a bow. If you look inside the piano you will see that small felt hammers hit the strings to make the sounds. It is a percussion instrument!

Making Musical Instruments

This chapter will help you to discover lots of different sounds by making your own instruments and then playing them. They are very easy to make. All you need to make music is a cardboard tube or drinks can, and a few bottle tops or a bath hat! Some of the instruments come from countries like Africa and Latin America, so it is a good chance to decorate them with really bright colours. If you make one of the fun shakers or rattles, it will feel like carnival time!

Maracas are filled with rice or beans and make a wonderful sound when shaken in the air.

Making Music Together

It is even more fun playing music in groups. Perhaps you and your friends can each make a different instrument to play. First try a rhythm game. Each of you choose a word and then play the rhythm (the beat) of that word on your instruments over and over again. Try to keep time with everyone else, then experiment by getting louder then softer, and slower then faster.

You could join in with your favourite pop song. Start with the percussion instruments to make the rhythm, then add a wind instrument like a kazoo to sing the tune. See how many different instruments you can use. Make up some music to describe a storm, a ghost story, or a trip to the zoo.

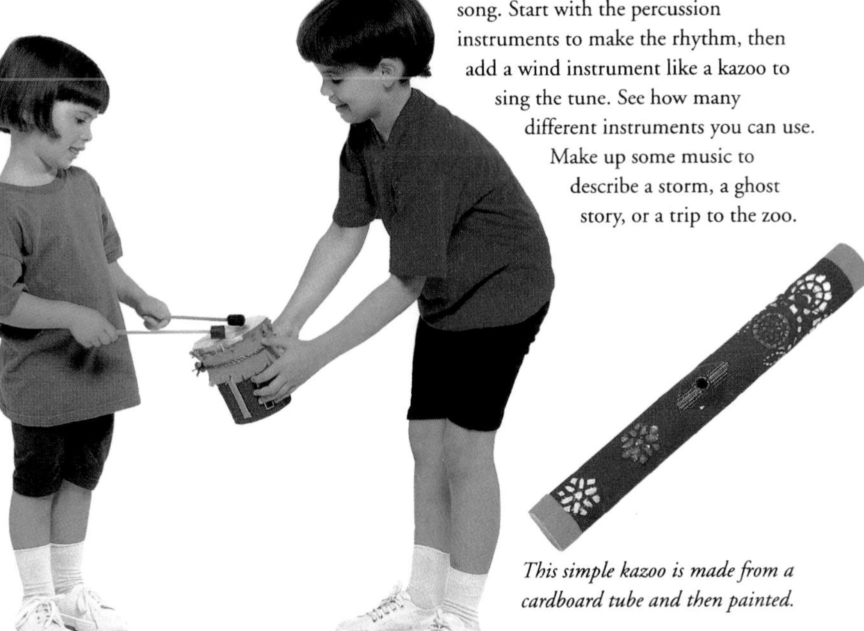

It is great fun to make music with someone else to help.

This simple kazoo is made from a cardboard tube and then painted.

Clashing Castanets

Castanets come from Spain, where they are used in flamenco dancing. The dancers stamp their feet and click their castanets in time to the music. It is very exciting to watch them. See if you can dance the same way. Izabella has made her castanets with metal pastry-cutters, so they make a wonderful sound. *Olé*!

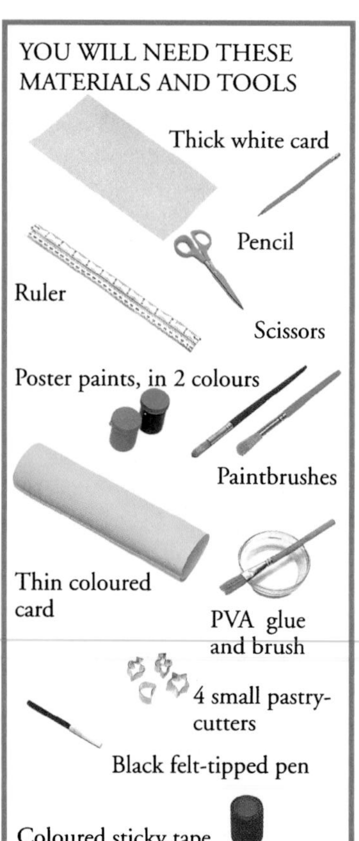

Put your thumb and middle finger through the yellow finger-holders and play away!

Making music

Clash the pastry-cutters together in time to the music. You can also play them by resting your hand on a table.

! Children may need help measuring out and cutting and scoring the card.

1 Draw a rectangle 20 cm (8 in) long and 7 cm (3 in) wide on thick white card. Draw two lines 4 cm ($1^1/_2$ in) apart down the centre of the rectangle.

2 Carefully cut out the rectangle. Bend the card along the centre lines. It helps if you score along the lines with the ruler first.

3 Paint one side of the card. Leave to dry, then paint the other side in a different colour. Leave to dry while you make the finger-holders.

4 Draw four small rectangles on thin card and cut out. Fold around into tubes to fit your middle finger and thumb, and glue together.

5 Decorate one side of the thick painted card. Draw around the pastry-cutters with a black felt-tipped pen to make outline shapes.

6 Reinforce the centre where the castanets bend with coloured sticky tape. This will make them last longer.

7 Glue the finger-holders onto the decorated side of the card. Place them about 1 cm ($^1/_2$ in) each side of the bend. Leave to dry.

8 Glue a pastry-cutter to the inside ends of each castanet. Use plenty of glue and let it dry properly.

Dustbin Drum

Drums are very old instruments. They are used for the rhythm in dance music and they help soldiers to keep in step when they march. Drums were also once used to send signals because you can hear them so far away. You can play your drum with bare hands or with beaters, like Jessica and Alice.

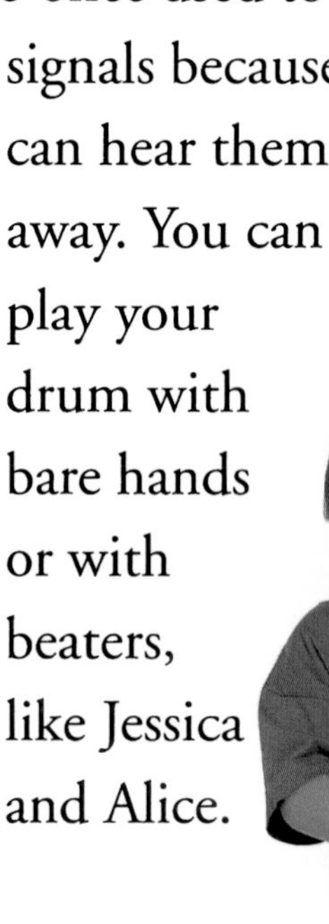

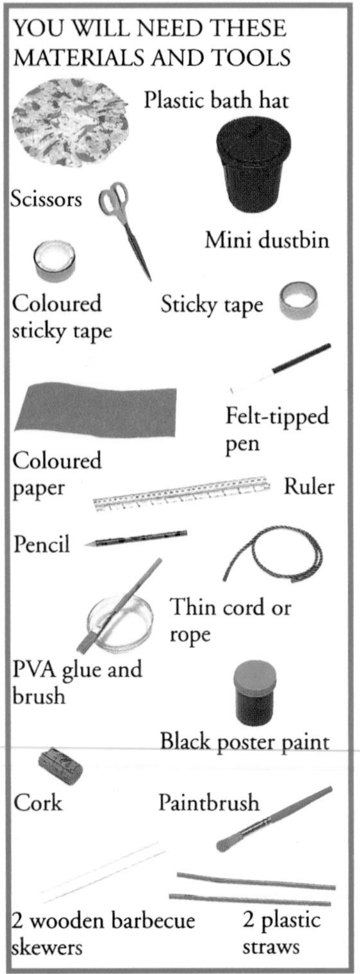

Making music

Do not hit the drum too hard. You will get the best sound if you hit it close to the edge. If you hit different parts of the drumskin, you will get different sounds. Try playing it with a pair of chopsticks or your hands.

! A grown-up should cut the cork in half with a craft knife and push the skewer into the corks, to make the beaters. Children may need help with scissors.

The finished drum looks very smart.

1 Cut the elastic out of the bath hat. Draw around a plate which is 5 cm (2 in) bigger all around than the top of the dustbin. Cut the circle out.

2 Decorate the dustbin with stripes of coloured sticky tape.

3 Stretch the plastic circle tightly over the open end of the dustbin. Stick in place with several small tabs of sticky tape.

4 Make sure the plastic drumskin is really tight, then tape right around the edge to hold it in place.

5 Cut a strip of coloured paper to fit around the dustbin top. Make small cuts on both sides for a fringe.

6 Glue the fringe around the top of the dustbin.

7 Tie the cord or rope around the centre of the fringe.

8 Ask a grown-up to cut the cork in half across the middle. Paint the corks black. Push the skewers through the straws, then ask a grown-up to push them into the corks.

Deep Box Bass

Bass instruments play the very lowest notes. This is because they are so large. The large box and the large hole mean there is plenty of space for the air to vibrate and make a deep, booming sound. Nicholas is plucking his box bass with his fingers, like a double-bass player in a jazz band.

Your box bass is all ready for a jazz session!

Making music

Hold the elastic with one hand and twang it with the other. You can change the sound by pressing the elastic in different places. Thick elastic makes a lower sound than thin elastic.

! A grown-up should cut the cork in half with a craft knife. Children may need help with scissors.

YOU WILL NEED THESE MATERIALS AND TOOLS

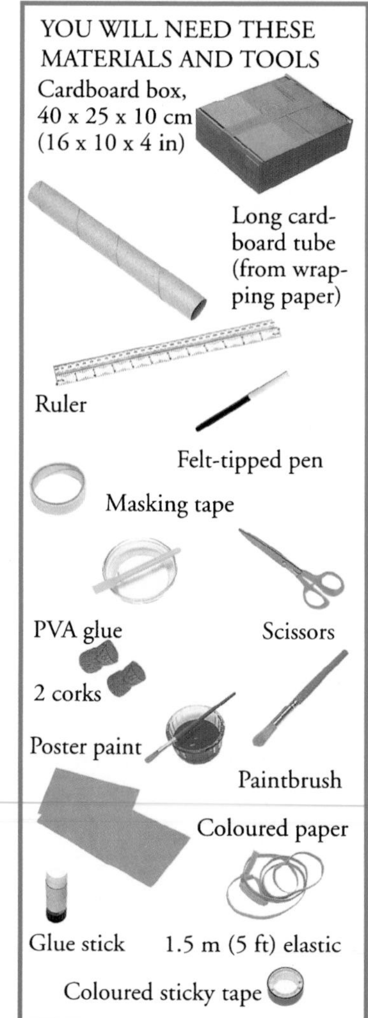

1 Draw around the cardboard tube to make a circle on the centre of the box top. Then draw around the roll of masking tape to make a larger circle on the box front. Position it as shown.

2 Carefully cut out both circles. Pierce the circle with the scissors, and make small cuts out towards the edge of the circle. Then cut around the edge of the circle.

3 Push the tube through the small hole. Glue and tape the tube in place. Ask a grown-up to cut a cork in half. Glue and tape one half as shown and the other below the large hole.

4 Paint the box and the tube, and leave to dry.

5 Draw musical notes on the coloured paper. Draw around a cork to make the circle shapes.

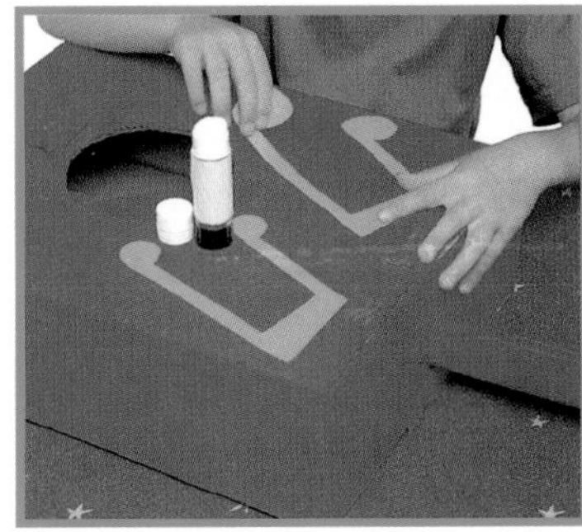

6 Cut out the notes and glue them onto the front of the box.

7 Ask a grown-up to cut an 8 cm (3 in) slit in the front of the tube. Tie the elastic around the bottom. Tie a double knot in the other end.

8 Decorate the box with tape. Stretch the elastic down the back of the box and back up the front. Slip the knot into the slit in the tube.

Singing Kazoo

This is a very unusual instrument. You sing through it and it makes your voice sound very strange. Indian musicians play a kind of kazoo which they hold against their throats when they sing. Lorenzo has covered his kazoo with stencils. This is a very easy and quick way to decorate things.

Making music

Sing through the hole in the middle of the kazoo. You can play any tune you like. Experiment with a smaller tube from a toilet roll, and see if it sounds different.

! A grown-up should make the hole in the cardboard tube and sticky tape. Children may need help with scissors.

Stencils are a good way to decorate any of the instruments.

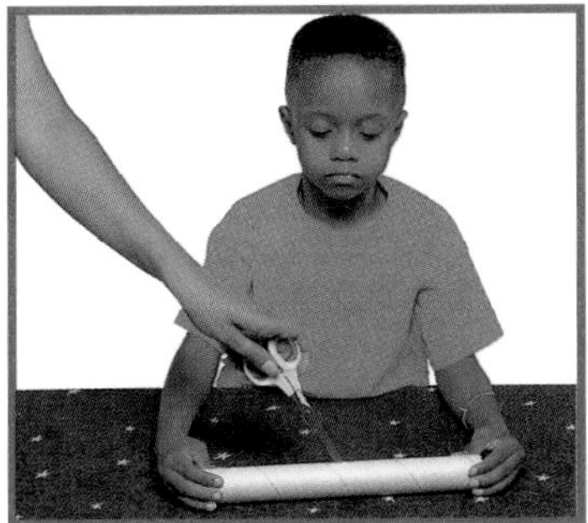

1 Ask a grown-up to make a small hole in the centre of the cardboard tube.

2 Use the end of a paintbrush to smooth the edges of the hole.

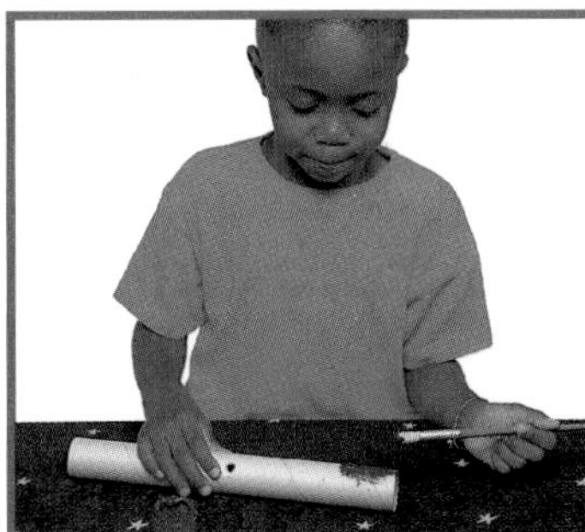

3 Paint the cardboard tube. Leave the paint to dry.

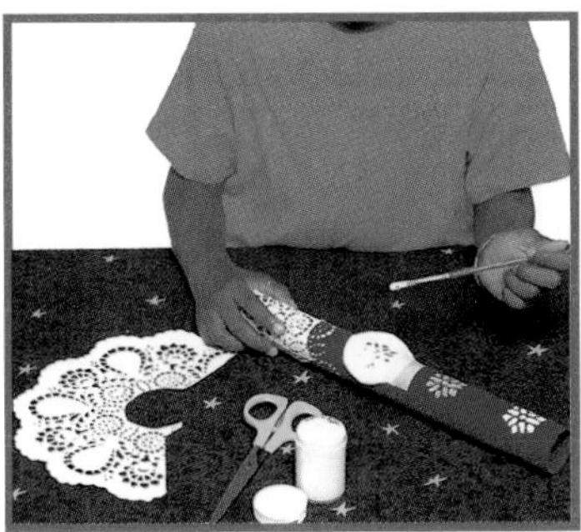

4 Cut flower shapes from the paper doily and use them as stencils. Stick them onto the tube with masking tape and paint over them. Leave the paint to dry, then remove the stencils.

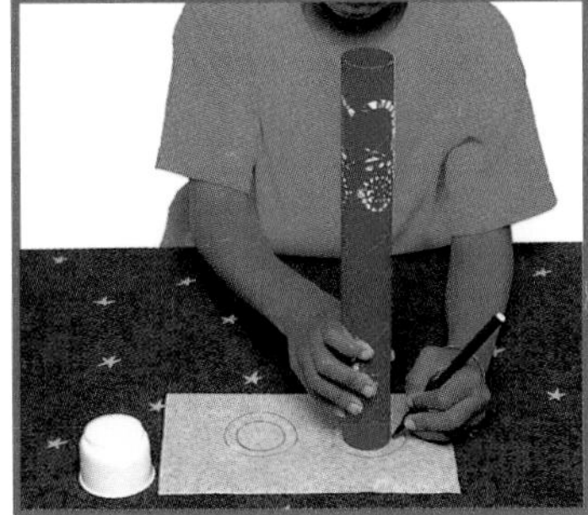

5 Draw two circles on the greaseproof paper. Draw around a cup or any round object that is slightly larger than the end of the tube. Now draw around the end of the tube to make a smaller circle inside each larger one.

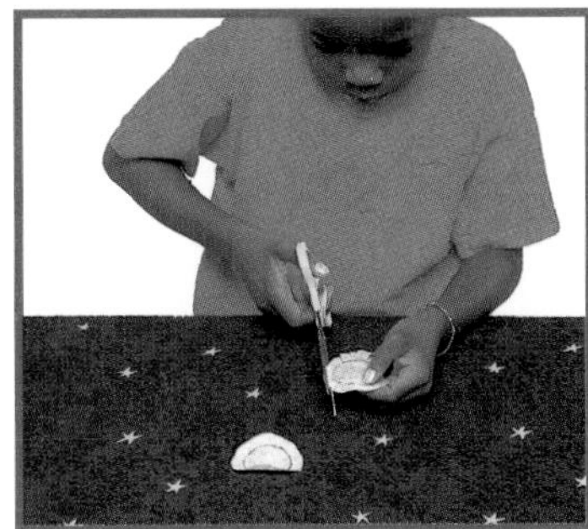

6 Cut out the large circles. Make small cuts between the large and small circles. This will give each circle a frill around the edge. Brush glue onto the frills.

7 Stretch the greaseproof paper circles tightly across the ends of the cardboard tube. Press the frills around the sides of the tube.

8 Glue ribbon around the ends of the tube. Stick a piece of coloured sticky tape over the hole. Ask a grown-up to pierce through the tape.

Tambourine Flower

Tambourines have been played since the Middle Ages. They were made of a circle of wood with very thin animal skin stretched across, and they had bells around the edge. Like castanets, tambourines are very popular in Spanish dancing – you could play them together. Leslie has painted his tambourine to look like a sunflower.

Instead of bottle tops, you could use beads or buttons. They will all make different sounds.

Making music

Hold your tambourine above your head and shake it. You can also hold it in one hand and tap it with the fingers of your other hand. You can even bang it against your knee.

! A grown-up should pierce the bottle tops with a corkscrew or other sharp object. Children may need help with scissors.

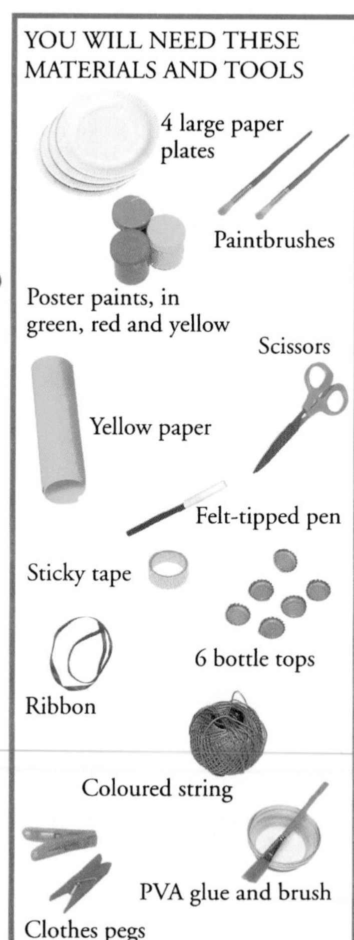

1 Using green paint, paint around the rim of one of the paper plates. Do not paint the middle. Leave the paint to dry.

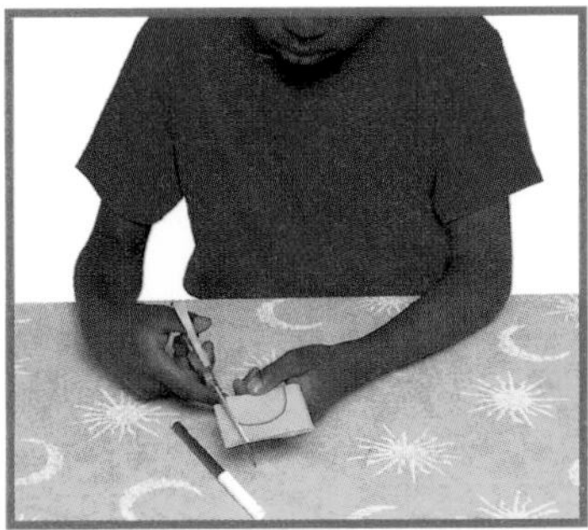

2 Cut a long strip of yellow paper. Fold the strip over and over. Draw a petal shape on the top layer and cut out through all the layers. Repeat to make 16 petals.

3 Tape the petal shapes around the unpainted circle in the middle of the plate.

4 Take another paper plate. Cut out the centre circle and paint it in red. Leave to dry.

5 Paint spots of yellow on the red circle. Paint the bottle tops red as well. Leave to dry.

6 Cut the ribbon into several pieces, each roughly the same length. Cut two pieces of string the same length and knot at one end. Ask a grown-up to pierce the bottle tops. Thread three onto each piece of string, tying a knot after each one.

7 Take the third paper plate. Glue three or four ribbons on each side. Glue the string on each side of the fourth plate. Glue the plates together.

8 Put clothes pegs round the edge, to make sure the plates stick together properly. Leave the glue to dry.

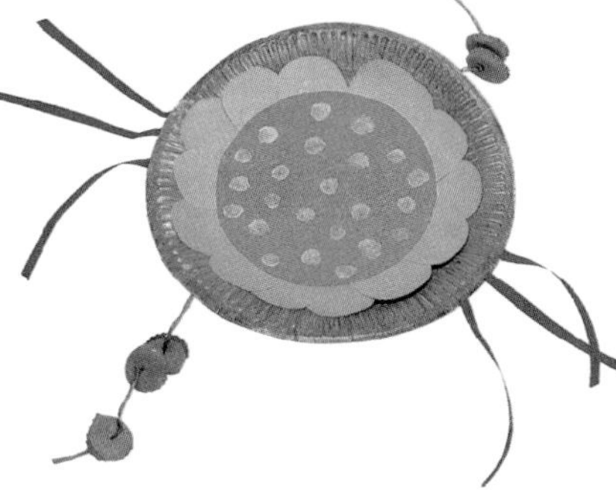

Shoebox Guitar

The guitar is probably the most popular instrument of all. It is easy to carry and you can play many different kinds of music on it. Jessica is plucking the elastic string on her guitar, just like a pop star. Electric guitars don't have boxes full of air like this one, so they need electricity to make them sound loud.

YOU WILL NEED THESE MATERIALS AND TOOLS

- Shoebox
- Pencil
- Ruler
- Long cardboard tube (from wrapping paper)
- Scissors
- Poster paints, in black and 3 colours
- Paintbrush
- 4 large rubberbands
- Plastic straw
- PVA glue and brush
- 1.5 m (5 ft) elastic

A guitar is a large box full of air. The air vibrates and makes the sound, which escapes through the hole.

Making music

Pluck the elastic string with one hand. With your other hand, press the elastic against the cardboard tube. If you press in different places, you can change the note. Try strumming the string with a coin instead of plucking it.

! Children may need help cutting out the circles. See the Introduction for an easy way of doing this.

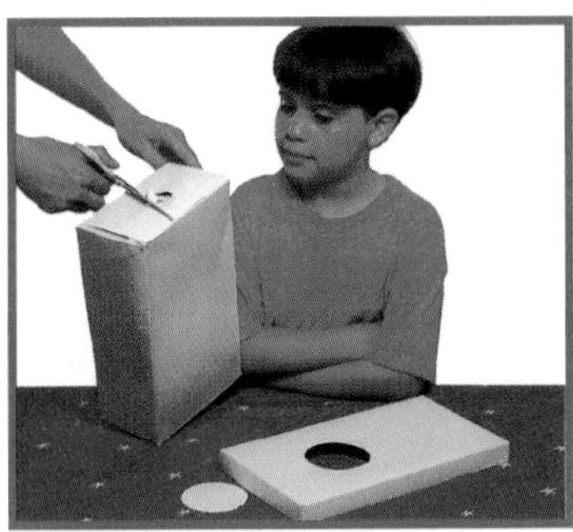

1 Draw a 10 cm (4 in) circle on the box lid. Draw around the tube on one end of the box base. Ask a grown-up to cut out the circles.

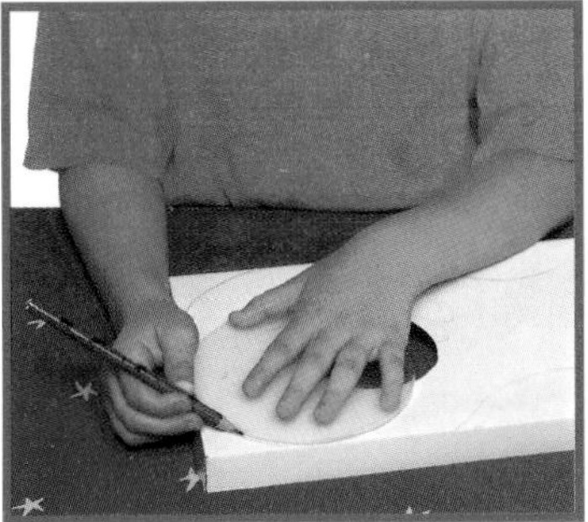

2 Draw a guitar shape on the lid of the box. Use a circular shape as a guide, or use a pair of compasses, if you like.

3 Outline the guitar shape in black paint. Fill in with coloured paint, then paint the rest of the box another colour. Paint the tube.

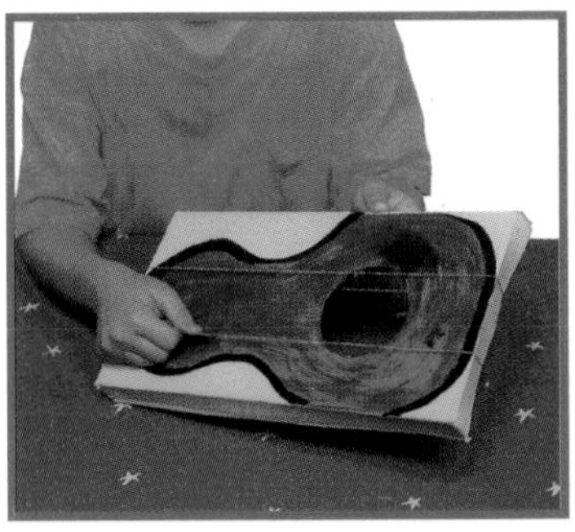

4 Stretch two rubberbands across the lid. Position them as shown, just on the edge of the hole.

5 Put the lid on the box. Hold it in place with two more rubberbands. Cut the straw in half. Slide the two pieces under the rubberbands at each end of the guitar. Glue in place.

6 Cut a slit about 8 cm (3 in) long at one end of the tube. Tie a knot in one end of the elastic. Make a loop in the other end and slide it over the end of the tube.

7 Push the tube into the hole in the box. Stretch the elastic around the back of the box and up around the front. Slip the knot into the slit in the tube.

Caxixi Rattle

The name of this rattle is pronounced "casheeshee". It comes from Latin America. You can fill it with anything that will make a good sound – try rice or beans, or sand. Alice has made a face for her rattle with scraps of paper and stickers. She has also given it a wonderful fringe.

! A grown-up should puncture the bottle and children may need help with scissors.

Shake your caxixi rattle in time to your favourite music.

Making music

Make two caxixi rattles and shake them together. Practise until you can keep in time to the rhythm of the music. Fill the bottles with different things to make different sounds.

YOU WILL NEED THESE MATERIALS AND TOOLS

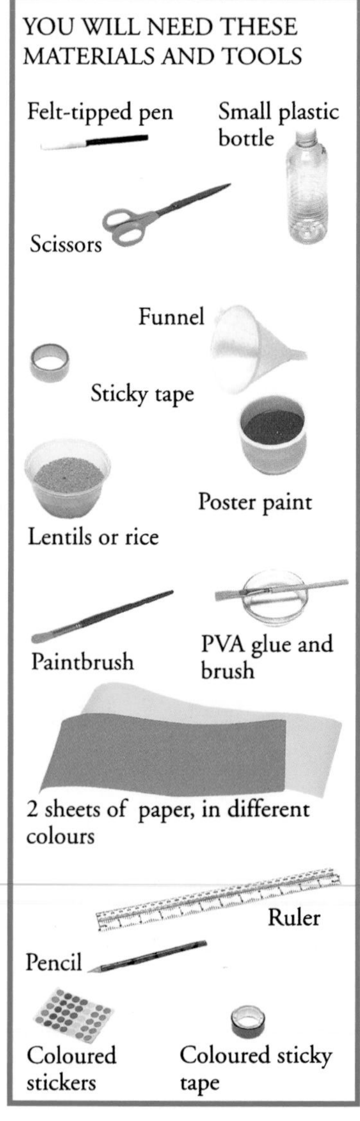

1 Wash and dry the bottle. Draw a line around the bottle about one-third from the top. Draw another line the same distance from the bottom.

2 Ask a grown-up to puncture the bottle with the point of the scissors. Then cut along both the lines you have marked.

3 Stick the top and bottom pieces of the bottle together with sticky tape to make a shorter bottle shape. Pour the lentils or rice into the bottle.

4 Mix the paint with glue and a little water and paint the top half of the bottle. Leave to dry.

5 Cut a strip from each of the coloured sheets of paper, long enough to wrap around the bottle.

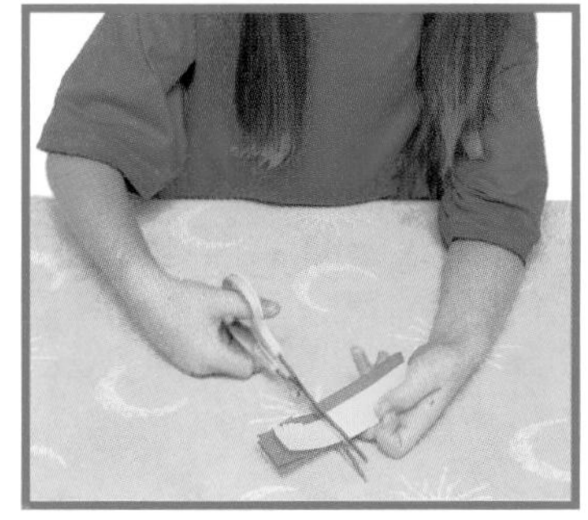

6 To make a fringe, fold the strips over and make plenty of small cuts halfway across the strips of paper.

7 Glue the fringe around the bottle. Hold it in place with coloured tape. Decorate your caxixi with a funny face using the coloured stickers, the paper and the felt-tipped pen.

This is a different caxixi shape made from a drinks can and decorated with star stickers and coloured sticky tape.

Saucepan Lid Cymbals

Saucepan lids make terrific cymbals. You can hit one with a beater, or clash them together as Benjamin is doing. Be careful not to bang them directly together – to do a proper cymbal clash, you move one cymbal up and one down. Real cymbals can turn inside-out if you hit them directly together! Cymbals are often played with drums in a drum kit.

YOU WILL NEED THESE MATERIALS AND TOOLS

- 2 matching metal saucepan lids
- Ribbon
- Coloured stickers
- Scissors
- Narrow and wide coloured sticky tape
- Large bottle-washer
- Wooden barbecue skewer
- Pan scourer
- Cork

If you want to decorate your saucepan lid cymbals, check with a grown-up first to make sure they don't mind.

Making music

Cymbals are often played very loudly, but they can also make a lovely, quiet sound. You can also hold a cymbal by its handle, or hang is from a piece of string, and strike it with one of your homemade beaters.

! A grown-up should cut the cork in half using a craft knife. Children will need help pushing the skewer into the cork.

1 Decorate the saucepan lids with coloured stickers. Arrange them in a circle, following the shape of the lid. Decorate the ribbon with stickers.

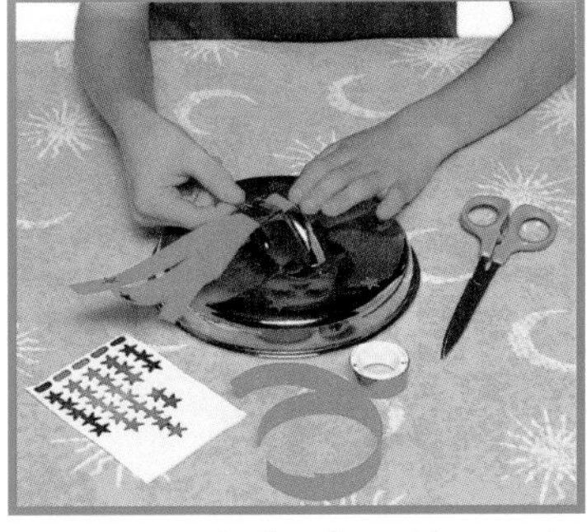

2 Decorate the handles with several strips of ribbon. Loop the strips around the handle and stick together with narrow coloured sticky tape.

3 Cover the rest of the handles with wide coloured sticky tape. Wind the narrow tape around the handle to make stripes.

4 Now make the first stick. Decorate the handle of the bottle-washer with coloured stickers and sticky tape.

5 Make the second stick. Push the wooden skewer through the middle of the pan scourer. Ask a grown-up to cut the cork in half. Push the sharp end of the skewer into one piece of cork.

6 Wind coloured sticky tape around the cork and the skewer where it comes out below the pan scourer. This will stop the pan scourer from slipping down the handle.

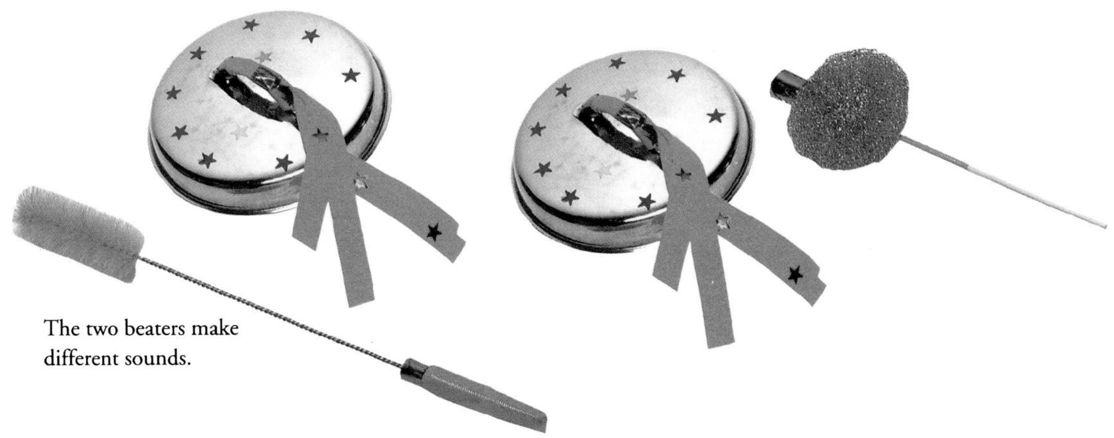

The two beaters make different sounds.

Snakey Maracas

Maracas are played by shaking them in time to the music. The rice inside rattles around to make the sound. Maracas are very popular in Africa and Latin America, where they are often made out of gourds. Nicholas has made his maracas out of papier mâché. This is wet newspaper mixed with glue. When it is dry, it sets hard so that you can paint it.

! Children may need help blowing up and tying the balloons, and with cutting the holes in the papier mâché.

When you play your maracas, the snakes will wriggle about and frighten everyone.

Making music

Shake both maracas together in time to the music. You can also play one maraca on its own. Hold it in one hand and roll it against the palm of your other hand.

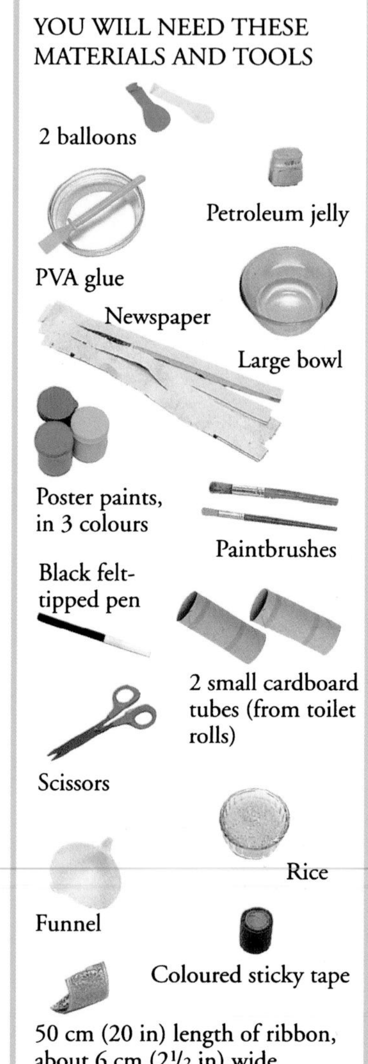

1 Blow up and tie the balloons. Cover them with petroleum jelly. Support the balloons in jars or mugs, otherwise they will bounce about.

2 Tear the newspaper into strips and squares. Soak them in glue. Cover the balloons with the strips. Leave to dry, then cover them with the squares.

3 Wait for the second layer to dry, then paint the balloons. Leave the paint to dry.

4 Now paint the cardboard tubes, using a different colour. Leave the paint to dry.

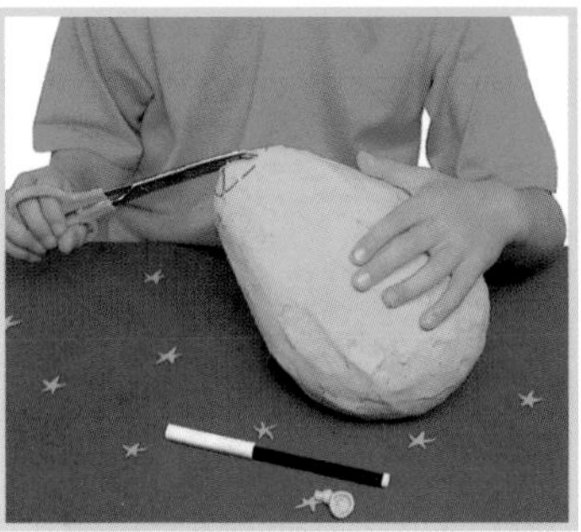

5 Draw around one of the cardboard tubes on the end of each balloon and cut out the circles.

6 Spread glue onto one end of each cardboard tube. Push them into the holes in the balloons for handles.

7 Pour the rice into the balloons through the handles. Seal the end of each handle with coloured sticky tape. Spread glue onto the handles, then cover them with ribbon.

8 Paint squiggly snakes to decorate the maracas. Use the black felt-tipped pen to draw the snakes' eyes and their forked tongues.

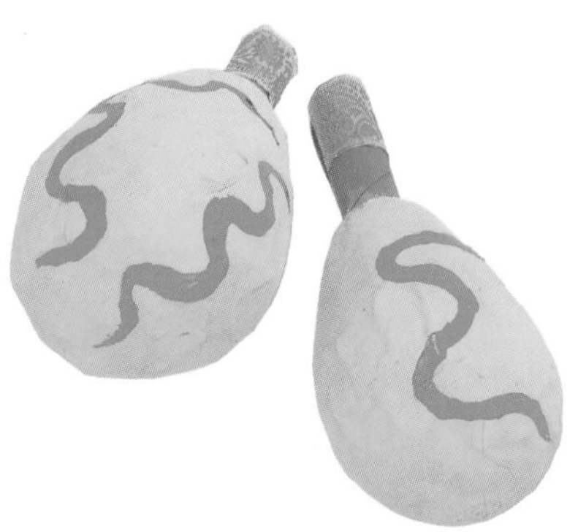

Bottle Xylophone

Bottles make wonderful musical instruments. To get different notes, you add more water. Play the xylophone with different sticks to make different sounds. You can also blow across the top of the bottles.

Gabriella has put coloured water in her xylophone bottles. This looks pretty and it also helps her remember the different notes.

! A grown-up should push the skewer into the cork. Never leave the coloured water in the bottles in case someone is tempted to try a taste. The water is NOT drinkable.

The different sticks make different sounds. What other sticks could you use?

Making music

See if you can play a simple tune like "Three Blind Mice". Add a little water to each bottle or pour some out until you get the notes right.

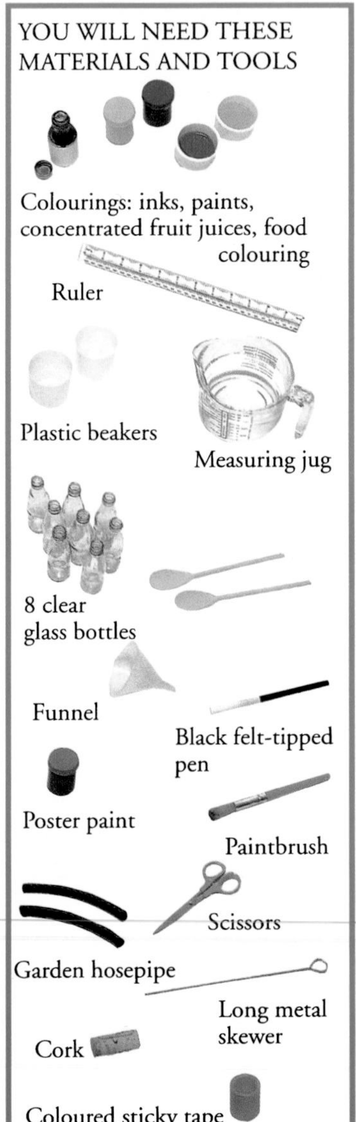

1 Mix seven different colours with water. Use inks, paints, concentrated fruit juices or food colouring.

2 Hit one of the glass bottles with a wooden spoon and listen to the sound it makes.

3 Mark 2 cm (3/4 in) from the bottom of the bottle. Use a felt-tipped pen.

4 Pour water into the bottle up to the mark. This is much easier if you use a funnel. Hit the bottle again – this time the sound will be lower.

5 Pour a different coloured water into each bottle. Raise the level of the water by 2 cm (3/4 in) each time. The bottle with the most water will give the lowest note.

6 Now try blowing across the top of each bottle. This time the bottle with the most water will give the highest note!

7 Paint the round ends of two wooden spoons. Cover the handles with hosepipe.

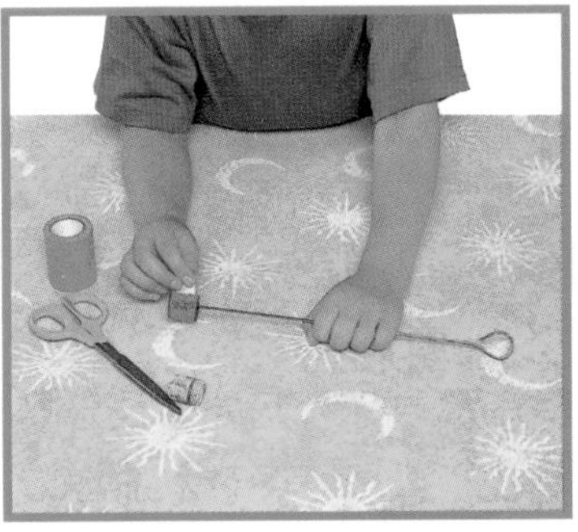

8 Make a different stick. Ask a grown-up to cut the cork in half and push in the skewer. Cover the cork with sticky tape.

Bugle Blow

The first bugles were used to send signals in battle or out hunting. Today bugles are used in the army, to wake everyone up in the morning! The soldier's bugle is a brass instrument but Claudius's bugle is made from a garden hosepipe. To get a good sound from this kind of instrument, you need a mouthpiece.

You will need plenty of puff to play your bugle.

Making music

Rest the rim of the mouthpiece on your lips and take a deep breath. Buzz your lips into the mouthpiece. To play higher notes, blow faster.

! Children may need help cutting and positioning the hosepipe.

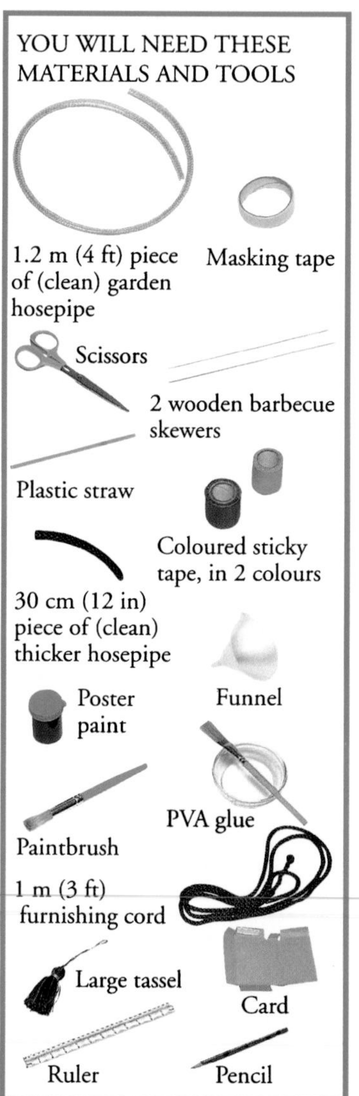

1 Bend the thin hosepipe into a circle so that the ends overlap as shown. Bind the circle together with two pieces of masking tape 8 cm (3 in) apart.

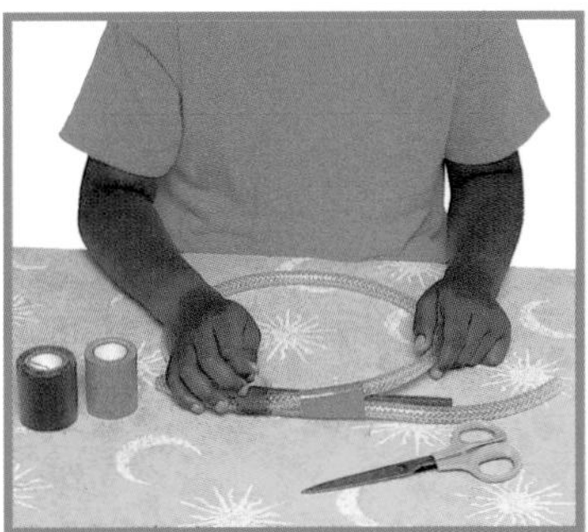

2 Push both skewers into the straw. Place the straw behind the join in the hosepipe and tape them together in three places.

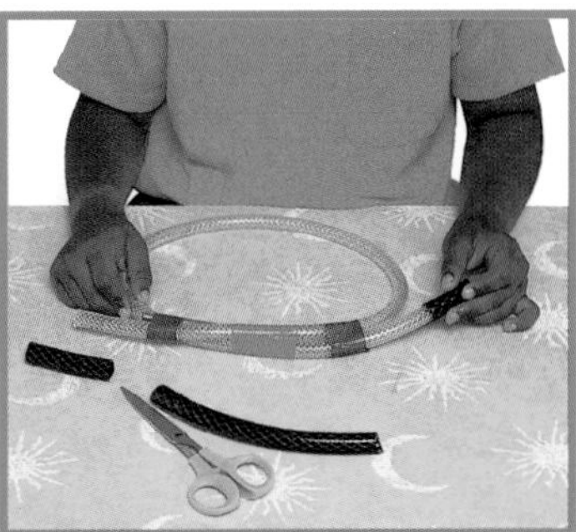

3 Cut a piece of thick hosepipe about 15 cm (6 in) long. Slide it onto one end of the hosepipe. Cut a shorter length and slide it onto the other end.

4 Mix the poster paint with the same amount of glue and a little water, and then paint the funnel. Push the funnel into the longer piece of thick hosepipe.

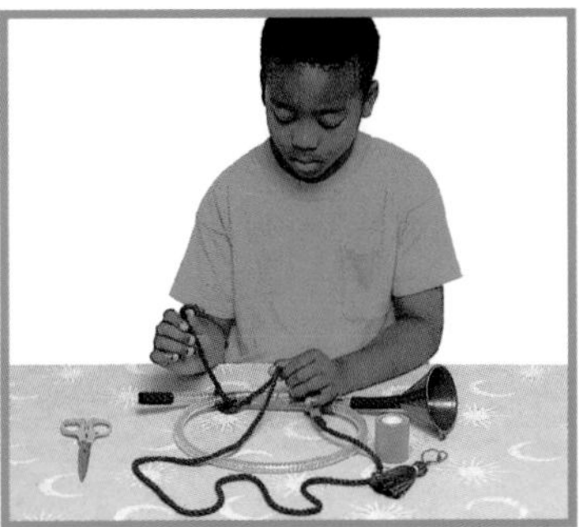

5 Tie the cord onto the bugle so that you can carry it across your chest. Fasten the tassel to the bugle.

6 Measure a square about 13 x 13 cm (5 x 5 in) on the card and cut out.

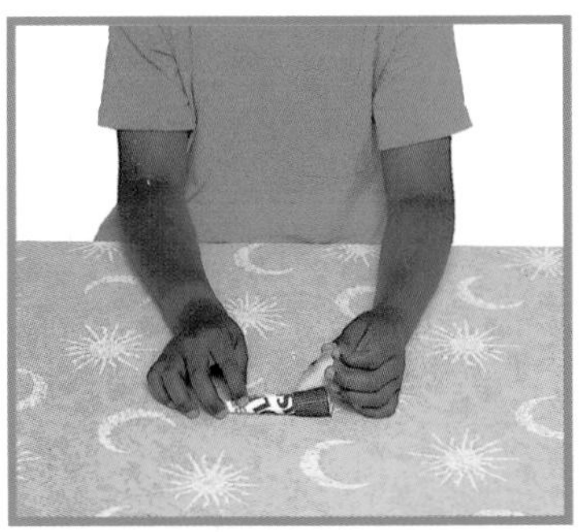

7 Roll the square into a cone shape and trim. Tape the cone together and tape over the sharp card edges.

8 Fit the cone into the mouthpiece end of the bugle.

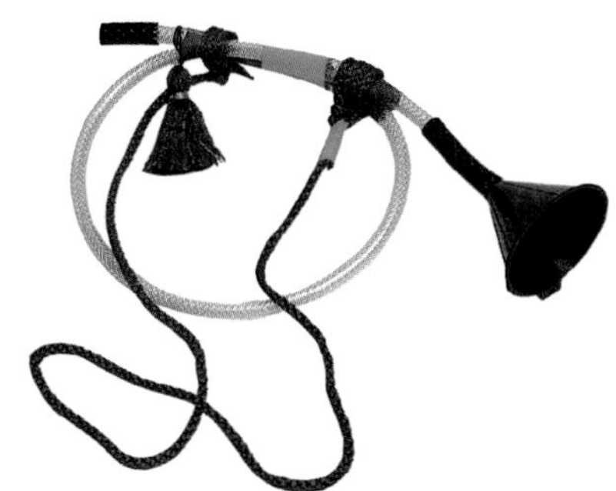

Flowerpot Chimes

You do not have to play these wind chimes yourself – if you hang them up the wind will play them for you. The best place to hang them is from a door frame or window frame. Ilaira likes to play her chimes herself, using wooden spoons. The flowerpots are very heavy, so you need a strong coathanger.

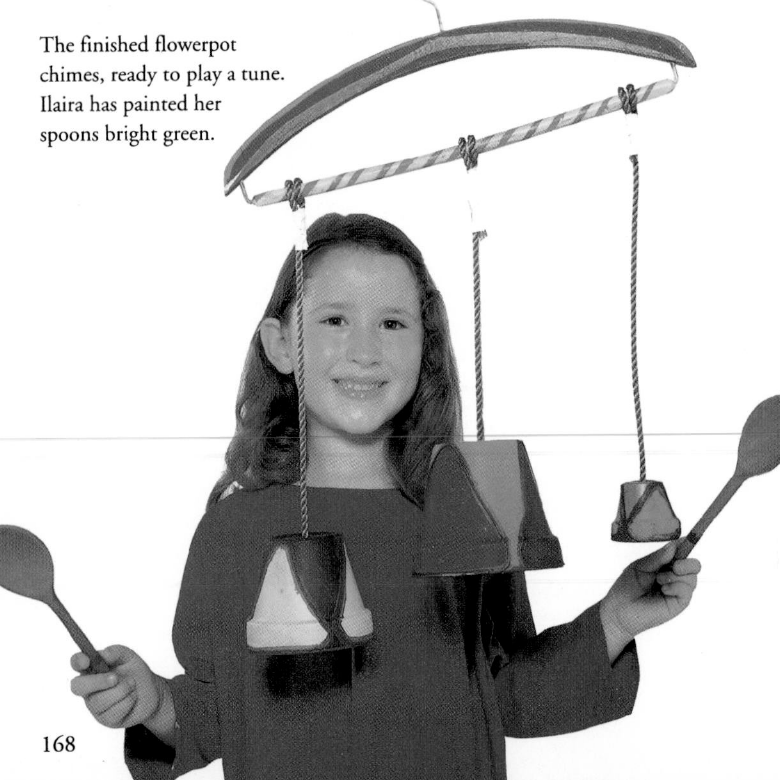

The finished flowerpot chimes, ready to play a tune. Ilaira has painted her spoons bright green.

Making music

Hit the flowerpots gently with the spoons. Does the small flowerpot sound different to the large one?

! A grown-up should make the holes in the corks and cut them in half with a craft knife. Children may need help with scissors.

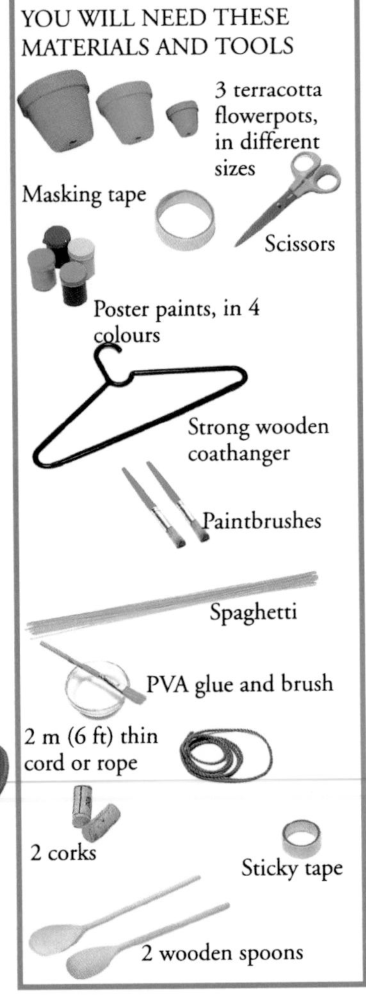

YOU WILL NEED THESE MATERIALS AND TOOLS

3 terracotta flowerpots, in different sizes
Masking tape
Scissors
Poster paints, in 4 colours
Strong wooden coathanger
Paintbrushes
Spaghetti
PVA glue and brush
2 m (6 ft) thin cord or rope
2 corks
Sticky tape
2 wooden spoons

1 Use the masking tape to make four triangle shapes on each pot. Paint above the tape in different colours. Leave to dry, then pull off the tape.

2 Tape along the edge of the painted area. Then paint below the tape in another colour. Leave to dry and remove the tape.

3 Decorate the coathanger. Use as many colours as possible to make it really bright. Paint the wooden spoons too, if you like.

4 Ask a grown-up to cook some spaghetti. Keep it soft in warm water until you glue it onto the pots. Hold the spaghetti in place with masking tape until the glue is dry.

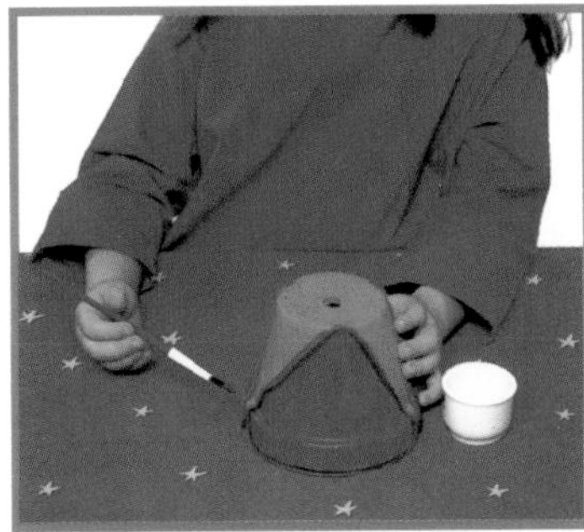

5 Mix the paints together to make brown and paint the spaghetti. Try not to paint the pots underneath. Leave to dry.

6 Cut the cord into three pieces. Ask a grown-up to make a hole in the corks and cut them in half. Thread a cork on each cord and tie a knot in one end.

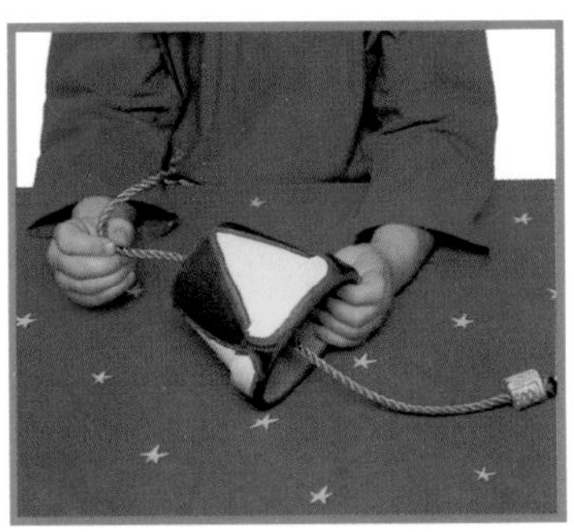

7 Thread the other end of the cord through the hole in the bottom of the flowerpot.

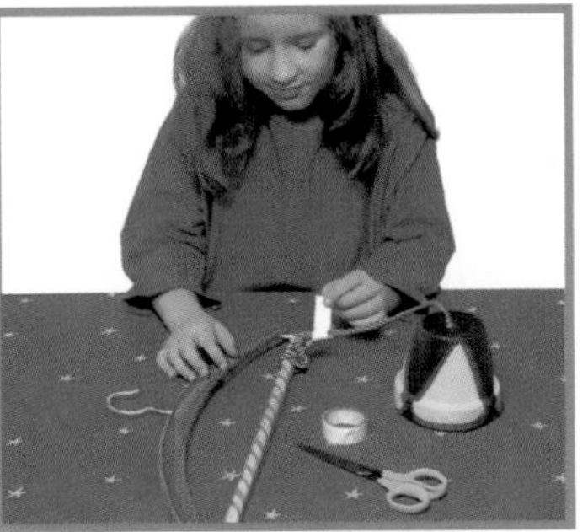

8 Tie each piece of cord to the coathanger. Tie a good knot, then bind the cord with sticky tape.

Twirling Japanese Drum

Different parts of the world have different kinds of music and instruments. Lorenzo's little Japanese drum has a handle that he twirls between his fingers. It makes a lovely rattling sound. When the drum moves fast, the paper swirls look as if they are spinning around.

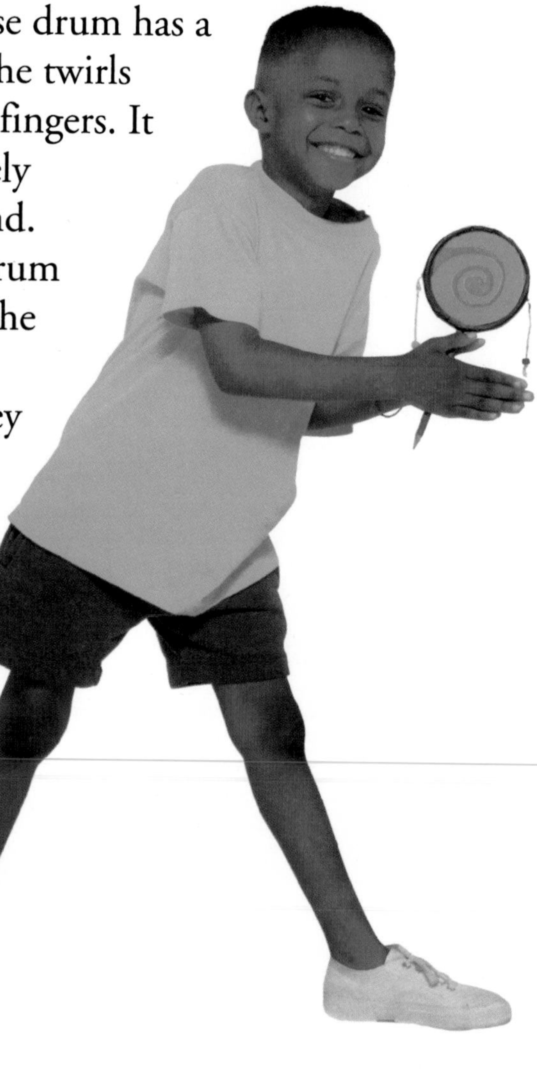

Making music

Hold the handle of the drum between your palms and twirl it backwards and forwards. The beads will fly up and hit the drum.

! A grown-up should make the holes in the side of the box lid and base. Children may need help with scissors.

YOU WILL NEED THESE MATERIALS AND TOOLS

Scissors

2 pieces of paper, in different colours

Round cheese box

Masking tape

Pencil

Black poster paint

PVA glue and brush

Paintbrush

String

Coloured sticky tape

Beads

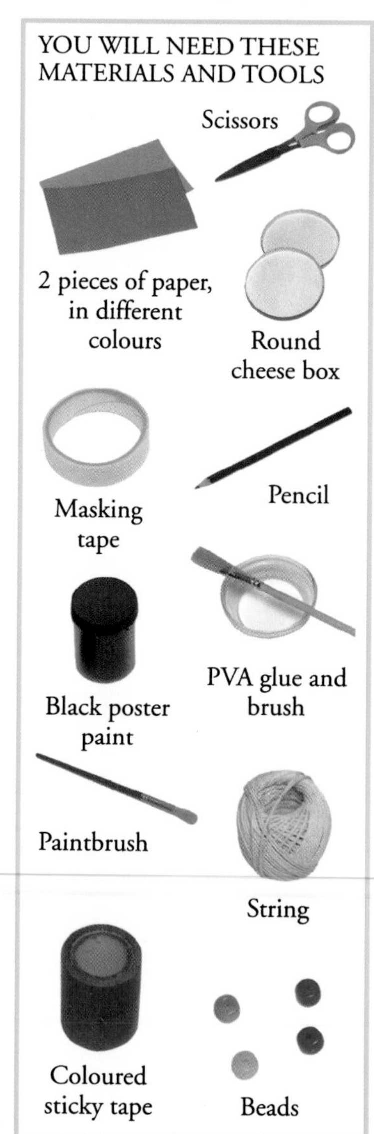

1 Draw twice around the box lid on one piece of paper. Cut out the circles. Cut them into swirls. Cut two circles from the other piece of paper.

2 Ask a grown-up to make a hole in the side of the box lid and one in the side of the base, large enough to push the pencil through. Put on the lid.

3 Push the pencil through the holes and secure it with glue and masking tape. Tape around the side of the box and paint the tape black.

4 Cut a piece of string about 30 cm (12 in) long. Tie a double knot at one end. Thread one or two beads onto the string, then tie another knot. Repeat at the other end of the string.

5 Spread glue over one side of the box. Lay the string carefully across the middle so that it is centred. Make sure that the same amount of string is showing on each side.

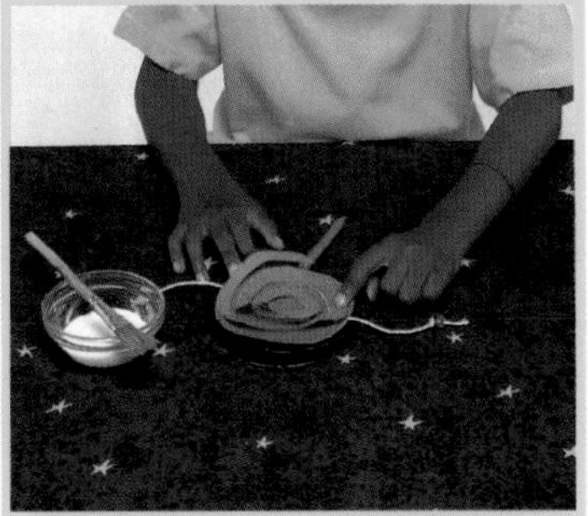

6 Cover the glue and string with one of the whole circles of coloured paper. Glue one of the paper swirls on top. Glue a paper circle and a swirl to the other side of the box. Leave to dry.

7 Decorate the pencil handle with coloured sticky tape. Leave some of the pencil showing to make stripes.

For a brighter effect, add extra strings to your drum. More beads, in different colours will also look good.

Party Fun

Introduction

Treasure chests are good for hiding presents in.

Protect your clothes if you are going to do something messy.

This chapter is full of great ideas for making your party extra special. The step-by-step projects cover all the ingredients of a good party: games, decorations, food and costumes.

Some of the projects here follow a theme. If you are excited by a particular theme, maybe you could make everything for your party follow the same idea. Some of the themes included in this book are Christmas, desert island, funfair, Halloween.

You can have as much fun preparing for a party as during it.

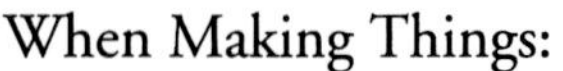

When Making Things:

1 Try to leave yourself plenty of time before the party.
2 Read through the instructions carefully.
3 Make a list of all the materials and tools you will need. You may need the help of someone older than you. This could be for finding or buying materials or tools.
4 Prepare your work space. Cover the surface you are working on, in case you spill anything. Make sure you have enough room.
5 Put on a smock or apron to protect your clothes. Or wear old clothes that are already stained.
6 When cooking wash your hands thoroughly.
7 Always clean up as you go along. Make sure anything that might spill is in a safe place.
8 At the end of a project thoroughly wash brushes in lukewarm water with a little detergent. Put lids on paints. Wipe surfaces.
9 Be extra careful with sharp tools, scissors or knives. Always make sure the tool is pointing down, away from your face. If you are unsure ask someone older for help.
10 If you're not sure what to do, always ask a grown-up for help.

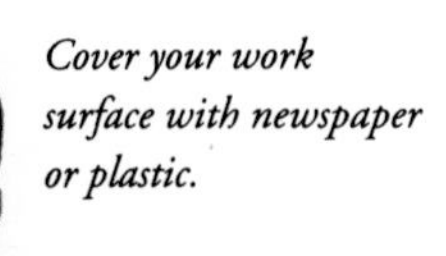

Cover your work surface with newspaper or plastic.

You can decorate a cake to match the theme of your party.

Materials

A lot of the materials used for party projects are the same ones you have been using for making things throughout this book, such as a ruler, pencil, scissors, glue and different types of paint.

Extra things that you will need include empty food cartons, such as egg boxes, yoghurt pots and cardboard boxes. You can get hold of them for free and keep collecting them for other projects. They are very useful for making things and as holders for keeping things still while painting.

There are many ways to decorate your objects to make them look special for a party: try shiny tinsel, brightly-coloured papers and stickers. Choose bright colours for your games, decorations and even your food and your party will be one to remember.

Whatever you are doing, look after your materials and equipment. Keep your tools in a box. And lay out any papers flat so that they don't get crumpled.
Have a good party!

Paper Chains

Paper chains are a must for every party. They are fun and easy to make. You can decorate your home by hanging them along walls and over doorways and they look great with balloons. You may need to hang them up with drawing pins, so make sure you ask a grown-up first. Aimee is making some special, patterned paper chains. Use as many bright colours as you want to. At Christmas use the festive colours of green and red.

YOU WILL NEED THESE MATERIALS AND TOOLS

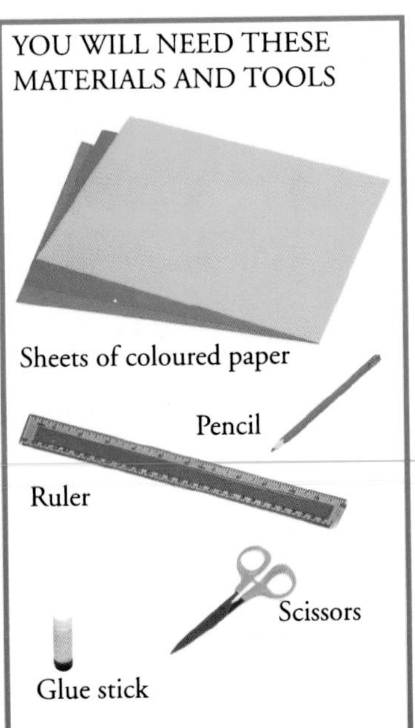

1 Using a pencil, draw lines lengthways down the sheets of coloured paper. Draw the lines a ruler's width apart (about 4 cm).

2 Draw a line across the paper, so that each rectangle on the coloured paper measures 25 cm.

3 Cut out the rectangles as carefully as possible. Aimee is cutting several sheets of paper together, to save time.

4 Make two piles of rectangles, with the same number in each pile. Fold all the rectangles in one pile in half. Draw a lattice pattern on them.

5 Cut out the pattern on all the rectangles in the pile. Keep the paper folded while you cut. Make sure the cuts are even.

6 Unfold your cut-out rectangle and stick it onto a plain rectangle from the other pile. Stick it on using a glue stick. Repeat this until you have made all the coloured rectangles into the links for your paper chain.

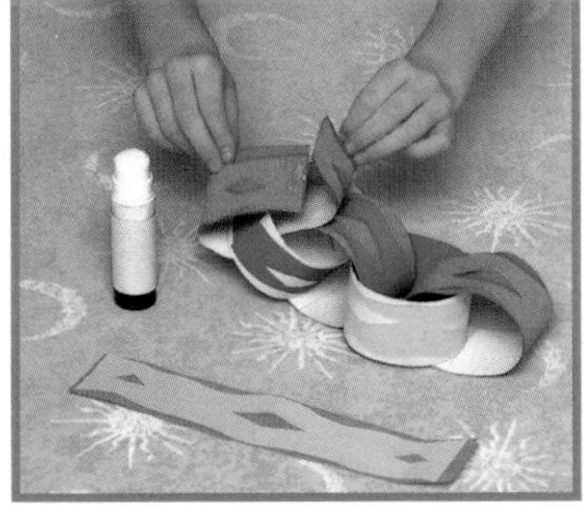

7 Stick the ends of the first link together. Put another link through the first one and stick the ends together. Repeat this with all your links.

You can make plain coloured links too, to mix and match.

"I Am Four" Badge

Deborah is making a badge to show everyone how old she will be at her birthday party. Make one for your age and wear it with your best party outfit. You could also start a collection for every birthday. Age badges make great presents, too! The badge is made from papier mâché, which is paper soaked in glue mixed with water.

Crafty collecting tip

Cardboard boxes are always handy to have around for making things. If you don't have any coloured paper, use pages from a magazine instead. Some of the colours are great for making flowers. Make sure you ask, before you cut up someone's magazine!

YOU WILL NEED THESE MATERIALS AND TOOLS

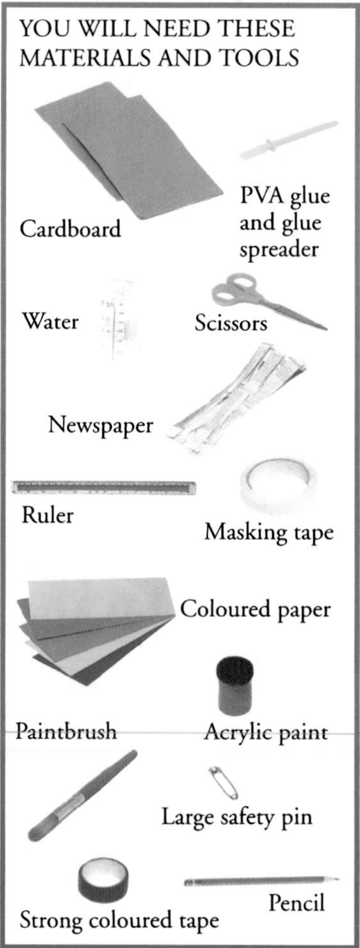

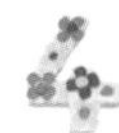

1 Draw your chosen number on cardboard. Cut it out carefully and draw around it onto three more pieces of cardboard. Cut out the numbers so that you have four cardboard numbers.

2 Prepare the papier mâché by mixing equal amounts of PVA glue and water in a bowl. Cut newspaper into strips, and leave them to soak in the glue and water.

3 Meanwhile, stick the four cardboard numbers together with glue. Then stick masking tape round them to hold them together.

4 Paint the badge with glue using the brush, and stick on a layer of wet paper strips. Leave to dry in a warm place and then stick on a second layer.

5 While the papier mâché is drying, cut out paper flowers from brightly coloured paper. Cut out circles for the centres of the flowers.

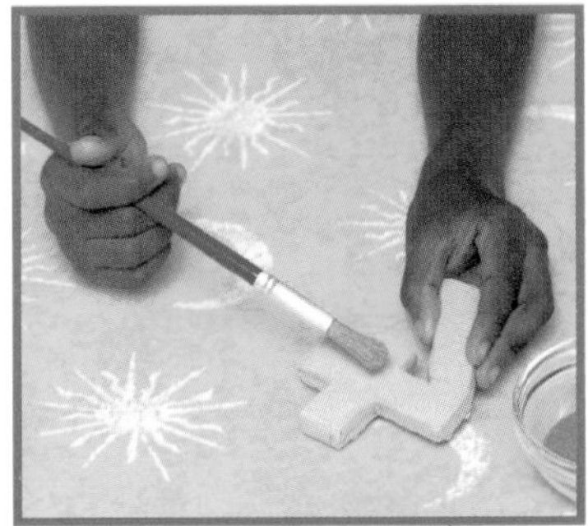

6 Paint your badge with acrylic paint. You might need to use two layers of paint to cover the newspaper. Leave to dry.

7 Glue on the paper flowers, then glue on contrasting circles for the centres. Leave to dry.

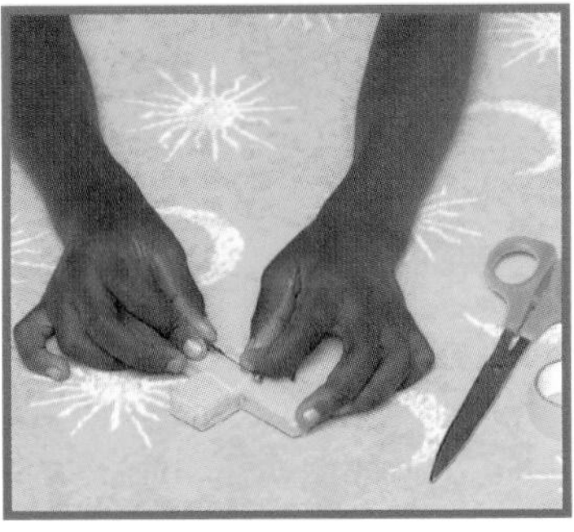

8 Use strong coloured tape to stick the non-opening side of the safety pin to the back of the badge.

Christmas Tree Hat

Nicholas has made a hat especially to celebrate Christmas. It shows the star of Bethlehem, which sits on the top of Christmas trees. He will definitely be the star of the party. You can make other hats, too, such as a sunshine hat or a flower hat for a summer party. Make the hat in the same way but with a big sun or flower instead of a star.

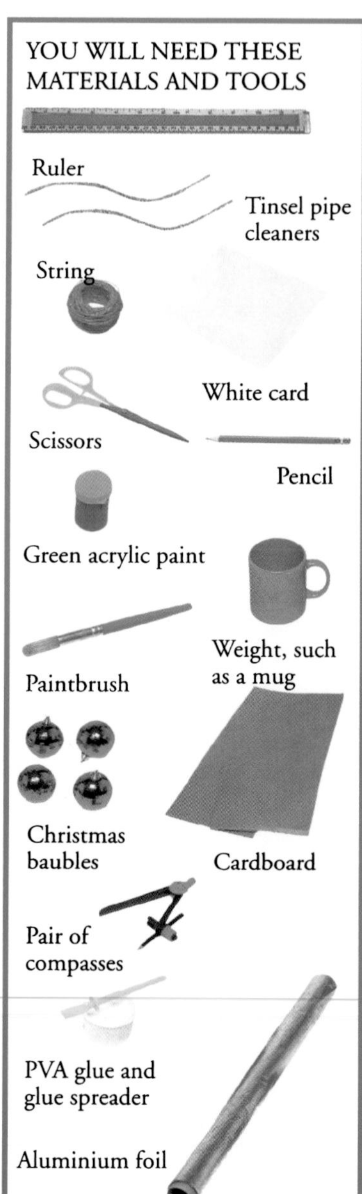

YOU WILL NEED THESE MATERIALS AND TOOLS

Ruler
Tinsel pipe cleaners
String
White card
Scissors
Pencil
Green acrylic paint
Paintbrush
Weight, such as a mug
Christmas baubles
Cardboard
Pair of compasses
PVA glue and glue spreader
Aluminium foil

1 Measure your head with the piece of string, then add 8 cm onto the length of the string.

2 Cut a piece of white card the same length as the string. Draw a dotted line down the centre. Draw a Christmas tree shape with tabs top and sides.

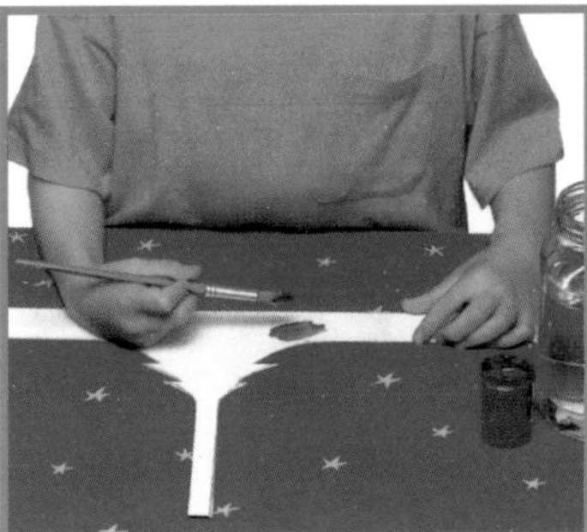

3 Cut out the tree shape with the tabs at the top and sides. Paint it green and leave it to dry.

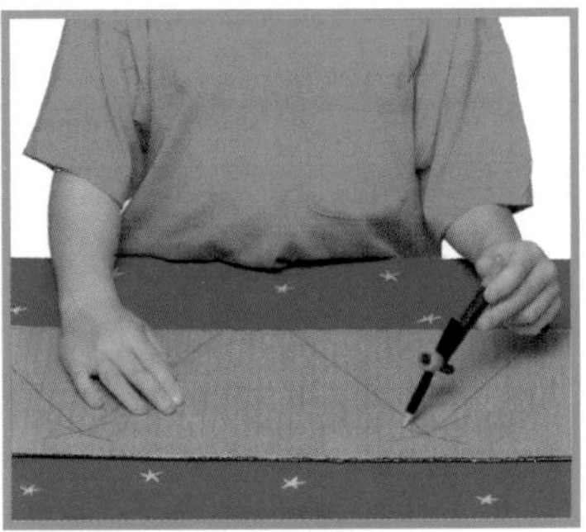

4 On a piece of cardboard, draw and cut out two triangles with 18 cm sides. Draw the bottom of the triangle first, then use the compasses to mark the top point.

5 Stick the two triangles together to make a star with six points. Glue aluminium foil onto the star and leave it to dry.

6 Glue the tab at the top of the tree to the back of the star. Leave it to dry under a weight, so the two pieces bond strongly together. Ask a grown-up to trim the tabs to fit.

7 Glue or tape the side tabs together, so the hat fits your head. Leave to dry. Tape tinsel around the hat.

8 Use tinsel pipe cleaners to tie Christmas baubles around the hat.

Treasure Chest

Aimee has made a treasure chest and she has filled it with lots of consolation prizes, so that each of her guests leaves the party with a going-away present. She has wrapped all the presents in gold paper, so that they look like treasure, and added bags of chocolate coins. The presents don't need to be big or expensive, just fun. She is going to hide her treasure trove until the end of the party, then everyone will play "hunt the treasure chest". The winner gets the first pick of the prizes.

Safety tip

When making holes with a pair of scissors, always make sure the blades are closed together and that you point the tip of them away from you.

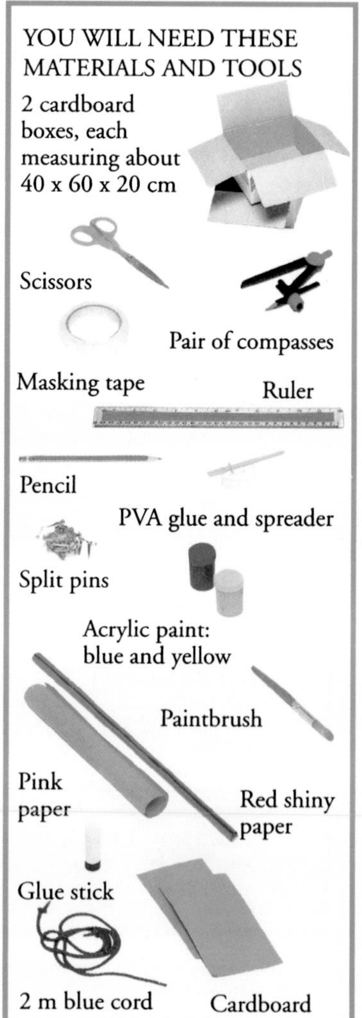

YOU WILL NEED THESE MATERIALS AND TOOLS

2 cardboard boxes, each measuring about 40 x 60 x 20 cm

Scissors

Pair of compasses

Masking tape

Ruler

Pencil

PVA glue and spreader

Split pins

Acrylic paint: blue and yellow

Paintbrush

Pink paper

Red shiny paper

Glue stick

2 m blue cord

Cardboard

1 Cut three of the flaps off one of the boxes, leaving one of the long flaps. This will be used later for the lid.

2 Cut up the second box, leaving the base, one long and two short sides. Draw a semicircle on each short side.

3 Use the compass to draw the semicircles, as shown in the picture for Step 2. Cut them out.

4 Fold up the semicircles to make the sides of the lid. Place the long side of the box in the middle and hold in place with masking tape.

5 Cut a 60 cm square of cardboard. Ask a grown-up to score the cardboard to help it bend. Glue it to the sides and secure with masking tape.

6 Cut the flap on the first box to make two hinges. Glue the lid onto the hinges and leave to dry. Stud with split pins, putting glue under each pin.

7 Paint the outside of the chest with blue acrylic paint. With the glue stick, stick on yellow stripes to create a barrel effect. Add a keyhole and pink skulls and crossbones.

8 Line the chest with paper. Pierce two holes in either side of the box base. Thread cord into each and knot, then glue onto the lid. Hold in place with masking tape until dry.

Palm Trees

Treasure Island parties are great for having adventures. You can dress up as pirates and sailors. Nicholas is making some palm trees to put on the table with all the party food. An adult could help you to make larger palm trees, to stick in the garden flower beds. All you need to do is make them with larger sheets of paper or stick several sheets of paper together.

Where to put it

Put your palm trees in places where they won't easily get knocked over!

YOU WILL NEED THESE MATERIALS AND TOOLS

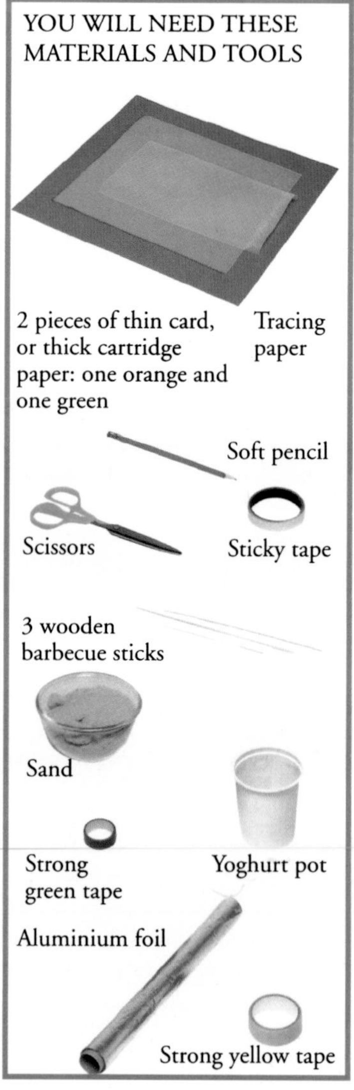

1 Draw a leaf 40 cm long and 20 cm wide on green card. Use the guide to help you. Fold the leaf in half and cut it out. Make three for each tree.

2 Roll the orange card into a long tube. Hold the tube firmly, so that it doesn't uncurl, and cut a fringe into the top edge of the roll.

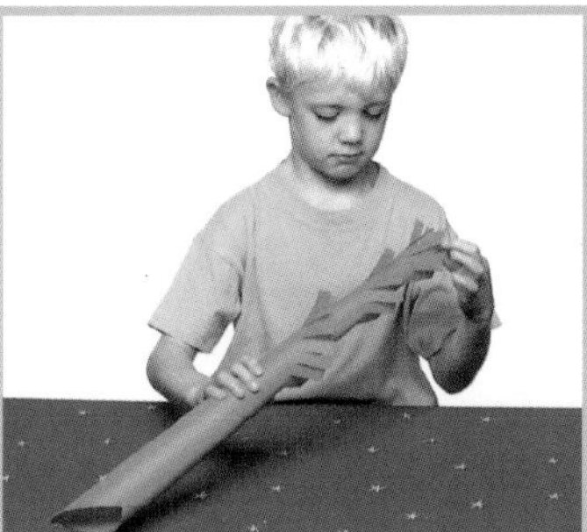

3 Still holding the tube firmly, gently pull out the inside edge of the card. Pull it right out to make the trunk of your tree.

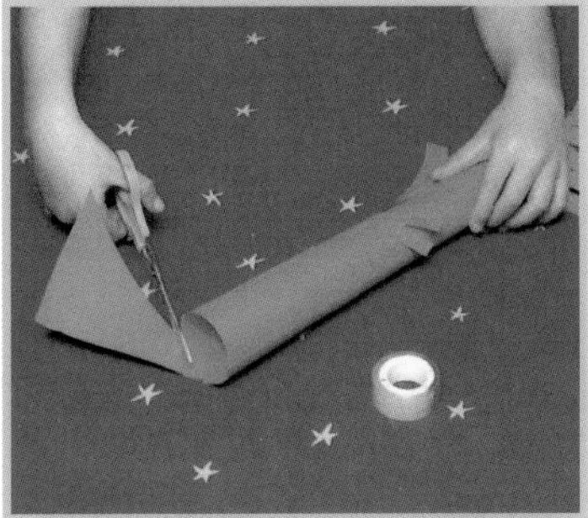

4 Use sticky tape to hold the trunk together at the base. Trim the base, so that the trunk can stand up straight.

5 Tape a barbecue stick down the middle of each palm leaf with green tape.

6 Snip two slits on opposite sides of the trunk, just big enough to take the stalk of the leaf. Make the slits 10 cm from the top of the trunk.

7 Slide a palm leaf into each slit. Push the third leaf into the top of the trunk and tape it in place.

8 Cover the yoghurt pot with aluminium foil. Stick stripes on it with yellow tape. Fill the pot with sand and push the palm tree into it.

Arty Party Wall

Making a fun wall is always a huge success at parties. Party goers can draw on it, and leave messages or their names. Here Christopher has drawn a picture of the sea, but you can choose any theme. Leave lots of crayons and pencils in jars next to the wall. You'll be left with a masterpiece.

Material brainwave

If you can't get hold of a large roll of coloured paper, buy some lining paper or simple patterned wallpaper from a decorating shop.

YOU WILL NEED THESE MATERIALS AND TOOLS

- Several sheets of coloured paper 
- Scissors 
- Pencils in different colours
- Glue stick 
- I large roll of paper, approximately 1 m square 
- Drawing pins 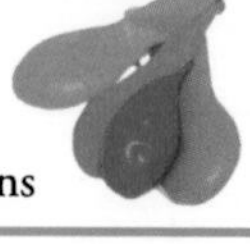
- Balloons 
- Strong black tape

1 Cut out long wiggly strips of green paper to make seaweed.

2 Draw the outlines of some fish onto coloured paper, using light pencils on dark paper. The fish should be quite large. Cut them out neatly.

3 Cut out eyes and patterns in coloured paper and stick them onto your fish with a glue stick.

4 Pin or tape your large sheet of paper to the wall. Decorate the corners with balloons. Ask a grown-up to help if you are using drawing pins.

5 Stick on your cut-out fish and seaweed. Arrange them so that they look nice, but leave room for other drawings too.

6 At your party, draw on lots of other creatures with your friends. You could write messages and add streamers to the decorations too.

Gone Fishing

Houw is making a fishing game. Each player has to hook up as many floating fish as possible when the music is on. The player who catches the most fish wins. This game is best played in the garden or kitchen, as it's easy to splash lots of water around. Houw has used washing-up bowls to make his fish ponds, but paddling pools are great as well.

Material note

The number of rods and bottles will depend on how many friends want to play. Make sure there are about three fish bottles per player.

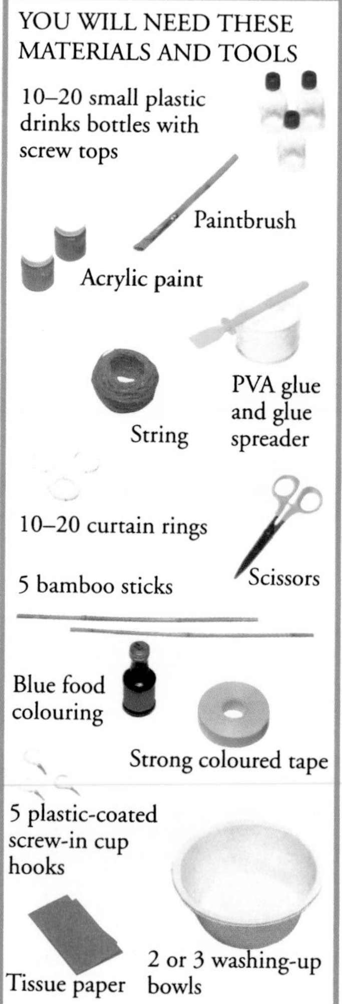

YOU WILL NEED THESE MATERIALS AND TOOLS

10–20 small plastic drinks bottles with screw tops

Paintbrush

Acrylic paint

String

PVA glue and glue spreader

10–20 curtain rings

Scissors

5 bamboo sticks

Blue food colouring

Strong coloured tape

5 plastic-coated screw-in cup hooks

Tissue paper

2 or 3 washing-up bowls

1 Wash the drinks bottles and soak off the labels. Leave to dry, then screw the lids back on. Paint fish shapes onto the bottles. Mix glue into your paint so that it sticks to the plastic.

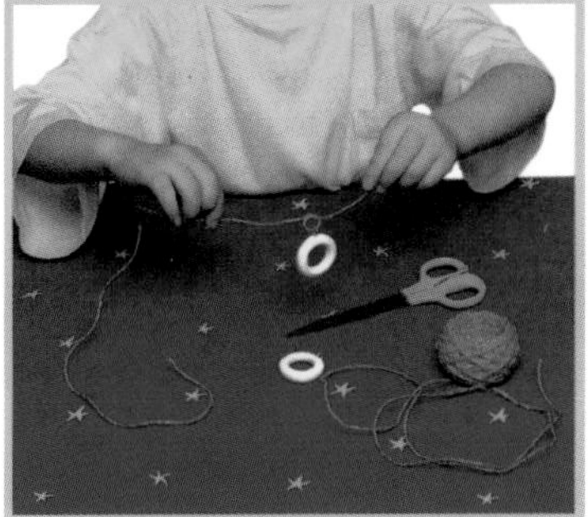

2 Cut string into lengths of 45 cm. Tie the end of each piece of string onto the hook in a curtain ring. Do this with as many curtain rings as there are bottles.

3 Tie the string onto the bottles with a double knot, so that the curtain ring dangles a bit.

4 To make the paint waterproof, mix a varnish of three parts glue to one part water. Apply two coats to the painted fish bottles. Leave the glue to dry between coats.

5 To make the fishing rods, decorate the bamboo sticks with bands of coloured tape.

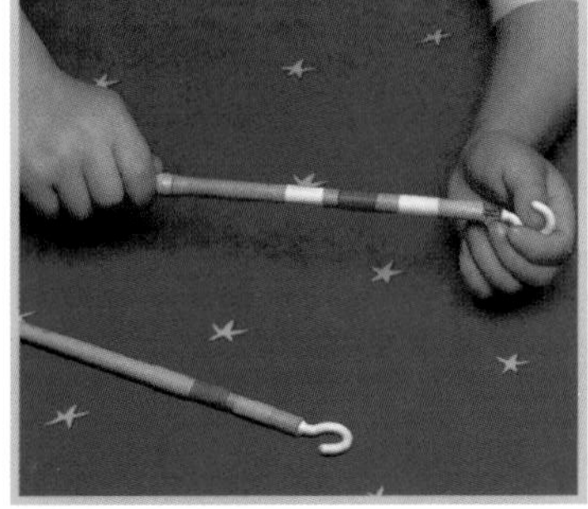

6 Screw a cup hook firmly into the end of each rod.

7 Wrap tissue around the bowls. Add food colouring to the water.

Coconut Shy

You don't need coconuts to make a coconut shy. Gaby is making her own version of the game you find in funfairs. Her game has lots of funny faces. To play, set your coconut shy on a table. Make sure there is space behind and in front. Mark a line in front where the players have to stand. Then try and knock the faces out of the pots with the little ball. Make sure the pots are weighted down and tied to the table. Have as many as you need – eight is a good number.

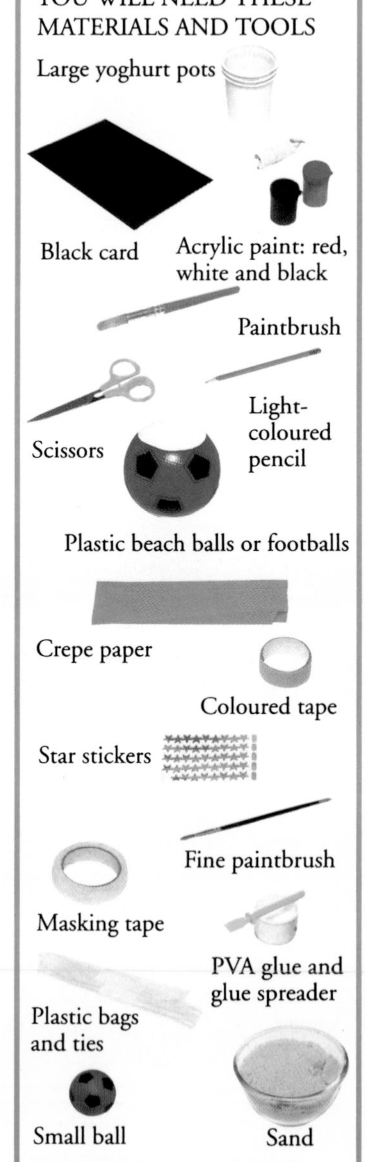

YOU WILL NEED THESE MATERIALS AND TOOLS

Large yoghurt pots
Black card
Acrylic paint: red, white and black
Paintbrush
Scissors
Light-coloured pencil
Plastic beach balls or footballs
Crepe paper
Coloured tape
Star stickers
Fine paintbrush
Masking tape
PVA glue and glue spreader
Plastic bags and ties
Small ball
Sand

1 Paint the sides of the yoghurt pots white. Leave to dry.

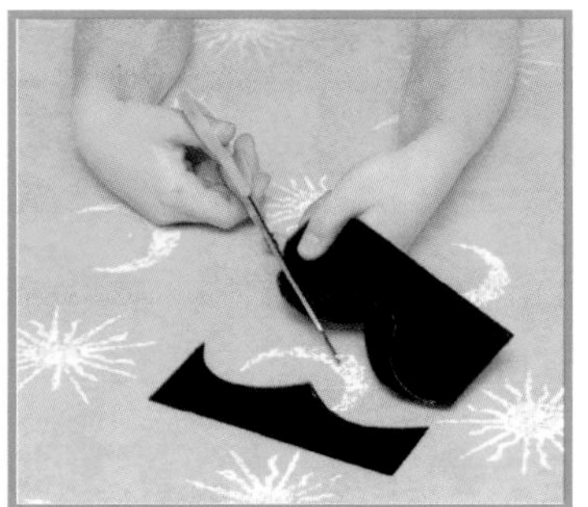

2 Draw a fun black moustache on black card with a light-coloured pencil and cut it out.

3 Paint a white circle onto your ball and leave it to dry. It is easier if you balance it on a yoghurt pot or mug so that it doesn't roll around.

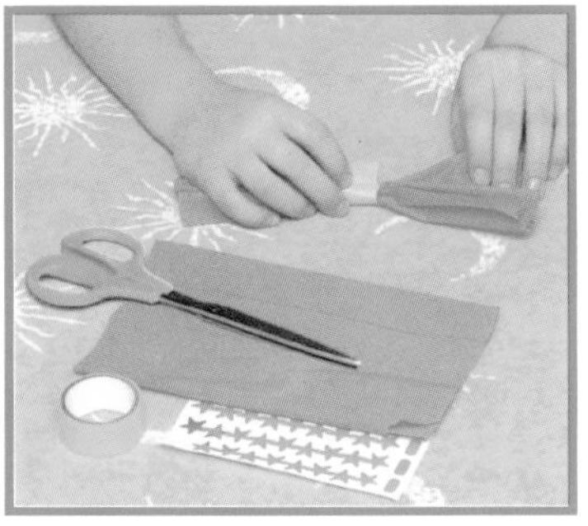

4 Whilst the ball is drying, make the bow tie. Cut crepe paper so that it measures 15 cm by 10 cm. Fold it several times. Tie the middle with a piece of tape and stick on some stars.

5 Paint a face onto the ball using a fine brush and black and red acrylic paints.

6 Once the paint on the yoghurt pots is dry, stick strips of masking tape on them, leaving 2 cm gaps. Paint the gaps with red acrylic paint and leave to dry.

7 Stick the moustache and bow tie onto the ball. Peel the masking tape off the yoghurt pots.

8 Fill a plastic bag with sand and twist a tie around the top. Place it in the pot and put the ball on top.

Apple Dunking

Apple dunking is a game traditionally played at Halloween, but is good to play at parties all year round. You have to get the apples out of the bowl without using your hands, as Moriam and Patrice are trying to do! It's great entertainment, but can get very wet, so wear something to protect your clothes. A plastic apron would be perfect. It's also a good idea to put your bowl on a table in the kitchen. Decorate the bowl to suit your theme. Happy dunking!

Finger paint

You can buy paint especially for finger painting, but acrylic paint is also fine. Have a cloth handy for cleaning up, as it can get very messy.

YOU WILL NEED THESE MATERIALS AND TOOLS

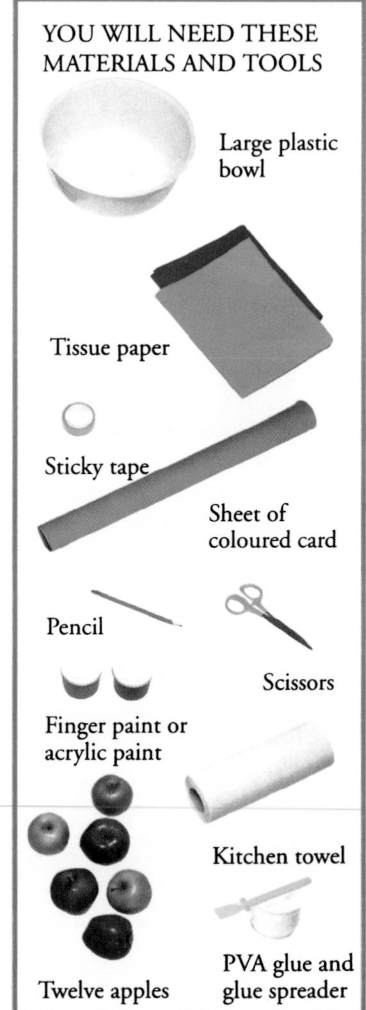

1 To decorate the bowl, stick a folded wad of tissue paper just under the edge of the bowl with sticky tape. Then gather the paper to fit round the bottom and tape it down. Do this with three more wads of tissue paper.

2 Draw an apple shape onto the card. Remember to use a pencil that will show up on the card.

3 Cut the apple shape out, then draw around it to make three more apples. Cut them out, too.

4 Finger-paint the apples with red dots. Keep a paper towel handy to wipe your fingers on, and wash your hands when you have finished.

5 Stick each apple onto the tissue paper with glue. Leave to dry.

6 Put the bowl on a waterproof table or floor and ask a grown-up to fill the bowl with water and all the apples.

Marzipan Dinosaur Cake

Marzipan is the delicious almond decoration you find on the top of birthday cakes. You can buy marzipan from any supermarket and it's easy to colour it with food dye. Decorate a ready-made cake for yourself or for someone in your family or a friend. Before you roll the marzipan, wash your hands.

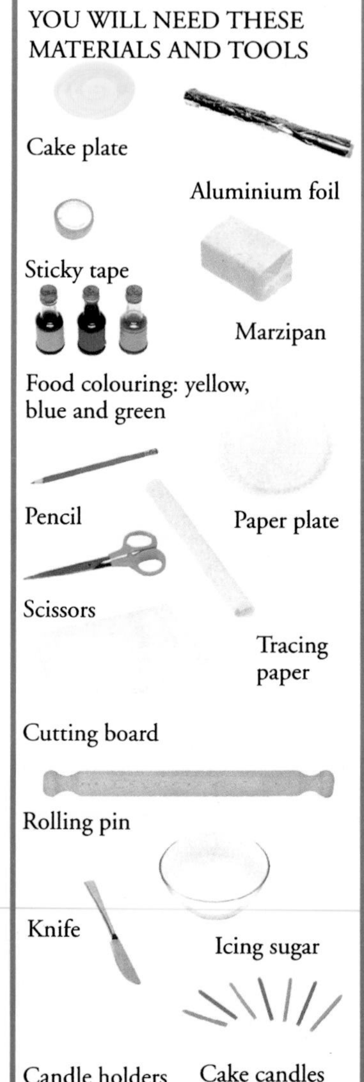

1 Cover the plate with aluminium foil and use a little sticky tape on the back to hold it.

2 Add food colouring to the marzipan, only a couple of drops at a time. Knead it in thoroughly.

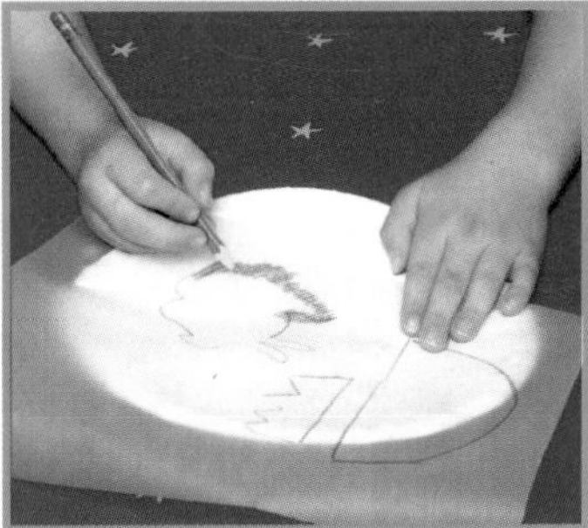

3 Trace the dinosaur template and transfer it onto the paper plate, using a soft pencil.

4 Cut out the dinosaur and the other shapes.

5 Roll out the marzipan until it is 5–10 mm thick. Sprinkle a little icing sugar onto the rolling pin and surface to stop the marzipan sticking.

6 Ask a grown-up to cut out the marzipan with a knife, using your card cut-outs as a guide.

7 Put the cake onto the plate covered in aluminium foil and carefully lay the marzipan on the cake. You can help the shapes stay in place by dabbing a bit of water underneath.

8 Push the candles into the holders, then decorate the cake with them. Light the candles and it's time to sing "Happy Birthday"!

Funny Faces Fairy Cakes

These are cakes you can either decorate before your guests arrive, or make into a game at the party. Lay out all the materials and see which guest can make the silliest face or the most imaginative object out of the cakes. Iza and Gaby have made funny faces with mad hair.

YOU WILL NEED THESE MATERIALS AND TOOLS

Paper plates

Silver doilies

Pair of compasses

Scissors

Crepe paper

Cup cakes and mini rolls

Mini coloured icing tubes

Silver ball decorations

Icing flowers

1 Put a silver doily on a paper plate. Using compasses, draw a slightly smaller circle on crepe paper and cut it out. Place it on top of the doily.

2 Place a cup cake and a mini roll on the plate. These will make the head and body.

3 Squeezing the mini icing tubes gently, pipe on the mouth, eyes and nose, using different colours.

4 Put silver balls on the eyes to make them sparkle.

5 To make the jacket, ice on stripes and buttons. Add icing flower decorations and silver balls.

6 Add some curly hair with a different colour of icing.

7 Add arms, hands and a skirt by piping coloured icing straight onto the pink paper. Add some icing flowers for the feet and your work of art is ready to eat!

A Magic Show

Introduction

So, you want to be a magician? Good! Because magic is fun. Actually, it is *great* fun. Making the tricks is fun, doing the tricks is fun and, most of all, entertaining people with magic is fun.

Some people, and books, say magic is very hard to do because it needs hour after hour, year after year, of never-ending practice. Well, in this chapter you will find lots of tricks that you will be able to do easily with only a little practice. And once you've learnt how to do all the projects shown here, you might go on to learn the more complicated secrets of magic.

Making Things For Your Magic

The Wand

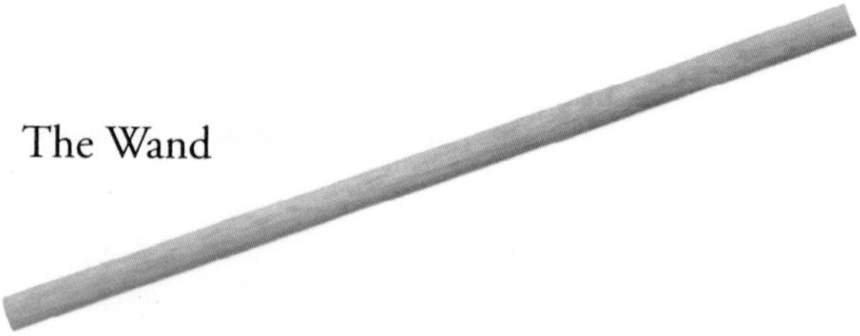

In order to practise magic, you need a few essential props. The most important of these is your wand. You can make one yourself. All you need is a 30 cm length of round wood, called dowel, some masking tape and black and white poster paints. Wrap masking tape around each end of the dowel and paint the wood in-between black. When the paint is dry, remove the tape and paint the ends white. Hey presto! The stick has magically become a wand, ready for you to do some brilliant tricks with.

The Magic Box

An essential prop is a beautifully coloured magic box. This box means you will be able to produce many things you need for your show, out of a box that seems to be empty!

1 First tape over the sharp edges of an empty 850 g baked bean tin. Then glue a rectangle of red card together at the edges, to make a tube wider and taller than the tin. For the outer box, join four identical pieces of stiff card together with masking tape. Ask a grown-up to help you cut out some holes in one piece for the front of the box.

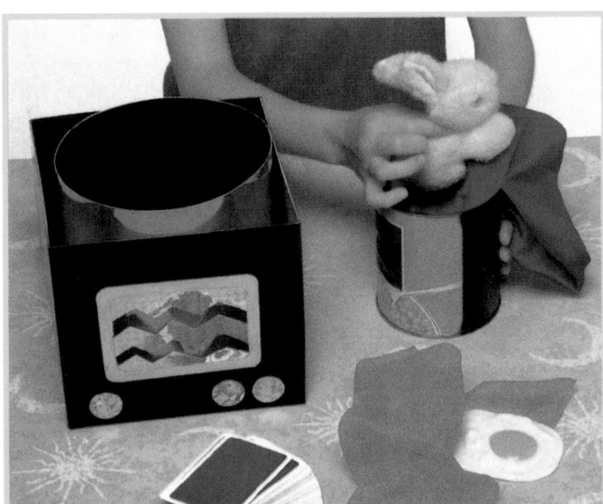

2 Here Lucy has decorated the box to look like an old-fashioned radio. Now paint half of the bean tin and the inside of the box with black poster paint. When the paint is dry, fill the tin with magical things.

3 Put the bean tin, filled with silk handkerchiefs, cards, a small pink rabbit and a plastic fried egg, inside the box. Can you see it? No? That is because you place it in the box with its black side facing the holes in the front, so when you lift out the red tube the box appears empty. After putting the red tube back over the bean tin, you can lift up the radio box, because it has no bottom, to show that it is empty as well.

4 This "illusion" means that Lucy can produce the hankies, cards and rabbit from an "empty" box. She can turn the tin around when it is inside the tube and lift it out, with the egg, to add a funny finish to her trick. Now, once she has put the tin and egg away, she can again show her audience that the tube and box are both empty. This time, as there is nothing left to hide, she can hold the tube and box up together.

The Hat

Every self-respecting magician has a top hat, and it is needed for many of the tricks in this book.

1 Ask a friend to measure around your head. Add 2 cm to the figure and cut a piece of stiff black paper to this length, and about 15 cm wide. Roll the paper into a tube and glue the edges together.

2 For the top of the hat, place the tube upright on a sheet of black paper and draw round it with a white crayon. Draw a second circle about 1 cm wider around the first circle and cut out the outer line. Cut small "V"s around the whole shape between the outer and inner circles. Glue the tabs downwards inside the top of the tube. To make the brim, draw round the shape of your hat onto more black paper. Draw a second circle 1 cm smaller than your tube and a third circle 5 cm larger. Cut out along these last two lines. Cut tabs again and glue them into the bottom of your hat.

3 A secret flap fixed inside your magician's top hat is perfect for hiding things. Cut out a round piece of stiff black paper to fit snugly down into the hat. Tape a flap onto the middle of it with masking tape. Paint the tape black and cut the flap into a semicircle so that it can be held against either side of the hat, with your fingers. If you briefly tip the opening of the hat towards the audience, anything hidden behind the flap will not be seen. They will just see blackness inside the hat and assume the hat is empty.

4 Add some ribbon to the hat to finish it off. Measure round the tube of your hat, and add 1 cm to this. Glue the ribbon round the hat just above the brim with a 1 cm overlap. A black or coloured bow tie will make you really look like a magician.

Performing

Performing magic is all about acting the part of the magician convincingly. When you are doing a trick you must try to believe that magic is really happening. If you believe it, so will your audience.

What to Say

What you say to your audience during your show is called your "patter". The most important thing is to be natural. Talk in your own way. Make up a story to go with the trick and add a few jokes if you would like to get a laugh.

Repeating Tricks

When you have done a good trick, people will ask to see it again. Don't be tempted to repeat it! Your audience might discover the secret of the trick the second time round.

Misdirection

This is the art of making your audience look where *you* want them to look. The audience will look where your eyes are looking or at your moving hands. If you are hiding a coin in your hand, don't look at that hand. Also, never say that a box or hat is "empty" or the audience will be suspicious. Quickly show them the inside and they will assume that it is empty.

Secrets

Always keep your magic secrets to yourself. Store your magic things out of sight, in a case or a closed box.

Appearance

Look smart and especially have clean hands and fingernails. Smile. Look happy. If you feel a little shy in front of an audience, try your tricks out in private first, and even in front of a mirror.

Mistakes

Sometimes things will go wrong (even the most famous magicians sometimes make mistakes!). Don't panic. If you can, correct things and carry on. If you can't, just smile and get the audience involved in another trick. Remember that your audience is there because they want to be entertained and they want you to do well. Practising your tricks in front of a mirror will help prevent the mistakes from happening.

Magic Secrets

Part of the skill of being a magician is keeping things to yourself. In order to show how to do things, we have taken photographs, but whenever you see the top hat symbol, this is a view that the audience should not see.

How Many Tricks?

Don't make your show too long. That way you will leave your audience wanting more and they will ask you for another show on another day. Plan a short show that has a beginning, a middle and an end. And don't forget – smile!

Magic Words

In magic there are many special words. Here are some useful ones for you to learn.

Effect What the audience sees.
Gag A joke or a funny story.
Gimmick or Fake A secret part of the prop that the audience does not see.
Illusion When something *seems* to happen but doesn't.
Load The things held in a secret compartment.
Palming Keeping something hidden in your hand.
Patter Your talk that goes with the trick.
Production Making something appear from nowhere.
Props The things you use for your tricks.
Routine A series of tricks or moves.
Shuffle To mix up cards in your hands.
Silks Silk handkerchiefs.
Sleeving Hiding something up your sleeve to make it vanish or ready to appear in your hand later.
Sleight of hand A clever movement of your hand to make magic.

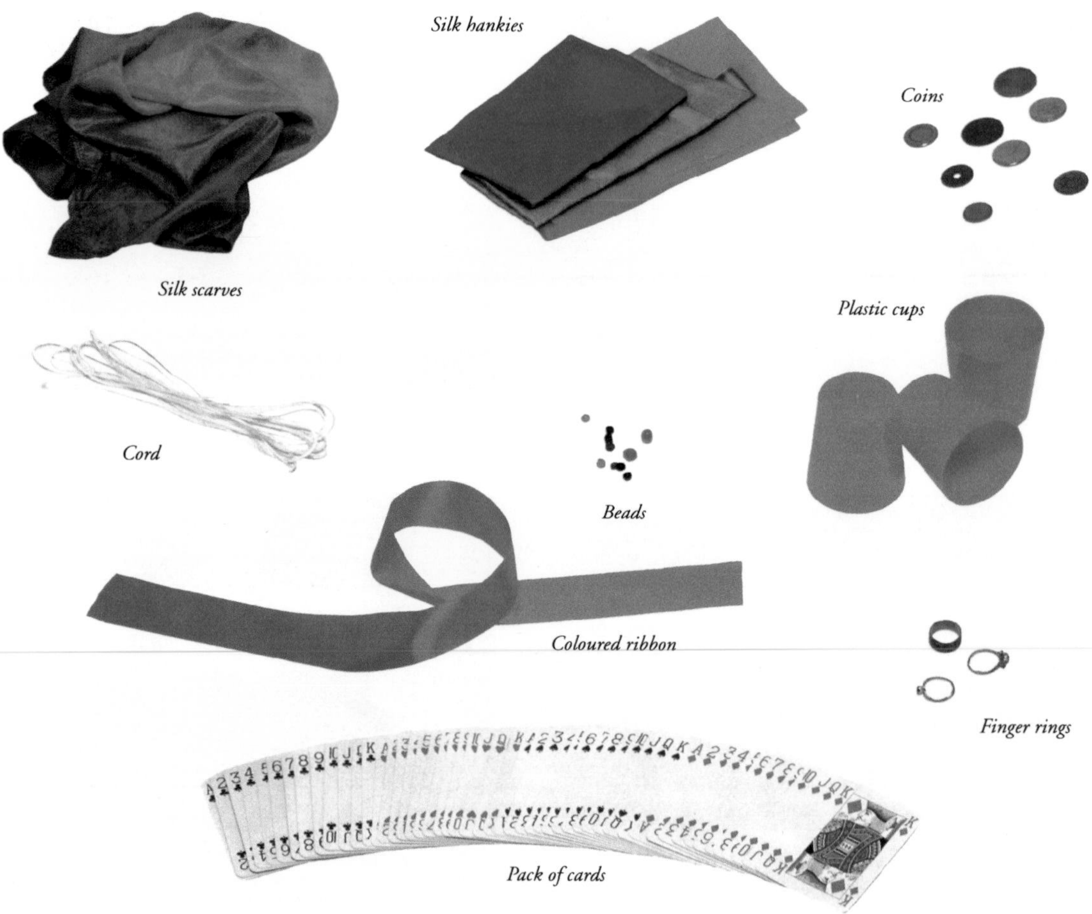

Silk hankies

Coins

Silk scarves

Plastic cups

Cord

Beads

Coloured ribbon

Finger rings

Pack of cards

STEAL To move something from its place secretly.
SWITCH To change one thing for another secretly.
TALK The sound that hidden objects might make – for example, rattle, click, etc.
TRANSPOSITION When something magically disappears from one place to reappear in another.
VANISH To make an object seem to disappear.

Materials

The materials that you will need are always listed. Gather them all together before you start. Work on a suitable surface. Wear an apron if you are painting or gluing, and tidy everything away afterwards. Allow time for paint and glue to dry before moving on to the next stage. Keep a collection of empty cartons, tubes and boxes, etc. Once they have been painted and decorated they are great for magic. Take great care when using scissors or other sharp instruments, and always ask a grown-up to help if you need to use a craft knife.

Black is a very useful colour in magic because a black object in black surroundings becomes almost invisible. So, if the instructions for a trick say to use black, then *do* use black. Finally, take your time and study the photographs and the text carefully. If a photograph shows someone doing a trick with their right hand and you prefer to use your left, don't worry. Just swap things over and do it your own way.

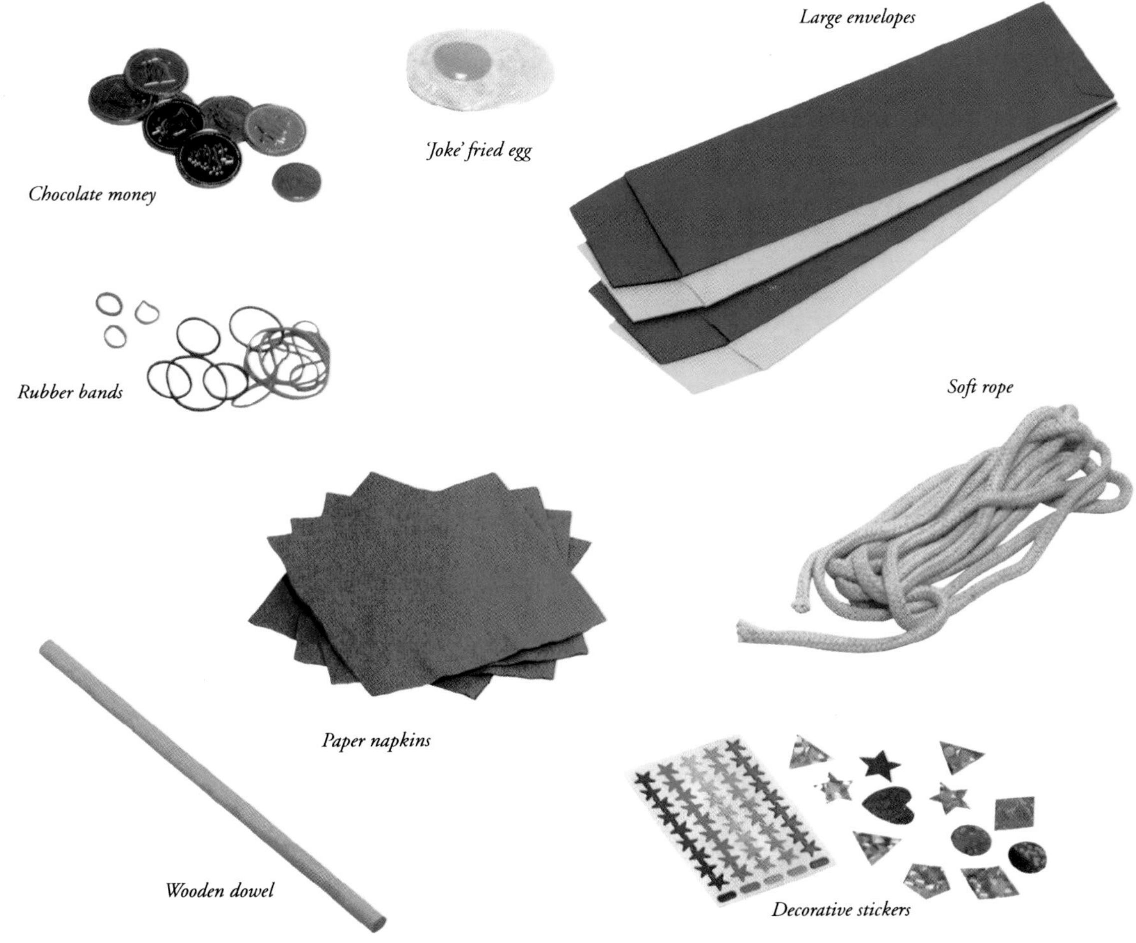

Chocolate money

'Joke' fried egg

Large envelopes

Rubber bands

Soft rope

Paper napkins

Wooden dowel

Decorative stickers

The Dirty Napkin Trick

Magic can have the most powerful effect when people are not expecting it. Here's a trick you could do during a meal. Sarah has this trick well under control. When the person opposite her has sat down and spread his paper napkin on his knee, she asks him for the napkin. She gives the excuse that she has noticed some tiny stains on it. To do the trick she tears off pieces from the centre of the napkin, explaining each time that, "this one's gravy, this one's ketchup", and so on. Finally she opens the napkin out to show that it is whole – without any bits torn out of it. This trick is a real reputation maker. Try it yourself.

YOU WILL NEED THESE PROPS

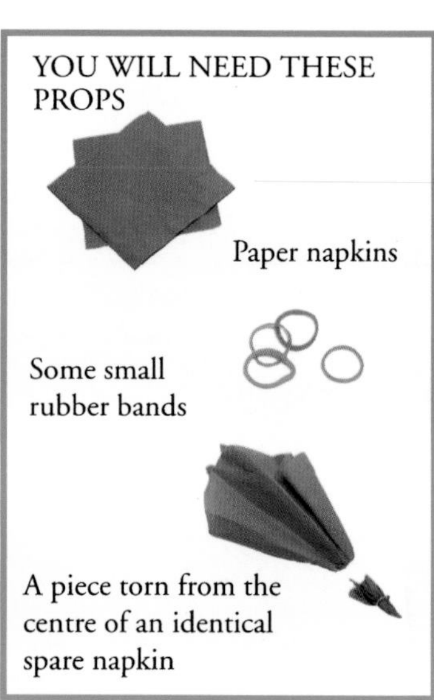

Paper napkins

Some small rubber bands

A piece torn from the centre of an identical spare napkin

Tip

Don't use your own napkin for the secret torn piece, as someone might ask to see it afterwards. When you tear off the pieces, remove the rubber band with one of them (see step 6).

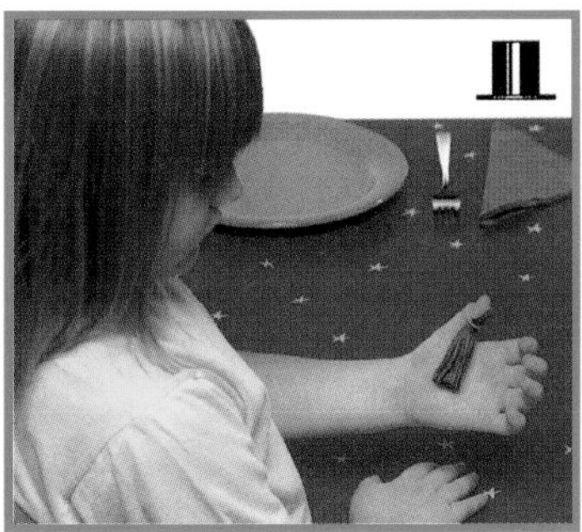

1 Secretly, under the table, attach the torn piece of napkin to the inside of your left thumb with the rubber band, so that it is hidden in your hand.

2 Borrow a napkin from another diner. No one will notice the torn piece as you reach across the table to take the napkin.

3 Spread the napkin over your left hand and point to the "stains" as you push the centre of the napkin into your hand.

4 The real centre, and the torn centre, are side by side. Here we can see under Sarah's napkin, but don't let anyone else see what is happening.

5 Take both the centres into your right hand. Turn them upside down and put them back into your left hand. Pull up only the torn piece.

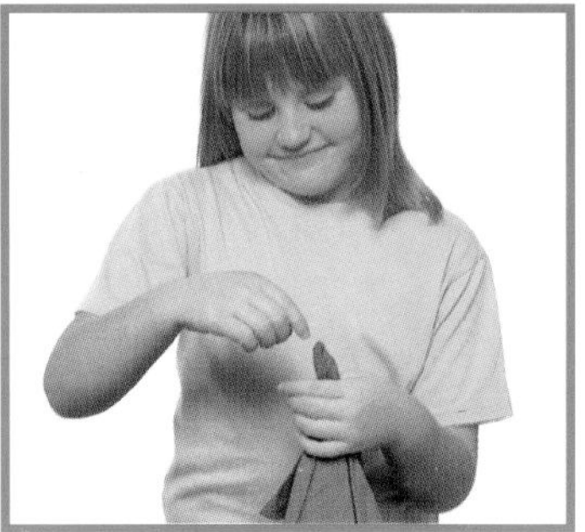

6 Tear off pieces, saying they are stained, and put them in your pocket. Remove the rubber band with one of the pieces.

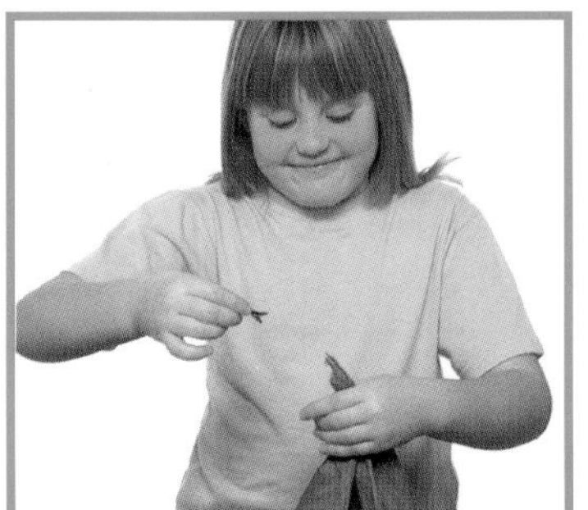

7 Really, you are tearing pieces from the extra piece in your hand. It will look as if you are tearing them from the centre of the napkin.

8 When it looks like you have thoroughly spoilt the napkin, calmly open out the real napkin to the amazement of everyone at the table.

Money from Nowhere!

Tip

For your special coin, to save it melting, carefully take the chocolate out of the foil and make it vanish, in your mouth! Replace it with a disc of cardboard and you can use the coin over and over again.

How about this for a trick? You are holding your empty top hat in one hand, then, with the other hand, you reach up and pluck a gold coin out of the air and drop it into your hat. Then you find another in the air, then another and another. Aribibia is finding coins all over the place, even behind people's ears! Finally he tips his hat onto the table and out pours a shower of golden coins. There are enough coins to hand out to friends after the show. When you do this trick, you will use a specially prepared coin, so make sure you do not give it away but keep it safely for next time.

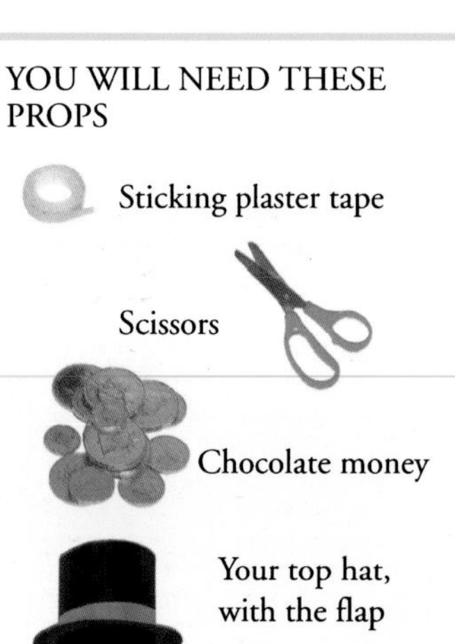

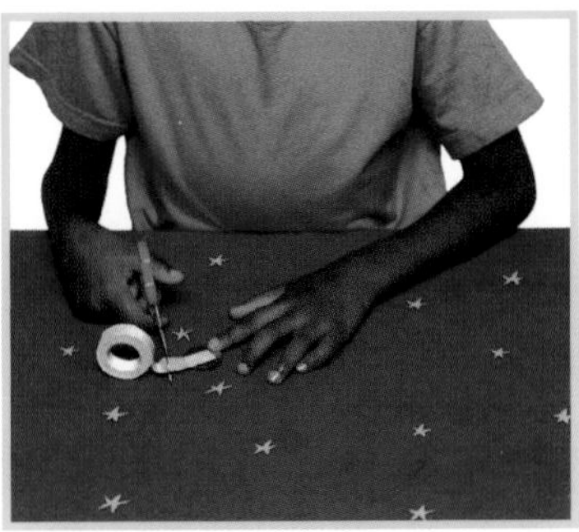

1 Before you start the trick, fix about 4 cm of sticking plaster to one side of your special coin, leaving about 2 cm hanging free.

2 Load one side of your hat flap with chocolate money. With the flap over the money, you can show your audience that the hat is "empty".

3 Hold the coin between your finger and thumb with the plaster stuck to your second and third fingers. Keep the back of your hand to the audience.

4 Hold your hand over the hat, and let the coin go. It will fall behind your fingers, but the audience will believe it has fallen into the hat.

5 Flick the coin up again, and catch it with your thumb. You've caught a coin from the air! Drop it into the hat. Repeat this action several times.

6 Shake the hat to rattle the coins that are already in it. The audience will be convinced that you have caught a hatful of coins from thin air.

7 Finally pour the coins onto the table to show just how many you have collected from thin air.

Magic Wands

It always looks good, in your show, to wave your wand whenever you wish the "magic" to happen. Nhat Han has also discovered some tricks that use the wand itself. She can make the wand "magnetic"; it will cling to her hand with, apparently, nothing holding it in place. She can, or so it appears, push the wand right into her leg and it doesn't hurt her. She can also make her wand stiff one minute and bendy the next. How does she do that?

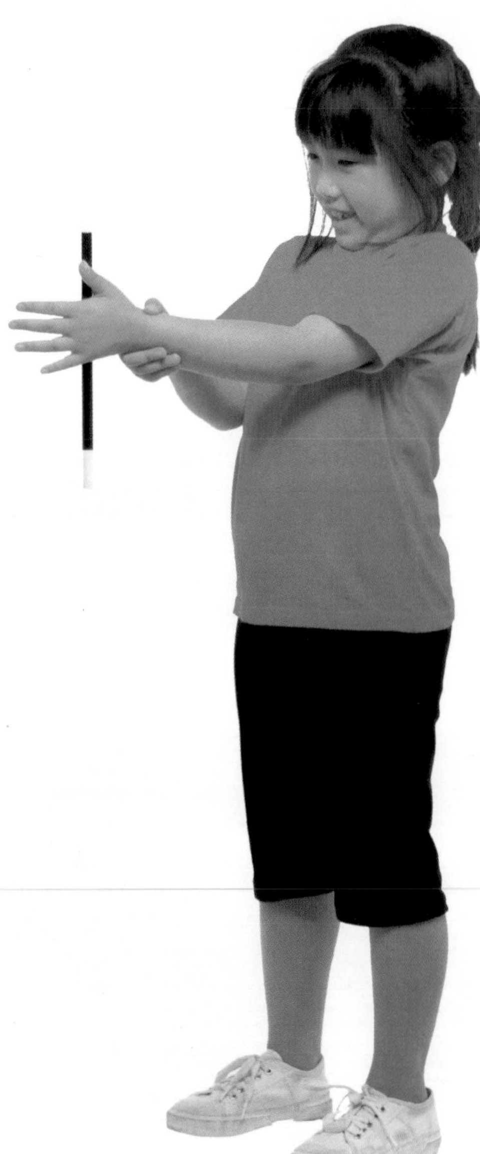

Magnetic Wand

1 If you are holding a wand and you open your hand, it falls to the floor. Oh, dear!

2 But if you are a magician, like Nhat Han, it will stay in your hand all by itself.

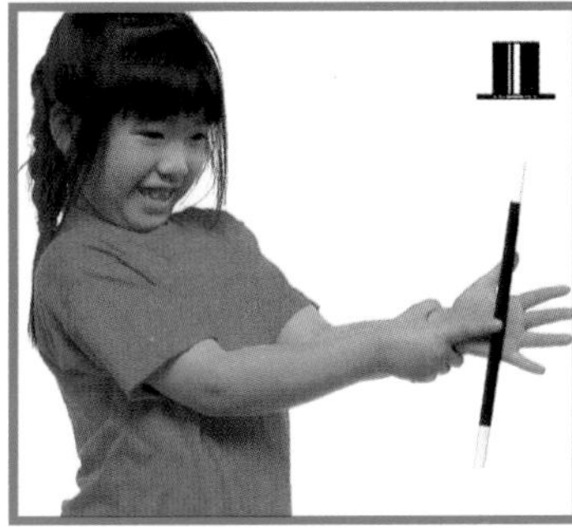

3 Look on the other side of her hand. Can you see her secret? Try it yourself.

Painless Wand

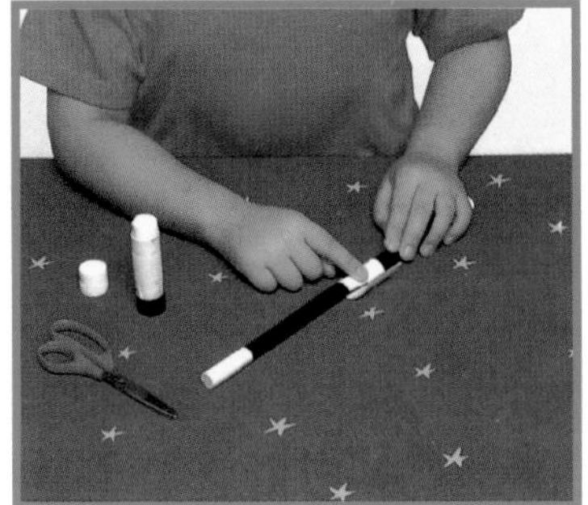

1 Nhat Han rolls up a piece of white paper and glues it to make a tube the same size as the tip of her wand.

2 Nhat Han has pushed the wand right into her leg! But it did not seem to hurt! How did she do that?

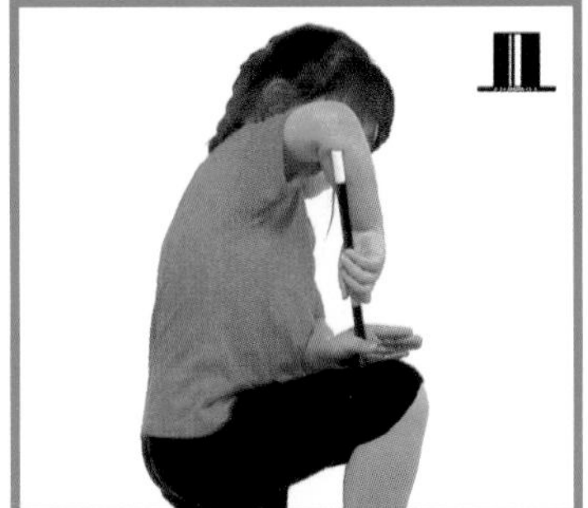

3 She hid the lower wand tip in her hand and pushed the paper tube down the wand with her other hand.

Wobbly Wand

1 Nhat Han is trying to bend her wand. It is definitely stiff.

2 Next, she holds it loosely between finger and thumb, about one third of the way down. When she moves it from side to side, it looks wobbly.

The Coin Fold

Tricks with money always get the audience's attention, especially if you make the money disappear and it belongs to someone in the audience! Alexander finds that the coin fold shown here is a very useful method for helping to make a coin vanish easily. But he had to practise hard to perfect his technique, especially making the coin reappear from Michelle's ear.

YOU WILL NEED THESE PROPS

Tip

Because the audience sees you wrap the coin in the paper, their eyes stay on the paper packet. This "misdirection" allows you to drop the coin into your hand.

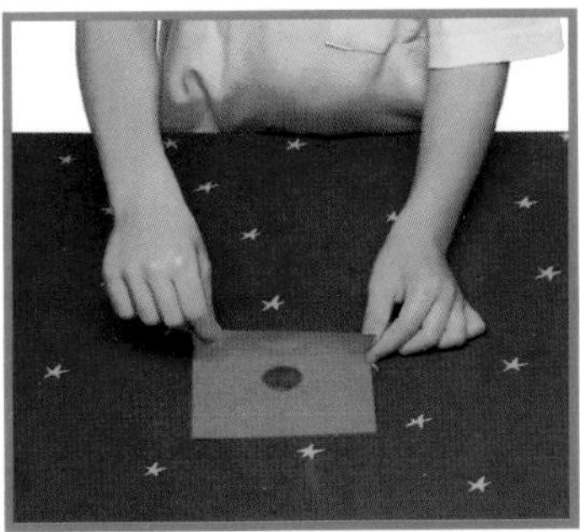

1 Place the coin in the middle of the paper and fold about one-third of the paper over it.

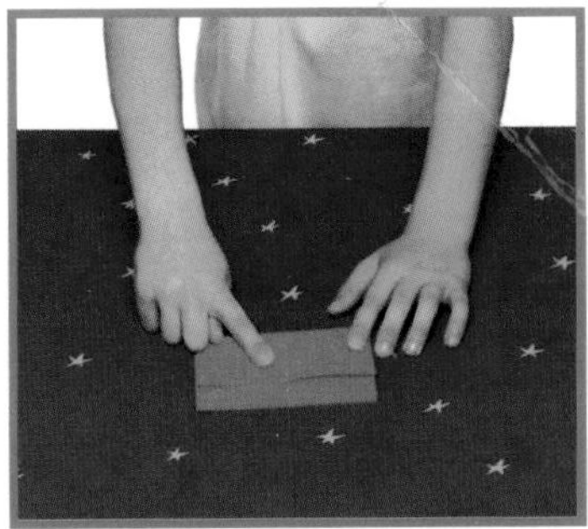

2 Press this down. It helps if you leave a coin-shaped impression in the paper.

3 Turn the paper and coin over, carefully, holding the coin in the fold of the paper, as Alexander is doing here.

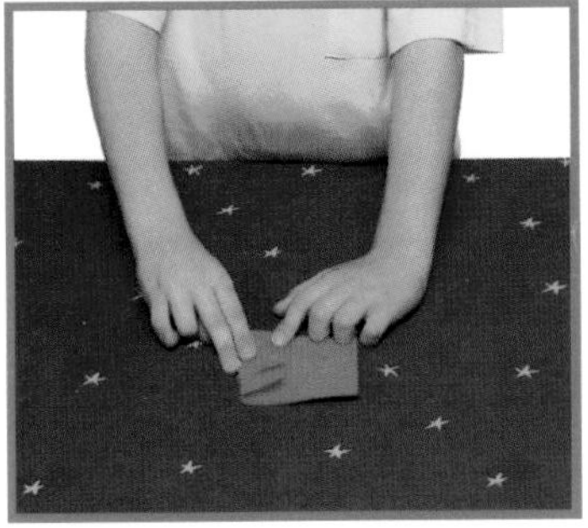

4 Fold over about one-third from one side.

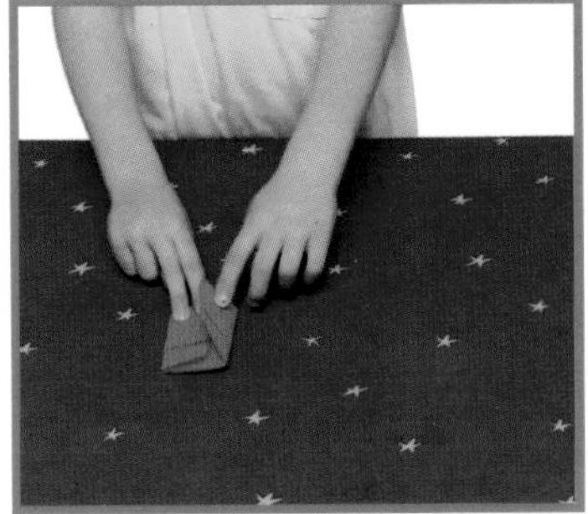

5 Then fold over about the same from the other side, so that the folds overlap.

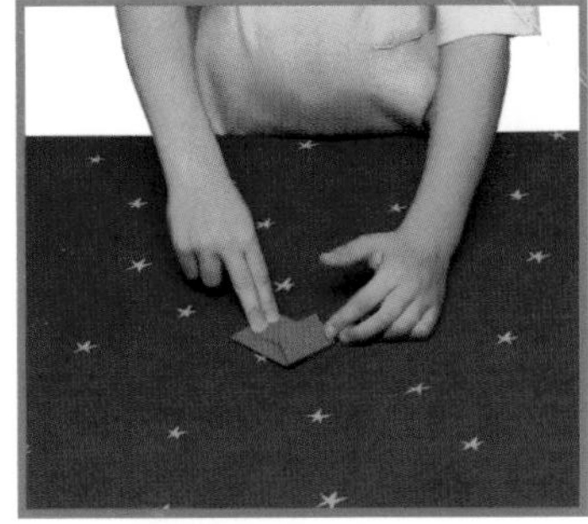

6 Now fold the flap at the top over the other folds. Put the package in your left hand and hold a corner of the flap with your left thumb.

7 Gently lift the package, so that the coin slides out of the secret gap and stays hidden in your hand. Hold it with your second and third fingers.

8 Now you can tear up the package in front of the audience. Or you can hand it to a friend to hold, and pretend to find the coin in her ear.

Cutting Coins

Here is a routine that uses the coin fold principle demonstrated in the previous trick, some misdirection and a technique called "sleeving" the coin. The trick is a bit complicated to do, and might need a lot of practice. But if you can do this trick successfully, everyone will be convinced that you really *are* a magician. You will need to wear a jacket, blazer or similar clothing, with an inside breast pocket. Look at the pictures carefully. Notice in particular how Lucy uses her eyes to draw the audience's attention to exactly where she wants them to look, while she is doing the secret move somewhere else.

Tip

Put the scissors in your breast pocket before you start the routine. Place them point down. If you borrow the coin, you could get the lender to sign it with a felt-tipped pen, or remember the date on the coin. This will prove that you are using only one coin.

All the time you are performing the trick, keep your eyes on the packet to misdirect your audience.

YOU WILL NEED THESE PROPS

Jacket with inside breast pocket

1 Borrow a coin and do the coin fold as described in Steps 1 to 7 in the previous trick. Keep the coin hidden in your right hand.

2 Reach into your breast pocket for the scissors, but first drop the coin into your sleeve. Keep your arm bent up, so the coin stays near the elbow.

3 Bring out the scissors and cut the packet into little pieces. The coin has vanished! (You know it is in your sleeve by your elbow.)

4 Make up another little packet, keeping your arm with the coin bent. The audience can see that your hands, and the paper, are empty.

5 Rattle the packet and listen to it. Look as if you can hear a coin in there. This misdirects the audience while you drop your left hand naturally to your side. Catch the coin with your fingers as it slides out of your sleeve.

6 Keeping the coin hidden, bring both hands together and quickly tear open the paper packet. The coin that was hidden in your fingers seems to come out of the empty packet.

Middle House Mouse

This trick is loosely based on what's probably the oldest magic trick in the world, the "cups and balls", which is over 2000 years old. When Wura performs the trick using fluffy mice, she tells a story about a mouse who only ever wanted to live in a middle house, never at the end of a row.

Tip

You do not have to use mice. Look in the shops for four identical novelty animals that fit in your cups or you could even make your own.

The beakers or cups need to be of flexible plastic, not china or metal.

To make the bases for your animals, draw around a beaker onto the cardboard. Ask a grown-up to cut out the circle so that it is just a little *smaller* than the mouth of the beaker.

Never ever show more than one mouse at one time. The audience must believe that there is only one.

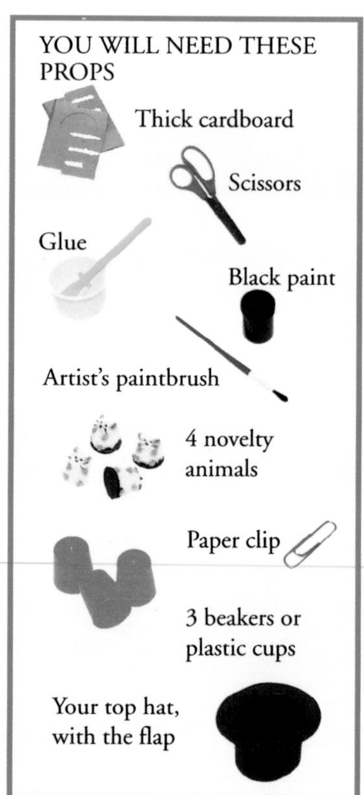

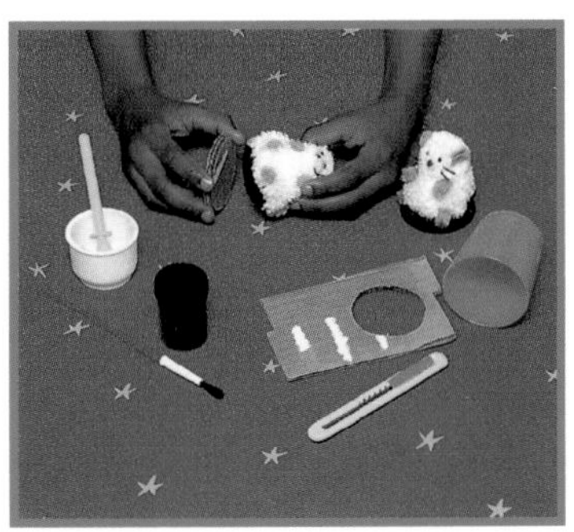

1 Ask a grown-up to cut out three circles to just fit inside a beaker. Paint them black. Leave to dry, then glue the circles onto the three mice.

2 Unbend the paper clip to make a hook at each end. Push one end into the fourth mouse. Hook it to your back before starting the trick.

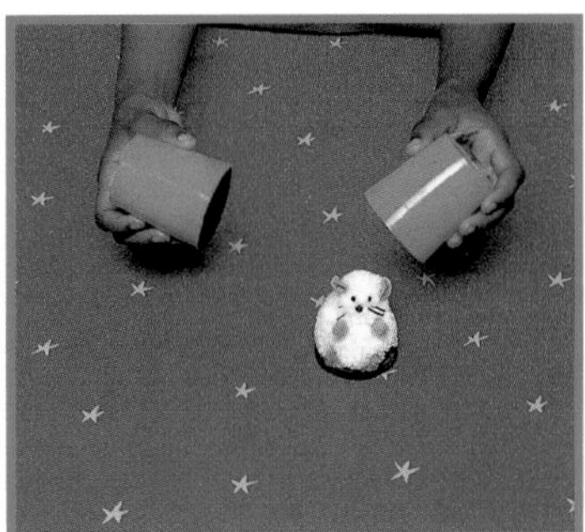

3 Practise lifting up a beaker with a mouse inside. If you squeeze the cup when you lift it, the mouse stays in the cup and seems to "disappear".

4 Now for the performance. Arrange three beakers, each with a mouse hidden inside, in a line. Show the audience only the middle mouse.

5 Squeeze the two end beakers gently as you lift them (to hold the mice inside) to show they are "empty".

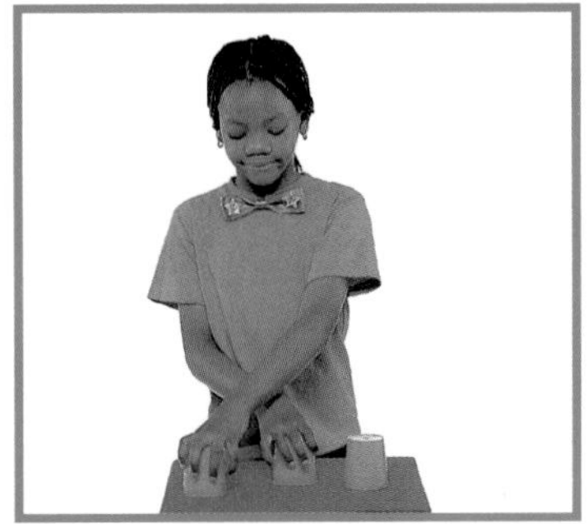

6 Swap the two end beakers with the middle one. Then lift the new middle beaker to show that the mouse has magically jumped back.

7 Swap the beakers again. Take the mouse from the end cup, and put it in your top hat. Lift the middle cup. The mouse has "jumped" back again!

8 Repeat until all the mice are in the hat, then show that the hat is also "empty". The audience will see where the mouse is when you turn round!

Postman's Wand

Gerald is demonstrating a really smart trick he has learnt. He puts his wand into an envelope, ready to post it. Then he performs a little magic, and "alakazam", the wand disappears from the envelope and then it reappears in a different envelope on the other side of the room.

Tips

Find some large envelopes that fit your wand, in different colours if possible or decorate them differently.

Make sure the envelopes stay in view at all times. Prop them up against the backs of two chairs if necessary.

Before you put the wand into the envelope, tap the chairs or tables with the wand. This proves that the wand is solid without your actually having to say so, which would seem suspicious.

YOU WILL NEED THESE PROPS

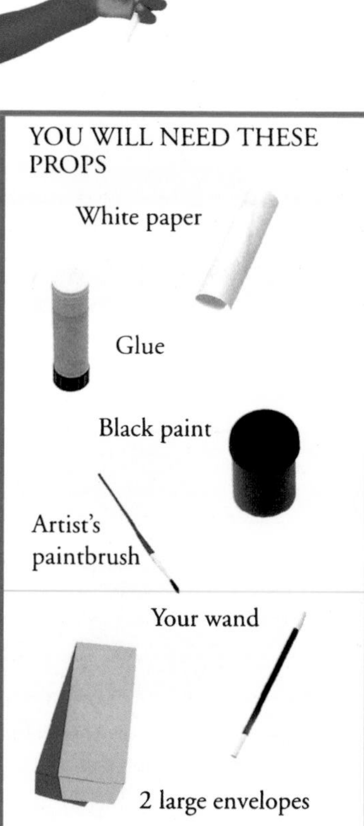

1 Roll up some paper and glue it to make a hollow paper wand. Paint it to look like a real wand. When the paint is dry, slide it over the real wand.

2 Show your audience the two empty envelopes and place them apart on two tables or chairs.

3 Put the wand into one envelope. Shake your head and take it out, secretly letting the real wand slide out of the paper one into the envelope.

4 Put the paper wand into the other envelope, saying, "I prefer it in this one". Now the trick is done, but the audience thinks it has just started.

5 So now it is all acting. Make a magical "swapping over" sign with your arms.

6 The audience saw you put the wand in the second envelope yet you can prove it is now empty by scrunching it up into a ball.

7 With a grand gesture, open up the first envelope to reveal your real wand, which has magically travelled through the air. Magician, take a bow.

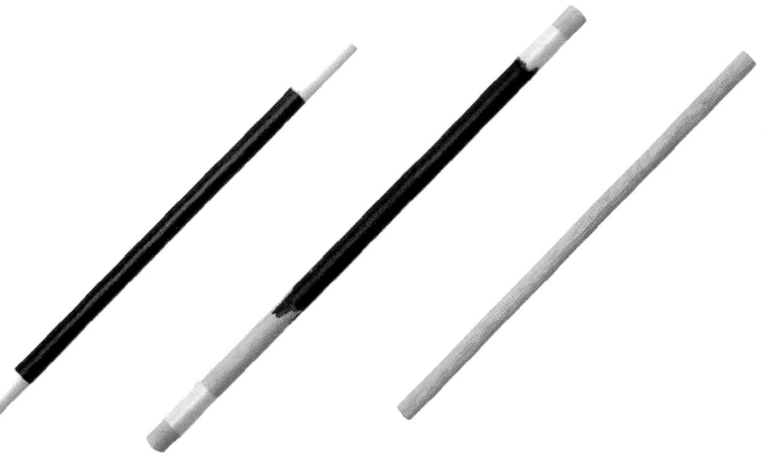

Back-flip Card

When people know you do magic, they will often ask to see a card trick. The trouble is, many card tricks involve complicated, finger-twisting moves. But try this: if you can put a pack of cards behind your back, turn the whole pack over and then turn just the top card over, you can do this trick. It is that easy. You have to have a reason for putting the cards behind your back, so explain that anyone can do a card trick when they can see the cards, but it takes a *real* magician to do it behind their back. Here, Michelle tries the trick out on Alexander.

Tip

When someone has chosen a card, ask them to show it to someone else (not you!). This helps to avoid them forgetting which card they chose, which would spoil the trick.

YOU WILL NEED THESE PROPS

Pack of cards

1 Shuffle the cards, then hold them like a fan, face-down in your hand. Ask a friend to take a card and remember it, but not to let you see it.

2 While talking about doing tricks behind your back, put the pack behind your back and turn it over. Pick off the top card.

3 Turn this card over and put it back on top of the pack. Do this quite quickly. Then bring the cards to the front again.

4 Hold the cards as a pack. All the cards are face up except the top one. Ask your friend to slide his card into the pack; keep the pack closed.

5 Put the pack behind your back again and pick off the top card.

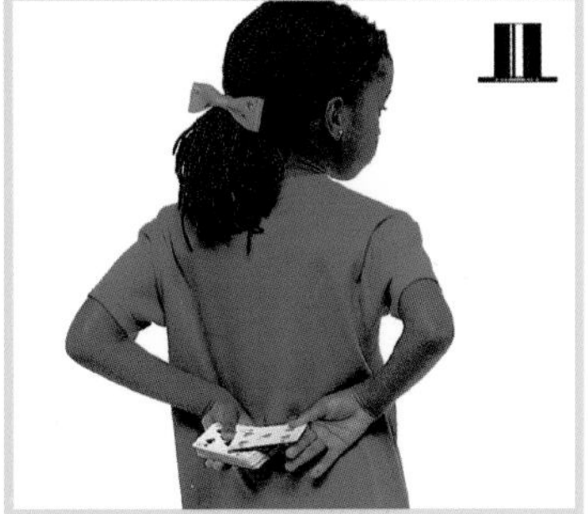

6 Turn over the top card and put it back on the pack. Then turn the whole pack over while you say you are trying to find your friend's card.

7 Bring the pack to the front again and spread them out. Hocus-pocus! One card is face up, and yes – it is the very card that was chosen!

Coin Through Hand

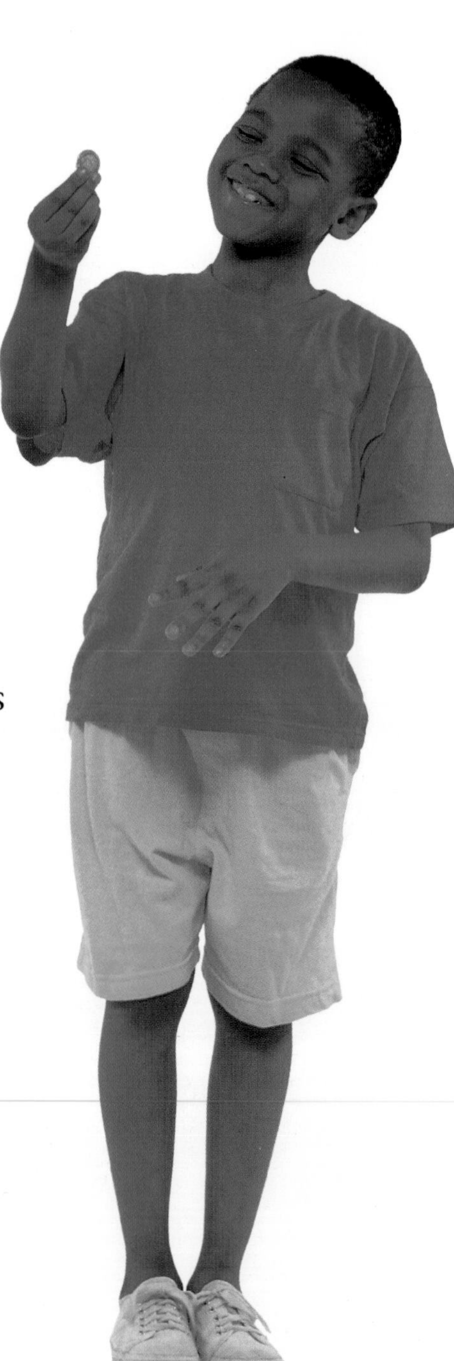

An impromptu trick is one that you can do anywhere with no preparation or "props". All you need for this impromptu trick is your hands and a coin, which you can borrow. It is also very easy to do and is the first coin trick real magicians usually learn. You can really "act" this one. The audience, at first, think they have caught you out, so they are even more surprised when the coin really does end up in your fist. Michael shows us how to do it.

YOU WILL NEED THESE PROPS

Coin

Tip

Use a medium to large coin, if possible. Small, light coins sometimes stick to your fingers and do not drop when you want them to.

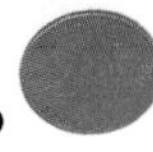

1 Hold the coin above your left fist, as shown, and announce, "I'm going to push this coin through the back of my hand".

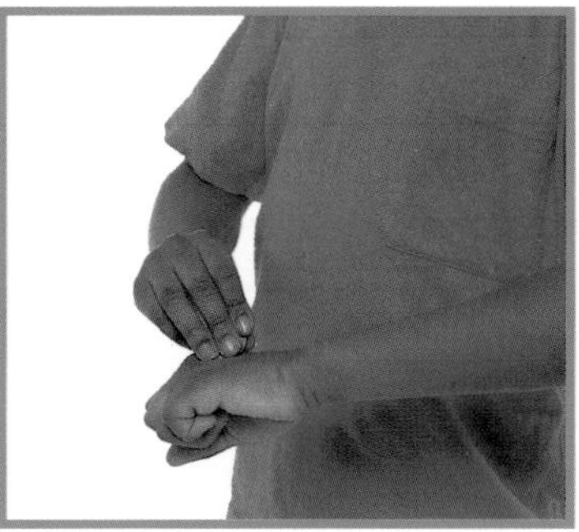

2 As you push the coin down, it slides up, out of sight behind your fingers. "There, it's gone through", you can say.

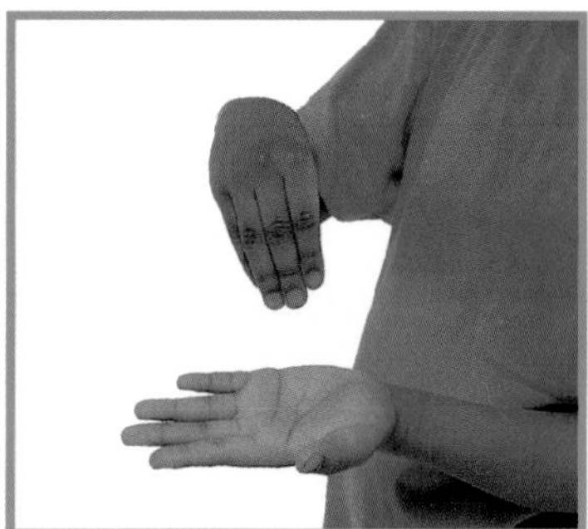

3 Open your fist and say, "Whoops! It must have got stuck, halfway". The audience, though, think they know where it is.

4 "I'll try again", you say as you do the sneaky bit. The sneaky bit is that, as you turn your left hand back over into a fist, your thumb almost brushes against the tips of the fingers holding the coin. Just at this point you let the coin slip out of your fingers, and you catch it in your left hand, which you make into a fist.

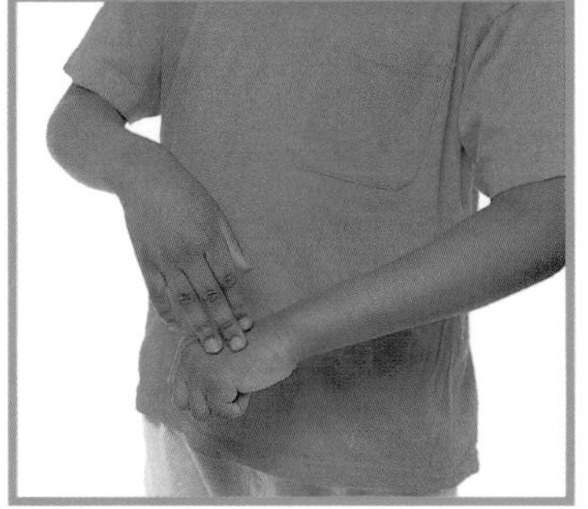

5 It all happens so quickly the audience believe it is still hidden behind your fingers, and you say, "I'll give it a harder push this time".

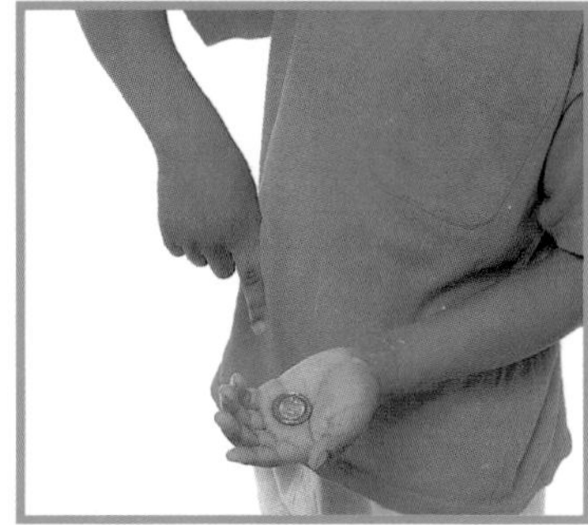

6 Now slowly turn your fist over and open it up. "Ah, there it is!"

Purple Hanky, Red Hanky

People in the audience love to come up and help during a show. For this trick, two assistants are needed. Nicola cleverly chose Scott, who was wearing a purple T-shirt, to hold the wrapped purple silk hanky, and Tope, who was wearing red, to hold the wrapped red silk hanky. Scott and Tope never let go of their parcels, but Nicola makes them keep changing sides. A wave of her wand and, "Hey presto", the hankies have changed places. Now, that *is* magic! How is it done? Well, the newspapers are not as ordinary as they seem.

Tips

If you choose volunteers who are wearing the same colours as your silk handkerchiefs, it is easier for the audience to follow the trick and for you to remember where the different silks are all the time.

When you tear open the parcel at the end of the trick, take care not to tear too deeply or you will expose the wrong silk.

YOU WILL NEED THESE PROPS

- 2 pairs of silk hankies in contrasting colours, such as red and purple
- Newspaper
- Glue stick
- Sticky tape
- Your wand

1 Before the show, lay out a silk handkerchief on a sheet of newspaper and spread glue round it (not on it!) with the glue stick.

2 Stick a second sheet on top. Do the same with a silk in the other colour. Make a secret mark on the papers, so you know which is which.

3 Fold up the sheets of newspapers and put them on your table, with your wand and the sticky tape. Show the audience the remaining two silks.

4 Wrap the red silk in the paper which has the purple one hidden inside, and make a rough ball shape.

5 Use sticky tape to hold the parcel together. Now wrap the purple silk in the paper with the red one inside, and hold it together with sticky tape.

6 Ask for two volunteers. Give the wrapped red silk to someone wearing red, and the wrapped purple silk to someone in purple.

7 Ask your volunteers to swap places while holding onto their parcels. Wave your wand in the air to make the magic work.

8 Tear open the outer layer of the "purple" parcel. Instead of a purple silk, you pull out a red one! And from the "red" you pull out a purple silk.

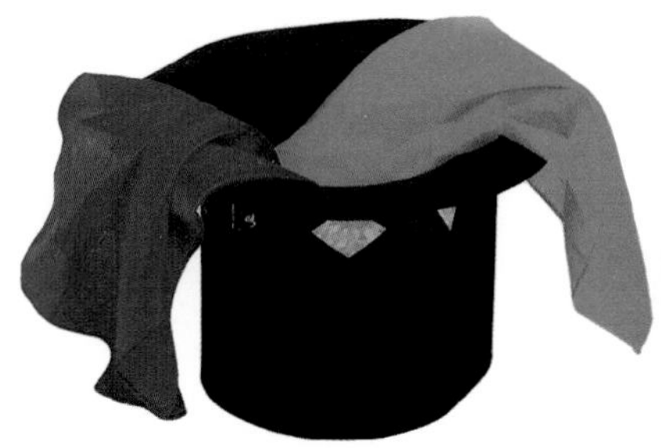

X-ray Wand and Ringing Up

Here are two special tricks using magic wands, but with a difference. The second trick uses your wooden wand, but the first one uses a hollow wand. Carl has made a hollow wand by rolling up a sheet of paper and painting it to look like a real one. The X-ray Wand routine is perfect for when you are showing a trick to just one friend, because you actually teach them how to do it. They will be amazed to see a hole right through their hand. Ringing Up is great fun because you can use a ring that you have borrowed from someone in the audience. People always enjoy seeing their own things behaving in strange magical ways.

YOU WILL NEED THESE PROPS

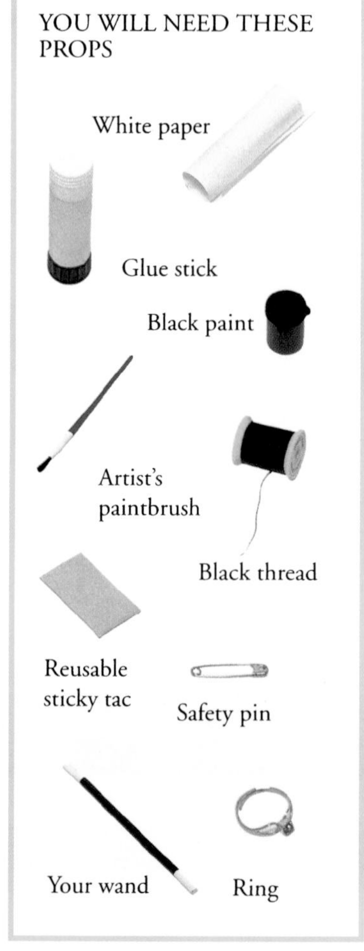

X-ray Wand

1 Roll and glue a sheet of paper to form a tube. Then paint it to look like a wand.

2 Hold the paper wand up to your eye and look through it, keeping both eyes open.

3 Place your other hand, open flat, about halfway along it, beside the wand.

4 Now you will see a hole right through your hand!

Ringing Up

1 Attach a black thread to your wand with sticky tac. Tie the thread to a safety pin; fix this to your waist. Put a ring over the wand to rest on your fist.

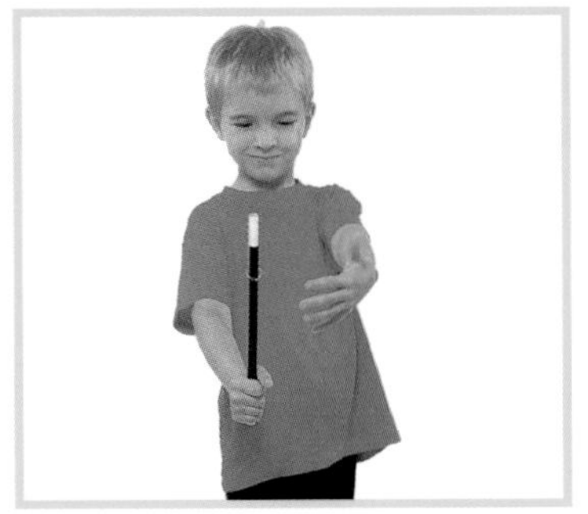

2 Wriggle your other fingers as you move the wand slightly away from yourself – the ring starts to rise. How?

3 As you move the wand forwards, the thread attached to the top of your trousers and to the wand moves higher, pushing the ring up the wand.

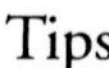

Time-bomb Escape

How would you like to do a really dangerous and "death-defying" trick to add drama and suspense to your show? Imagine, then, being tied up in a time-bomb and escaping with only seconds to spare. You could pretend to be like Houdini, who was one of the greatest magicians and escapologists of all time. Before you start, ask a grown-up to make a small hole on each side of the box, about halfway up, for the ropes to go through.

Tips

Decorate your box to make it look really dangerous!

Once you are shut in the box, get the audience to count down from 30 to 1 and then, if you have not escaped, to shout "Bang".

With practice, you will find you can free yourself from the ropes in only a few seconds, but do not jump out too early. The effect is much more dramatic if you leave it until there are only two or three seconds to spare!

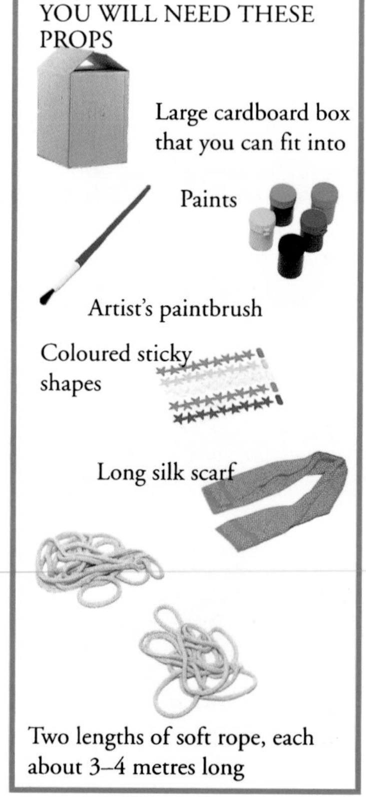

1 Ask one of your assistants to tie your hands with the scarf. Tie the scarf round one wrist, then the other next to it, firmly, but not *too* tightly.

2 Then ask your assistants to loop a rope over each of your arms. They must hold on firmly to the ends of the ropes, not letting go until the trick is completed. You will be trapped!

3 Climb into the box with an assistant standing guard on each side. Ask them to push the free ends of the ropes out through the small holes in the sides of the box, and then keep hold of them.

4 Squat down inside the box and tell your assistants to close the flaps. Now they can start the countdown with the audience: 30, 29, 28...

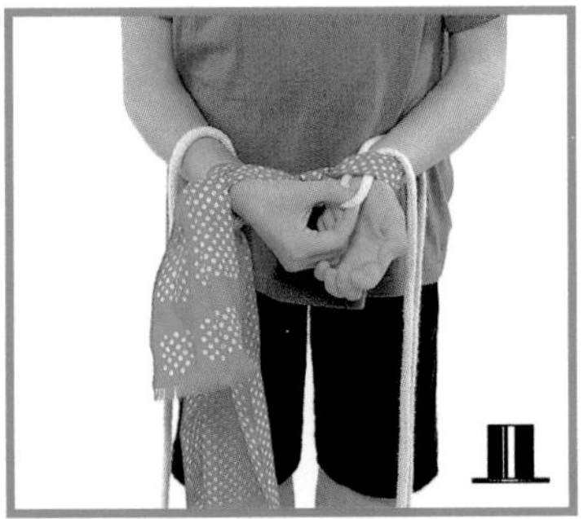

5 Even though you are tied up, you will be able to work the rope free. Pull a loop of the rope down the inside of your wrist under the silk scarf.

6 Push the loop back over your hand and let it slide up the back of your wrist. That hand is free. Now do the other one.

7 With only a few seconds of the countdown to spare, jump up like a jack-in-the-box, holding your arms in the air to show they are free.

Growing Things

Introduction

Gardens and gardeners come in many shapes and sizes. You can be a gardener too, whether you live on a farm with a large garden or in an apartment with some space on a windowsill for a few plants.

Growing things takes time and patience, but the rewards are worth waiting for. There are lots of other things for you to be getting on with while your seeds are germinating under the soil. Once you see the first green shoots appear you will know that a plant really is going to grow and you are already a gardener!

Pot marigolds

In this chapter we show you how to grow lots of different plants yourself, with perhaps just a little help from a grown-up. There are plants that grow very fast and produce something to eat, like mustard and cress. Some plants take longer to grow but give you special treats, like strawberries. Other plants are grown just for fun, like vegetable tops and a coconut head. So, whether you choose to grow giant sunflowers that take all summer, or sprouting seeds for your salad that are ready in just a few days, you will find out all you need to know by following what the children are doing in the pictures.

Strawberries

Different plants grow, then flower and die with the seasons.

Vegetable tops

Daffodils like the crisp, cold springtime sunshine while nasturtiums thrive in the baking hot summer sun, needing no shade and very little water. Some plants live through the winter, growing new flowers each summer. Others live only for one season but make seeds that will grow into new plants the following year. Houseplants usually come from parts of the world where the weather is warmer all year round, but they grow very happily indoors in countries with cooler climates.

How Plants Begin to Grow

Plants start growing in many different ways and it is important to know how to treat each type. Look at the list below to find out how plants can be grown.

Seeds

A seed needs water to soften its outer shell, and then the new plant sends a root downwards into the soil and a stem upwards, towards the light. The tiniest seeds just need to be scattered on top of the soil, but the larger ones have to be buried. Usually seeds are planted as deep as they are thick. So measure a seed between your fingers and you will know how deep it has to go into the soil in order to grow properly.

Seeds

Bulbs, corms and tubers

These are thick, fleshy and roundish in shape. A bulb looks like an onion – in fact if you planted an onion it would grow leaves and flowers! They all produce new plants which will grow in the right conditions. Some need icy cold winters underground and others should only be planted when the weather gets warmer. Daffodils grow from bulbs, begonias from corms and dahlias from tubers.

Bulbs

Tubers

Corms

Grow a new plant from a stem cutting

Cuttings

Some plants need very special conditions to make their seeds grow, but you can still grow some new plants from cuttings. Take a piece of the healthy full-grown plant, and stand it in water or compost in a warm place. It will grow roots from its stem and you will soon have a strong little plant. Some plants can be grown from leaf or root cuttings as well.

Plantlets

Some fully-grown plants send out long runners which grow miniature plants at their ends. These send down roots of their own if they rest on the soil, and eventually the runners will die back to leave a separate new plant. Strawberries and spider plants grow in this way.

Grow a new plant from plantlets

Caring for Your Plants

Your seeds, bulbs, cuttings and plantlets will only grow into healthy adult plants if you look after them carefully. This doesn't need to take a lot of time, but you do need to remember to look at them every few days to check that they are doing well.

Watering

Watering your plants is a lot of fun, but if you give them too much they will rot and die. Try to keep the soil damp but not wet. When you press it with your finger, you should be able to feel the moisture without a little pool of water forming. If your plants do dry out, stand their pots in a saucer or bowl of water rather than pour on water from above. This way the soil will gradually soak up water to feed the thirsty roots.

Test the soil to see if it needs more water

Weeds

If you do your gardening outdoors, you may find that other little plants also begin to grow where you haven't planted any seeds. Ask a grown-up to show you what weeds look like, and try to keep your garden weed-free. It seems cruel to pull out healthy little plants, but if you leave them they will spread very quickly and stop your plants from getting the light and moisture that they need to grow. So pull them up before they grow big enough to flower and make more seeds to grow more weeds.

Pests

These are creatures that we don't want around us, and in the garden they include greenfly, caterpillars, snails and slugs. They love eating juicy new plants but luckily there are some other creatures that like eating them. Ladybirds love greenfly, but they can't always eat them up quickly enough so you may have to do something. Try adding a small amount of washing-up soap to a spray bottle filled with water and then use it to spray the greenfly on your plants. If you have a problem with slugs and snails, you can sprinkle ashes or sand around your lettuces as they don't like the feeling of sliding over it. Caterpillars need to be removed by hand and – if you don't mind doing it – just drop them into a jar of water. Otherwise, set them free somewhere far away from your precious plants.

If the soil is dry, stand the pot in a bowl of water

Spray a plant with soapy water to get rid of greenfly

Important!

Remember that even the most expert gardeners sometimes have failures, when plants don't grow, or pests become a big problem. If this happens to you, try not to feel discouraged. The best thing to do is to try something new so that you always have some gardening on the go!

Latin Names

Every plant has a special Latin name that tells you exactly what it is. Just like we have our Christian names and surnames, a plant has a family name first and its own name second. The names are often difficult to say, but if you take a few letters at a time you will be able to join them up and say something in Latin. When they are printed in a book, Latin names appear in italics, like this: *Helianthus debilis. Helianthus* is the family name for sunflowers, and *debilis* is the special name given to a small, or dwarf, type of sunflower.

Glossary

Here are some special gardening words that you may not know but will see mentioned in the projects.

Alpine A rock garden plant.
Annual A plant that completes its life cycle in one year. It starts by growing from a seed and finishes by making new seeds.
Compost A special soil mixture or rotted-down garden and kitchen waste that feeds the plants so they grow well.
Crocks Broken pieces of clay flowerpot. They are used in the bottom of pots to help with drainage.
Cutting A piece of plant (leaf, stem or root) which can be used to grow a new plant.
Germination The first stage of growth from seed to plant.
Node A stem joint, where new stems and leaves grow.
Mulch A layer of chopped up leaves, bark or other plant matter. It is spread on top of the soil to stop it drying out and to prevent weeds from growing.
Propagating Growing new plants by different methods, including taking cuttings.
Runner A creeping stem which grows roots and produces new plants.

Mulches stop the soil drying out so quickly

New umbrella plants are grown from cuttings

Spider plants grow runners

Finding What You Need

A garden centre can be very large and confusing when you only need a few small things to start you off. Here is a basic list of useful gardening materials and tools. You will be able to get some of the equipment mentioned here from toy shops, too, such as a small plastic watering can, a scoop to use as a trowel and a sieve, which are often sold for playing with in sandpits.

Trowel You will need a small trowel for filling flowerpots with compost and for digging holes in the garden.
Watering can A can with a sprinkler will be best for gentle watering. Remember that water is very heavy to carry, so choose the size of can that you will be able to lift easily when it is full.
Sieve This is useful for sprinkling a very fine layer of compost over your newly-sown seeds.
Flowerpots These should always have a drainage hole in the bottom. They come in lots of different sizes, made from either clay or plastic, and they usually have matching saucers to stop drips. You can decorate clay pots at home or buy plastic ones in lots of fun colours. Don't forget to collect some pretty outer containers too. Clay pots need a layer of crocks or pebbles adding to them before the compost. This helps them to drain better after watering.
Peat pots These are special types of flowerpots which are usually used for planting seeds. When the new plant has started to grow the plant and its pot can be planted in a larger flowerpot. The peat pot will gradually dissolve in the compost.
Seed trays These are useful for planting lots of little seeds or for standing pots of seeds in. You can also use foil dishes used for freezing food.

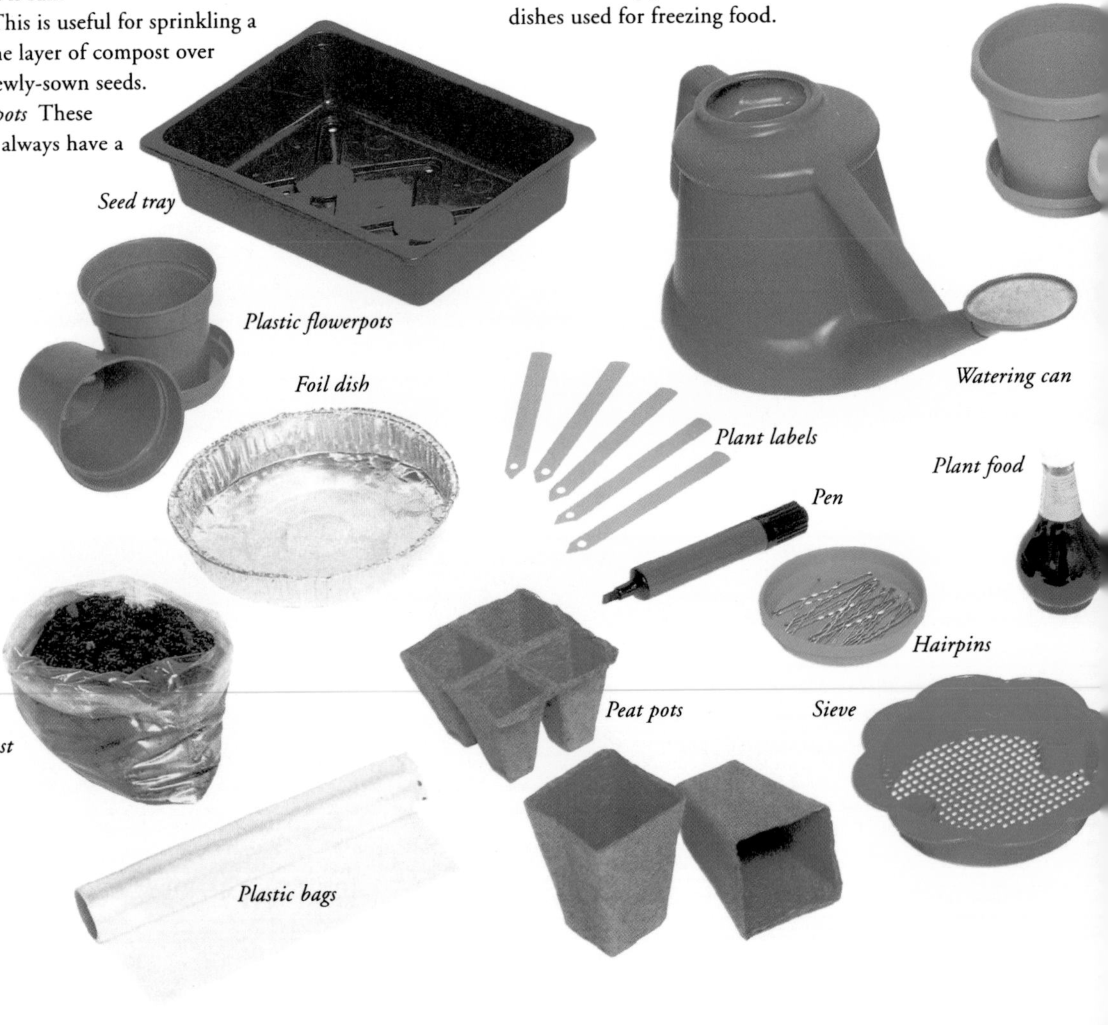

Seed tray

Plastic flowerpots

Foil dish

Compost

Plastic bags

Watering can

Plant labels

Plant food

Pen

Hairpins

Peat pots

Sieve

Compost Specially prepared soils that we buy in bags are called composts. There are lots of different mixtures that suit some types of plant better than others. Seed and cutting compost will give you the best chance of success with new plants. Houseplant compost is useful for indoor gardeners. Cactus compost is good for succulents. Any all-purpose compost is good for general growing, and it comes in bags of all sizes.

Plant food Some plants need more "food" than they can get from compost alone while they are growing. Always ask a grown-up to help you measure out the correct amount of special plant food, following the instructions on the bottle or packet.

Crocks and pebbles These are used to provide better drainage in the bottom of clay pots. You can also sprinkle a layer of pebbles or gravel on top of the compost. This both looks nice and is good for the plants as it helps to keep the soil moist.

Canes and string Some plants grow tall and their stems need to be supported to stop them bending or breaking.

Hairpins These are used to pin baby plantlets growing on the end of runners into compost so that they form roots.

Plant labels and pen Always label your plants so you can remember what you are growing in different pots.

Seeds, bulbs etc There are usually more than you need in a packet, so before buying any ask grown-up gardeners, like your parents, grandparents or neighbours, whether they can spare you a few of their left-over seeds or bulbs. Gardeners always like to share things.

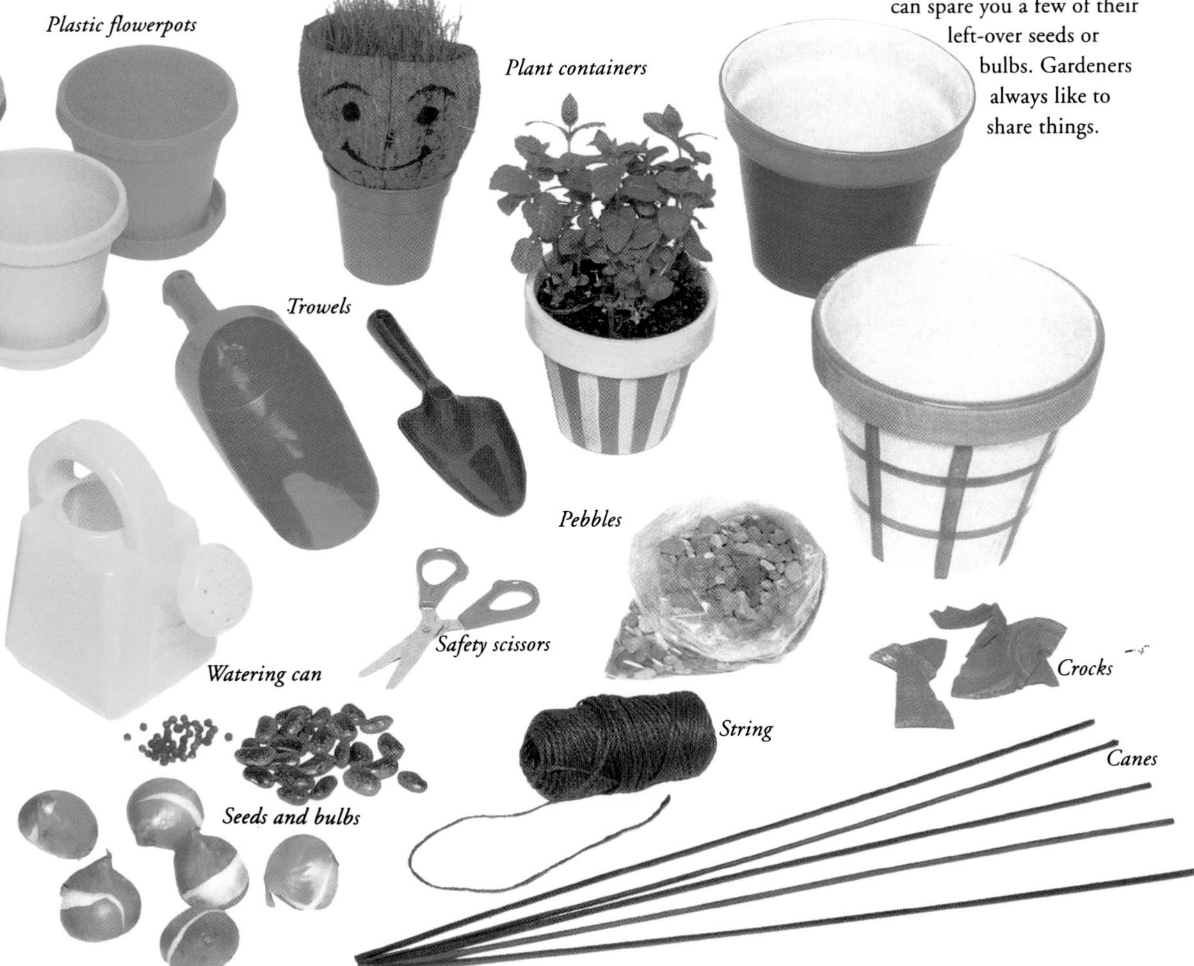

A Sunflower Race

You have to look up to see a sunflower, because they are the tallest and the biggest flowers that we grow in our gardens. It's great fun to have a sunflower race with your friends or family. Roxy and Dominic are having a sunflower race. Follow the step-by-step photographs to see who won.

Tasty pickings

The flower centres of sunflowers are sometimes as large as dinner plates and packed with tasty seeds. These seeds can be eaten raw once the husks have been removed, or the whole flowerhead can be dried and hung out to feed the birds in winter. In hot countries you can see whole fields of huge sunflowers that are grown to make cooking oil and margarine.

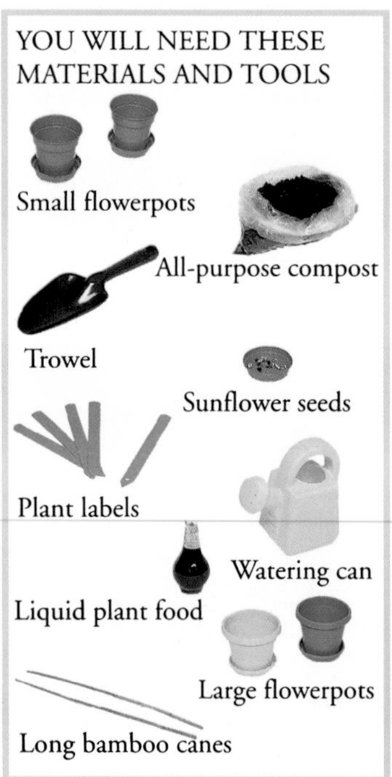

1 Fill some pots with compost and press in the sunflower seeds.

2 Water the pots and cover them with black plastic, or put them in a dark place to germinate.

Size is Not Everything

If you really love sunflowers but have no space to grow the very tall ones, don't worry – you can grow the smaller types. Buy a packet of sunflower seed called *Helianthus debilis*. Sow the seeds into peat pots and then move them into medium-sized flowerpots or a space in the garden, if you have one. They will grow about 80 cm (2ft 8 in) tall, and are just as beautiful.

3 When the seeds germinate and you can see a bit of green, move the pots into the light.

4 When the seedlings are big enough to handle, they can be moved into bigger pots. To help them grow strong and tall you will need to give them a liquid feed once a week. Ask a grown-up to help you with this.

Above: As the plants grow you will need to move them into even larger pots or plant them in the garden. They will need canes to support them.

Some of the plants will be bigger than you are. Measure each one to find the winner of the great sunflower race. This one is a dead heat!

Juicy Strawberries

Strawberry plants have very pretty pink or white flowers with yellow centres, and when the petals drop the fruits begin to grow. They are green at first and then white. As they get bigger and juicier, and ripen in the sun they gradually turn a shiny bright red. If you can bear to wait you will find that the riper they get, the sweeter they taste.

How do baby strawberry plants grow?

Strawberry plants send out long thin stems called runners and baby plants form at their ends. They are fed by the root system of the parent plant through the runner. But if these babies come to rest on soil, they put down roots of their own and no longer need the parent plant to keep them alive. Tania is going to start off some baby strawberry plants and grow herself a mouthwatering treat.

Below: Delicious juicy strawberries – well worth waiting for.

1 Fill the small flowerpots with potting compost and gently firm it down.

2 Place your pots around the parent plant so that a baby plant rests in each of the pots. Push a hairpin into the compost over the runner.

3 Water all the pots. Remember to check the compost each day to be sure it never gets too dry.

4 When the plants have rooted you will see tiny new leaves beginning to sprout.

5 If the baby plants feel firm in the compost, you can now cut the runners.

6 As your plant grows it will need more space, either in the garden or a larger pot.

Cascading Strawberries

If you only have a small space for growing your fruits, a strawberry pot is useful and pretty. It is a tall pot with little "balconies" all the way around it. The idea is to fill the whole pot with compost and plant a small strawberry baby in each of the openings. Water each one and plant the biggest strawberry plant in the top of the pot. When the plants begin to grow they will cover the pot and strawberries will hang down in the sun to ripen.

7 Remember to water your strawberry plant regularly. If it's kept too dry, the fruit will shrivel.

Coconut Head

This coconut head looks so funny that you'll have to be careful who you show it to – everyone will want one! They are so easy to do, and as the grass grows you will be able to change the hair-style of your coconut head. You could also try sowing mustard and cress for a really curly hair-style. Follow the method shown by Dominic and Alex.

Nuts about hair

You can buy grass seed in small amounts from most hardware stores or garden centres, and just 50 g (2 oz) will grow a really good "head of hair" for your coconut. You will have to ask a grown-up to saw or break the top off your coconut, because the shells are really hard. If you haven't eaten fresh coconut before or drunk coconut milk, try some – it's really tasty! Put some out for the birds as a treat.

1 Ask a grown-up to take the top off your coconut. Pour out the milk and ask someone to help you remove the flesh – it's quite difficult.

2 Stand the coconut shell in a flower-pot to stop it falling over, and draw a face on it with a chunky marker pen.

3 Fill your coconut with compost, pressing it down gently.

4 Scatter grass seed thickly over the top of the compost.

5 Sieve a thin layer of compost over to cover all the seed. Press down gently again.

6 Water and cover with a black plastic bag, or put in a dark place until the seeds have begun to grow.

7 When green shoots appear, stand the coconut in the light and water when it looks dry. When the grass has grown over the rim of the coconut, it is ready for its first haircut.

Above: Before and after! If you keep snipping the grass as it grows, it will get thicker and thicker!

Desert Bowl

Succulent plants come from very dry countries where there is hardly any rain at all. Succulent means juicy or filled with sap. To stay alive these clever plants use their roots to suck up any moisture that is in the sandy soil, and they store it in their thick stems or leaves. Try planting up a container with five different types of succulent plants like Joshua and Ilaira have done, and create your own desert environment.

Propagating succulents

Baby plants form on the edges of leaves or on the sides of stems and these can be planted in their own small flowerpots. Succulent plants that you have grown like this make nice presents, and because they grow on indoor windowsills, they suit everyone.

Some succulent plants – known as cacti – are spikey, or covered with fine hairs that sting if you get them in your fingers. Avoid the ones that can hurt you because there are many more safe succulents to choose from.

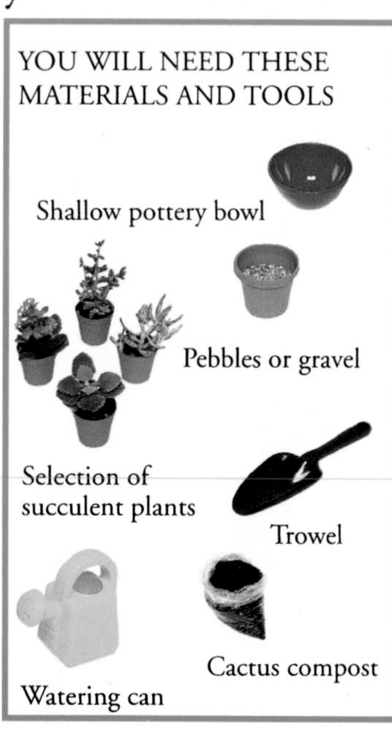

1 Fill the bottom of the bowl with a 5 cm (2 in) layer of gravel.

2 Before you plant your garden, plan where the plants will look best by placing them in the bowl and moving them around in their individual pots.

Alpine Garden

There is another sort of tiny garden you can grow in a pottery dish or shallow round flowerpot. An alpine garden needs gritty soil and pebbles for good drainage. A pet shop will sell small bags of gravel or grit because it is used in fish tanks. Mix equal quantities of grit and compost and put at least five little alpine plants in your dish. Most garden centres have a special area for alpine plants, and there are plenty to choose from.

3 Remove each plant from its pot very carefully. Take your time, as succulents are brittle and bits fall off quite easily.

4 When all the plants are in the bowl, fill all the spaces around the roots with cactus compost, and gently firm the plants in place.

5 Give the plants a little drink, but not too much. Remember that succulents live in sandy places and deserts, and hate to have wet roots.

6 To finish your succulent garden, spread gravel over the surface.

Right: Keep your desert bowl on a sunny windowsill – succulents love the warmth and light.

Jolly Geraniums

Geraniums are lovely, bright flowering plants that live outside in the sunny weather. In the winter they can be brought inside to live on a sunny windowsill. Their flowers are either red, white or pink and they have pretty shaped leaves – some of them are scented. Rub a leaf between your fingers to discover their surprising smells of rose, lemon, pineapple or peppermint!

Taking a cutting

The best way to grow your very own geranium plant is to find somebody who owns a nice bushy geranium, and ask them to take a cutting for you. Tania is going to start a plant from a cutting. Just follow the step-by-step instructions, and you will be able to grow one too.

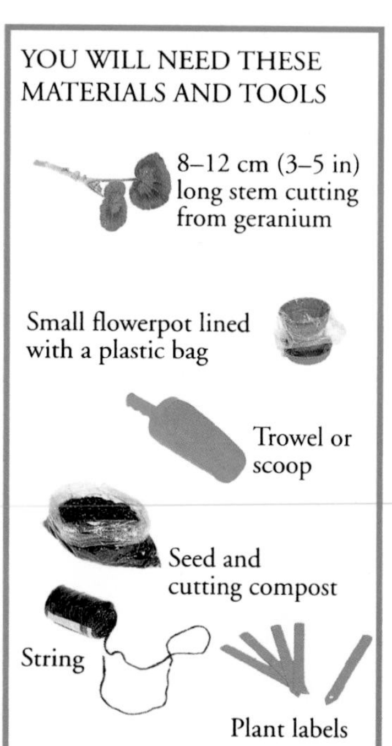

1 Ask a grown-up to take a cutting from a non-flowering shoot of a big geranium plant. Cut the stem just below a node or leaf joint.

2 Take off all leaves except for the small ones at the top.

3 Line a small pot with a plastic bag and fill with moist (but not wet) compost. Seed and cutting compost is the best type to use.

4 Make a hole in the compost for your cutting with a finger. Put the cutting in the hole. Press the compost down gently around the cutting to hold it in place.

5 Lift the edges of the plastic bag, gather it up and tie it around the stem of the cutting with string. Take care not to damage the stem by tying it too tightly.

6 Fold the top of the bag back down over the pot, write a label for your plant and place your pot on a light, but not too sunny, windowsill. After ten days your cutting should have rooted. When it has grown new leaves, lift up the plastic bag and you will see new roots in the compost. You can now remove the bag and plant the geranium in a larger pot.

Above: What an achievement. Your very own plant from a cutting.

Crazy-Shaped Mustard and Cress

Once you have learned how to grow mustard and cress, you can make all sorts of shapes and patterns with your plants. Try animals and faces, or even your own name. Mustard and cress are fun to grow and delicious to eat in salads and sandwiches.

How to grow mustard and cress

Mustard and cress are two of the easiest and quickest plants you can grow. They don't need flowerpots or compost, just cotton wool and water. Sprinkle the seeds onto damp cotton wool and water them each day – as Alex and Reece are doing here. Within a week the little plants will be growing strongly and one week after that you can harvest them with a pair of scissors and then eat them. Your mustard and cress will taste just as good as the type you can buy from shops.

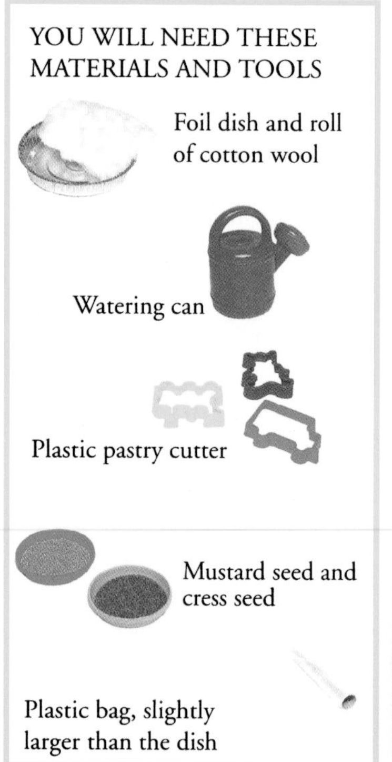

1 Line a foil dish with a layer of cotton wool.

2 Pour on water, until all the cotton wool is damp.

3 Place the plastic pastry cutter in the centre of the dish.

4 Very carefully, scatter mustard seeds inside the cutter.

5 Now scatter the cress seeds all around the rest of the dish.

6 Place the dish in the plastic bag and put it in a dark place. Check the dish each day to see if the seeds have germinated. When they have, remove the plastic bag and place the dish on a light windowsill.

7 Add a little water to the dish each day – just enough to keep the cotton wool wet. When the plants are as tall as your little finger, you can cut the mustard and cress and put them in a salad or sandwich.

Mustard and Cress "Eggheads"

You can grow mustard and cress in eggshells. Save the shell from your boiled egg and line it with damp cotton wool. Sow the seed thickly and wait for your "egghead" to grow its hair. Use felt tipped pens to draw a happy face on the shell, and trim the mustard and cress into a nice "hair-style".

Creepy-Crawly Spider Plants

Spider plants are stripey and spikey and hang down like spiders' legs. They are happy to sit on an inside windowsill or you can put them in special hanging baskets. They will hang down from the ceiling, just like real spiders!

Happy houseplants

In warm countries spider plants grow outdoors, but in cooler places they are mainly grown as houseplants. All they need is some light and water. They will even let you know when they are thirsty, by turning a lighter shade of green. A happy spider plant sends out long stems that have baby plants on the ends, and these can be potted up and grown into new spider plants. Reece will show you how to grow new plants from spider plant runners. Just follow the step-by-step guide here.

YOU WILL NEED THESE MATERIALS AND TOOLS

- Several small flowerpots and saucers
- Trowel
- Houseplant compost
- Spider plant with babies
- Hairpins
- Watering can
- Safety scissors

1 Fill the small flowerpots with compost.

2 Press the compost down using the base of another pot.

Other Plants with Babies

The common name of the *Tolmiea menziesii* is the piggyback plant, because new young plants form on the leaves of the parent plant. Just take the leaves with babies on and pin them onto the surface of a pot of compost, using a hairpin. Water and leave in a sunny place. The little plants will soon root and begin to grow. Then you can move them into their own pots.

3 Place the pots around the parent plant, so that a baby plant rests comfortably in each of the pots.Use the hairpins to hold the baby plants firmly in place.

4 Water all the plants. Remember to check the pots each day to make sure that they don't get too dry.

5 When the plants have rooted you will notice new leaves beginning to sprout. Now you can carefully cut the runners.

Right: Finally, the reward for all your care – a new spider plant.

Chocolate-Pot Plant

Can you believe your nose? This lovely plant smells exactly like chocolate! It is a very special sort of cosmos daisy that is bought as a small plant and, if it is kept out of the cold, it will flower again next year.

What a wonderful smell!

To make the smell of chocolate even stronger and more delicious, Dominic and Alex have used a special mulch to cover the soil. This mulch is made from cocoa shells after the cocoa beans have been removed to make chocolate. It has a lovely chocolate smell and is also good for the soil!

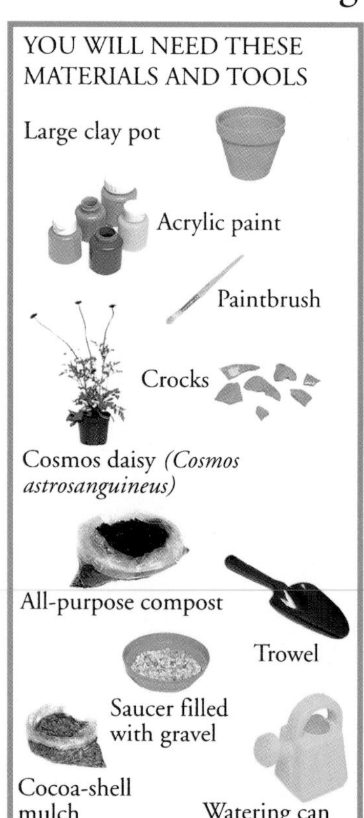

Right: A chocolate-pot plant would be a lovely and unusual present for someone special – if you can bear to part with it.

1 Use a round paintbrush to paint coloured dots all around your flowerpot.

2 When the paint has dried, put some crocks in the bottom, so that the drainage hole does not clog up.

3 Remove your plant from its pot very carefully. If its roots have started to curl around inside the pot, gently loosen the roots as Alex is doing here.

4 Put the plant into the decorated pot and fill all around the roots with compost, pressing down the edges until the plant is firmly in position.

5 Cover the soil around the plant with a thick layer of cocoa-shell mulch.

6 Stand the pot on the saucer filled with gravel and water the plant thoroughly.

7 Press the flower petals gently between your fingers to release a delicious chocolate smell.

8 After all that hard work, and the tempting smells, a real chocolate was irresistible.

More Surprising Smells

A lemon balm plant will grow very quickly. Plant it in a medium-sized flowerpot in all-purpose compost. When you rub the leaves between your fingers, a lovely lemony smell is released. Another surprising plant is one of the sages, *Salvia elegans*. It has a mouthwatering smell of pineapple. There is a mint and a geranium that have a pineapple smell too.

Sprouting Seeds-Jam-Jar Salads

You won't need a garden, or even a windowsill to grow these delicious, crunchy salad sprouts. All you need is a jam jar with some air holes in the lid and some seeds and beans. What could be simpler?

Healthy harvest

If you go to a healthfood shop where they weigh out their own grains and pulses, you will be able to buy small amounts of all kinds of suitable seeds for sprouting. Aduki beans, mung beans, brown lentils, sunflower seeds, chickpeas, sesame seeds and alfalfa seeds are all easy sprouters. You will need to have a jam jar for each type, because every seed germinates at a different speed. A tablespoon of seeds or beans should make about 170 g (6 oz) sprouts. Laurence and Josie will show you exactly what to do.

YOU WILL NEED THESE MATERIALS AND TOOLS

Jam jars

Sieve

Chickpeas, mung beans and alfalfa seeds

1 Wash some jam jars and their lids. You need a separate jar for each type of seed or bean you are using.

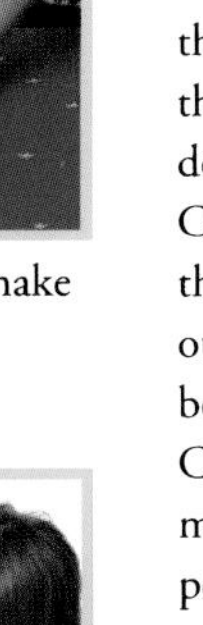

2 Ask a grown-up to help you make holes in the lids.

Chinese-Style Beansprouts

The beansprouts that are sold in supermarkets are mung beans that have been germinated in water and kept in the dark. Try growing beansprouts in the same way as salad sprouts, but don't move them into the light. Change their water regularly, and when they look thick and juicy take them out and rinse in a sieve. The beansprouts can be used to make a Chinese stir-fry. Ask a grown-up to mix them up with slivers of carrot, peas, sweetcorn and a bit of oil. They only need to cook for 5 minutes. Add a dash of soy sauce for a tasty meal!

3 Put a tablespoonful of seeds or beans in each jar.

4 Rinse the seeds then cover them with lukewarm water.

5 Put the lids on the jars and turn them upside-down, so that most of the water drains away. Put the jars in a warm, dark place for three days.

6 Take them out every morning and evening, and give them a good rinse with cold water, draining each time as in Step 5. After three days, transfer the jars to a warm windowsill, and continue to rinse them out twice a day.

7 When the seeds have roots and leaf-tips they are ready to eat. Empty them into a sieve and rinse once more under the cold tap. A delicious crunchy salad snack grown in a jam jar!

Vegetable-Top Forest

Rosie and Tania are making up a miniature "forest" using several different vegetable tops. To make it look more realistic they have scattered compost and birdseed under their "trees" and grown some undergrowth. Dinosaurs or jungle animals could prowl about, hiding behind trees or sneaking through the long grass!

From roots to shoots

Beetroot, turnips, swedes, parsnips and carrots are all root vegetables because they grow under the soil. Unless we grow them ourselves, we never see what their leaves look like. But there is a way to grow the leaves from the vegetable tops that we usually throw away. Just stand the top of a root vegetable in a saucer of water, and leaves will begin to sprout from the top!

YOU WILL NEED THESE MATERIALS AND TOOLS

Selection of root vegetable tops

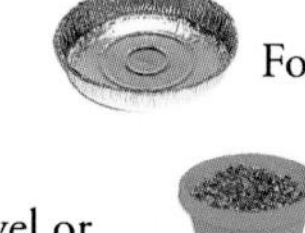

Foil tray

Gravel or small pebbles

Watering can

Compost

Birdseed or grass seed

1 Ask a grown-up to cut the tops off a variety of root vegetables for you. Vegetables like kohl-rabi, beetroot and turnips need half of the root, others just the top 3 cm (1 in).

2 Arrange the vegetable tops quite close together in a foil tray.

3 Surround them with gravel which will look like the forest floor.

4 Pour in 1 cm ($^1/_2$ in) of water and place on a sunny windowsill.

5 Add a little more water each day to make sure the roots don't dry out.

6 When the leaves are about 8 cm (3 in) tall, sprinkle the compost and birdseed or grass seed over the gravel, and water.

Weed Jungle

There is another type of forest that you can grow very quickly – a weed jungle. You have probably heard grown-ups complaining about how fast weeds grow in the garden. They grow even faster if you care for them! Half fill a shallow freezer tray with garden soil or compost. Use a spoon to dig up all sorts of small weeds, and plant them in your tray. Put the tray in a warm place and water when it is dry. Soon you will have a real jungle of leaves and flowers – a perfect home for small model jungle animals.

Left: Within a week you will have grown your own vegetable-top forest.

Upside-Down Umbrella Plants

Why are they called umbrella plants? Because their stems look like the skeletons of umbrellas. How do they make new plants? Upside-down! Have a look at how Joshua and Ilaira are propagating a new plant on the next page, then try it for yourself.

Getting your feet wet

Umbrella plants love water. It is almost impossible to over-water them! This is because they belong to a family of water-loving reeds. They can grow to around 1.3 m (4 ft) tall and love sharing your bathroom where the air is always humid, and also warm in winter. Try growing them in a glass tank filled with water and pebbles.

YOU WILL NEED THESE MATERIALS AND TOOLS

- Umbrella plant *(Cyperus alternifolius)*  
- Small glass tank 
- Gravel or small pebbles 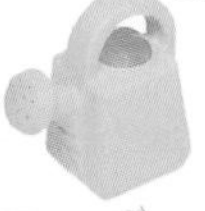 
- Watering can
- Safety scissors 
- Flat-bottomed glass dish
- Flowerpot  
- Trowel
- Houseplant compost

1 Take the plant out of its container and stand it in the glass tank, on a bed of gravel.

2 Fill all around the umbrella plant with gravel or stones, to the top of the compost.

3 Fill the tank with water to the top of the gravel. Umbrella plants grow naturally in shallow water at the river's edge, and enjoy having wet feet!

4 To make new plants, cut off a flowerhead with 5 cm (2 in) of stem attached. The flowerheads need to be "mature". If they have brown tufts coming out from their centres they are just right for propagating.

5 Give the leaves a "haircut", so that they are about half their original length.

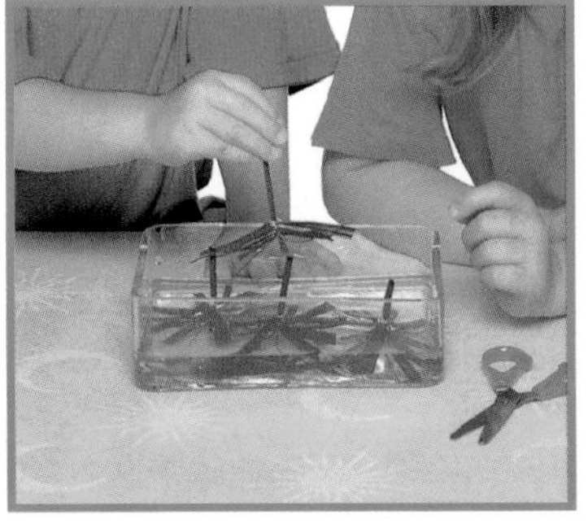

6 Fill the flat-bottomed dish with water and float the flowerheads upside-down on the surface.

7 When they have grown some roots, plant them in pots filled with houseplant compost.

More Water-Loving Plants to Grow

If you have a patio or a garden, you could grow some water-loving plants in a small tub, or washing-up bowl. Some plants just float on the water, needing no stones or soil. The water violet is very easy to grow. If you know someone with a garden pond, ask for some small bits from their plants.

Above: A brand new umbrella plant.

Lazy Summer Afternoons

Nasturtiums and pot marigolds are two plants for lazy gardeners! They need very little care – in fact they thrive and produce more flowers in poor-quality soil. So don't pamper them – they just don't like it. Follow the steps shown in the photographs to find out how it's done.

Pretty useful

Nasturtium flowers range from yellow to deep red, and marigold flowers are bright orange or yellow. Nasturtium flowers can be eaten raw. They have a peppery taste, and some supermarkets sell packets of the flowers that would turn a plain salad into a party dish. Marigolds are not eaten but they are used to make soothing skin lotions and healing ointments. Their petals were once used to colour cheeses, custards and cakes, too.

Neither of these plants likes to have its roots disturbed, so Dominic and Roxy are starting them off in little peat pots. The plants can be potted on in these because the peat will gradually dissolve into the new compost.

YOU WILL NEED THESE MATERIALS AND TOOLS

- Peat pots
- Trowel
- Garden soil, or all-purpose compost
- Nasturtium and pot marigold seeds
- Plant labels
- Seed tray
- Black plastic bag
- Watering can
- Two large flowerpots and saucers

1 Fill the little peat pots with garden soil or compost.

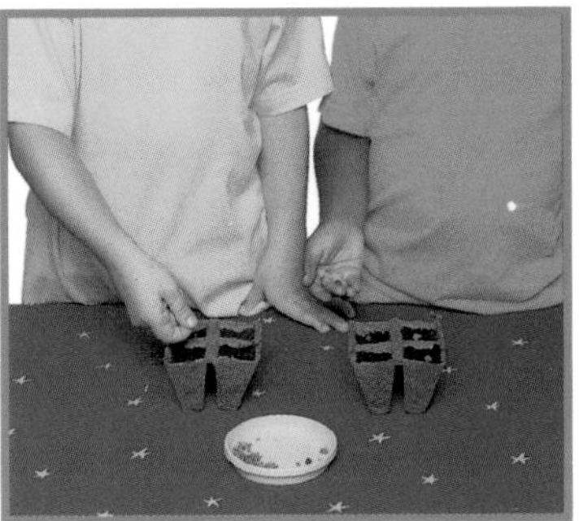

2 Either sow one nasturtium or two marigold seeds in each pot, and gently firm them in.

3 Write a label for each kind of flower and put it in the pot.

4 Stand the pots in a seed tray and water them until the pots turn dark brown all over.

5 Cover the pots with a black plastic bag until the seeds have germinated and you can see green shoots. Then move them into a light place.

6 When the seeds are 5–8 cm (2–3 in) tall they can be planted in bigger pots. Break off each peat pot, and plant the pot with the seedlings.

7 Both marigolds and nasturtiums will produce seeds on their flower-heads when the petals have dropped. Let these dry and save them in labelled packets for next year's flower crop.

Above and right: The orange-yellow colour of marigold and nasturtium flowers are especially summery. You could transfer your plants to a windowbox for a pretty outdoor display of colour.

Modelling Fun

Introduction

Modelling is not just about making sculptures of animals or people, it is also about creating useful things like pots and plates. Even jewellery can be fashioned from modelling material and then decorated. In ancient cultures, nearly everything needed for cooking or for serving food was made from clay. The clay was then baked to make it hard.

The ancient Greeks used clay to make beautiful pots, called urns, in which they collected water and stored food. Many of these pots were decorated with patterns or pictures and then painted.

Types of modelling materials

In Modelling Fun, we use several different types of modelling material. There are projects that use a material that hardens when baked in the oven, a special drying material that hardens without baking, and a plastic type that remains soft so that it can be used over and over again.

There are also projects made with salt dough. This can be made at home by using the recipe that follows. All the other types of modelling materials can be bought in toy, craft or hobby shops.

Always store your modelling materials in sealed plastic bags or airtight containers. This will keep them clean and ready for future use. Drying modelling material will harden if it is left out in the open air.

What you can make

Your friends will be astounded when they see the weird and wonderful things you have made using the projects in Modelling Fun. There is a Grinning Cat, a Snappy Crocodile and a friendly dinosaur. There are also Heart and Star Rings and a Heart Throb Bracelet, Coiled Pot and Plate, a pirate's Treasure Chest and a Space Rocket. The project that will doubly impress your friends is the Spotty Clock. Not only does its salt dough clock face look terrific, but it tells the time!

After making a few of the models shown here, why not design some of your own? You could create some more characters like Wonder Boy and write a play about their adventures. Once you have learned the knack of making animals, you could create your own miniature wildlife park or farmyard. There is no end to the amount of crafty modelling fun you can have.

Safety

There are a few rules to follow when preparing and baking your models.

1. To cut a piece of modelling material, use a butter knife or the bladed end of a plastic modelling tool. Modelling materials are soft – there is no need for sharp cutting utensils.
2. Always ask an adult to turn on the oven and set the temperature. An adult should supervise placing the baking tray into the oven and removing it. When doing these things and transferring the baked items to a cooling rack, always wear a pair of oven gloves. Do not touch the baked items until they have had time to cool down.
3. Keep hot baking trays and modelling materials out of reach of young children.

Materials and equipment

Acrylic paint This is a water-based paint that comes in a range of vibrant colours.
Baking modelling material This material hardens when it is baked in an oven. It comes in a range of colours. Always read the instructions on the packet.
Baking tray You will need a baking tray when using baking modelling material.
Biscuit cutters These are used to cut interesting shapes from modelling material. Use either plastic or metal ones.
Chopping board Use a plastic chopping board to protect tabletops when modelling. Wash thoroughly after use.
Cooling rack After the salt dough has baked in the oven, place it on a cooling rack to cool before painting.
Drying modelling material This white or terracotta modelling material will harden in about 24 hours without baking. Always read the instructions on the packet.
Fine sandpaper Before the baked salt dough is painted, rough edges are smoothed by rubbing sandpaper over them.
Modelling tool The most useful modelling tool has one pointy end and one flat end. This tool can be used for carving and sculpting.
Oven gloves These must be worn when removing a baking tray from the oven and when handling hot salt dough models.
Parchment paper This prevents the salt dough sticking to the baking tray when it is baking.
Plastic modelling material This inexpensive and reusable material comes in lots of bright colours. It does not harden, so the models are less permanent.
PVA glue This is strong glue for joining surfaces but it can also be mixed with water to make a varnish for your models.
Rolling pin This is for rolling salt dough flat. Before using, dust the rolling pin with flour to stop the dough sticking.
Tall, thick glass Use a thick glass for rolling out baking, drying or plastic modelling material. Do not use a wooden rolling pin – these materials will stick to it.
Varnish If you do not want to make a varnish with PVA glue, you can buy ready-made varnish from art and craft shops.

Acrylic paints
Drying modelling material
Modelling tool
Masking tape
Paintbrush
Cardboard and coloured card
Baking tray
Tall, thick glass
Chopping board
Biscuit cutters
Baking modelling material
PVA glue
Plastic modelling material
Fine sandpaper
Plastic bags
Oven gloves
Varnish
Parchment paper
Rolling pin
Cooling rack

Basic Techniques

These basic techniques apply to baking, drying and plastic modelling materials.

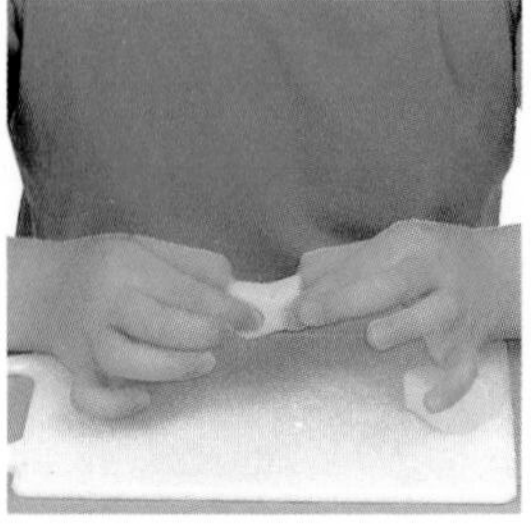

To soften modelling material, hold it in your hands. Their warmth will soften it and make it easy to model.

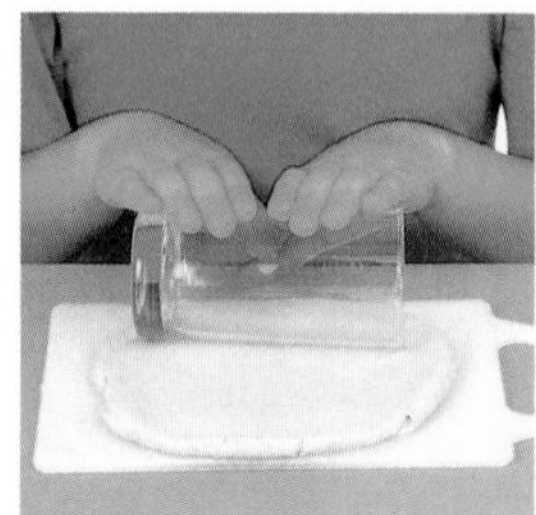

To roll out modelling material, apply even pressure and use a thick glass to get a smooth surface of the right thickness.

Shaping materials

To shape modelling materials you can use your hands to make round or oval balls, and snakes and sausages. The secret to modelling with your hands is to be patient and to mould the material gently. If you press too firmly, ball shapes will become blobs and snakes will be uneven. To make textures, smooth joins or to cut modelling materials, it is best to use a modelling tool. For small, detail work like adding features to a face, a cocktail stick is perfect. You can also shape modelling material by moulding it on to a plate or around a cup.

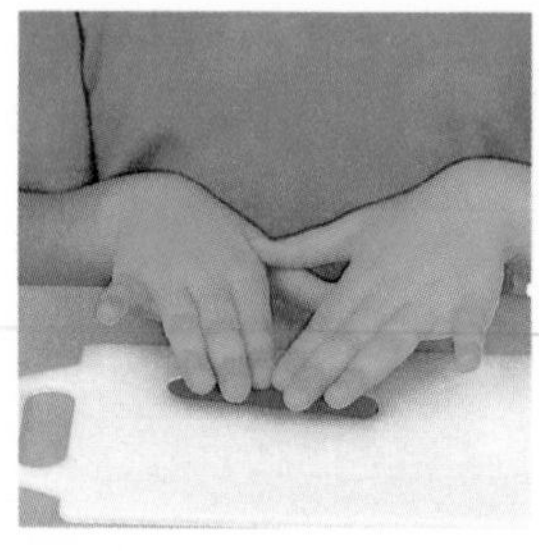

To make snake and sausage shapes, roll the modelling material back and forth under the palms of your hands and fingers. Move your hands along the material to make it even.

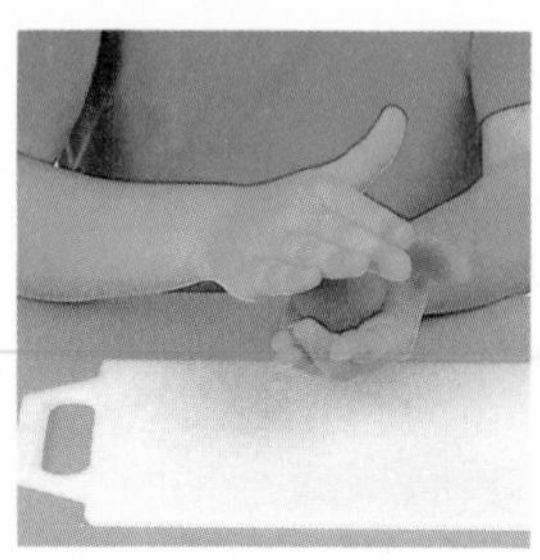

To make a round ball, gently roll a piece of modelling material between your flattened palms. Cut the ball in half with a modelling tool or butter knife to make dome shapes.

Attaching limbs

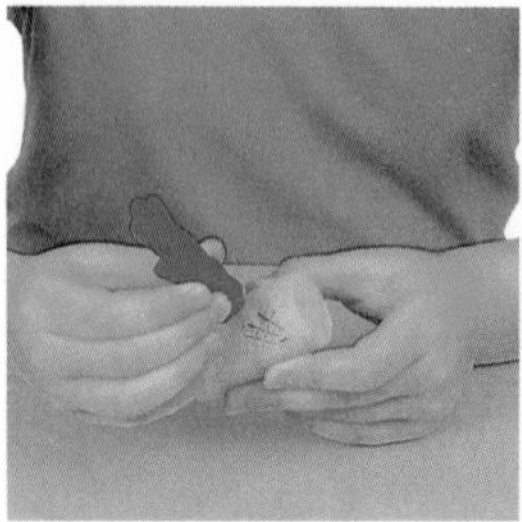

One way of securely fixing limbs to a body is to score lots of fine lines on both pieces. Press the pieces together and smooth the join using a modelling tool.

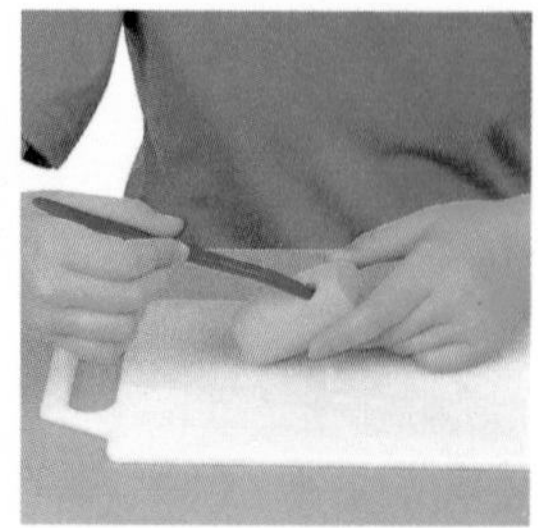

An alternative method is to make a hole in the body with the thin end of a modelling tool. Shape the end of the limb into a point and push it into the hole firmly.

Keeping colours separate

To stop plastic modelling material colours being mixed together, tape sheets of white paper on to your work surface or chopping board. Roll or model only one colour of material on each sheet. After finishing a model, put the paper aside and use it the next time you use the same colour.

How to Make Salt Dough

For some of the projects you need to make a quantity of salt dough.

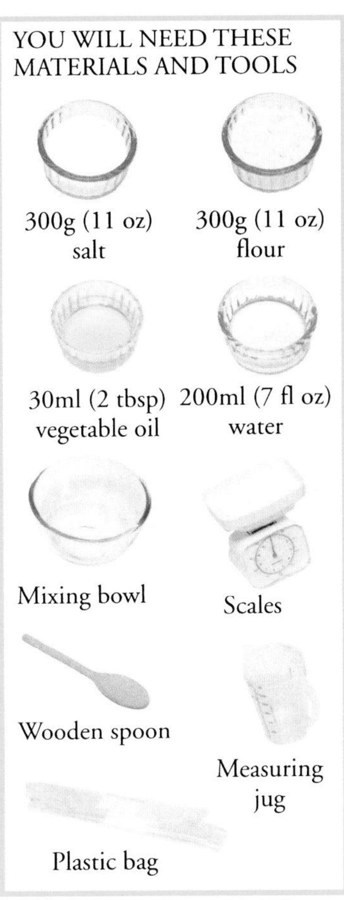

1 Use the scales to weigh the correct amount of flour and salt. Put the flour and salt in the bowl. Mix them together using the wooden spoon.

2 Measure 200ml (7 fl oz) of water in a measuring jug. Pour the water gradually over the flour and salt and mix well.

3 Pour the oil over the mixture and mix it in well. When all the oil has been absorbed, remove the dough from the bowl and place on a clean surface that has been sprinkled with flour.

4 Knead the dough with your hands until it is firm, then put it in a plastic bag or wrap it in plastic food wrap. Place the dough in the refrigerator for 30 minutes before you use it.

Handy hint

If you do not use all the salt dough you have made, store it in an airtight container or a plastic bag and put it in the refrigerator. When you want to use it again, simply sprinkle it with flour and knead it. This will soften the salt dough and make it easy to work with.

Remember that models made with salt dough will be fragile, so handle them with care.

Wiggly Snake Frame

Snakes alive! This fun picture or mirror frame will catch everyone's attention. It is bound to be a great hit. Hiss!

Handy hint

The length of the snakes will vary according to the size of your frame. Do not forget that you will have to make two long and two short snakes for a rectangular picture frame.

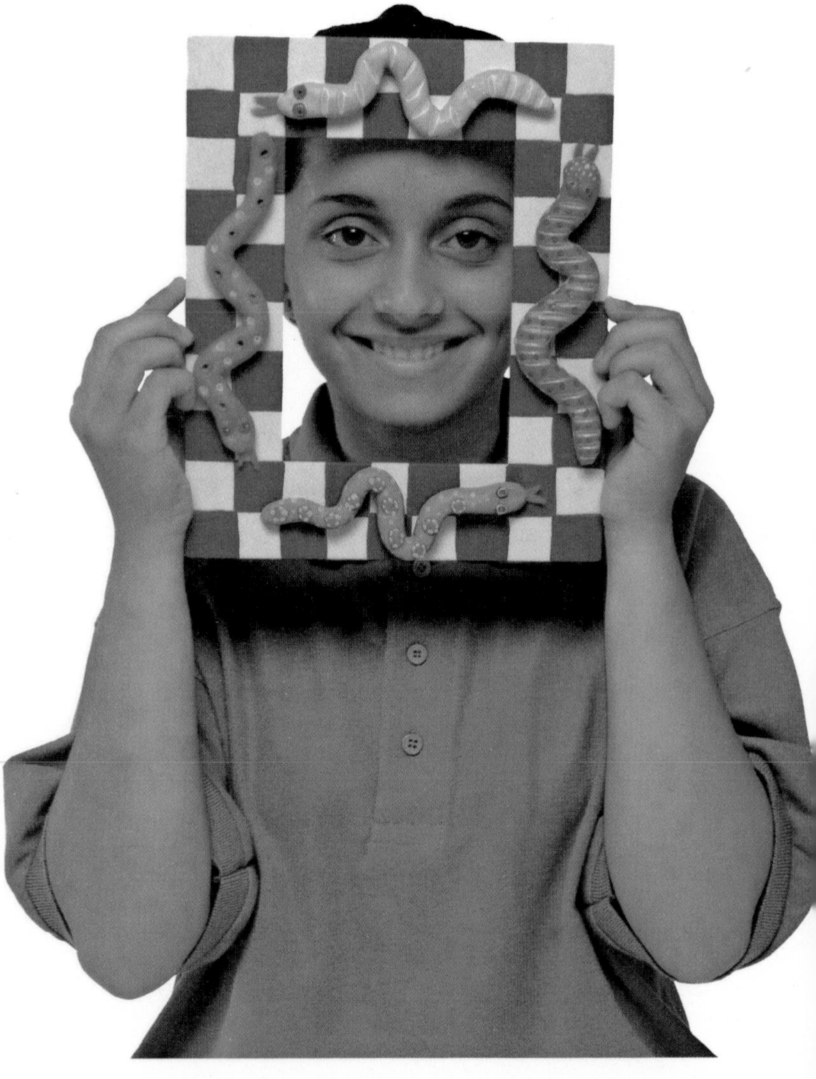

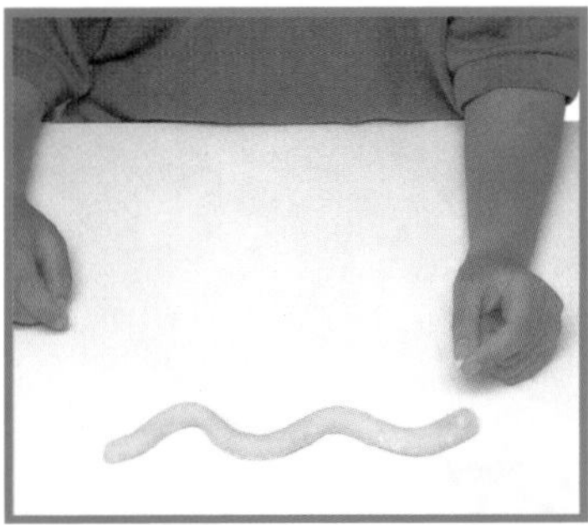

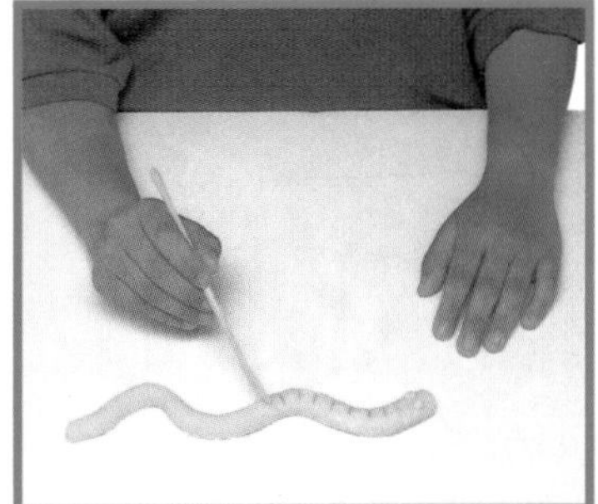

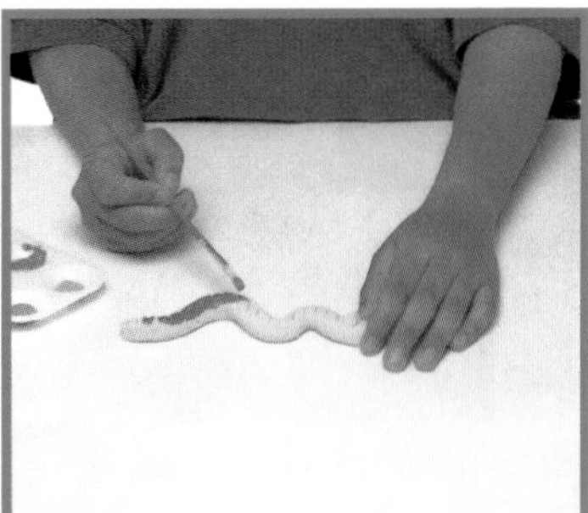

1 Roll out a piece of salt dough and bend it into a wiggly shape. Roll two small balls of salt dough for the eyes and attach them to one end of the snake. Make three more snakes in exactly the same way.

2 Decorate each snake with spots, zigzags or stripes using the modelling tool. Place the snakes on a piece of parchment paper on a baking tray and bake them for about four hours at 120°C/250°F/Gas ½.

3 Ask an adult to remove the hardened snakes from the oven with a pair of oven gloves and to place them on a cooling rack. When cool, lightly rub the snakes with sandpaper before painting and varnishing them.

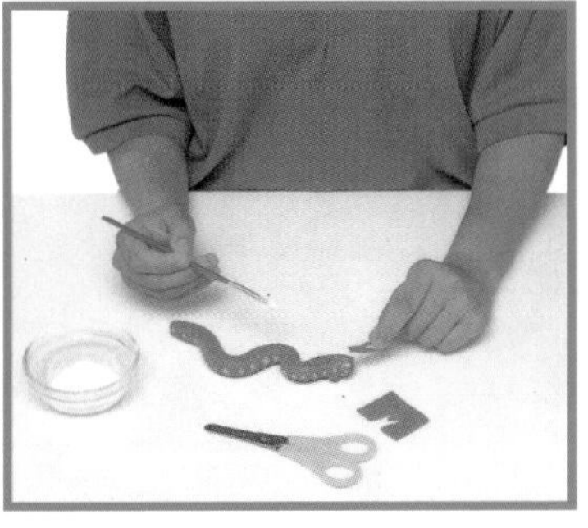

4 To make a tongue for each snake, use scissors to cut Y-shaped pieces of coloured felt. Glue a tongue to the underside of each snake's head. The forked section should protrude from the front of the head.

5 Use a pencil and ruler to draw a chequer-board pattern on to the front and sides of the frame. Paint the frame using two colours, as shown. To finish, glue the snakes on, one on each edge of the frame.

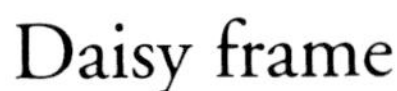

Daisy frame

If snakes gives you the shivers, then decorate your frame with salt dough daisies. Follow the steps for Wiggly Snake Frame, but use biscuit cutters to make the daisies and the centres.

This cheerful picture frame will add colour to any shelf or wall. You could paint the flowers and decorate the frame to match your room. These daisy shapes would look great on round or oval frames, too.

Space Rocket

This rocket is made using a rocket-shaped cardboard base covered with colourful plastic modelling material. Not only does this method make the model stronger, it means that you can be more inventive when you design your own deep-Space explorer.

YOU WILL NEED THESE MATERIALS AND TOOLS

Coloured pencil
Thick cardboard
Scissors
Ruler
Masking tape
Chopping board
Modelling tool
Tall, thick glass
Plastic modelling material (white, black, purple, green, orange, yellow)

'Mission control to Space Rocket commander, are you ready for blast off? We are starting countdown.'

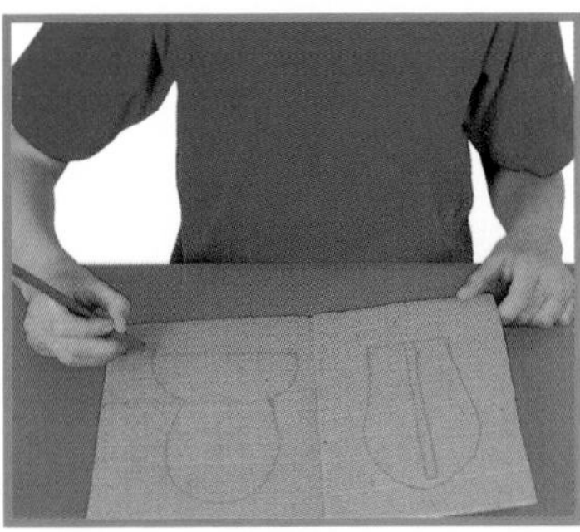

1 On a piece of thick cardboard, use the pencil to draw two tongue-like shapes 20cm x 8cm (8in x 3in). On one of the shapes mark a 3mm ($^1/_{16}$in) wide slit, as shown. On the other, draw semi-circular fins on either side.

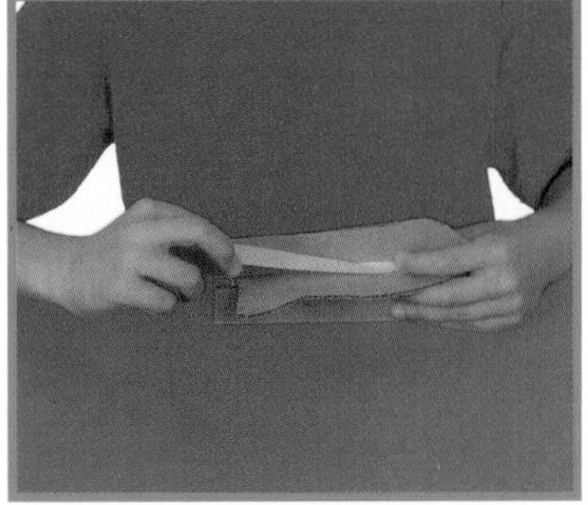

2 Cut out both pieces and the slit. Slot the finned piece into the slit so that the rocket will stand upright. If the model leans to one side, trim the base to straighten it. Fasten the joins with masking tape.

3 Roll out pieces of plastic modelling material in different colours. Mould these firmly on to the card base, pinching the joins together securely. Use the modelling tool to trim the edges and draw markings.

4 When the rocket is covered with modelling material, press on flattened balls of modelling material to make windows and rivets.

5 Mould an astronaut from white material. Make a hole in a window and press the astronaut into the hole.

Once you have constructed your first Space Rocket, you can go on to design a whole fleet of rockets, Space labs or alien Space ships. It is best not to make the cardboard base too large because the amount of modelling material needed to cover it will keep your craft Earthbound.

Sun and Star Pot

This pot is made from slabs of modelling material. The slabs are joined by smoothing the inside seams with a modelling tool. When the pot is complete, smooth the outside seams. This pot is ideal for storing small valuables. To make a nest of pots, make two more pots – one smaller and one larger than your Sun and Star Pot.

YOU WILL NEED THESE MATERIALS AND TOOLS

Chopping board
Tall, thick glass
Ruler
Drying modelling material
Acrylic paints
Modelling tool
PVA glue
Paintbrush

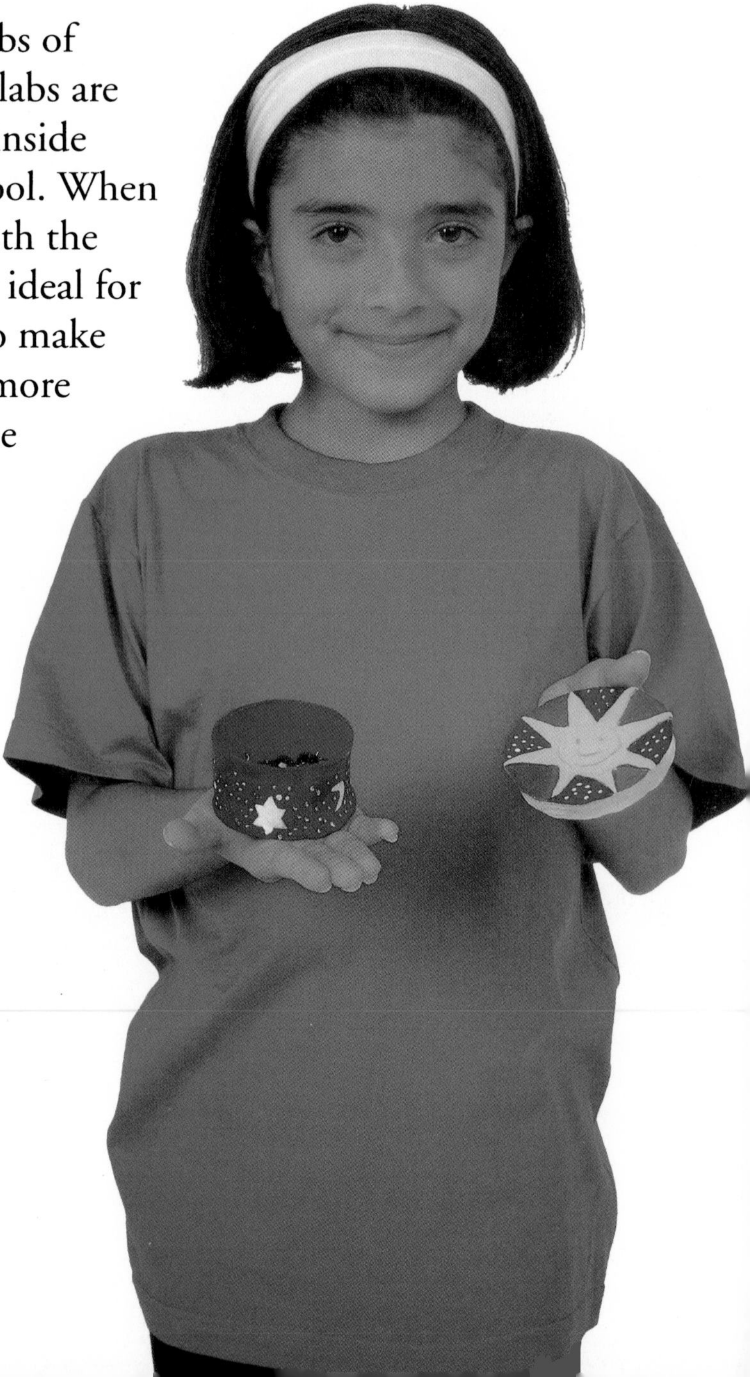

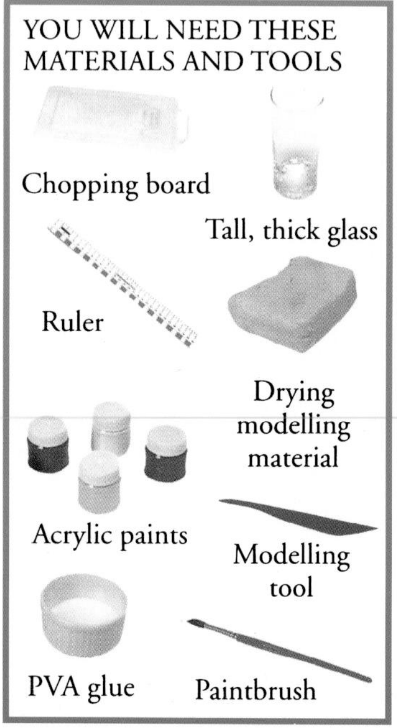

1 Roll a large slab of material until it is 5mm (1/4in) thick. Use an up-turned glass to cut out two circles. Cut out two strips, one 25cm x 5cm (10in x 2in) and one 25cm x 2cm (10in x 3/4in).

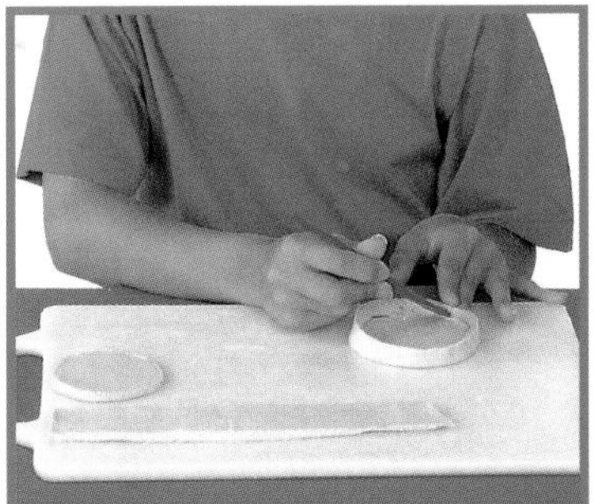

2 To make the lid, roll out one of the circles until it is 5mm (1/4in) wider than the other circle. Score around the side of the lid before pressing on the narrow strip. Bind the edges together.

3 Score the side of the remaining circle and carefully wrap the wider strip of material around it. Support the sides of the pot as you bind the edges together and smooth the joins.

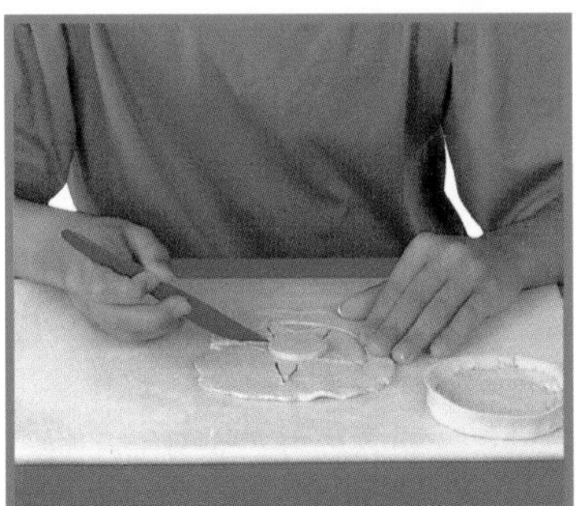

4 Press an upturned glass on to rolled out material to make the outline of a circle. Into the centre, place a small circle of material. Carve the Sun's rays around it using the modelling tool.

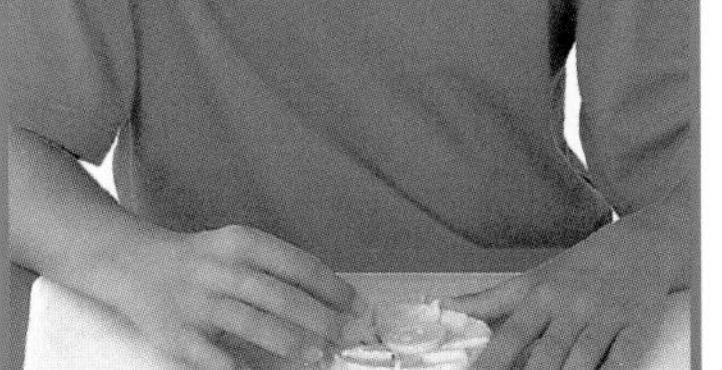

5 Cut out the Sun with the modelling tool and position it on the flat, upper surface of the lid. Place the lid on the up-turned glass to dry. Allow the pot and the lid to dry for 12 hours before turning them over to dry for further 12 hours.

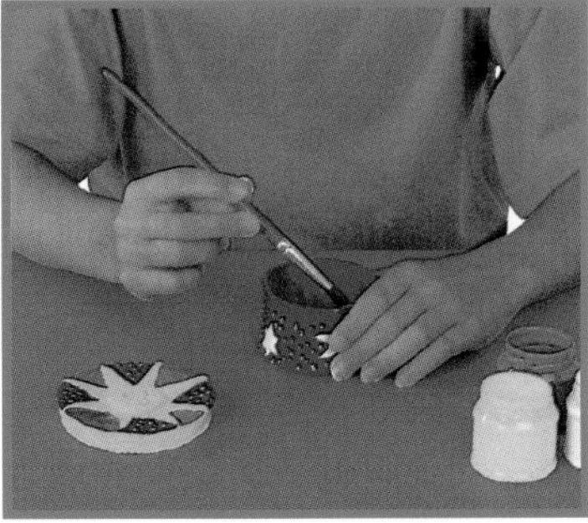

6 Paint and decorate the insides and outsides of the pot and lid. When dry, apply a varnish of 8 parts PVA glue to 1 part water.

Painting tips

❖ Paint the inside and outside of the pot first. While this is drying, paint the top and the bottom of the lid yellow. Decorate the pot with stars and then go on to complete the lid with the blue and green paint. To finish, paint stars on the lid.

❖ To make the stars and moons really shine, sprinkle gold or silver glitter on to the wet paint.

❖ If you are into astrology, you could paint star signs around the side of the pot or on to the lid.

Spotty Clock

Watch time tick by on this Spotty Clock. The only special items you require to make this working clock are a pair of clock hands and clock workings. These can be bought in specialist hobby and craft shops. Check which size battery is required and read the assembly instructions for the kit carefully.

YOU WILL NEED THESE MATERIALS AND TOOLS

Salt dough (see recipe)
Rolling pin
Modelling tool
Baking tray
Oven gloves
Cooling rack
Varnish
Fine sandpaper
Paintbrush
Acrylic paints
Parchment paper
Round pastry cutter
Clock hands and workings

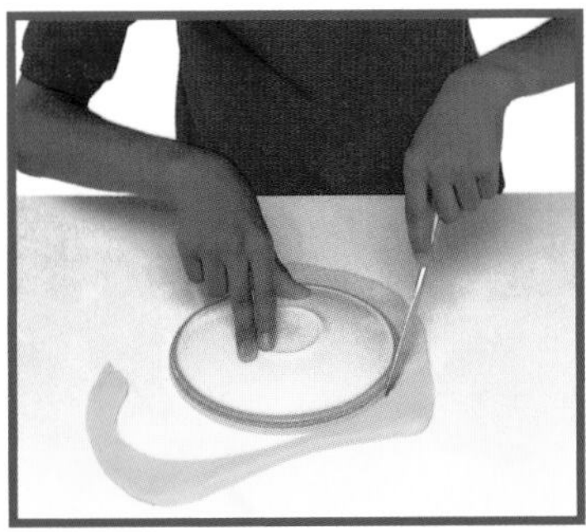

1 Roll out a piece of salt dough to 1cm (1/2in) thick. Place a plate on the dough and cut round it. Find the centre of the circle and make a small hole. Make sure the clock workings will go through this hole.

2 Roll out another piece of salt dough to about 5mm (1/4in)thick and cut out 12 circles of dough with the round pastry cutter. Stick four circles of dough on to the clock face with a dab of water to mark 12, 3, 6 and 9. Use the remaining circles to decorate the clock face. Bake the clock face on a baking tray lined with parchment paper for about five hours at 120°C/250°F/Gas ½.

3 Ask an adult to remove the hardened salt dough from the oven with oven gloves and place it on a cooling rack. When cool, smooth the edge of the clock face with sandpaper. Paint the clock face a light colour before painting the circles in contrasting colours. It is good idea to paint the circles for 12, 3, 6 and 9 in the same colour. Paint a line around the edge of the clock face.

4 Mark the four points of the clock face by painting on the numbers. When dry, apply a coat of varnish. Attach the clock hands and workings following the instructions on the kit.

This is just one way of decorating the clock face. You may like to use stars, squares, diamonds, hearts or flower shapes. These shapes and many more can be made with fancy biscuit cutters. It is important that the shapes are not too large or too thick. If they are too thick, the hands will not be able to move around the clock face.

Snappy Crocodile

This fantastic crocodile is made from a special modelling clay that hardens when baked in the oven. This means that Snappy will be flashing its fangs at passers-by for years to come. Just like a real crocodile, Snappy has pointy teeth and stays cool by keeping its mouth open.

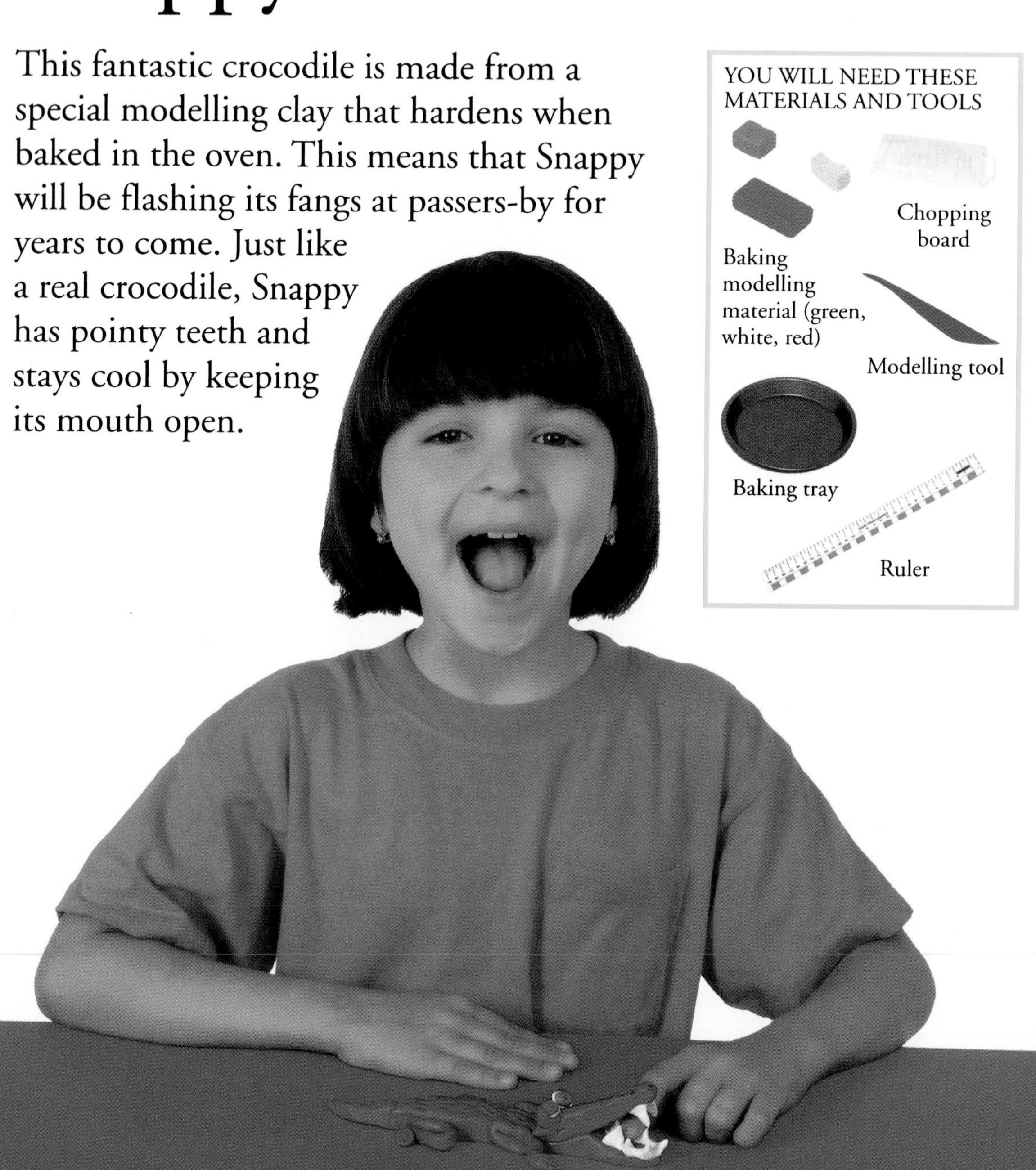

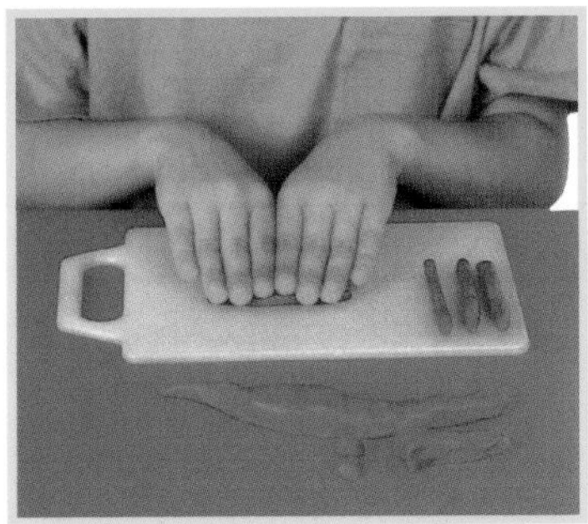

1 Roll one sausage 15cm (6in) long, another 6cm (2½in) long and four more 5cm (2in) long. Roll two balls for the eyes. Shape the two large sausages to make Snappy's body and upper jaw.

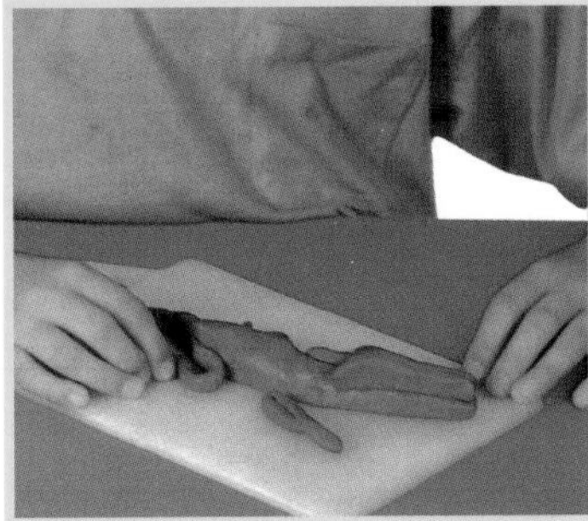

2 Press the jaw and legs into position. Bend the back legs to look like those of a real crocodile. Fold the front legs so that they are thicker at the top. Smooth the joins with your fingers.

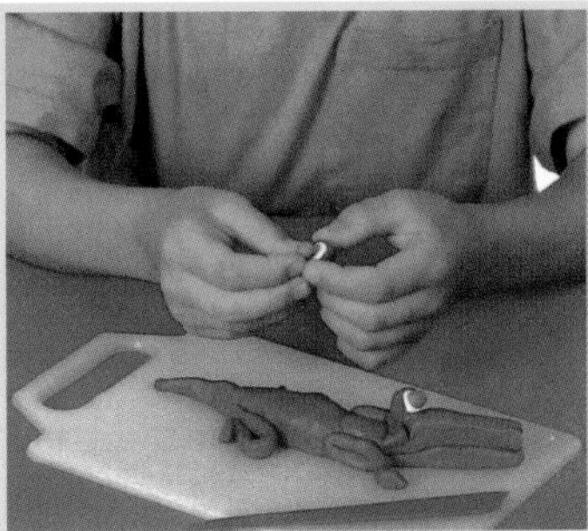

3 Press a ball of white material on to each of the small green balls. Press a little red material on top to complete the eyes. Position the eyes to cover the join between the jaw and body.

4 Cut four rectangular strips of white modelling material. Carefully carve small triangles from the strips to make pointed and jagged teeth. Position them neatly along Snappy's jaws. Press them firmly into position.

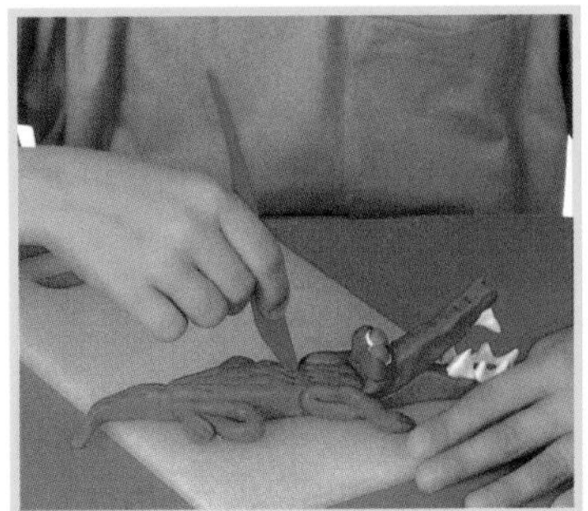

5 Use the modelling tool to mark scales on the crocodile's back. Place your masterpiece on a baking tray. Ask an adult to put it in the oven and to bake it according to the instructions on the packet.

Toothy reminder

Snappy's brilliant white teeth could act as a reminder for you to clean your teeth. To transform Snappy into the most ferocious toothbrush holder in the world, just make sure that when modelling its mouth the opening is wide enough to fit a toothbrush.

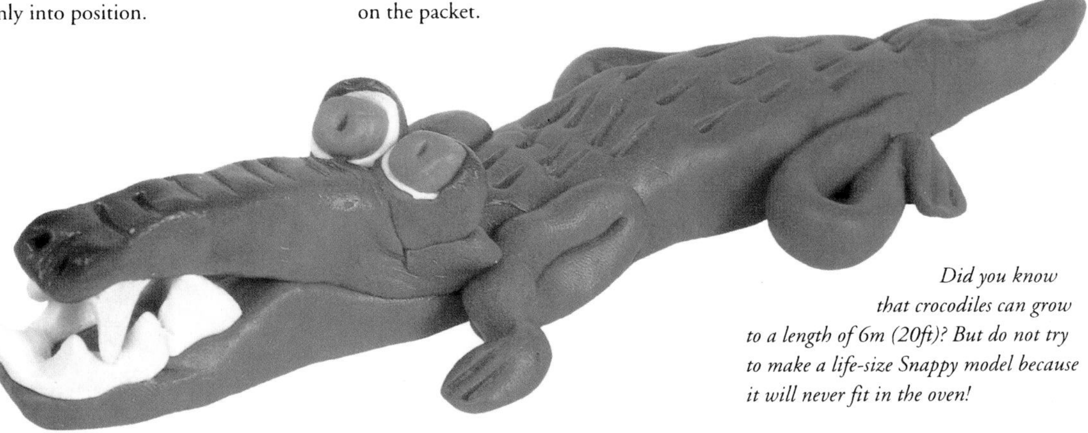

Did you know that crocodiles can grow to a length of 6m (20ft)? But do not try to make a life-size Snappy model because it will never fit in the oven!

Coiled Plate

This plate is for decoration only! Remember to use an ovenproof plate for the mould.

YOU WILL NEED THESE MATERIALS AND TOOLS

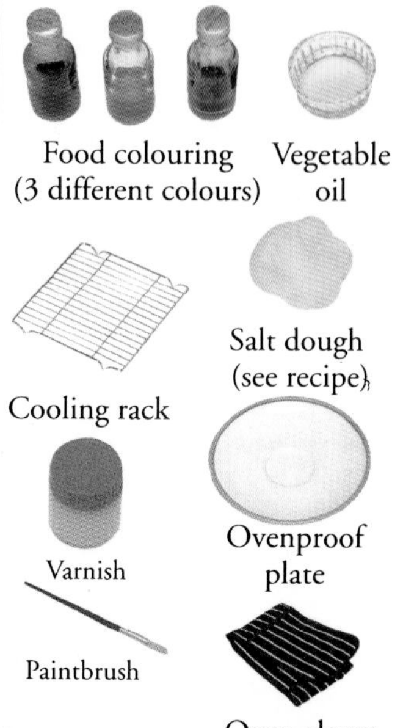

Food colouring (3 different colours)
Vegetable oil
Salt dough (see recipe)
Cooling rack
Ovenproof plate
Varnish
Paintbrush
Oven gloves

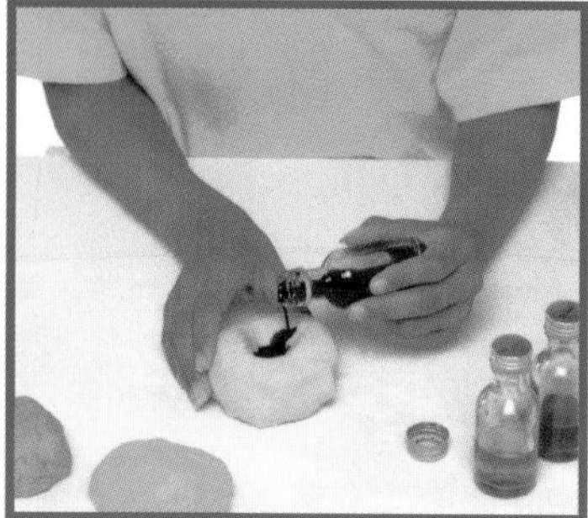

1 Divide the dough into three balls. Make a well in the centre of each ball and add three drops of food colouring to each. Each ball will be a different colour. Knead them on a floured surface to spread the colouring evenly. Lightly oil the ovenproof plate.

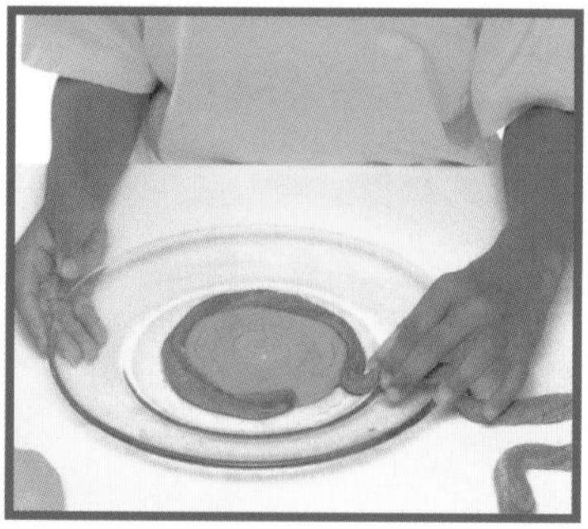

2 Roll the balls of dough into long, thin sausages. Place the end of one sausage at the centre of the ovenproof plate and coil it around. Join the next sausage to the end of the first piece and continue coiling. Do the same with the remaining sausage.

3 Decorate the edge and centre of the plate with small balls of coloured dough. Bake the plate in the oven for six hours at 120°C/ 250°F/Gas 1/2. Ask an adult to remove the hardened salt dough from the oven with oven gloves and transfer to a cooling rack.

When cool, give your Coiled Plate a shiny finish by applying a coat of varnish.

Snake Pot

This little storage pot looks like a sleeping snake curled around on itself.

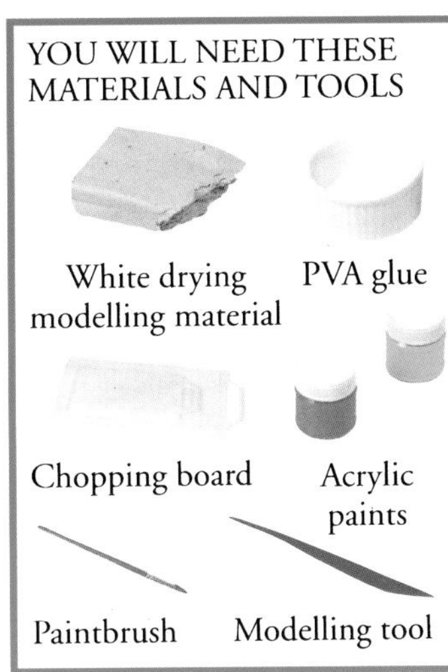

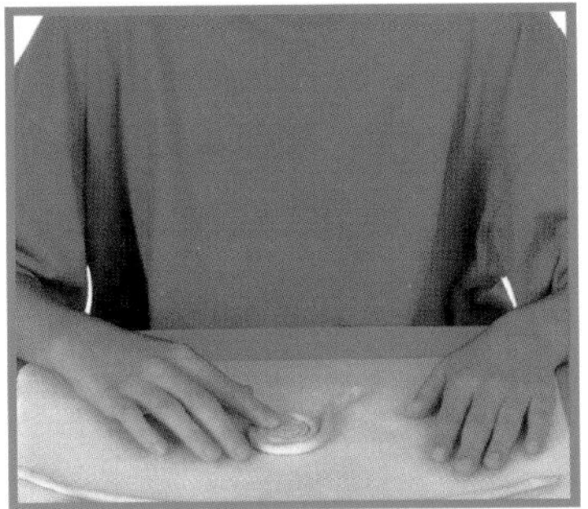

1 Cut three pieces of drying modelling material and roll each into a snake. Make each one as long as possible but not too thin. Tightly coil one of the snakes into a flat circle. This will be the base of the pot. If there are any gaps, gently press them together. Bind the joins with the modelling tool.

2 Build the walls of the pot by coiling a snake on top of the outer edge of the base. Smooth the ridges on the inside of the pot. Continue coiling with the second snake. When you have finished, shape the end to make the snake's face. Use the modelling tool to carve a pattern around the edge.

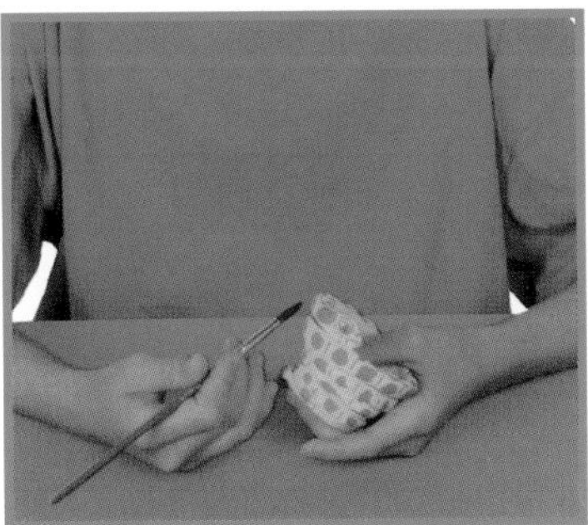

3 Allow the pot to dry for about 12 hours on each side before painting it yellow with red spots. To finish, apply a varnish made of 8 parts PVA glue and 1 part water.

The Snake Pot is the perfect place to store small treasures or even pocket money. No one would dare touch it for fear of disturbing the sleeping snake!

Handy hint

If you want to make a larger coil pot to use as a pencil holder, roll the snakes a little thicker. If you need more snakes to complete your pot, bind the snakes together and keep coiling.

Wonder Boy

Like all great superheroes, Wonder Boy wears a dashing cape and has superhuman powers. You could build a whole story world about Wonder Boy's thrilling adventures from modelling material. Your hero could save a city of skyscrapers from the rampages of monsters and dinosaurs!

YOU WILL NEED THESE MATERIALS AND TOOLS

Modelling tool

Chopping board

Plastic modelling material (green, orange, white, red, yellow)

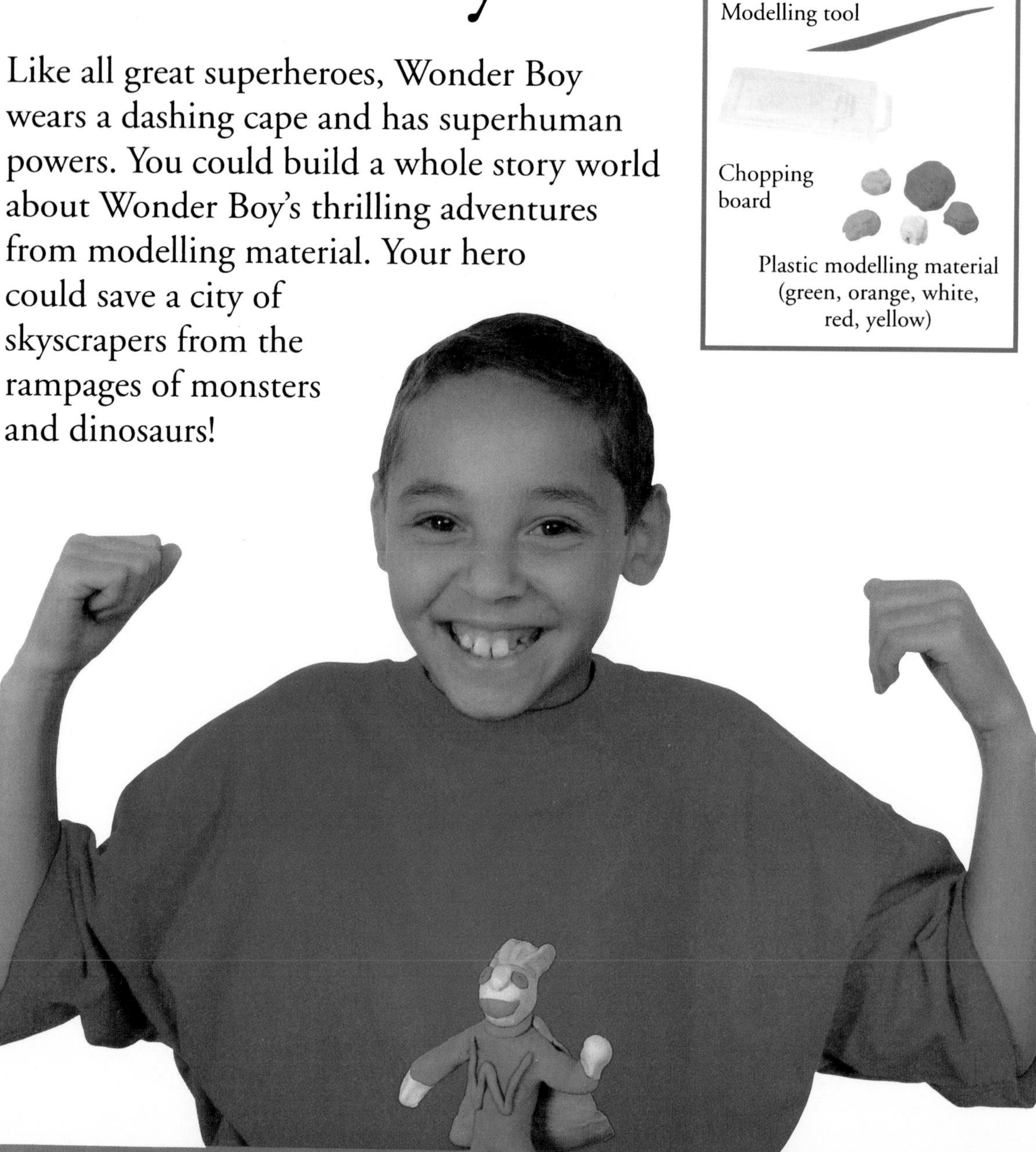

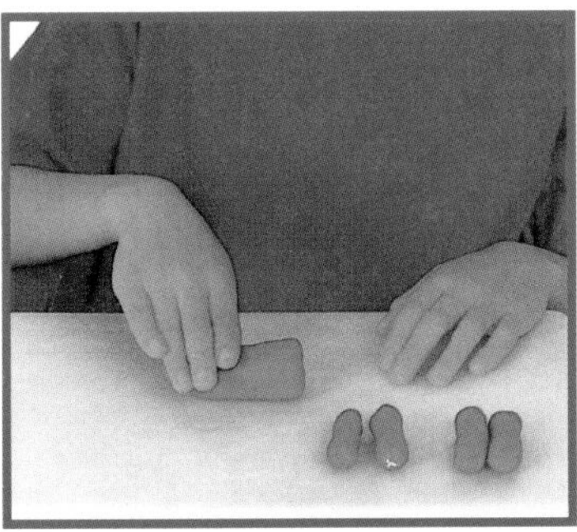

1 Roll out four small sausages and one large sausage from green modelling material. The large sausage will be the superhero's body, so it should be narrow at the top and wide at the bottom.

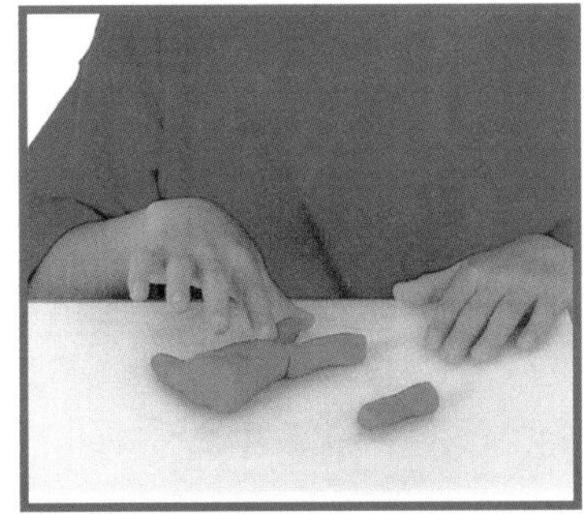

2 Firmly press the four small sausages on to the body to make the legs and arms of Wonder Boy. Use your fingers to carefully bind and smooth the joins. Make sure that your model can stand.

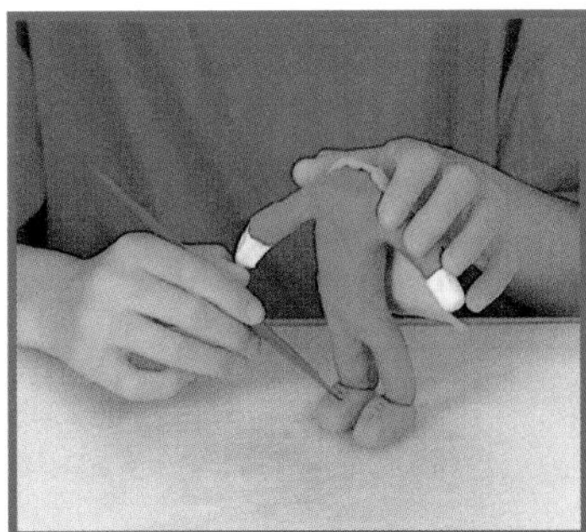

3 Roll out orange modelling material and shape it to make a cloak. Shape two white balls to make fists, and two red balls to make a pair of shoes. Press the pieces into position and decorate.

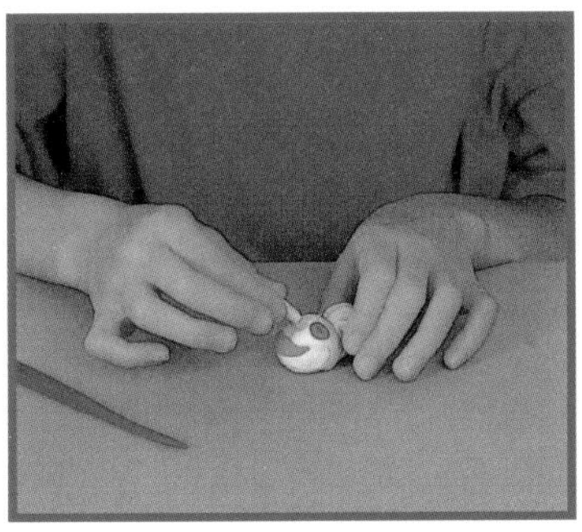

4 To make the face, roll a ball of white material. Use scraps of modelling material to make the eyes, mouth and nose. Carve a piece of yellow material for the hair and press it into position.

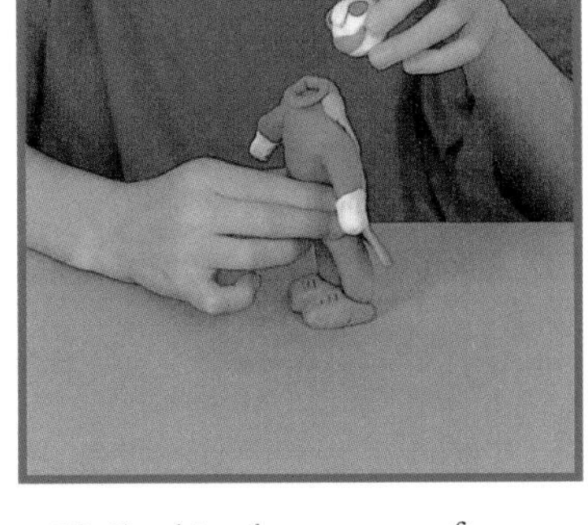

5 Roll a thin, short sausage of green material, shape it into a small circle and position it where the head will go. Press the head firmly on to the body and smooth the join. Lay Wonder Boy gently on to his back.

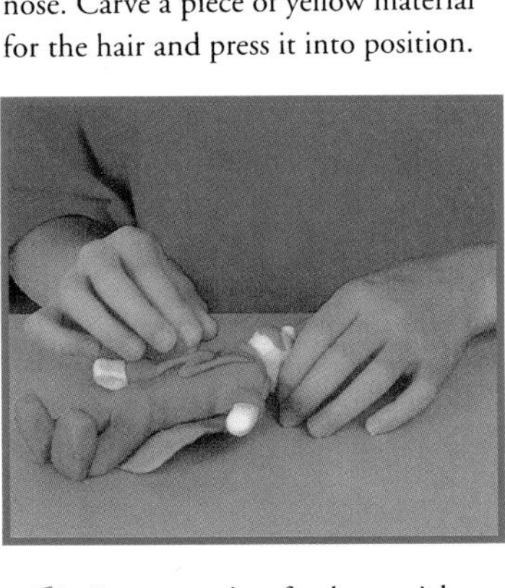

6 Roll out a snake of red material. Press it on to Wonder Boy's chest in the shape of the letter 'W'.

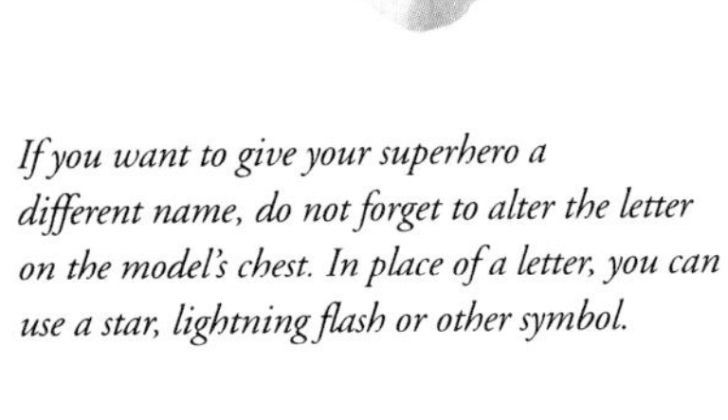

If you want to give your superhero a different name, do not forget to alter the letter on the model's chest. In place of a letter, you can use a star, lightning flash or other symbol.

Family of Pigs

These three little pigs would make lovely ornaments for a shelf or window ledge. They would be the perfect gift for someone who collects models of pigs. Sows can have up to ten piglets in a litter, so make as many as you like!

YOU WILL NEED THESE MATERIALS AND TOOLS

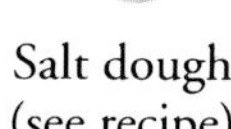

Salt dough (see recipe)

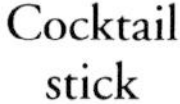

Cocktail stick

Parchment paper

Oven gloves

Fine sandpaper

Baking tray

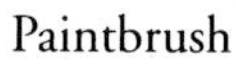

Paintbrush

Acrylic paints

Cooling rack

Varnish

These pigs have been painted pale pink, but you could paint them any colour you like or even decorate them in wild patterns. You may even like to give each pig a name that could be painted on to the side of its body.

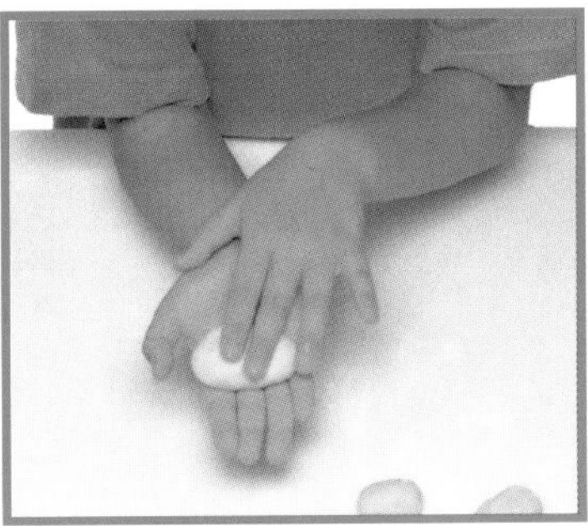

1 Roll pieces of dough to make three oval shapes of different sizes. Shape one end of each oval into a pig's face and use a cocktail stick to mark eyes and nostrils. Attach two small triangles of dough on to each head for the ears.

2 Roll a small piece of salt dough into a long strip for each pig's tail and stick one on to the back of each pig with a dab of water. Gently bend it into a coil shape. Place the pigs on a baking tray lined with parchment paper.

3 Form 12 stumpy, round legs from small balls of salt dough. Try to make the legs the same size. Place them on the baking tray with the pigs' bodies. Ask an adult to bake them in the oven for five hours at 120°C/250°F/Gas ½.

4 When cool, join four legs on to each body with salt dough and a dab of water. Place the pigs back in the oven at the same temperature for two hours.

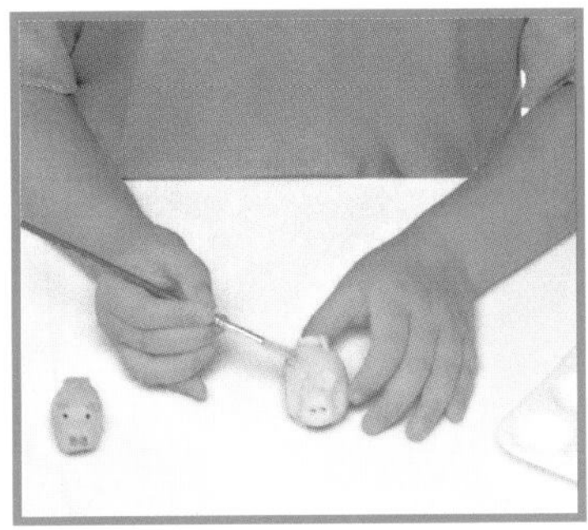

5 Allow the finished pigs to cool on a rack before smoothing any rough parts with sandpaper. To finish, paint and varnish your Family of Pigs.

! SAFETY

Always ask an adult to help you set the oven temperature. Wear oven gloves when placing the baking tray in the oven and when removing it. A pair of tongs or an egg slice will make it easy and safe to transfer hot items from the baking tray on to the cooling rack. Allow plenty of time for your models to cool.

Treasure Chest

This treasure chest is a great place to keep small and precious things. It is made of drying modelling material that slowly hardens when left in the air. The skull and crossbones on the front is the traditional sign of a pirate ship.

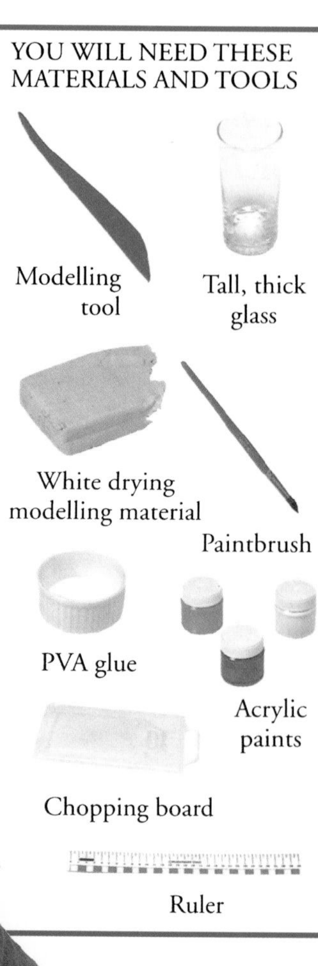

Handy hint

Roll out the modelling material for the base and sides of the chest to about 5mm (¼in) in thickness. If the material is rolled too thinly, the sides of the chest may collapse.

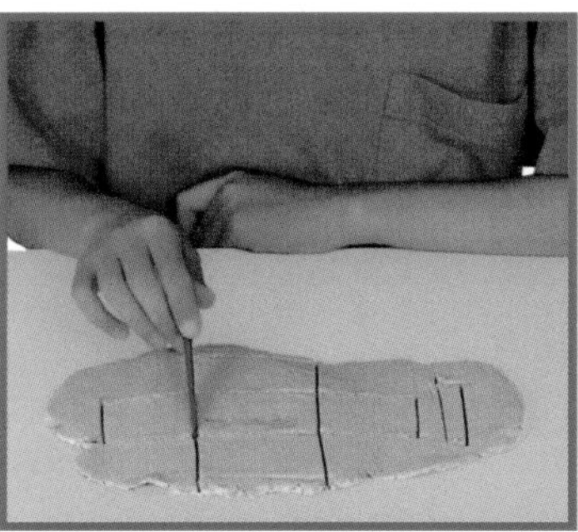

1 Roll out the material. Cut out two sides and a base each 6cm x 4cm (2½in x 1½in), and two more sides each 4cm x 4cm (1½in x 1½in). Cut a strip 8cm (3in) long for the lid strap.

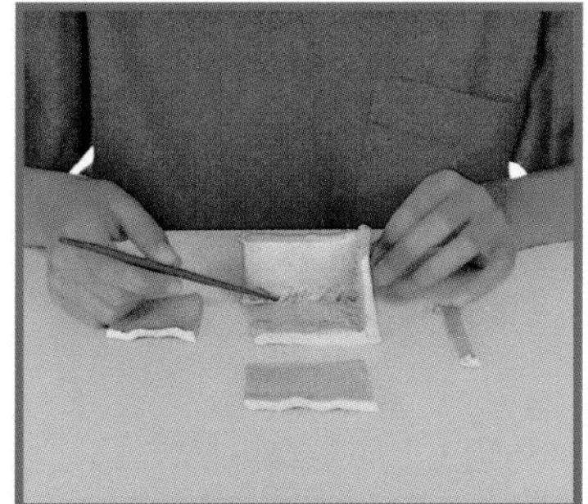

2 Score around the sides of the base with the modelling tool. Position the first side and smooth the inside join. Position the remaining sides and smooth the inside joins.

3 When all the sides are in place, smooth the outside edges with the tool. Use the point of the tool to make dots in the modelling material to create the effect of studs.

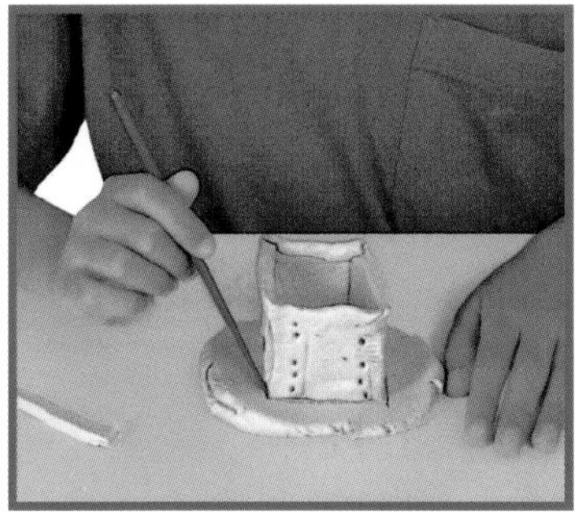

4 Roll out another piece of modelling material and place the chest on it. Cut around the chest so that the rectangle for the lid will be exactly the same size as the base of the chest.

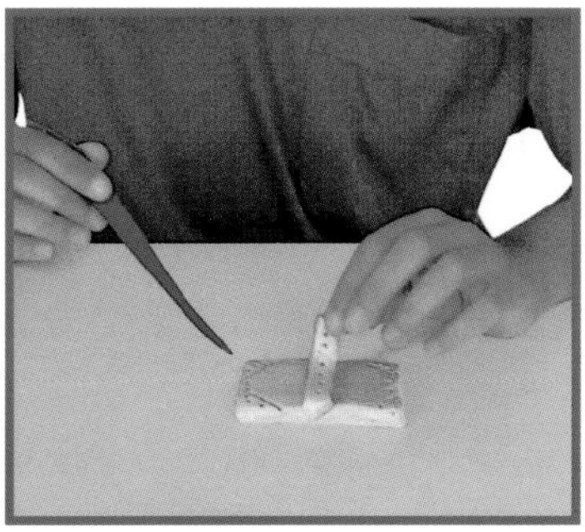

5 Decorate the lid and fix the strap on to the lid. Place the lid on the chest. Decorate the chest with a skull and crossbones cut from modelling material. Allow the chest to dry for 24 hours.

6 When the chest is dry and hard, paint it inside and outside with acrylic paints. Allow the paint to dry before applying a coat of varnish made from 8 parts PVA glue to 1 part water.

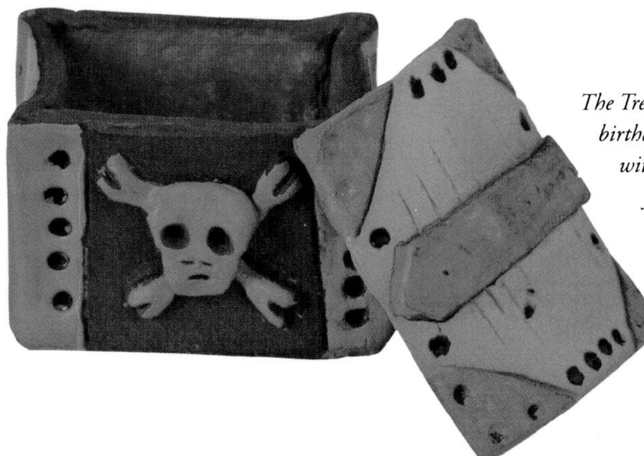

The Treasure Chest would make a wonderful birthday or Christmas gift for a friend if filled with chocolate coins wrapped in gold foil. If you want to use your Treasure Chest to store small, fragile valuables, line the treasure chest with cotton wool.

Grinning Cat

This grinning cat looks very pleased with itself. You can almost hear it purring! This model is very simple to make because the cat's legs are curled tightly under its body. Do not make the tail too thin or it will break.

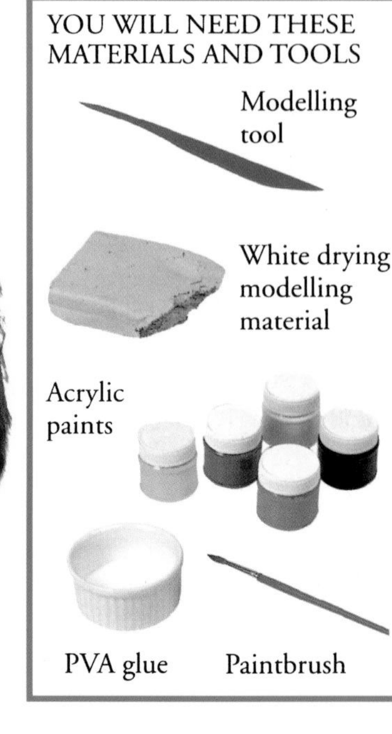

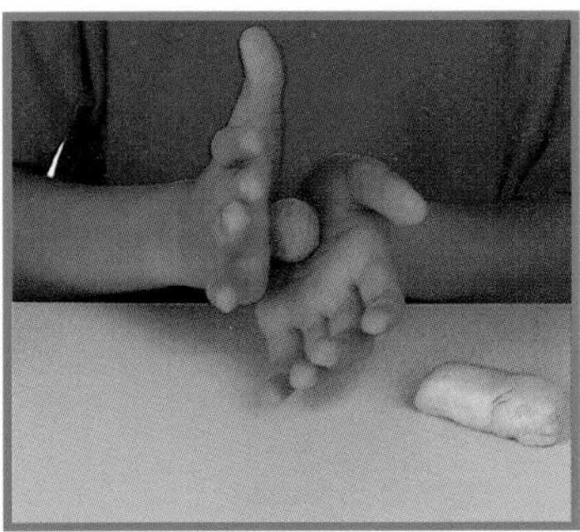

1 Roll a ball of white drying modelling material between your palms to make the head. Then roll a thick sausage 6cm ($2^1/_2$in) long and $2^1/_2$cm (1in) wide for the cat's sleek body.

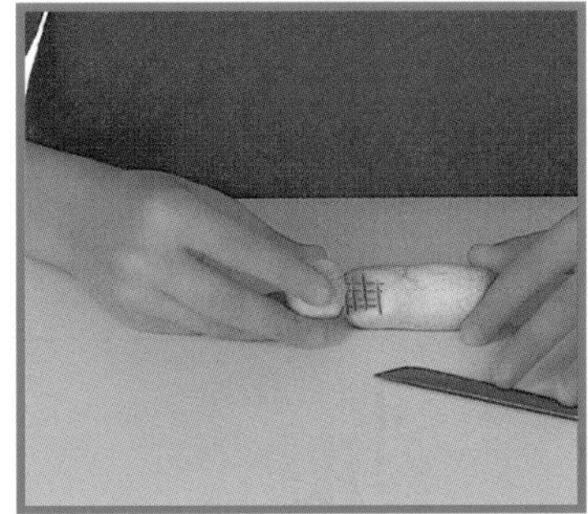

2 To fix the head on to the body, score the bottom of the head with the modelling tool and press the head firmly on to the body. Smooth the join with your fingers.

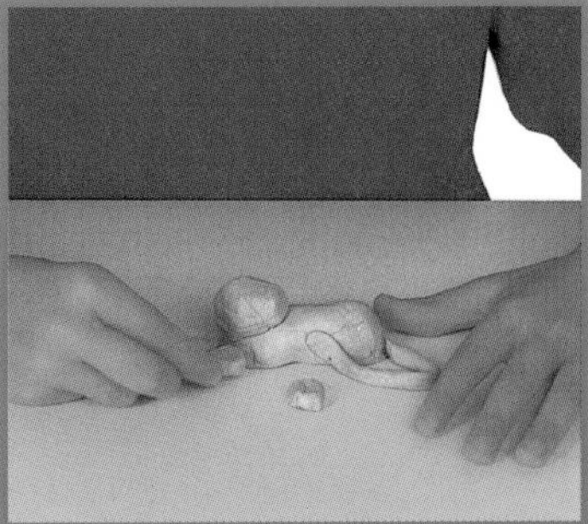

3 Cut and shape two pieces of modelling material to make the front paws. Press them into position. Make a tail and press it on to the body. Curl the tail around the body.

4 Flatten a small piece of modelling material with the palm of the your hand. Use the blade of the modelling tool to cut out two small triangles for the cat's ears.

5 Use the modelling tool to carve the features of the cat. You might want to practise this using a piece of leftover material. Allow the cat to dry for about 12 hours before starting to paint it.

6 Carefully paint the cat and use only the very boldest colours. Allow the paint to dry thoroughly before applying a varnish made of 8 parts PVA glue and 1 part water.

Paperweight Cat

Because Grinning Cat does little more all day than sit around looking pleased with itself, it would make a great paperweight. A paperweight stops sheets of paper from being blown around and lost. To make Paperweight Cat, all you have to do is make a larger and therefore heavier model. You will need to allow 24 hours for drying before painting.

Heart and Star Rings

These rings are great fun and easy to make. To make heart and star templates, draw the shapes on to card and cut them out.

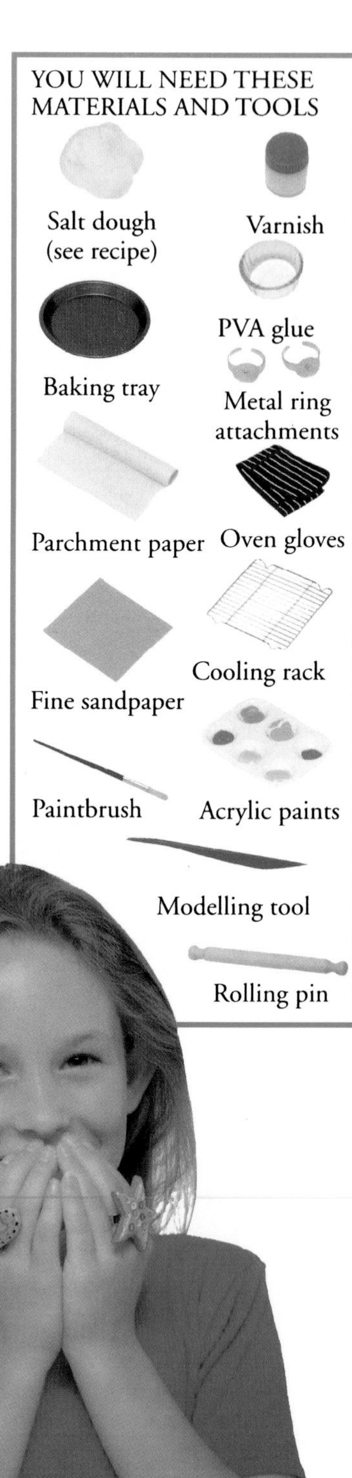

1 Roll out a piece of salt dough 1cm (1/2in) thick. Place the heart and star templates on the dough and cut around them. Place the shapes on a baking tray lined with parchment paper and bake them for about four hours at 120°C/250°F/Gas ½.

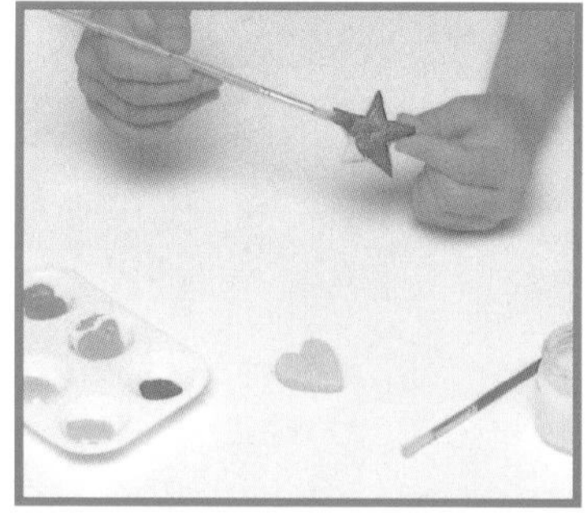

2 When the shapes have hardened, remove the tray from the oven (using oven gloves) and transfer them to a cooling rack. Once they have cooled, smooth rough edges with sandpaper before painting your rings. When dry, apply a coat of varnish.

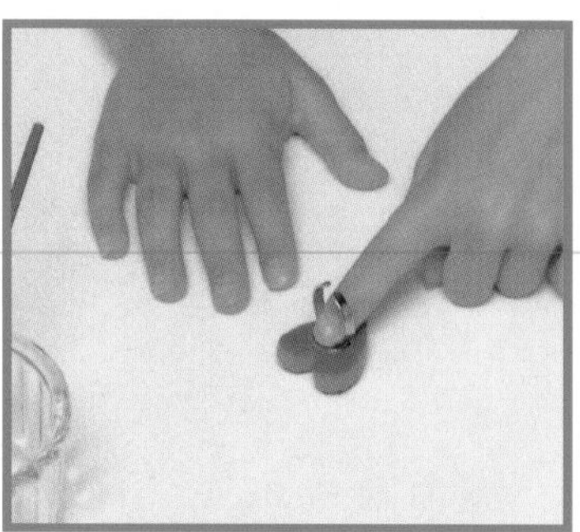

3 Glue a ring attachment on to the back of each shape and leave the glue to dry before trying on the rings.

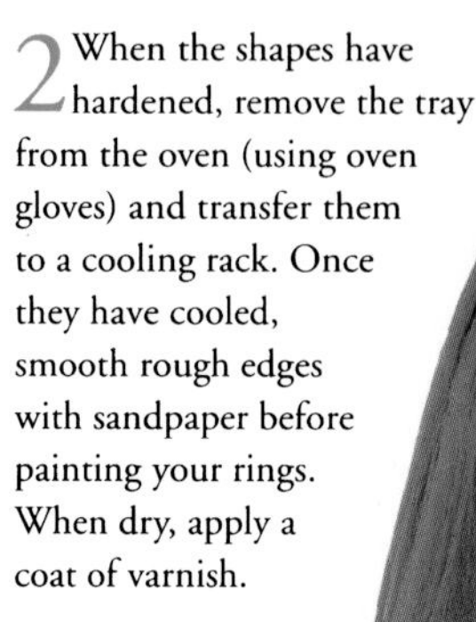

These rings are so easy to make you will soon be wearing one on each of your fingers!

Heart Throb Bracelet

Dress up for a party and wear this fun bracelet. You could make other bracelets with stars or flowers.

YOU WILL NEED THESE MATERIALS AND TOOLS

- Salt dough (see recipe)
- Card
- Rolling pin
- Biscuit cutter
- Varnish
- Parchment paper
- Baking tray
- Oven gloves
- Cooling rack
- Paintbrush
- Fine sandpaper
- Acrylic paints
- Scissors
- Glue

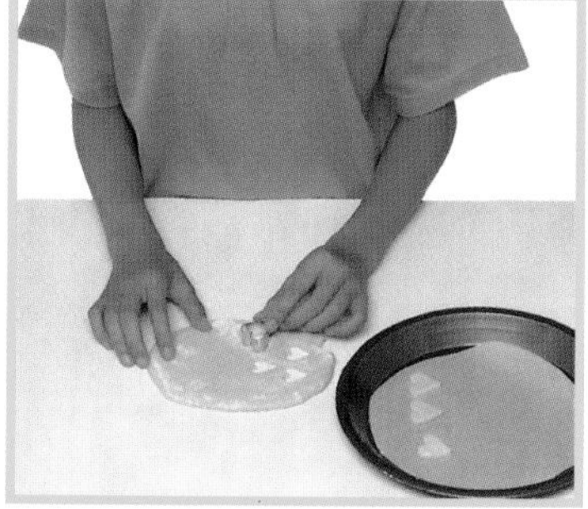

1 Roll out a large piece of salt dough to about 1cm (½in) thick. Using a heart-shaped biscuit cutter, cut out five hearts. Place the hearts on a baking tray lined with parchment paper and bake them in the oven for about four hours at 120°C/250°F/Gas ½.

2 Ask an adult to remove the tray from the oven using oven gloves and to transfer the hardened shapes to the cooling rack. When cool, smooth the edges with sandpaper then paint the hearts in lots of bright colours. When dry, apply a coat of varnish.

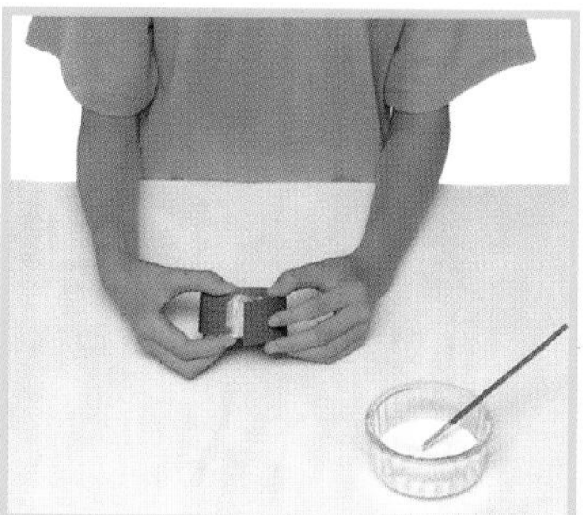

3 Cut a strip of card 20cm x 5cm (8in x 2in). Check that it will fit easily over your wrist before gluing the ends.

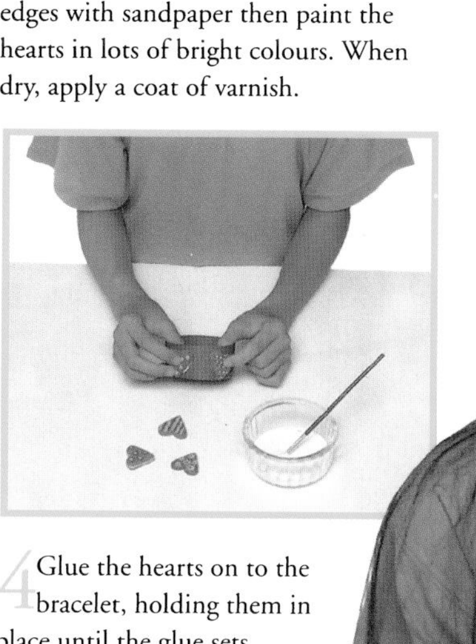

4 Glue the hearts on to the bracelet, holding them in place until the glue sets.

Tyrannosaurus Rex

The Tyrannosaurus Rex is back and it is living in your bedroom! This cheery model of the scariest dinosaur of all has big feet, scaly skin and a winning smile! The Tyrannosaurus Rex is just one type of dinosaur, why not try making the three-horned Triceratops or inventing your own fantastic reptile?

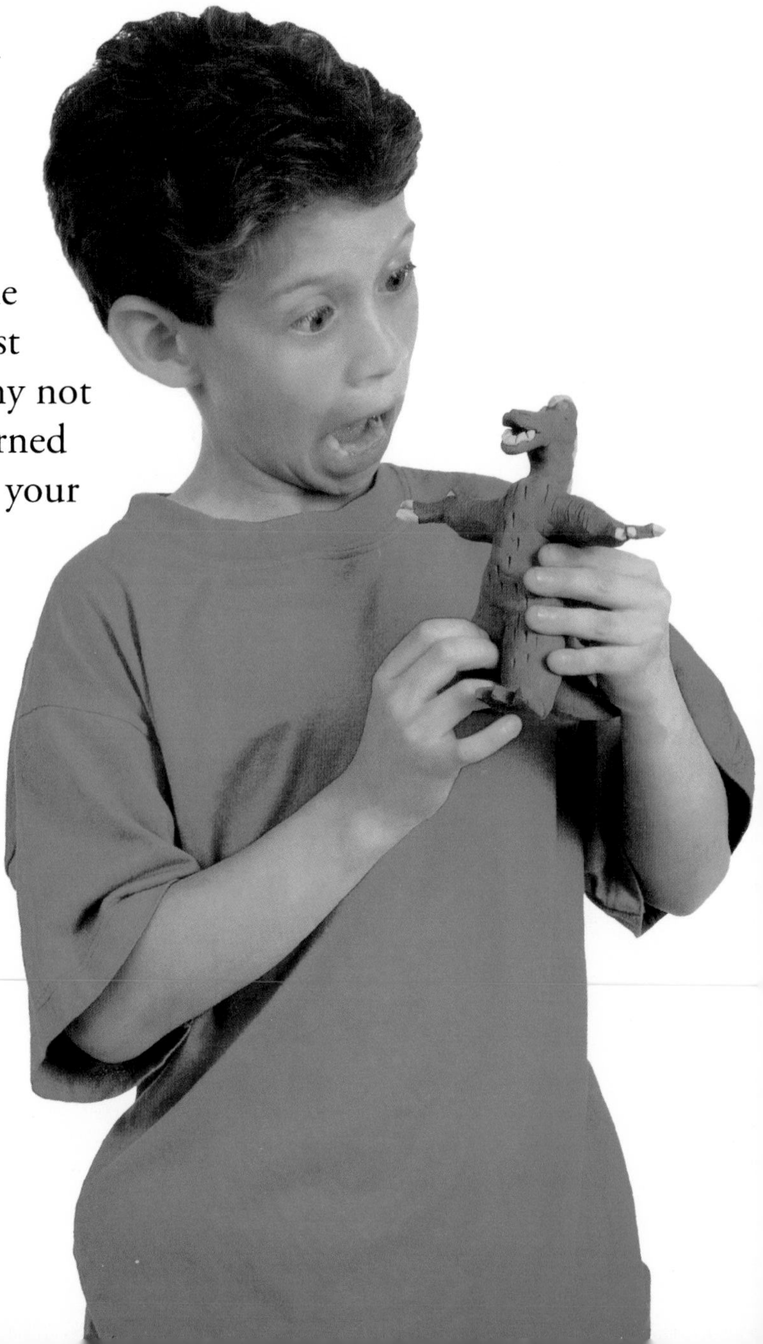

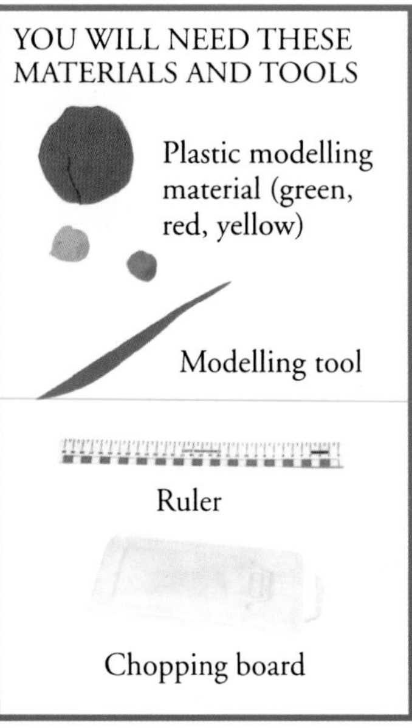

1 Roll five sausages 5cm x 2cm (2in x 3/4in) for the limbs and body. For the head and neck, mould one lump 2cm x 2cm (3/4in x 3/4in) and two smaller lumps. For the tail, roll an 8cm (3in) sausage and cut a strip 5cm (3in) long.

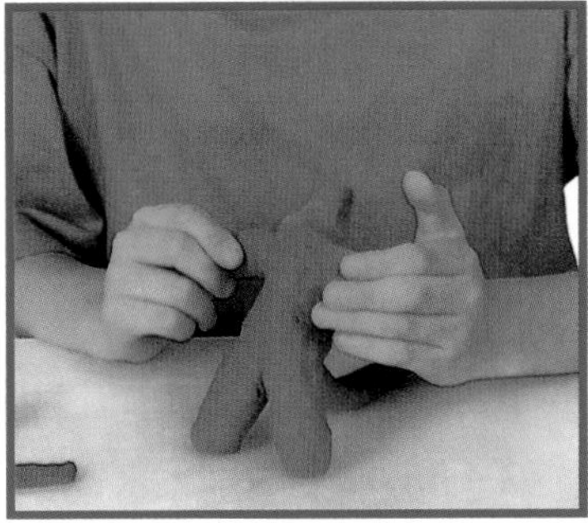

2 Bind the arms, legs, body and tail of the dinosaur together. Use one of the small lumps for a neck. Shape the two remaining lumps into a head. Roll the larger lump into a thick sausage and press the smaller lump on top.

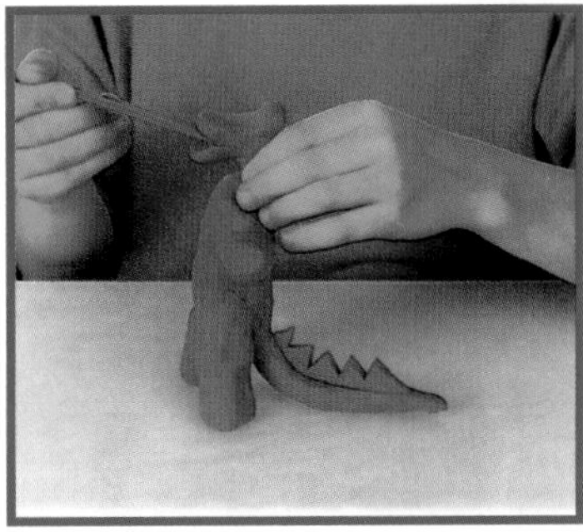

3 Use the tool to carve triangles in the strip of material. Press it on to the tail. Make an opening for the mouth by levering the modelling tool up and down. Take care not to push the dinosaur's head off!

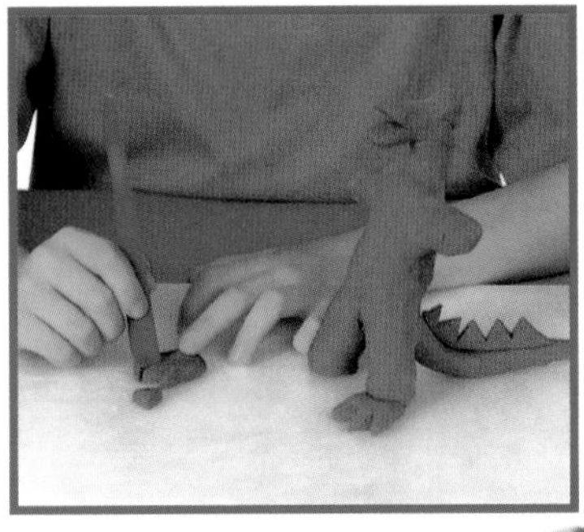

4 Roll out four thick slabs of green material for the feet and hands. Carve the toes and fingers before pressing them into position.

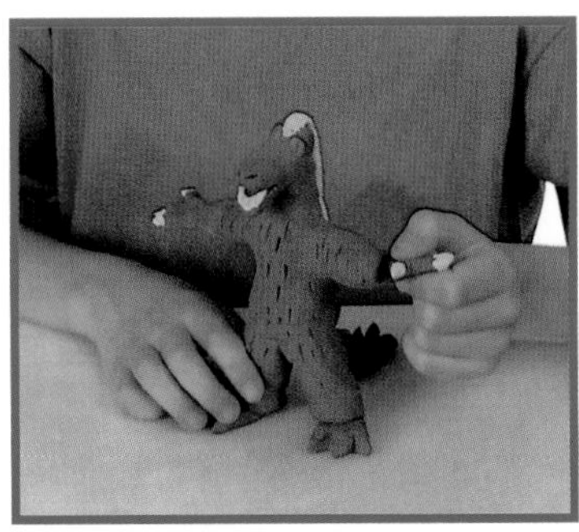

5 Shape red material to make the eyes, and yellow material for teeth, claws and the stripe down the dinosaur's back.

The finishing touch is to texture the surface of your model to create T Rex's scaly reptilian skin. You can do this with the pointy end of your modelling tool or with a cocktail stick.

Queen Chess Piece

The Queen is one of the most important pieces in the game of chess. As a sign of her royal position she holds an orb and sceptre and wears a crown. For an extra special touch decorate the crown with gold and red glitter glue. If you are a keen chess player you could design and make a complete set of pieces.

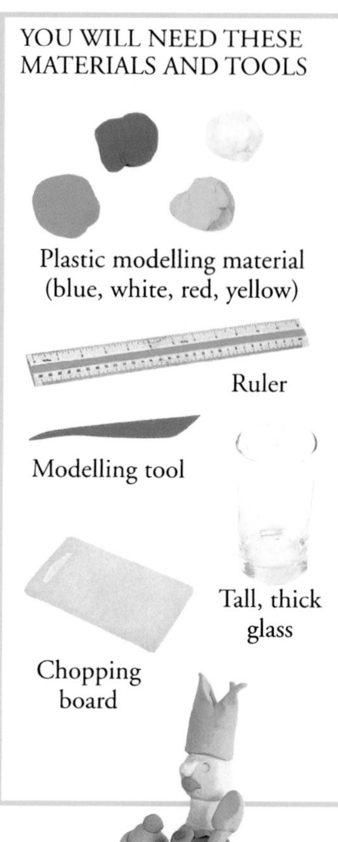

1 To make the body of the queen, roll a thick sausage of blue modelling material to measure 13cm long and 5cm wide. To make the base of the chess piece, roll a ball 5cm wide from the same material. Your fingers are the best tool for this job.

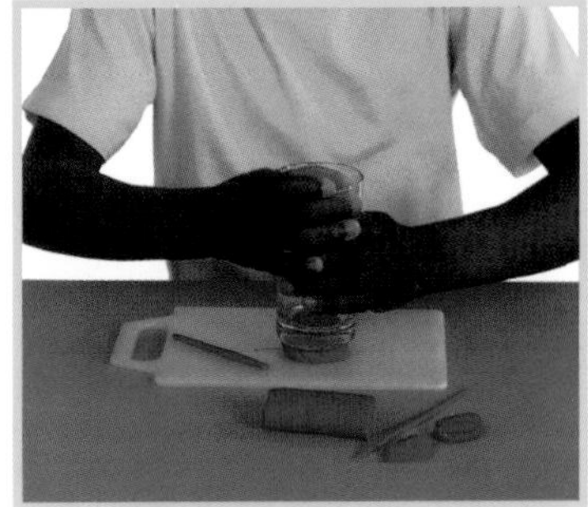

2 Roll a thin snake of blue modelling material 14cm long. Trim both ends of the body with a modelling tool. This will give the final piece a neater appearance. Flatten the ball with the bottom of the glass to form a flat round base. Press firmly and gently.

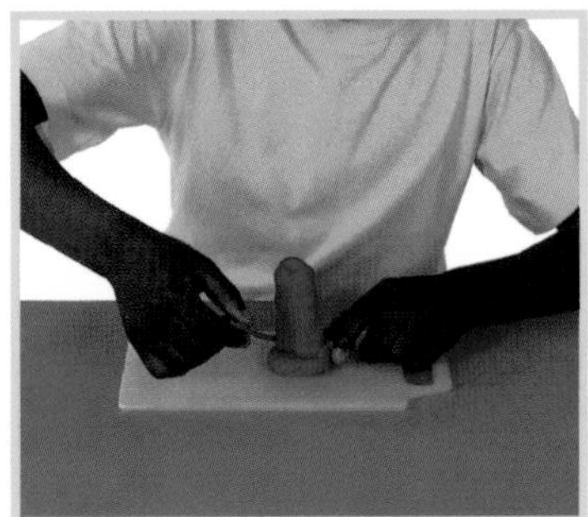

3 Roll the body unevenly so that it is thinner at one end. Press the fatter end on to the base. Wrap the thin snake of modelling material around the join and press to keep it in place.

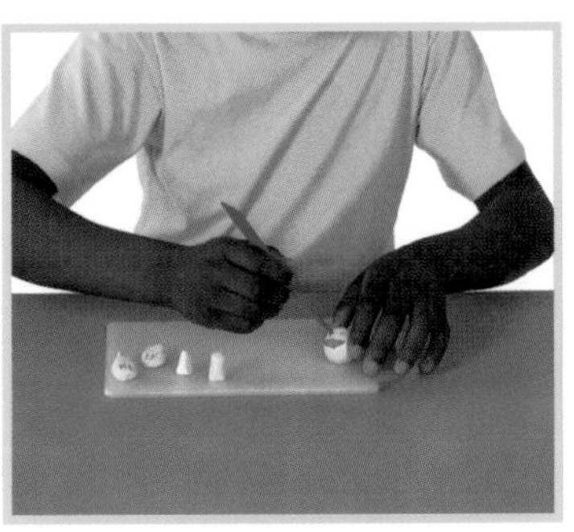

4 Clean the chopping board. Make a head, neck, two hands and a nose in white material. Make a pair of lips in red material. Press lips and nose on to the face and mark eyes with the tool. Attach the neck.

5 Make a hole on either side of the body. Shape the hands so that they will fit snugly into each hole. Press the neck and head on to the body. Add the yellow crown, orb and sceptre. Then trim with red.

You can make the Queen chess piece from drying modelling material if you would like a long-lasting model. Finish the piece by painting and then varnishing it.

T-shirt Painting

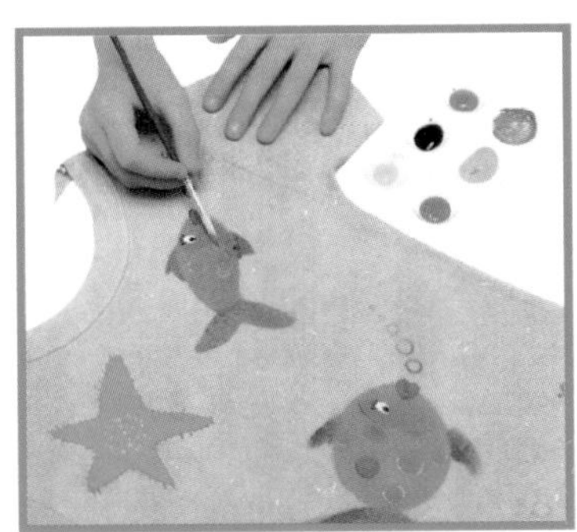
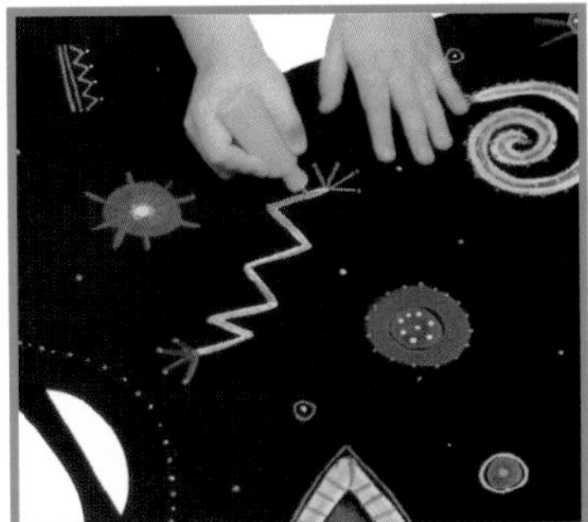

Introduction

Decorating T-shirts with fabric paints, glitter and material is fun and very easy to do. In no time at all you will be creating stylish and wacky T-shirts for yourself, friends and family.

T-shirt Painting shows you how to prepare the T-shirts for painting as well as how to use different types of fabric paints to achieve brilliant effects. It is also bursting with ideas. There are T-shirt designs for sports fans, disco dancers, animal lovers and aspiring astronauts. There is even a T-shirt design for bug collectors – this one will give you goosebumps!

Many of these designs can be used for a fancy dress outfit or for school plays. All you need to complete the outfits are leggings or shorts, a hat and a bit of face painting.

Most of the projects are simple to do. A few are more difficult and use special techniques. If you have never done any fabric painting before it might be a good idea to start on one of the easier projects like Swirly Spots, Glitzy Stars, Crazy Spiral or Basketballer.

The colours and types of fabric paints used in the designs are only suggestions. Change them to create different effects and to suit the clothes you will be wearing with the T-shirt. The ultimate design is really up to you. Feel free to modify patterns and to come up with your own ideas.

Glitzy Stars would also look great on a dark blue or black T-shirt. This design is simple and quick to do.

Disco Dazzler is painted with fluorescent fabric paint that glows under ultra-violet light.

Safety

❖ Always keep fabric paints and sharp utensils out of the reach of small children.

❖ Read the instructions on fabric paint packaging before you start painting. Follow the manufacturer's guidelines for preparing the T-shirt, mixing and applying paints and for drying wet paint. Some manufacturers will also recommend washing or ironing the painted T-shirt before wearing it.

❖ Ask an adult to iron the T-shirt and to supervise the use of sharp tools.

❖ If you splash fabric paint on to your clothes, soak them immediately in lots of cold water. Keep rinsing the garments until the fabric paint is removed. Then wash the clothes in warm, soapy water.

This T-shirt is fun and practical. It has three pockets made of felt fabric. The pockets are sewn on with embroidery thread.

Materials and Tools

These are the materials and tools you will need to complete the projects that follow.

Chalk fabric marker This is a special white chalk that is used for drawing outlines on to dark coloured T-shirts.
Fabric glitter This is special glitter that can be fixed to fabric with fabric glue. It is very fine, so use it carefully.
Fabric glue This glue will stick pieces of fabric together. Always use a special brush for applying fabric glue.
Fabric marker pen A fabric marker pen looks like a normal felt-tip pen, but it is designed to be used on fabric.
Fabric paint Fabric paint is applied to fabric and will not wash out. Read the instructions on the container before using it.
Fluorescent fabric paint Under ultra-violet light, this paint will glow. It comes in many bright colours.
Glitter fabric paint This sparkly fabric paint comes in a tube or squeezy container. Always read the instructions on the packaging before using glitter fabric paint.
Hairdryer You will need a hairdryer with a low heat setting to dry puffa fabric paint. Ask permission before using a hairdryer.
Pearl fabric paint This fabric paint dries with a special sheen. It comes in a squeezy container.
Puffa fabric paint When dried with a hairdryer, this paint puffs up. It comes in a squeezy container. Always follow the manufacturer's instructions when using puffa fabric paint.
Sponge You can buy an inexpensive sponge from a chemist shop. A sponge dipped in fabric paint and gently pressed on to fabric makes an interesting texture.
Sticky-back hook and loop dots These dots stick to each other when pressed together.
Stiff card. Large pieces of card are inserted into the body and sleeves of a T-shirt to stop wet fabric paint seeping through. You can buy sheets of thick card or use cardboard from recycled packaging and boxes.
T-shirt For the projects you will need cotton T-shirts. There are designs for short and long sleeved styles.

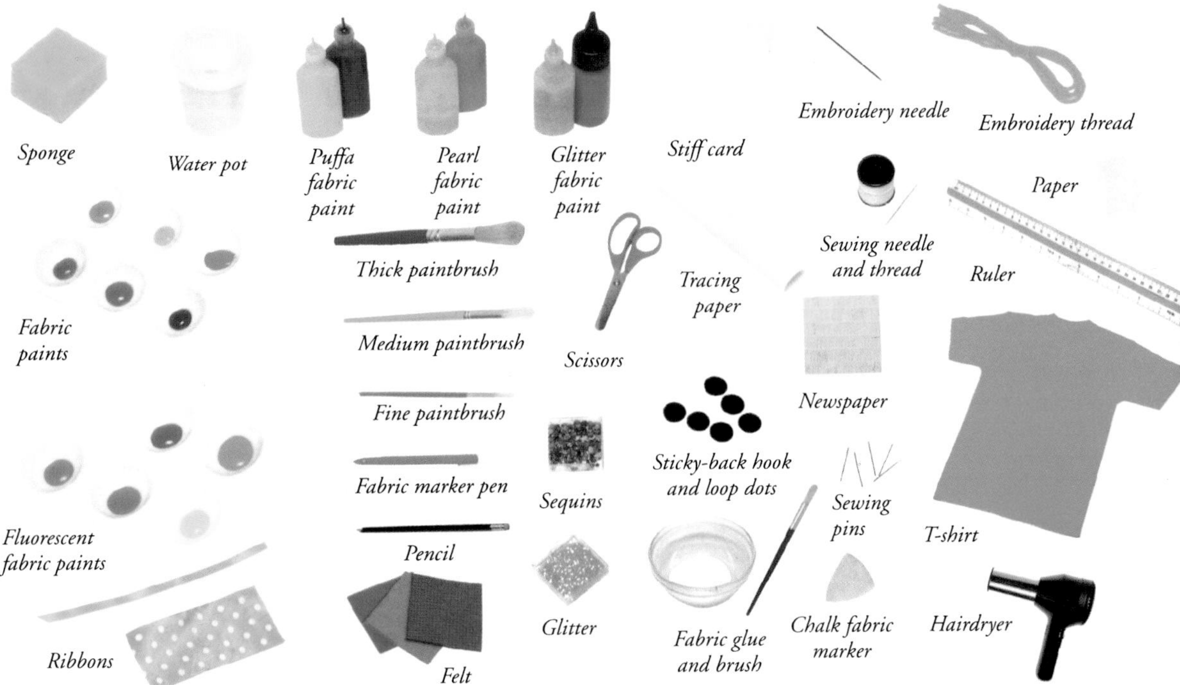

Getting Started

Before you can start painting, you must prepare the T-shirt and perfect your design. The more time you spend getting these things right, the more spectacular the results will be.

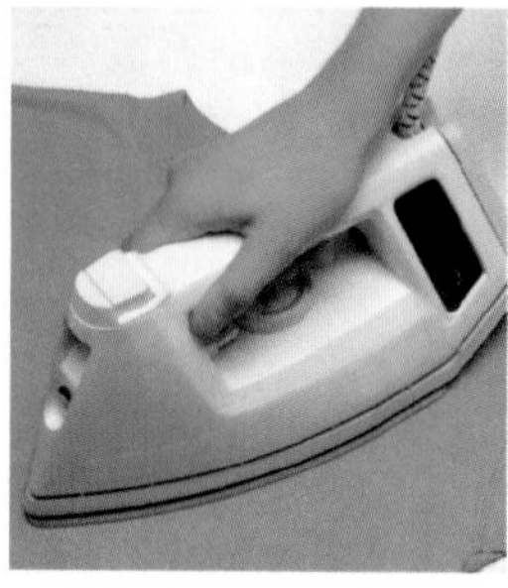

If you are using a new T-shirt, wash and rinse it to remove excess dye. When the T-shirt is dry, ask an adult to iron it to smooth out creases.

To stop fabric paint seeping through the T-shirt, insert pieces of stiff card into the body and sleeves. The pieces of card should fit snugly into position.

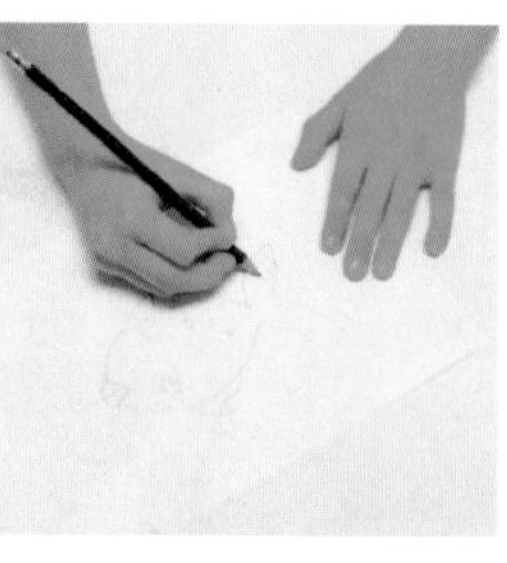

Draw roughs of your design on a piece of paper before drawing it on the T-shirt. Fabric marker pen, like fabric paint, cannot be washed out.

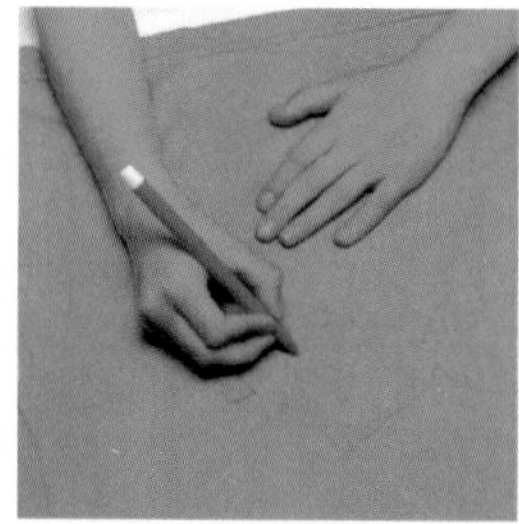

When you are happy with your design, draw it on to the T-shirt. Use a fabric marker pen on light coloured T-shirts. and a chalk marker on dark T-shirts.

When you are ready to start painting and have gathered all the necessary materials and tools, you must cover the work surface with a large sheet of wipe-clean plastic or lots of sheets of newspaper. It is also a good idea to protect any nearby furniture. Fabric paint can splatter, especially if you are flicking a brush loaded with fabric paint to get a special effect. Protect your clothing with an apron and old shirt – fabric paint will not wash off.

Painting tips

Fabric paints come in many wonderful colours and textures, but it is not necessary for you to have everything to create stunning designs on a T-shirt.

Fabric paint colours, just like normal acrylic or poster paint colours, can be mixed together to make other colours. This means, for example, that you can mix blue puffa fabric paint with yellow puffa fabric paint to make green puffa fabric paint. You can also mix glitter fabric paint colours together to make other colours.

To make fabric paint colours lighter, add white fabric paint to the colour or simply add a little water. Fabric paint colours can be made darker by adding a little black fabric paint.

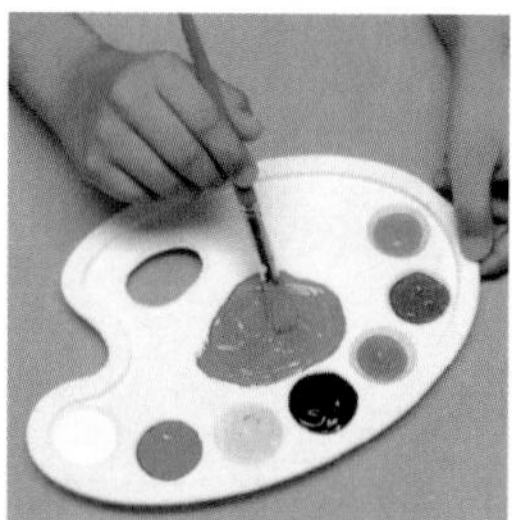

How to mix colours:
yellow + blue = green,
yellow + red = orange,
red + blue = purple.

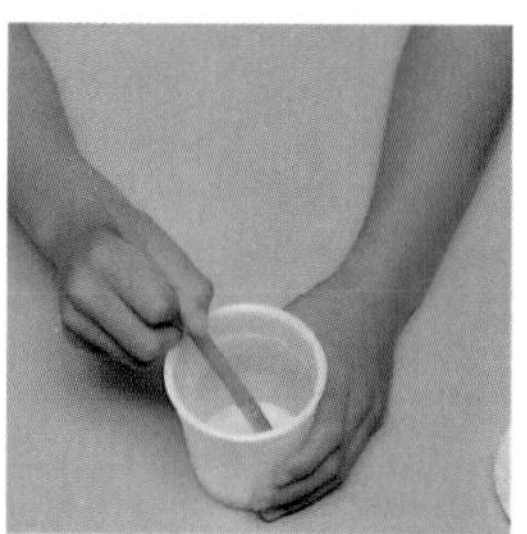

Mix large quantities of a colour in a water pot or small bowl. Add a little water to paints to make them go further.

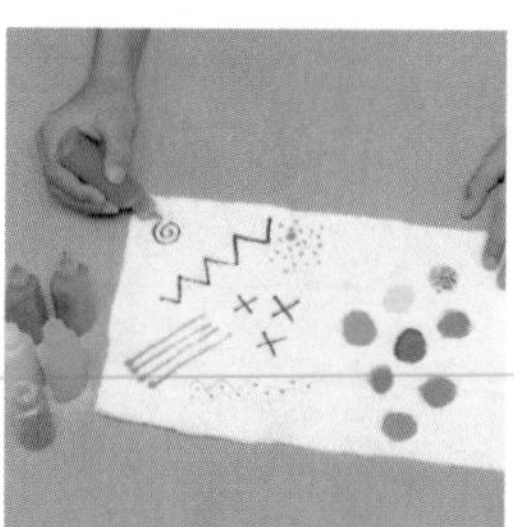

Before painting the T-shirt, try out the techniques and the colours on a piece of leftover fabric. This is especially important when using fabric paints in squeezy containers.

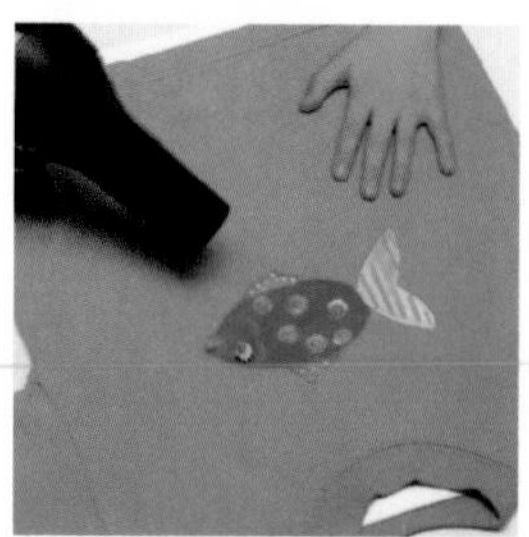

Puffa paint only puffs up when it is dried with a hairdryer, set on low heat. Before drying other fabric paints with a hairdryer, check the instructions on the paint container.

Stencils and Templates

You will need to make stencils and templates to complete some of the T-shirts.

Noughts template for Noughts and Crosses

Paw stencil for Muddy Puppy

Crosses template for Noughts and Crosses

Puppy template for Muddy Puppy

Noughts and Crosses

This T-shirt is great fun. Well, it is not often that an item of clothing doubles up as a board game, is it? Wear it when you are travelling long distances and you will never be bored.

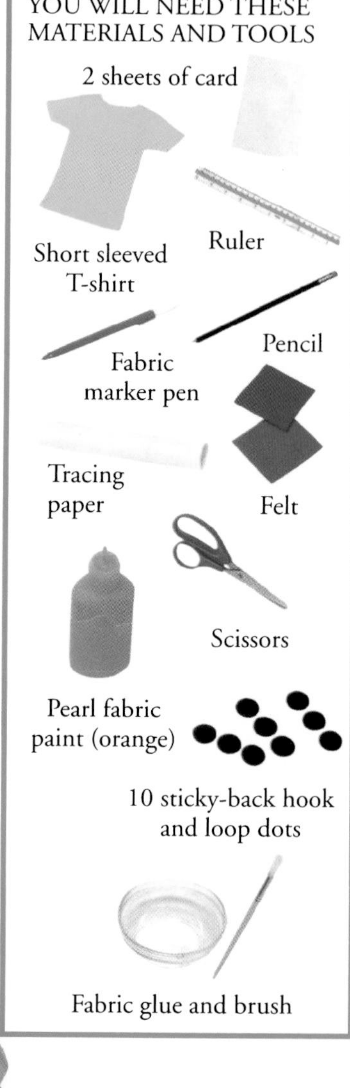

Three noughts in a row means that the boy has won this game of Noughts and Crosses.

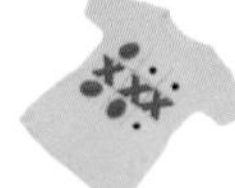

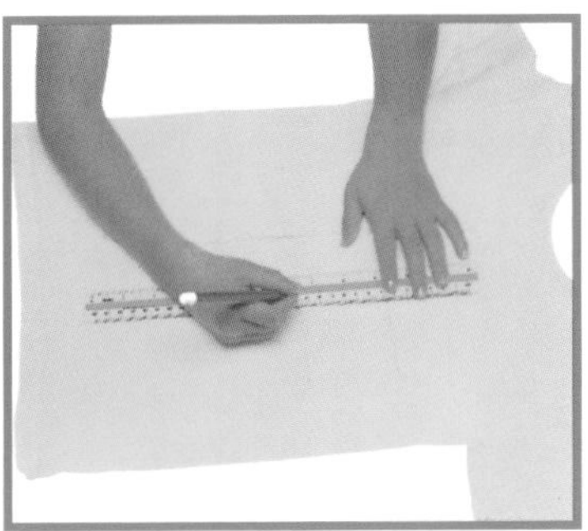

1 Insert a piece of card inside the body of the T-shirt. The card should fit snugly. Use a ruler and fabric marker pen to measure and draw the Noughts and Crosses grid. The lines should be 24cm ($9^1/_2$in) long and 8cm (3in) apart.

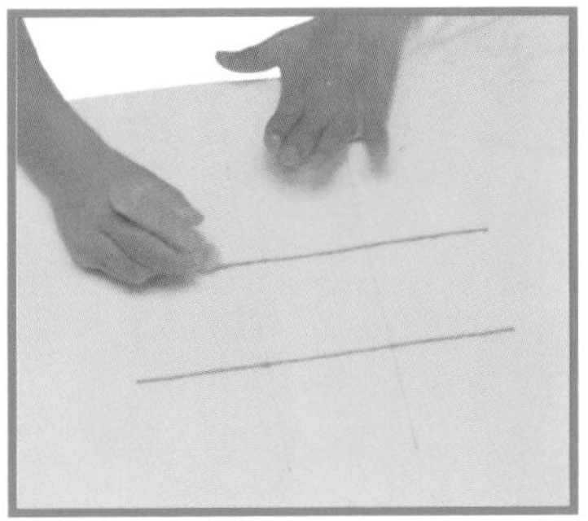

2 Go over the lines with orange pearl fabric paint in a squeezy tube. Move the tube evenly and smoothly along the lines – otherwise the pearl paint will form blobs. Allow the pearl paint to dry thoroughly before continuing.

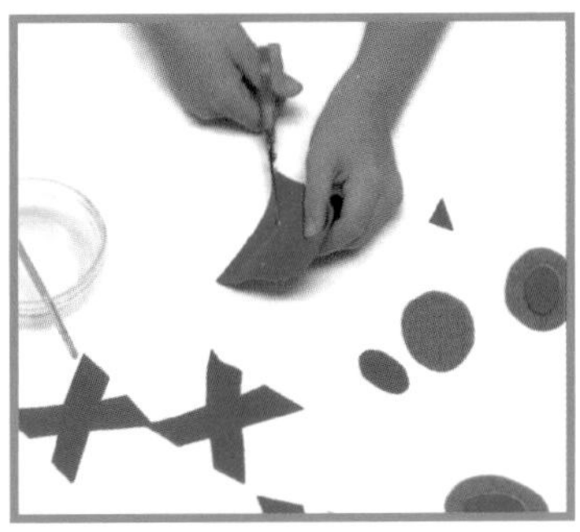

3 Trace and cut out the nought and cross templates in the Introduction. Place the templates on to the felt and draw around them. You will need five red noughts and five blue crosses. Cut out the shapes. Also cut out five small blue ovals and glue these on to the noughts with fabric glue.

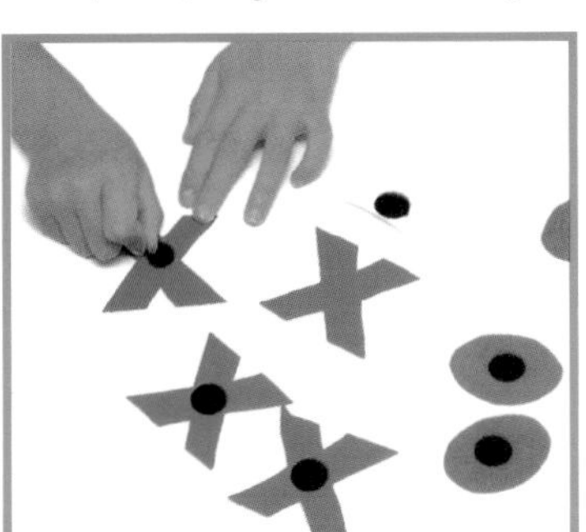

4 Remove the backing from the hoop side of a hook and loop dot. Press the sticky surface on to the back of one of the felt shapes. Repeat for all the remaining shapes.

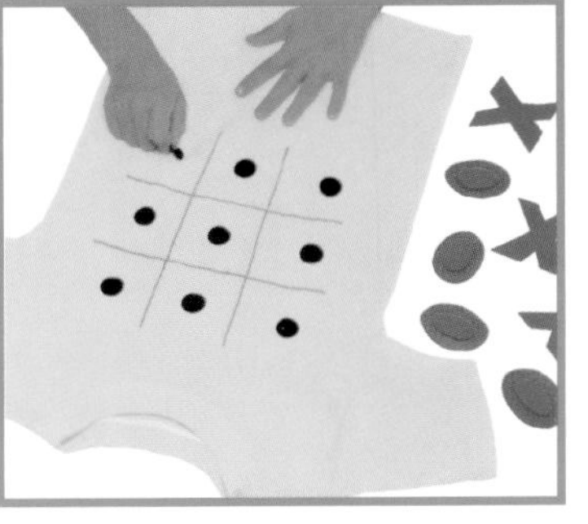

5 Remove the backing from the remaining dots (these will all be looped-sided dots) and press them firmly on to the centre of each square on the grid.

Do not forget to remove the noughts and crosses before washing the T-shirt.

6 You are now ready to play Noughts and Crosses. Have fun!

Sea Life Fantasy

When you look at this T-shirt you can almost smell the salty air, hear the crash of the waves and see the schools of brightly coloured fish darting backward and forward in a pale blue ocean. In this design there are only two species of marine life, but you could also add crabs, shells, coral and fronds of seaweed.

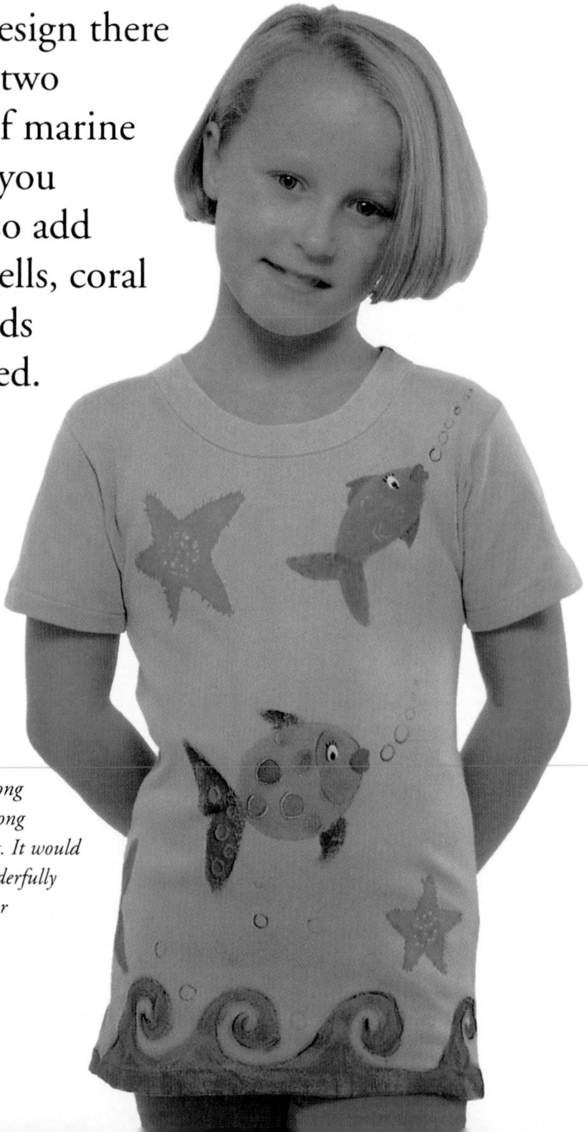

This T-shirt could also be painted on to a long sleeveless vest or long sleeved sweatshirt. It would also make a wonderfully relaxing image for a pillowcase.

Handy hint

It is good idea to practise your design for this T-shirt on paper before you start drawing it on to the T-shirt. If you have trouble drawing fish or star shapes, trace them from a book or magazine. The underwater world is a fascinating one so if you want to get more ideas for painting your T-shirt, have a look in an encyclopedia or other reference book.

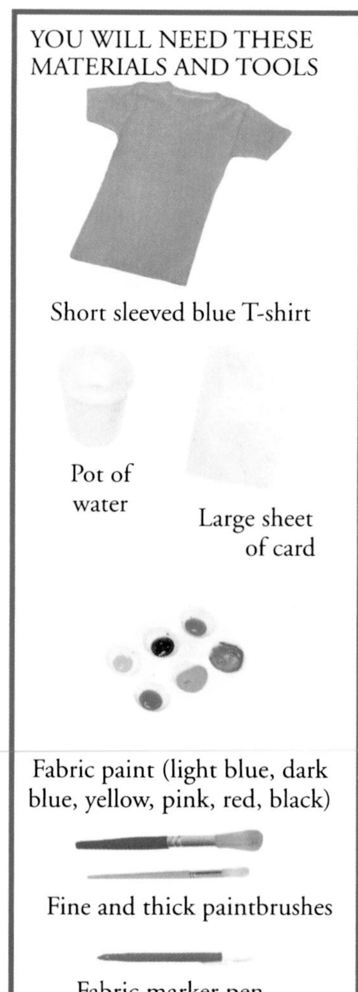

1 Insert the piece of card inside the body of the T-shirt. Use the fabric marker pen to draw the outlines of the fish, starfish and waves on to the front of the T-shirt.

2 Paint the waves with light and dark blue fabric paint using the thick brush. Do not worry if the paint does not go on smoothly – an uneven texture will look more realistic.

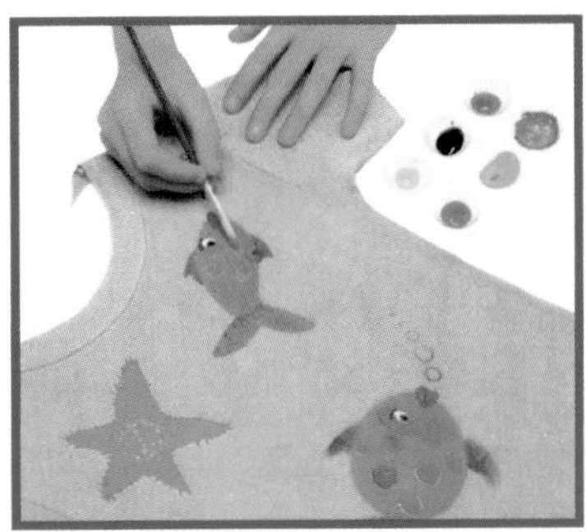

3 Paint the fish in shades of blue, green, pink and red. The green can be made by mixing yellow and blue. Use the fine brush to paint the lips and eyes. Paint black bubbles coming from their mouths. Mix red and yellow to make orange. Paint the starfish with the orange paint.

4 Allow the fabric paint to dry. Turn the T-shirt over, making sure that the piece of card is still in position. Use the fabric marker pen to draw another fish on to the back of the T-shirt. Continue the pattern of the waves.

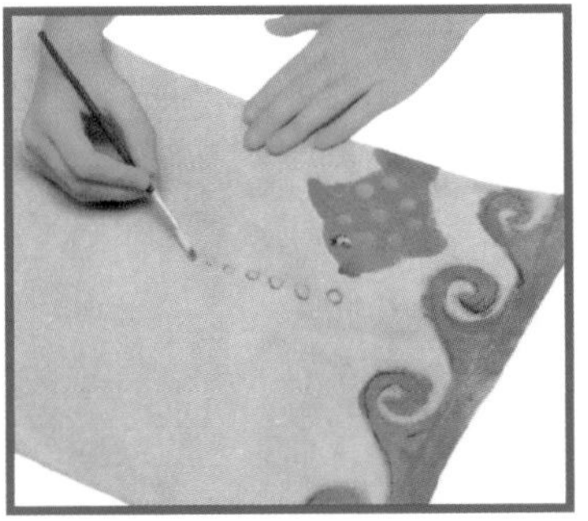

5 Use the thick brush to paint the waves with light and dark blue fabric paint. Wash the brush before painting the fish pink with yellow spots. Paint features on to the fish's face and bubbles coming from its mouth.

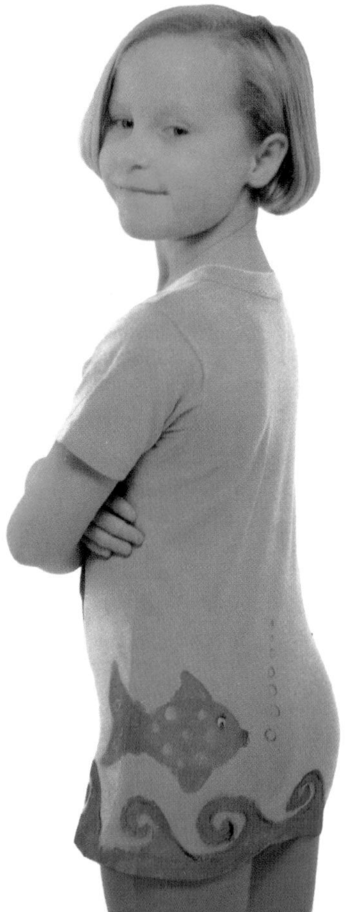

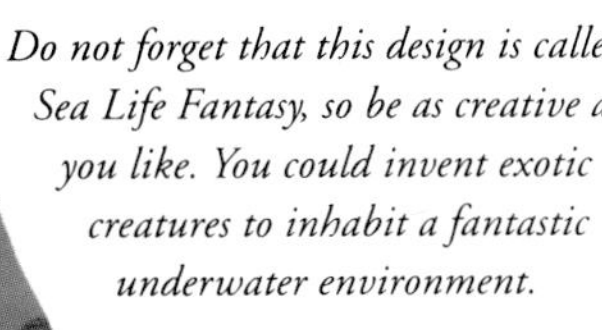

Do not forget that this design is called Sea Life Fantasy, so be as creative as you like. You could invent exotic creatures to inhabit a fantastic underwater environment.

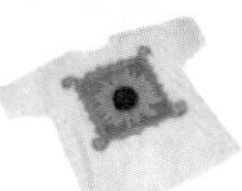

Sunny Sunflower

On the Sunny Sunflower T-shirt you can show off your artistic flair for colour, shape and texture. In fact, your painting will be so good that it will be framed in gold. But there is something missing from this painting – the signature of the artist.

YOU WILL NEED THESE MATERIALS AND TOOLS

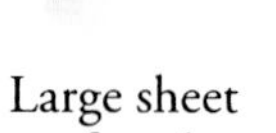

Large sheet of card

Short sleeved T-shirt

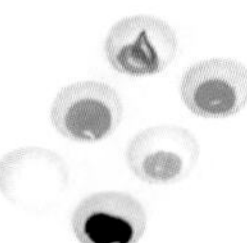

Fabric paint (black, yellow, red, orange, light blue, gold)

Fabric marker pen

Glitter fabric paint (gold)

Pot of water

Medium paintbrush

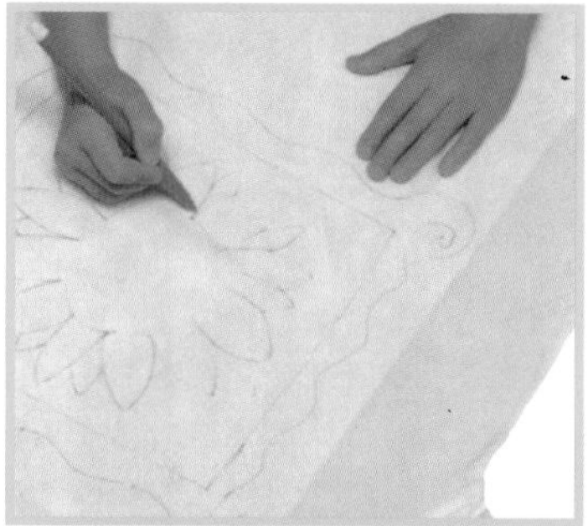

1 Insert a piece of card inside the body of the T-shirt. Use the fabric marker pen to draw the outline of the sunflower and the fancy picture frame.

2 Paint the centre of the sunflower with black fabric paint. Use shades of yellow, red and orange to paint the petals. Allow the paint to dry.

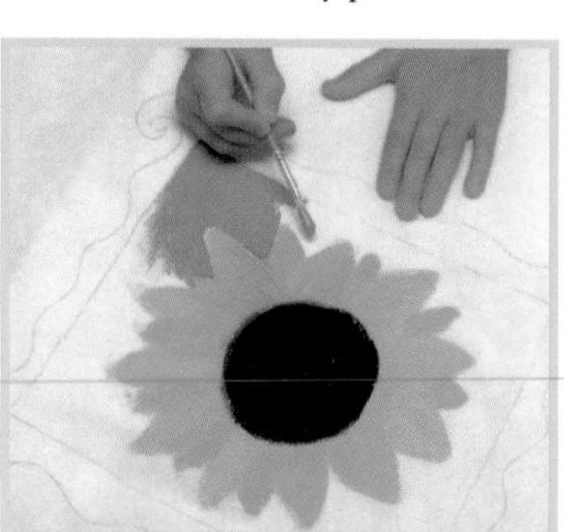

3 Use a sky blue fabric paint for the background of your sunflower painting. Take care not to paint over the petals or into the frame. Allow the paint to dry.

4 Using a clean brush, paint the picture frame with gold fabric paint. For the final artistic touch, decorate the gilt frame with swirls of gold glitter fabric paint.

Optical Illusion

This design is inspired by an artist called Escher. He was famous for his paintings of bizarre optical illusions. In his paintings nothing was ever as it should be – water flowed uphill and darting fish would become birds before your very eyes.

YOU WILL NEED THESE MATERIALS AND TOOLS

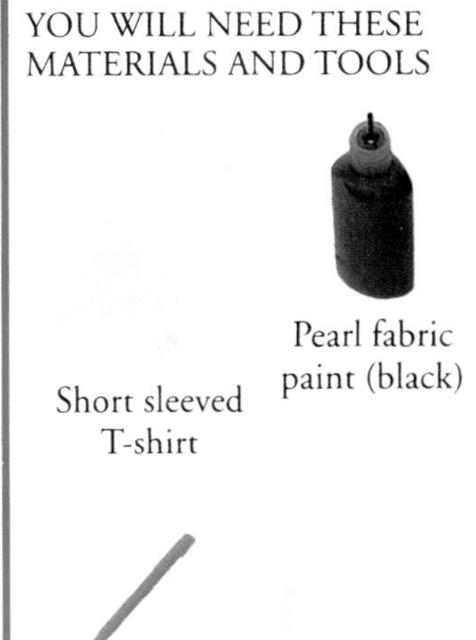

Short sleeved T-shirt

Pearl fabric paint (black)

Fabric marker pen

Large sheet of card

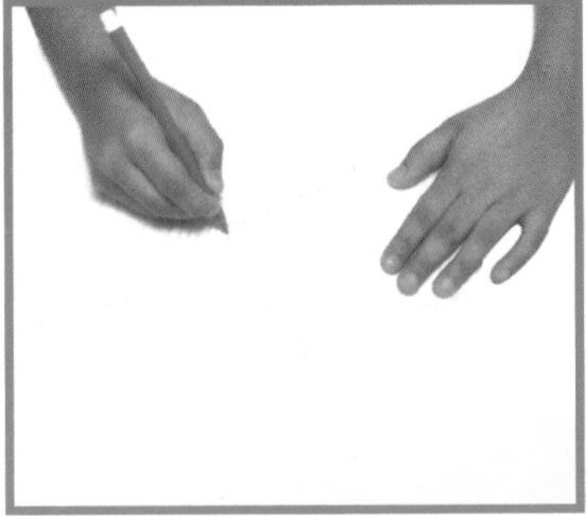

1 Insert a piece of card inside the body of the T-shirt. Use the fabric marker pen to draw a large rectangle on to the front of the T-shirt. Draw more rectangles inside the large rectangle.

2 Go over the design with black pearl fabric paint in a squeezy container. If you are using a new container of pearl fabric paint, cut the nozzle close to the top so that you can paint fine lines.

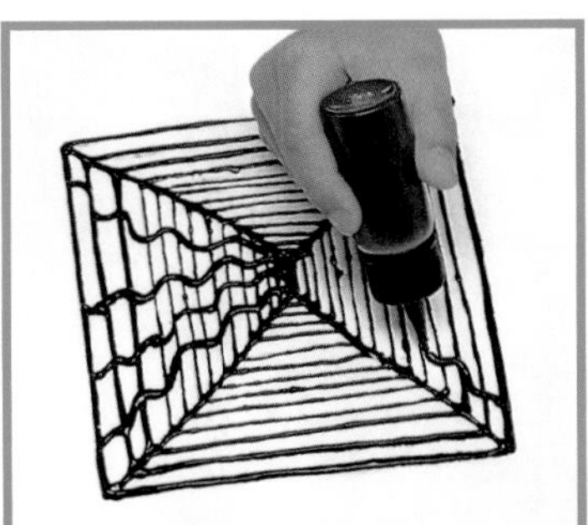

3 Paint lines with black pearl fabric paint from each corner to the middle. Then paint black wiggly lines in the two side triangles, as shown.

To make your Optical Illusion really convincing, divide each line in the bottom triangle into rectangles using the black pearl paint. The rectangles will get smaller as they get closer to the centre. Paint alternate rectangles black to make a checkered pattern.

Bug Collector

Aargh! Do not look now but there are spiders and insects crawling all over you. The Bug Collector T-shirt is not for the squeamish – it is for the enthusiastic mini-beast collector who really wants to bug his friends and family. You can invent your own creatures, or better still, copy them from real life!

This is the perfect T-shirt to wear to a fancy dress party. To make it even more horrifying, stick plastic spiders and other insects on to the T-shirt with double-sided sticky tape. Do not forget to remove your eight- and six-legged plastic friends before you put the T-shirt in to be washed.

YOU WILL NEED THESE MATERIALS AND TOOLS

Long sleeved T-shirt

Pot of water

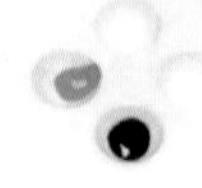

Fabric paint (black, red)

Black pearl fabric paint

Large sheet of card

Fine and medium paintbrushes

Fabric marker pen

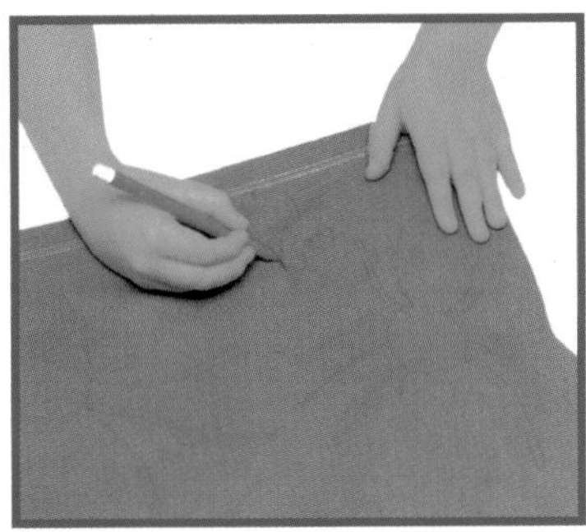

1 Insert pieces of card inside the body and sleeves of the T-shirt. Use the fabric marker pen to draw three very large spiders on to the front of the T-shirt. Draw two or three spiders on to each sleeve.

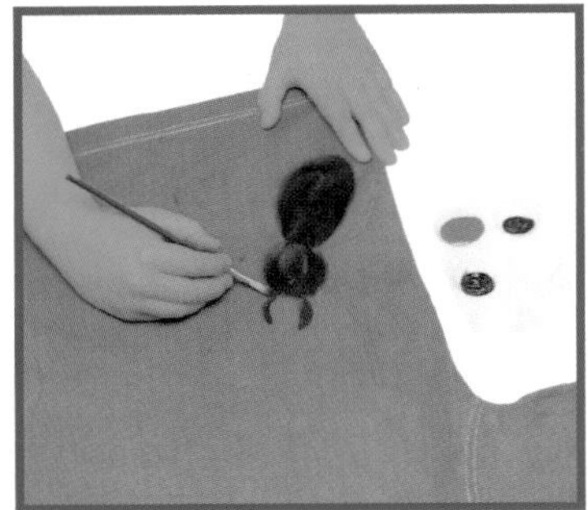

2 Use the medium brush and black fabric paint to paint the spiders' heads, bodies and fangs. To paint the black jointed legs, use the fine brush. Wash the brush before painting the spiders' eyes red.

3 Dip a finger into black fabric paint and press it on to the T-shirt to make the body and head of a small insect. Repeat until you have covered the front and sleeves of the T-shirt with mini-beasts. Allow to dry.

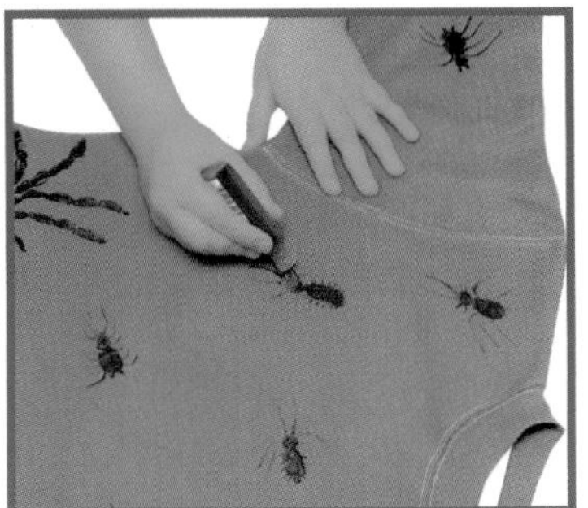

4 To paint legs on the small bugs, use black pearl fabric paint in a squeezy container. Allow the paint to dry thoroughly. If you like, you can paint more spiders and bugs on to the back of the T-shirt.

Potato stamp mini-beasts

To make repeated designs, like small spiders or insects, you can make a stamp with a halved potato. Etch the outline of an insect's body into a cut surface of the potato with a blunt pencil. Ask an adult to cut away the potato from around the shape with a sharp knife. Dip the stamp lightly into fabric paint and press it on to the T-shirt. Keep stamping until you have covered your T-shirt. Paint the legs using black pearl fabric paint. When dry, this paint has a raised and textured finish.

Swirly Spots

The Swirly Spots design is simple to draw and you can use as many colours as you like. The fabric paint must be dry before you decorate the spots with glitter fabric paint.

YOU WILL NEED THESE MATERIALS AND TOOLS

- Large sheet of card
- Short sleeved T-shirt 
- Medium paintbrush
- Pot of water
- Fabric marker pen 
- Fabric paint (red, black, pink, blue, white) 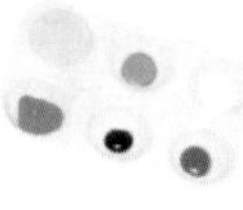
- Puffa fabric paint (purple, red, yellow, orange, blue) 
- Hairdryer 
- Glitter fabric paint (silver)

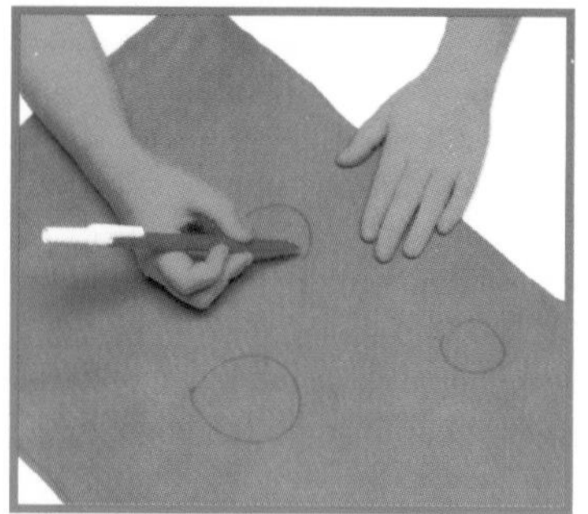

1 Insert pieces of card inside the body and sleeves of the T-shirt. Use the fabric marker pen to draw circles on to the front of the T-shirt. Draw circles on to the sleeves as well.

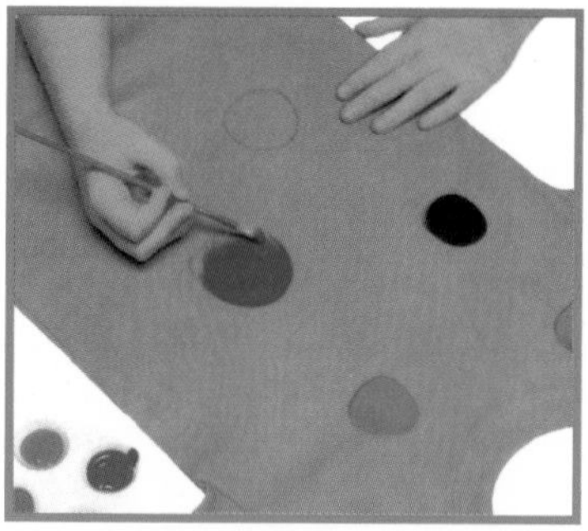

2 Use the medium brush to paint the circles different colours. Do not forget to wash the brush when changing colours. Allow the fabric paint to dry thoroughly before starting the next step.

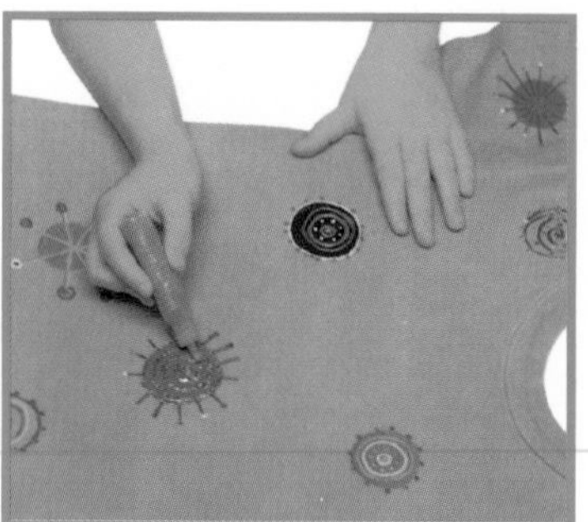

3 Use purple, red, yellow, orange and blue puffa fabric paint to decorate the circles with swirls, lines and dots. Dry the puffa fabric paint with the hairdryer. This will make the puffa paint puff up. To finish, decorate some circles with silver glitter fabric paint.

When using fabric paints in squeezy containers, keep the nozzle moving smoothly over your design. If the nozzle stays in one place too long, the paint will form blobs.

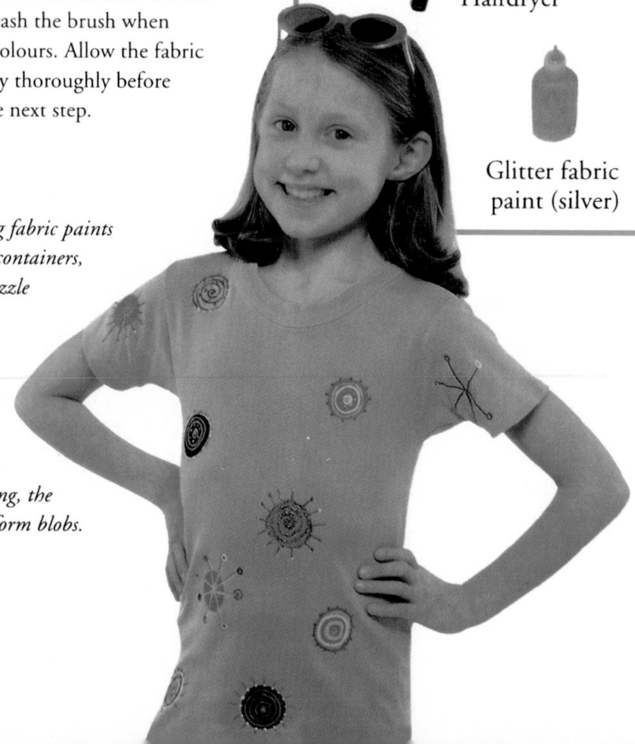

Glitzy Stars

This twinkling T-shirt is perfect for a party. The glitter and sequins will make the stars sparkle under lights. Special fabric glitter can be bought in hobby and craft shops.

YOU WILL NEED THESE MATERIALS AND TOOLS

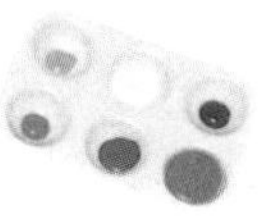

Fabric paint (blue, yellow, white, red, pink, green)

Short sleeved T-shirt

Glitter fabric paint

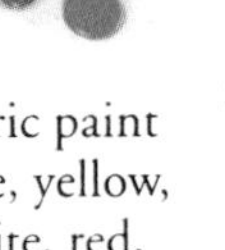

Fabric marker pen

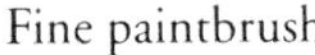

Fine paintbrush

Sequins

Fabric glitter

Large sheet of card

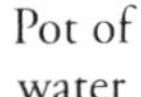

Pot of water

Pearl fabric paint (yellow)

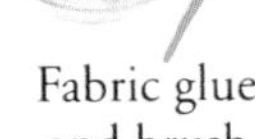

Fabric glue and brush

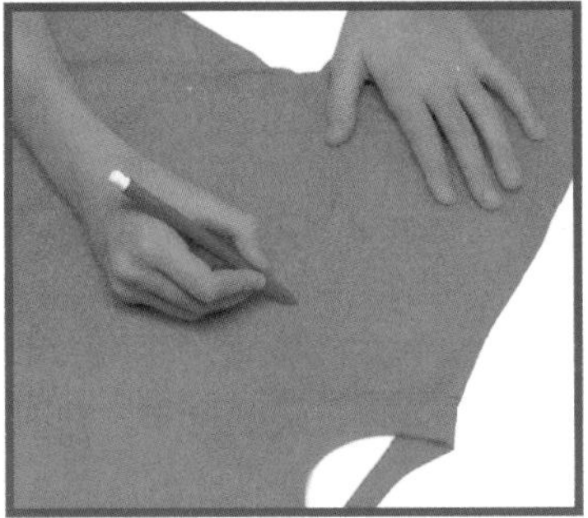

1 Insert a piece of card inside the body of the T-shirt. Use the fabric marker pen to draw the outlines of stars all over the front of the T-shirt. Make some stars large, others small.

2 Use the fine brush to paint the stars with blue, green, red, yellow and pink fabric paints. When dry, paint around the edges of the stars with yellow pearl fabric paint and gold glitter fabric paint. Decorate the stars with dots of yellow and gold.

3 Now it is time to add some real sparkle to this starry T-shirt. Paint the stars with fabric glue. While the glue is still wet, sprinkle on fabric glitter and sequins. When dry, gently shake the T-shirt over a sheet of newspaper to remove excess glitter and sequins.

If you would like to decorate the back of the T-shirt, wait for the front of the T-shirt to dry before turning the T-shirt over. Check that the card is still in place before repeating steps 1, 2 and 3.

Disco Dazzler

Wear this wild T-shirt to be the centre of attention. The patterns will positively glow in the dark under ultra-violet light. This is because they have been painted using fluorescent fabric paint.

YOU WILL NEED THESE MATERIALS AND TOOLS

- Short sleeved black T-shirt
- Pot of water
- Hairdryer
- Large sheet of card
- Medium paintbrush
- Chalk fabric marker
- Fluorescent fabric paint (yellow, blue, pink, orange, green)
- Puffa fabric paint (orange, yellow, purple, red)

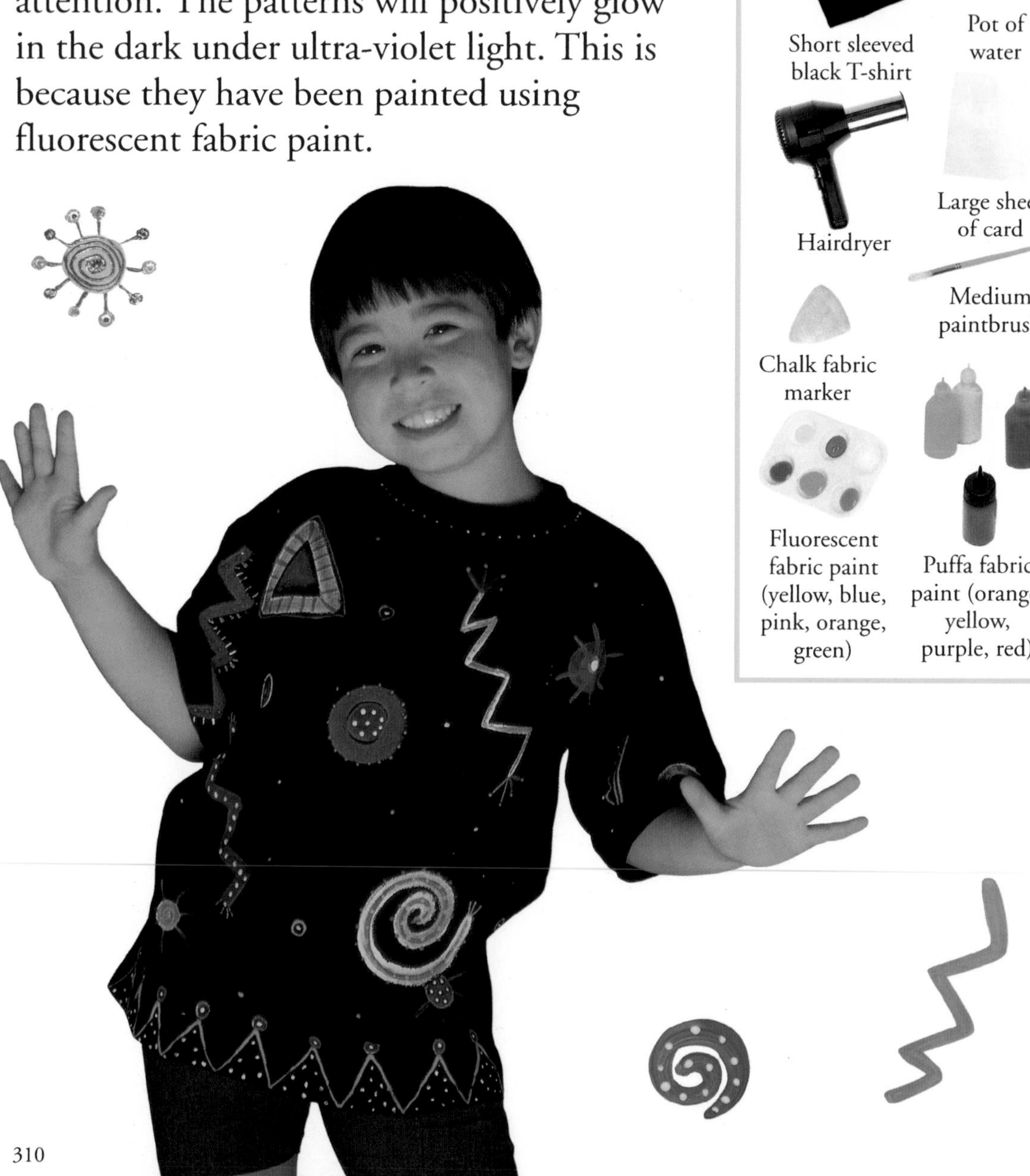

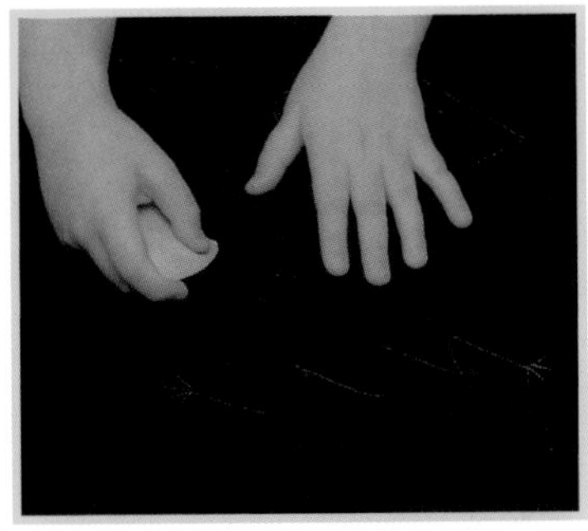

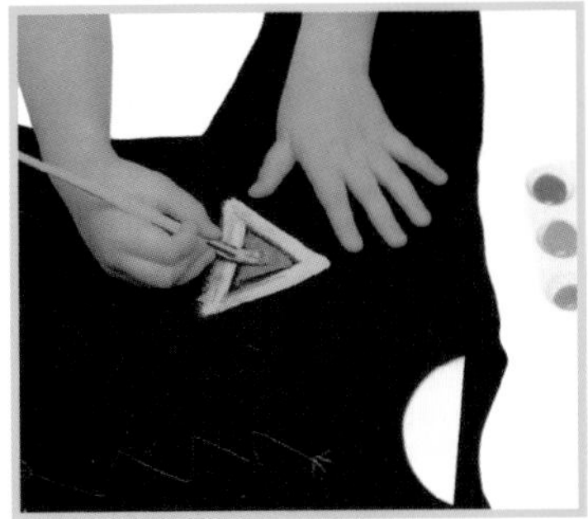

1 Insert pieces of card inside the body and sleeves of the T-shirt. Use the chalk fabric marker to draw the outlines of triangles, spirals and zigzag patterns all over the front and the sleeves of the T-shirt. Draw a zigzag pattern along the bottom edge of the T-shirt.

2 Use fluorescent yellow, blue, pink, orange and green fabric paint to fill in the outlines. To make other colours, simply mix different colours together on a palette. Allow the fabric paint to dry before painting patterns on to areas already painted.

3 Decorate the T-shirt with dots and squiggles of orange, yellow, purple and red puffa fabric paint. You can make your patterns as wild as you like. To make the puffa fabric paint puff up, dry it with a hairdryer. Set the hairdryer to its coolest setting.

4 Go over the zigzag at the bottom of the T-shirt with orange puffa fabric paint. Use other puffa fabric paints to add circles and dots. Once again, use the hairdryer set to its coolest temperature to dry the puffa fabric paint. Allow your T-shirt to dry thoroughly before hitting the disco and dazzling all your friends.

Dazzling colours

Though this design looks great in fluorescent fabric paint colours, it can also be done using brightly coloured plain fabric paints. Even though these paints will not glow-in-the-dark, your T-shirt will still be the envy of all at the disco. But if you like a bit of glitz and glitter, why not use glitter fabric paint or fabric glitter?

If you want to continue the zigzag pattern on the back of the T-shirt, wait for the front to dry before turning the T-shirt over. Before starting to paint check that the card is still in place.

Pockets of Fun

Handy hint

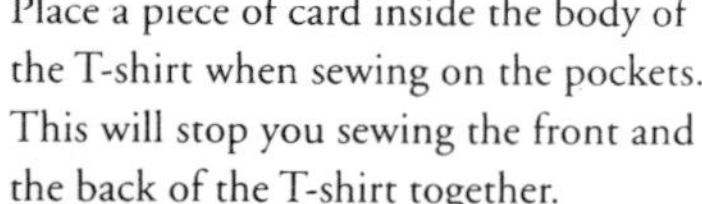

Place a piece of card inside the body of the T-shirt when sewing on the pockets. This will stop you sewing the front and the back of the T-shirt together.

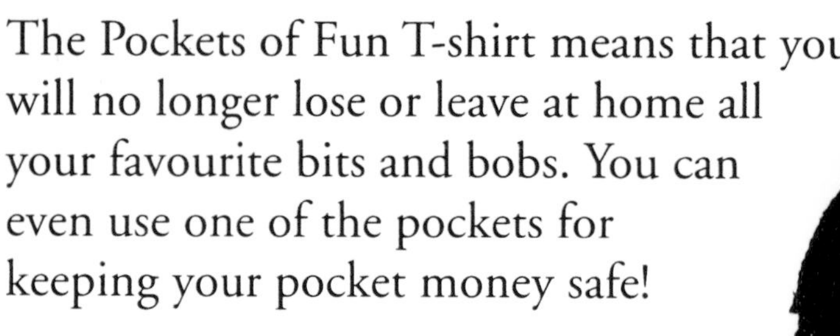

The Pockets of Fun T-shirt means that you will no longer lose or leave at home all your favourite bits and bobs. You can even use one of the pockets for keeping your pocket money safe!

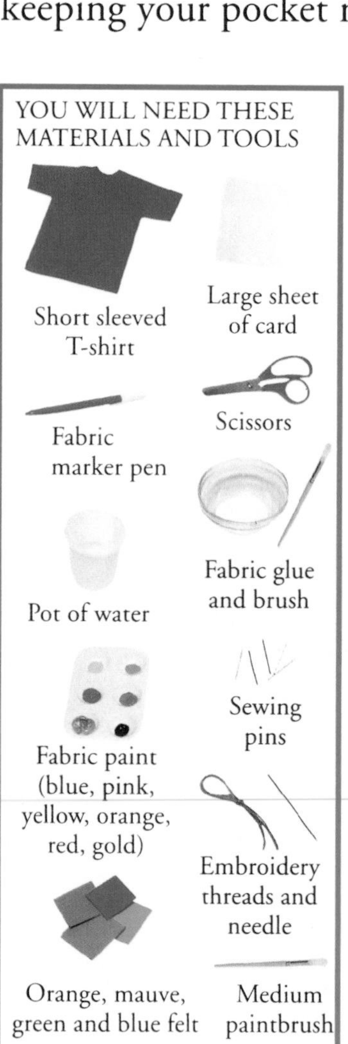

YOU WILL NEED THESE MATERIALS AND TOOLS

Short sleeved T-shirt

Large sheet of card

Fabric marker pen

Scissors

Pot of water

Fabric glue and brush

Fabric paint (blue, pink, yellow, orange, red, gold)

Sewing pins

Embroidery threads and needle

Orange, mauve, green and blue felt

Medium paintbrush

1 Cut three pockets and three decorative strips from the orange, mauve, green and blue felt. The strips must be long enough to fit neatly along the top edge of each pocket. Glue a strip on to the top of each pocket with fabric glue.

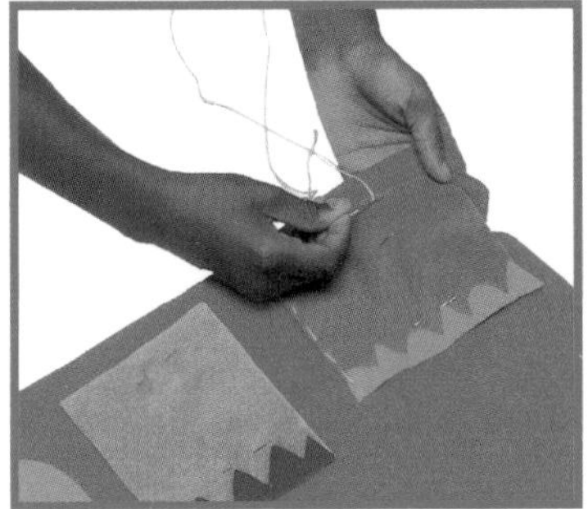

2 Position the pockets along the bottom of the T-shirt with pins. Thread the needle with embroidery thread and tie a knot in the end. Use thread that is a different colour from the pocket. Sew the pockets on to the front of the T-shirt using big stitches.

3 Use the fabric marker pen to draw the outlines of sweets, coins and dice just above each pocket. Here are ideas for other items you could draw on your Pockets of Fun T-shirt – pencils, rubbers, jewellery, sunglasses, favourite toys, lipstick and hair clips.

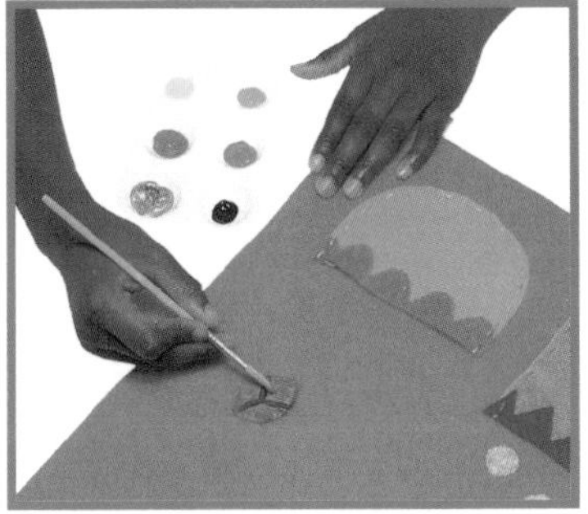

4 Insert a piece of card into the body of the T-shirt. Paint the dice and sweet wrappers in bright colours. Use gold fabric paint for the coins. Allow fabric paints to dry thoroughly.

If you like you can also decorate and outline the pockets using pearl fabric paint in a squeezy container.

Sewing tips

1. To tie a knot, form a loop near end of the thread. Pass the free end of the thread through the loop then pull on the thread.
2. To sew, push the needle up through the fabric and pull till the thread tightens. Move the needle forward then push it down through the fabric. Keep pushing the needle up and down until the pocket is stitched on.

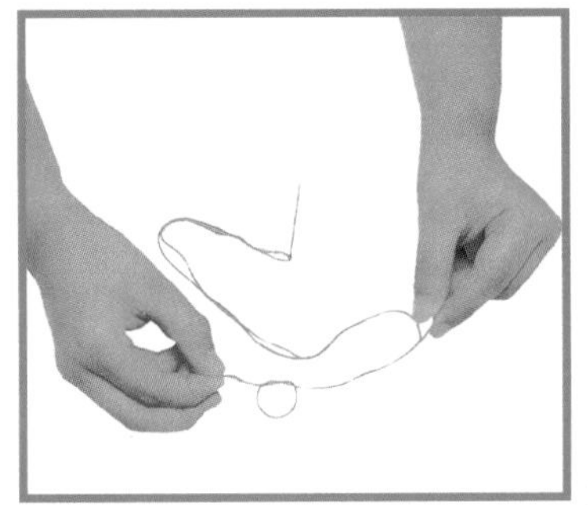

1

2

Basketballer

If you can slam dunk and dribble, then this is the T-shirt design for you. Why not get friends together to form a basketball team? You can have a different number each and choose your own team colours.

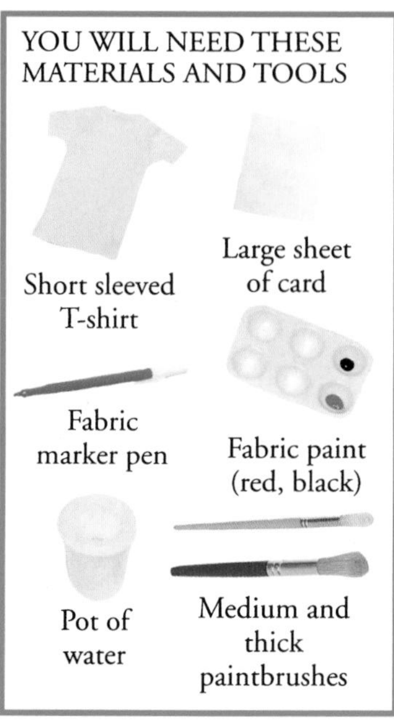

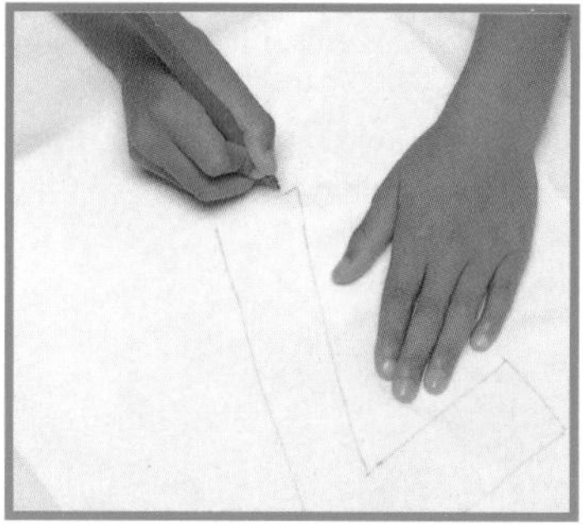

1 Insert card inside the body and sleeves of the T-shirt. Use the fabric marker pen to outline the number 7 on to the front. Draw two bands along the edge of each sleeve front.

2 Use the thick brush to fill in the outline of the number and the bands on each sleeve with red fabric paint. Allow the paint to dry. Use the medium brush to paint a black line around the number and above the red band on the sleeve.

3 Paint the ribbing around the neck of the T-shirt with black fabric paint. When dry, use the medium brush to paint the narrow red line. Allow to dry. Turn over the T-shirt and repeat steps 1, 2 and 3.

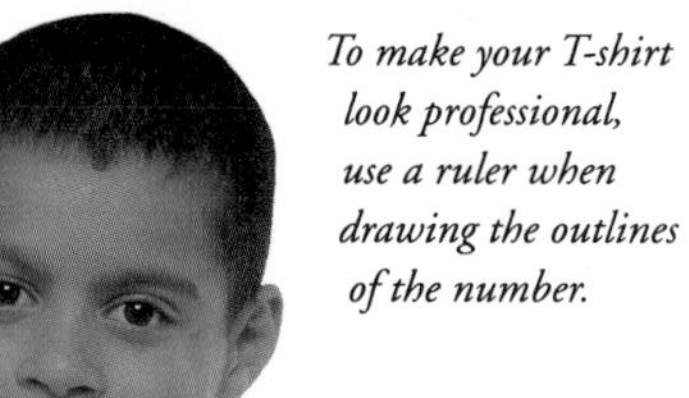

To make your T-shirt look professional, use a ruler when drawing the outlines of the number.

Skeleton

This T-shirt is perfect for a fancy dress party. All you need to complete your nightmare outfit is a black cap, black leggings and a pair of black gloves. Make up your face with white face paint and black eye shadow.

YOU WILL NEED THESE MATERIALS AND TOOLS

Long sleeved black T-shirt

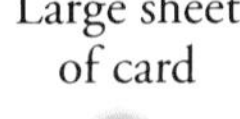

Large sheet of card

Chalk fabric marker

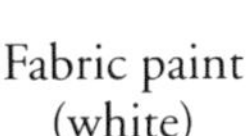

Fabric paint (white)

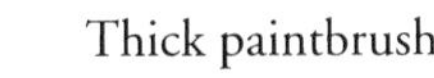

Thick paintbrush

Pot of water

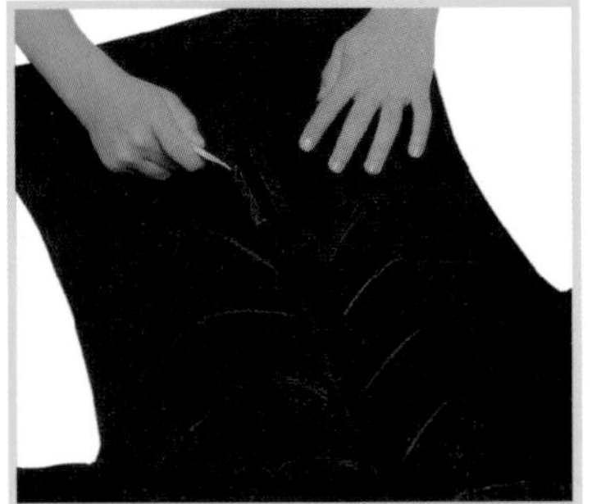

1 Insert card inside the T-shirt body and sleeves. Use the chalk fabric marker to draw outlines of the shoulder blades, rib cage, spine and hips on to the front of the T-shirt. Draw outlines of the arm bones on to both sleeves.

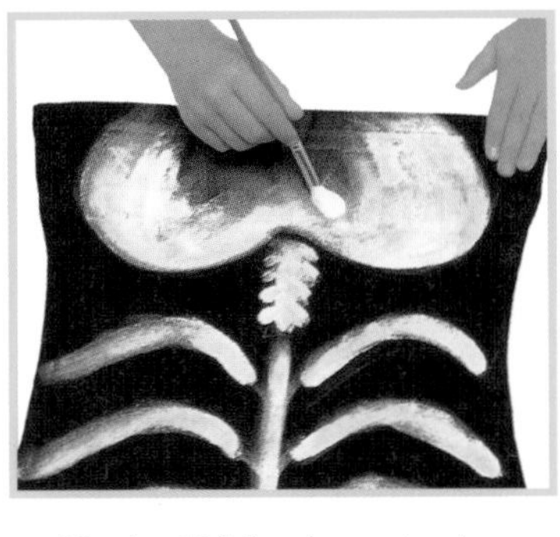

2 Use the thick brush to paint the bones on the front of the T-shirt with white fabric paint. To make the bones really white, do two coats. Allow the paint to dry between coats.

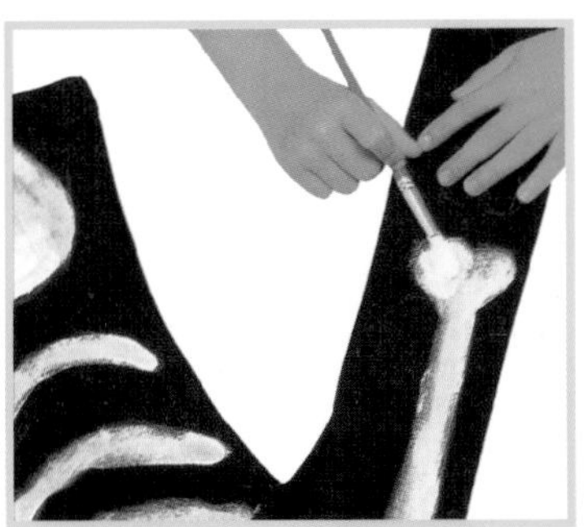

3 To finish off, paint the bones on both sleeves. Leave the white fabric paint to dry thoroughly between coats. All you have to do now, Bones the Skeleton, is wait for a full Moon!

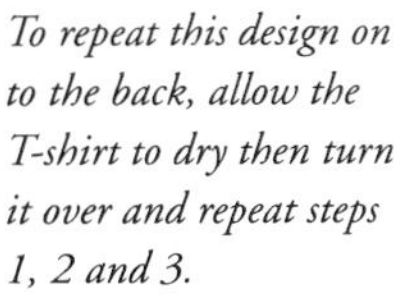

To repeat this design on to the back, allow the T-shirt to dry then turn it over and repeat steps 1, 2 and 3.

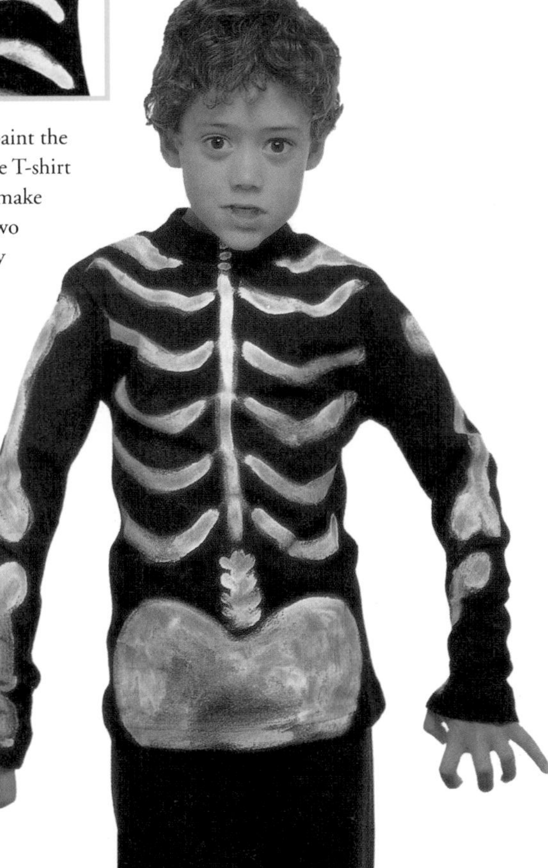

Crazy Spiral

The Crazy Spiral T-shirt is simple to do, even if you are new to fabric painting. Draw the outline of the spiral as large as you can to make it easy to paint and to decorate. You can add smaller spirals to the design or paint a spiral on the back of your T-shirt, too.

Handy hint

To stop the T-shirt moving around when you are drawing the outline or painting your design, fix the T-shirt to your work surface with masking tape. Lay the T-shirt out flat, making sure there are no uneven surfaces or bumps, before taping.

YOU WILL NEED THESE MATERIALS AND TOOLS

- Short sleeved T-shirt
- Large sheet of card 
- Fabric marker pen 
- Fine, medium and thick paintbrushes 
- Glitter fabric paint (green, purple)
- Pot of water 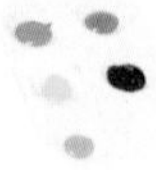
- Fabric paint (black, orange, yellow, light blue, green) 
- Pearl fabric paint (yellow, orange, purple)

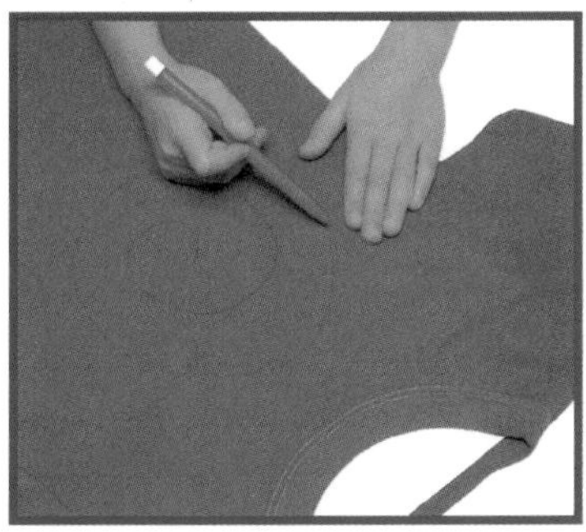

1 Insert pieces of card inside the body and sleeves of the T-shirt. Use the fabric marker pen to draw a large curly spiral on the front of the T-shirt.

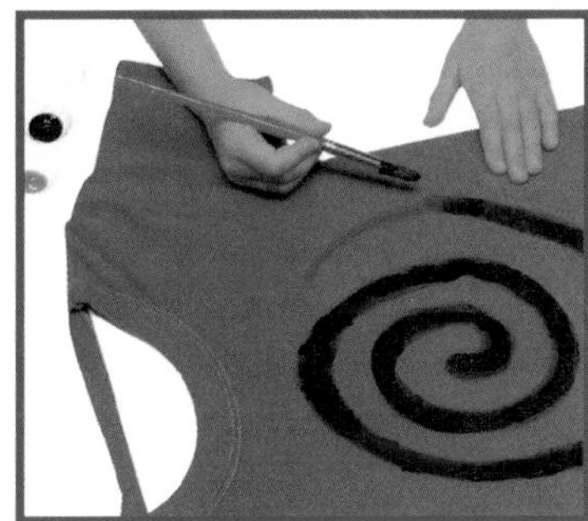

2 Paint the spiral with black fabric paint using the thick brush. Allow the paint to dry thoroughly before starting the next step.

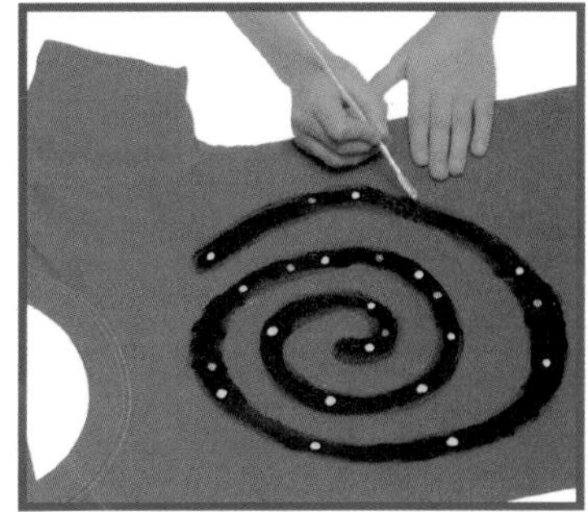

3 Decorate the spiral with orange, yellow, light blue and green dots of fabric paint. Do this using the medium brush. Allow the paint to dry.

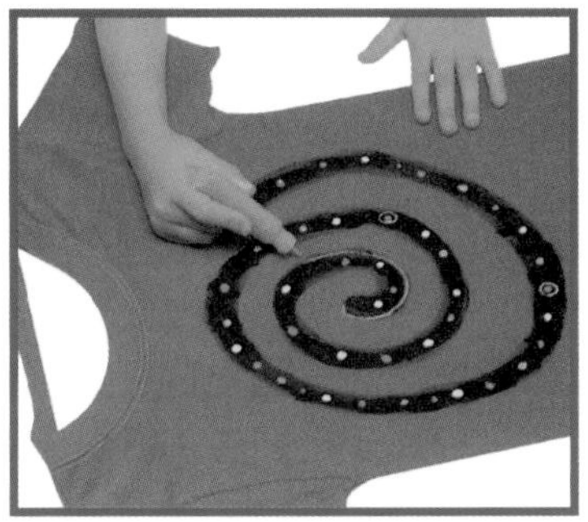

4 Draw circles around some of the dots using yellow pearl fabric paint. Go around the outline of the spiral with orange and purple pearl fabric paint.

5 Make dots of yellow pearl fabric paint inside the spiral. Cover the front of the T-shirt with green glitter fabric paint dots. To finish, dot the sleeves with purple glitter fabric paint.

Choosing your own colours

The colours used on this design are suggestions only – you can choose any combination of colours you like. You could paint the design using only yellows and oranges, or shades of pink and red. Make sure before you start that your colours will stand out against the colour of the T-shirt.

Space Trekker

This T-shirt goes where no other T-shirt has gone before. Its glowing fluorescent yellow after-burners will be seen by alien beings in every far-flung galaxy and planet. But all Space Trekkers should make sure that they know how to get back to Planet Earth!

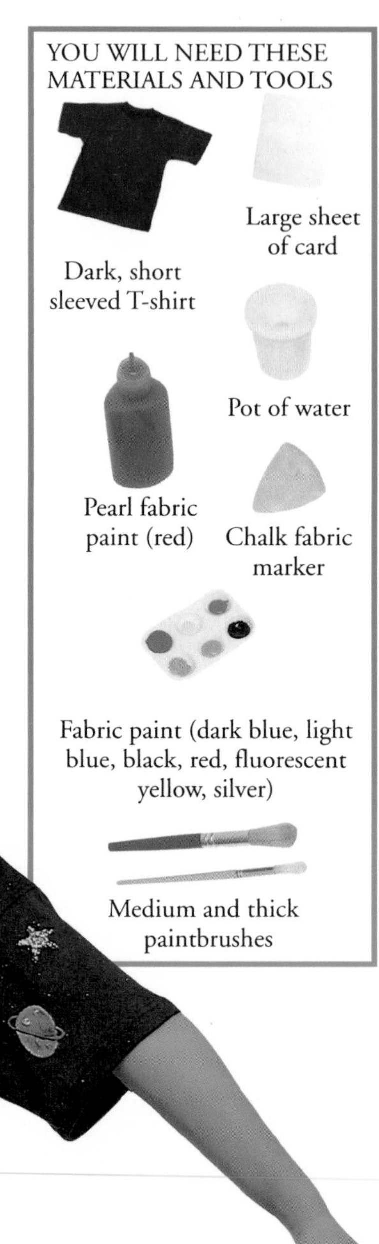

YOU WILL NEED THESE MATERIALS AND TOOLS

- Dark, short sleeved T-shirt
- Large sheet of card
- Pot of water
- Pearl fabric paint (red)
- Chalk fabric marker
- Fabric paint (dark blue, light blue, black, red, fluorescent yellow, silver)
- Medium and thick paintbrushes

This Earth-bound Space Trekker dreams of blasting off in his rocket and crashing through the Earth's atmosphere. He wants to discover the secrets of the Solar System and find out about life on other planets.

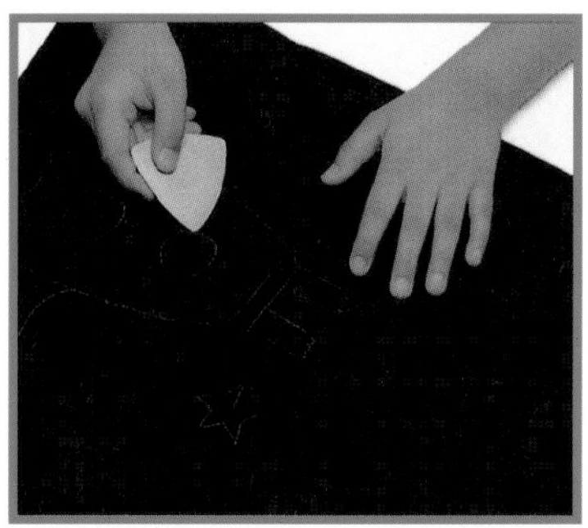

1 Insert card inside the body and sleeves of the T-shirt. Use the chalk fabric marker to outline the planets, stars and rocket. Draw only the end of the rocket on to the front of the T-shirt.

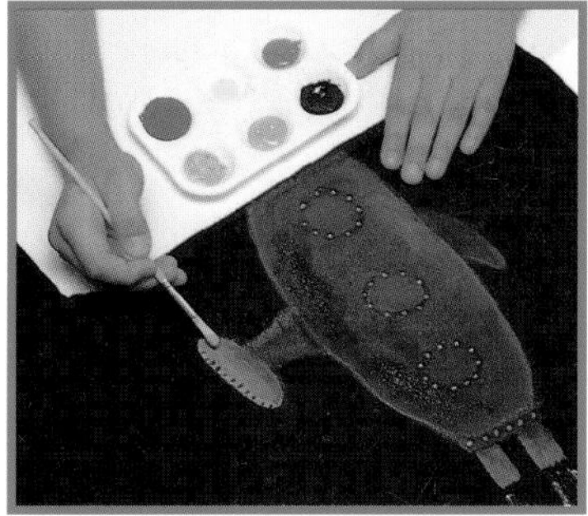

2 Use the medium and thick brushes to paint the rocket with dark blue, light blue, black and red fabric paint. Use fluorescent yellow fabric paint for the rivets and after-burners. Paint the top of the rocket silver.

3 Paint the stars with silver fabric paint. Use plain and fluorescent fabric paints for the planets. When dry, make a ring around each planet with red pearl fabric paint. Use the pearl fabric paint to add details to the rocket.

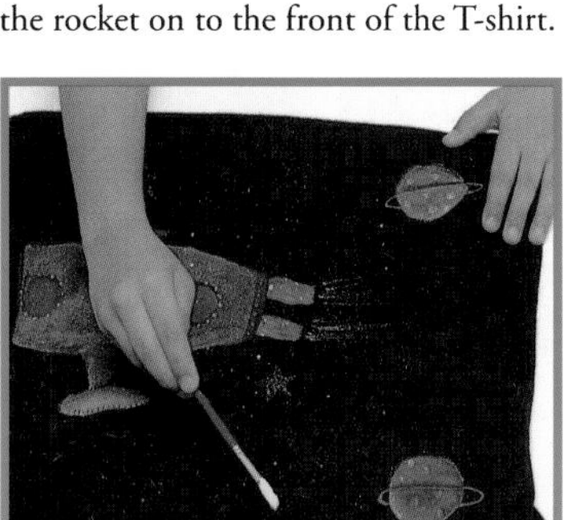

4 To make galaxies of stars, dip the thick brush in yellow fluorescent fabric paint and then flick the brush at the T-shirt. Allow to dry.

5 Turn the T-shirt over. Use the chalk fabric marker to draw the nose of the rocket to line up with the section on the front. Paint the rocket and stars as before.

Paint the Solar System

Imagine how impressed your teacher would be if you painted the Solar System on to your Space Trekker T-shirt. You know that the Earth looks like a green and blue ball from Outer Space, but do you know what the other eight planets look like? To find out about Mercury, Venus, Mars, Jupiter, Saturn, Uranus, Neptune and Pluto, find some pictures in a reference book.

Muddy Puppy

Oh, no! Someone has let the puppy walk all over this T-shirt with its muddy paws! Surely such a naughty puppy does not deserve to be given a big, juicy bone! To stop the puppy covering everything with mud, it has been given a fancy pair of socks to wear.

This boy just cannot believe what the Muddy Puppy has done to his white T-shirt. To find out for yourself, look on the next page.

YOU WILL NEED THESE MATERIALS AND TOOLS

Short sleeved T-shirt

2 sheets of card

Scissors

Pot of water

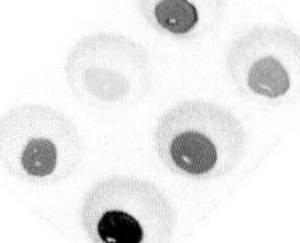

Fabric paint (brown, black, white, turquoise, red, pale blue, yellow)

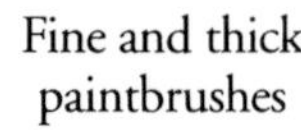

Fine and thick paintbrushes

Fabric marker pen

Pencil

Fabric glue and brush

Tracing paper

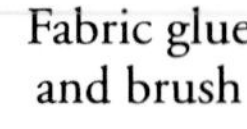

Sponge

Narrow yellow ribbon

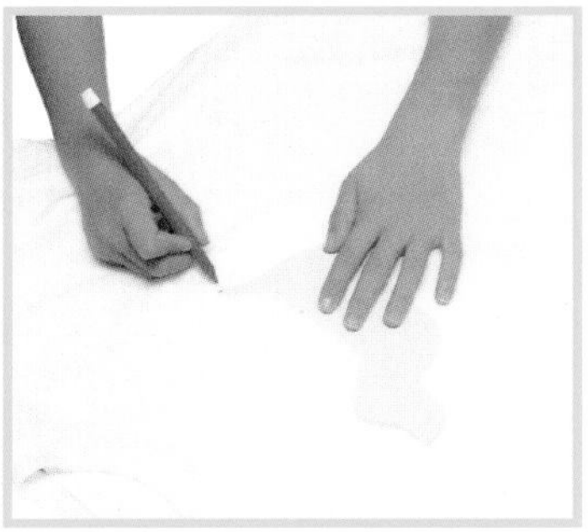

1 Insert card inside the T-shirt body and sleeves. Trace the puppy template in the Introduction. Place the template on to the front of the T-shirt. Draw around it with the fabric marker pen.

2 Paint the dog brown using the thick brush. If you do not have brown paint, make some by mixing together blue, red and yellow. Allow to dry before starting the next step.

3 Use the fine brush to paint black spots on to the body. Continue using the black paint for the ear, tail, shoes and bone. Add features to the face and decorate the socks, shoes and collar.

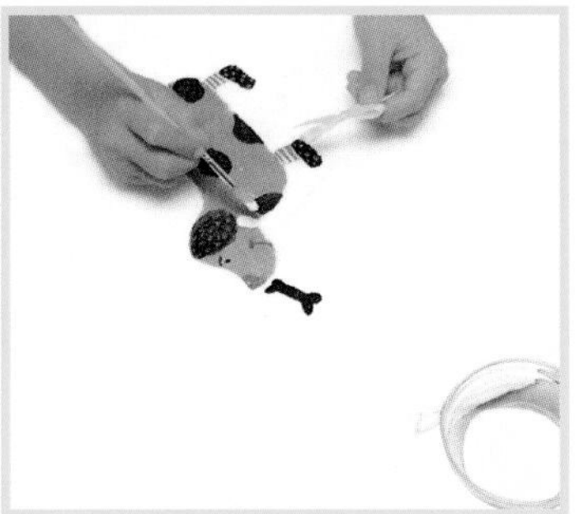

4 When the paint is dry, tie the ribbon into a small bow. Fix the bow on to the collar with fabric glue. Hold the bow in position until the glue is dry.

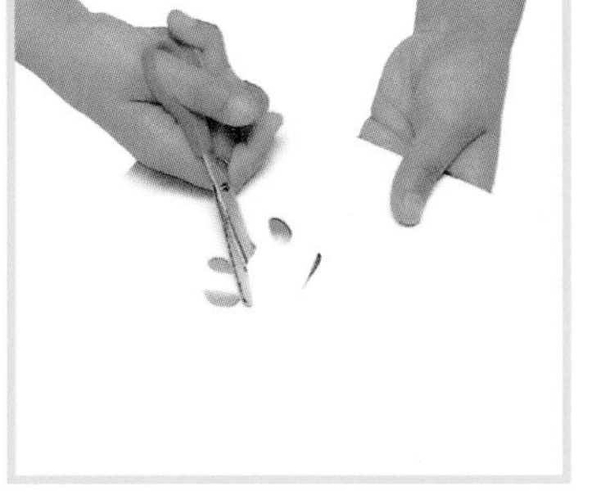

5 Trace the paw print stencil in the Introduction. Cut out the stencil, as shown. Turn the T-shirt over, checking that the pieces of card are still in position.

6 Hold the stencil on the T-shirt. Dab the stencil with brown fabric paint. Lift off the stencil. Repeat until the back of the T-shirt is covered with prints.

Stencilling is an easy way to create a repeat pattern. Look through magazines and books to find ideas for other stencils. You could use this same simple technique to cover a T-shirt with cars, flowers, aeroplanes, hearts, stars or even lots and lots of muddy puppies!

Birthday Present

Why not make this T-shirt as a birthday gift for a friend? They could wear it to their own party! It is important that the painted ribbon is identical to the real ribbon. To achieve this, you may have to mix fabric paints together to make the right colour.

YOU WILL NEED THESE MATERIALS AND TOOLS

Large sheet of card

Ruler

Short sleeved T-shirt

Fabric marker pen

Scissors

Fabric paint (green, white, pink)

Pot of water

50cm (20in) of wide, green ribbon

Sewing needle and sewing thread

Medium and thick paintbrushes

As a special treat you could use green, red and gold to paint a Christmas version of the Birthday Present T-shirt. In place of the spotty green ribbon, use a glittery gold ribbon. The dots on the T-shirt could become bunches of holly.

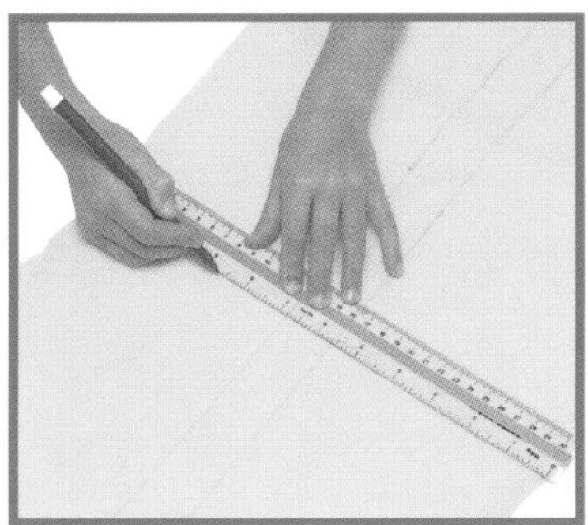

1 Insert pieces of card inside the body and sleeves of the T-shirt. Use the ruler and fabric marker pen to draw two parallel lines down the centre of the T-shirt and two parallel lines across the T-shirt.

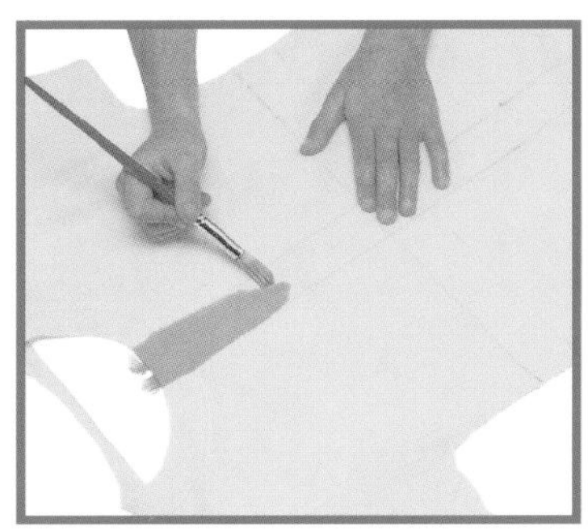

2 Paint the area inside the lines with green fabric paint. Do this with the thick brush. These are the pretend ribbons on the present. Make the edges of the ribbon as straight as possible. Allow to dry.

3 Use the medium brush to decorate the painted ribbon with small dots of white fabric paint. Wash and dry the brush before changing fabric paint colours. Cover the rest of the T-shirt with larger pink dots. Allow to dry.

4 Cut a V-shape from both ends of the ribbon to give a neat finish to the birthday present bow.

5 Tie the ribbon into a bow. Thread the needle and tie a knot in the end. Position the bow where the painted ribbons cross and sew it into place.

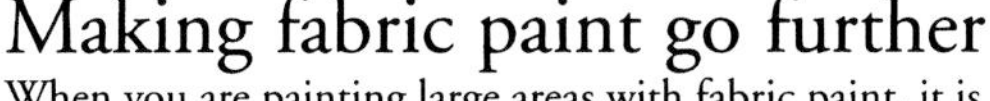

Making fabric paint go further

When you are painting large areas with fabric paint, it is a good idea to add a little water to the fabric paint. This will make your fabric paints last longer and make them easier to apply. It will also make the colour slightly lighter and may take longer to dry. The more water you add, the lighter the colour will become. Do not make the fabric paint too runny or it will drip all over the place.

Hungry Cat

This hungry cat is dreaming of a seafood feast. If the dream does not come true, the cat's contented purr will become a moaning miaow. Does the cat get its wish? Look at the back of the T-shirt to find out...

YOU WILL NEED THESE MATERIALS AND TOOLS

- 2 sheets of card
- Pencil
- Scissors
- Pot of water
- Short sleeved T-shirt
- Fabric marker pen
- Sponge
- Medium and thick paintbrushes
- Embroidery needle
- Black embroidery thread
- Tracing paper
- Fabric paint (blue, white, black, red, yellow, orange, pink)

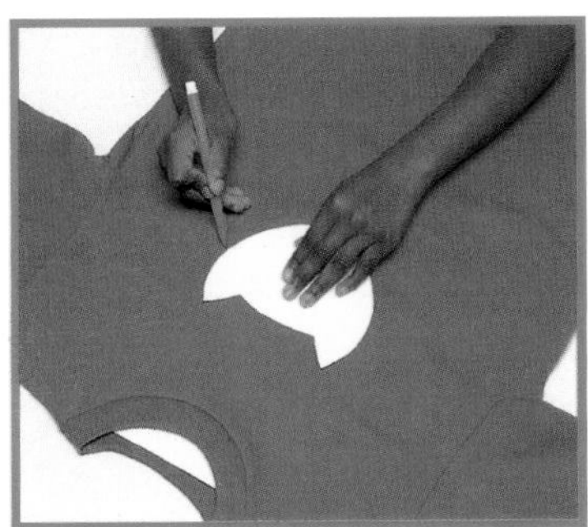

1 Insert a piece of card inside the body of the T-shirt. Make a cat template, like the one shown here. Place the template on to the front of the T-shirt and draw around it with the fabric marker pen.

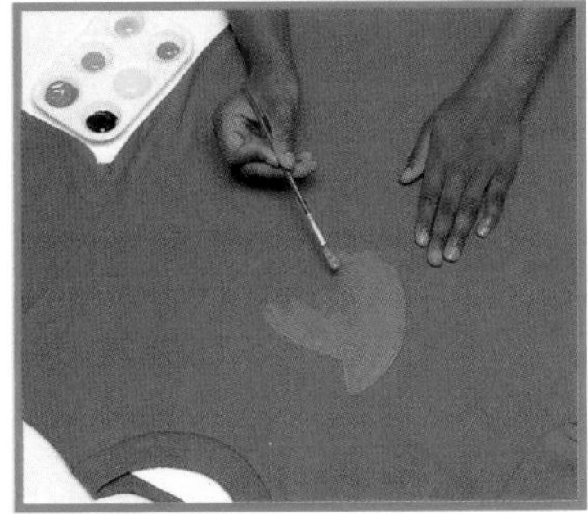

2 Use the thick brush to paint the cat's face with blue-grey fabric paint. To make this colour, mix blue, white and black fabric paints. Add more white to this colour to paint the cat's markings on to its face.

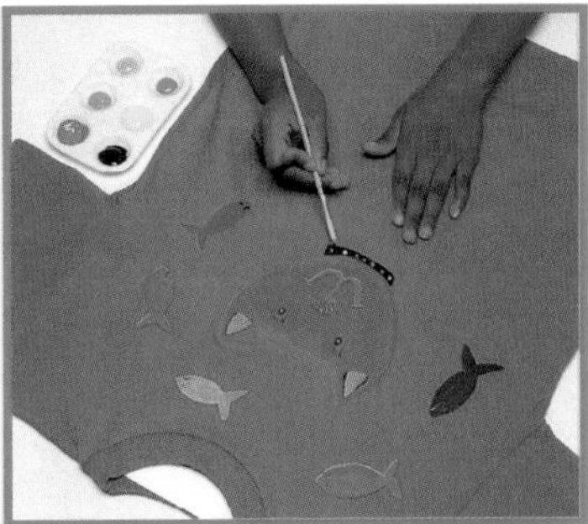

3 Draw five fish using the fabric marker pen. Paint the fish different colours. This hungry cat is dreaming of its fishy lunch, so give it a happy and contented face. Paint and decorate the cat's fancy collar.

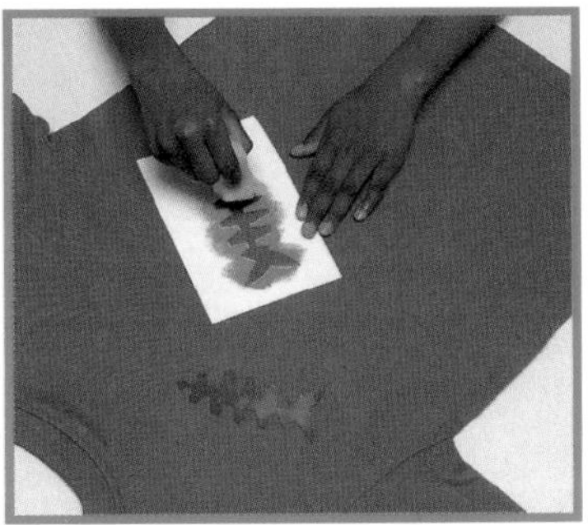

4 Make the stencil for the fish skeleton, as shown here. When the fabric paint is dry, turn the T-shirt over. Place the stencil on to the back of the T-shirt and dab it with a sponge dipped in red fabric paint. Lift off the stencil. Stencil on four more fish skeletons in different colours.

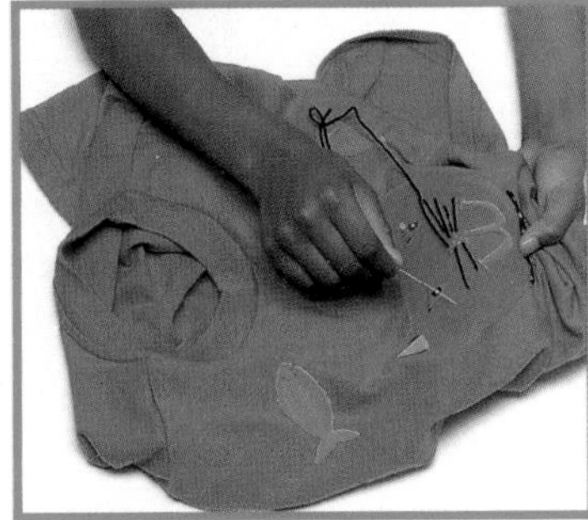

5 When the fabric paint is dry, remove the card and turn the T-shirt over again. Thread the needle with black embroidery thread and tie a knot at the end. Sew four long stitches on either side of the cat's nose to make whiskers.

...oh dear, poor little fish! The cat has been satisfied – for the time being.

Friendship Bracelets

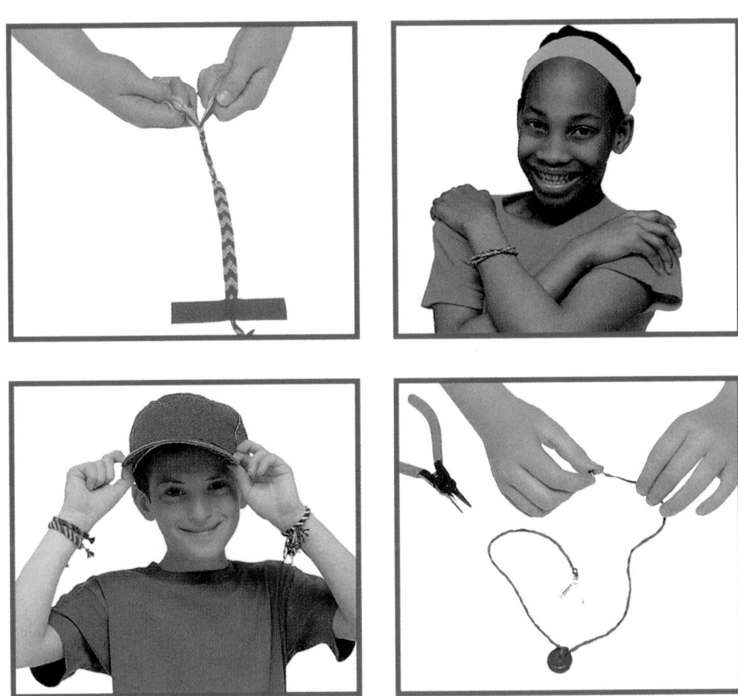

Introduction

Friendship bracelets are a symbol of friendship, which is why they make such fun presents for your friends and family. You could make matching friendship bracelets for you and your best pal, or weave a bracelet, anklet or necklace using the colours of your favourite sports team. But there is one more good thing about friendship bracelets – anyone can wear them – teenagers, young children and even adults!

Make them anywhere

Braiding and weaving friendship bracelets can be done anywhere – outside in the garden, on holidays, at the kitchen table or at friends' houses. You do not need to carry around big bags of equipment – all you need are threads, tape, scissors, beads and a smooth work surface. This means that friendship bracelets are also very inexpensive to make.

It is a good idea to store your braiding materials in a bag or small box. This will keep everything clean and ready for when you want to have a bit of fun.

This Hippy Headband is made using the same braiding techniques that are used to make friendship bracelets.

Practice makes perfect

Some of the bracelet designs we show you are quite complicated. They may use many threads, and the knotting and braiding techniques may be a little fiddly. But there are also many designs that even novice braiders will be able to perfect first time.

If you are having trouble making a particular bracelet, do not give up – try again after reading the instructions through and looking closely at the photographs. Your patience will be rewarded when you wear your own hand-made bracelet and all your friends want to know where you bought it!

Experiment with colours

Once you have the knack of braiding and beading, let your imagination run wild and design your very own range of jewellery and accessories. You will soon be experimenting with your own combinations of colours and adding beads and decorations to your bracelets. You will also discover lots of new and exciting threads that will add unusual textures to your designs.

It is very easy to knot colourful beads into friendship bracelets and necklaces.

Materials

These are the materials and tools you will need to complete the following projects.

Beads These come in a wide variety of different sizes, colours, textures and patterns. Tiny or small beads usually have very small holes, so it is easier to thread them on to fine sewing thread, or to sew them on to items using needle and thread. Medium and large size beads are perfect for using with thicker yarns. Metallic beads are shiny and add an extra sparkle to your handiwork.
Cotton knitting yarn This type of yarn is very chunky. Use cotton knitting yarn when you want to make a thick bracelet or anklet. It is available in many bright colours.
Electrical tape This is a strong sticky tape. It is very good for fastening threads to a work surface. You can buy it from electrical and hardware shops.
Hair clip This hair accessory has a metal clip that grips the hair. The top of the hair clip is made of plastic.
Jewellery clamp A jewellery clamp can be fastened over the knot at each end of a friendship cord to finish it off. Jewellery fasteners can be attached to clamps.
Jewellery fastener This is a releasable metal clasp that can be used to secure a bracelet or necklace.
Metal rings These small metal loops are used to attach jewellery fasteners to jewellery clamps.
Pliers Use small jewellery pliers or fine-nosed pliers to open and close metal rings and to secure jewellery clamps. Many types of pliers have a cutting edge, so always ask for adult help when you use pliers.
Soft embroidery thread This is a thick thread that is ideal for friendship bracelets. It comes in many vibrant colours.
Stranded embroidery thread As its name suggests, this cotton thread is made up of many strands. It is very good for making patterned and knotted friendship bracelets.
Sunglasses attachments These rubber loops are used to attach sunglasses to a strap. Buy them from specialist bead shops.

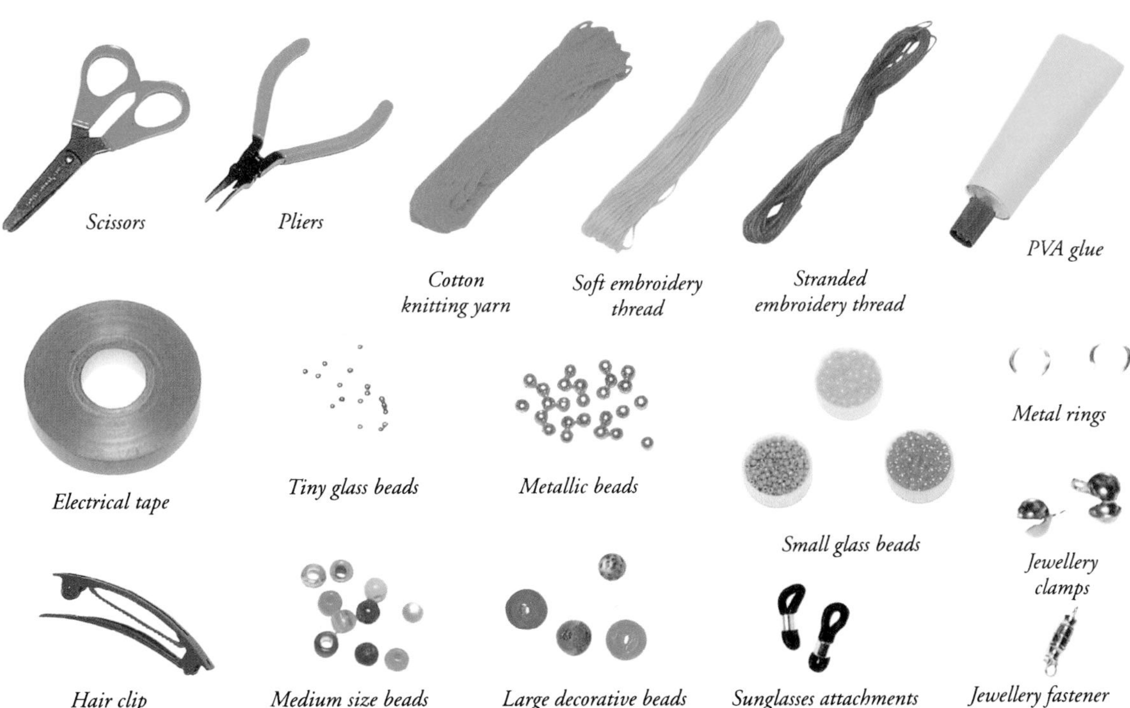

Scissors *Pliers* *Cotton knitting yarn* *Soft embroidery thread* *Stranded embroidery thread* *PVA glue*

Electrical tape *Tiny glass beads* *Metallic beads* *Small glass beads* *Metal rings* *Jewellery clamps*

Hair clip *Medium size beads* *Large decorative beads* *Sunglasses attachments* *Jewellery fastener*

Basic Techniques

Starting off

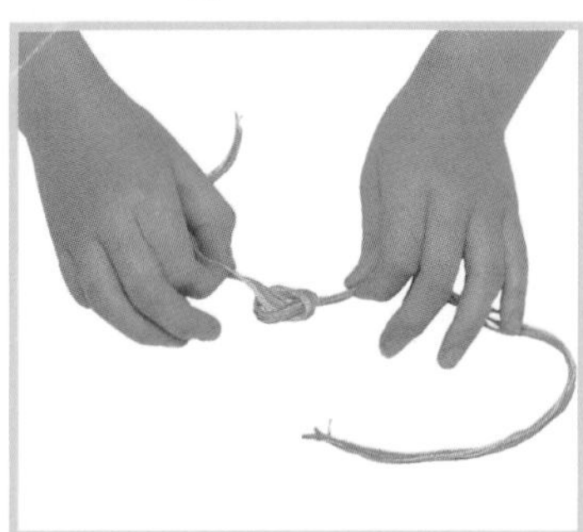

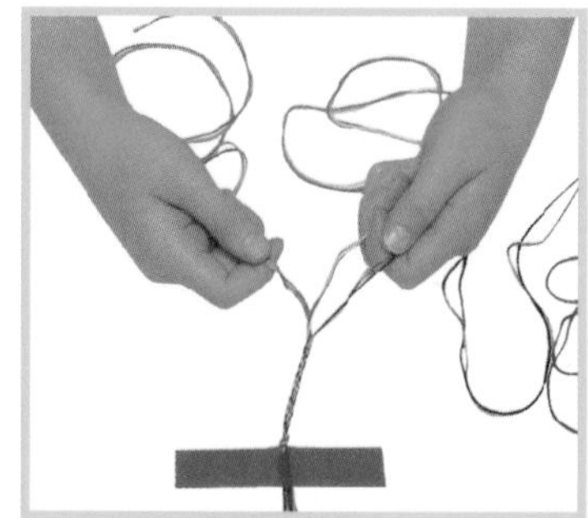

1 Cut the threads to the required length. Check that you are using the right type of thread and have the correct number of threads in each colour. Gather the threads and line up the ends. Tie the threads together with a knot near one end. Each project will tell you exactly where to tie the knot.

2 Secure the threads to your work surface using a piece of electrical tape just above the knot. Press the tape firmly over the threads so that the threads do not come lose. A breadboard, laminated tray or piece of stiff card make excellent portable surfaces on which to do your braiding.

3 Some projects will then ask you to plait a 5cm (2in) length before you start braiding. Try to keep an even pressure on the threads when plaiting so that it remains straight. Secure the end of the plaited section to your work surface with electrical tape. Press the tape firmly over the plait.

Finishing off

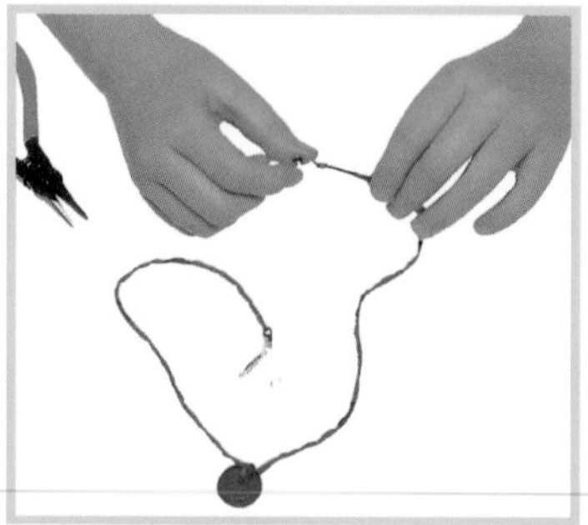

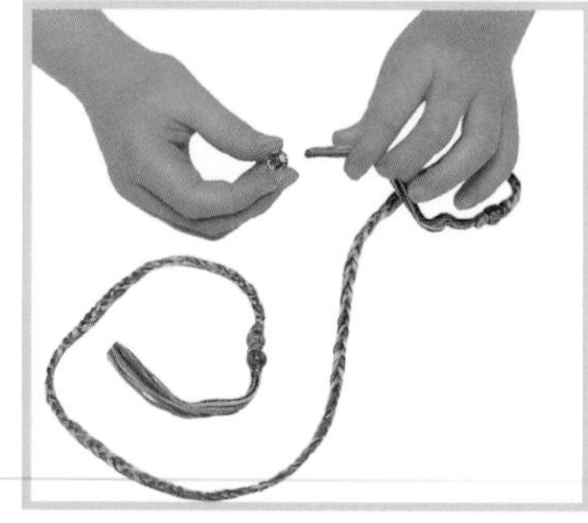

To finish a bracelet - divide the threads at the end of the braid into three even groups and plait together. This plait should be the same length as the one at the other end of the bracelet. Tie a knot at the end of the plait before threading on beads. Keep the beads in place with another tight knot. Trim the threads.

To finish a necklace - tie a tight knot at the end of the braid. Use pliers to close a jewellery clamp over the knots at both ends of the braid. Open the metal rings using pliers and attach a metal ring to each clamp. Separate the sections of the jewellery fastener and attach one section to each ring. Close the rings.

To finish a headband - tie a tight knot close to the end of the braid and thread beads on. You can thread beads on to each thread or use a large bead through which all the threads will pass. To hold the beads in place, tie another knot. The knot must be large enough to stop the bead falling off.

Tying off

Tying on a bracelet - ask a friend to help tie a double knot. If there is no one around to help, you could tie the bracelet around your ankle instead.

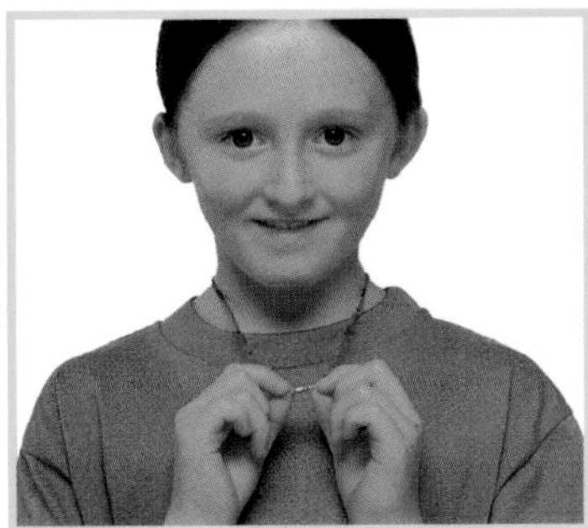

Fastening a necklace - place the necklace around your neck with the opened fasteners at the front. To line up the clasps, look in a mirror.

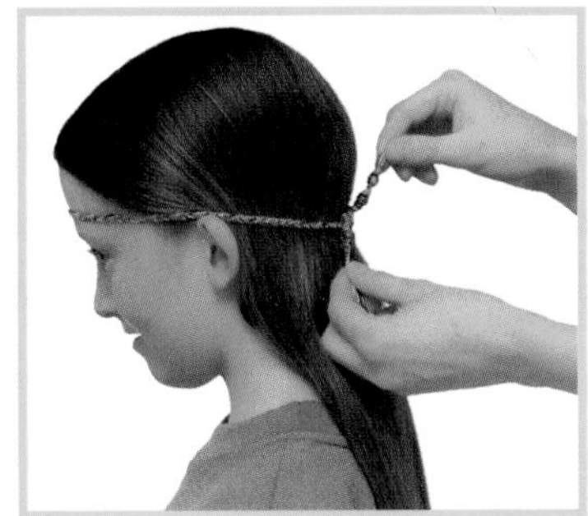

Tying on a headband - if you cannot do it yourself, ask a friend to tie the ends in a double knot or in a bow at the back of your head.

Braiding tips

The first thing you must do before starting a friendship bracelet design is to carefully read through the instructions and look at the photographs. The second thing to do is make sure you have the right thread and have carefully measured out the lengths needed. Double-check that you have the right number of threads in the right colours.

If you are doing a complicated design it can help to use the same coloured threads as used in the project. Then, when you have mastered that braiding technique, you can go on to make the bracelet, necklace or anklet using your own wonderful colour combinations.

To give your bracelets the professional look, try to keep the tension on the threads even. An uneven tension will make the bracelet twist and buckle.

Using your imagination

The colours and beading ideas used in these projects are just to get you started. There is really no end to the sorts of things you can do to make your friendship bracelets totally unique. Here are some ideas that you might like to try.

❖ Tightly knot together leftover lengths of thread and trim excess threads. When you braid with these multi-coloured threads you will create a bracelet of many colours. These lengths of thread are also useful when trying out a new braiding technique.

❖ Beads with very small holes, buttons and sequins can be sewn on to a completed bracelet using ordinary sewing needle and sewing thread.

❖ Use textured or glittery threads in your designs.

Looking after your materials

❖ To keep your leftover threads in order, wind them around rectangles of thick card. To stop them unravelling, insert the thread ends into a small slot cut into one edge of the card.

❖ To keep your scissors sharp, do not use them to cut paper.

❖ Store your beads and jewellery equipment in lidded containers. This will stop you losing them and, more importantly, will keep them out of reach of young children.

Twisty Bracelet

This bracelet is almost like mixing a palette of coloured paints. But instead of using paints, you are twisting threads together to make new colours.

YOU WILL NEED THESE MATERIALS

Stranded embroidery thread

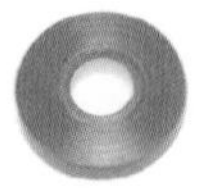

Electrical tape

Scissors

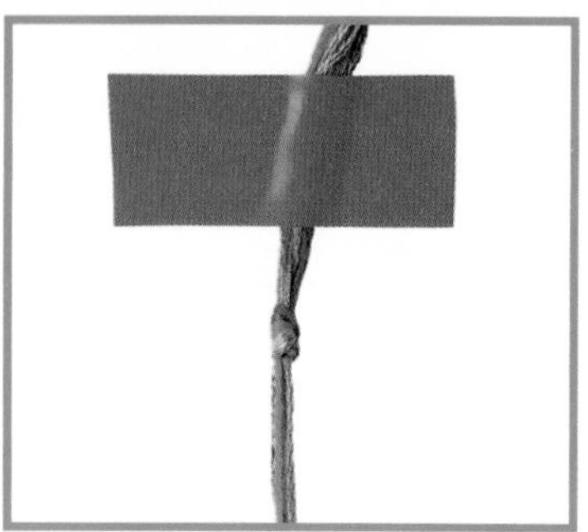

1 You will need six threads of different colours, each 70cm (27in) long. Tie them in a knot, 10cm (4in) from the top of the threads. Fasten them on to your work surface with electrical tape just above the knot.

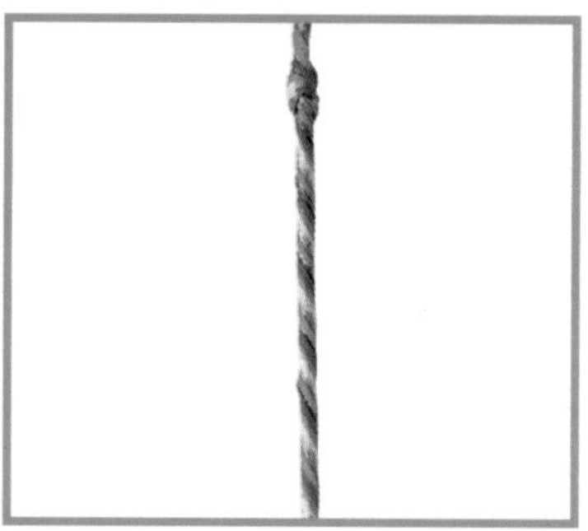

2 Hold the ends of the threads together and twist them together in the same direction until they feel tight. The threads will start to get shorter.

3 Pull the twisted length straight and place your finger in the centre of it. Fold the twisted length in half and carefully remove your finger. As you do this, the twisted threads will wind around each other.

Handy hint

Be sure to hold on tightly to the twisted braid. If you let go before you have secured it with a knot, the twist will unwind.

4 Remove the electrical tape and tie a knot in the free end. Tie this knot as close to the end as possible. Trim any uneven threads with scissors. To fasten the bracelet around your wrist or ankle, push the knot through the loop at the other end.

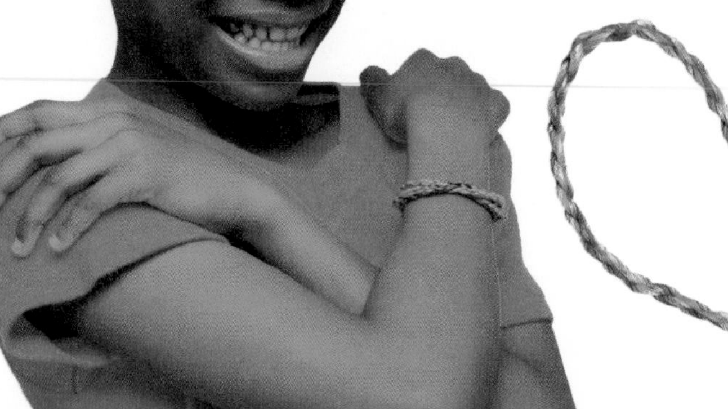

Hippy Headband

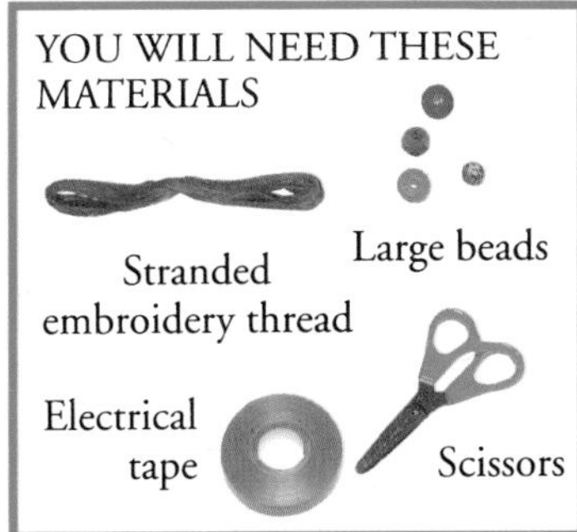

Dress up as a happy hippy and wear this colourful band around your head. The more threads you use, the wider the plait will be. Why not make a bracelet to match?

1 Cut 12 lengths of thread, each 150cm (60in) long. Tie them in a knot 15cm (6in) from the top of the threads and fasten them on to your work surface with a piece of tape just above the knot.

2 Divide the threads into three groups, each with four threads. Continue plaiting the threads until the band is long enough to fit around your head. Try to keep the tension on the threads even or the plait will twist.

3 Tie the threads at the end of the plait in a knot. Remove the tape.

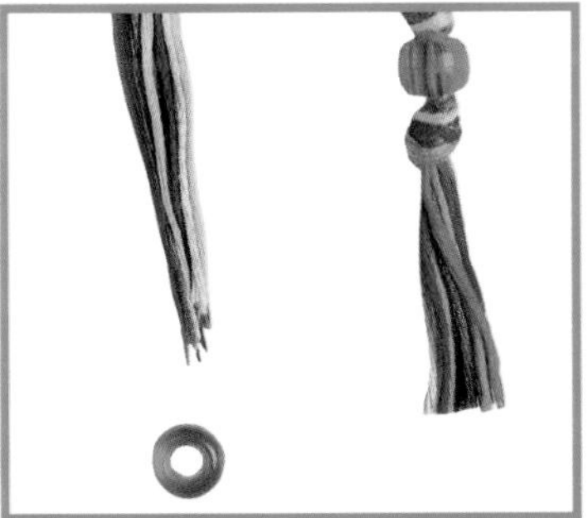

4 Thread beads on to both ends of the headband and secure with knots. Thread another bead on to each end and tie another knot. Trim any uneven threads. To make a bracelet to match, cut 12 threads, each 40cm (16in) long. Then follow steps 1 to 4.

To make it easy to thread the beads on to your headband, wrap a little tape around the end of the threads. This will keep the threads together and stop them from fraying.

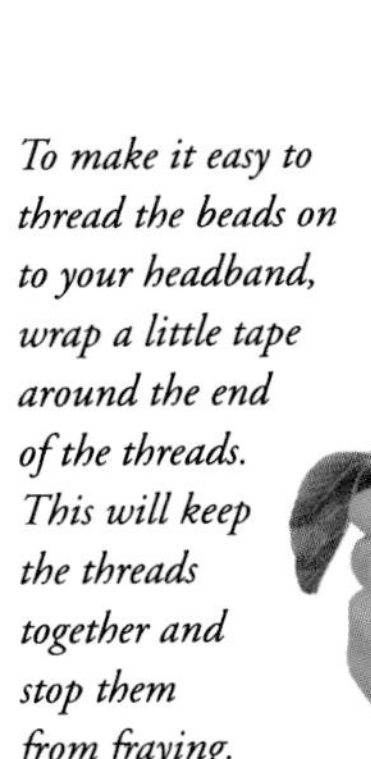

Jungle Bracelet

This bracelet is inspired by the colours you would see on an African safari. So when choosing your threads, look out for brown, ochre and yellow. You could choose your own theme, such as a rainbow, a sunset or a season, and select colours to co-ordinate with that theme.

YOU WILL NEED THESE MATERIALS

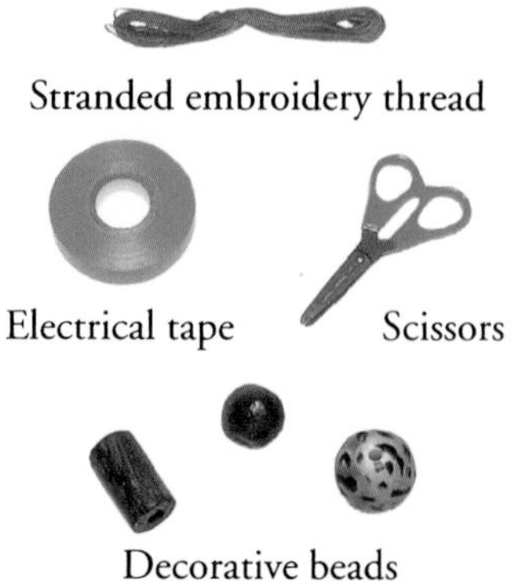

Stranded embroidery thread

Electrical tape

Scissors

Decorative beads

1 Cut three threads of one colour and two of another, each 100cm (40in) long. Tie the threads in a knot, 15cm (6in) from the top. Fasten the threads to the work surface with tape just above the knot. Lay out the threads, as shown.

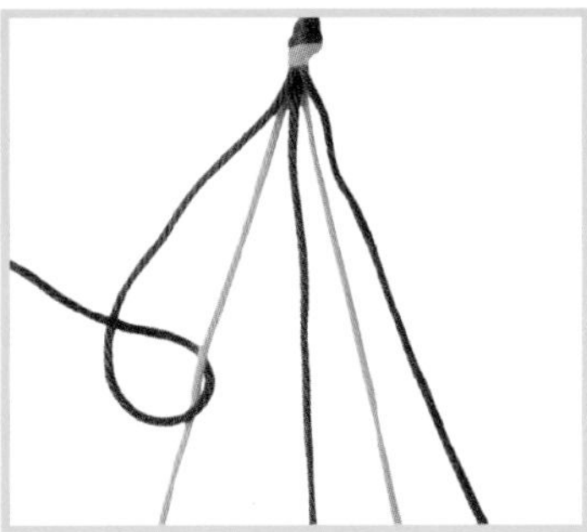

2 Start with the thread on the far left (in this project it is a brown thread). Take this thread over the orange thread on the right, back under the orange thread, through the loop and over itself. Pull gently to make a knot and repeat.

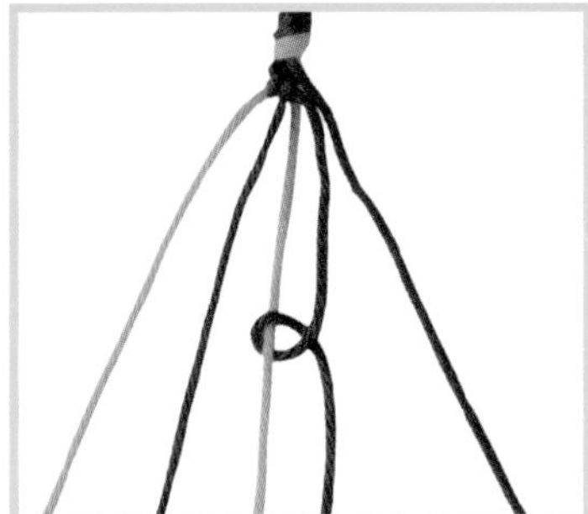

3 Continue the same knotting technique as shown in step 2, making two knots on each of the remaining threads on the right, until you get to the end of the first row. The brown thread will finish on the right.

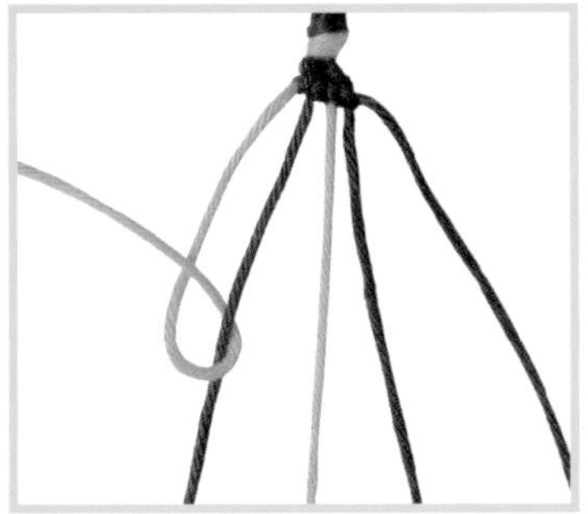

4 Take the new thread on the far left (an orange thread) and make a new row of knots as shown in steps 2 and 3.

5 Continue knotting the bracelet until it is the right length to fit around your wrist or ankle. Tie the threads in a knot to secure the braid.

Easy way to learn

If you have never made friendship bracelets before it may help if you use the same colour threads as used in the photographs. This will make it much easier for you to follow the steps and use the correct threads. When you have mastered a braiding technique, then you can go on to create one using your favourite colours.

6 Plait the loose threads for 5cm (2in) and tie the end of the plait in a knot. Thread a bead on to each thread. Secure each bead with a knot.

These Jungle Bracelets have been made using different colour combinations.

Woven Bracelet

YOU WILL NEED THESE MATERIALS

Cotton knitting yarn

Electrical tape

Scissors

This popular style of friendship bracelet uses a very easy weaving technique. If you want to make a really wide bracelet, weave two bracelets and then sew them together using embroidery thread and needle.

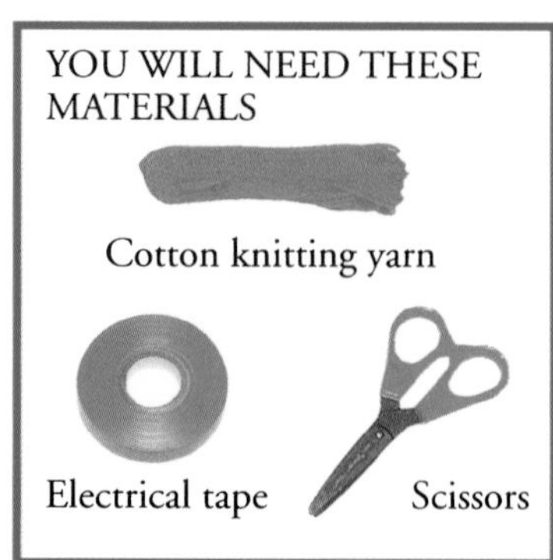

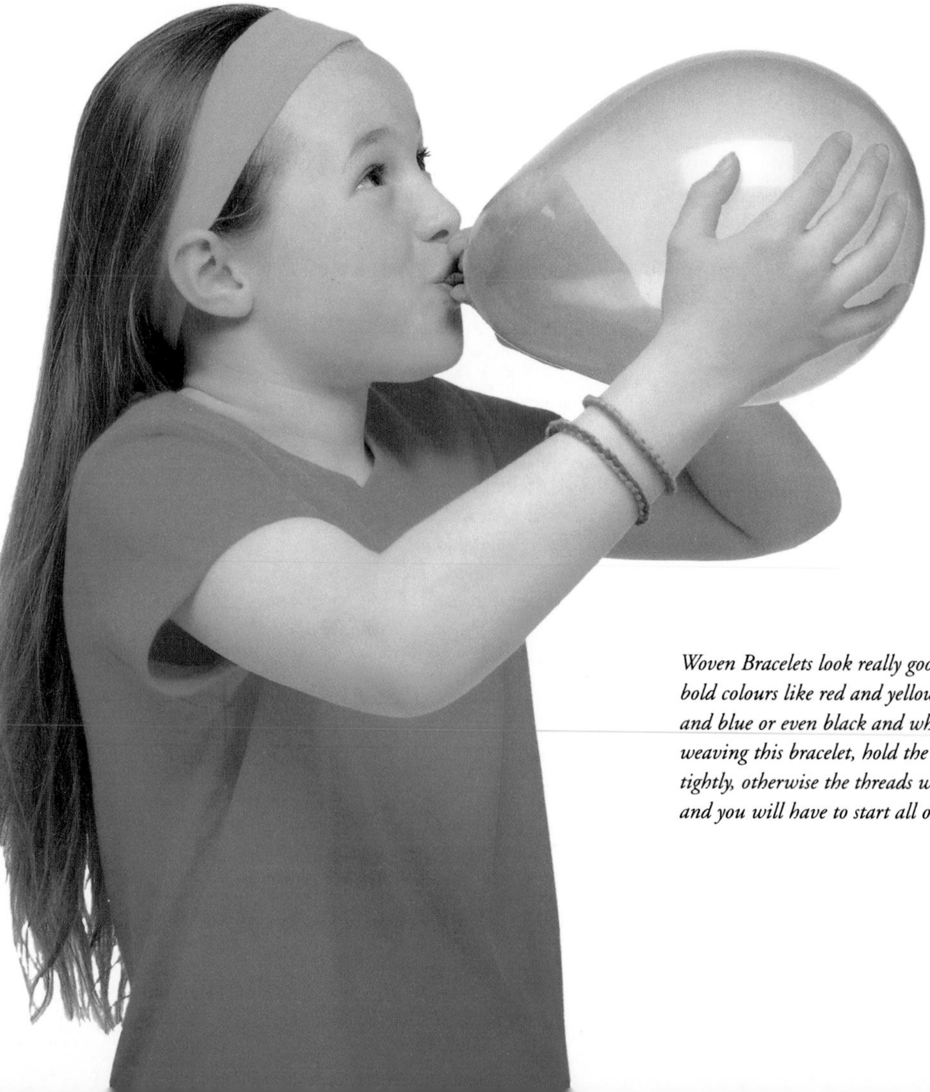

Woven Bracelets look really good in strong, bold colours like red and yellow, purple and blue or even black and white. When weaving this bracelet, hold the threads tightly, otherwise the threads will unwind and you will have to start all over again!

1 Cut two threads in one colour and two in another, each 80cm (31in) long. Fold them in half and tie the ends by the fold in a knot, 5cm (2in) from the top. Fasten the threads to your work surface with tape close to the knot. Arrange the threads in colour pairs.

2 Start with the far right pair of threads (in this project they are blue) and take them under the blue pair and purple pair next to them, then back over the purple pair. Leave them in the middle, as shown.

3 Take the pair of purple threads on the far left that you have not used yet. Take these threads under the purple and blue pairs next to them, then back over the blue pair. Leave the purple pair in the middle.

4 Pull the pairs of threads up tightly to the top. Then go back to the blue pair of threads on the far right and repeat steps 2 and 3 until the bracelet is long enough to fit around your wrist.

5 Tie the threads in a knot at the end of the weaving. Snip the looped threads at the top of the braid. You can leave the ends as they are or plait them.

Woven belt

If you have lots of patience and reams of chunky cotton yard or knitting wool you can make a woven belt. Take your waist measurement and cut lengths of yarn that are three times the size of your waist measurement. If you want long lengths of loose threads at the ends, cut them a little longer. Make your woven belt following the instructions for Woven Bracelet.

Funky Bracelet

This chunky bracelet uses ten strands of knitting yarn. You have to hold the threads firmly, or the weaving will be uneven.

YOU WILL NEED THESE MATERIALS

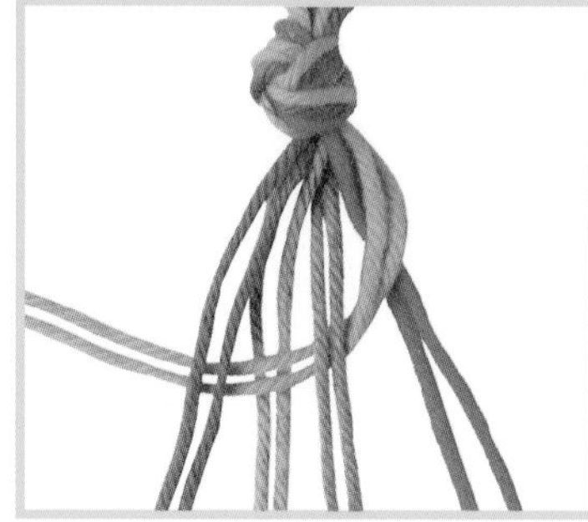

1 Cut five different coloured threads, each 80cm (32in) long. Fold the threads in half and tie in a knot, 5cm (2in) from the fold. Fasten the threads to your work surface with tape above the knot. Lay the threads out as shown.

2 Start with the far right pair of threads (in this project they are yellow) and weave them over the pink pair, under the blue pair, over the green pair and under the purple pair. Pull the yellow threads up tightly and leave on the left.

3 Take the pink pair and weave them over the blue pair, under the green pair, over the purple pair and under the yellow pair. Pull the pink threads up tightly and leave on the left.

4 Repeat steps 2 and 3 with each new pair of threads on the far right, until the braid is the right length. Tie the end in a knot and cut the top loop.

To make a Funky Bracelet or anklet for a special occasion, you could replace two coloured threads with glittery gold and silver threads.

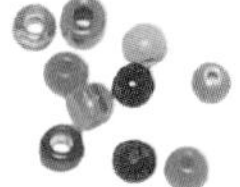

Hair Wrap

These braids look great! Take it in turns with a friend to do each other's hair. Finish off the braid with two beads tied on to the end.

YOU WILL NEED THESE MATERIALS

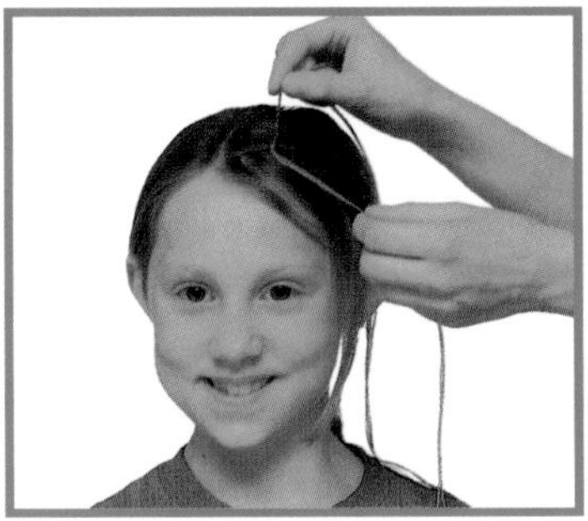

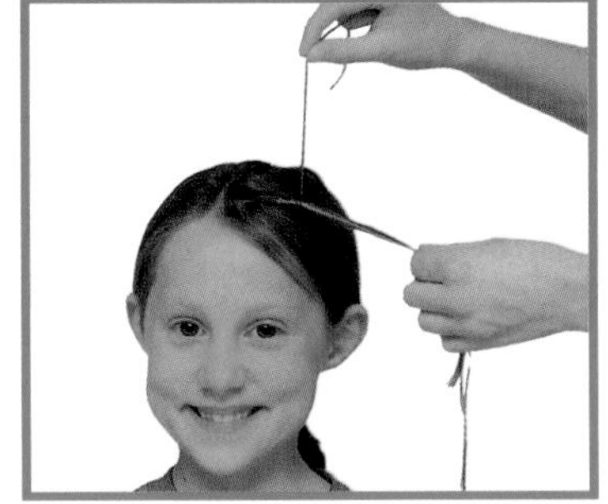

1 Cut three lengths of different coloured thread, twice the length of the hair you are braiding. Take a 1cm (1/2in) section of hair and knot the centre of the threads around the hair, close to the scalp.

2 Hold the section of hair away from the head. Select one of the coloured threads and start winding it tightly around the hair and the other threads. The loops of thread should lie very close together.

3 When you have wound as much as you want of the first colour, start winding a thread of another colour in the same way. Keep alternating the colours until you reach the end of the hair.

4 To finish off, thread a few beads on to the end of the hair and tie a knot in the thread to stop the beads falling off. Knot the threads around the hair to stop the wrap unravelling. When you want to remove the wrap, cut off the knot and beads at the end of the wrap and unwind the threads.

Stripes Galore Bracelet

Handy hint

This bracelet consists of wide stripes in three colours, but you can also braid it using six threads of different colours. The stripes will be narrower, but your bracelet will be much more colourful. To make this really stripy bracelet, choose six threads of contrasting colours and follow the instructions in steps 1 to 6.

This is one of the most popular styles of friendship bracelet and, if you are a beginner, it is a good one to start with. The more threads you have, the wider the bracelet will be. The more colours you use, the brighter it will be.

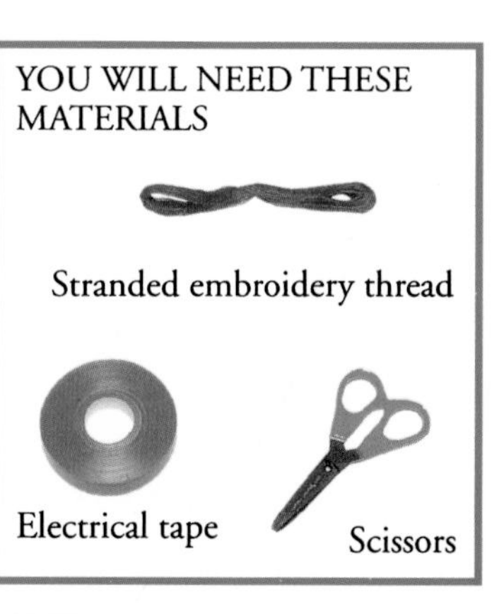

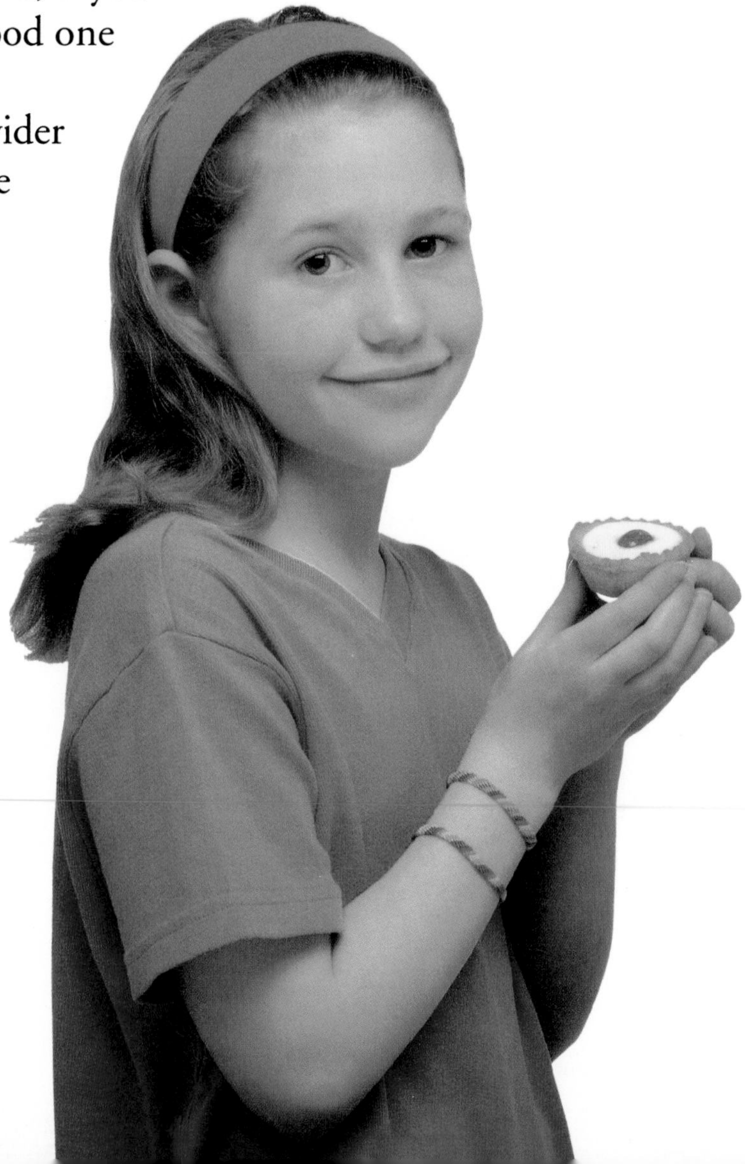

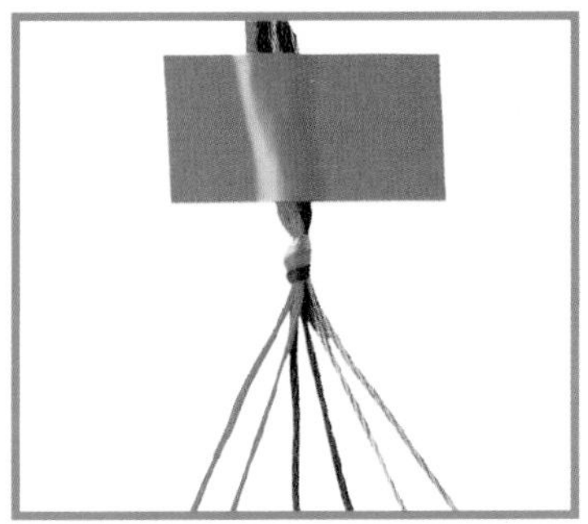

1 Cut six threads, two of each colour and each 100cm (40in) long. Knot them together, 10cm (4in) from the top of the threads. Fasten the threads to your work surface with tape, close to the knot. Lay the threads out as shown.

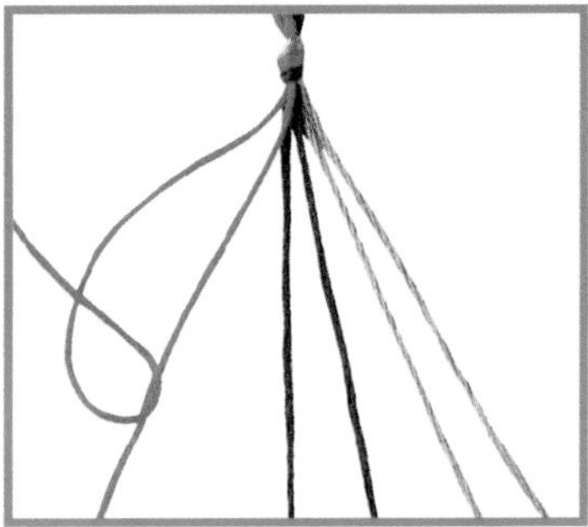

2 Start with the thread on the far left (in this project it is a pink thread). Take the thread over the pink thread next to it, then back under the pink thread, through the loop and over itself. Pull the thread gently to make a knot.

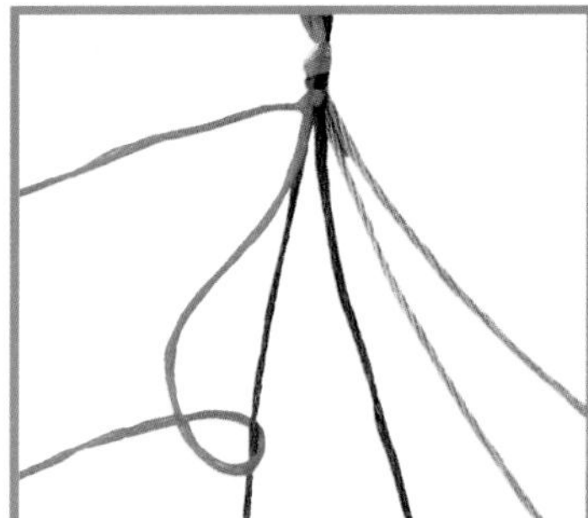

3 Repeat step 2. Still using the same thread, make two knots on the purple thread. Continue to knot the remaining purple and green threads with the pink thread in the same way until you reach the end of the first row.

4 Go back to the new thread on the far left, which is another pink thread, and repeat steps 2 and 3 to make another row. Now the new thread on the far left will be a purple thread. Knot it in the same way.

5 Continue knotting each new far left thread over the other threads to build up stripes of the three different colours. Keep braiding until the bracelet is the right length to fit around your wrist or ankle.

6 Tie the threads at the end of the braid in a knot. Plait the loose threads at both ends of the bracelet for 6cm (2½in) and secure the plaits with knots. Carefully trim any uneven threads with scissors.

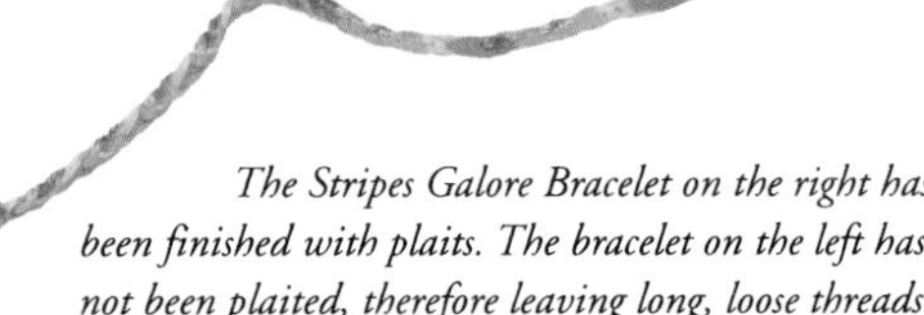

The Stripes Galore Bracelet on the right has been finished with plaits. The bracelet on the left has not been plaited, therefore leaving long, loose threads.

Stripes and Beads Bracelet

This bracelet has beads threaded into it to add extra sparkle, colour and texture. Use small or medium size beads, but make sure the hole of each bead is large enough for the thread to fit through.

Handy hint

It is a good idea to sort out which beads you are going to use before you start braiding the bracelet. It is hard enough keeping hold of the right threads without having to fumble around in a jar of beads at the same time.

YOU WILL NEED THESE MATERIALS

Soft embroidery thread

Electrical tape

Scissors

Small and medium beads

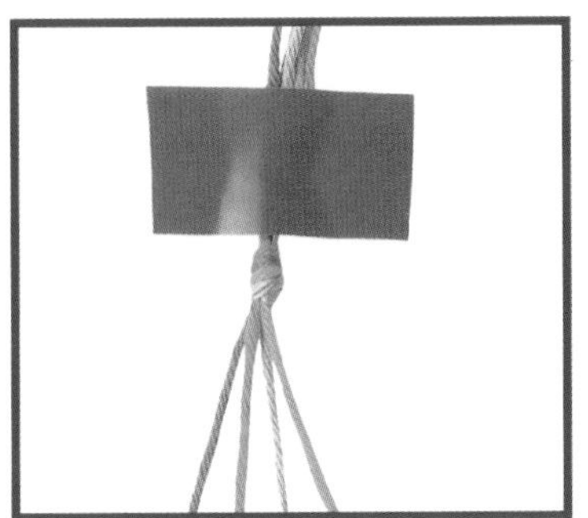

1 You will need four threads 100cm (40in) long. Tie the threads in a knot, 10cm (4in) from one end. Fasten them to the work surface with tape above the knot. Lay threads as shown.

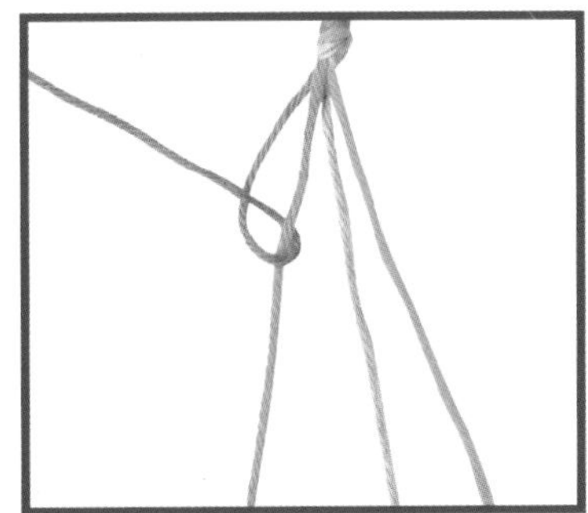

2 Take the thread on the left (a purple thread) over the pink thread next to it and back under, through the loop and over itself. Pull the thread to make a knot. Repeat to make another knot.

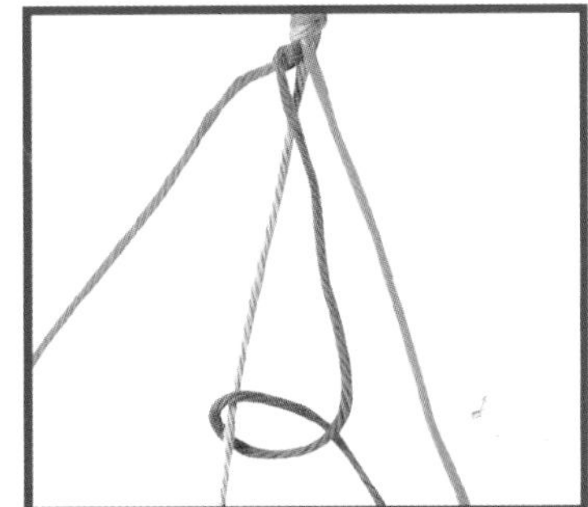

3 Make the same knots on the blue and the orange threads using the purple thread. You will now have finished the first row and the purple thread should be on the right.

4 Go back to the new thread on the left (a pink thread) and thread a bead on to it. Knot the pink thread following steps 2 and 3.

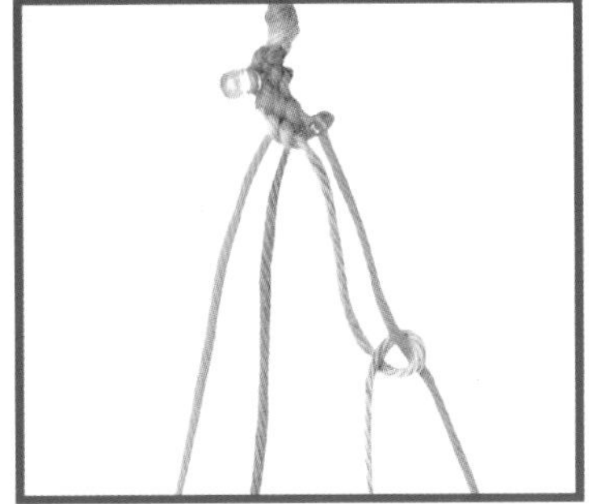

5 Go back to the new colour on the left (a blue thread). Knot this thread over the first two threads (orange and purple) and, before you knot it over the pink, thread a bead on to the pink thread and then knot the blue thread over it. This knot will secure the bead.

Fraying threads

The ends of the threads become quite ragged when threaded through beads. To prevent this, wrap a small piece of sticky tape around the ends of each thread before you start braiding.

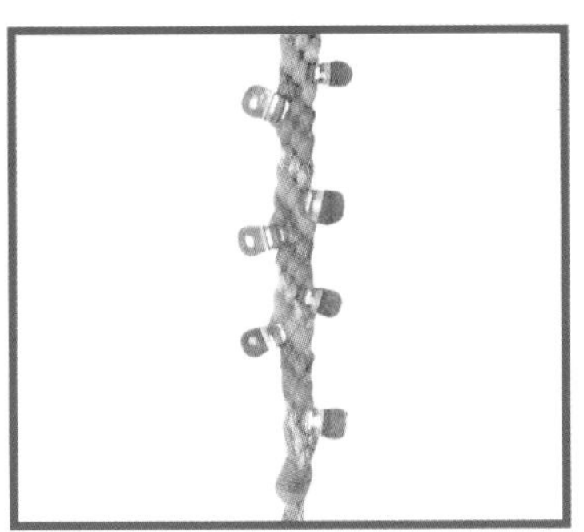

6 Continue to knot and thread on beads until the bracelet is the right length. Tie the threads in a knot.

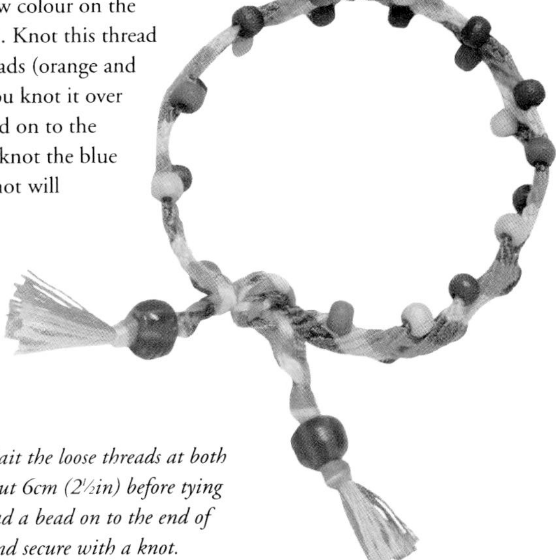

To finish, plait the loose threads at both ends for about 6cm (2½in) before tying knots. Thread a bead on to the end of each plait and secure with a knot.

Noughts and Crosses

The Noughts and Crosses bracelet will really impress your friends! It looks terrific in black and white, but could also be braided using the colours of your favourite football team.

YOU WILL NEED THESE MATERIALS

- Soft embroidery thread
- Electrical tape
- Scissors

1 You will need eight pieces of thread in two colours, each 100cm (40in) long. Tie the threads in a knot and plait them for 5cm (2in). Fasten the threads to the work surface with tape at the end of the plait. Lay out threads as shown.

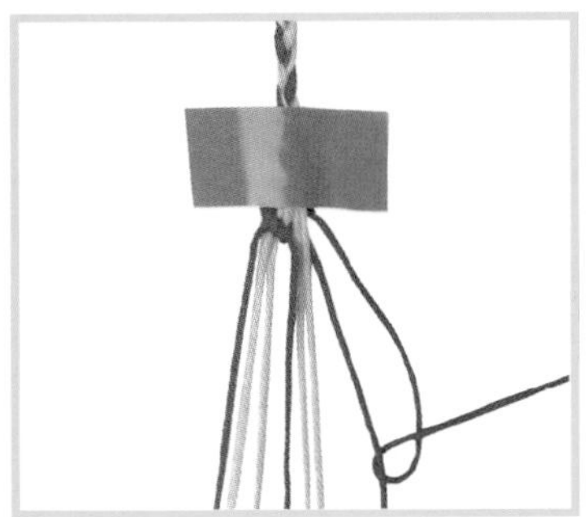

2 Take the thread on the far left (in this project it is purple) and tie two knots on each of the three threads to its right. Leave the purple thread in the middle. Repeat with the purple thread on the far right.

3 Take the purple thread on the middle right and knot it over the middle left thread. Do two knots. Repeat steps 2 and 3 using the three outer pairs of threads. Start with the outermost thread on the left.

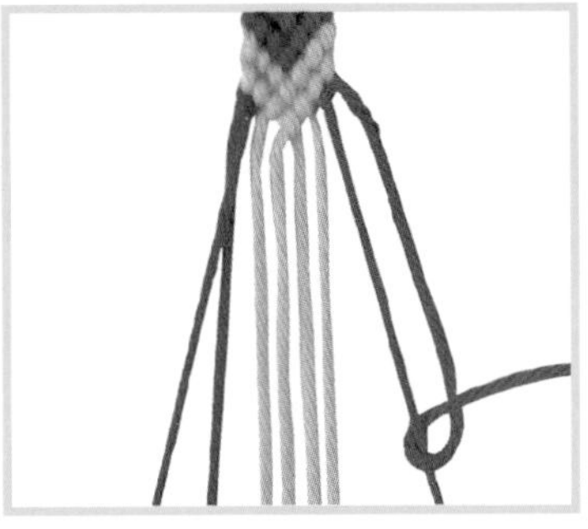

4 Knot the far right purple thread over the purple thread next to it. Do two knots. Repeat with far left purple thread.

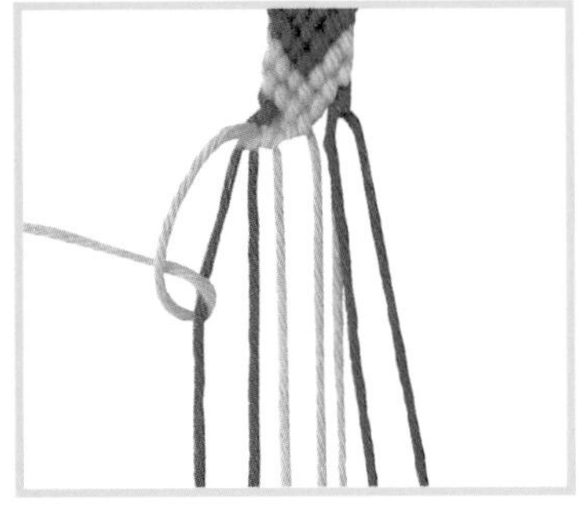

5 Using the fourth thread from the left, do three knots on each of the threads to its left. Repeat with fourth thread from right.

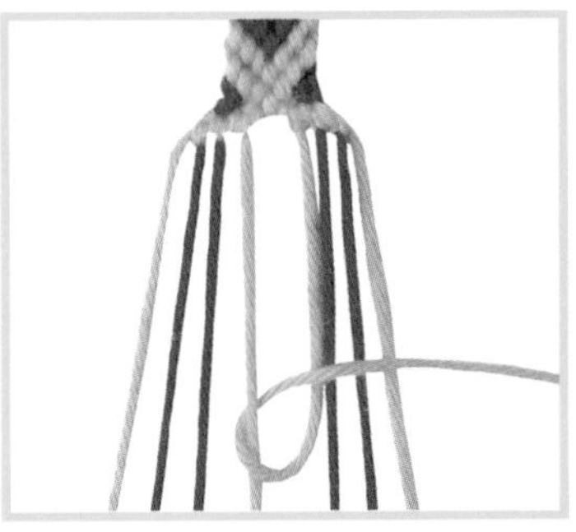

6 Knot the new middle right thread over the middle left thread, twice. Repeat step 5 to make a cross. Repeat steps 5 and 6 using the purple threads. Knot the middle left pink thread over the thread to its left, twice.

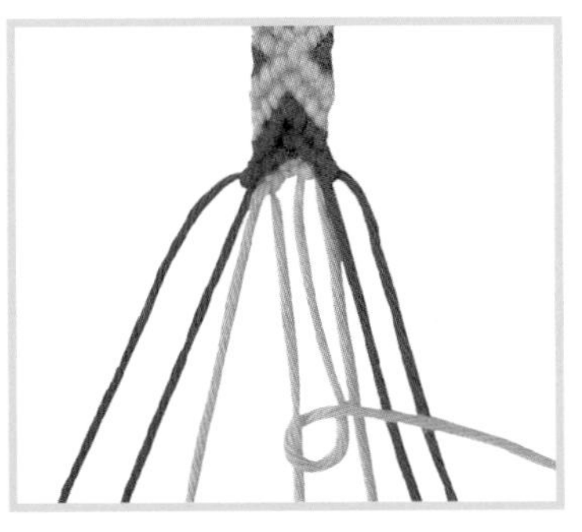

7 Knot the middle right pink thread over the thread to its left, twice. Next, knot the middle right thread over the middle left thread, twice.

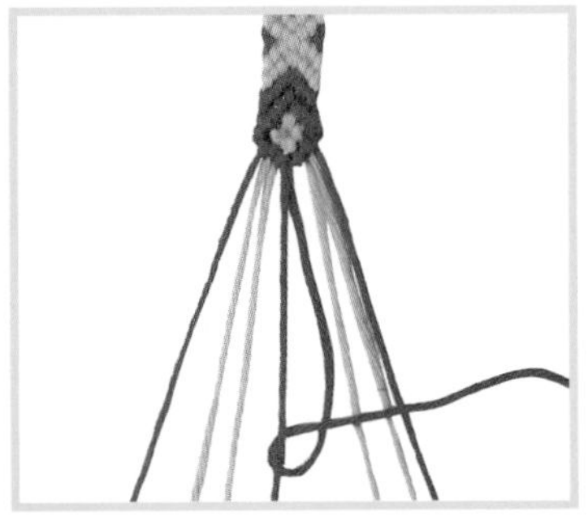

8 To complete the design, repeat from step 2 onwards until your bracelet is the right length. To finish, plait 5cm (2in) and tie a knot and trim the ends.

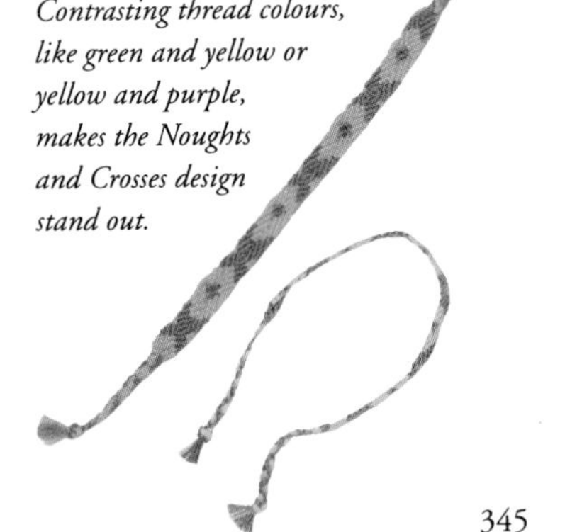

Contrasting thread colours, like green and yellow or yellow and purple, makes the Noughts and Crosses design stand out.

Stripy Beaded Hair Clip

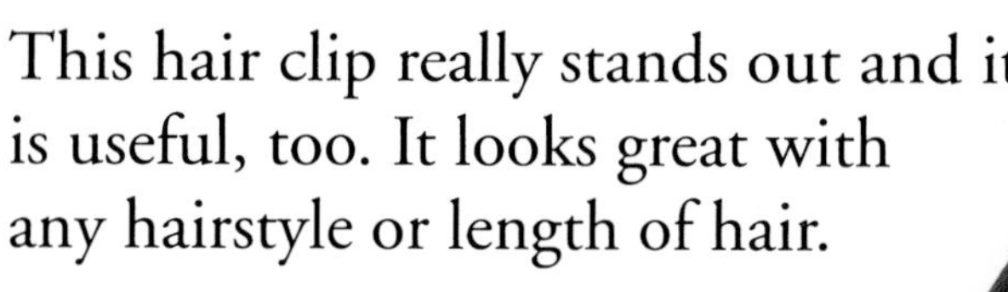

This hair clip really stands out and it is useful, too. It looks great with any hairstyle or length of hair.

Handy hint

To put dangling beads on to the other end of your braid, carefully undo the knot at the top of the braid. Trim the threads to the same length as those on the other end and then follow the instructions in step 5. Glue the braid to the top of the hair clip, making sure that the braid is centred on the hair clip.

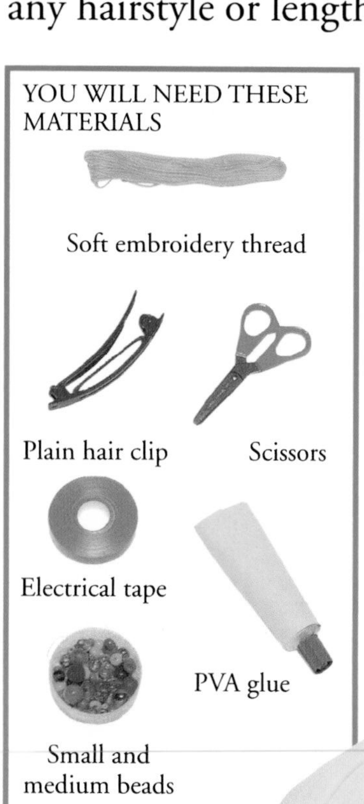

1 Cut ten lengths of thread, two of each colour and each 80cm (32in) long. Tie the threads in a knot, 15cm (6in) from the top. Tape threads to the work surface. Lay threads, as shown.

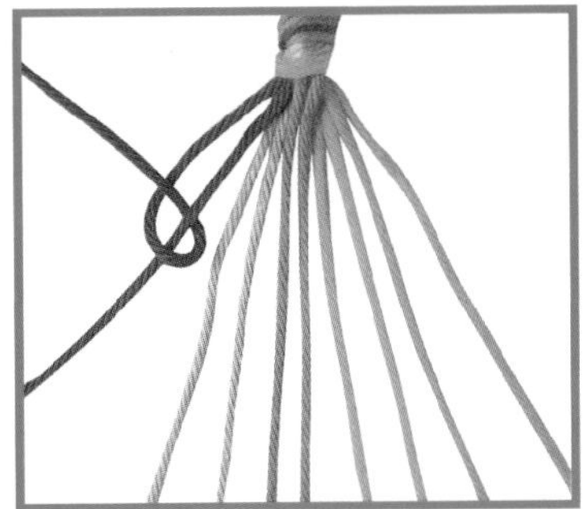

2 Take the dark blue thread on the left over the pale blue thread next to it, back under the thread, through the loop and over itself. Pull the thread gently and repeat the knot.

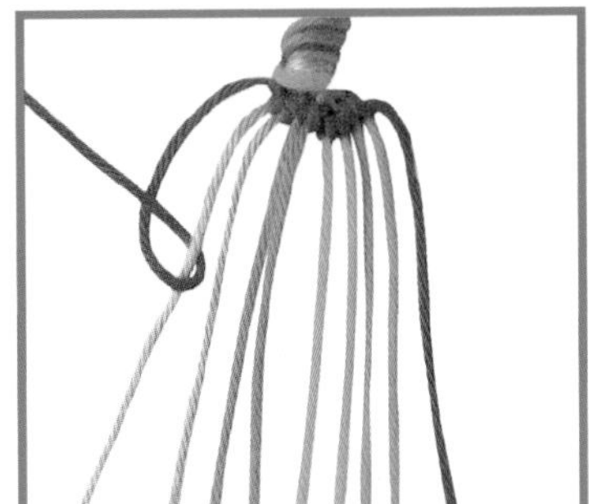

3 Do the same knots on the other threads in the row until the thread you started with is at the end of the row. Go back to the new thread on the far left (another dark blue thread) and repeat the knotting technique explained in steps 2 and 3.

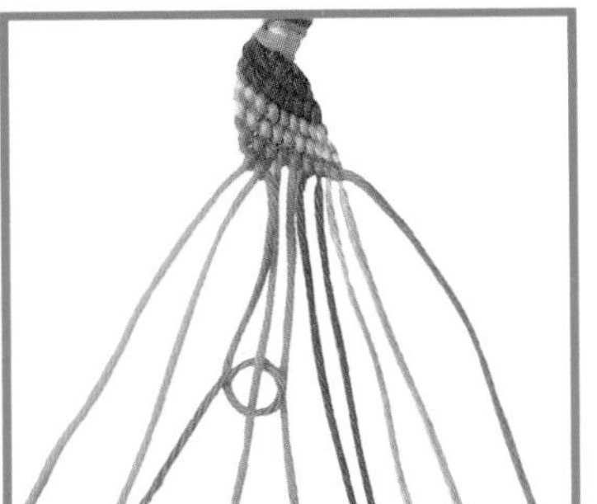

4 Continue knotting the rows with each new far left thread, building up stripes of different colours, until the braid is the same length as the hair clip.

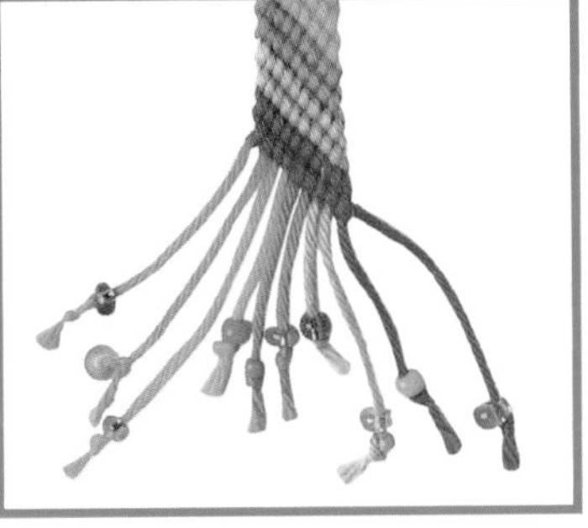

5 Thread small beads on to the end of each thread. Tie a knot on each thread to stop the beads falling off.

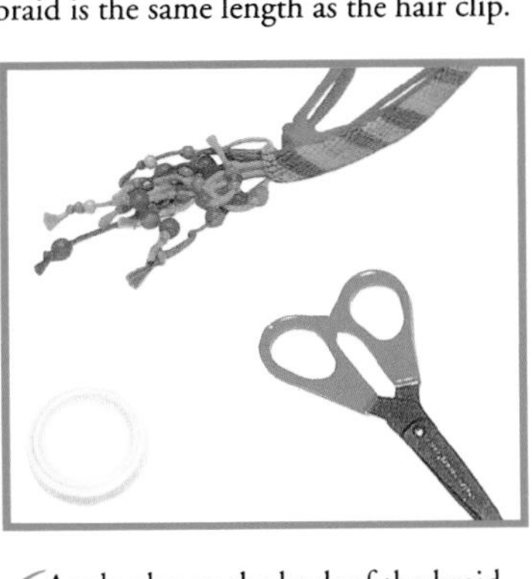

6 Apply glue to the back of the braid and stick it to the top of the clip. Fold the knotted end of the braid to the underside of the clip and glue.

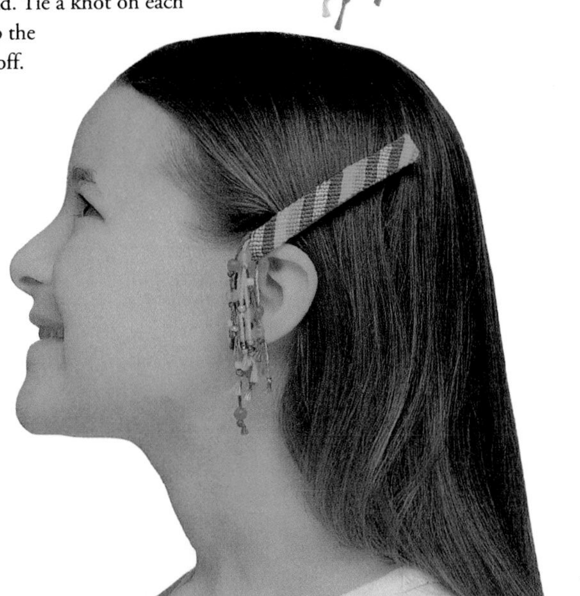

Knotty Dotty Necklace

Choose lots of your favourite beads to knot into this colourful necklace, or select one really beautiful big bead to knot halfway along the necklace. If you do not have a jewellery fastener to secure your necklace around your neck, tie the ends in a knot.

Handy hint

Before you start braiding, check that the holes in the beads are large enough for the thread to pass through. Craft and hobby shops sell beads made specially for braiding.

YOU WILL NEED THESE MATERIALS

Stranded embroidery thread

Pliers

Scissors

Electrical tape

Jewellery fastener

2 metal rings

2 jewellery clamps

Small and medium beads

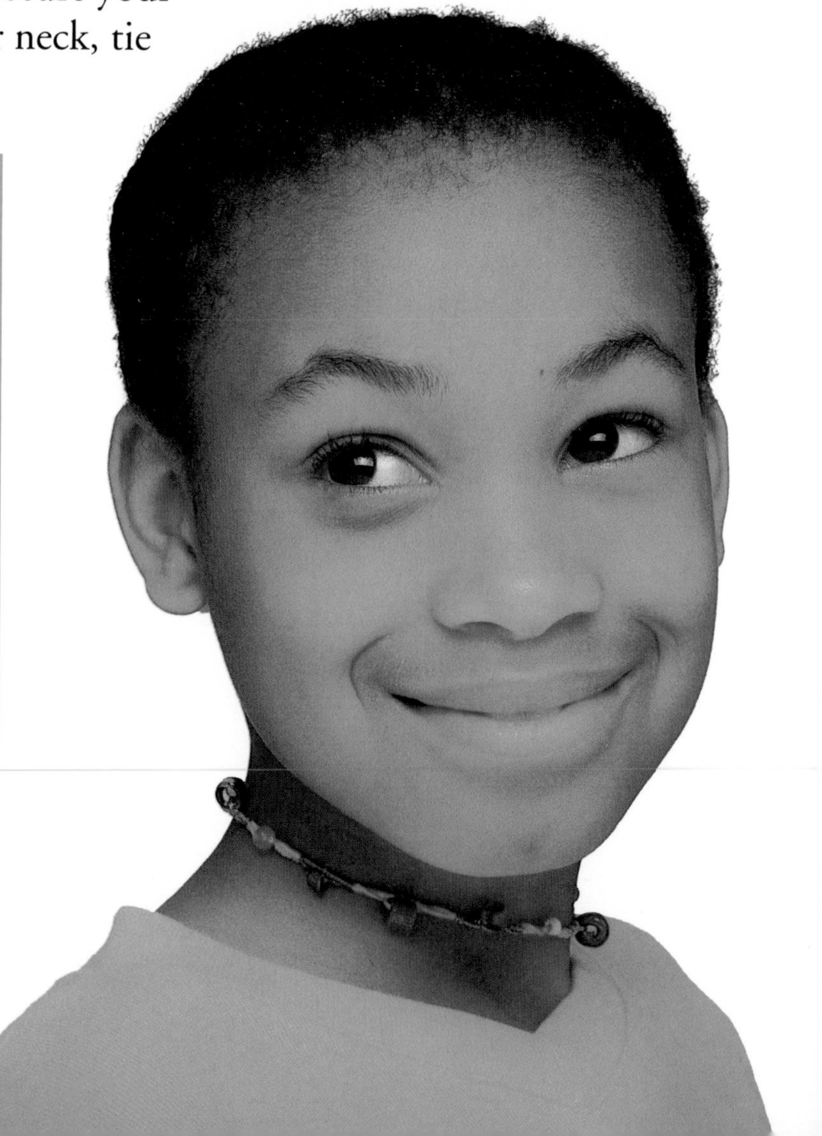

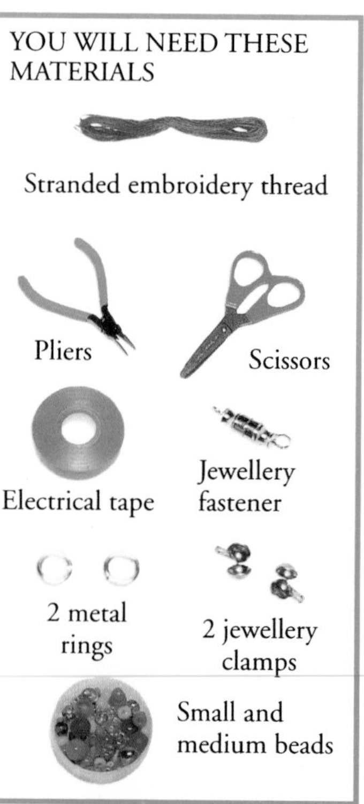

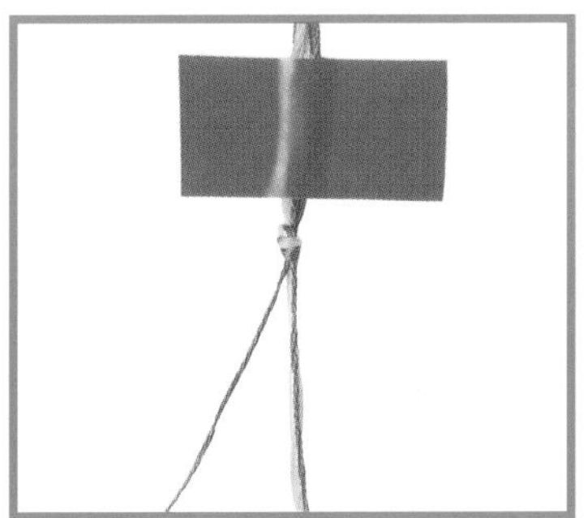

1 Cut four threads, two of each colour and each 150cm (60in) long. Knot the threads 10cm (4in) from the top. Tape them to the work surface above the knot. Lay the threads, as shown.

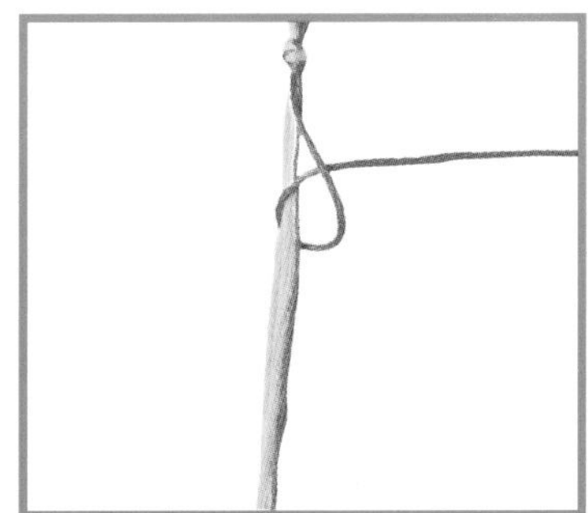

2 Start with the thread that is out on its own (a blue thread). Take it over the other threads, then under them and through the loop. Pull this thread up tightly while holding the other threads.

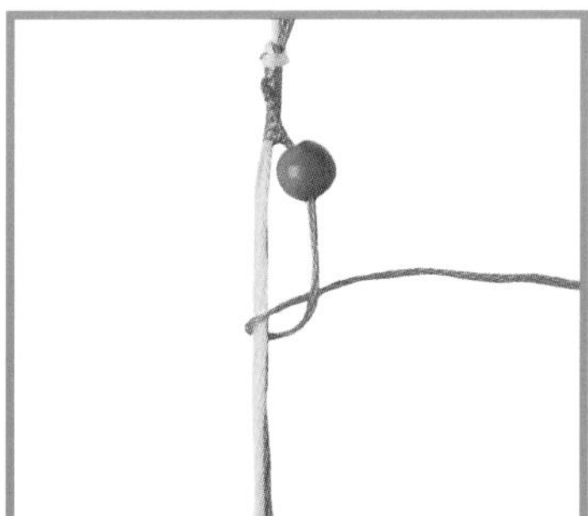

3 After you have knotted a row of about five knots, thread a bead on to the blue thread and then continue to make a few more knots. It is now time to start working with a new thread.

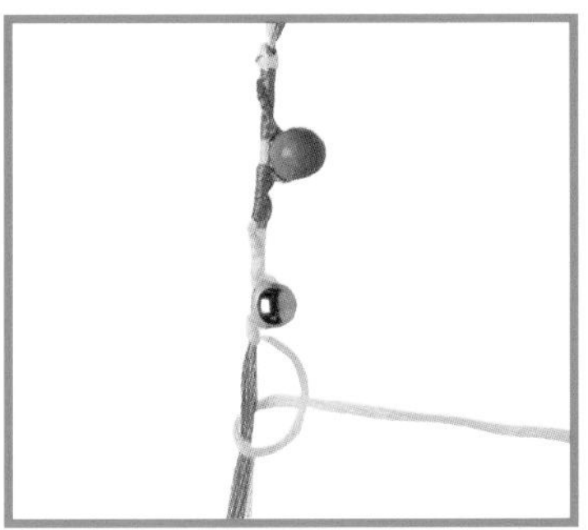

4 Make a new row of knots with the new thread. After five knots, thread on a bead.

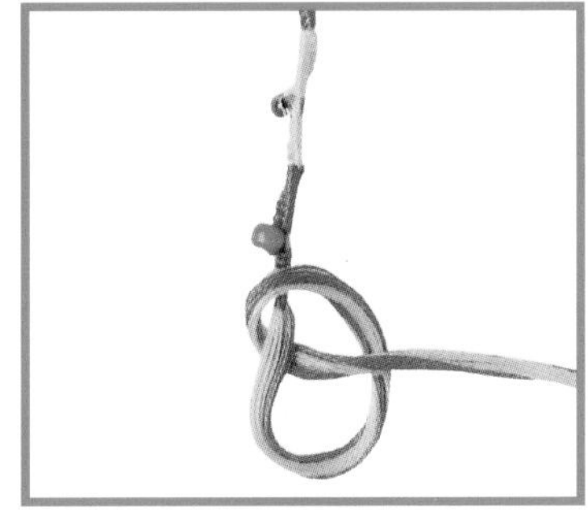

5 Continue making rows of knots and adding beads in this way until the necklace is the length you want. Tie all the threads together in a knot.

Long necklace

You can also make a longer version of the Knotty Dotty Necklace by simply doubling or even tripling the length of the yarns. Do not forget that you will also need lots more beads to decorate your necklace.

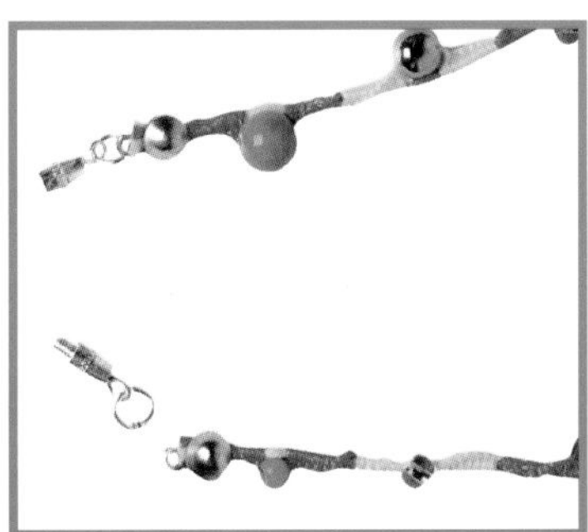

6 Trim the threads close to the knot at each end. Attach a jewellery clamp over each knot and a metal ring to each clamp. Then attach half the jewellery fastener to each of the metal rings.

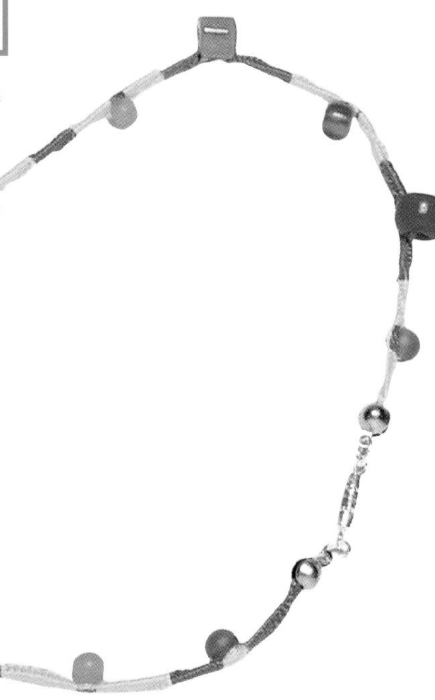

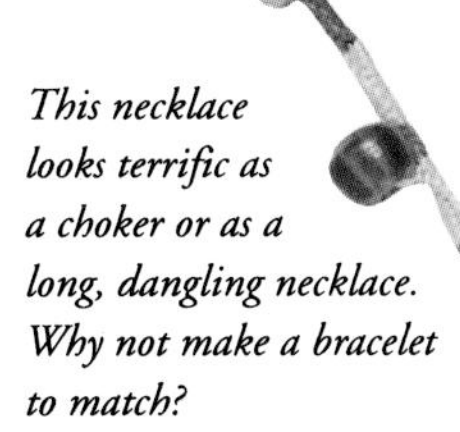

This necklace looks terrific as a choker or as a long, dangling necklace. Why not make a bracelet to match?

Sunglasses Strap

This Sunglasses Strap is very useful and great fun to wear. When you do not want to wear your sunglasses, you can hang them around your neck. You could make Sunglasses Straps for all the members of your family or as gifts for friends.

Handy hint

Some types of jewellery clamps and rings are made of very tough metal. It may be necessary to ask an adult to help you open and close these pieces of equipment using a pair of fine-nosed pliers or jewellery pliers.

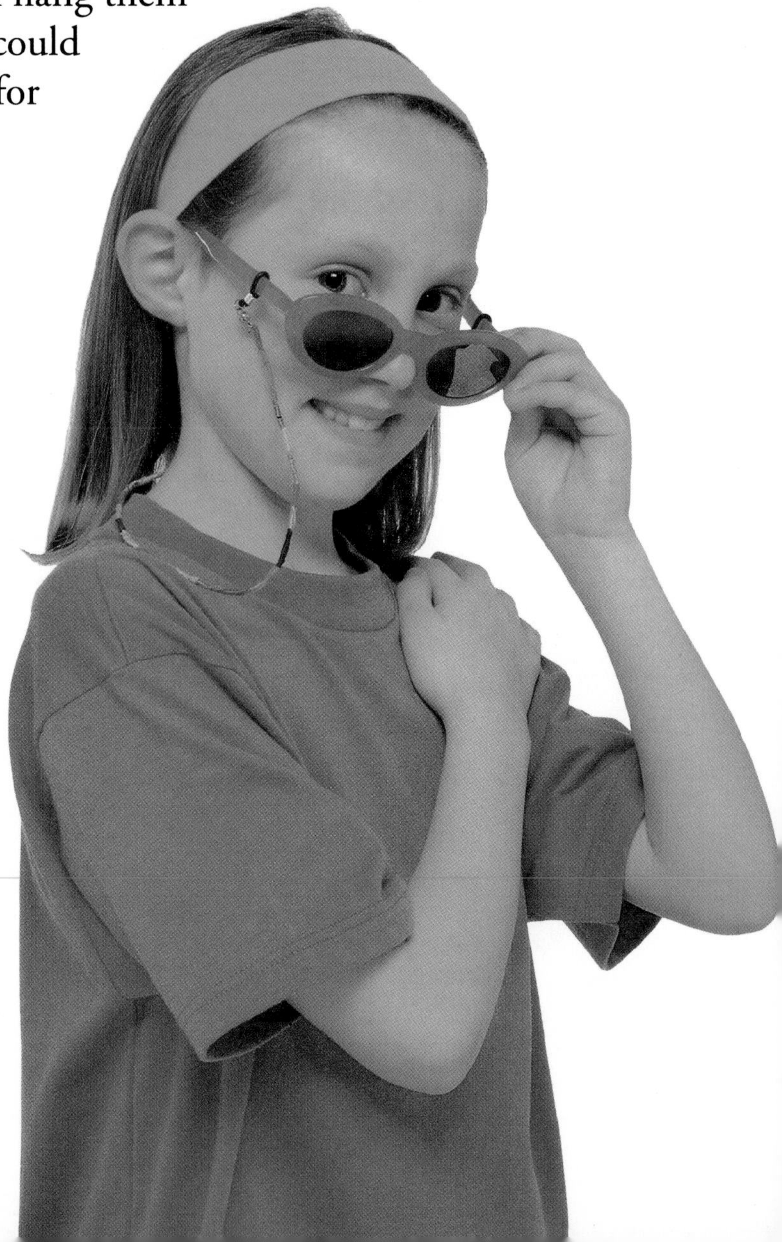

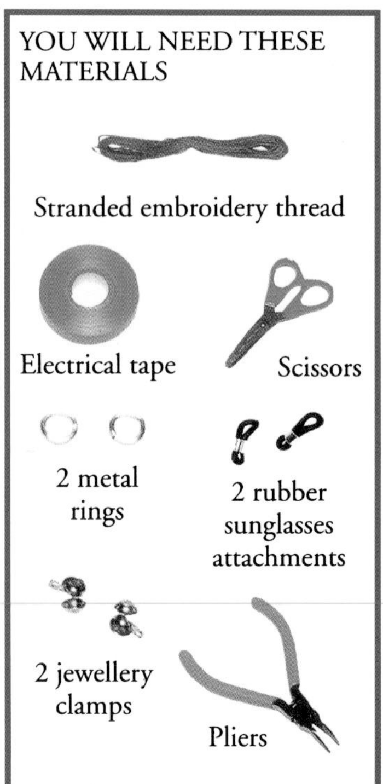

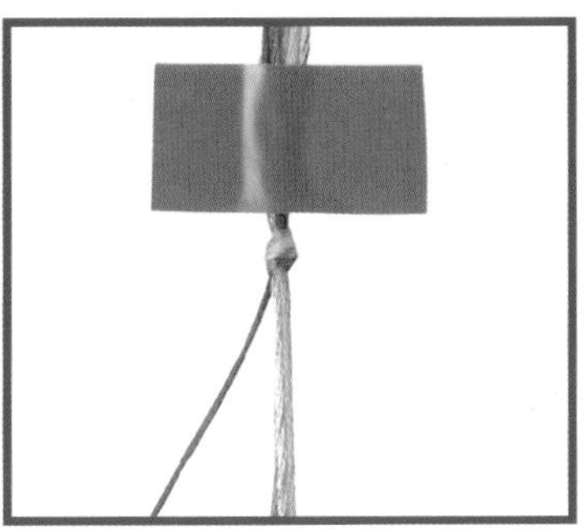

1 Cut six strands of thread, each 200cm (80in) long. Knot the threads together, 5cm (2in) from the top. Tape them to the work surface.

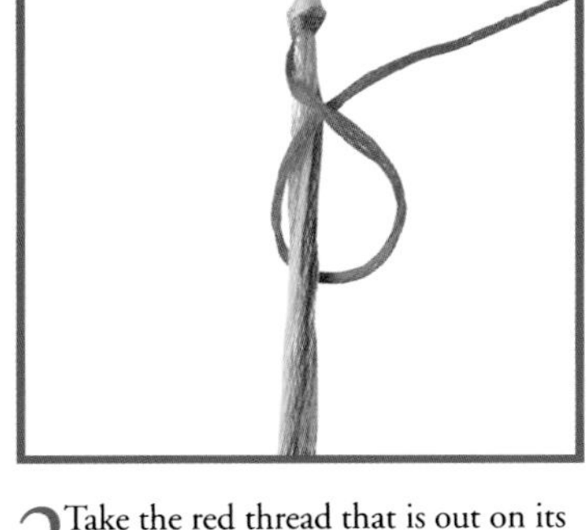

2 Take the red thread that is out on its own and put it over the other threads, then under them and through the loop. Pull the thread up tightly.

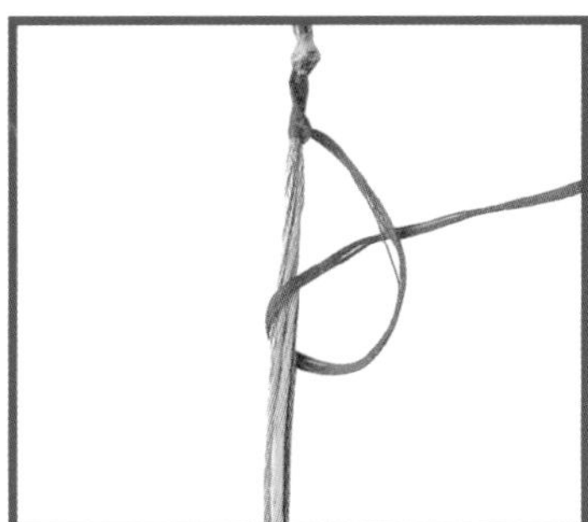

3 Continue knotting this single thread over the others until you have as much as you want of that colour and want to change it.

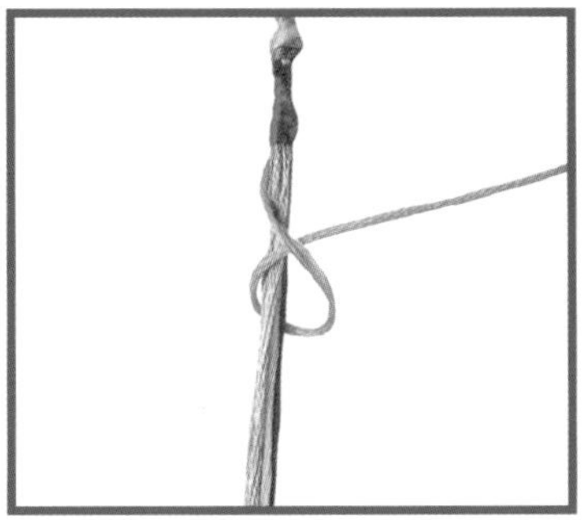

4 Take a new thread and place the red thread with the others. Make a row of knots as shown in step 2. Continue knotting in this way and changing the thread colour as often as you wish.

5 When the knotted cord is about 70cm (28in) long, tie the threads in a tight knot close to the braid. Trim the loose threads very close to the knot at each end. Take care that you do not cut into the knots themselves.

6 Attach a jewellery clamp over each knot and close the clamps. Attach a metal ring to each clamp and a rubber loop to each ring.

Using other styles of braid

Many of the other braiding techniques shown can also be used to make the Sunglasses Strap. Whichever Friendship Bracelet design you choose, allow at least 200cm (80in) of each thread. If you choose to make a wide strap, you may need to use larger jewellery clamps and metal rings.

To attach the strap, thread the rubber loops over the arms of your sunglasses and tighten the loops around the arms.

Boxes and Bands Bracelet

Handy hint

Use only two different coloured threads for this bracelet. If you use more, the clever boxes and bands design will not stand out.

This is quite a difficult bracelet to make. If you are not pleased with your first attempt, keep practising until you become an expert.

YOU WILL NEED THESE MATERIALS

Soft embroidery thread

Electrical tape

Scissors

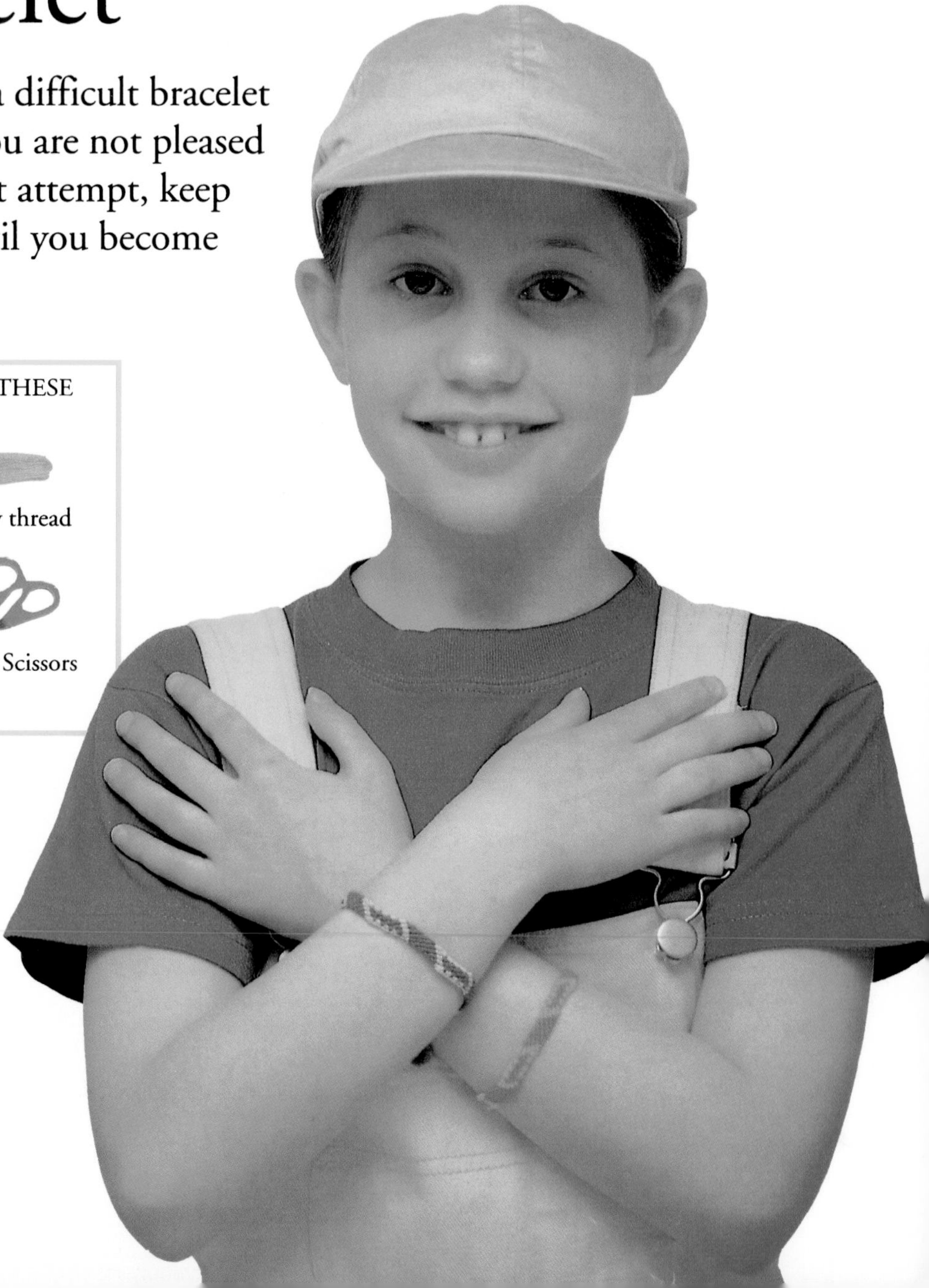

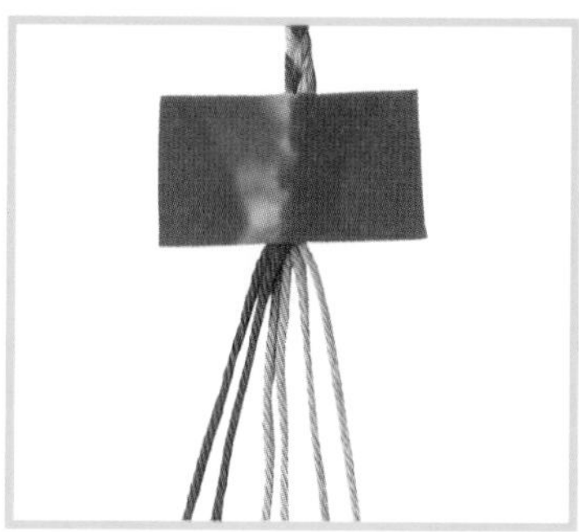

1 Cut two threads in one colour and four in another colour, each 100cm (40in) long. Knot threads and plait for 5cm (2in). Tape threads to work surface.

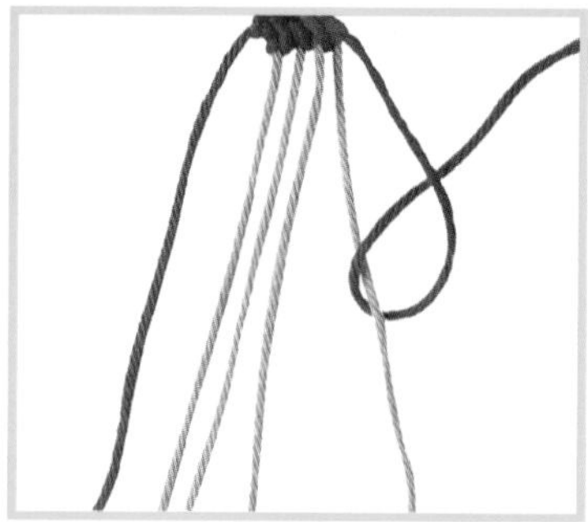

2 Arrange threads as shown in step 1. Knot the far left thread (dark blue) over the threads to the right. Do two knots on each thread.

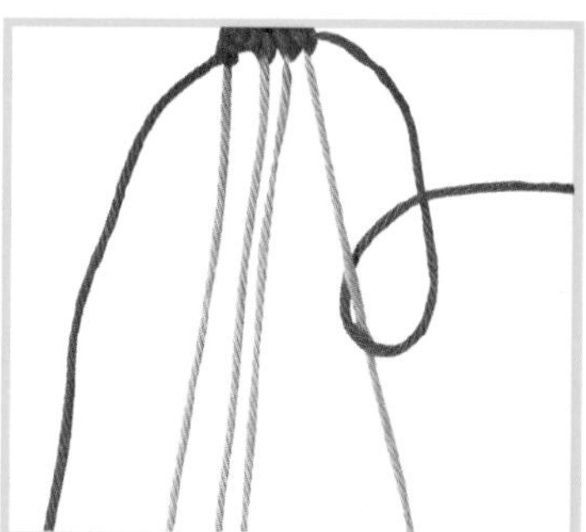

3 Knot the far left thread (also dark blue) over the pale blue thread and do two knots. Repeat, knotting the far right thread over the thread to the left.

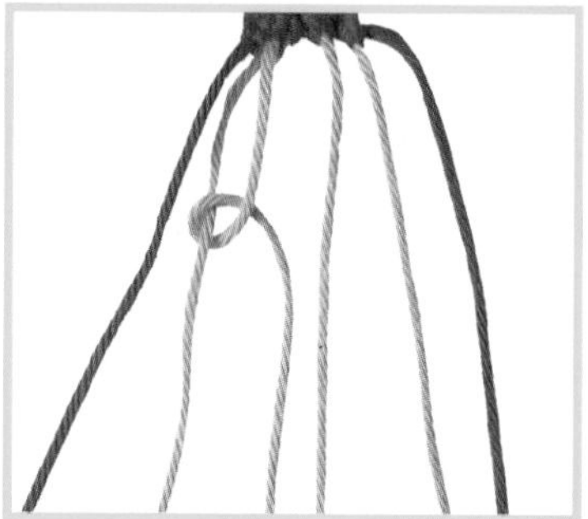

4 Knot the pale blue thread (second on the left) over the thread to the right. Do two knots. Then do one knot over each of the other pale blue threads.

5 Repeat steps 3 and 4 until you have woven four rows of pale blue threads inside a box of dark blue threads. Take care to braid the right thread each time.

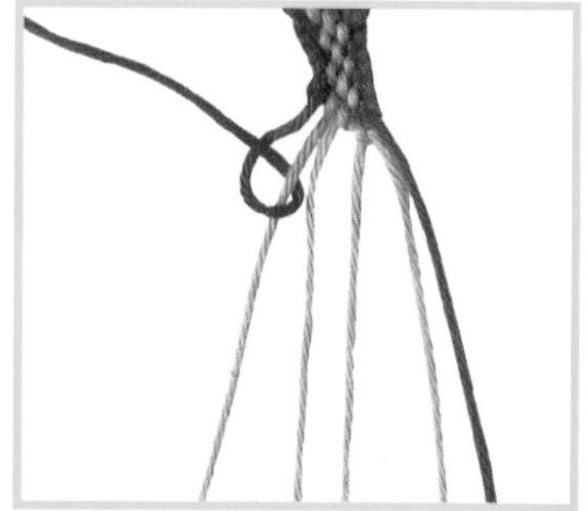

6 Take the dark blue thread on the left and knot it over the pale blue thread next to it. Do two knots and return the thread to the starting position. Do the same with the dark blue thread on the far right.

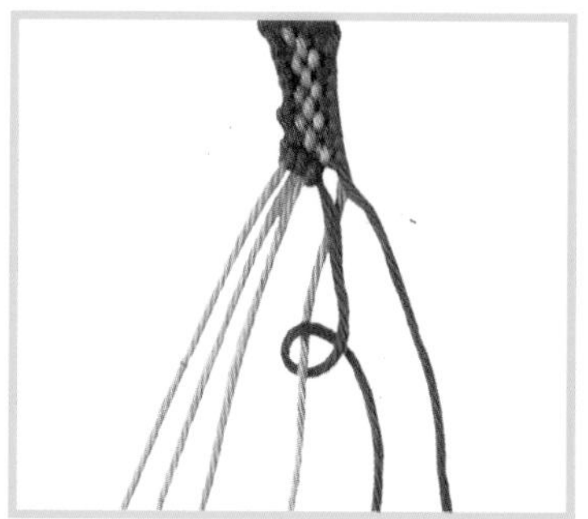

7 Knot the far left dark blue thread over all the threads on the right. Now knot the far left pale blue thread over all the threads on the right until you get to the end of the row.

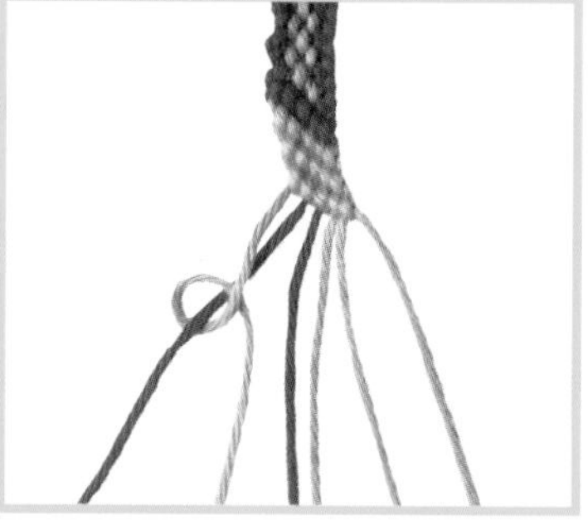

8 Continue knotting the far left thread over the other threads until there is a dark blue thread on either side of the pale blue threads. Repeat steps 2 to 8 until the bracelet is the right length.

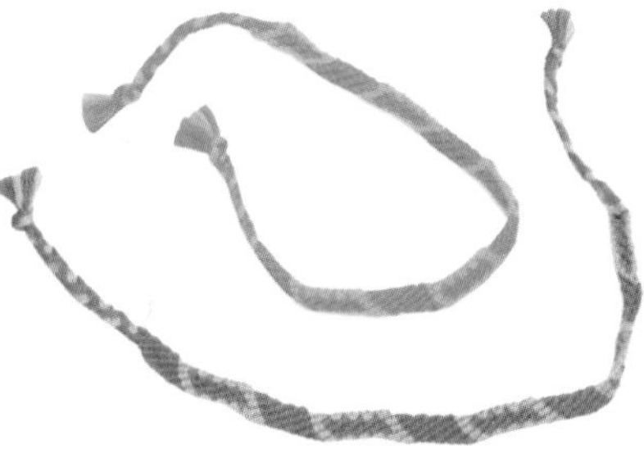

To finish your Boxes and Bands Bracelet, plait 5cm (2in) and then tie the threads into a knot. Trim the threads at both ends to the same length.

Arrow Bracelet

YOU WILL NEED THESE MATERIALS

Soft embroidery thread

Electrical tape

Scissors

You can make the Arrow Bracelet using two, three or four different coloured threads. Choose colours to match your best outfit or, if you are making this for a friend, choose his or her favourite colours. To make a thicker Arrow Bracelet, use more threads.

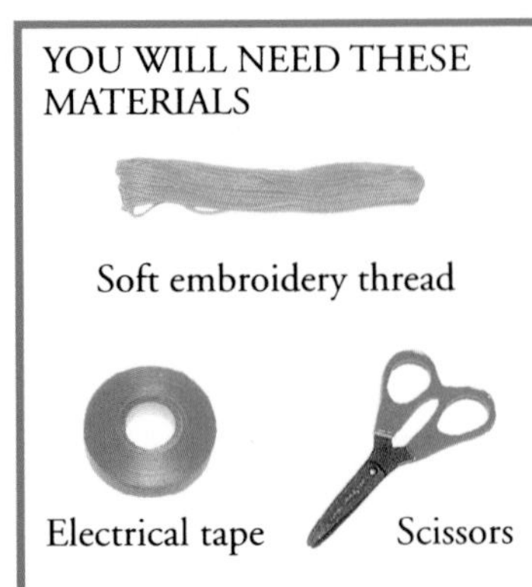

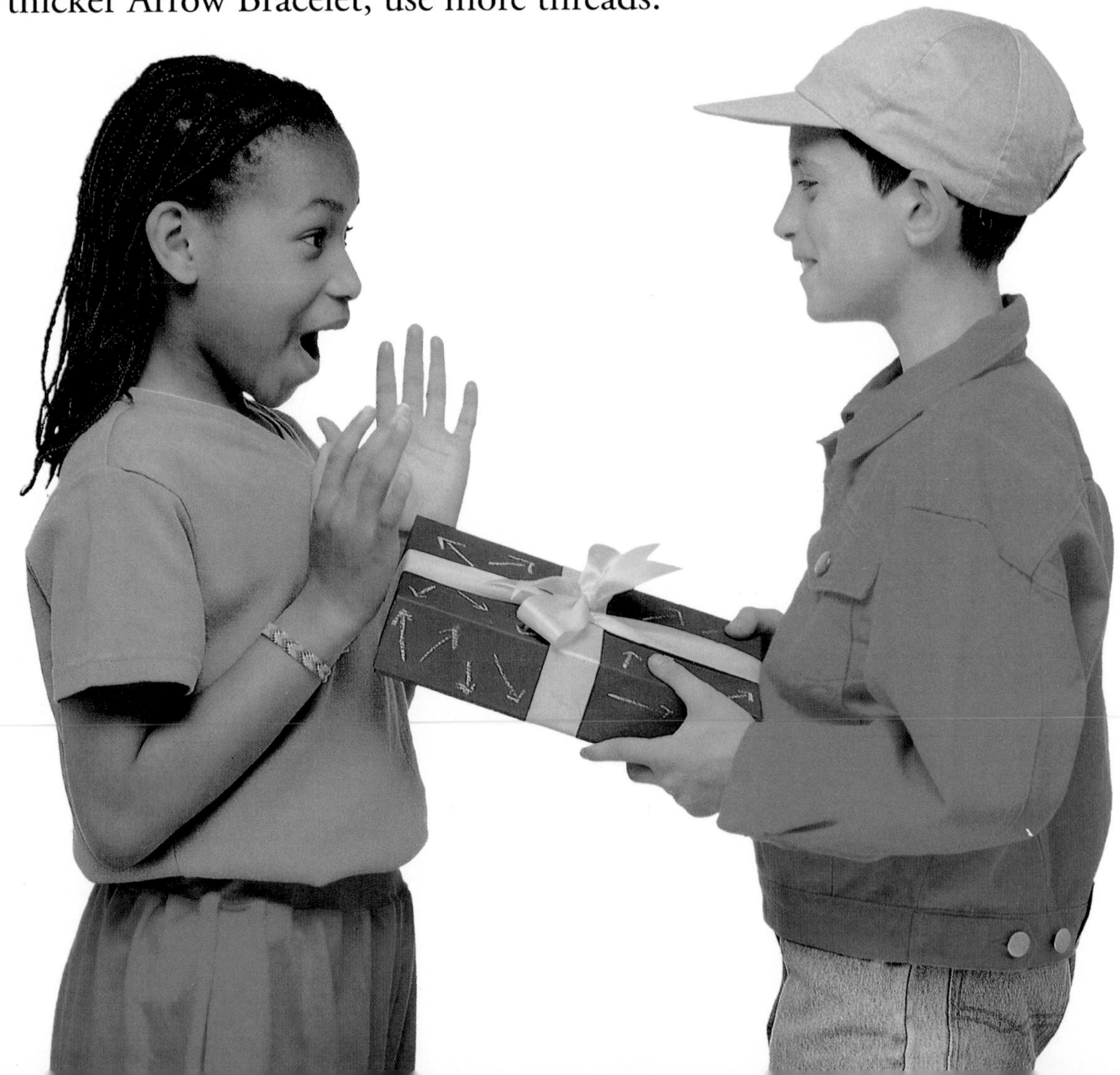

1 Cut eight pieces of thread, four of each colour and each 100cm (40in) long. Knot the threads 5cm (2in) from the top and tape threads to your work surface. Lay the threads out, as shown.

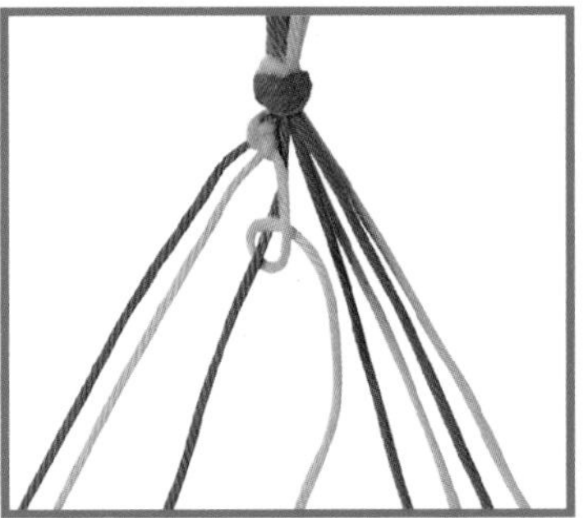

2 Start with the thread on the far left (in this project it is orange) and do two knots on each of the three threads next to it on the right. Leave the orange thread in the middle.

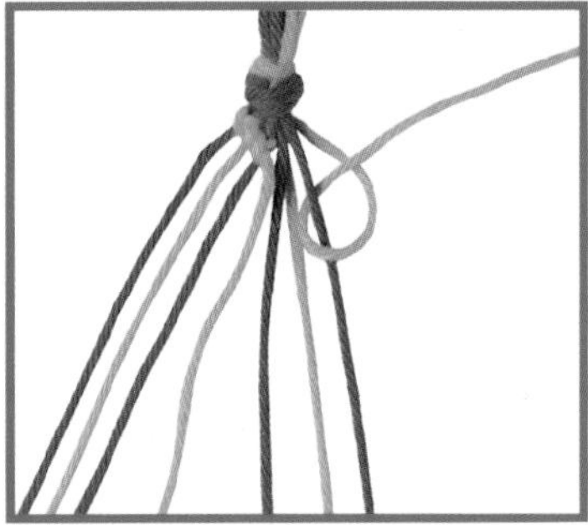

3 Now take the orange thread on the far right and do two knots on each of the three threads next to it on the left. Leave the orange thread in the middle.

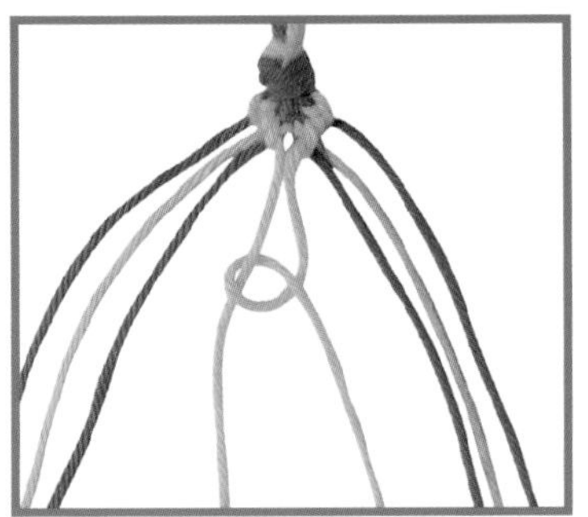

4 Take the middle right orange thread and make two knots over the orange thread on the left.

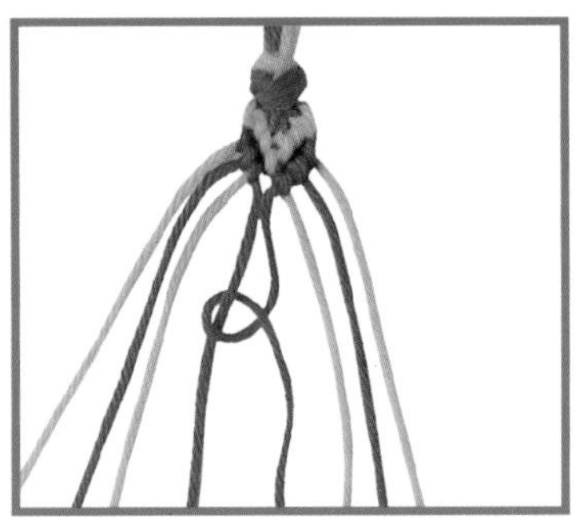

5 Repeat steps 2, 3 and 4, knotting blue and orange alternately until the bracelet is the right length.

6 Plait the threads for 5cm (2in) and secure with a knot. Trim any uneven threads with scissors.

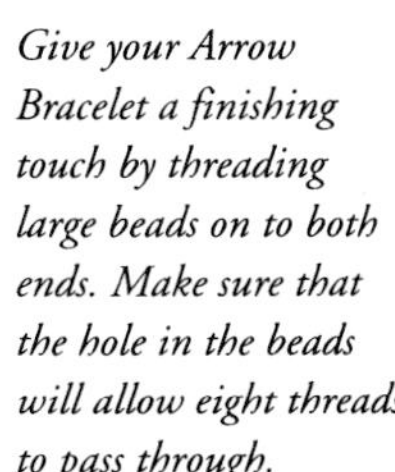

Give your Arrow Bracelet a finishing touch by threading large beads on to both ends. Make sure that the hole in the beads will allow eight threads to pass through.

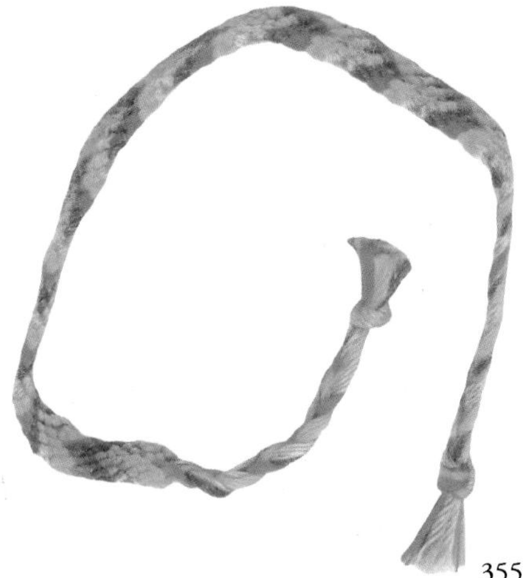

Fabulous Hairstyles

Introduction

This style uses the basic techniques to create a simply spectacular look. The ribbons are the final touch!

Doing your hair is such fun, and you will be surprised to see how easy it is to create different styles. There are lots of things you can do whether your hair is straight, wavy or curly, short or long. All you need is a brush and comb, and as many brightly coloured ribbons, beads, bows, covered bands and fancy hair clips as you can find.

Getting started

Firstly, assemble all the materials and accessories you will need. Then find somewhere to set up your hair salon. Ideally you need a table, chair and a large mirror. Ask for permission before you start rearranging furniture and also ask an adult to help set up a mirror, if necessary.

It is also a good idea to ask a friend to join you. A friend can not only do the plaits and ponytails at the back of your head, your friend can also tell you just how wonderful you look with your new hairstyle. Having your own hair done is only half the fun – the other half is doing someone else's hair!

Basic techniques

Before you start on the exotic hair styles like Crimping Crazy, Wonder Waves and Beaded Plaits, it is a good idea to practise the basic techniques. The basic techniques include the Perfect Ponytail, High Ponytail, Bouncy Bunches and the Simple Plait. When you have mastered these, then even the most complicated styles will be easy to do.

Mini plaits look great with beads threaded on to the end.

It is also important that you comb and brush your hair correctly. Tugging and pulling roughly on your hair will only damage it. Brush your hair with a gentle brush to smooth it and to make it easy to style. To remove knots or tangles, use a wide-toothed comb. Separate out the section of tangled hair and start combing from below the tangle and gradually work your way up the section of hair until the tangle disappears. Never try to force a comb through a knot from above – it will tear your hair.

Making a centre or side parting in your hair is easy with a wide-toothed comb, but making the parting straight requires practice. Your hairstyles will look really professional if the parting does not wiggle around like a snake!

Everyone's hair is different and some hair types are better suited to some hair styles. To work out which styles work best for you is simply a matter of trial and error. If you have flyaway hair, for example, cover a bristle brush with a silk scarf and stroke it over the hair. The static electricity that makes hair wispy will magically disappear. To flatten hair that sticks up, wet your hands with water and smooth them over your hair.

Materials

Here are the materials and equipment you will need to set up your hair salon. To create the hairstyles, you do not need a hairdryer or any type of hair gel or lotion. If you go on to create other hair designs and need things like a hairdryer or hair gel, always ask an adult for permission.

Beads Plaiting, or braiding, beads have a large hole through which a fine plait can be threaded. They come in lots of different colours and can be bought in craft and hobby shops.
Brush You will need a brush with widely spaced soft bristles. The bristles can be made from nylon or a natural fibre. Keep your brush clean by running a comb through it to remove hairs. Some brushes can be washed under running water. It is always best to have your own brush and comb.
Covered bands You need lots of these towelling or yarn covered stretchy bands. Unlike ordinary rubber bands, these bands will not damage your hair. They come in lots of different sizes, thicknesses, colours and textures. You can buy inexpensive packets of assorted covered bands in supermarkets, department stores and chemists.
Fabric curlers These soft curlers are easy to use and much more comfortable to wear than other types of curlers. You can buy them in department stores and chemist shops.
Hairband Use one of these to keep your hair off your face. All hairbands are made of flexible plastic, but some are padded with a soft material and covered in fabric, cord or ribbon.
Hair grips These are sometimes called Kirbigrips or hair slides, and they are used to keep a small section of hair in place. They are made of sprung metal and have plastic, rounded tips so that they do not damage your hair or hurt your scalp. They come in different sizes and colours.
Ribbons You really cannot have too many ribbons when styling your hair. Start collecting ribbons of different widths, colours, textures and patterns.
Scrunchy This is a loop of elastic covered by a wide strip of fabric. You can buy scrunchies in lots of different sizes.
Thick cord To bind a plait you use a thick cord, or cording, that can be bought on rolls or by the metre (yard) in craft and fabric shops. Cord without a shiny, smooth finish is the easiest to use as it will not slide off the plait.
Thread To put beads on to plaits you will need to use a thick thread like an embroidery thread. Embroidery threads or similar come in lots of colours. There is even a glittery thread.
Wide-toothed comb This comb has large spaces between the teeth and is good for untangling knots. Always rinse after use.

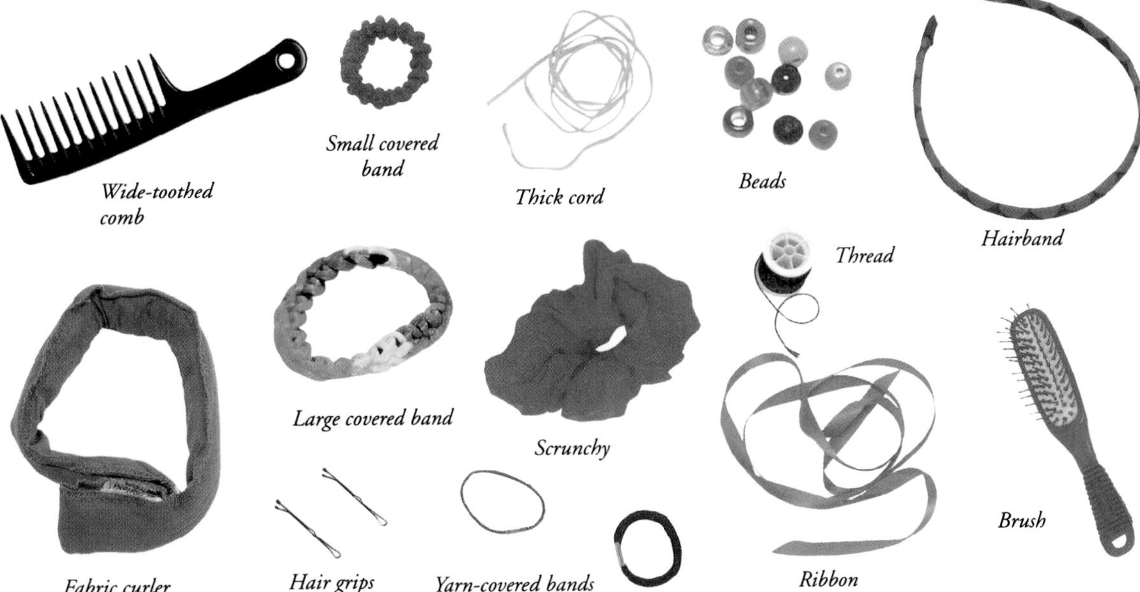

Accessories

Hair accessories are used to decorate your hair rather than to create a style. They are the finishing touch to ponytails, plaits and bunches. Even a simple hair clip can turn an ordinary plait into something special.

Chemist shops and department stores are full of colourful and beautiful hair accessories. Some are expensive, others are very inexpensive. When choosing a hair accessory make sure that it is the right sort for your hair and for what you want it to do. Some hair slides and grips, for example, are made for long or thick hair; others for fine or short hair. Always try to select hair accessories that will coordinate with your favourite outfits or with other hair accessories you want to use.

You do not even need to buy special hair accessories, you can design and make your own using all sorts of unusual materials. Pictured below are hair accessories decorated with uninflated balloons, fabric flowers from a florist, tiny ribbon flowers from a haberdashery shop, and varnished sweets.

Here are some other unusual materials that you could use when designing and decorating your own unique range of hair accessories: colourful raffia, string, shells, beads, embroidery thread, papier mâché, tiny toys and dolls, crêpe paper (but do not get it wet), plastic bags, gift-wrapping ribbon, strips of leftover fabric, and dried pulses and pasta.

To start making hair accessories you will need something to decorate (a plastic hairband, a plain plastic-backed hair slide or hair grip), PVA glue and brush, sewing needle and thread, and your imagination. To get you started you could make the Glitzy Hairband on the next page.

If you think that creating fabulous hairstyles is lots of fun, wait till you start making your own hair accessories!

Tortoise-shell hair clip

Fabric sunflower attached to a hair grip

Velvet bow and fancy button hair slide

Dingly-dangling hair grip

Hair grips decorated with a tiny fabric flower and narrow ribbon

Plastic hair grip decorated with sweets

Stretchy band decorated with balloons

Chiffon fabric scrunchy

Fabric-covered bendy band

Covered stretchy band with piglet

Stretchy narrow band decorated with beads

Fabric rose and nylon netting rosette attached to hair grips

Glitzy Hairband

Create your own designer hair accessory by simply sewing an assortment of brightly coloured beads on to a padded hairband.

YOU WILL NEED THESE MATERIALS

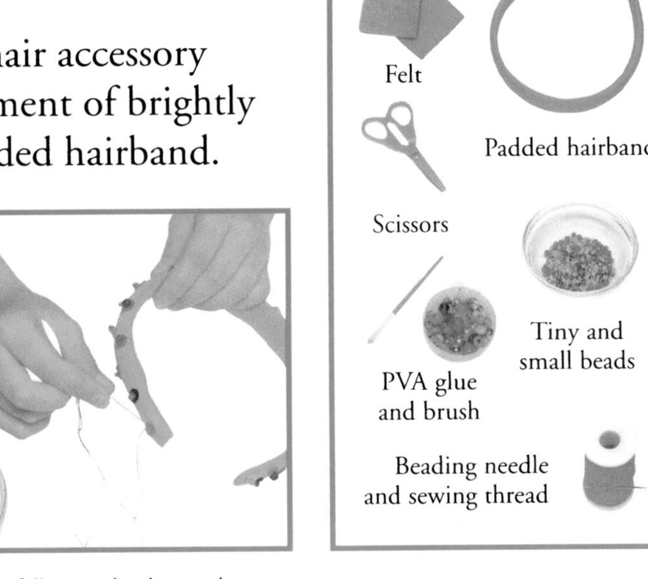

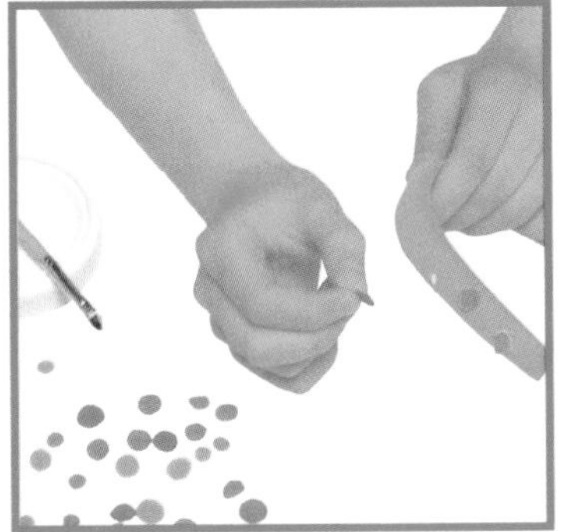

1 Cut out small dots of felt in lots of different colours. Dab a small spot of glue on to the padded hairband where you want each dot to be. Stick the felt dots on and let the glue dry.

2 Carefully sew a bead on to the centre of each felt dot. Do two or three stitches. Then knot the thread around the bead. Cut the thread as close as possible to the knot. Do the same for all the remaining beads.

3 To make a different style of hairband, select a mixture of beads that match the colour of the hairband, or create a rainbow effect by sewing your beads in rows of one colour. Use sparkly beads and a black hairband to make a special occasion hairband.

Perfect Ponytail

A ponytail is one of the easiest styles to do. It keeps hair tidy and stops it getting into a tangle when playing sports or swimming.

YOU WILL NEED
Scrunchy
Brush

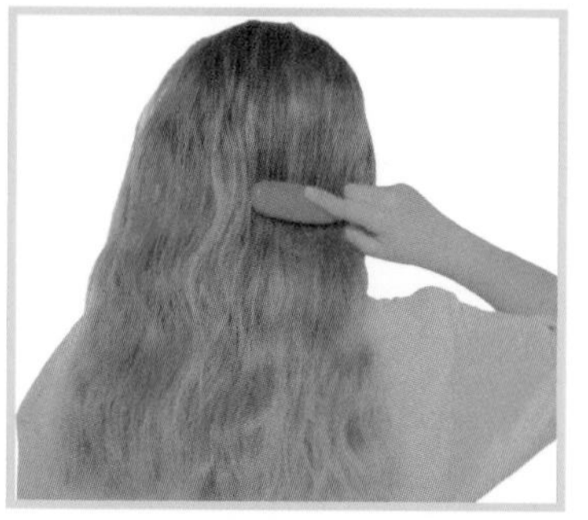

1 Brush your hair straight back off your face using long sweeping strokes to make sure there are no knots. Tease any knots out by brushing gently from the bottom.

2 Place the scrunchy around your wrist. Pull your hair together with your hands at the back of your head. Your hair should go over the top of your ears.

Hair care hint

Scrunchies are very good for holding your hair in place because they do not tear or damage the hair. Ordinary rubber bands can tear your hair when they are removed. If you have very silky or fine hair, it may be necessary to hold the hair in place with a small, yarn-covered elastic before finishing with a large, colourful scrunchy.

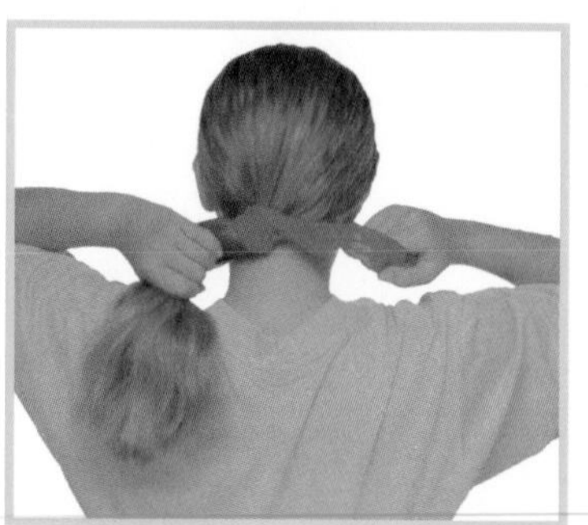

3 Hold your hair in place using the hand on which the scrunchy is wound. Use the other hand to slip the scrunchy off the wrist and over the ponytail. Keep holding the hair while the scrunchy is twisted, as shown.

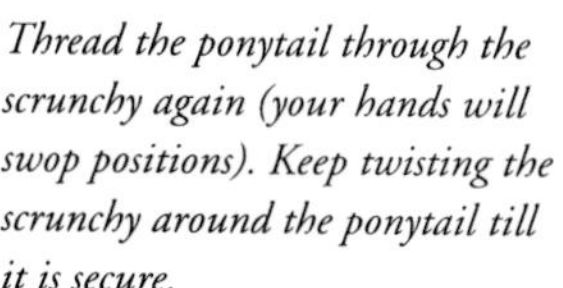

Thread the ponytail through the scrunchy again (your hands will swop positions). Keep twisting the scrunchy around the ponytail till it is secure.

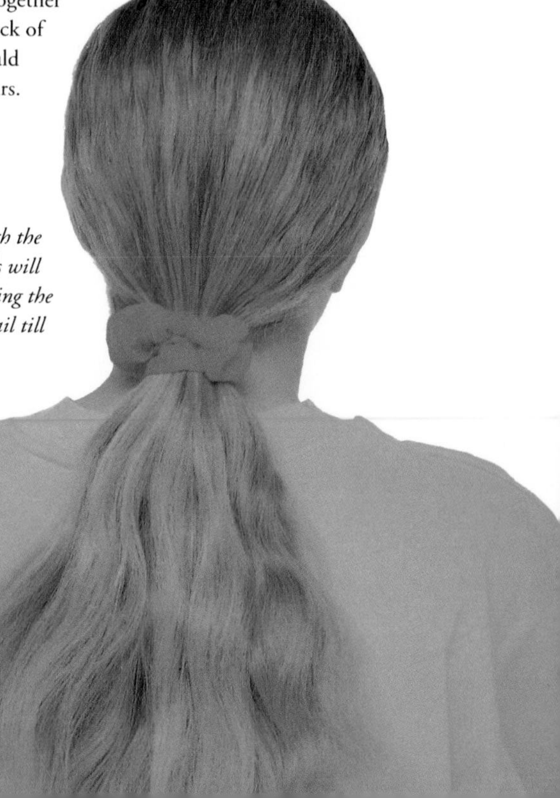

High Ponytail

A high ponytail, right on the top of your head, makes you instantly taller. This is a glam style that is great for parties and discos.

1 Tip your head forwards and brush your hair from the back of your neck right to the ends. Make sure there are no tangles or knots. It is easiest if you use a brush with wide spaces between the bristles.

2 Take hold of your hair with one hand. Run the fingers of your other hand through your hair to make it smooth. Hold your hair and lift your head up.

3 Put a scrunchy over the knuckles of one hand, then pull your hair though the scrunchy. Twist the band and pull your hair through again. Repeat until the scrunchy holds your hair securely.

4 Twist on two more scrunchies above the first one. These will give your ponytail lots of height and make you look really tall. You can use scrunchies in matching or contrasting colours.

To finish, use hair grips to pin the fabric flowers in place. You can buy fabric or net flowers in the sewing departments of large stores or in craft shops.

Pony Princess

Here the top section of your hair is smoothed back into a ponytail halfway down the back of your head. It is then combined with the rest of your hair to make another ponytail.

Handy hint

A fabric-covered bendy band is made from a long flexible strip of wire that is sewn into the edge of a strip of fabric. To make the topknot in the band, put the band around your head and then twist the the ends together.

YOU WILL NEED

Brush

4 covered bands

Fabric-covered bendy band

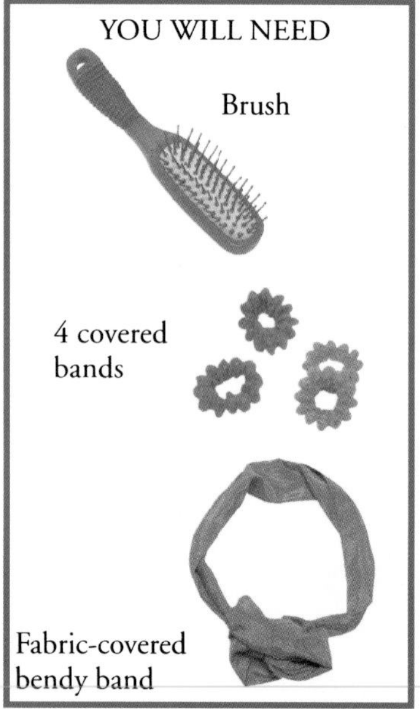

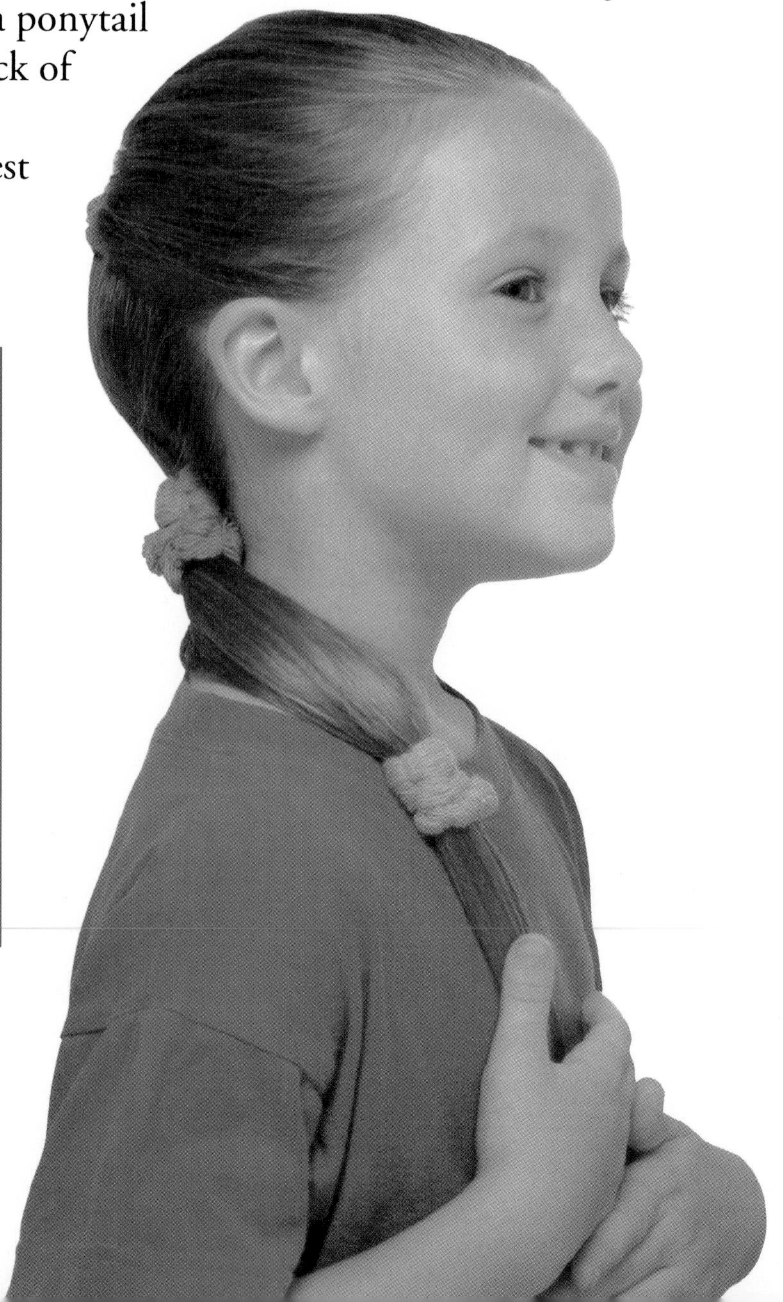

You can wear your Pony Princess ponytail hanging down your back or, if you have very long hair, draped over your shoulder.

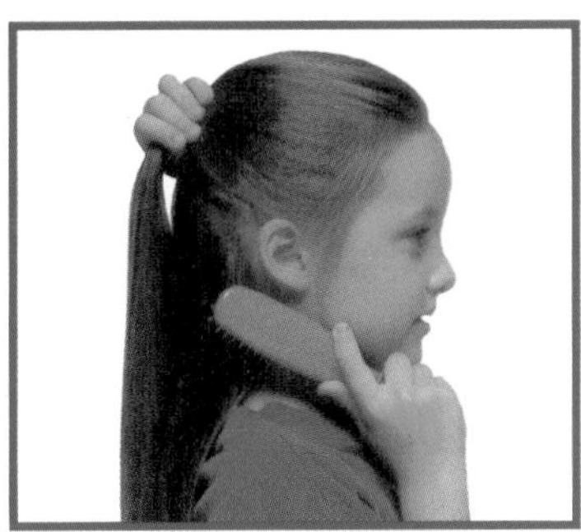

1 Brush your hair so there are no tangles or knots. Then use your thumbs to divide off the top section of your hair, as shown. Hold this section tightly with one hand.

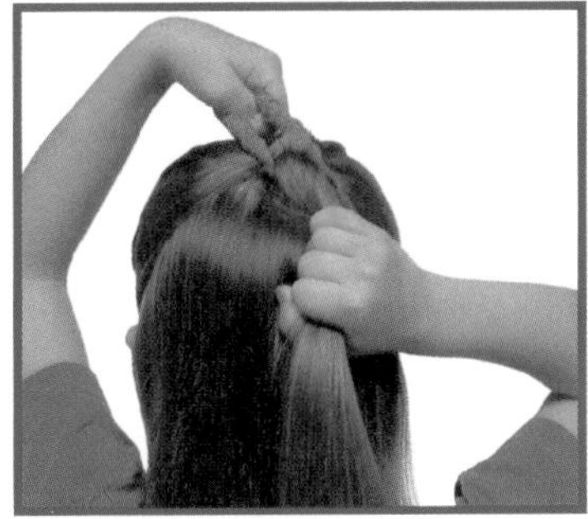

2 Use a towelling-covered band to secure this top section of hair. You may need to twist the band once or twice so that it is tight enough to hold the hair properly.

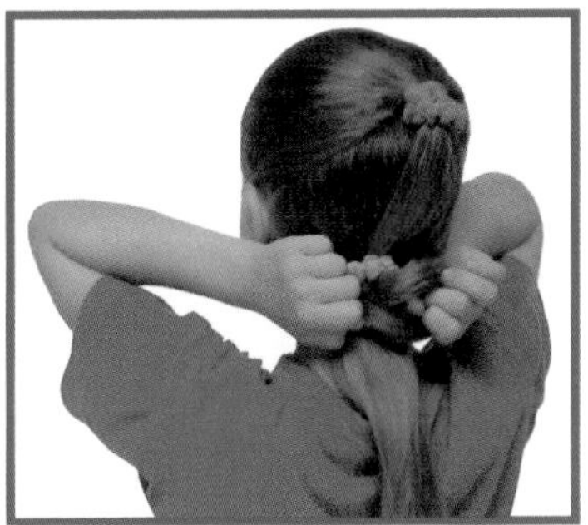

3 Gather all your hair together at the nape of your neck and secure it in another towelling band of a different colour. You may need to twist it again so it is tight enough to stay in place.

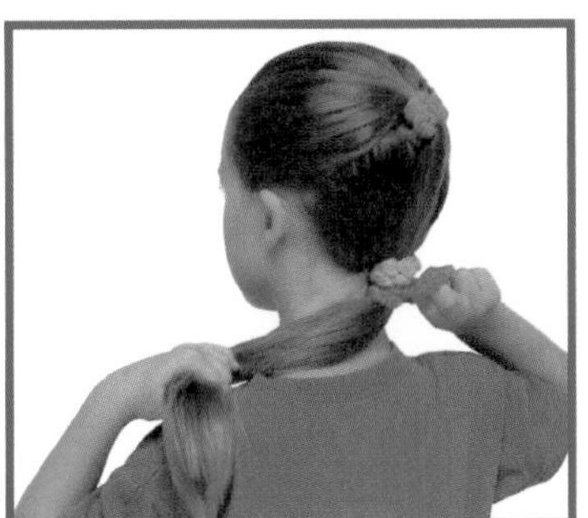

4 Take another coloured band and do the same thing again. The bands should sit neatly next to one another, so push them together.

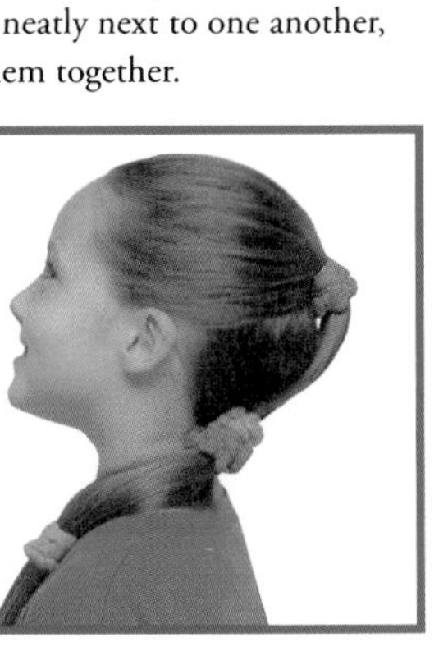

5 Add another coloured band about halfway down the ponytail. Brush or comb the end of the ponytail to make it smooth.

To finish, place a fabric-covered bendy band round the back of your head. The band can go over or under the ponytail. Bring the ends of the band to the front of your head. Twist the ends together to make a topknot.

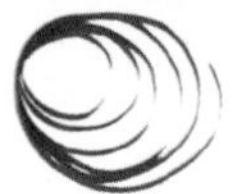

Topsy Turvy Ponytail

A topknot is great if you are growing out your fringe because it can catch all those little ends that tend to stick out or fall over your eyes.

Handy hint

Twist the ribbons together for a really unusual hairband, and choose colours that match your clothes. To stop the ribbons slipping, it may be necessary to secure them with small hair grips placed just behind each ear.

YOU WILL NEED

Brush

2 hair scrunchies

2 long lengths of narrow ribbon in different colours

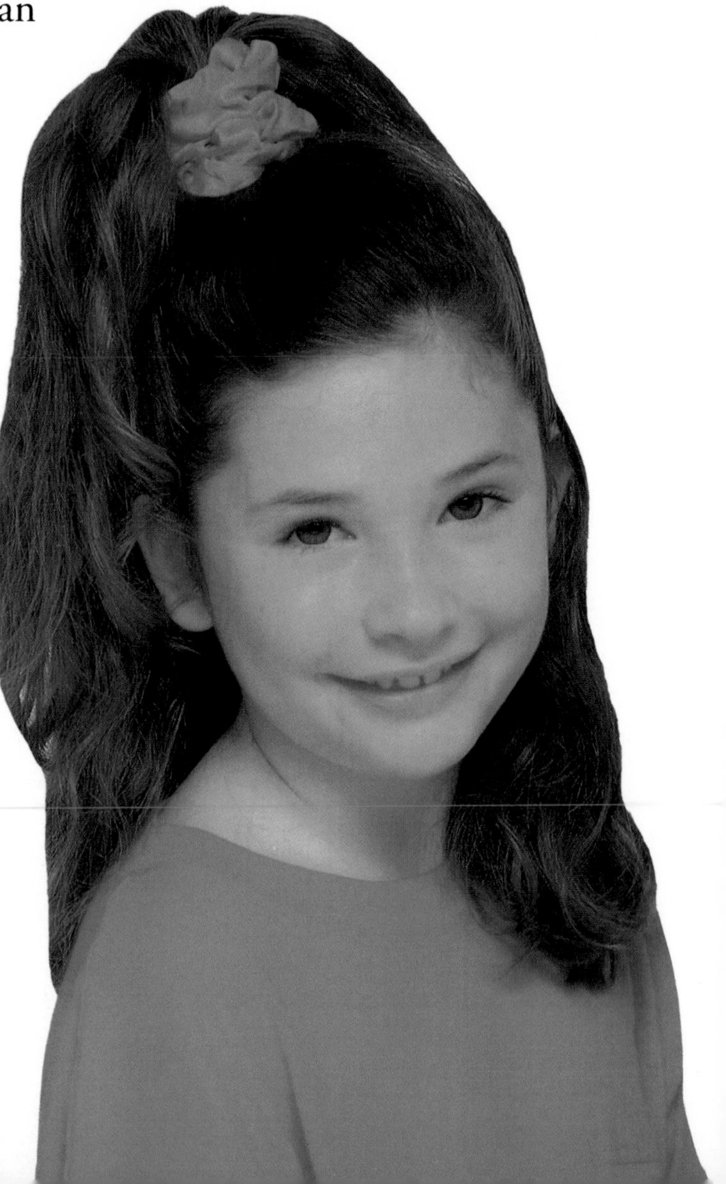

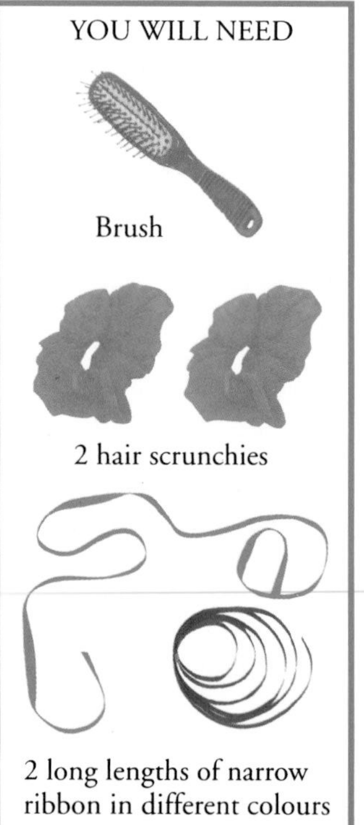

1 Brush your hair through to remove any tangles or knots. Use the thumb of each hand to divide off the top section of the hair from your ears up to the top of your head.

2 Push a scrunchy or other type of fabric-covered band over the fingers of one hand so that it rests on your knuckles. Clasp the topknot of hair in your other hand.

3 Slip the scrunchy over the hair. Twist the scrunchy and then pull the ponytail through the scrunchy. Repeat until the scrunchy holds the hair securely.

4 Add a second scrunchy and twist it around the top of the first scrunchy. This will give the Topsy Turvy Ponytail height. If the first scrunchy was large and thick, you may not need to add a second scrunchy.

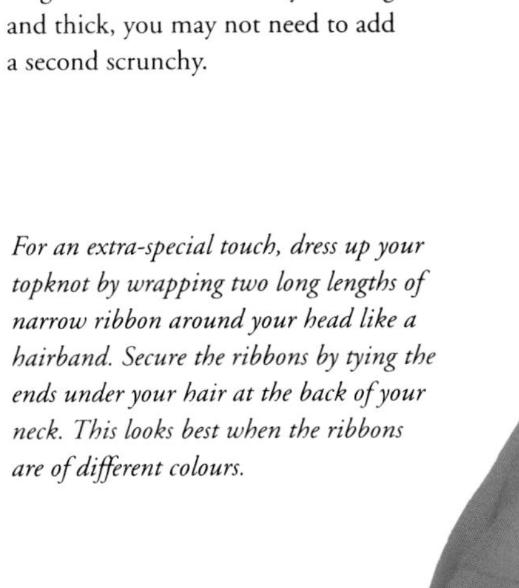

For an extra-special touch, dress up your topknot by wrapping two long lengths of narrow ribbon around your head like a hairband. Secure the ribbons by tying the ends under your hair at the back of your neck. This looks best when the ribbons are of different colours.

Bouncy Bunches

Any length of hair can be scooped up into pretty bunches. Tie the bunches with bright ribbons in fun colours and patterns for school, and add fairy bows for party time.

1 Part your hair in the middle from front to back. Put a covered band over one hand, so that it sits on your knuckles. Hold one half of your hair in the other hand.

2 Slip the bunch through the covered band, holding your hair tightly with one hand. Use your thumb to pull the band tight and then twist it.

3 Put your fingers through the loop in the band and pull the bunch through. Do this again until the band is tight enough to hold your hair.

4 Tie a short piece of ribbon round the bunch, then make a bow. Repeat for the other side. To finish, slide two fairy bows on either side of the centre parting at the front.

Banded Bunches

Keep your bunches tidy by wrapping bands of colour round them all the way to the bottom. Finish off your hairstyle with a pair of madcap decorated bands.

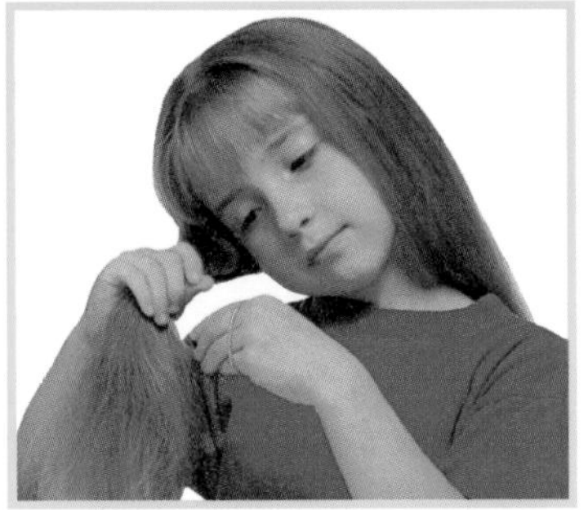

1 Part your hair in the middle from front to back. Put a plain band over one hand so it sits on your knuckles, then slip it over one section of hair. Twist it back over the bunch until it is tight. Repeat for the other bunch.

2 Take two bands (we used ones decorated with piglets) and slip one over each bunch. You may need to twist the bands twice so that they hold each bunch tightly.

3 Take two more plain bands and slip a bunch through each band, about 5cm (2in) from the first band. These bands should be a different colour to the decorated bands.

4 Take more plain bands (in a different colour to the last ones) and add them to your bunches, always about 5cm (2in) from the last band. Continue until you run out of hair or covered bands!

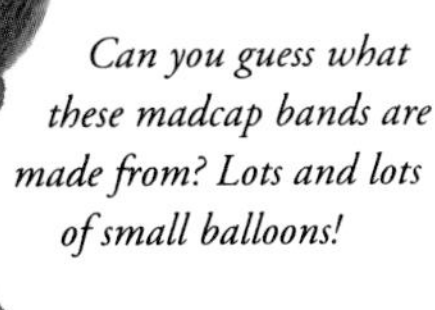

Can you guess what these madcap bands are made from? Lots and lots of small balloons!

Be-Bop Bunches

High bunches like these are really easy to do on bobbed or shoulder-length hair. You can twist ribbon around a small section of hair for a really snazzy look!

1 Part your hair in the centre and brush your hair so it is really smooth. Take a small section at one side and brush again. Experiment to see how large a section you would like to use.

2 Tie this small section of hair in a covered band. We used crocheted silky bands in a rainbow of colours. You can use your favourite bands but make sure they are not to thick or large.

3 Twist the band and wrap it around the bunch until it is tight enough to hold the bunch in place. Repeat for the other side.

4 Divide off a small section of the hair from one of the bunches and slip the end of the ribbon halfway through the covered band. To keep the ribbon in place, tie it on to the band. Twist the ribbon around your hair and tie the ends in a knot and then a bow.

Hair care tip

To keep your hair shiny after shampooing, always use cool water for the final rinse.

Teeny Bopper

You can use bouncy curls and waves to create lots of styles. The Teeny Bopper style makes it look as though your hair is much thicker than it really is!

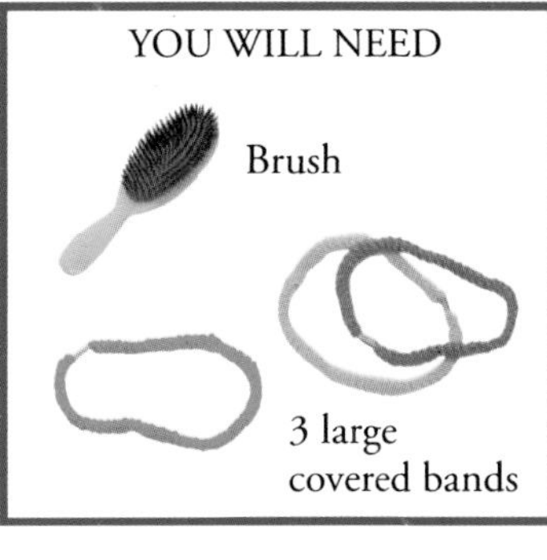

YOU WILL NEED

Brush

3 large covered bands

1 Lift a section of hair from the front to the top of your head, and then use a bristle brush to smooth the front of your hair. Do not brush through the length of your hair or you will pull the waves out.

2 Take a large covered band (one that will wrap round lots of times) and use it to secure the top section of hair. Make sure this is right in the middle, because you do not want your topknot to be lopsided.

3 Separate out a section of hair from one side of your head. Fasten it with another large, covered band in a different colour. Loosen the waves with your fingers, but do not brush your hair.

4 Do exactly the same with a section of hair on the other side of your head. Do not forget to use a different coloured band!

This girl is ready to dance. When she dances, her curls will bounce and bop!

Simple Plait

A three-stranded plait, also called a braid, is a lot easier to do than it looks. Plaits are really useful for keeping your hair under control, especially when swimming.

YOU WILL NEED

1 Part your hair from centre front to the nape of your neck. Divide one half of your hair into three equal sections and hold the back and front outer sections.

2 Cross the back section over the centre section. Use your fingers to make sure that the other two sections remain separate. Pull gently on the back section as you cross it over.

3 Cross the front section over the centre section. Gently pull all three sections evenly as you work, so that the plait is straight.

4 Now you can see how the plait is beginning to form. Carry on plaiting by crossing the back section over the centre section, and the front section over the centre section.

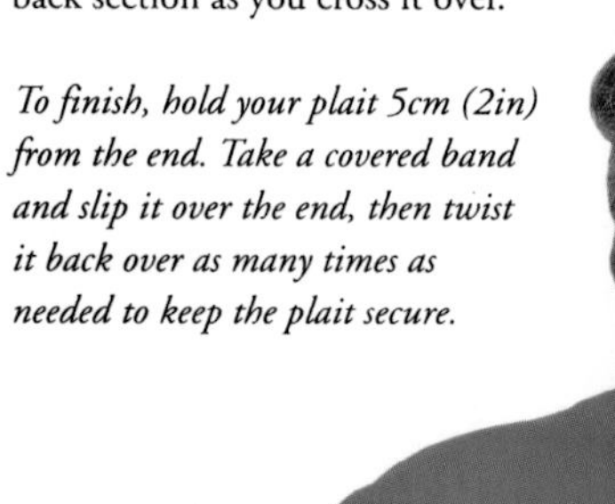

To finish, hold your plait 5cm (2in) from the end. Take a covered band and slip it over the end, then twist it back over as many times as needed to keep the plait secure.

Triple Twist

This is a perfect style if your hair is thick and wavy. A ponytail is divided into three sections and each section is plaited. Then these plaits are braided to make one plait.

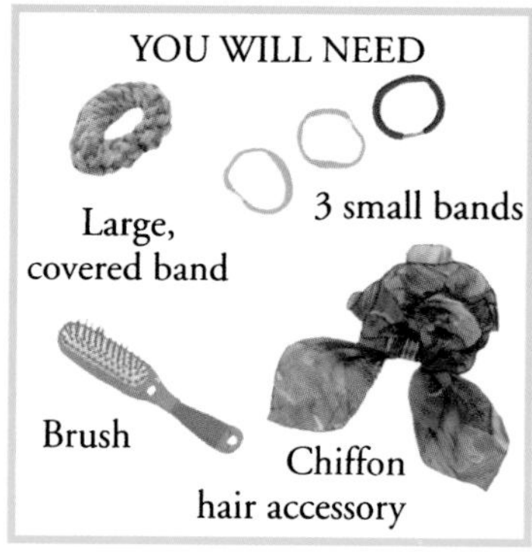

1 Brush your hair into a low ponytail at the nape of your neck using a wide bristled brush. Make sure the front and sides are really smooth. Secure the ponytail with the large, covered band.

2 Divide the ponytail into three equal sections. Take the first one and plait it from top to bottom. If your hair is long enough, bring the plaits over to the front of your shoulder.

3 When you get to the end of the plait, secure it with a small band. Plait the other two sections in exactly the same way. You now have three plaits to work with.

4 Take the three single plaits and plait them together in the same way as before. Your hair will form into a thick plait that looks like a twist of hair.

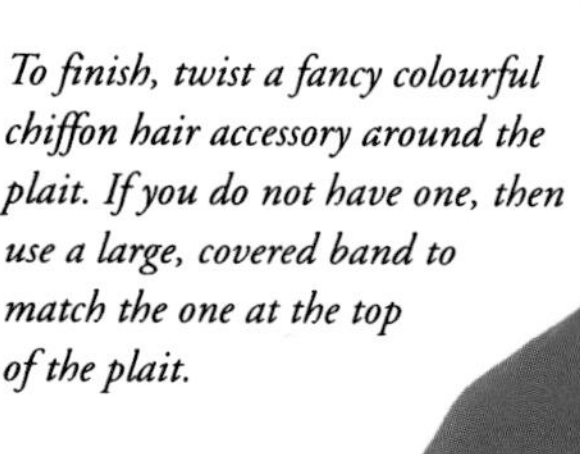

To finish, twist a fancy colourful chiffon hair accessory around the plait. If you do not have one, then use a large, covered band to match the one at the top of the plait.

Pretty Plaited Flips

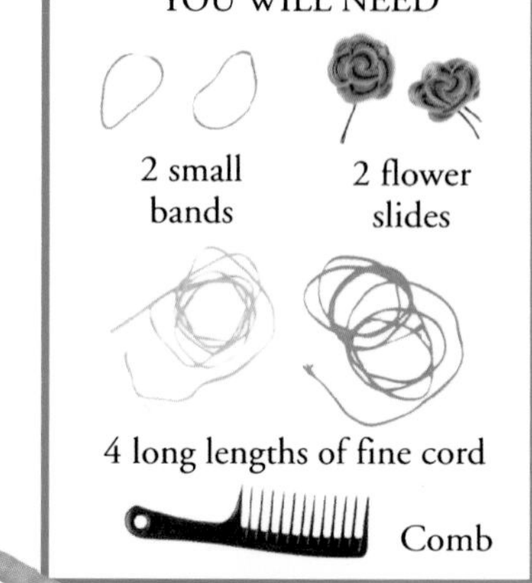

This style is inspired by the North American Indians. In their culture, men and women plait their hair and then bind the plaits with cord.

When choosing the cord to bind your plaits, avoid those with a very shiny, smooth finish. These cords are difficult to knot and they will slip off the plait.

1 Part your hair in the centre, and then plait the hair on one side from the roots to the ends. Keep the tension even so that your plait is straight.

2 Secure the end of the plait with a covered band, twisting it back over until it holds the plaits tightly. Do the same with the remaining hair.

3 Take a piece of cord and, starting at the top, bind the plait by wrapping the cord tightly round it. Keep the circles of cord close to one another.

4 Halfway down the plait, change the colour of the cord. Hold the ends of the first and second colours against the plait and bind the new colour tightly round the ends. Continue binding until you reach the end of the plait.

5 Secure the end of the cord by tucking it into the covered band that holds the plait together.

Add flowers or matching slides to either side of your head, at the front or above the plaits.

Racy Ribbons

Plaits look really good if you include ribbons as you go. At the ends, tie each ribbon into a bow for a really beautiful cascade of colour.

YOU WILL NEED

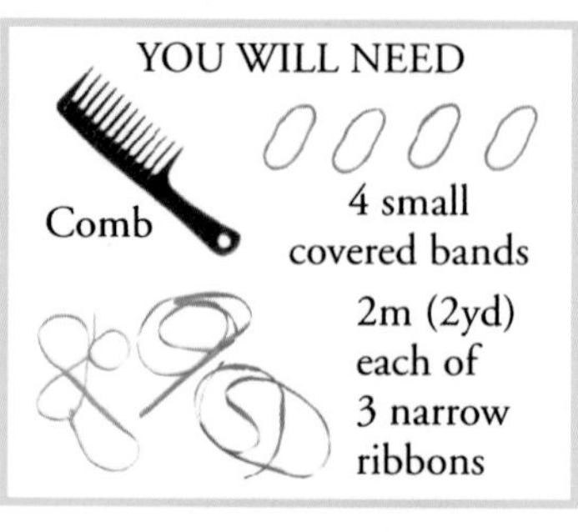

1 Part your hair in the centre and brush it through. Gather up the hair at each side and use a covered band to secure in bunches. Make the bunches at about ear level. Cut the ribbons in half.

2 Take three lengths of ribbon, each of a different colour. Pull the ends halfway through the band, then tie them on to it once. Make sure the ends are even.

3 Divide the hair into three sections and put two matching pieces of ribbon with each one. Plait the hair as normal but include the lengths of ribbon into the plait.

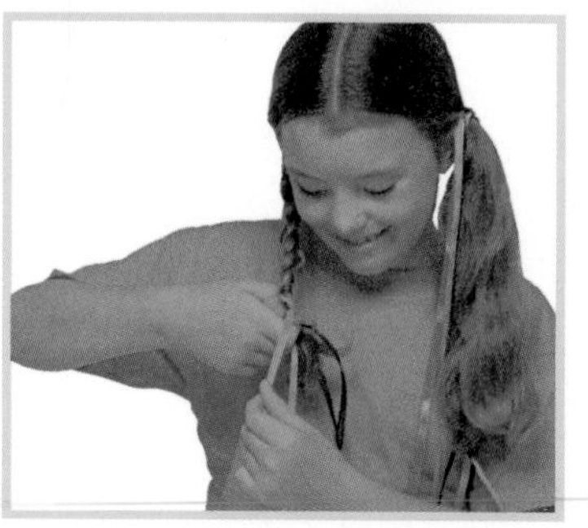

4 Secure the end of the plait, including the ribbons, in a small, covered band. Now take each pair of matching ribbons and tie them in a bow. Plait and tie the other side.

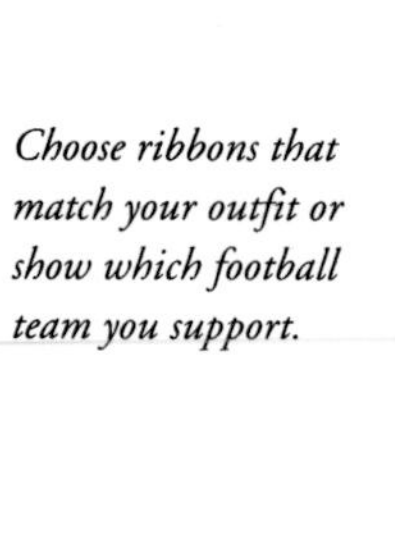

Choose ribbons that match your outfit or show which football team you support.

Ribbon Roll

It is easy to make very curly hair look neat and tidy if you plait a high ponytail with ribbon and twirl it into a roll.

YOU WILL NEED

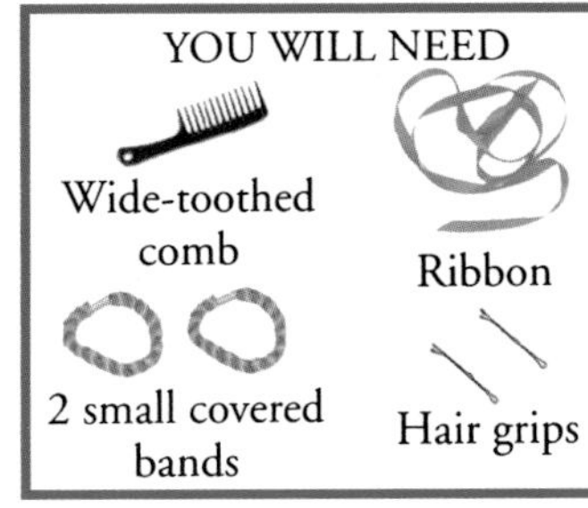

1 Use a comb with widely spaced teeth to help you smooth your hair up on to the top of your head. Hold your hair with one hand and put a small, covered band over the other hand. Twist the band round your hair a number of times to secure the ponytail.

2 Plait the ponytail from the top right down to the ends. Secure the ends with another small, covered band. You could leave your hair just like this if you wanted to.

3 Take a length of the ribbon and slip one end under the covered band at the top of your head and pull through, so the ends are even. Bind the ponytail with the ribbon right down to the ends.

4 Take the ends of the ribbon and plait in one hand and roll the lot round on itself to make a bun. Use one or two hair grips to secure the bun in place. Leave the ends of the ribbon to fall free.

The Ribbon Roll looks very classy. It is the perfect hairstyle for a special occasion like a wedding or fancy party.

Beaded Plaits

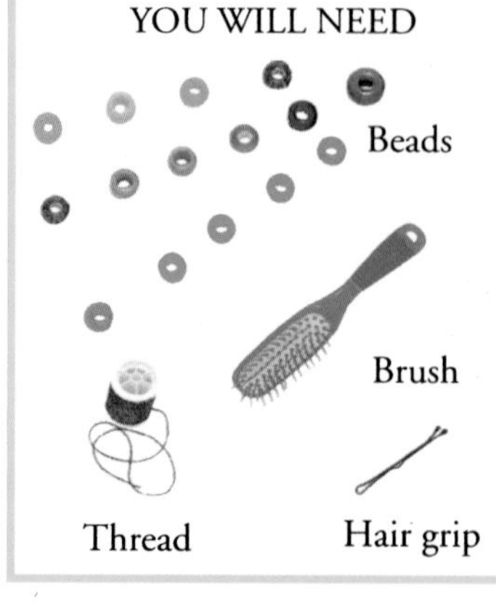

Fine plaits with beads threaded through the ends look spectacular. Bead just a few plaits around your face or ask a friend to help you do them all over your head.

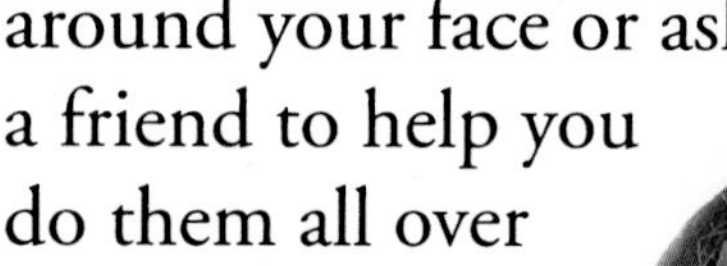

Safety!

Make sure you always keep your hair beads in a safe place away from babies or small children, who may think they are sweets.

Add colourful beads – as many as you wish – to brighten up your hair.

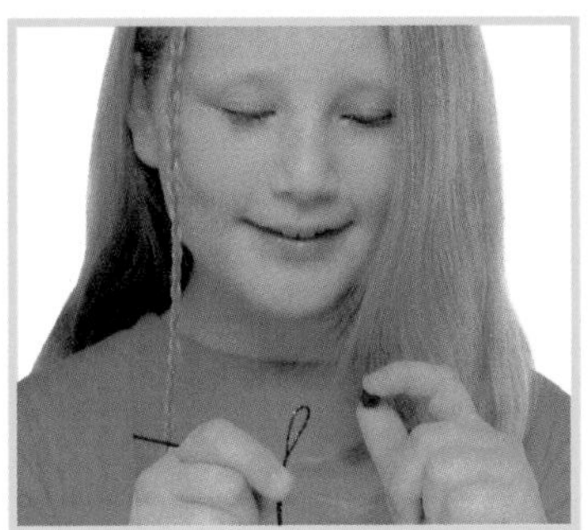

1 Plait a small section of hair down one side of your face. Secure the ends with a hair grip. Fold an 18cm (7in) piece of glittery thread to make a loop.

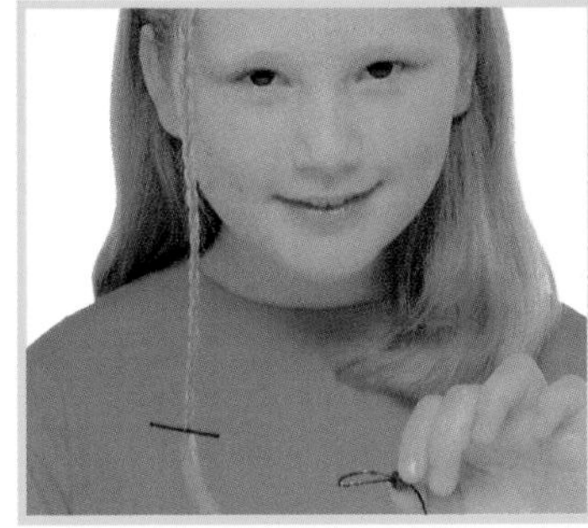

2 Pass the looped end of the glittery thread through the centre of the bead. This is easy if the bead has a large hole in the centre.

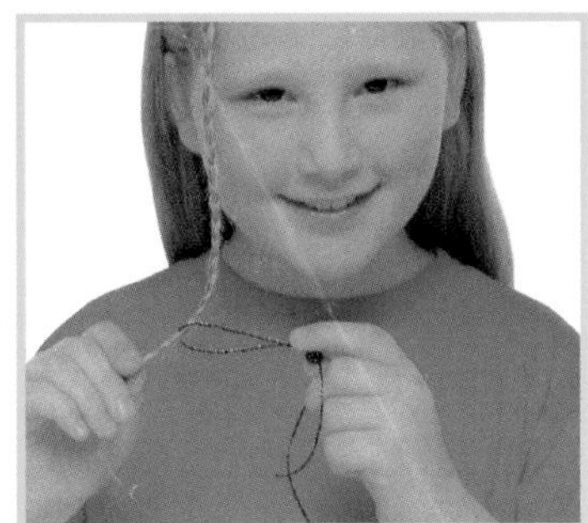

3 Remove the hair grip and pass the end of the plait through the loop of thread. Make sure you keep a firm hold on the bead, so that it does not fall off.

4 Push the bead towards the plait, then pull on the ends of the thread. This will pull the plait through the hole in the bead. Continue pulling until the end of the plait comes through the bead.

5 Wrap the thread round and round the end of the plait, making sure the strands lie flat. Carry on until you have covered about 1cm (1/2in) of hair below the bead.

Beads galore!

To put more than one bead on each plait, complete up to step 4 and then thread another bead on to the glittery thread. Push the bead towards the plait and then pull on the thread so that the plait comes through the hole in the bead. Repeat as many time as you like before following steps 5 and 6.

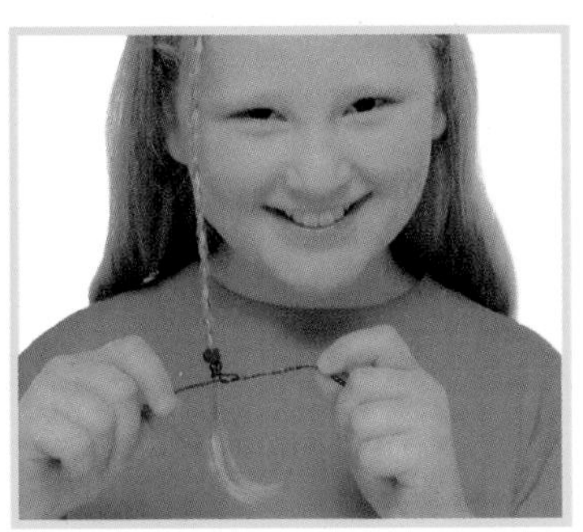

6 Cross over the ends of the thread, then tie a tight knot close to the plait. Trim the threads but be careful not to trim your hair!

Beaded plaits look best if the beads on each plait are level.

Plaits and Bows

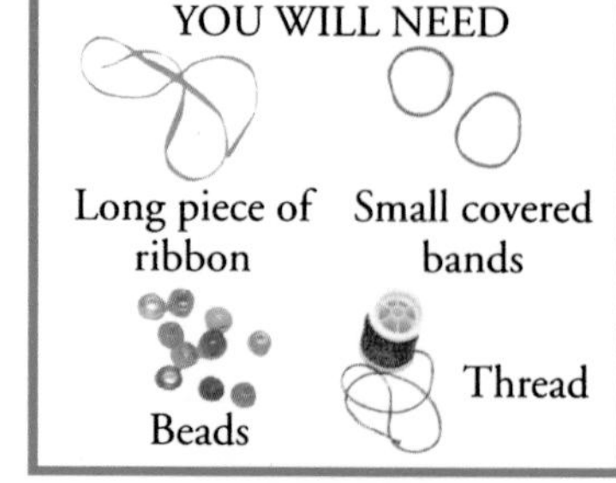

Simple plaits can be tied at the back of the head in a pretty bow, while tiny front plaits can be decorated with small beads.

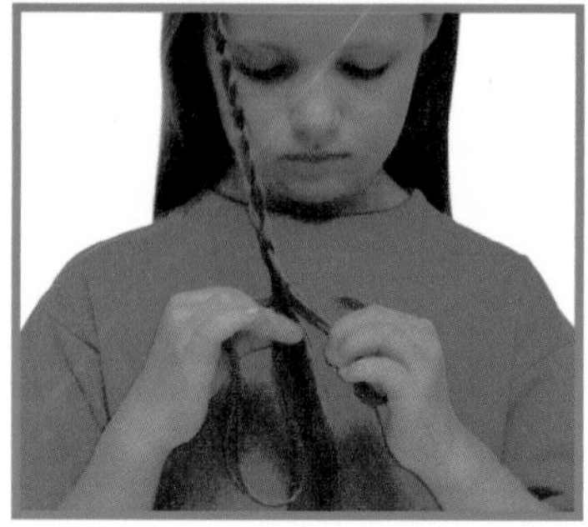

1 Part your hair in the centre, then take a small section of hair from one side. Start plaiting near the roots and work all the way down to the ends. Secure the ends with a covered band.

2 Take a small section of hair from the other side of your head and plait in the same way. Secure the ends in a covered band, twisting and wrapping the band round until it holds tight.

3 Take the braids round to the centre of the back of your head. Tie them together with a long piece of ribbon and loop it into a bow. Leave the ribbon ends dangling.

4 Plait two more sections of hair, so that each one hangs in front of an ear. Thread three different-coloured beads on to each plait (see Beaded Plaits). Try to match some of the beads to the colour of the ribbon.

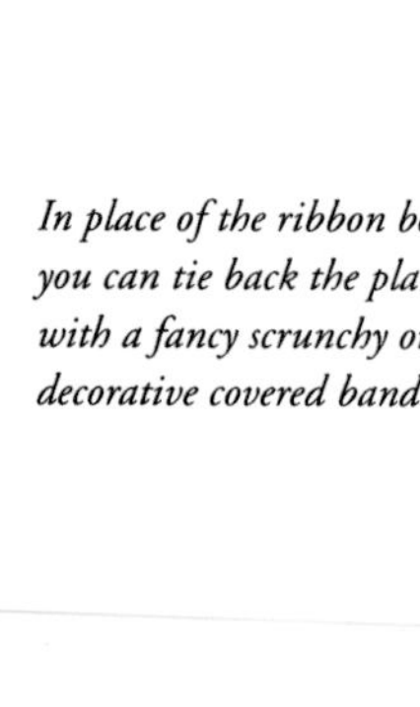

In place of the ribbon bow you can tie back the plaits with a fancy scrunchy or decorative covered band.

Bound Plaits

YOU WILL NEED

Lengths of ribbon in different colours

Thread

Medium-length or long straight hair can be plaited then wrapped with different coloured ribbons for a really wild style.

1 Take small sections of hair and plait them tightly from roots to ends. You may need a friend to help you plait the hair at the back.

2 Secure the end of each plait by winding fine, colourful thread two or three times around each plait. Secure with a firm knot and trim threads.

3 Fold a length of ribbon in half. Tie the ribbon to the top of the plait. The ends should be even. Bind the plait by crossing the lengths of ribbon over and over, first at the front of the braid, then at the back.

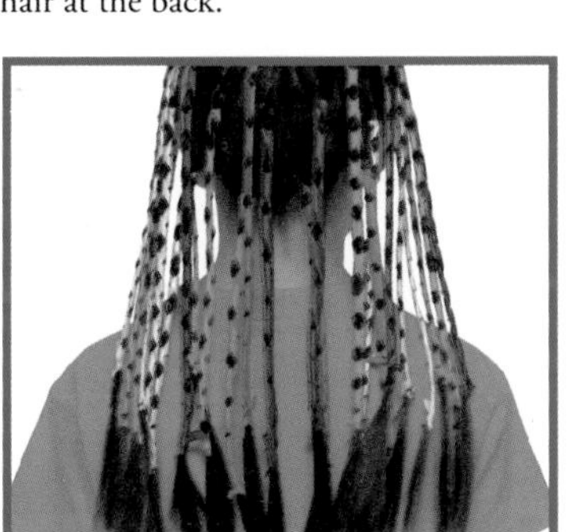

4 Continue binding until you reach the end of the plait. Tie the ends of the ribbon in a tight knot. Repeat until you have bound all your plaits. You will need a friend to help you bind the plaits at the back of your head.

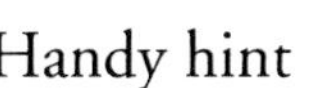

Handy hint

For each plait you will need a length of narrow ribbon that is three times the length of the plait.

Crimping Crazy

Hair care hint

When unravelling the plaits be gentle and patient. If you pull roughly on your hair you will damage it. Untangle any knots by starting at the hair ends and working upwards with a wide-toothed comb.

If you use only a wide-toothed comb on your crimps, they should last until you next wash your hair.

You do not need a crimping iron gadget to create soft ripples in your hair – all you have to do is plait your hair in lots of fine plaits. You will need to leave the plaits in overnight to set so do not leave this fabulous hairstyle to the last minute!

YOU WILL NEED

- Wide-toothed comb
- Thread
- Hairband
- Fabric flowers

1 Divide your hair into fine sections and braid it from the roots to the ends, making the plaits even and quite tight. The smaller the sections are, the finer the finished crimp will be.

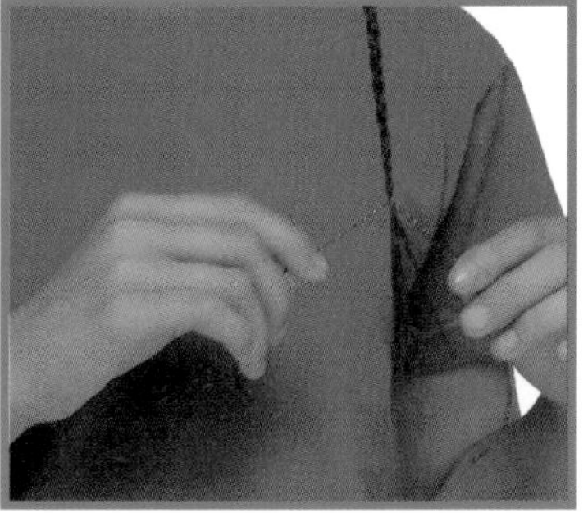

2 Secure the end of each plait with a piece of thread, wrap it around two or three times and then tie the ends into a little knot. If you prefer, you can use very small covered bands.

3 Leave the plaits in overnight to set your hair into lots of soft ripples. You can lightly mist your hair with water if you wish but do not go to bed with wet hair.

4 In the morning carefully unravel each braid, loosening it with your fingers as you go.

5 You can leave your hair loose and flowing or keep it off your face with a hairband. For a special occasion make two small ponytails at the front and tie on fabric flowers with cord or ribbon.

Wonder Waves

Straight hair can be changed into a mass of waves by using fabric curlers. You can leave the curlers in overnight, but even after a few hours you can achieve wonderful results.

Handy hint

You will get tighter and curlier Wonder Waves if your hair is just slightly damp when you put the curlers in. The easiest way to dampen your hair is with a water mist sprayer, but ask for permission before you borrow one. Never go to bed with wet hair.

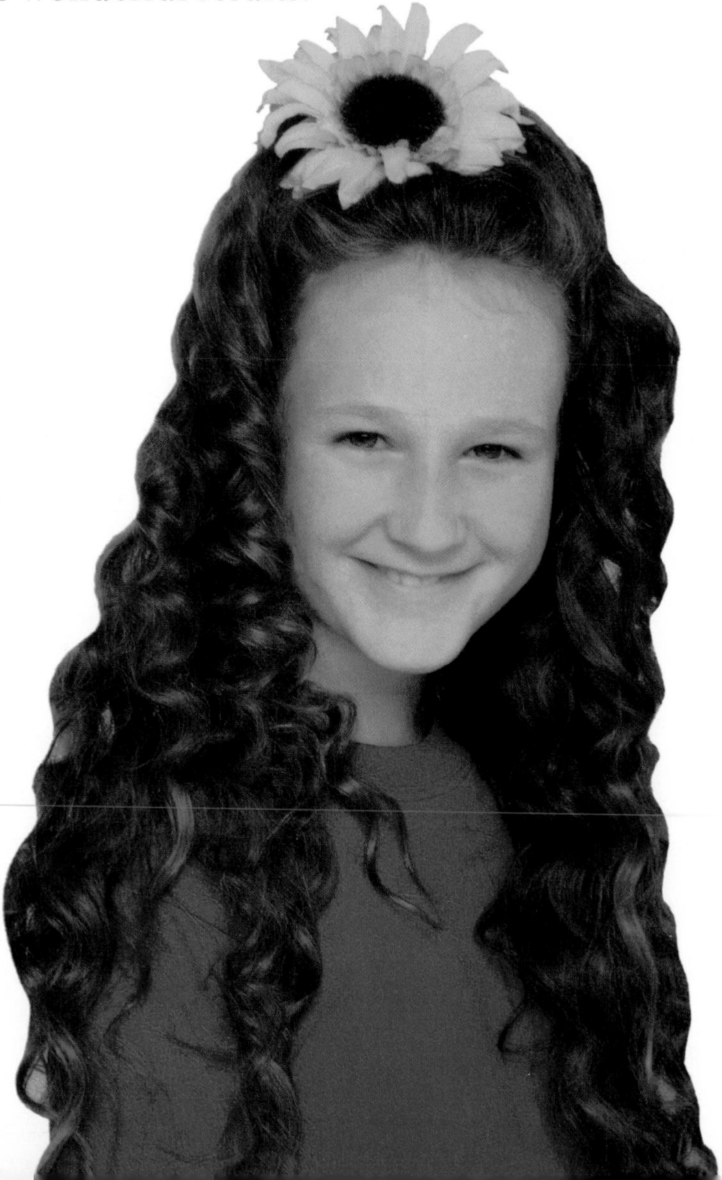

To make your lustrous locks look even more wonderful, tie a small ponytail at the top of your head. Secure with a covered band and use a hair grip to pin a brilliant fabric flower to the front of the ponytail. Fan out the ponytail so that it falls naturally around the sides and back of your head.

1 Take a fabric curler and fold it in half to grip a section of hair between the two pieces. Pull the curler right down to the bottom of the hair.

2 Wind the fabric curler up the hair from the ends towards your head. Do this slowly and make sure you do not let go of either end of the curler.

3 When you can wind no further, hold the ends of the curler and bring them together. Cross the ends over to lock the curler in place.

4 Repeat all over your head. Remember, the bigger the sections of hair you wind, the looser the wave will be. For really tight curls, take only small sections and use lots of curlers.

5 Leave your curlers in overnight. They are very soft, so they are comfortable to sleep in.

To reveal your Wonder Waves, gently undo and remove each curler. Use your fingers to 'rake' through each wave. You will look amazing!

Magical Masks

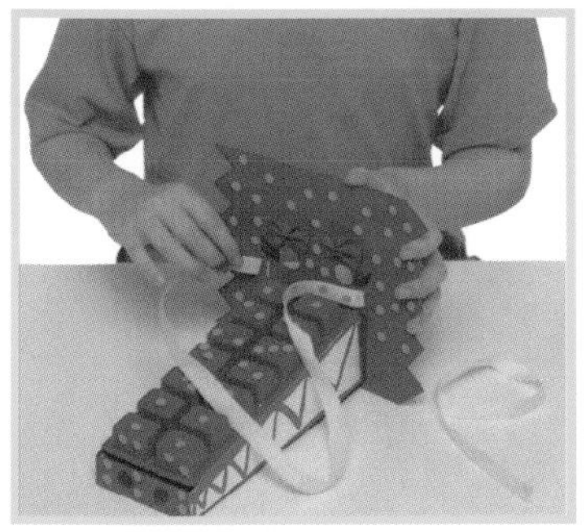

Introduction

The very scary Wicked Witch mask!

Masks are used to transform people and for disguise. In many ancient cultures, masks were an important part of religious and social customs. The person wearing the mask could become a god or a spirit. But masks are also important in modern culture. They are used in the re-enactment of special events, in the theatre and for fun. Japanese theatre relies on the actors wearing masks to portray certain characters, and could you imagine a street carnival without people wearing funny masks? There are even special parties, called masquerade balls, to which everyone must wear a mask.

You can make a mask to wear to a party, for dressing-up or to wear in a school play. Masks also make great wall decorations.

The Fancy Dress Masks that follow are both easy and fun to make. Card, fabric and papier-mâché are good basic materials, but you can also use items such as an ice-cube tray, an old tennis ball or pan scrubbers. In fact, almost anything can be used in mask-making. Following are some basic techniques that will help you to make some wonderful masks.

The Venetian Mask makes the wearer look most mysterious.

Fitting a mask

To make eye and mouth holes in the right positions on your mask, you need to know the distance between your eyes and the distance from your nose to your mouth. Start out by tracing around a pair of glasses or swimming goggles on to your mask. Then measure the distance from the bridge of your nose to your mouth. Measure and mark this distance on your mask.

Cutting eye holes

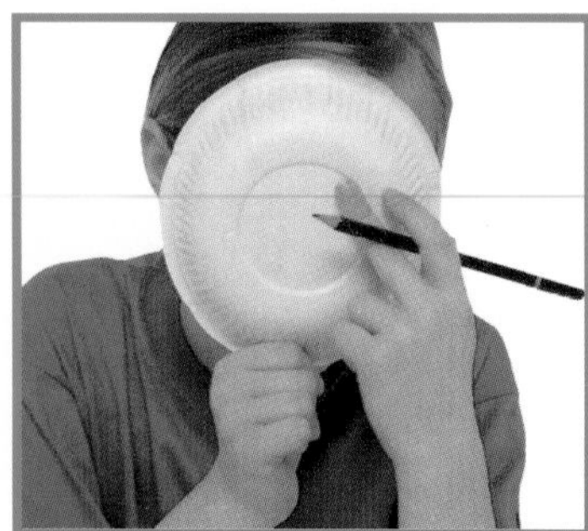

1 Hold a paper plate in front of your face. Carefully feel where your eyes are using your fingers.

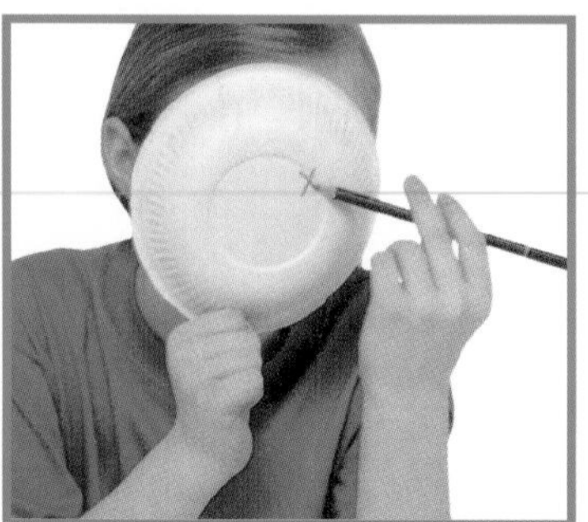

2 When you have found where your eyes are, mark the position of each one on the paper plate with a pencil.

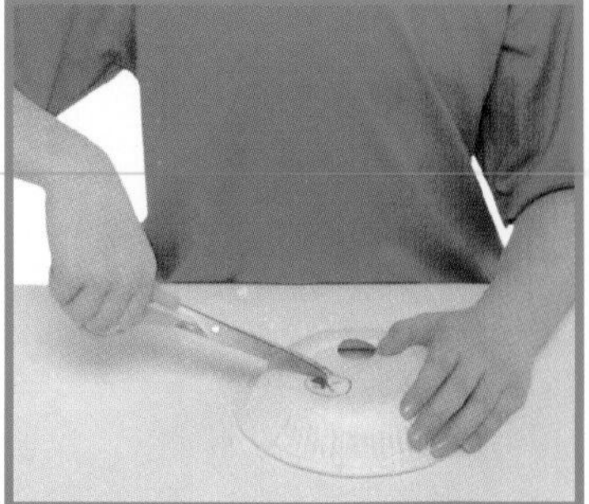

3 Draw two circles around the marks. Make a hole in the centre of the circles, then cut around the outlines.

Cutting a mouth

To cut out a mouth from a paper plate or card mask is easy if you do this simple trick.

Draw the outline of the mouth on to the back of a paper plate or card. Fold the mask in half so that the centre of the mouth is on the fold. Cut across the fold, following your outline. This will make sure that the cut-out mouth is even on both sides of your mask.

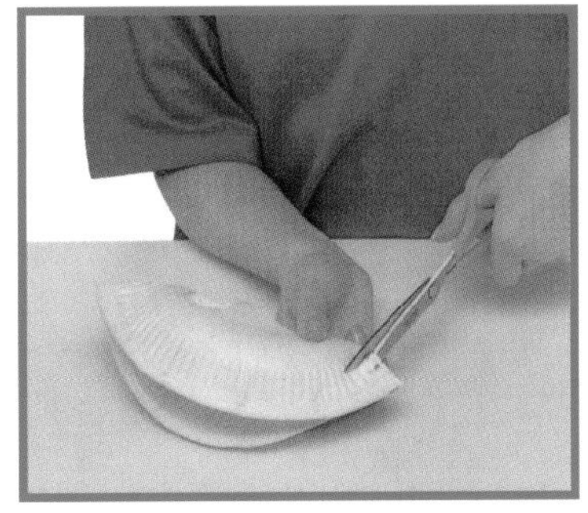

This mask is two masks in one. Open out the Hungry Wolf mask to reveal the Unlucky Lamb.

Attaching straps and ties

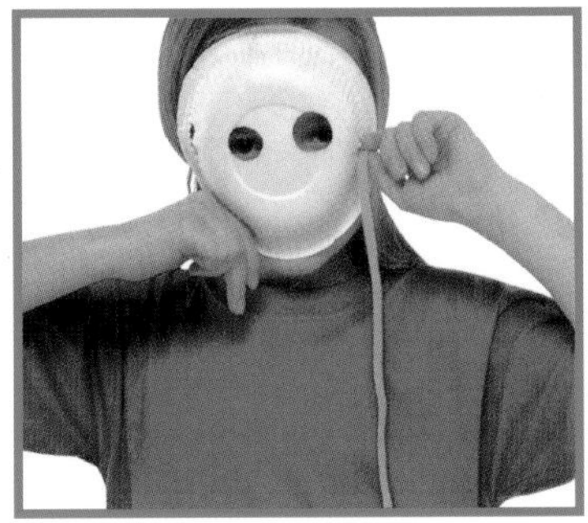

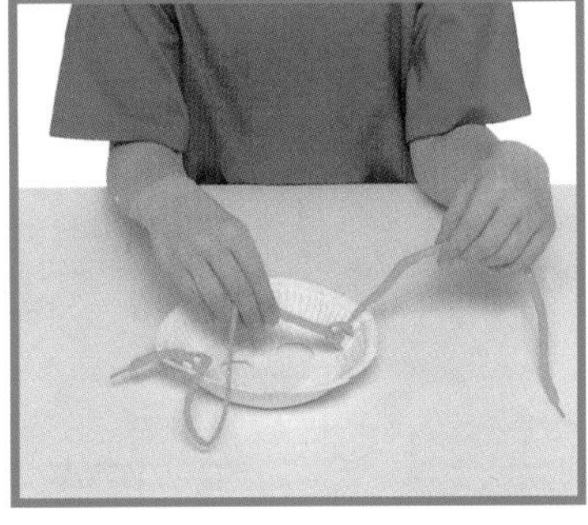

1 Cut two small holes on each side of the mask. Attach a strap to one side and place the mask on your face. Run the strap around the back of your head. Pinch the strap with your fingers when it makes contact with the second side.

2 Take the mask off, but do not let go of the strap – keep it pinched between your fingers. Put a mark on the strap where it is pinched between your fingers. Thread the strap through the second side and tie firmly at the mark.

3 Another way of attaching a strap is to glue it to the back of the mask. Mark the middle of a 1m (1yd) long strap and position the mark in the centre of the mask just below the eye holes. Allow to dry before wearing the mask.

There is something very fishy about this mask.

Safety tips

❖ Keep glues, sharp utensils and pointed objects well out of the reach of young children.

❖ Never put sharp or pointed objects near your eyes. When trying on a mask for the first time, check that there is no wet paint or glue on the back of the mask. Also check that there are no sharp edges. It is a good idea to stick clear sticky tape around the edges of masks made with a foil baking trays. Put tape around eye, nose and mouth holes as well.

❖ Plastic food wrap and plastic bags should never be used to decorate a mask.

❖ Ask an adult to trim the points and remove splinters from wooden skewers or garden sticks before using.

Materials

These are the main materials and items you will need to complete the Fancy Dress Mask projects.

Basket A round, cane or straw basket is best. It should be about the same size as a large plate.
Cotton wool You can use either cotton wool balls or a roll of cotton wool.
Corrugated card This thick brown card has ripples on one side and is smooth on the other. For some projects you can use corrugated card recycled from boxes. Other projects require a large sheet of corrugated card. It can be purchased in rolls or sheets from stationery and craft shops.
Disposable kitchenware This includes things like paper plates, plastic cups and foil baking trays or pie plates. Some of these items can be recycled from empty food packaging.
Fabric You can use a large piece of leftover plain or printed fabric or buy an inexpensive remnant from a fabric shop.
Funnel A small plastic funnel is available from hardware and kitchen shops. It can be used to make a nose for a mask.
Ice-cube tray Even an everyday item like a rectangular, plastic ice-cube tray is invaluable in mask-making. As you will not be able to reuse the tray, use an unwanted tray or buy one.
Newspaper You need sheets of newspaper to cover your work surface, and strips of newspaper for making papier-mâché.
Pan scrubber This is a round pad of twisted plastic or metal thread that is used to clean pots and pans. You can buy it in lots of bright colours or in a shiny copper or silver colour.
Pipe-cleaners You can find pipe-cleaners in art and craft shops. They come in various lengths and colours. To make the masks, you need an assortment of coloured, stripy and glittery ones.
Shoelaces These are used to make ties for your masks. You can paint or buy shoelaces to match the colour of your mask.
Sponge Use a felt-tip pen to mark out the shape you want on an ordinary bath or kitchen sponge, then trim with scissors.
String You will need fine, plain or coloured string to make ties for your masks.
Swimming goggles If you do not already have any swimming goggles, they are easy to find at sports shops. Goggles are fun to use in a mask, and make a cheap substitute for safety goggles too. Wear goggles whenever you are cutting something that may fly up into your eyes.
Tap hose This is used on the end of a kitchen tap to direct the stream of water. You can buy a plastic tap hose in a hardware or kitchen shop. Use it to make a nose for a mask.
Tennis ball If you are making a large mask, such as the Spanish Giant, an old tennis ball cut in half and painted makes a great pair of eyes. Ask an adult to help you cut the tennis ball, as it can be quite tricky to do.

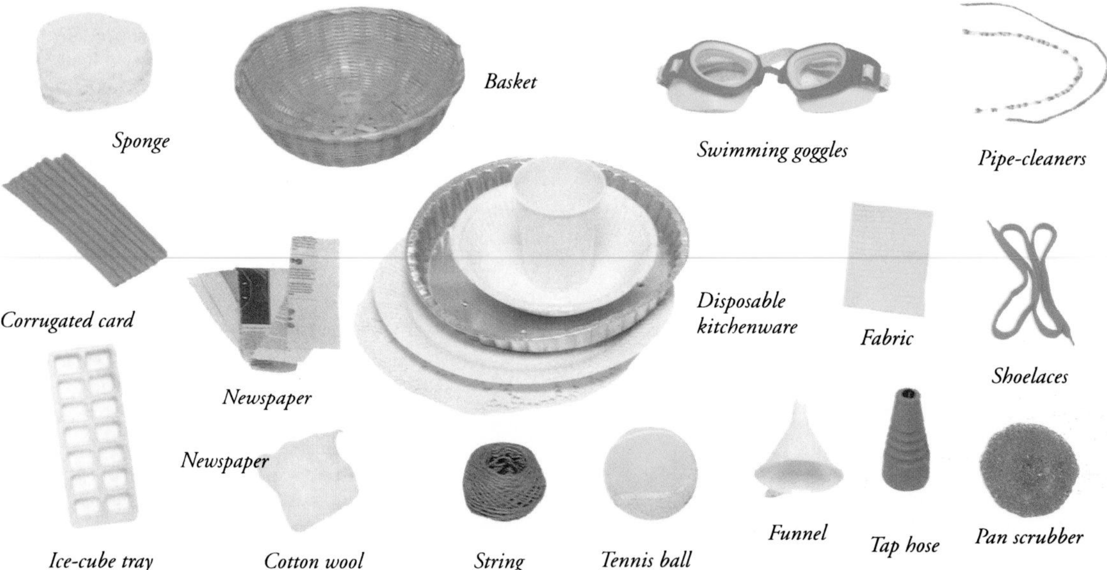

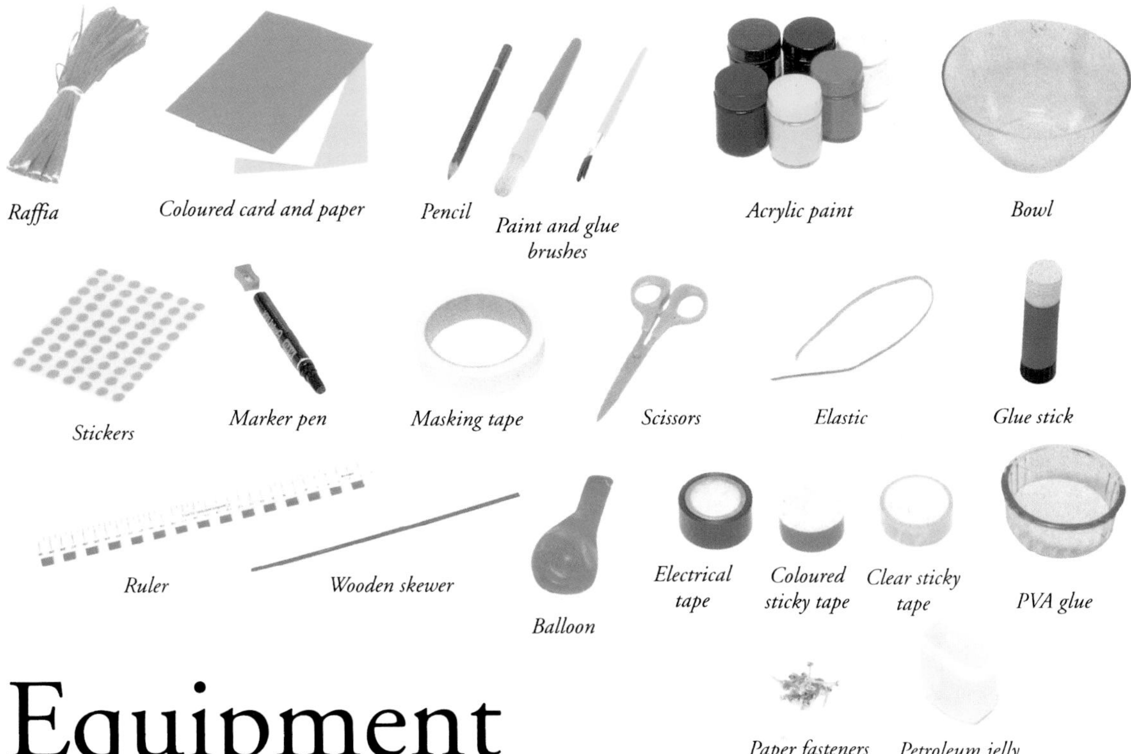

Equipment

Acrylic paint This is a water-based paint that comes in lots of bright colours. You can also use poster paints.
Balloon You will need an ordinary round balloon to use as a mould for making a papier-mâché mask.
Coloured card and paper Use either scraps of leftover card or paper, or buy sheets from a stationery shop.
Elastic To tie a mask firmly around your head you can use a length of narrow elastic. This can be bought in fabric shops. In place of elastic, use shoelaces, string or ribbon.
Electrical tape This is also called insulating tape, and it can be bought in hardware shops. It comes in various widths and in lots of bright colours.
Glue stick This is great for sticking a piece of paper to a flat surface. Smooth out lumps before leaving it to dry. Always replace the lid, as glue sticks dry out.
Masking tape This is useful for holding things in place while glued surfaces dry. Masking tape can be painted over.
Paper fasteners These are small, shiny metal pins with a round head and two legs. When the legs are pushed through paper or other items and opened, they fasten the items together.
Petroleum jelly This white or creamy jelly is very greasy. It is applied to a balloon before it is covered with papier-mâché. It prevents the papier-mâché from sticking to the balloon.
PVA glue This glue is also known as wood glue, school glue or white glue. PVA glue is a strong glue that can be used to bind paper, card, fabric, plastic or wood surfaces.
Raffia This flat, ribbon-like material is made from the leaves of a palm tree. It comes in tied-up bundles and in lots of bright colours. Buy it in craft shops or stationery shops.
Scissors If possible, you should have two pairs of scissors, one for cutting fabric and the other for cutting paper.
Stickers Use stickers in all sorts of colours, shapes and sizes as a quick way of decorating a mask.
Sticky tapes You can use clear, coloured or patterned sticky tapes to make Fancy Dress Masks.
Wooden skewers These narrow, round, pointed sticks are about 30cm (12in) long and can be bought in supermarkets. You can also use garden sticks or split canes, but ask an adult to cut them to the required length.

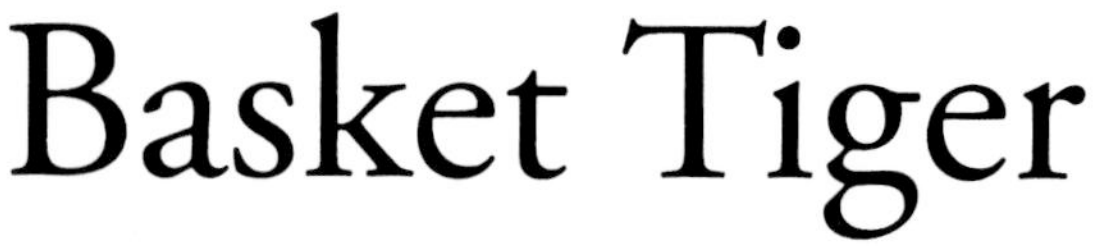

Basket Tiger

The idea for this mask is inspired by traditional African masks, many of which looked like wild animals. Just like a real African mask, this mask is made using a natural material – a basket made from cane. Clay and wood were also used to make masks.

YOU WILL NEED THESE MATERIALS AND TOOLS

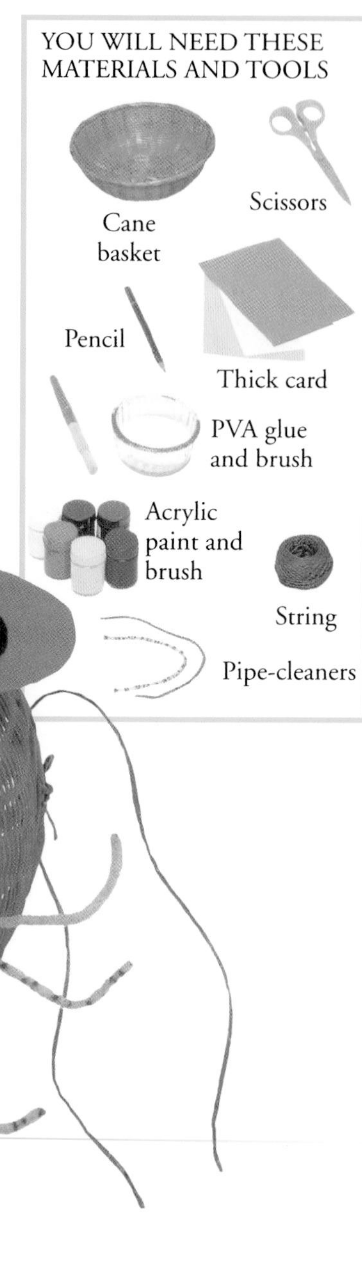

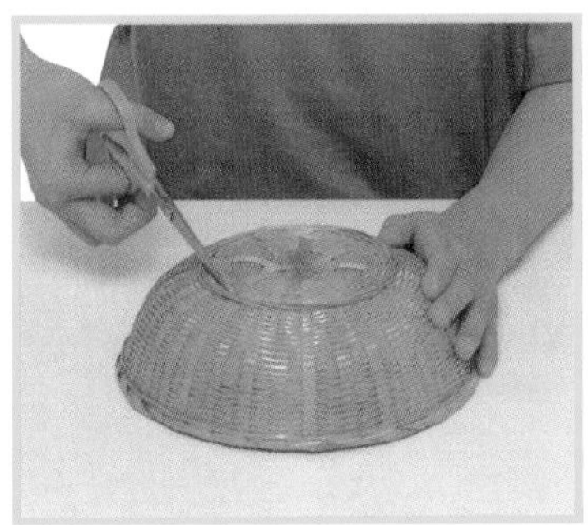

1 Cut a round hole in the bottom of the basket using a pair of scissors. You may need to ask an adult to help you do this. When cutting the hole, do not put your fingers under the basket.

2 Place the basket on the sheet of coloured card. Draw around the hole. This will become the face of the tiger. Remove the basket and draw an ear on either side of the face.

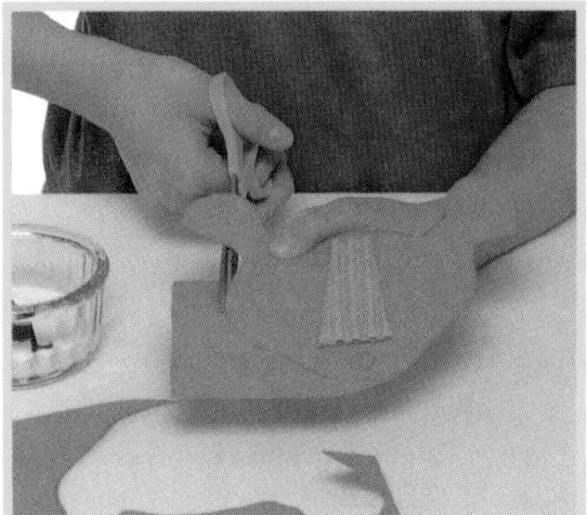

3 Cut out the face and ears. Draw and cut out a nose from a scrap of thick cardboard. Glue the nose on to the face and leave to dry. Draw, then cut out eye and mouth holes.

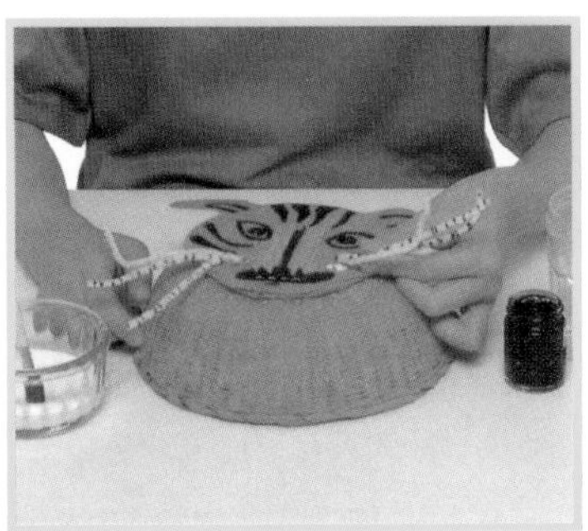

4 Apply glue to the back of the face and press it firmly in position over the hole in the basket. Leave to dry. Paint the basket and face orange. When dry, paint the tiger's features with black paint. Glue pipe-cleaners on either side of the nose for whiskers. Allow the glue to dry thoroughly before starting the next step.

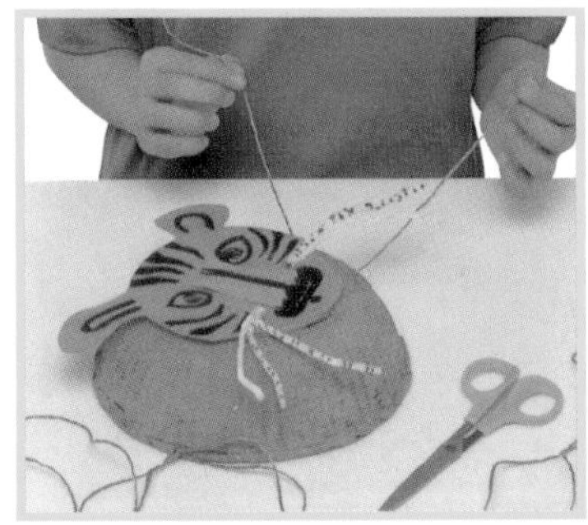

5 Thread string through gaps in the basket, on each side of the mask. Tie the mask securely around your head.

Basket animals

A cane or straw basket and card can be used to make a whole zoo of animals. Follow the instructions for Basket Tiger but modify the face, ears, nose and colouring to make a monkey, a lion, an elephant or a bear. Basket masks would be perfect to use in a school play.

The Basket Tiger mask is easy and quick to make. To act like a real tiger you must growl and move quietly with great stealth.

Venetian Mask

Venice is famous for its Carnival, when everyone dresses up in colourful costumes and fancy masks. This mask is not tied around your head – it is simply fixed to a wooden stick. A Venetian lady would hold the mask to her face when she wanted to be mysterious, and lower it to reveal her beauty.

Handy hint

If you find that PVA glue is not strong enough to hold the wooden skewer securely to the mask, use sticky tape or masking tape as well. It is also a good idea to wind tape around the bottom and the top of the skewer to keep the pipe-cleaners in place.

YOU WILL NEED THESE MATERIALS AND TOOLS

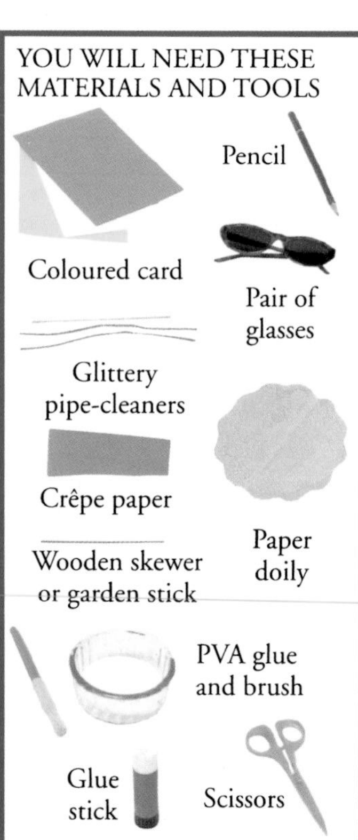

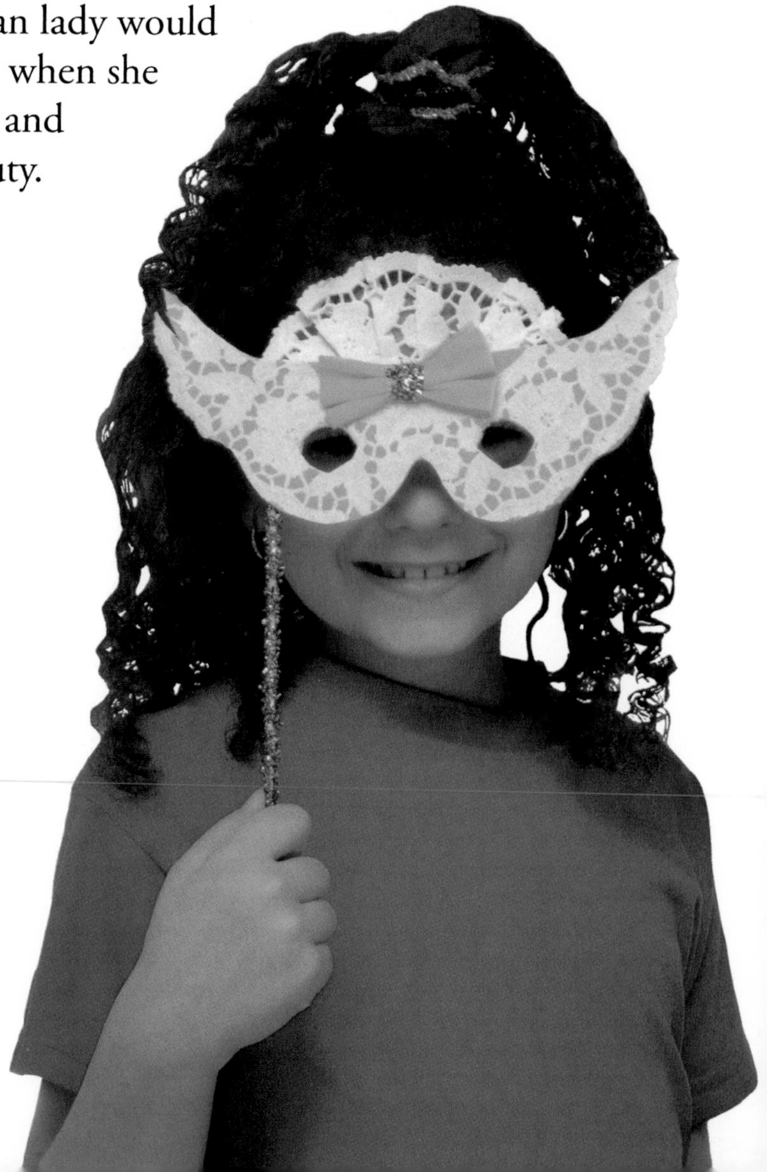

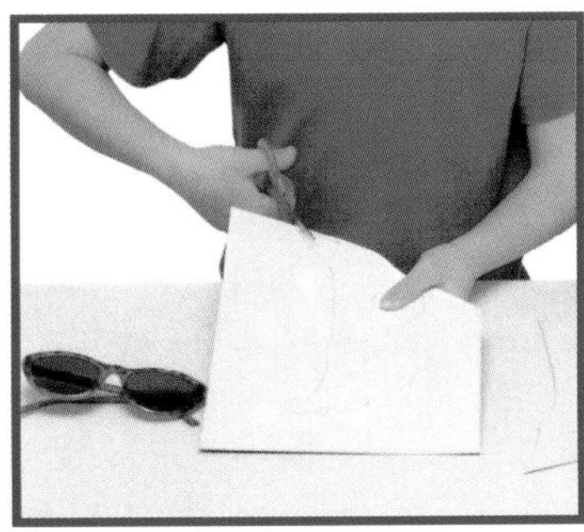

1 Place a pair of glasses on to the card and draw around them with a pencil. Add on to your outline the fancy curves on both sides of the mask. Cut out the card with scissors.

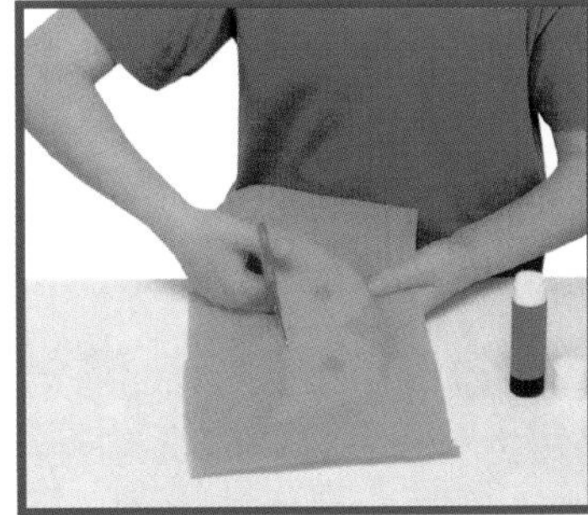

2 Apply glue to the front of the card with the brush and place a large piece of crêpe paper on top. Smooth out the crêpe paper. When the glue is dry, trim around the edges with scissors.

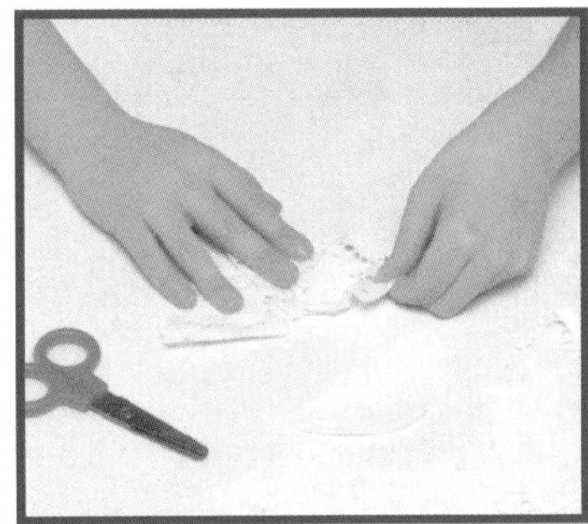

3 Fold the paper doily in half and cut out the semi-circle in the middle. Unfold the doily and cut in half following the fold line. Pleat one half of the doily so that it looks like a fan.

Safety!

Be careful when moving around wearing a mask. Your vision may be restricted by the size of eye holes in the mask. Take extra care when there are wooden sticks attached to the mask.

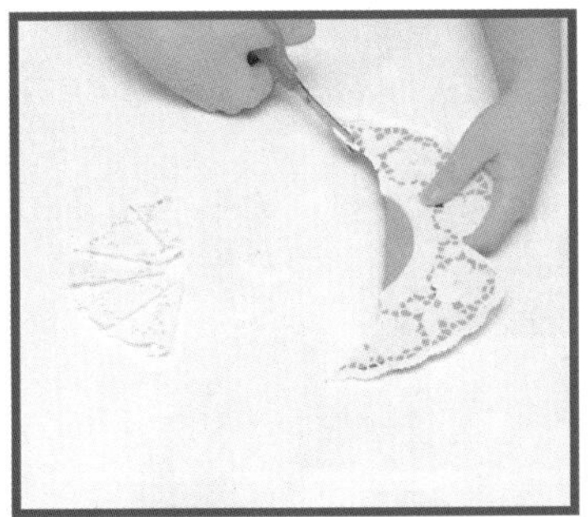

4 Glue the other half of the doily to the front of the mask with paper glue. The cut-out semi-circle should be at the top of the mask. Trim around the edges so that it fits the mask perfectly. Glue the pleated doily to the top of the mask. Draw eye holes on to the front of the mask, then cut them out.

5 Ask an adult to trim any sharp ends from the wooden skewer or garden stick. Tightly wind pipe-cleaners around the skewer to cover it completely. Fix the skewer to the back of the mask with PVA glue and leave to dry thoroughly. Cut a rectangle of crêpe paper and wind a pipe-cleaner around the middle to make a bow. Glue the bow on to the mask, as shown. Allow to dry.

You can really let your imagination run wild when decorating your Venetian Mask. The Venetians certainly do when designing their masks for the Carnival. You could add sequins and glitter, or even paint the doily gold!

Easter Rabbit

Make this fun rabbit mask to wear on Easter morning. Its plump, white cheeks are made from bath sponges. To make the whiskers you can use wooden skewers or plastic straws.

YOU WILL NEED THESE MATERIALS AND TOOLS

Pipe-cleaners
Coloured card
Scissors
Pencil
PVA glue and brush
Glue stick
Black felt-tip pen
Two bath sponges
Six wooden skewers or plastic straws
Small pieces of black and white paper
Ruler

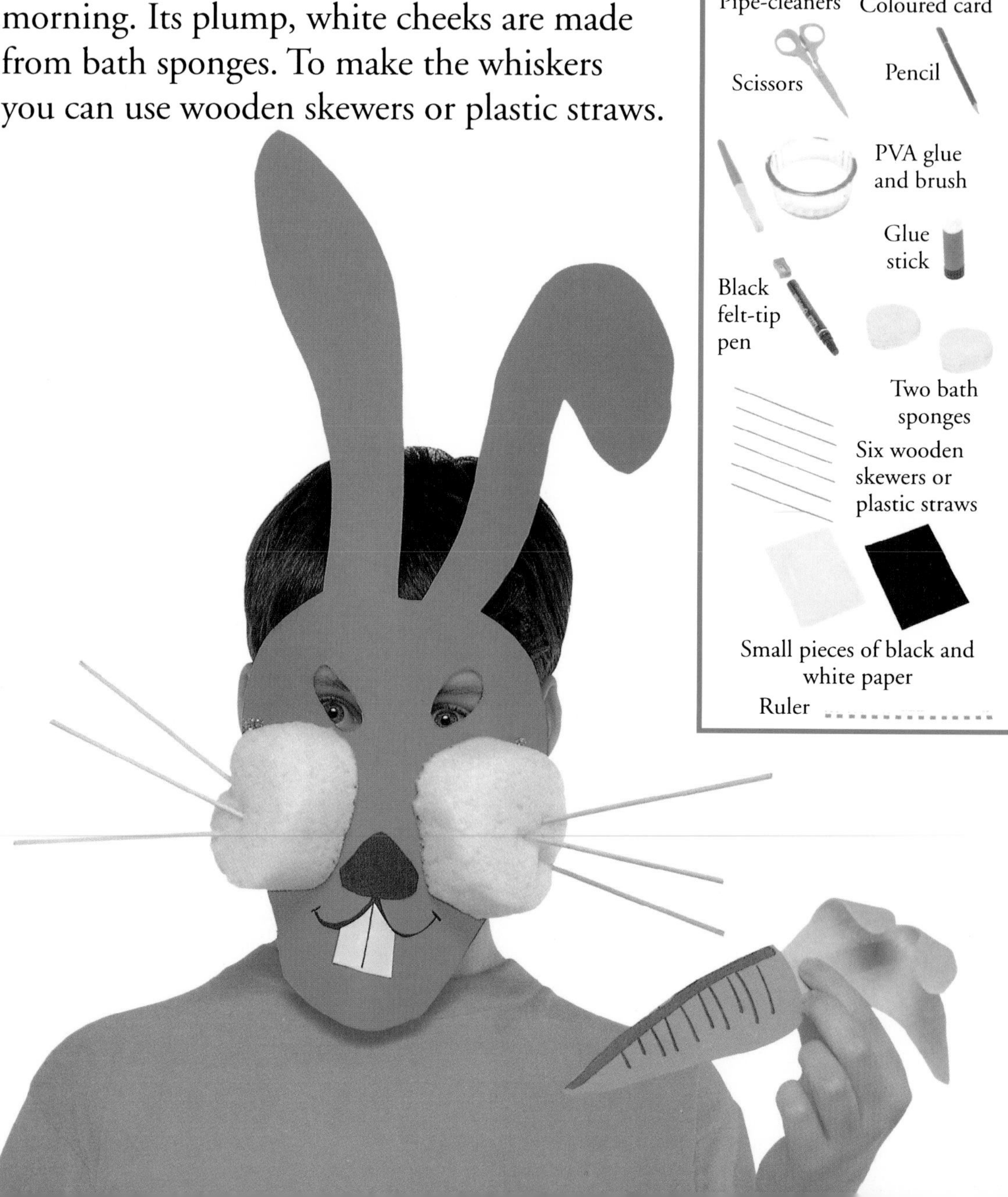

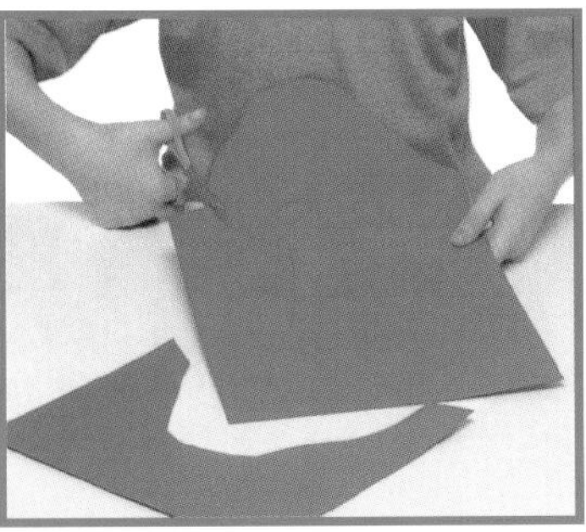

1 Draw and cut out a rabbit's face and ears, measuring 30cm (12in) wide and 60cm (24in) long, from thin coloured card. Cut out two eye holes.

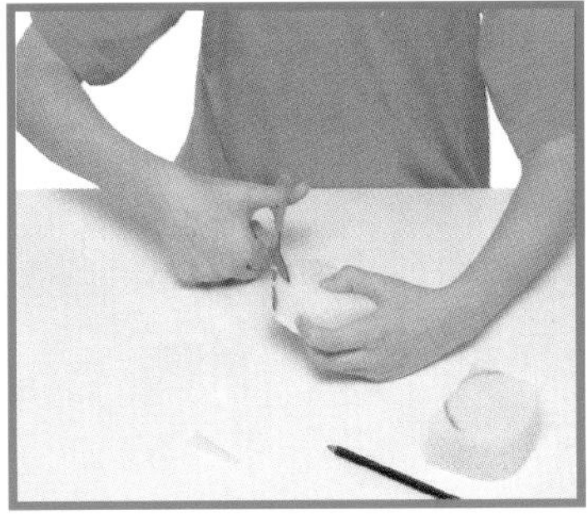

2 To make the rabbit's cheeks, draw a large circle on both bath sponges and cut them out. Make the circles as large as possible, then trim them to fit.

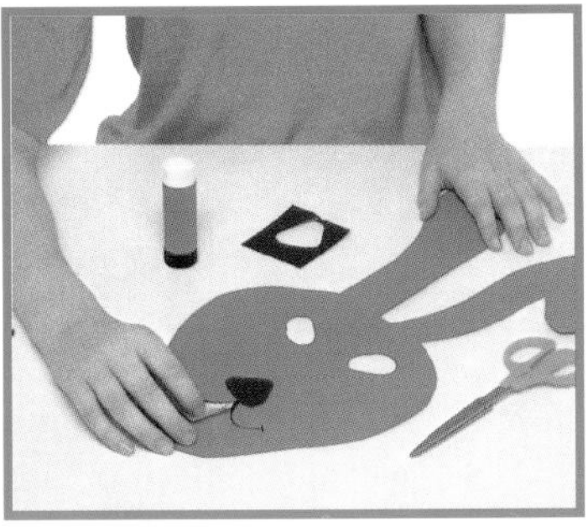

3 Draw a mouth with the felt-tip pen. Cut out a nose from black paper and a pair of teeth from white paper. Glue them on to the mask.

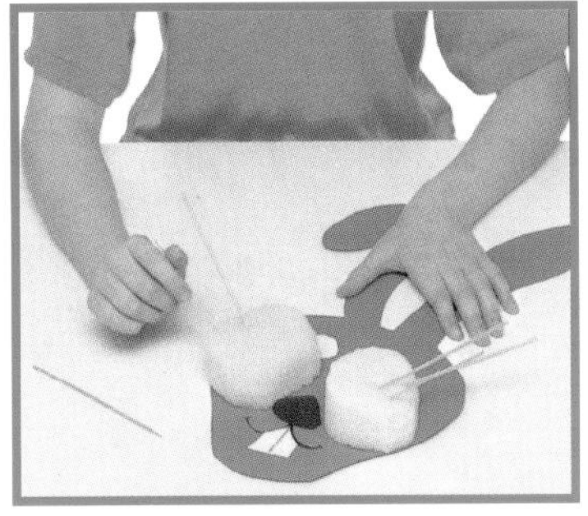

4 Glue on the sponge cheeks using PVA glue. The sponge will absorb the glue, so apply lots. Allow plenty of time for the glue to dry. Ask an adult to cut the pointy ends off the skewers. Dab a little PVA glue on to one end of each of the skewers. Insert three skewers into each sponge for the whiskers. If the whiskers are too long, ask an adult to trim them.

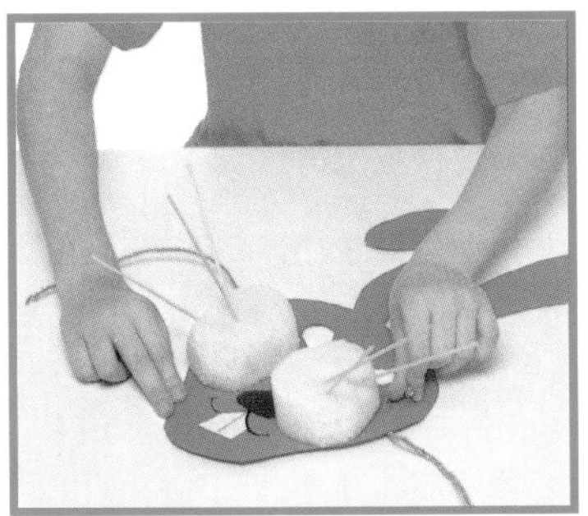

5 Make a small hole on either side of the mask. Thread a pipe-cleaner through each hole and twist the end to hold it in place. To wear the mask, hook the pipe-cleaners around your ears.

Painting your mask

If you want to paint the rabbit's furry grey face you will need – black, white and red paints, a mixing palette, water pot, and fine and medium paintbrushes. It is best if you paint the mask before gluing on the cheeks, nose and teeth.

To help you get the colours and fur just right, refer to a photograph of a rabbit in a book or magazine.

To start, mix together black and white paint to make a pale grey colour. Use the medium paintbrush to paint the front of the mask, but do not paint the ears. Mix a little more black into the grey to make it darker. Use this colour to paint lots of short, fine lines radiating outward from the cheeks. While this dries, paint the ears pink. You can make pink by mixing white and red paint. Paint the edges of the ears grey. Paint lots of short, fine white lines, also radiating outward from the cheeks. When dry, finish making the mask.

Wicked Witch

Make yourself a naughty witch disguise to wear to a Halloween fancy dress party. To complete your awful transformation, make a broomstick from twigs and branches and wear a black cloak over your shoulders.

Handy hint

If you cannot find a plastic funnel to use for the witch's nose, form a cone from a piece of card.

To make a cone, cut out a circle 15cm (6in) wide. Cut the circle in half. Bend one half so that the straight edges overlap. Join the edges with tape. Trace around the base of cone on to the plate. Draw a slightly smaller circle inside the outline. Cut out the small circle. Make shorts snips up into the base of cone. Fold out these flaps and push the cone into the hole. Glue the flaps to the back of the plate.

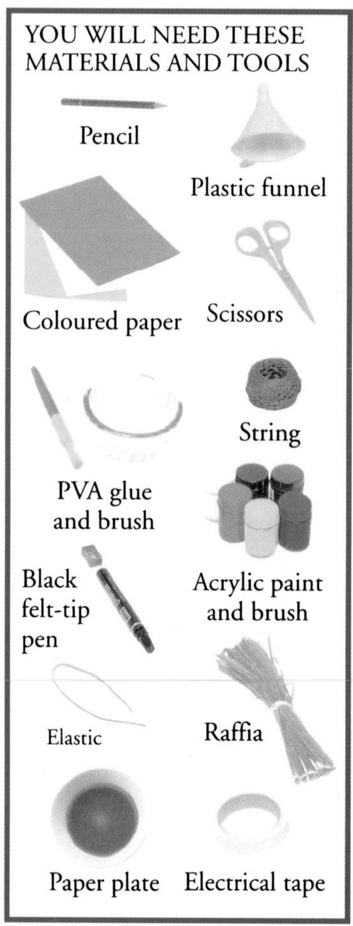

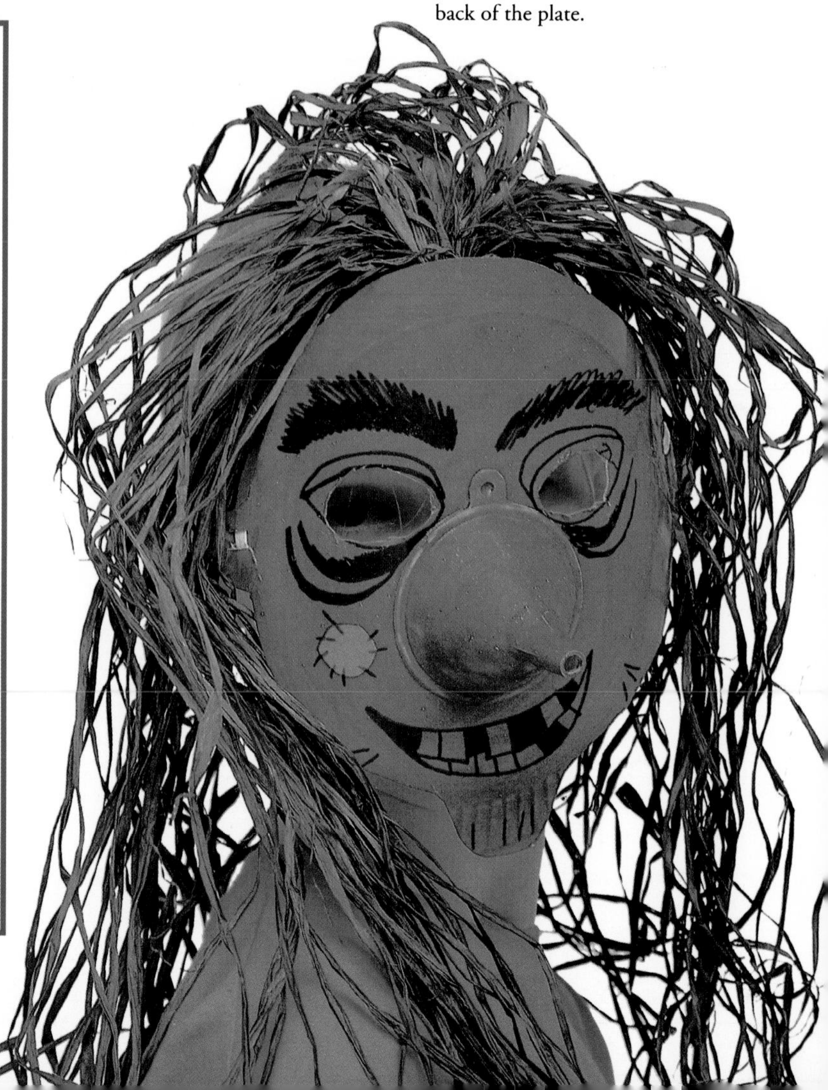

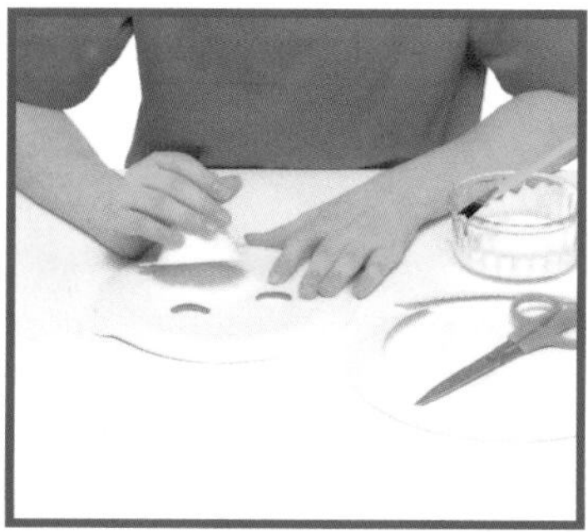

1 Draw a witchs face with a pointy chin on to the back of a paper plate and cut it out. Cut out holes for eyes. Place the funnel in the centre of the plate and trace around it. Cut out the circle, slightly inside the drawn line. Glue the funnel over the hole.

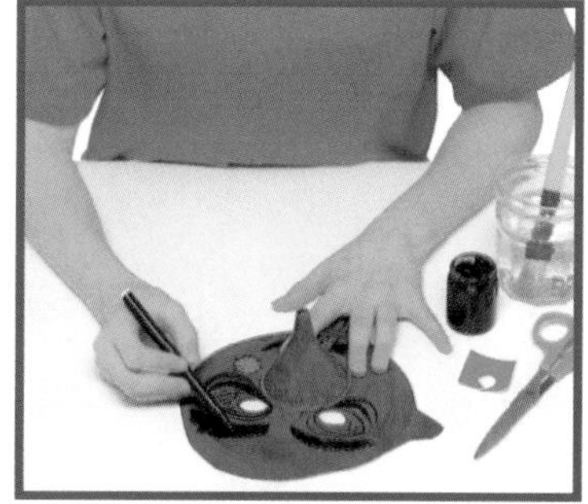

2 Mix a little PVA glue into green paint – the glue will help the paint stick to the funnel. Paint the face and funnel green. Cut out a small circle of red paper and glue it to one cheek to make a wart. Draw and colour in other features with a black felt-tip pen.

3 Undo the bundle of raffia and cut it into long lengths for the witch's hair. Tie the lengths of raffia together at one end with a piece of string. Use a piece of electrical tape to fix the bundle of raffia to the back of the plate.

4 Make a hole on each side of the mask. Thread a long length of elastic through one hole and tie it on. Put the mask on your face. Cut the elastic to the right length and knot it on to the other hole.

If this gruesome, green mask does not scare your friends and family, then nothing will. To really play the part of a witch, make up some spooky spells and carry around a pot full of plastic spiders and frogs!

Crazy Glasses

These glasses are inspired by the ones you find in joke shops. Crazy Glasses will really let you make a spectacle of yourself!

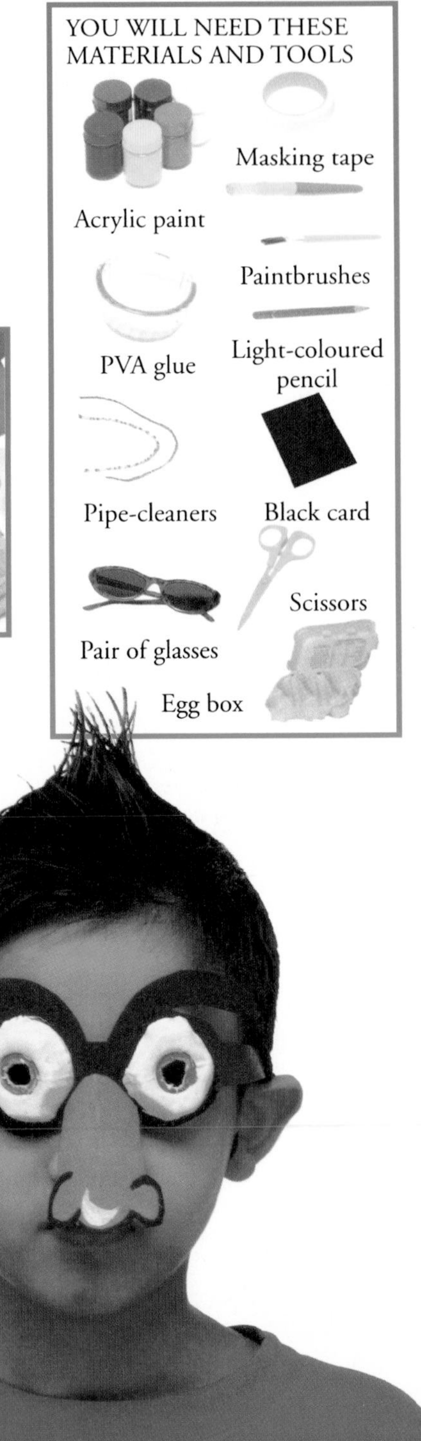

1 Draw a glasses shape on the black card. Use the pair of glasses as a guide for size and for the shape around your nose. You will need to use a light-coloured pencil or the outline will not show up. Cut around the outline.

2 Cut out two of the compartments from an egg box to make the eyes. Make a hole in the centre of each one for you to see through. Cut a piece of card from the lid of the egg box for the nose. Paint them and leave to dry.

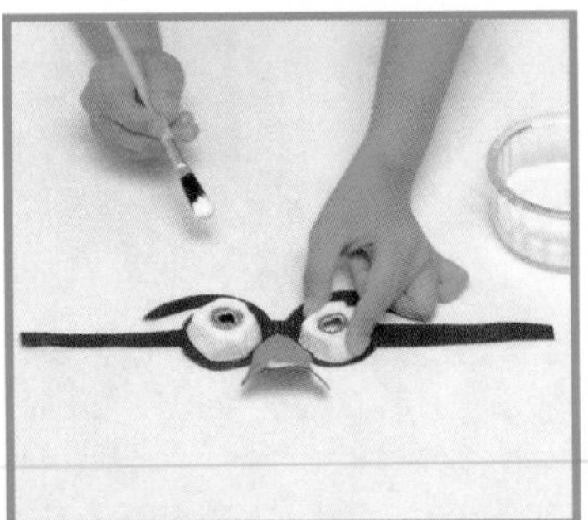

3 When dry, glue the eyes and nose on to the frame of your Crazy Glasses with PVA glue. To make sure the nose is firmly fixed, use masking tape to hold it in position. While the glue is drying, prop up the nose with a pencil. Paint two pipe-cleaners black and leave to dry.

To finish, apply PVA glue to the ends of both arms of the Crazy Glasses. Wind a black pipe-cleaner several times around each glued area and leave to dry. Bend the pipe-cleaners round your ears to keep your crazy specs in place.

Fish Focals

Masks can be made using almost anything! Here, a pair of swimming goggles is used to make a very fishy mask.

YOU WILL NEED THESE MATERIALS AND TOOLS

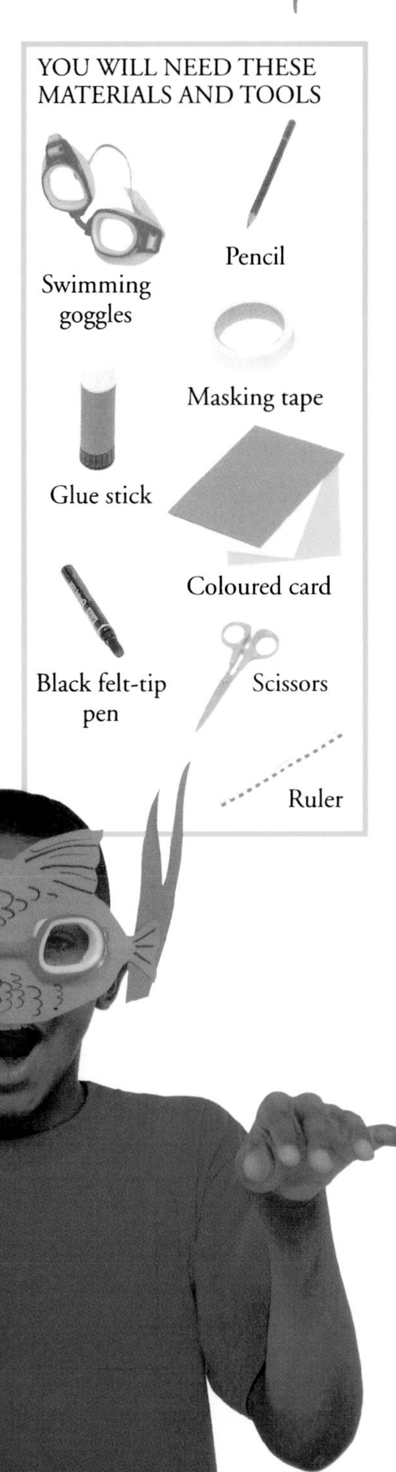

Swimming goggles
Pencil
Masking tape
Glue stick
Coloured card
Black felt-tip pen
Scissors
Ruler

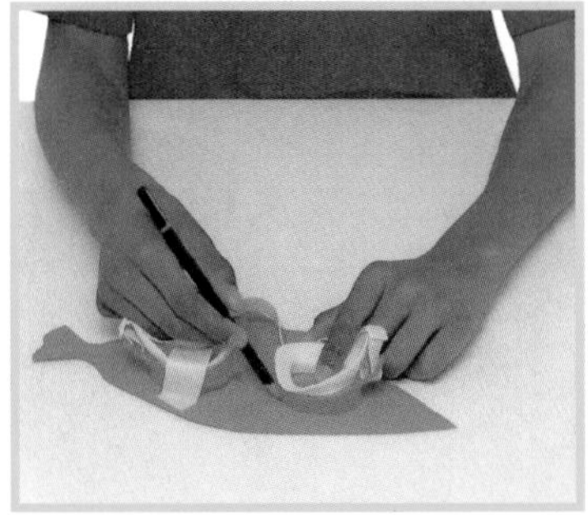

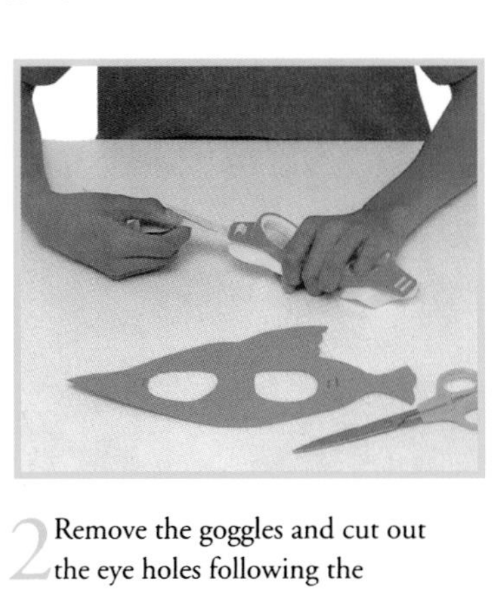

1 Draw a fish shape 25cm x 10cm (10in x 4in) from card. Cut it out. Place the swimming goggles on to the fish and draw around the outline. To make this easy, hold the goggles in position with masking tape. Also cut from different coloured card, a small circle for the eye and fronds of seaweed.

2 Remove the goggles and cut out the eye holes following the lines you have drawn. Cut four small vertical slits, two on the outside edge of each eye hole. Make sure the slits are large enough to fit the strap on the goggles. Remove the strap from your goggles.

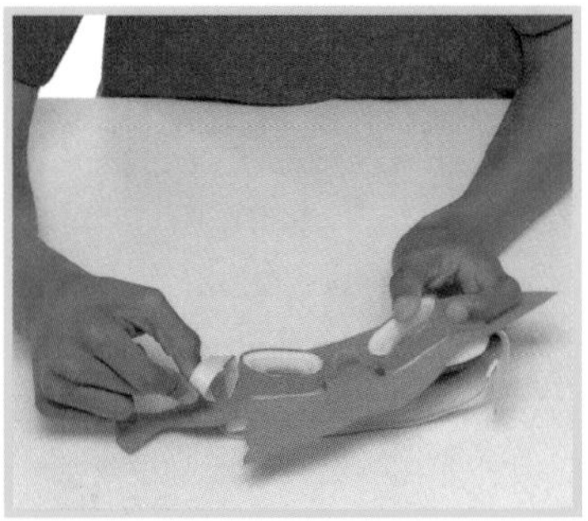

3 Push the swimming goggles into the holes of the Fish Focals. If they do not fit, make the eye holes on the mask at little larger. Reattach the strap to the goggles by threading the strap through the slits in both goggles and the mask.

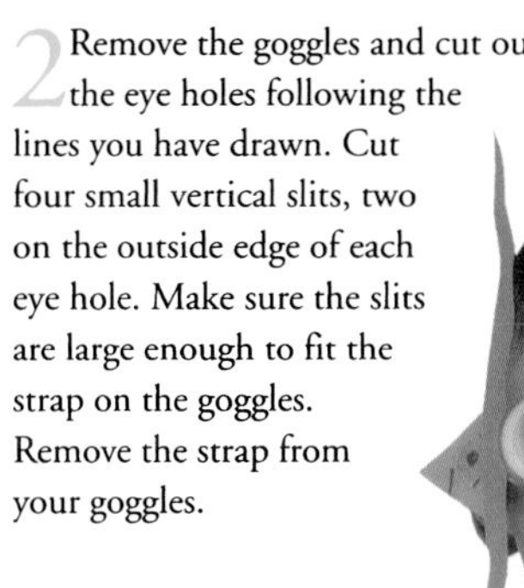

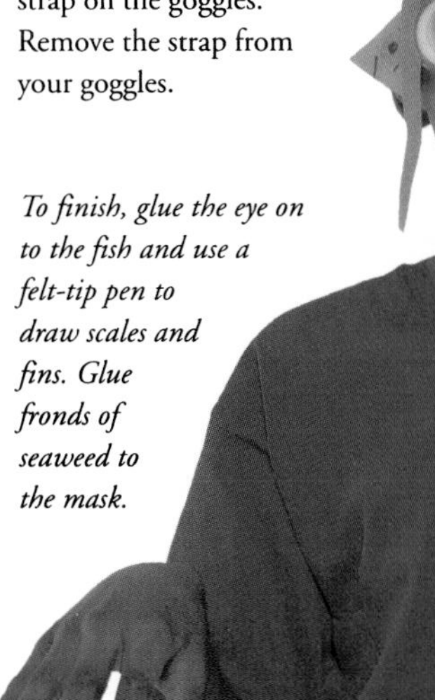

To finish, glue the eye on to the fish and use a felt-tip pen to draw scales and fins. Glue fronds of seaweed to the mask.

Hungry Wolf, Unlucky Lamb

This type of mask is called a transformation mask because it changes from one animal into another. It comes from the north-west coast of America. This mask tells the story of an unlucky lamb eaten by a wolf.

YOU WILL NEED THESE MATERIALS AND TOOLS

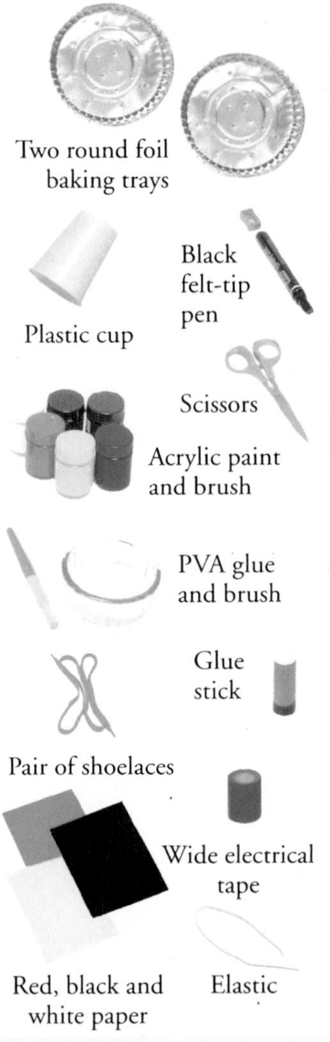

Two round foil baking trays

Plastic cup

Black felt-tip pen

Scissors

Acrylic paint and brush

PVA glue and brush

Glue stick

Pair of shoelaces

Wide electrical tape

Red, black and white paper

Elastic

'Watch out Lamb, the Hungry Wolf is about, and he cannot wait to gobble you up!'

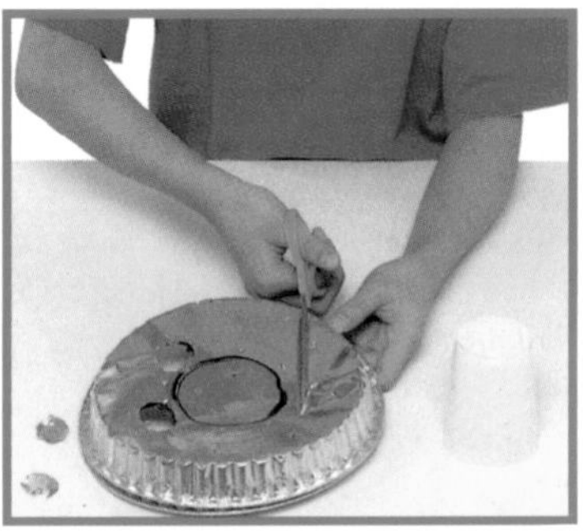

1 Place an upturned plastic cup into the centre of one of the baking trays. Draw around the cup with the black felt-tip pen. Remove the cup. Inside the circle, draw a hole for your nose. Then draw eye and mouth holes. Cut out the nose, eye and mouth holes.

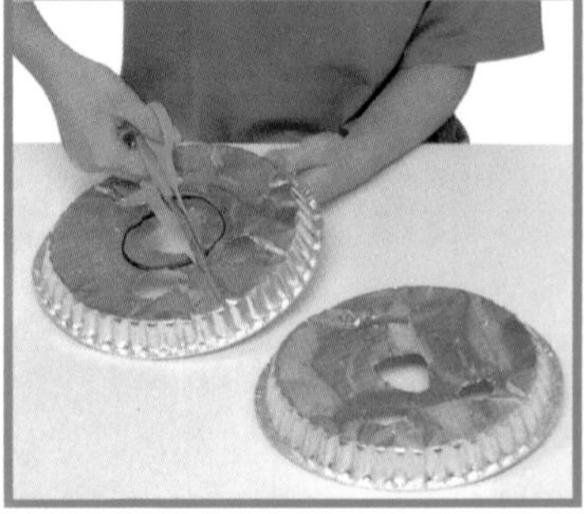

2 Place the cut tray inside the other tray and trace around the nose, eye and mouth holes. Separate the trays and cut around the lines. Take the tray with the outline of the circle in the middle and cut it in half, straight down the middle between the eye holes.

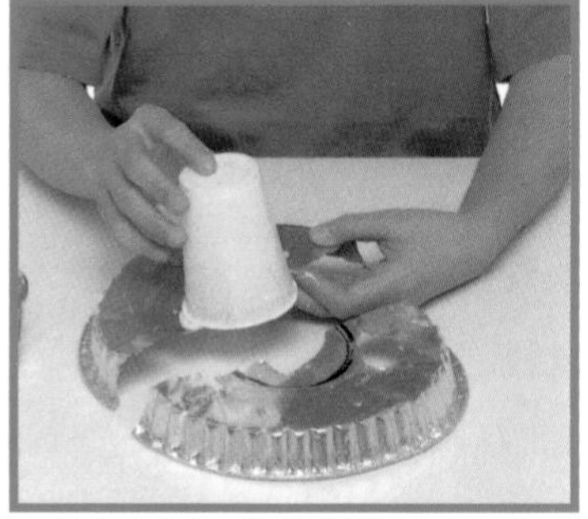

3 Use PVA glue to stick the upturned plastic cup on to the back of one half of the halved tray. Position the cup on the felt-tip line. Do not worry if the glue spreads – PVA glue is invisible when dry. Allow plenty of time for the glue to dry thoroughly.

4 To paint foil, always add a little PVA glue to the paint colour before applying. Paint both halves of the halved tray red. Cut out red, black and white paper to make a pair of pointed ears, sharp white fangs and large oval eyes for the wolf. Paint the end of the cup black. Paint the other tray white. Use red and black paint to add the lamb's features. Paint a blue tear on the lamb's cheek. Allow the masks to dry.

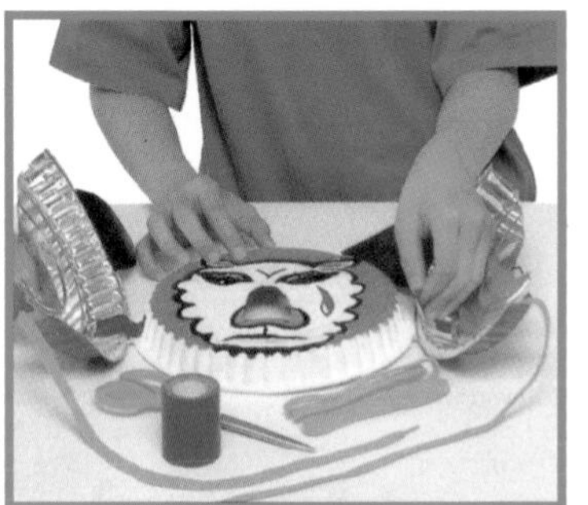

5 Place the two halves of the wolf mask on top of the lamb mask – the eye and mouth holes must line up. Use masking tape to hinge the wolf masks to the lamb mask. Open the mask and make hinges on the inside. Paint over any visible tape. Tape a shoelace to the bottom of each half of the wolf mask. Tie the laces to keep the mask closed. Make a small hole through both masks on each side. Try on the mask before cutting and tying on the elastic strap.

To reveal the Unlucky Lamb mask, undo the shoelace tie at the front. The blue pieces of electrical tape show how the shoelaces are attached and where the hinges are placed.

Coco the Clown

If you enjoy the circus, then you will love this jolly mask. Use colourful or shiny pan scrubbers to make the clown's wild hair.

Handy hint

To make Coco's hair you can use copper- or silver-coloured pan scrubbers or brightly coloured plastic ones in yellow, green, purple, red or blue. Use different coloured pan scrubbers to make Coco's hair really wild! You can buy pan scrubbers in supermarkets or hardware shops.

YOU WILL NEED THESE MATERIALS AND TOOLS

- Pencil
- Two paper plates
- Scissors
- PVA glue and brush
- Raffia
- Acrylic paint and brush
- Electrical tape
- 6 paper fasteners
- 6 pan scrubbers
- Elastic
- Small plastic lid

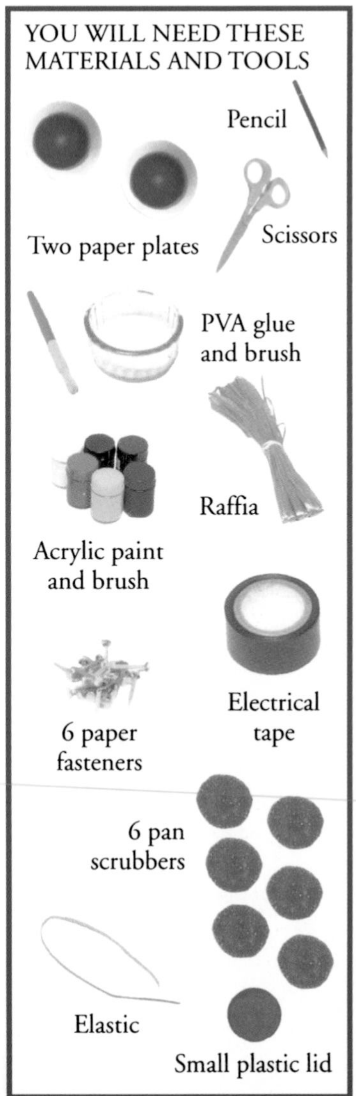

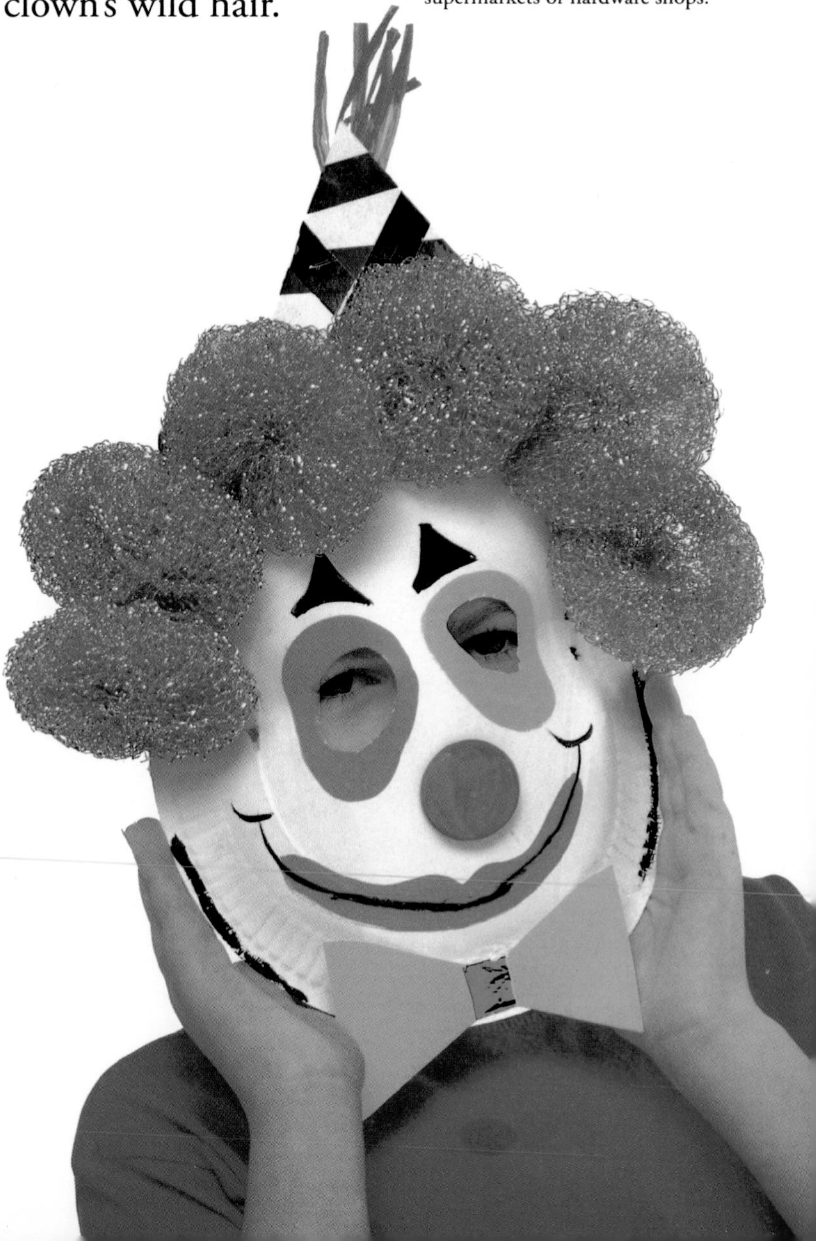

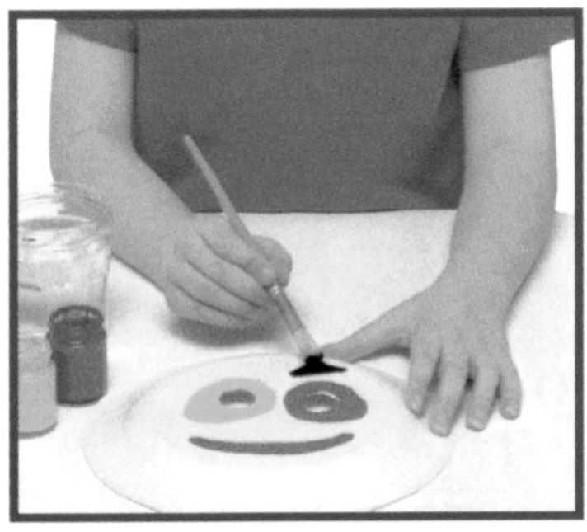

1 Hold one of the paper plates up to your face and ask an adult to mark eye holes. Cut out the eye holes. On the back of the plate, paint your clown face. Allow the paint to dry.

2 Draw a triangular hat and bow tie on the remaining paper plate. Cut them out. Paint and decorate the hat and bow tie with paint and coloured electrical tape. Finish the hat with a tassel of raffia. Attach the raffia with electrical tape.

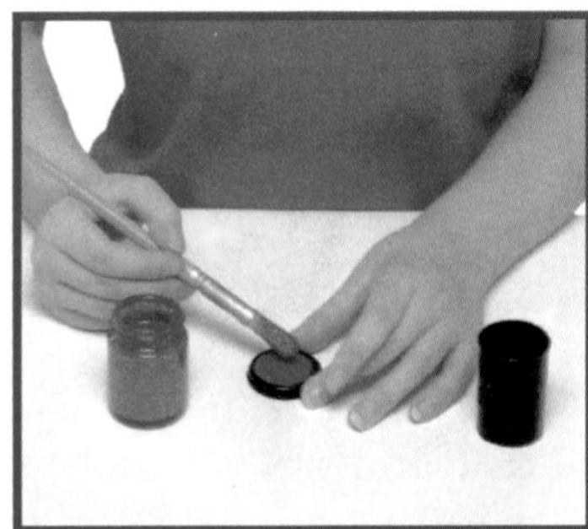

3 To make the clown's nose, use the plastic lid from a tube of sweets or plastic juice container. Mix a little PVA glue into some red paint and paint the nose. When dry, glue the nose on to the clown's face. Use PVA glue to stick on the hat and bow tie. Allow glue to dry.

4 Push a paper fastener through a pan scrubber and position it near the top edge of the plate. Push the paper fastener through the plate and flatten the fasteners. Attach the remaining pan scrubbers in the same way. Make a small hole in each side of the mask. Tie the elastic to one hole, then fit the mask before tying the elastic to the other hole.

Clown outfit

To make a clown outfit very quickly, attach colourful pan scrubbers down the front of a T-shirt and to the front of your shoes. Electrical tape is also great for jazzing up a pair of plain jogging pants. Use it to make stripes, checks and wacky patterns.

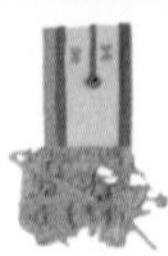

Bush Spirit Mask

The idea for this mask comes from the Pacific island of Papua New Guinea. It is made for ceremonies that celebrate the bush spirits, or Kovave. This card and fabric mask is a simple version of the real one. The fringe at the bottom of the mask covers the wearer's shoulders and gives the effect of a bird's body.

YOU WILL NEED THESE MATERIALS AND TOOLS

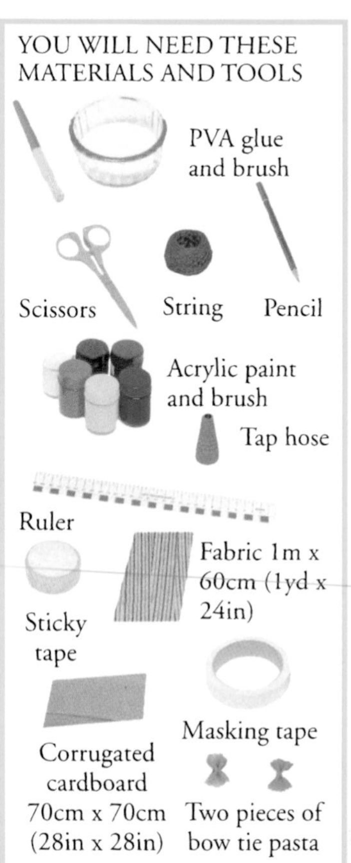

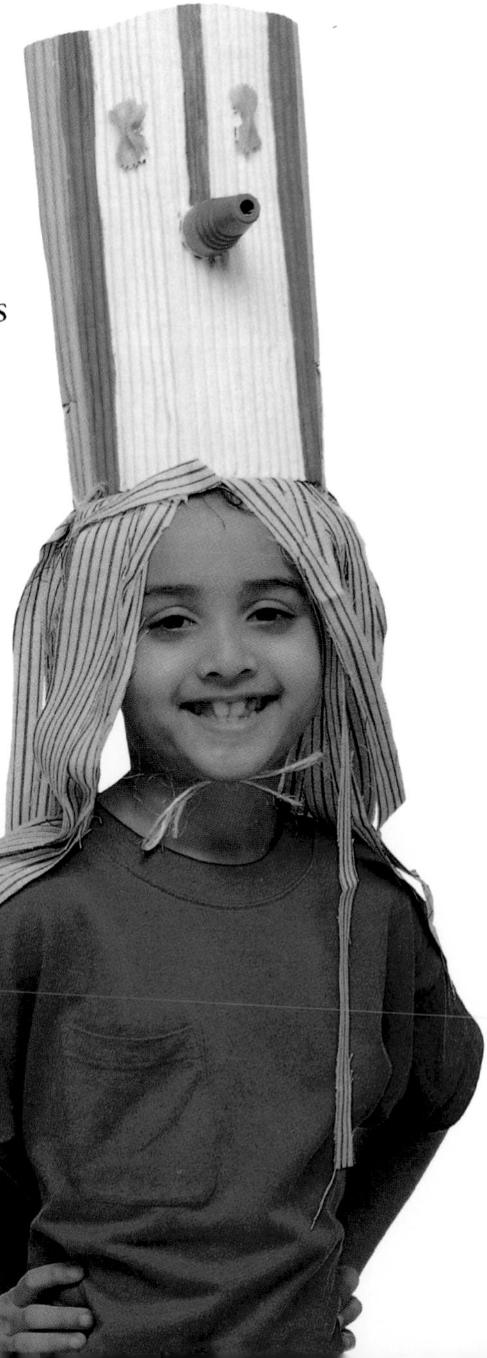

Drape the strips of fabric over your shoulders and across your face. Then you can start to strut and move like a bird.

1 Fit the piece of cardboard around your head and fix the join with masking tape. The rippled side of the cardboard should be facing out.

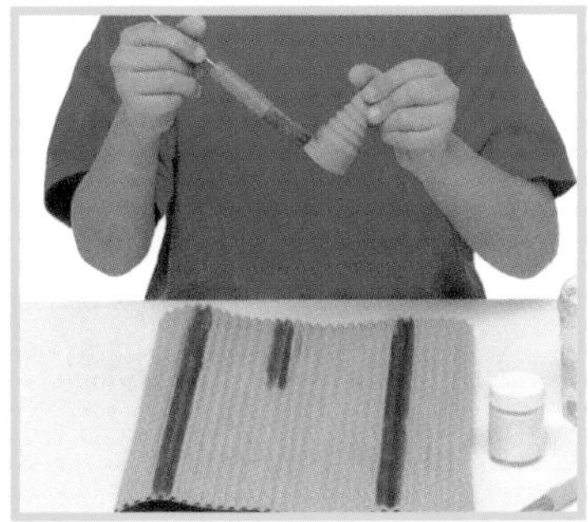

2 Glue the cardboard at the join. Leave it to dry and remove the masking tape. Paint the tap hose brown, adding some PVA glue to the paint so that it sticks to the plastic. Paint brown stripes on to the cardboard. Paint between the stripes white.

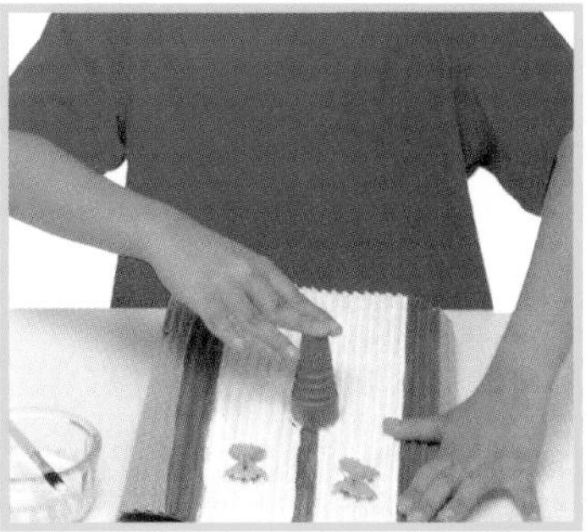

3 When the paint on the tap hose is dry, fix it to the cardboard with PVA glue to make the bird's beak. Use plenty of glue and do not worry about spills – PVA glue is invisible when dry. Glue on pasta pieces for the eyes. Allow the glue to dry thoroughly.

4 To make the fringe, cut the fabric into 2cm (3/4in) wide strips. Attach one end of the strips to a 70cm (28in) length of sticky tape. Overlap the strips. Glue the fringe inside the bottom edge of the mask.

5 Make a small hole on each side near the base of the mask. Knot a piece of string to each hole and tie under the chin.

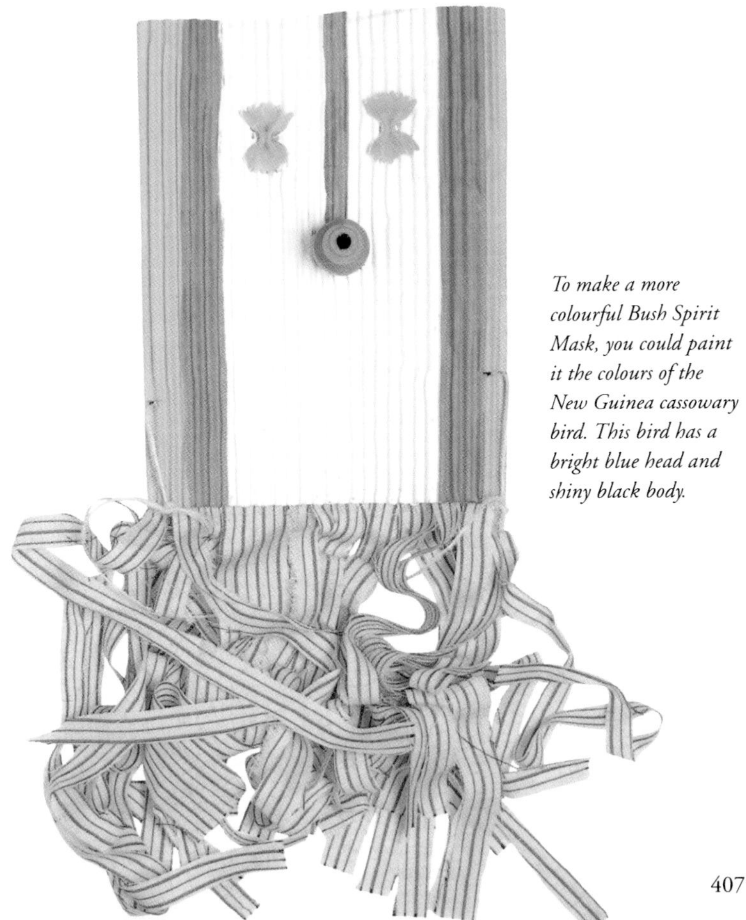

To make a more colourful Bush Spirit Mask, you could paint it the colours of the New Guinea cassowary bird. This bird has a bright blue head and shiny black body.

Beaky Bird

This mask has a beak that opens and closes. The idea comes from the ceremonial masks made by Native American Indians.

YOU WILL NEED THESE MATERIALS AND TOOLS

Scissors

Coloured and white card

PVA glue and brush

Pencil

Acrylic paint and brush

Newspaper

Ruler

Strong sticky tape

Masking tape

Wide electrical tape

Bowl

Wooden skewer or garden stick

Elastic

Papier-mâché

Papier-mâché involves gluing small squares or strips of newspaper on to a shape, mould, to make it stronger or to change its shape.

To make the glue, mix together equal quantities of PVA glue and water in a dish. Dip the newspaper pieces into the glue and smooth them on to the shape until it it covered. Allow to dry before applying a second layer of papier-mâché.

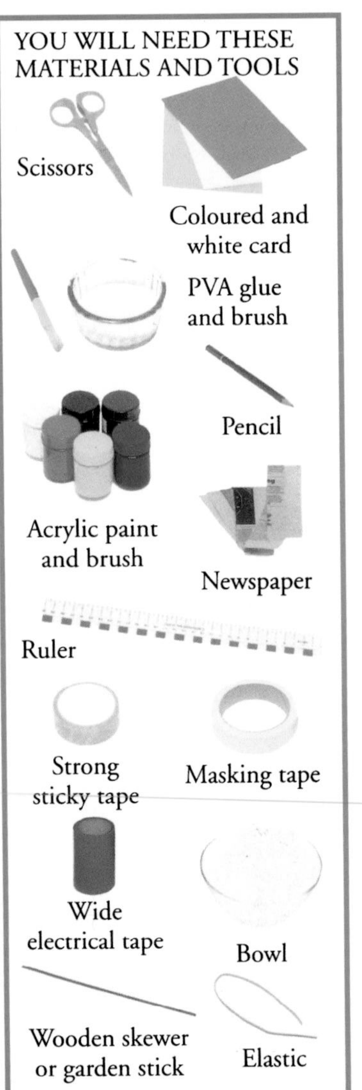

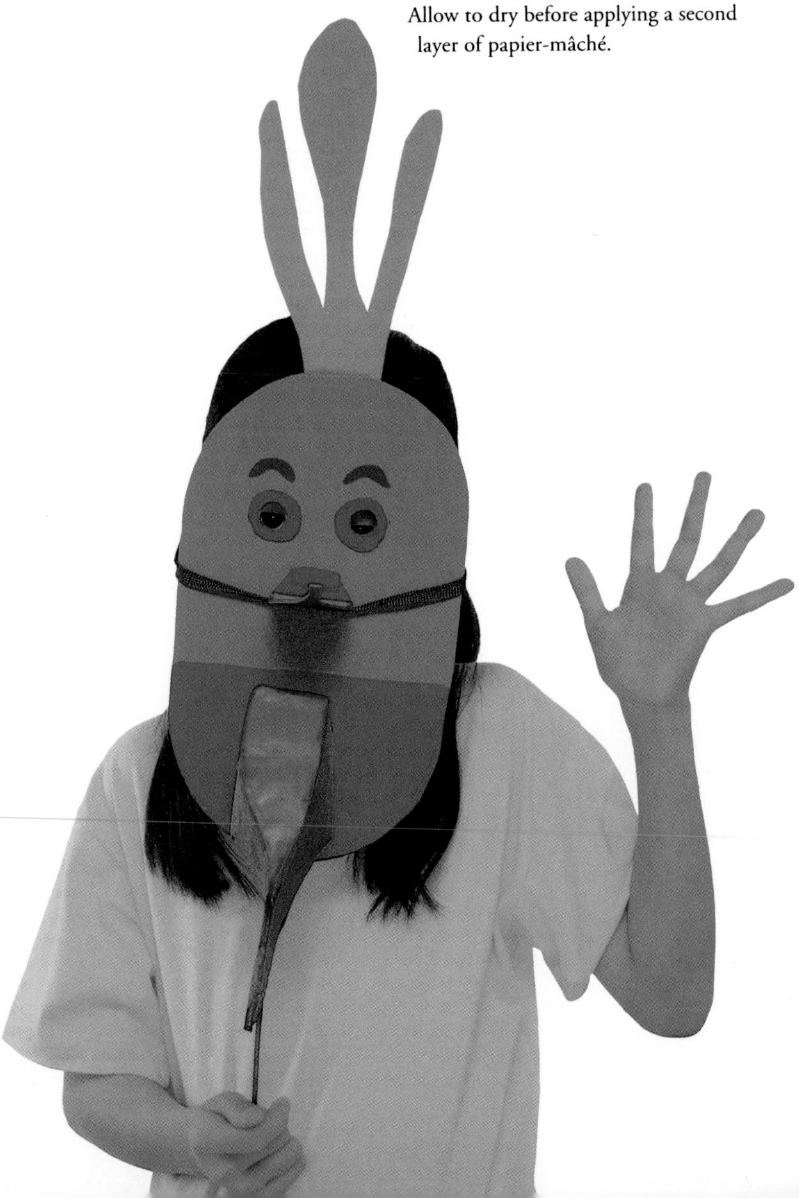

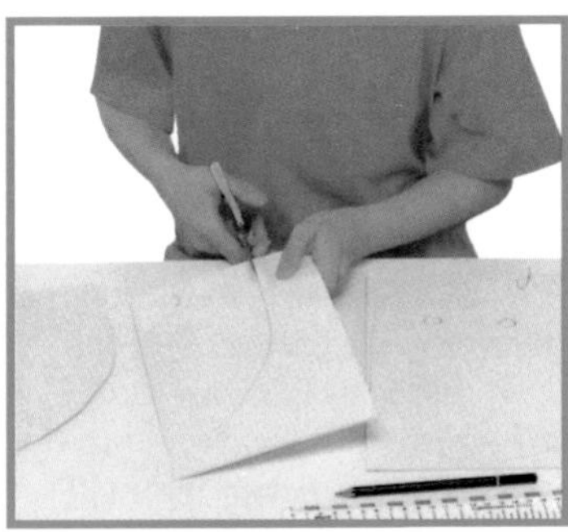

1 Draw on to card one lozenge shape for the face 30cm x 10cm (12in x 4in), two triangles for the upper beak 15cm x 3cm (6in x 1¼in) and two rectangles for the lower beak 15cm x 8cm (6in x 3in). Cut out all the pieces.

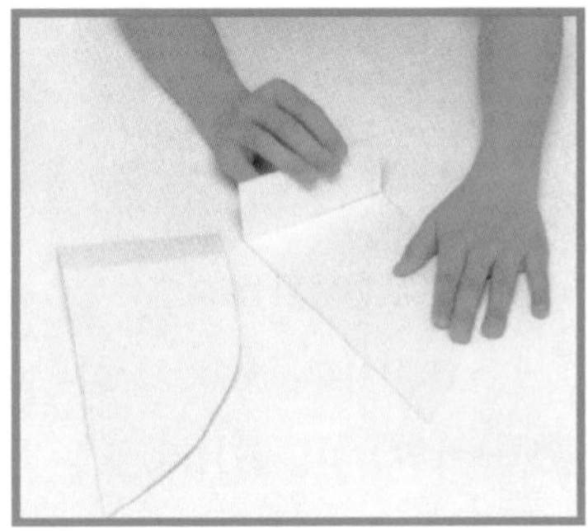

2 To make the beak, trim the two rectangles (for the lower beak) to match those shown above. Use scissors to score a fold line along the short edge of all four beak pieces. Bend each piece along the fold line to form a small flap.

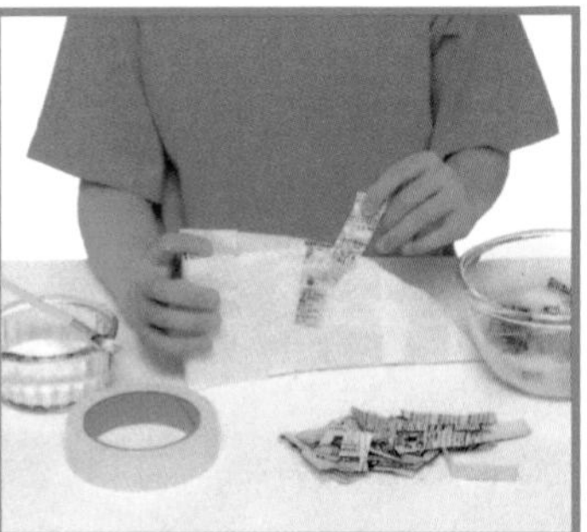

3 Use masking tape to join the curved edge of the lower beak pieces. Take one of the upper beak triangles and tape its long edges to the long edges of the lower beak. Fold the flaps inward and tape over the hole. The shape should resemble the bow of a boat. Cover the beak with papier-mâché. When dry, tape the skewer to the front of the beak. Do two more layers of papier-mâché.

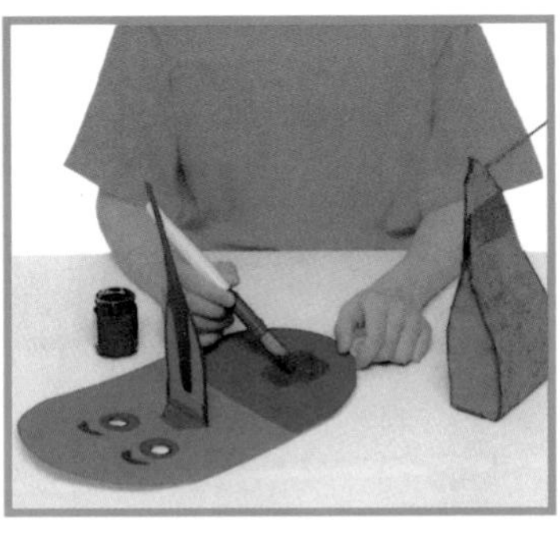

4 Glue the flap of the remaining upper beak piece on to the face. When dry, paint the face and beak.

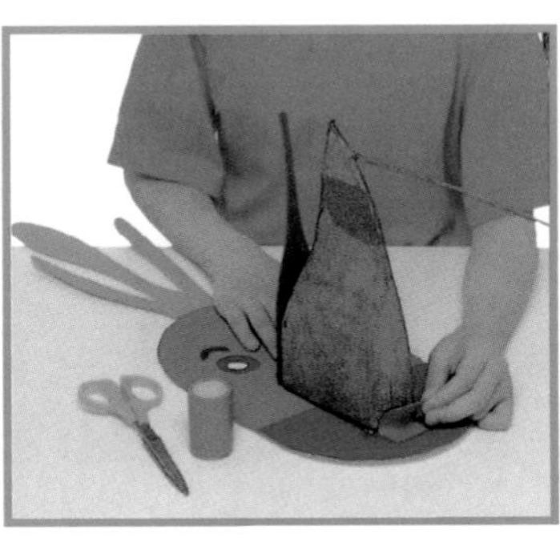

5 Cut out a plume from card and glue it to the back of the mask. Hinge the bottom of the lower beak on to the mask with electrical tape.

To finish, make a small hole on both sides of the mask. Tie a length of elastic to each hole. When you are ready to make Beaky Bird squawk and talk, tie the elastic at the back of your head and use the skewer to move the lower beak up and down.

Talking House

Not all masks are of animals or humans. You can also create wonderful illusions using masks of inanimate, or non-living, objects. The Talking House mask is one of these very clever illusions. Once you have made the Talking House, see how many other objects you can turn into funny masks.

Handy hint

To create a really convincing illusion, make a costume to wear with your Talking House mask. If you dress in green and tape cotton wool bushes on to your T-shirt, your house will become the house on the hill. To create the illusion of a beautiful garden outside your house, wear a flowery shirt. Make a path to the front door with yellow electrical tape.

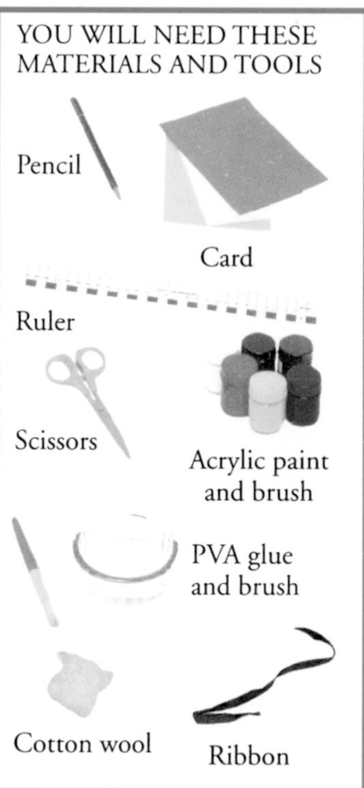

If you and your friends all make Talking House masks, you would have the whole street talking!

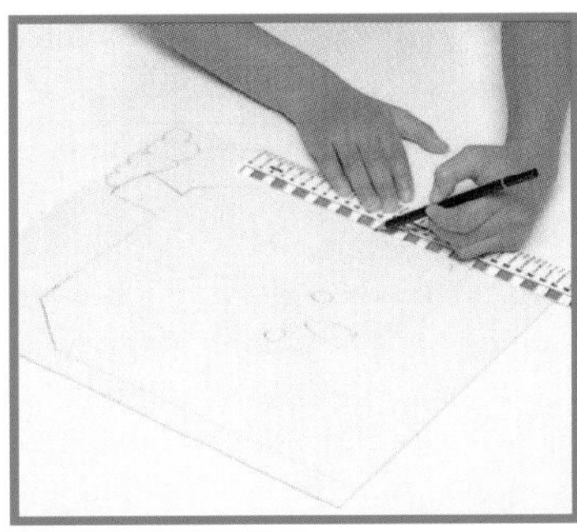

1 Draw a house (with a smoking chimney) 25cm x 30cm (10in x 12in) on a piece of card. Draw in two eye holes and a hole for your nose.

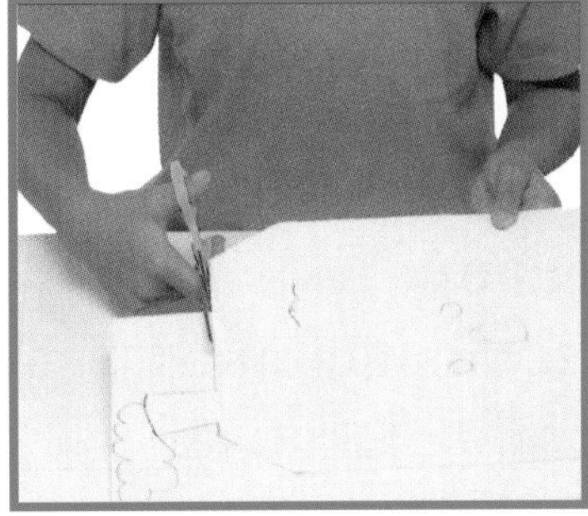

2 Cut out the house shape. Cut out the holes for the eyes and the nose.

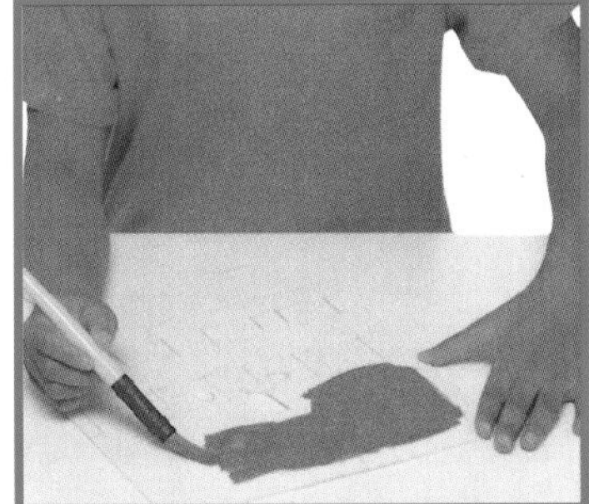

3 Paint the house red. When dry, paint rows of bricks and roof tiles in yellow. Paint window and door frames and the trunk of a tree black.

4 Tease some cotton wool to resemble billowing smoke and glue it to the chimney. Lightly dab the cotton wool with grey paint. Repeat to make the top of the tree, but lightly dab the cotton wool with green paint.

5 Make two holes just above the eye holes. Thread a long piece of ribbon through the holes, as shown.

Add as many details to your house as you like. You could even make a Talking House that is exactly like your own house!

Spotty Crocodile

There is a long tradition in mask-making of using everyday materials from around the home. With this crocodile mask, an ice-cube tray takes on a new life!

YOU WILL NEED THESE MATERIALS AND TOOLS

- Masking tape
- Thin card
- Ruler
- Pencil
- Scissors
- PVA glue and brush
- Plastic ice-cube tray
- Acrylic paint and brush
- Coloured sticky dots
- White fabric tape
- Two pieces of bow tie pasta

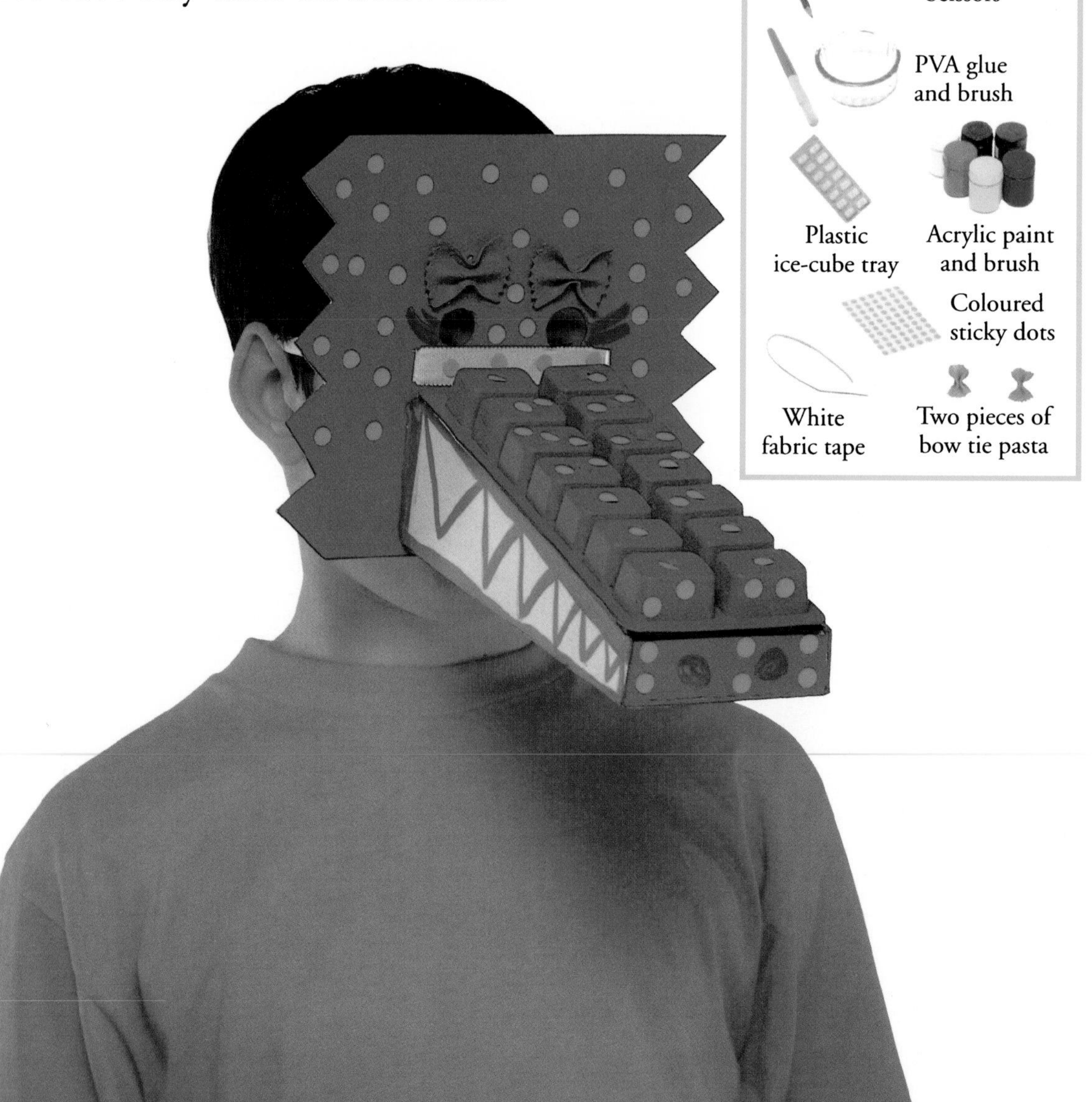

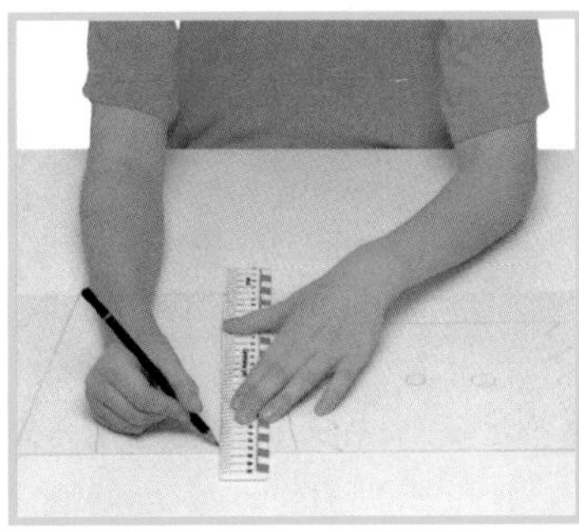

1 Draw a 20cm (8in) square on card. Draw eye holes, and a zigzag line down two edges. Do two tracings of the ice-cube tray on to card. Add tabs, the same depth as the tray, to every side of both tracings. Make the tabs on the long sides of one tracing, wider at one end.

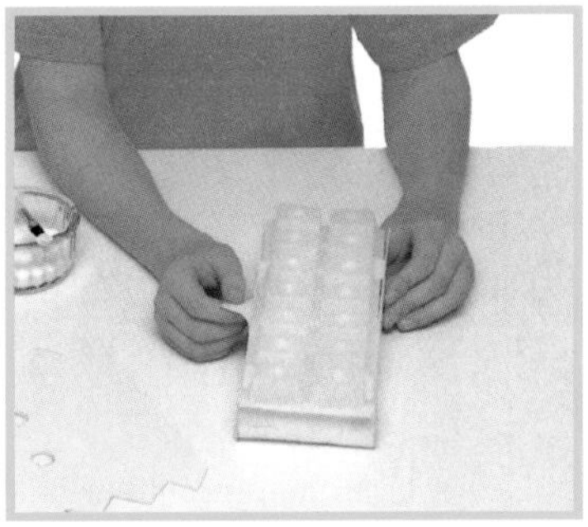

2 Cut around the outlines and cut out the eyes. Make fold lines by scoring all lines on the snout with scissors. Make the lower jaw by folding and gluing the tabs together. When dry, glue the ice-cube tray on top of the snout. Use masking tape to keep things in position while the glue dries.

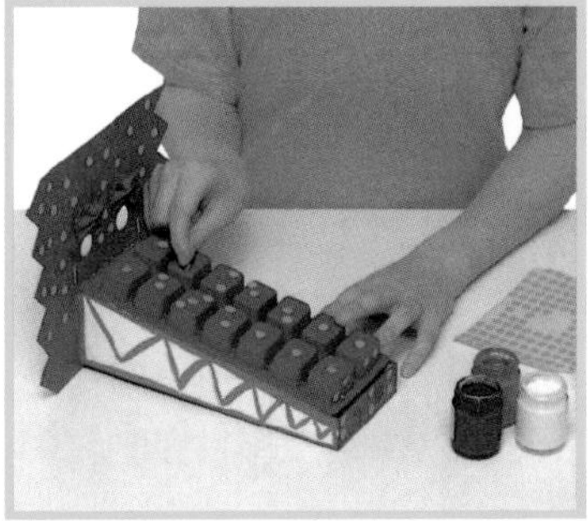

3 Glue the snout to the face. Carefully cut two slits in the face just above the snout, as shown. Glue pasta above the eyes. Paint Spotty Crocodile's face and the top and front of its snout blue. Paint the sides of the snout white and mark teeth in red. When dry, cover the crocodile with coloured sticky dots.

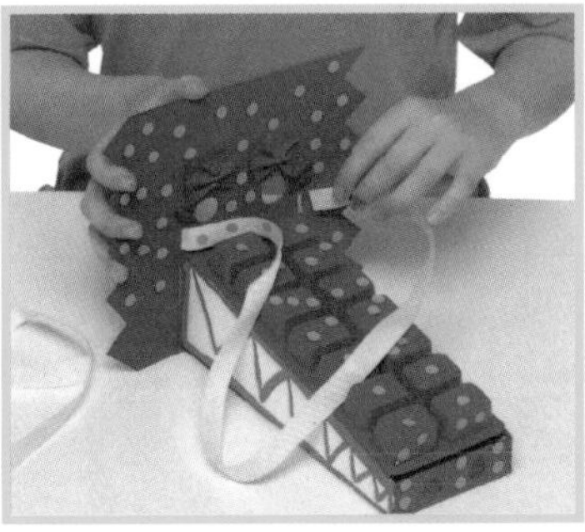

4 Thread the fabric tape through the slits, as shown. The tape will show, so decorate it with a line of sticky dots. Tie the tape around your head.

Animals with snouts

This method of creating a long snout using card, can be used to make other long-snouted animals like horses, giraffes or even dogs. To adapt this snout for other less-snappy creatures, simply make the rectangles shorter and the sides wider. You can add ears and horns by simply cutting them out of card and gluing them on to the face. Then all you have to do is paint and decorate your animal mask!

To make your crocodile mask look more realistic, find a photograph in a book and copy the colours. If you make two identical crocodile masks, you and a friend could play SNAP!

Spanish Giant

This mask is made to sit on top of your head. Nylon netting fabric falling from the mask covers your face. Masks like this one are used in Spanish carnivals and are often two or three times the size of a person.

Handy hint

When painting the face, make sure you leave enough space under the mouth so that the base can be trimmed. If you prefer, you could fit the mask and make holes for the elastic before you start painting.

To trim the mask, use scissors. If you find the papier-mâché too hard to cut, ask an adult to help.

YOU WILL NEED THESE MATERIALS AND TOOLS

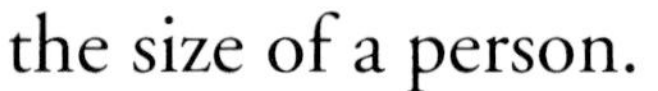

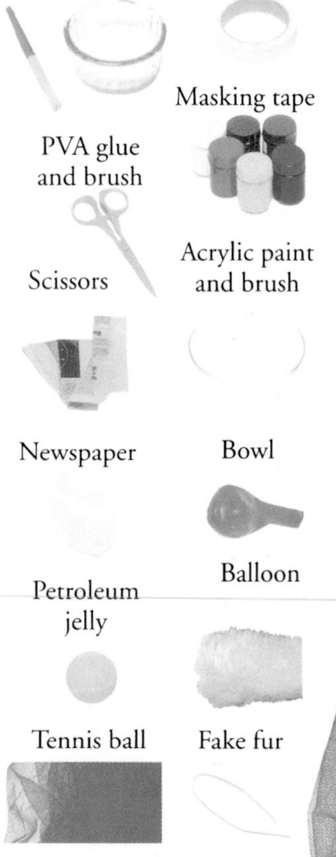

PVA glue and brush

Masking tape

Scissors

Acrylic paint and brush

Newspaper

Bowl

Petroleum jelly

Balloon

Tennis ball

Fake fur

Nylon netting

Elastic

1 Inflate the balloon and tie a knot in the end. Cover the balloon with petroleum jelly. Make papier-mâché glue by mixing equal amounts of PVA glue and water. Glue strips of newspaper over the balloon to cover it. Do three layers.

2 Leave the papier-mâché somewhere warm to dry. When it is hard and thoroughly dry, deflate the balloon by snipping off the top of the balloon. Pull the balloon out of the papier-mâché shell and discard the balloon.

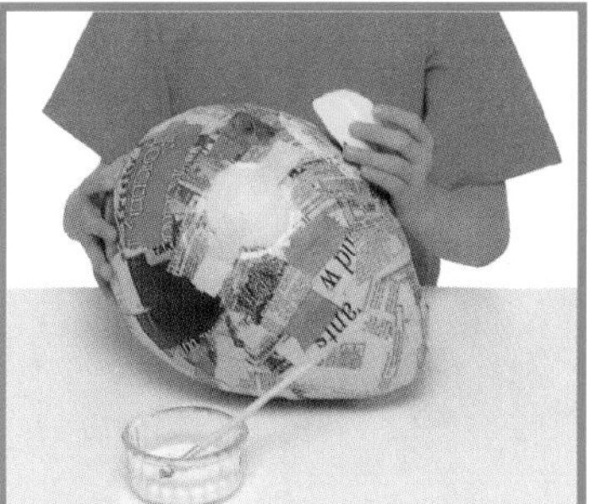

3 Ask an adult to help you cut an old tennis ball in half. Glue the halves on to the papier-mâché shell for the eyes. Use plenty of glue and hold the halved balls in place with masking tape while the glue dries.

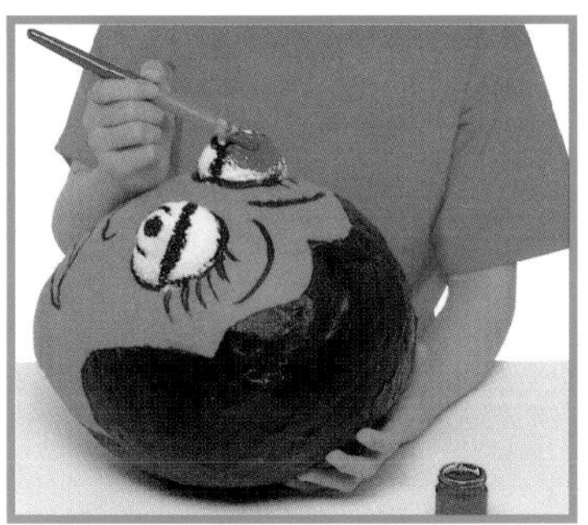

4 Paint the mask. Use a thick brush to paint large areas and a thin brush to paint details. Some areas may need two coats. Allow to dry.

5 Trim the base of the mask so that it sits on your head. Make holes near the base of the mask. Attach elastic to one hole. Get a friend to hold the mask on your head while you fit the elastic strap under your chin. Pull on the elastic to get a snug fit, then tie the elastic to the hole.

6 Tape layers of nylon netting inside the base of the mask. Glue on a strip of fake fur to make a collar.

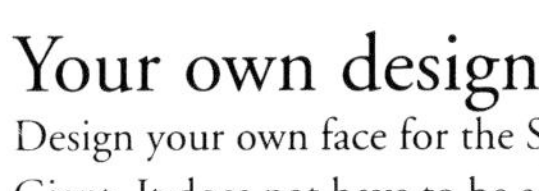

Your own design

Design your own face for the Spanish Giant. It does not have to be a woman, it could be a scary monster, a funny clown or an alien. You could even paint your own face on to the mask!

Face and Body Painting

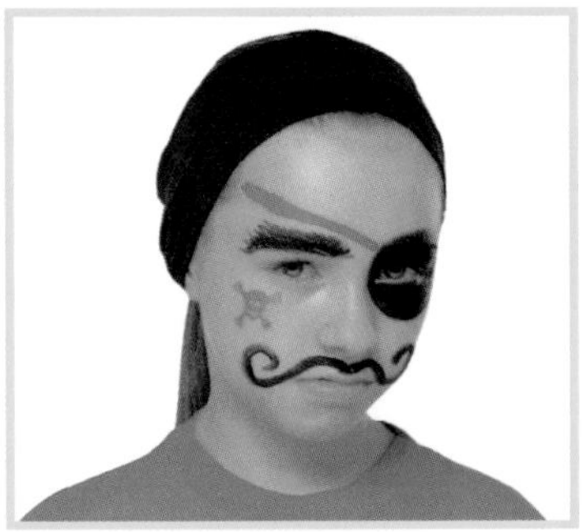

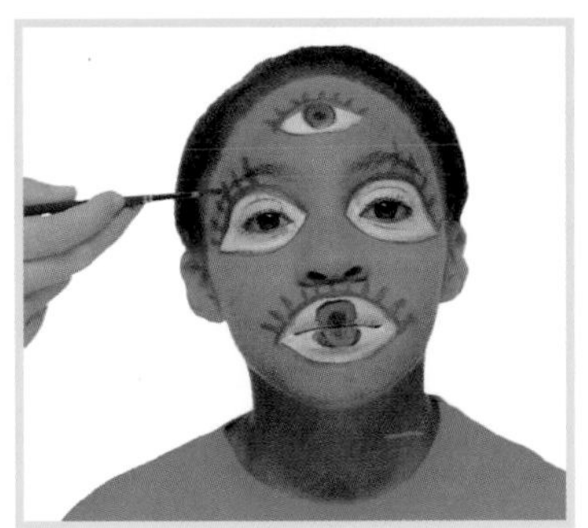

Introduction

Face and body painting has a tradition that goes back thousands of years. In many ancient cultures, face and body painting was used to camouflage tribespeople when they went hunting. In other societies, face and body painting was an important part of religious ceremonies and cultural customs.

In our society today, we use face and body painting mostly to have fun and to entertain. You can face paint yourself for special occasions, fancy dress parties, school plays or to go to a wonderful street carnival. Even putting on ordinary make-up is a form of face painting.

When your friends see your Spotty Puppy face painting, they will all want it done!

Become anyone you want

Face painting can transform you into someone, or even something, entirely different. With little more than a collection of face paint colours, sponges and brushes you can become a Prowling Leopard, a Spotty Puppy, a Disco Diva or even a many-eyed alien.

Body painting

There is no reason for the face painting fun to stop at your neck. You can also paint your body and limbs using exactly the same materials. Watch your hands being transformed into a proud Stag, a very rare species of Octopus, a Little Devil and even a Digital Soccer star. Once you realize the possibilities and how easy it is to create some very funny characters, there will be no stopping you!

The only difference between face and body painting, is that body painting can take longer. So, be patient and try not to laugh when a ticklish spot is being painted.

You can paint just one hand or your whole body. This funny character is the very rare pentapus. It is an octopus with only five tentacles.

Someone to help

It is very difficult to do your own face and body painting. The best idea is to ask a patient friend or adult to help. You can always promise your make-up artist that you will paint their face or body in return.

Before you get out the face paints and brushes, read through the information on Basic Techniques on the following pages. This information will show you how to achieve stunning effects and a professional finish.

To give Super Robot's face a metal-like finish, it has been painted with silver face paint.

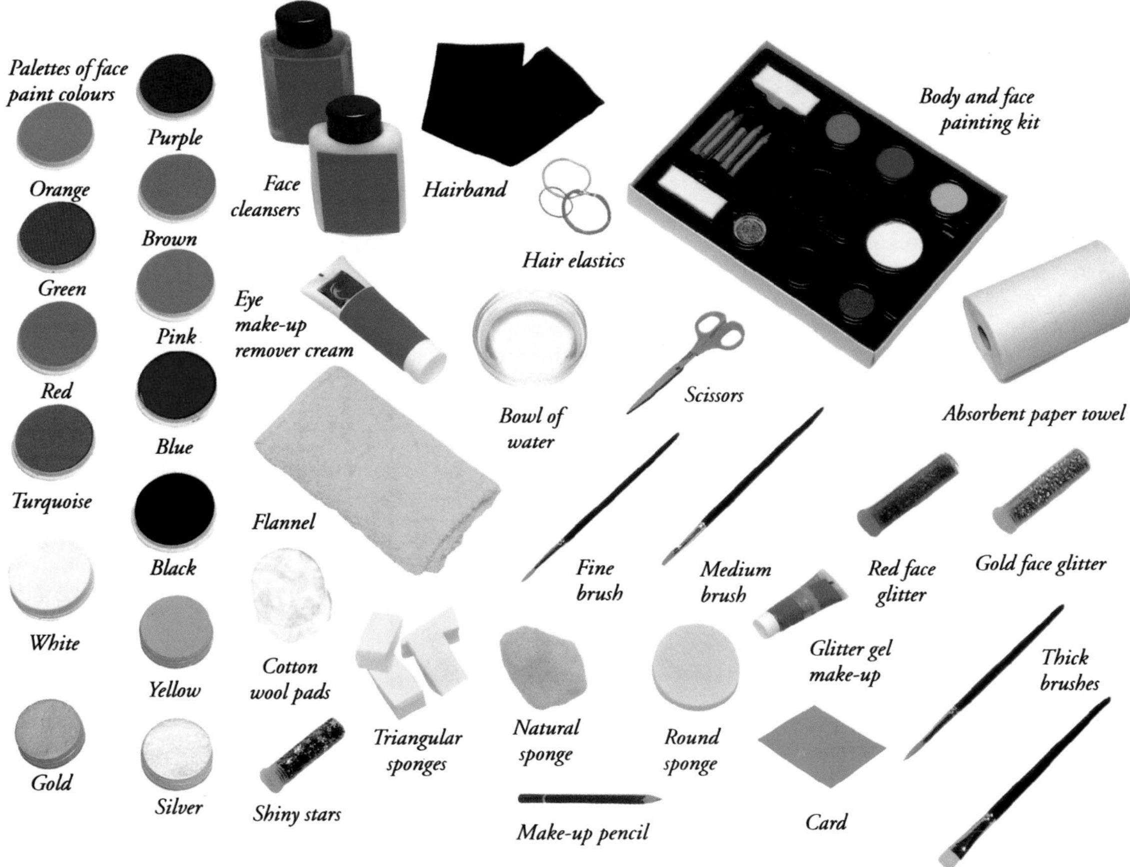

Materials

Brushes You can buy special make-up brushes, or you can use good quality watercolour brushes. You will need three brushes to complete the projects in this book – a fine, a medium and a thick brush.

Face glitter This is specially made to be used on the face. It is available in speciality shops.

Face paints These are available in kits or in individual palettes. Buy professional face paints because they are easy to use, give a very good finish and are long-lasting.

Flannel and absorbent paper towel Use these for wiping away excess paints from your face.

Glitter gel make-up This is a clear, gel make-up that contains coloured glitter.

Make-up remover creams and cleansers These lotions will remove face paint without stinging. Always ask an adult before using any type of make-up removing product.

Natural sponge You can buy an inexpensive natural sponge in chemist shops and in some supermarkets. The texture of this sponge makes it ideal for creating a dappled effect.

Round sponge This smooth, round sponge is used for applying a base coat of face paint.

Shiny stars These tiny stars are made specially to be used on the face. They come in tubes and can be bought in theatrical shops. Stars can be glued to the face with special face glue.

Triangular sponges These are standard make-up sponges. It is a good idea to have two or three so that you do not have to wash them every time you change face paint colours.

Basic Techniques

Before you start, protect clothing with an old shirt or towel. It is a good idea if the make-up artist protects his or her clothing too. Cover the work surface with absorbent paper towels and lay out your materials. Always have a bowl of water handy.

Dip the brushes and sponges into water to dampen them before loading them with face paint. Always wash brushes when changing colours. When the water becomes discoloured, replace it with clean water.

How to apply the base colour

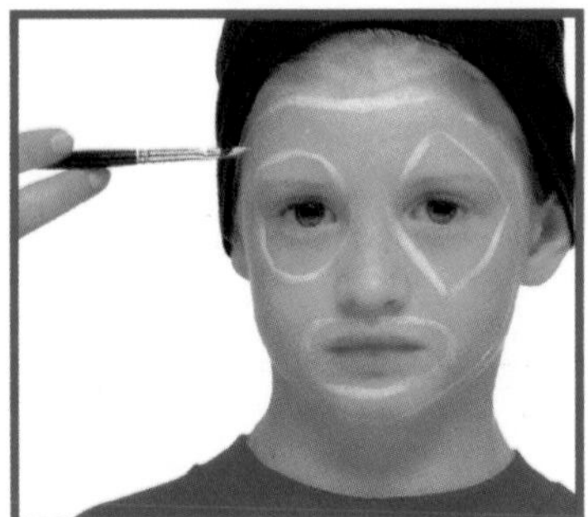

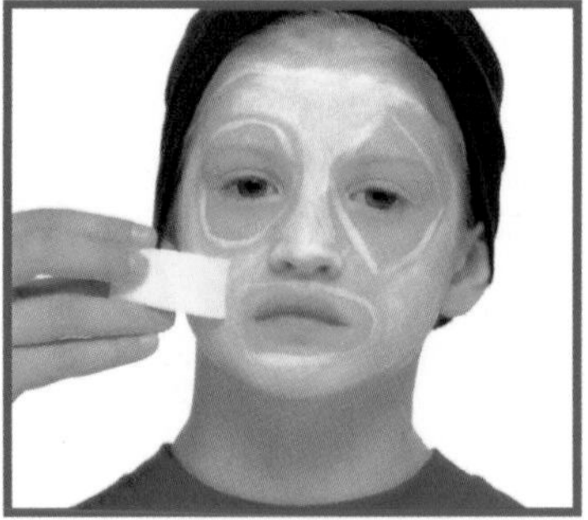

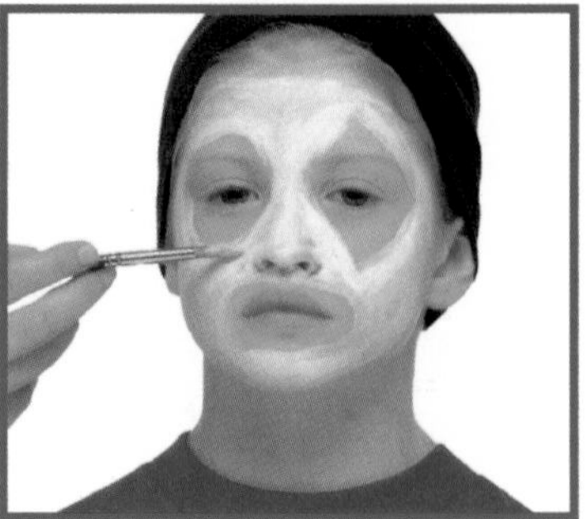

1 Use a medium or thick brush to paint the outline of a circle around the face and any other features. Paint the outlines in the base colour. The instructions will always state which colour should be used.

2 Dampen a round or triangular sponge in water. Rub the sponge gently around the face paint palette a few times to load sufficient colour on to the sponge. Fill in the outline with base colour.

3 When the outline is filled in, use a brush to neaten the edges. Use the sponge to get an even finish. In some cases, a second base coat will need to be applied to achieve this. Allow the face paint to dry between coats.

How to apply a two colour base

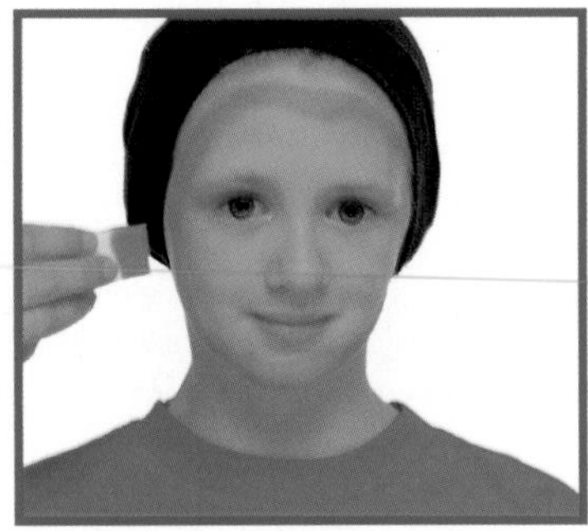

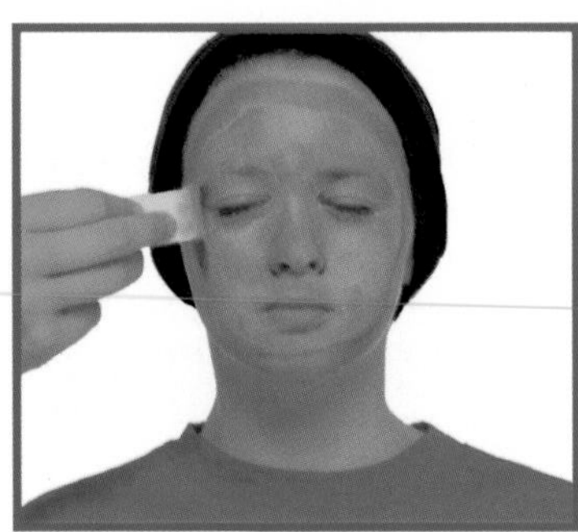

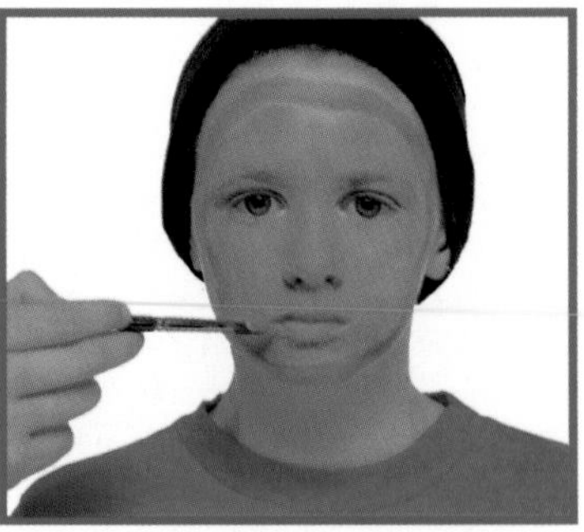

1 Outline the face using a triangular sponge or a round sponge folded in half. The instructions will always state which colour to use.

2 Use a clean sponge to apply the second colour. This colour will go inside the outline. To make the colours merge, go over with a damp sponge.

3 When the outline is filled in, use a fine or medium brush to neaten the edges. Use the brush also to touch up gaps around the nose, eyes and mouth.

Body painting

The technique for applying a base colour or second colour to the body or limbs is the same as for face painting.

Before starting body painting, put on the clothes you want to wear. Pulling clothes over the body painting may smudge it. Protect these clothes with an old shirt or towel. Always cover the work surface or floor with lots of absorbent paper towel or kitchen cloth.

Remember when wearing body paint that it will rub off on to furniture, clothes and anything you handle.

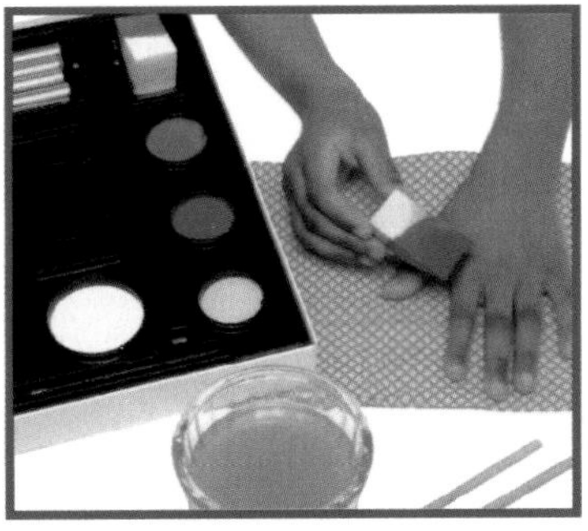

Lay out a cloth. Apply the paint with a dampened sponge.

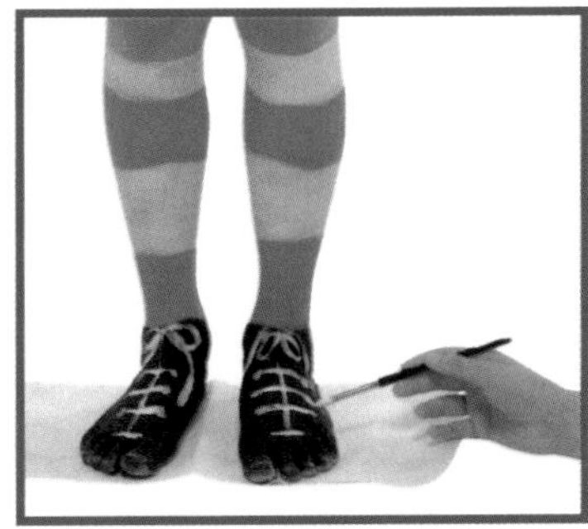

Allow the base to dry before applying the second colour.

Removing make-up

Face and body paints can be easily washed off with mild soap and water. There is no need to rub hard.

Glitter gel make-up, face glitter, shiny stars and make-up glue are best removed using make-up remover creams and cleansers applied to cotton wool. Use special eye make-up remover cream to clean the sensitive skin around the eyes.

Always check with an adult before using any type of make-up remover, cleanser or cream.

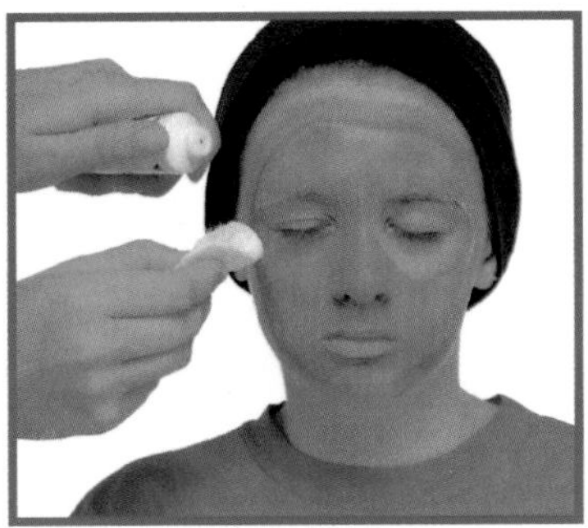

Close your eyes when face paint is being removed from around the eyes.

Dry your face and remove any traces of face paint with an old towel.

Safety tips

It is a good idea to buy proper face paints. They will be more expensive than some alternatives, but they are easier to apply and therefore gentler on the skin. Some face paints are specially made for sensitive skins.

When you have finished face painting, gently rinse the surface of the palette under water. Wipe around the edge of the palette with a paper towel to remove excess face paint before replacing the lid.

If you do these things your face paints will remain clean, moist and ready to use.

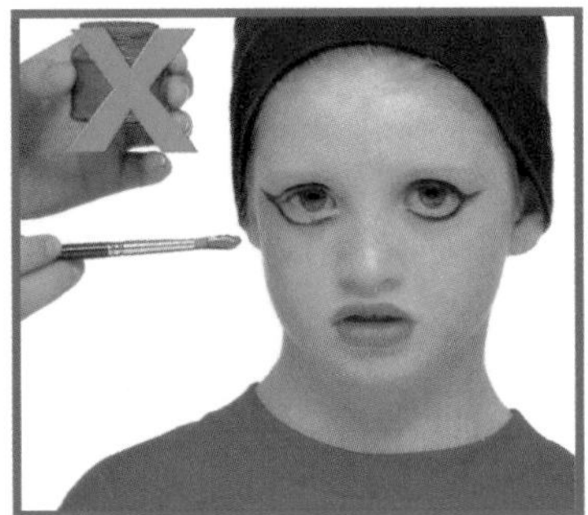

You must never use craft paints, felt-tip pens, crayons, craft glues or other stationery items on your face. They may cause an irritation.

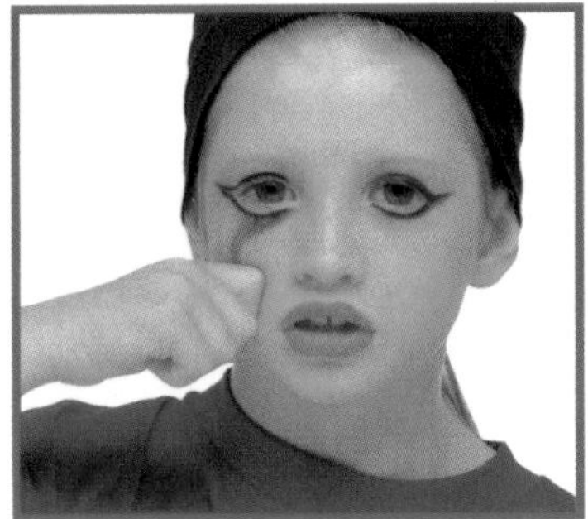

Try not to accidentally touch wet face paint as it will cause the paint to smudge. Even when dry, face paint will smudge if it is rubbed.

Sea World

Would you like to be transformed into a living marine fantasy? It is easy and lots of fun. The crab painted around your mouth will twitch every time you smile or talk. When you blink your eye, the fish will look as though it is moving.

Handy hint

It is a good idea to wear an old towel around your neck and shoulders while your face is being painted. The towel will protect your clothes. It also provides your make-up artist with a handy place to wipe paint smudges from his or her hands and fingers.

Do not use a good towel – some dark face paints may leave a faint mark.

YOU WILL NEED THESE MATERIALS

Absorbent paper towel

Bowl of water

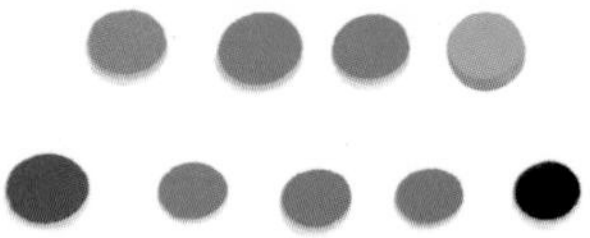

Face paints (brown, turquoise, orange, yellow, blue, pink, red, green, black)

Triangular sponge

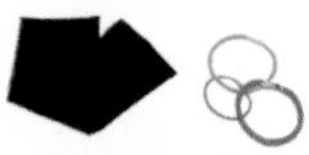

Hairband or hair elastics

Fine and thick brushes

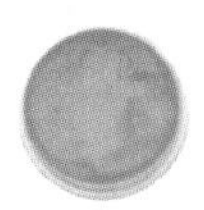

1 Tie the hair back. Paint a brown outline of a fish around one eye and on one cheek. Do this with the fine brush. Paint a turquoise circle around the face. Fill the circle using the sponge.

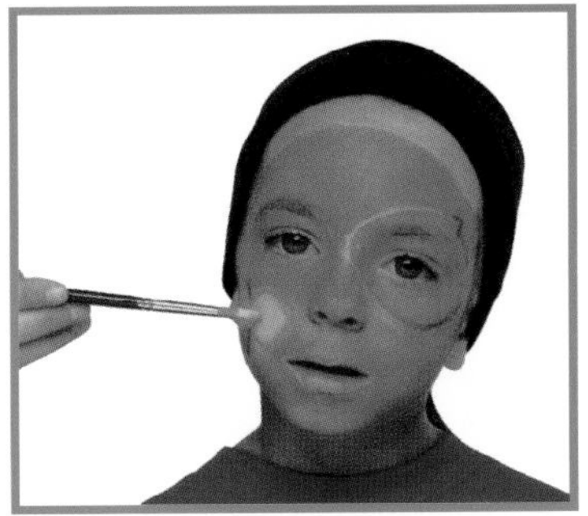

2 When the turquoise face paint is thoroughly dry, use the thick brush to paint one fish a glowing orange colour and the other a bright yellow. Allow to dry.

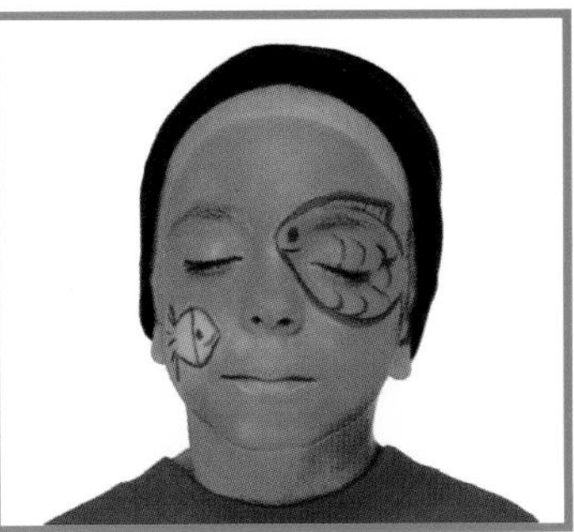

3 Paint the eyes, mouth, scales and fins on to the fish, using blue face paint and a fine brush. You must sit as still as possible while this is being done as it is quite fiddly!

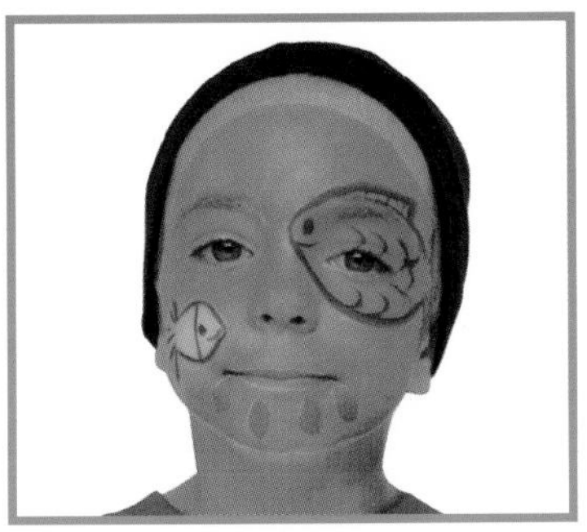

4 Break into a smile while your lips are being painted pink. Paint four pink crab claws just below the lower lip. The fine brush works best for detail work like this.

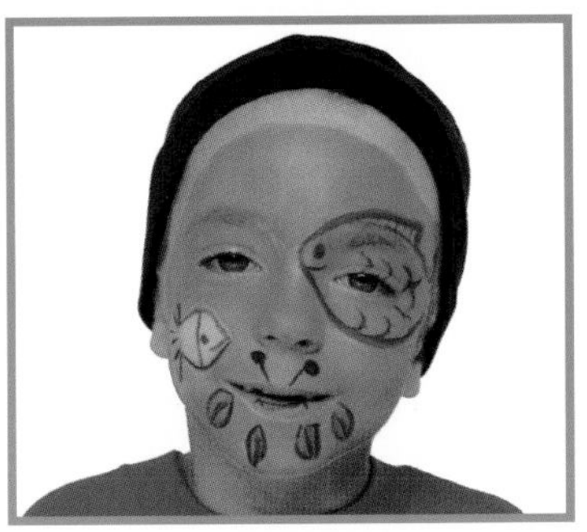

5 Use blue paint and a clean fine brush to outline and decorate the claws. Paint the face of the crab on the lower lip and draw in the stalks. Paint the crab's eyes red.

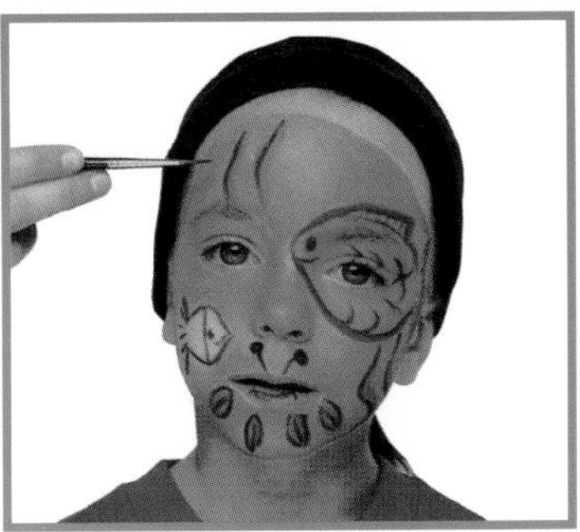

6 Use the fine brush to paint wavy green fronds of seaweed on to the forehead. To make the seaweed stand out, outline it in black face paint.

Underwater outfit to match

There is no need to spend money or lots of time making an outfit to go with your face painting. All you really need are sea-blue T-shirt and leggings, sheets of card, felt-tip pens, scissors, double-sided sticky tape and your imagination!

Draw some fishy, underwater-type creatures or vegetation on to card with the felt-tips pens. These drawings can be as large or as small as you like as long as they will fit on your T-shirt. Cut out the shapes. Press a piece of double-sided sticky tape to the back of each shape. Peel off the protective backing and press the shape on to your T-shirt.

Here are some ideas to get you started – tropical fish with trailing fins, a pod of dolphins, corals, shells and seaweeds. You could even include a pirate's treasure chest. When your Sea World fantasy is over, simply peel the pieces of card off your T-shirt.

Super Robot

This robot has supernatural abilities. Its radar vision can detect when enemy craft are approaching. The reflective metal helmet protects the robot during intergalactic battles. To make the helmet, cover a large, empty cereal box with aluminium foil.

YOU WILL NEED THESE MATERIALS

Round sponge

Hairband or hair elastics

Absorbent paper towel

Bowl of water

Fine and medium brushes

Face paints (silver, purple, blue, black)

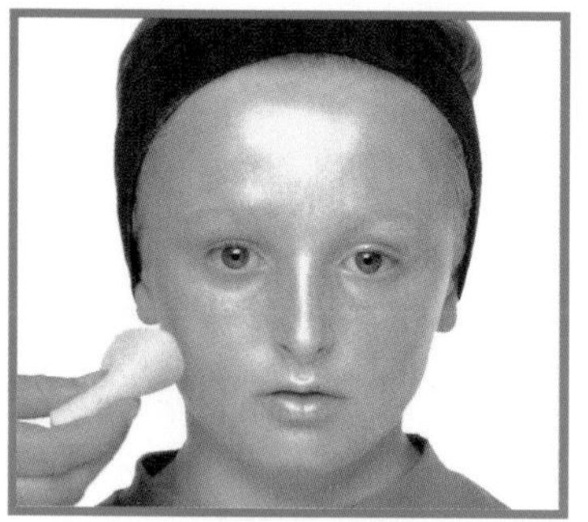

1 Tie the hair back. Close your eyes and mouth while your face is painted with the silver face paint using the round sponge. To make the silver stand out, apply two coats. Allow to dry.

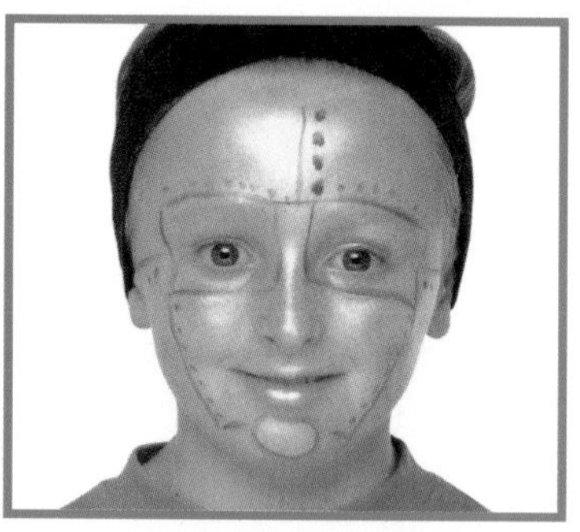

2 Use the fine brush to paint purple lines on to the face, as shown. Paint small purple dots beside the lines using the tip of the fine brush. This is the robot's reflective metal casing.

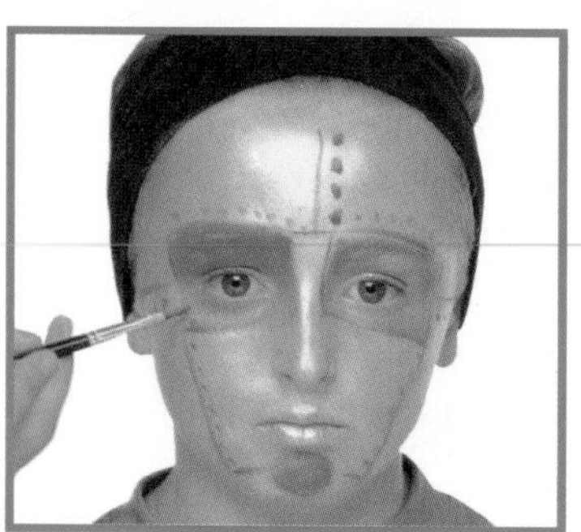

3 Paint the circle below the mouth with blue face paint using the medium brush. Then fill in the outlines around the eyes with blue face paint.

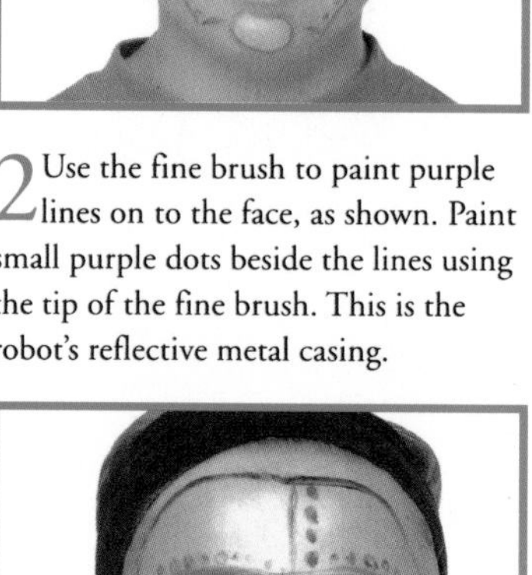

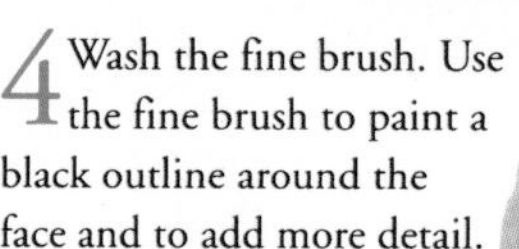

4 Wash the fine brush. Use the fine brush to paint a black outline around the face and to add more detail.

Pirate Peta

Welcome aboard landlubbers and meet one of the nastiest villains that ever sailed the high seas. This pesky, painted pirate has a black eye patch, curly moustache, pointy goatee and Jolly Roger tattoo. Peta's nose is pink because she does not wear sunblock.

YOU WILL NEED THESE MATERIALS

Natural sponge

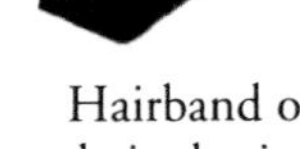

Hairband or hair elastics

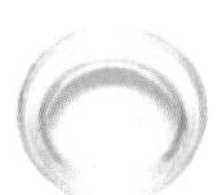

Bowl of water

Absorbent paper towel

Fine and medium brushes

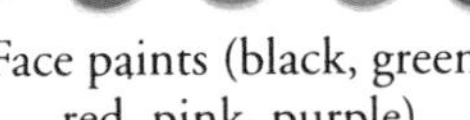

Face paints (black, green, red, pink, purple)

1 Tie the hair back. Use black face paint and the fine brush to paint the moustache. It is a good idea to start at the centre of the lip and work outwards. Stay still while this is being done.

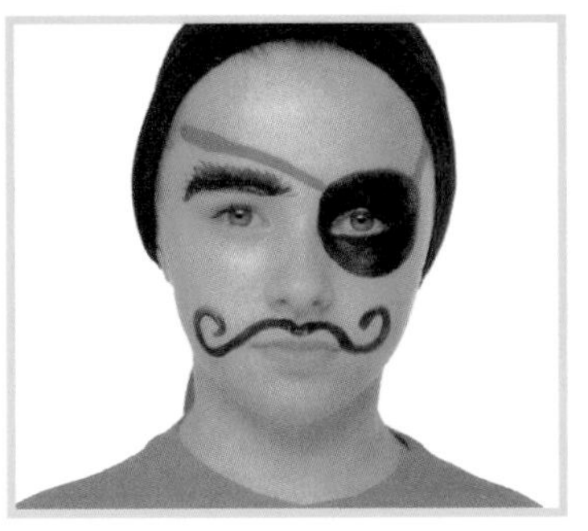

2 Paint the outline for the eye patch with the fine brush. Close your eye while the outline is filled with black. Paint a bushy eyebrow. Then paint the green straps for the eye patch.

3 Paint the skull and crossbones tattoo with red face paint and the fine brush. Use the medium brush to paint the pointy, black goatee.

4 Use the natural sponge to dab the nose with pink face paint. Then dab purple face paint over the top of the pink.

A costume for Pirate Peta is easy to put together. All you need is a plain or striped T-shirt, a pair of baggy trousers, a sword, a rope and a head scarf.

Halloween Witch

Witches are an essential part of the Halloween tradition. This witch is a horrible shade of green – perhaps she ate someone nasty! She has a wrinkled face and lots of hairy warts. No wonder she does not look happy! To feel right at home in the role of a witch, why not make a broomstick from long twigs and have a spider for a pet?

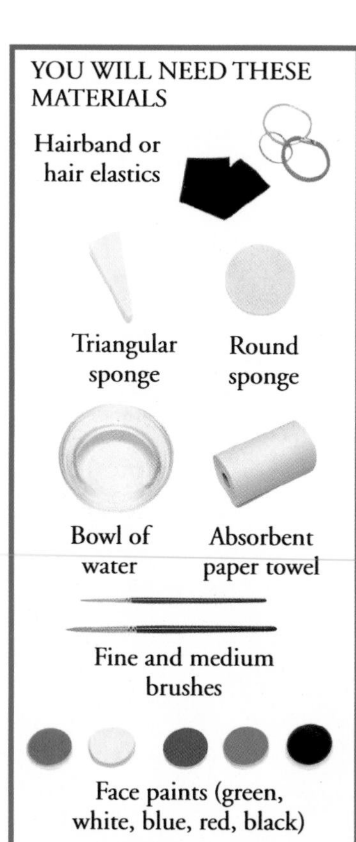

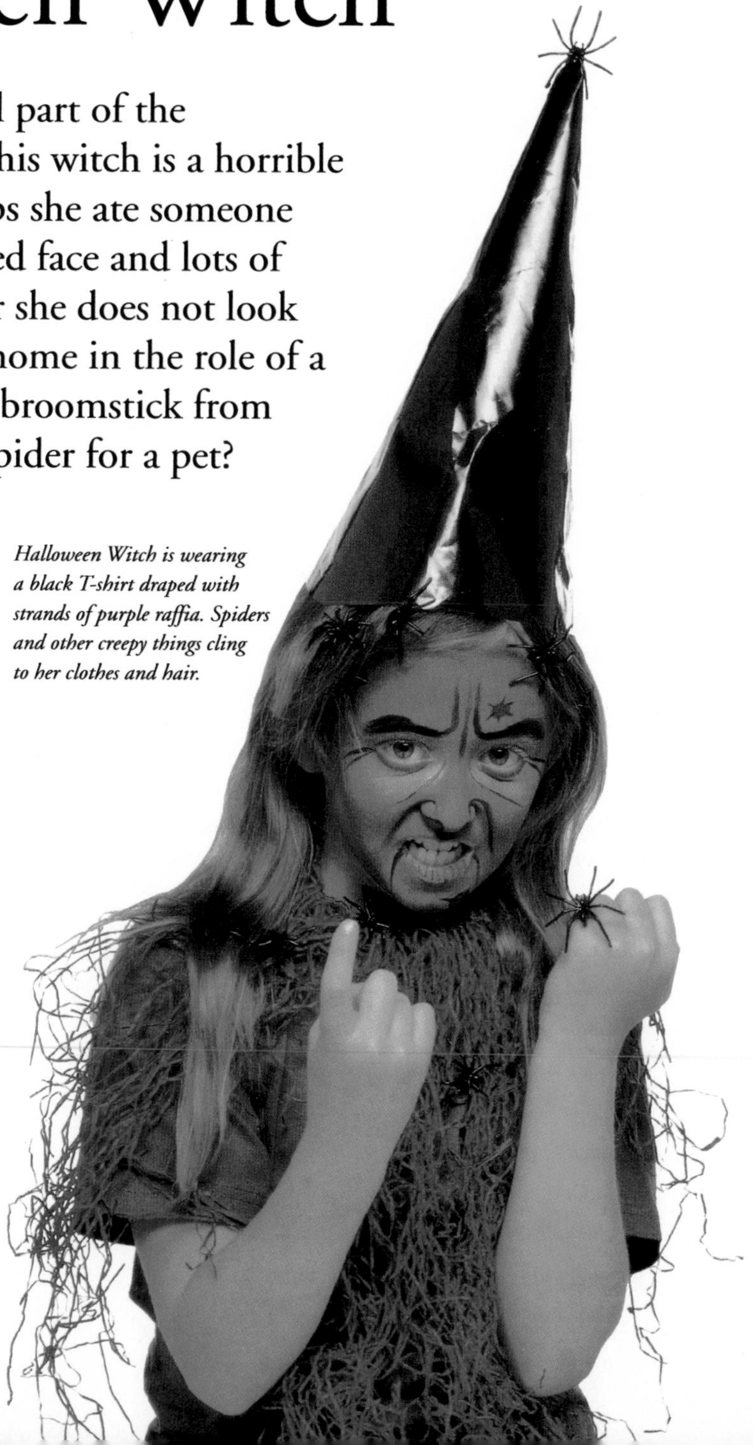

Halloween Witch is wearing a black T-shirt draped with strands of purple raffia. Spiders and other creepy things cling to her clothes and hair.

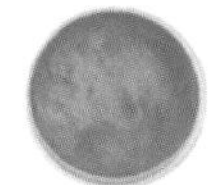

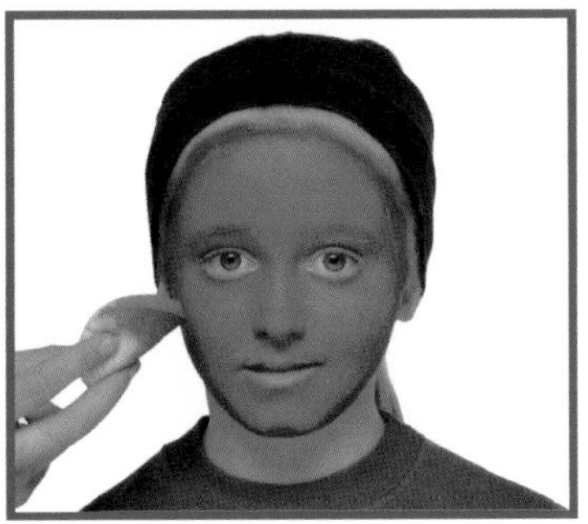

1 Tie the hair back. Use the triangular sponge to make a purple outline around the face. Fill the outline with green face paint using the round sponge. Blend the colours with the round sponge.

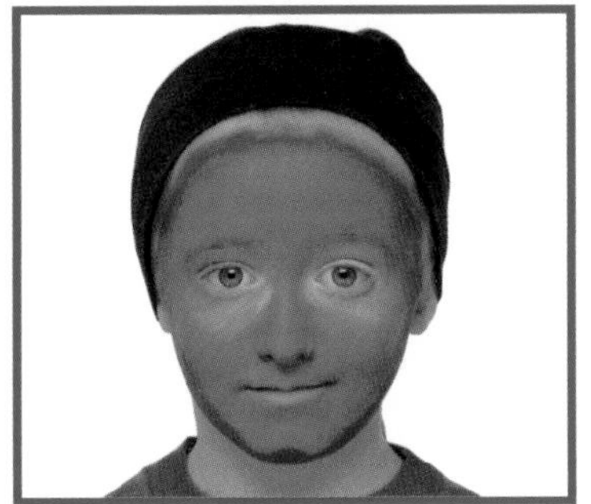

2 Before the green face paint dries, use the medium brush to paint above and below the eyes with white face paint. Dab this on quickly with the round sponge so that it will mix with the base colour.

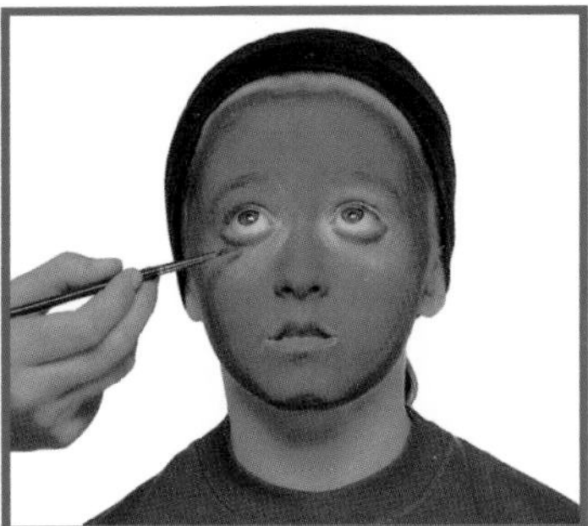

3 Mix white and blue face paints to make light blue. Paint the lower lip light blue using the medium brush. Look up towards the ceiling and keep your head still while a red line is painted under both eyes.

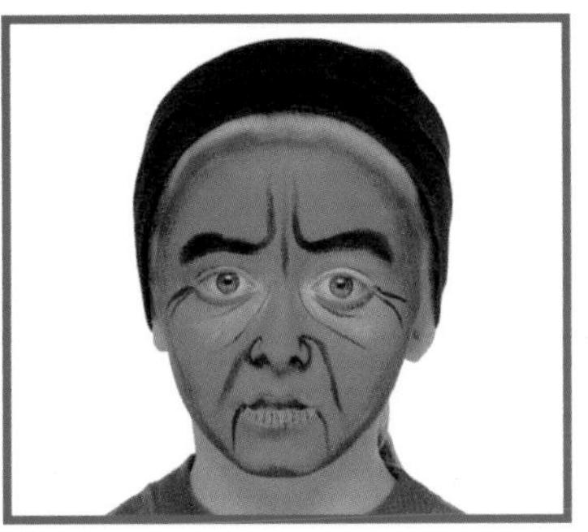

4 Paint black bushy eyebrows and wrinkles. Paint creases on the lips. Witches rarely smile, which is why they have deep frown lines.

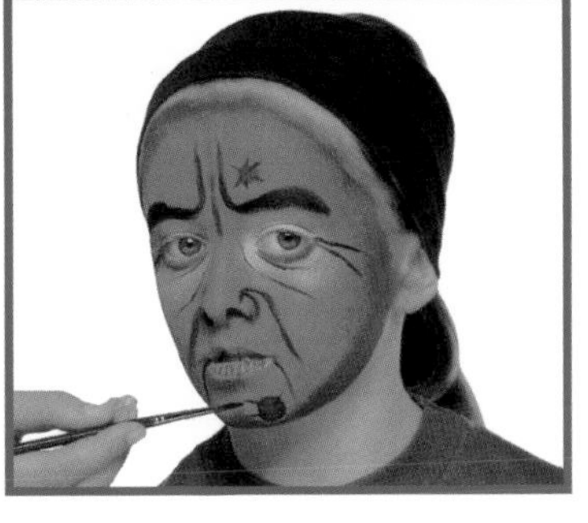

5 Use the tip of the fine brush to paint red circles on the chin and forehead. Clean the fine brush before outlining the circles in black. Keep using the fine brush to paint black hairs sprouting from the warts.

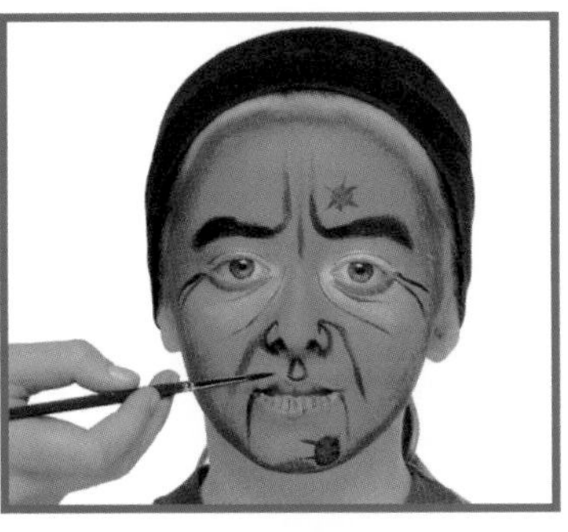

6 Use the fine brush and black face paint to accentuate the lines under the nose and add other gruesome features.

Bind together lots of twigs and branches to make a broom. Halloween Witch needs a broomstick for getting about and for sweeping up around the cauldron!

Spotty Puppy

There is only one thing more adorable than a puppy... a spotty puppy. The face painting for this extra cute canine is easy to do. It is perfect for someone trying their hand at face painting for the very first time.

If Spotty Puppy is going to a fancy dress party, she had better behave. No jumping on the furniture or chewing everything in sight!

YOU WILL NEED THESE MATERIALS

Hairband or hair elastics

Natural sponge

Round sponge

Bowl of water

Absorbent paper towel

Fine and thick brushes

Face paints (pink, white, black)

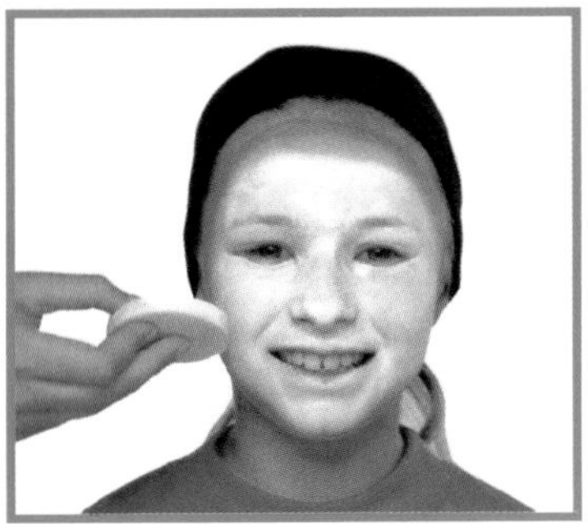

1 Tie hair off the face. Use a thick brush to paint a thick pink circle around the edge of the face. Close your eyes and mouth while your face is being painted white with the round sponge. Do two coats if necessary.

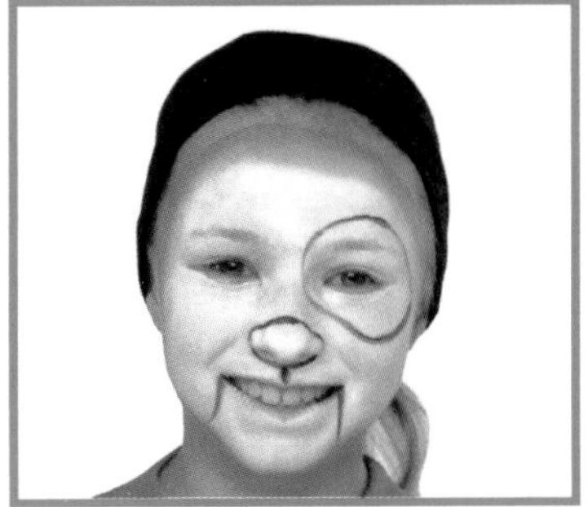

2 Use the fine brush to paint a black circle around one eye and around the nose. Paint a black line from the base of the nose to the upper lip. Paint two black lines from the corners of the mouth to the jawline.

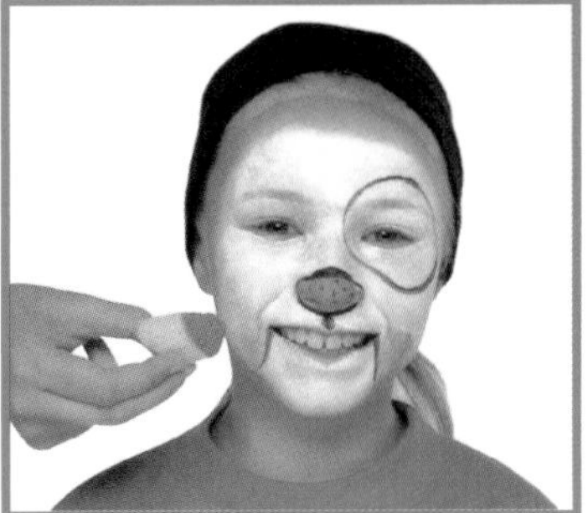

3 Colour the nose pink using the thick brush. Paint black dots on the nose with the fine brush. Dab pink face paint on either side of the mouth with a natural sponge. The sponge will create a dappled effect.

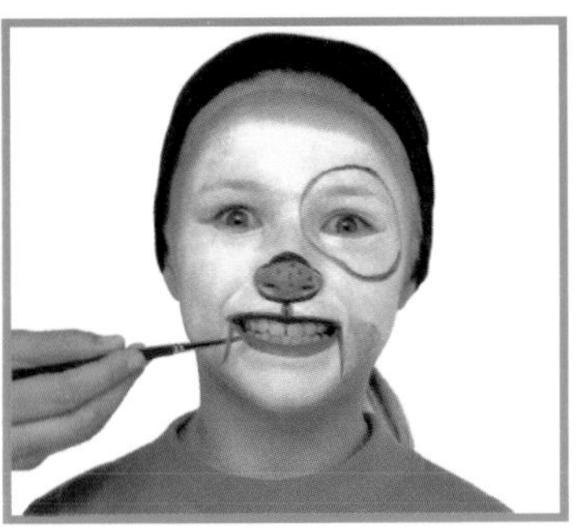

4 Make a smile while your lips are being painted. Use the fine brush to paint the upper lip black. Then paint the lower lip red.

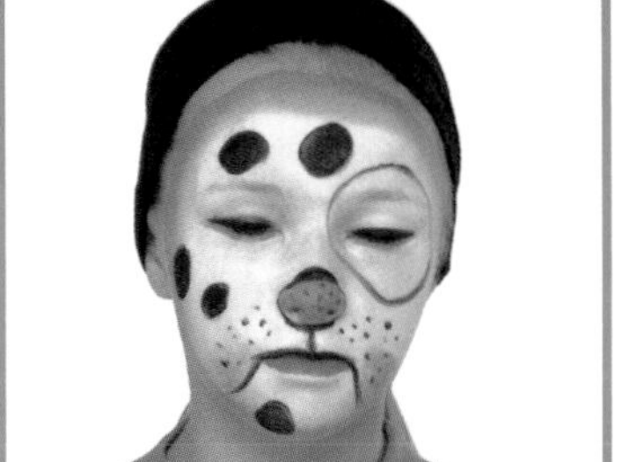

5 Use the fine brush to paint black dots on to the cheeks. Paint circles on to the forehead, cheeks and chin with the fine brush. Paint the circles black. Close your eyes while a line is painted on to both eyelids.

To make the outfit, cut out circles of paper and stick them to a T-shirt and headband with double-sided sticky tape. Instead of painting your hands, you could wear socks covered with paper spots on your hands.

6 Paint the back of the hands white using the round sponge. Paint black lines on the fingers and four circles.

Octopus

This is a very rare and unusual species of octopus because it only has five tentacles instead of eight. Perhaps it should be called a pentapus – 'penta' meaning five. If you let pentapus get wet, he will disappear!

YOU WILL NEED THESE MATERIALS

Kitchen cloth

Bowl of water

Triangular sponge

Medium brush

Face paints (blue, red, black, white)

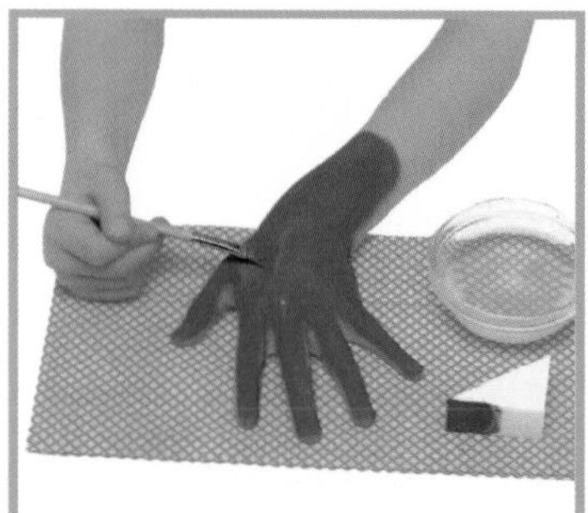

1 Lay a kitchen cloth on your work surface. Apply blue face paint to your hand with the triangular sponge. Leave to dry for a few minutes, then apply another coat with the medium brush. Leave to dry.

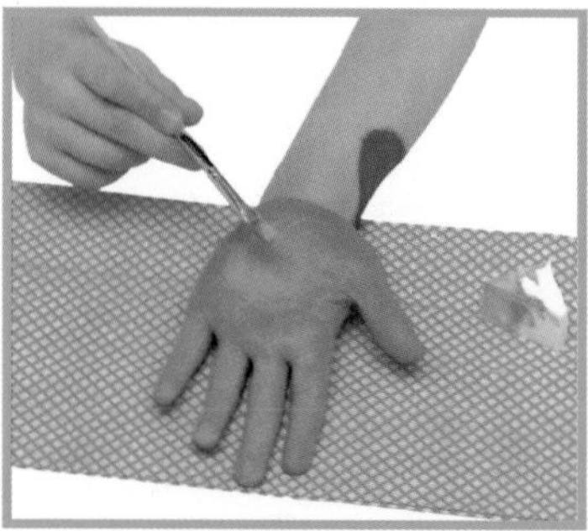

2 Turn your hand over and paint the palm pink. To make a strong pink colour, mix red and white face paints. Apply the pink using the sponge. Apply a second coat with the medium brush.

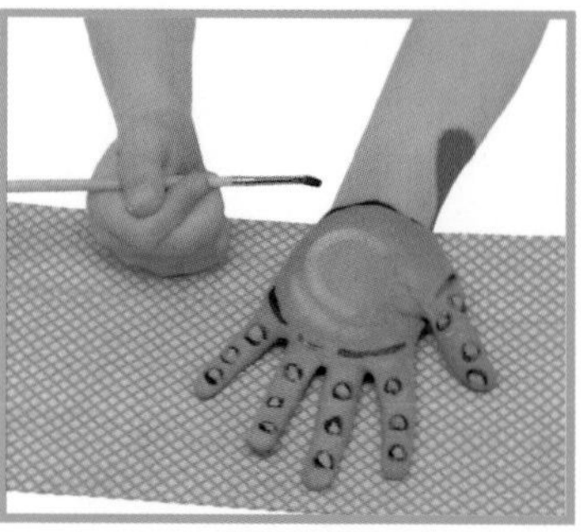

3 With the medium brush, paint white dots on your fingers. Leave to dry for a few minutes. Outline the white dots (suckers) with a fine line of black face paint.

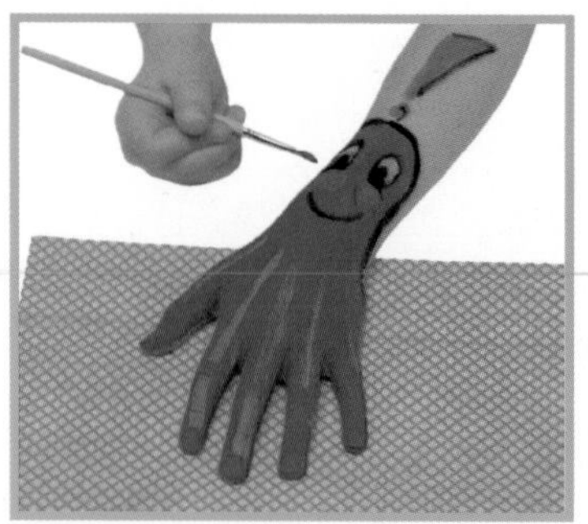

4 When the paint is dry, turn over your hand and paint the face of the octopus on to the blue background. Paint red lines down the fingers and an exclamation symbol (!) above the head.

Make a mini-stage for Octopus to perform in by decorating an empty cardboard box with paint and paper. You will need to leave the top of the box open so that you can put your hand on to the stage. Cut the front of the box to resemble draped stage curtains.

Stag

This painted hand puppet captures the elegant beauty of a proud stag. The antlers are formed using the little finger and first finger. Pinch together the two middle fingers and thumb to make the head.

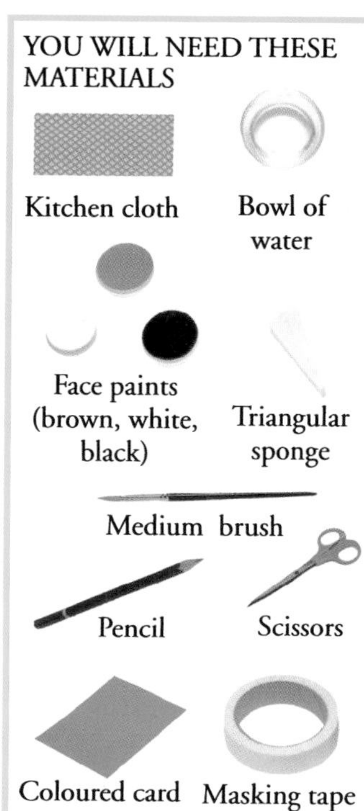

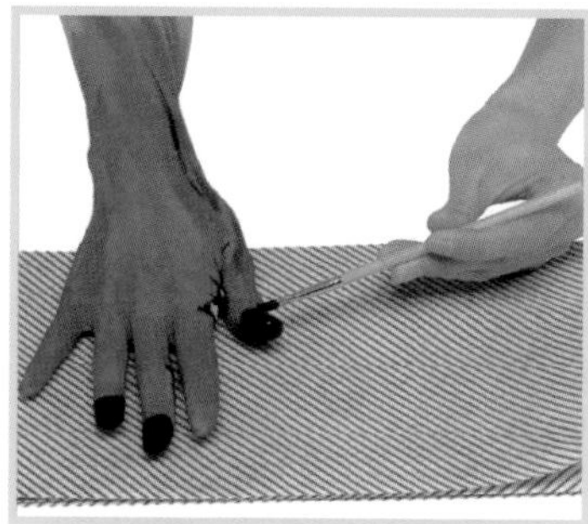

1 Rest your hand on a kitchen cloth. Apply brown face paint with the sponge. Leave to dry. Use the brush to apply streaks of light brown face paint. Paint the ends of your thumb and two middle fingers black.

2 Pinch your fingers together to make the stag's head and antlers. Paint the the eye white, as shown. Outline the eye with black and paint eyelashes.

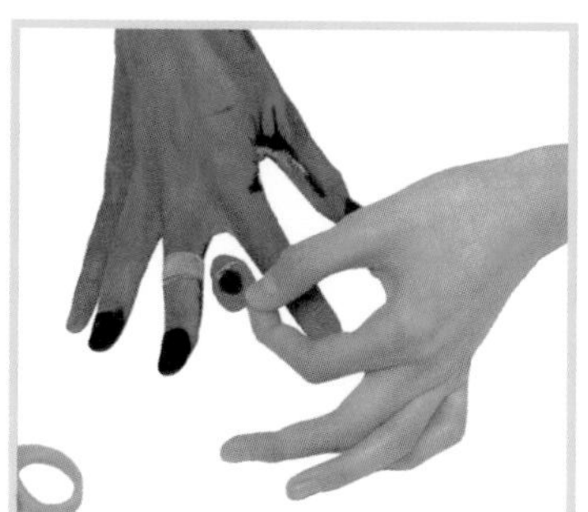

3 Cut out a 2cm (3/4in) circle of blue card to complete the eye. Paint a black dot in the middle. Tape the eye on to your middle finger using masking tape, as shown. Paint over the tape.

To finish, draw two antlers on to card. At the base of each antler draw a narrow strip 5cm (2in) long. Cut the antlers out. Wrap the strips around your fingers and tape the ends.

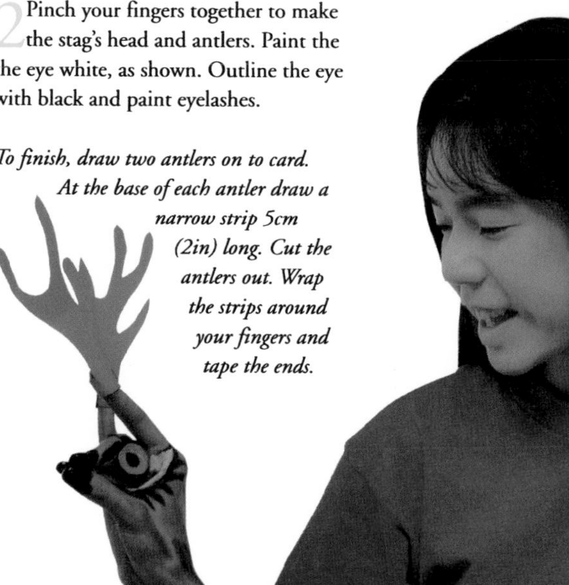

Flowering Tree

This body painting of a tree is so realistic you could almost hide undetected in a tropical jungle. Even the flowers winding their way up the trunk are exotic looking. If you moved your arms as though they were branches swaying in the wind, your camouflage would be complete.

YOU WILL NEED THESE MATERIALS

- Hairband or hair elastics
- Absorbent paper towel
- Triangular sponge
- Bowl of water
- Fine, medium and thick brushes
- Face paints (brown, red, yellow, green, blue, pink)

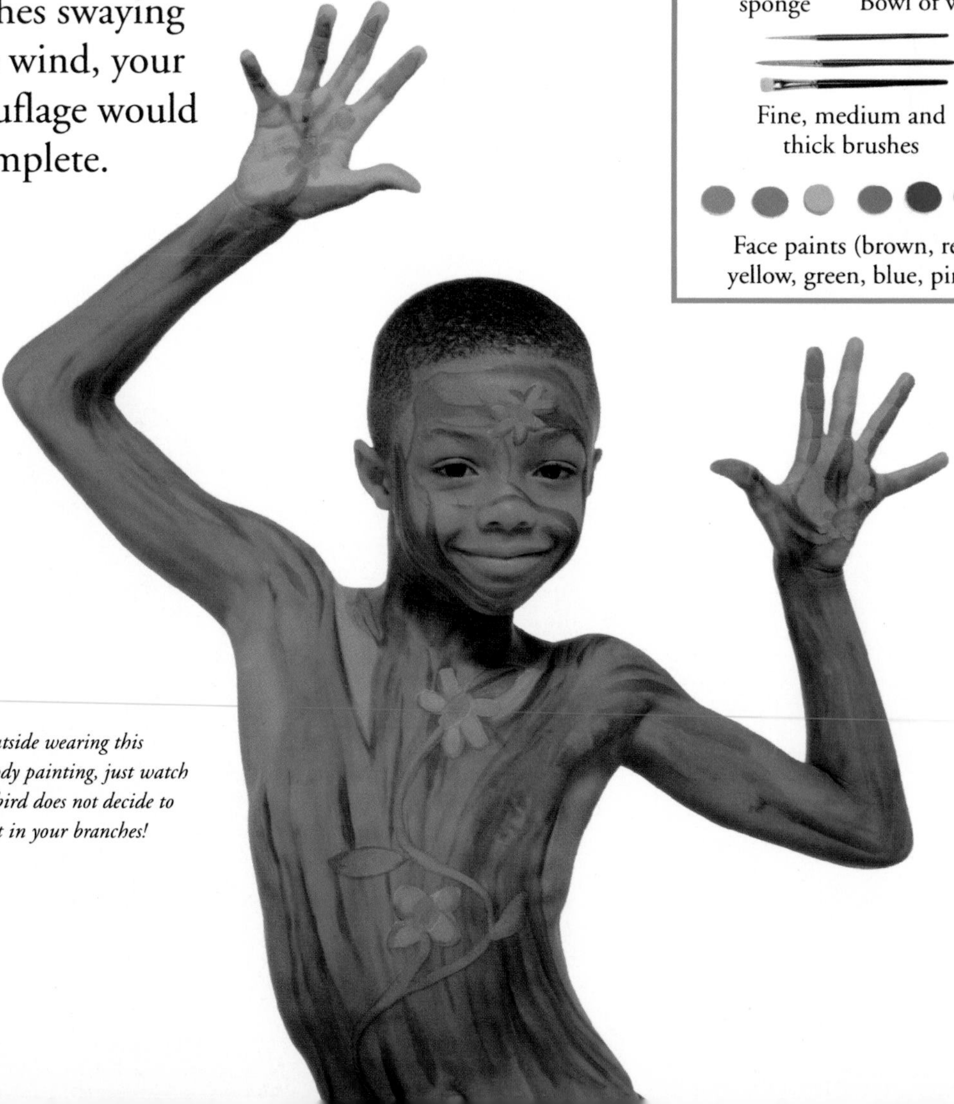

If you go outside wearing this fantastic body painting, just watch out that a bird does not decide to make a nest in your branches!

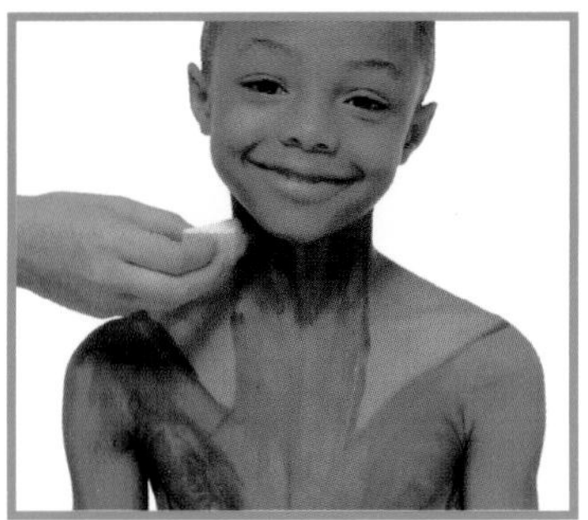

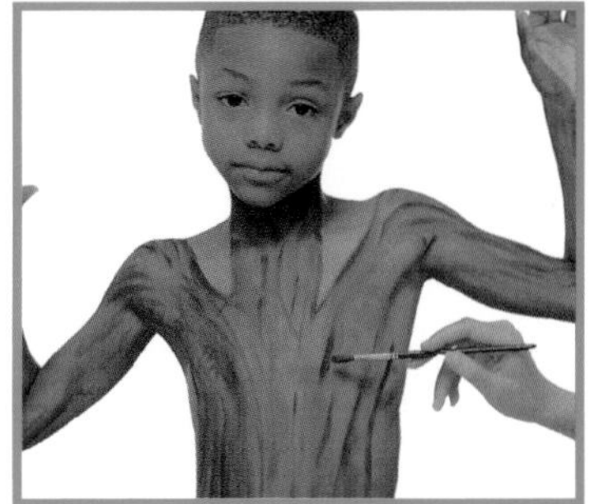

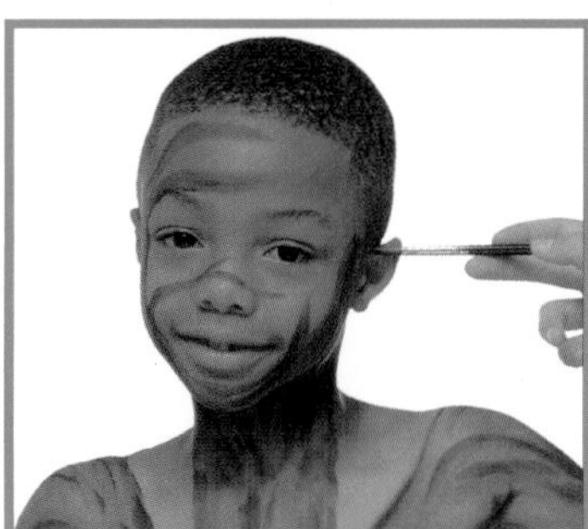

1 Tie the hair back. Use the medium brush to paint the brown outline of the tree trunk on to the chest and back. Use the sponge to fill in with brown face paint. Make shades of brown by adding red or yellow to brown.

2 Paint the front and the back of the arms (the branches) in the same way. Extend the paint on to the hands but taper it to resemble the end of a branch. Do the texture of the bark using dark brown face paint.

3 Use the thick brush and brown face paint to paint branches up the neck and on to the face. Make the branches twist and turn. Allow the paint to dry thoroughly before starting the next step.

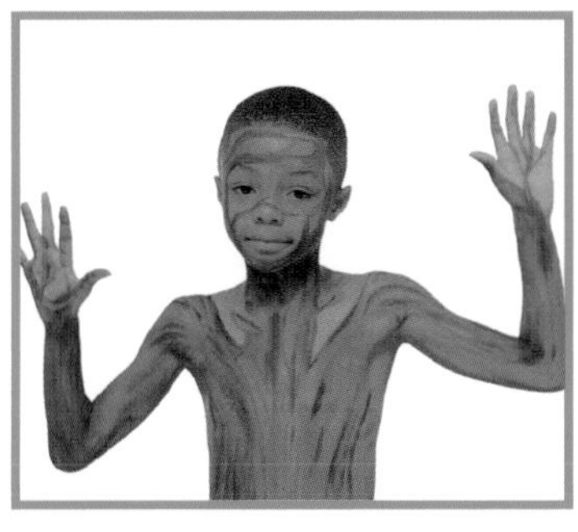

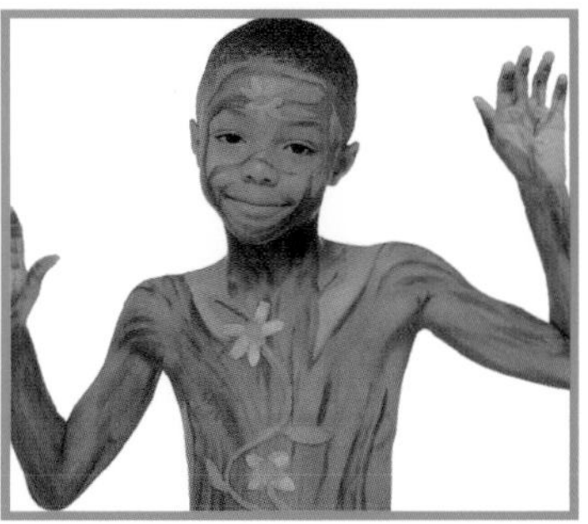

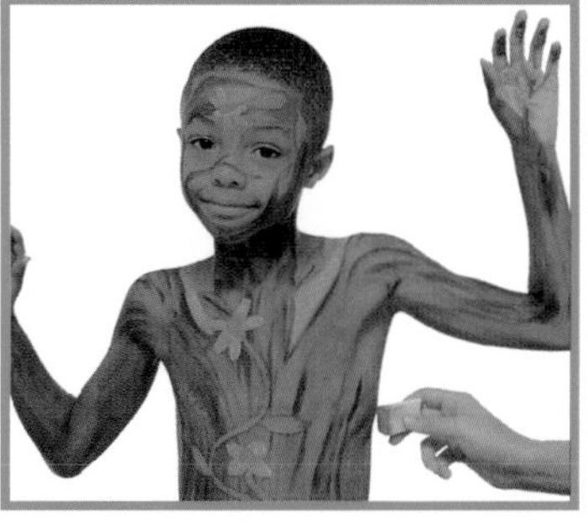

4 Wash the brush and sponge. Squeeze the sponge to get rid of excess water. Draw outlines for the leaves in green face paint. Fill in the outlines using the thick brush.

5 Paint a green stem spiralling up the trunk and linking all the leaves. Paint the flowers blue using a thick brush. Do two coats. When dry, paint the centres pink.

6 Use the clean sponge to paint in the background sky. This means filling in the unpainted areas with blue face paint. Apply it unevenly to look like a cloudy sky.

Making face paints go further

When you are painting a large area, like a person's body, with face paints always apply the paints with a triangular, round or natural sponge. Before dipping the sponge into the paint, dampen it in a little water. This will make the face paint go on easier and also make it go further. To even out face paint, dampen the sponge and wipe it gently over the area where the colour is concentrated.

You can mix face paint colours just as you would ordinary acrylic or poster paints. If you only need a little amount of a mixed colour, do the mixing on the lid of the palette. For large amounts of a mixed colour, use a smooth plate. To add sparkle to your face paint colours, mix in glitter gel make-up, face glitter or sequins.

Disco Diva

To dazzle all the other dancers at the disco, add a sparkle or two to your face with glitter gel make-up. It comes in lots of colours, so choose your favourites. Glitter gel make-up is easy to use, but it can be a little messy.

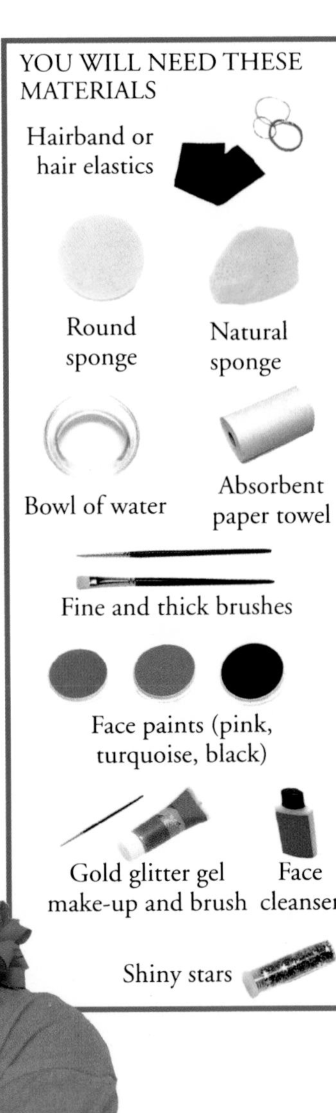

A diva is someone who is excellent at doing something. A Disco Diva is someone who knows all the dance moves and how to make them!

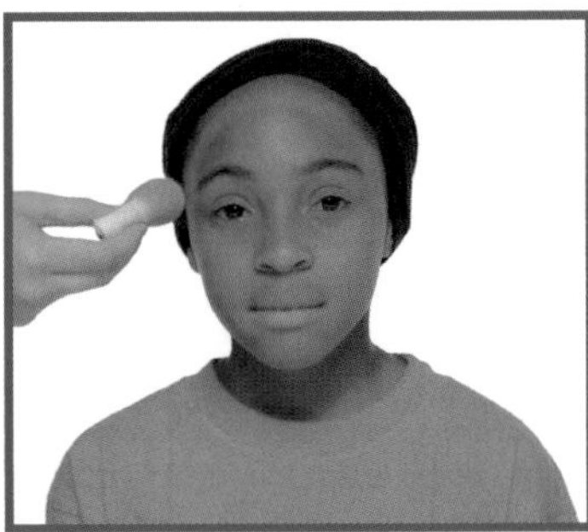

1 Tie the hair back. Apply a wide circle of pink face paint around the edge of the face using a damp round sponge. Do not worry if the circle is not perfect – the edges can be neatened with the fine brush.

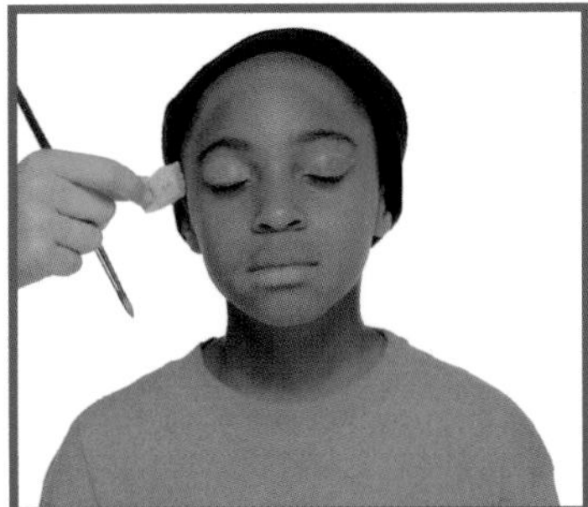

2 Paint a turquoise line with the fine brush from the inside corner of each eye up to the end of each eyebrow. Fill in with turquoise using the thick brush. Blend in the colour with a damp natural sponge.

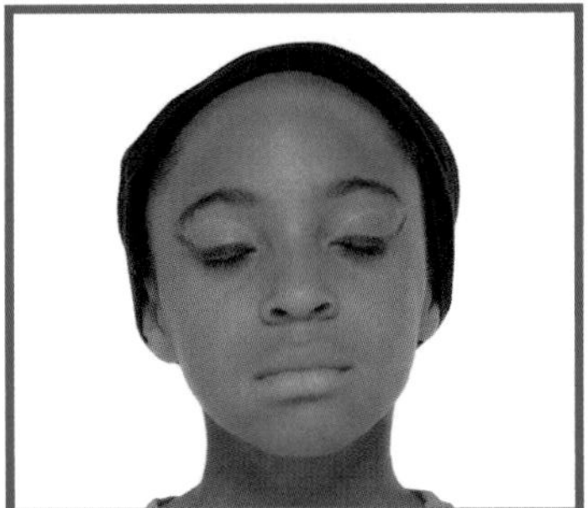

3 When the face paint is dry, paint two thin black lines on to the eyelids, as shown. Start the line from the inside corner of each eye and move outwards. Keep your eyes closed until the paint has dried.

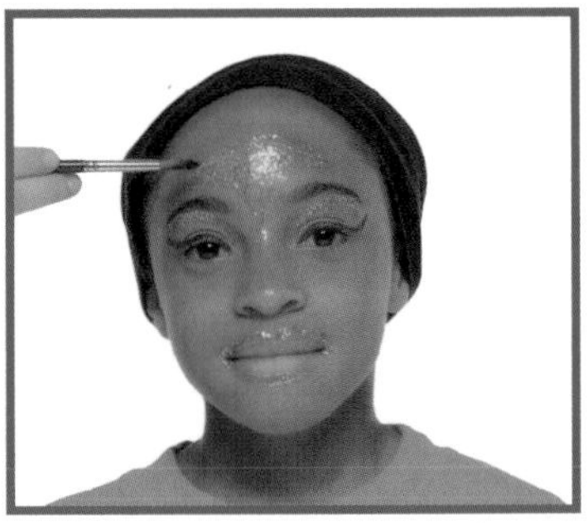

4 Use the glitter gel brush to paint the gold glitter gel on to the forehead, nose, eyelids and around the mouth. Glitter gel make-up is quite runny so apply it sparingly and carefully. When dry, apply another coat if necessary.

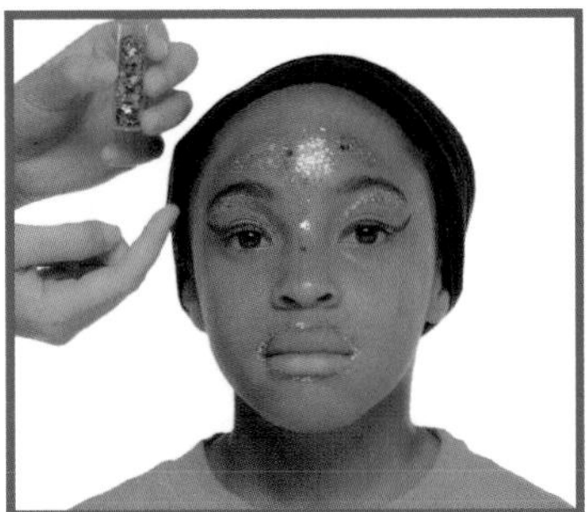

5 While the glitter gel is wet, gently press some stars on to the forehead and nose. Do not put lots of stars in one place, they will fall off. If the gel dries before the stars are in place, apply some more gel.

Sparkling extras

This would be a great time to spray your hair with a glitter hair spray. To remove the sparkling dust, rinse or brush your hair. You can buy glitter hair spray in specialist theatrical shops and some chemist shops.

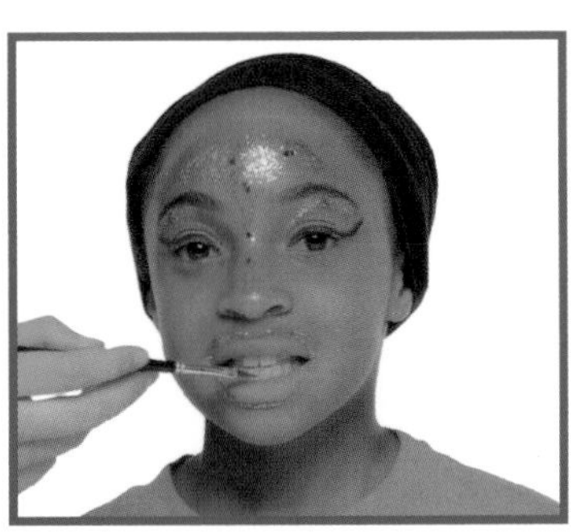

6 Stretch your lips into a broad smile while bright pink face paint is applied to your lips with the thick brush. You have every reason to smile, Disco Diva, because you are ready to go dancing!

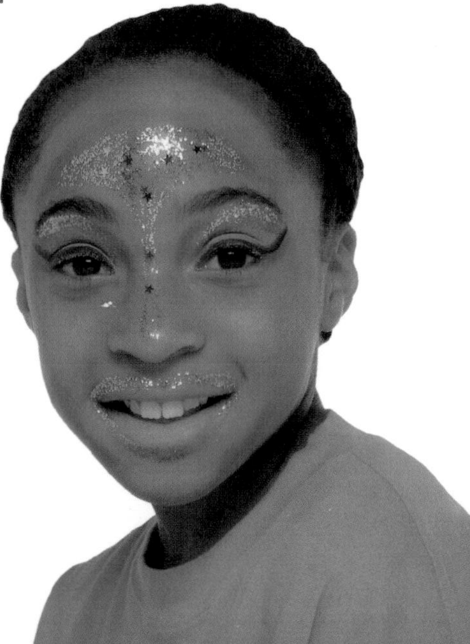

Prowling Leopard

Face painting is a great way to be transformed into an animal, especially an exotic jungle creature like this sleek, spotted leopard. To make your face look lean, mean and hungry, the outline around the face is a special shape.

YOU WILL NEED THESE MATERIALS

- Hairband or hair elastics
- Bowl of water
- Absorbent paper towel
- Face paints (yellow, orange, black, red, brown)
- Fine, medium and thick brushes
- Round sponge

Handy hint

If you use face paint on your hands, do not forget to keep your hands away from water. Even small splashes of water will wash away face paint.

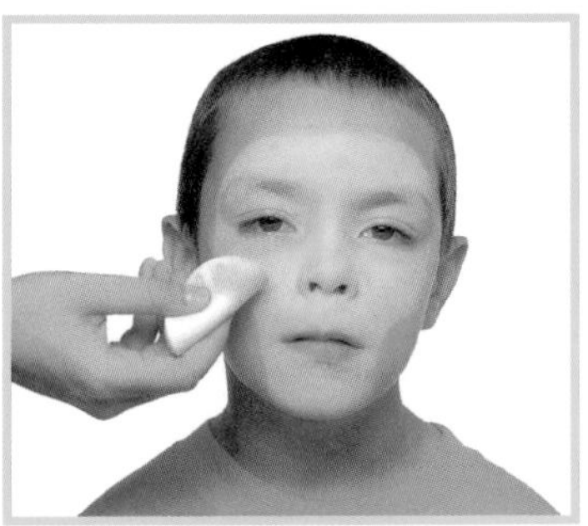

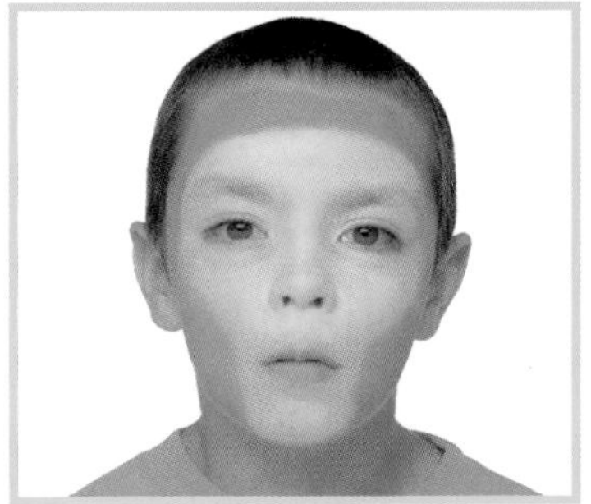

1 Tie the hair back. Paint a yellow circle around the face with a medium brush. Fill in the circle with yellow face paint applied with a round sponge. Try to apply the face paint smoothly and evenly.

2 Use the thick brush to paint an outline around the face in orange face paint. Shape the outline, as shown. Neaten the edges with the fine or medium brush. Allow the base colour to dry thoroughly before continuing.

3 Close your eyes while black lines are painted on your eyelids. A fine brush will be needed for this. Paint the nose and the upper lip with black face paint. Paint the line that runs from the upper lip to the nose.

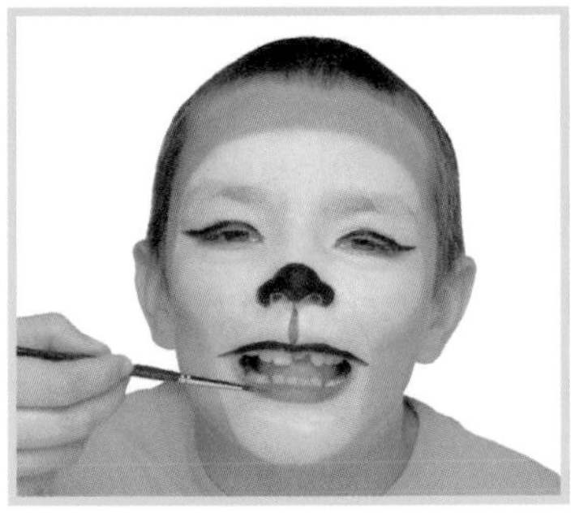

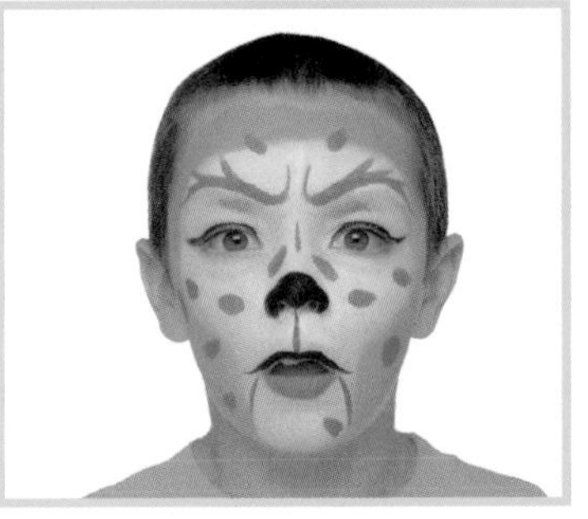

4 Even leopards can raise a smile so that their lower lip can be painted bright red. A fine brush will be needed to paint the lips.

5 Use the fine brush to paint the sweeping eyebrows, spots and lines on the face brown. Try to do this as neatly as possible.

6 Paint tiny brown dots below the nose with the fine brush. Paint lines from these dots to make the leopard's whiskers. Growl!

Look out, leopard about!

To make yourself a really convincing leopard takes a little more than just face paint. You will have to prowl like a leopard – silently – and growl like a leopard. It also helps if you dress like this sleek lord of the jungle.

To make the ears, cut two oval shapes from orange card. Fold along the bottom to form a flap. Draw a line in felt-tip pen on each ear, as shown. Apply special make-up glue to the base of the flaps and press them on to your forehead. Adding spots to an orange T-shirt (and even jogging pants or leggings) is easy. Simply cut yellow circles from card and use double-sided sticky tape to attach them to the front and back of the T-shirt.

You can either paint the paws using face paint or wear a pair of gloves or socks on your hands. You can decorate the gloves or socks with circles and strips of card. Attach the card with double-sided sticky tape.

Fake Tattoo

A tattoo is simple to do when it is done with face paint. Better still, it will wash off with soap and water. Tattoos can be painted anywhere on your body. This tattoo consists of a banner, a heart and your initials.

YOU WILL NEED THESE MATERIALS

Bowl of water

Absorbent paper towel

Face paints (purple or black, red, green)

Fine and thick brushes

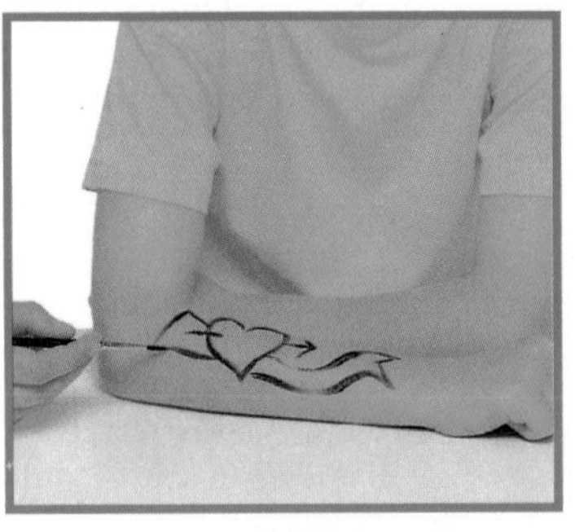

1 Paint the outline of the tattoo in purple or black using the fine brush.

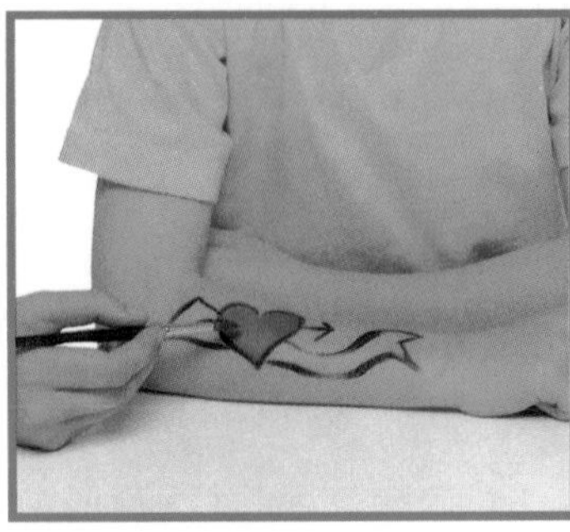

2 Allow the outline to dry before painting the heart red. Do this with the thick brush.

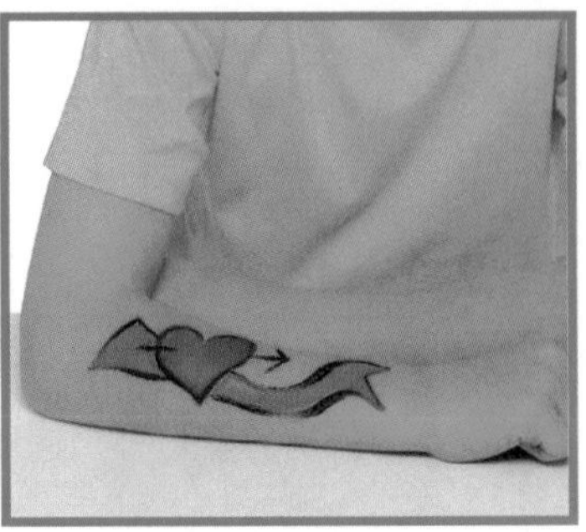

3 Clean the thick brush before using it to paint the banner green. Do two coats, if necessary.

Be more adventurous and artistic with your tattoo by including images of animals, flowers, cars, ships or even your favourite pair of roller skates.

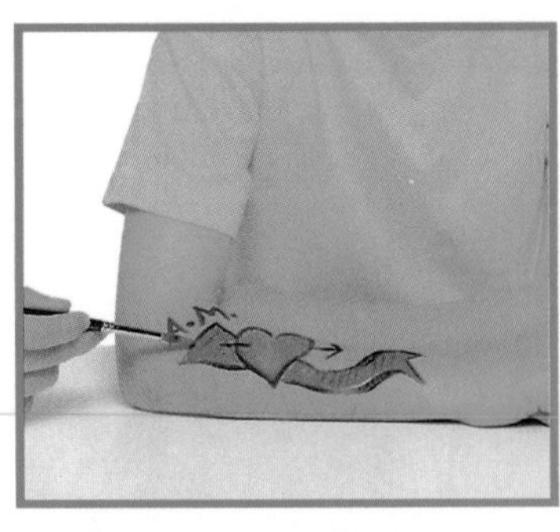

4 Paint the initials in purple or black face paint using the fine brush. Clean the fine brush. Decorate the banner with thin red stripes using the fine brush.

Jewels Galore

Use face paints to create fantastic jewellery. Do it for fun or to jazz up a fancy dress costume. Imagine how amazed your friends will be when you turn up at a party dripping with diamonds, rubies and sapphires!

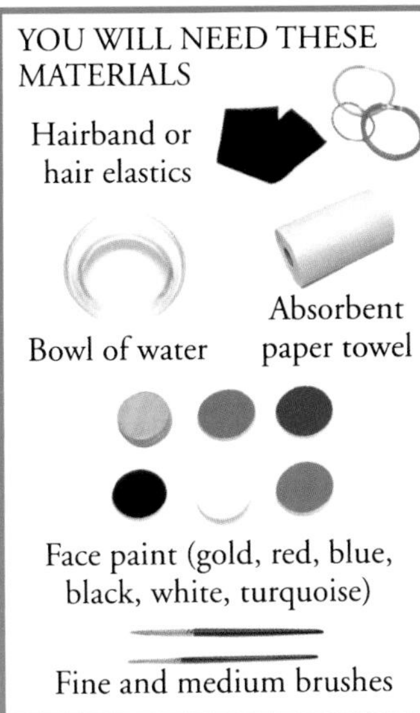

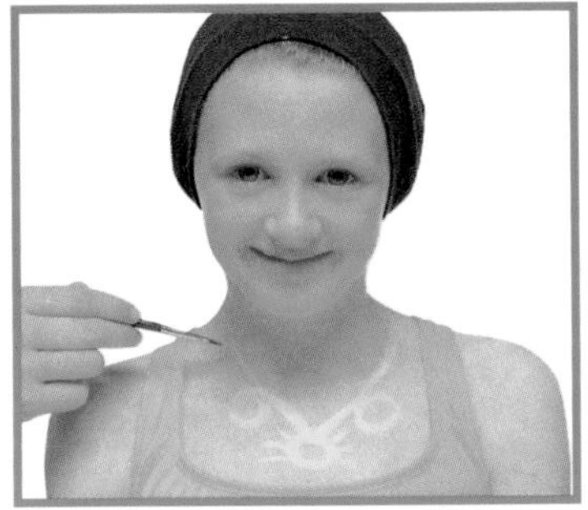

1 Tie the hair back. Paint the outlines of the necklace in gold face paint using a medium brush. Do two coats, if necessary.

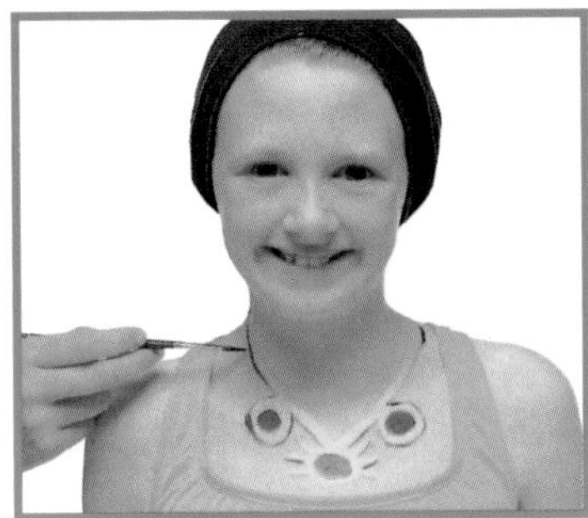

2 Fill in the outlines with red and blue face paints. Paint a thin black line around the necklace and pendants with a fine brush.

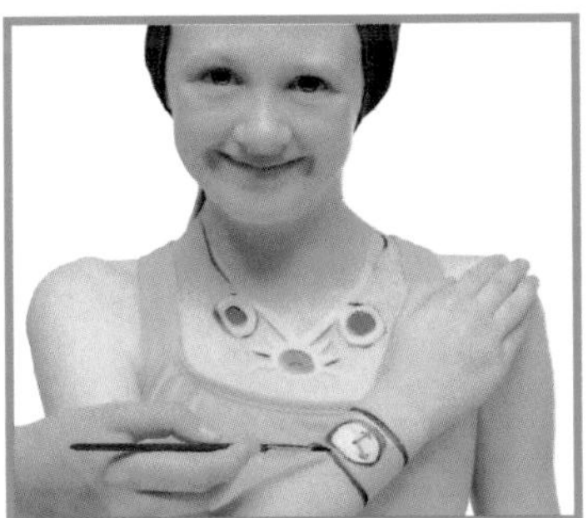

3 Paint a gold band around the wrist, then paint the outline for the watch face and straps black. Use the fine brush to paint the watch face white and the clock hands turquoise.

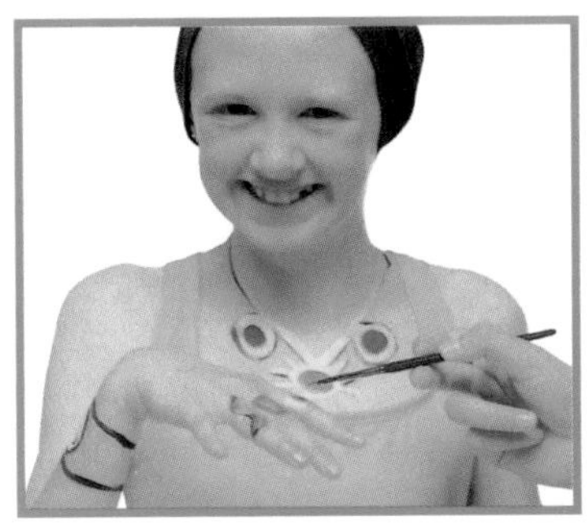

4 Use a clean fine brush to paint the gold outlines of rings on to the fingers. Allow to dry before painting exquisite turquoise, ruby and sapphire gems on to the rings.

Handy hint

Gold face paint is a bit more expensive than other colours. If you do not have gold face paint, use yellow instead.

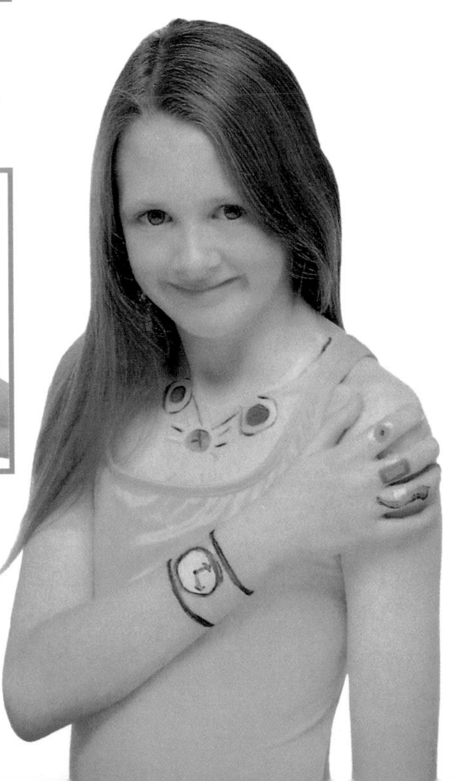

Football Hero

You do not have to buy your football team's strip – you can paint it on! Body painting is lots of fun especially when the paint is being applied to ticklish spots! Try not to laugh too much or you will end up with socks covered with wiggly lines. Remove body paint under the shower and dry yourself with an old towel.

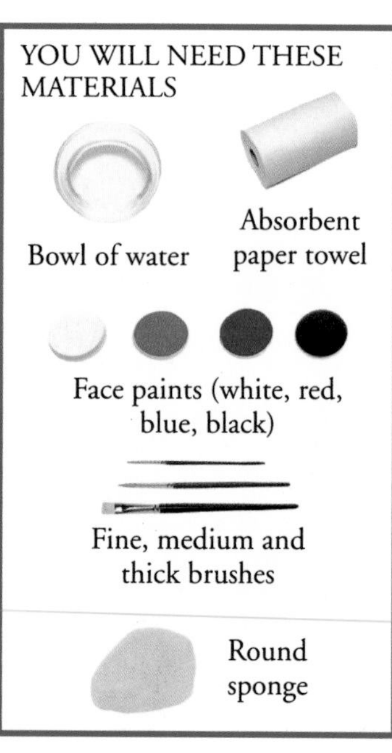

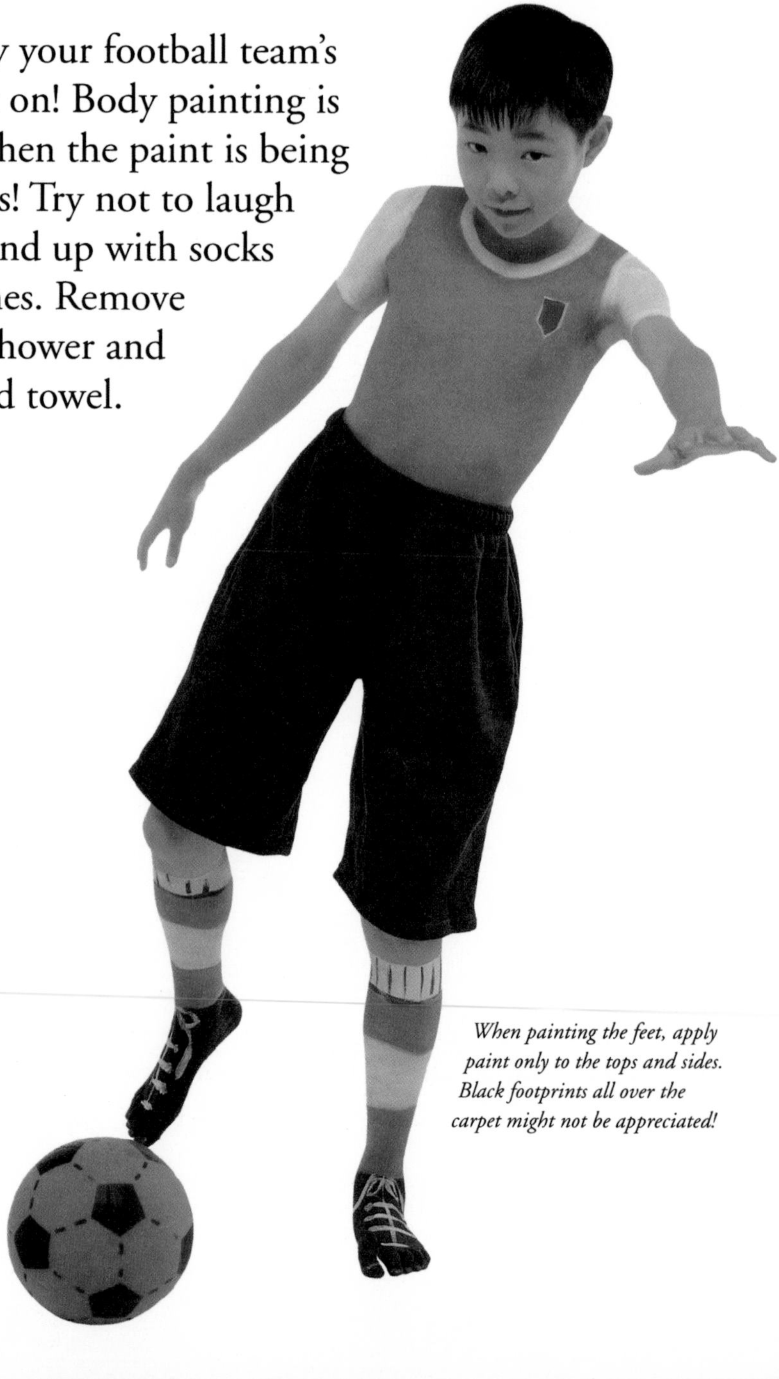

When painting the feet, apply paint only to the tops and sides. Black footprints all over the carpet might not be appreciated!

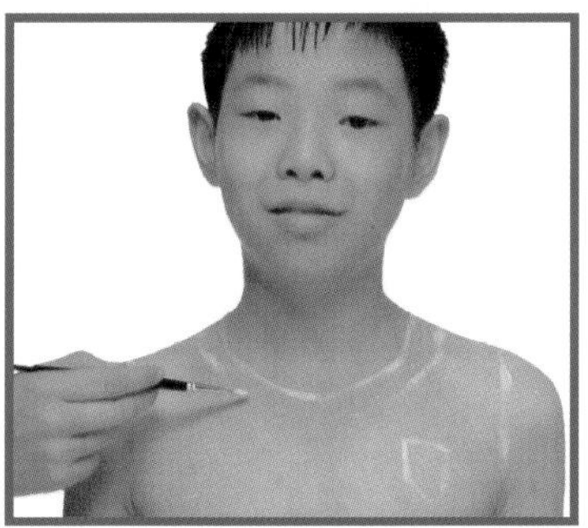

1 Make an outline on the chest and back in white face paint of the front and the back of the football shirt. This is best done with a medium or thick brush. Do not forget to paint the outline of the team's badge.

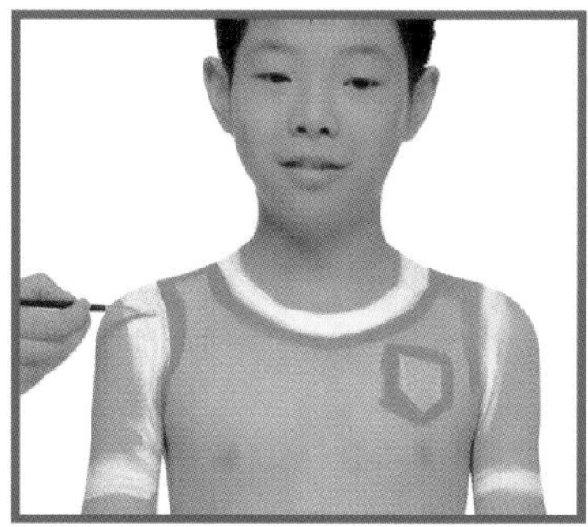

2 Use the thick brush to paint broad red lines inside the white outlines. Paint a red line around the waist. In white face paint, go over the outline to make the collar. Paint the sleeves white with a thick brush.

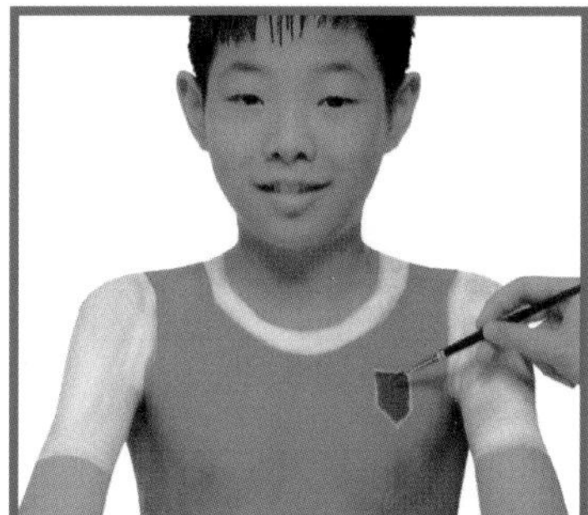

3 Use the round sponge to paint the rest of the shirt. To make the face paint go on easily, slightly moisten the sponge before applying the face paint. Paint the details on the badge using a fine brush.

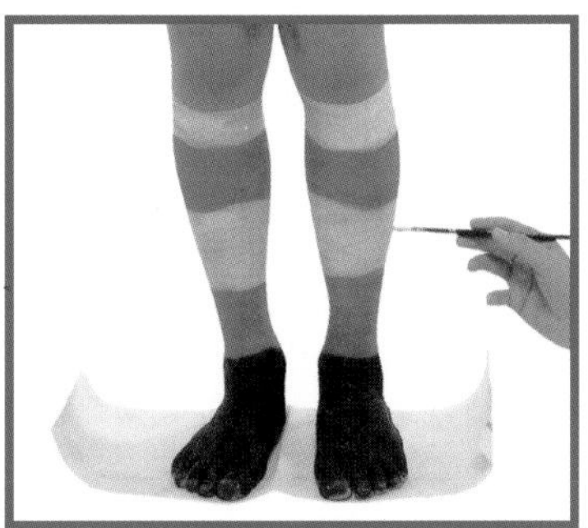

4 Wash the sponge thoroughly and cover the floor with absorbent paper towel. Paint the tops of the feet black using the clean sponge. Use a thick brush to paint red and white bands around both legs.

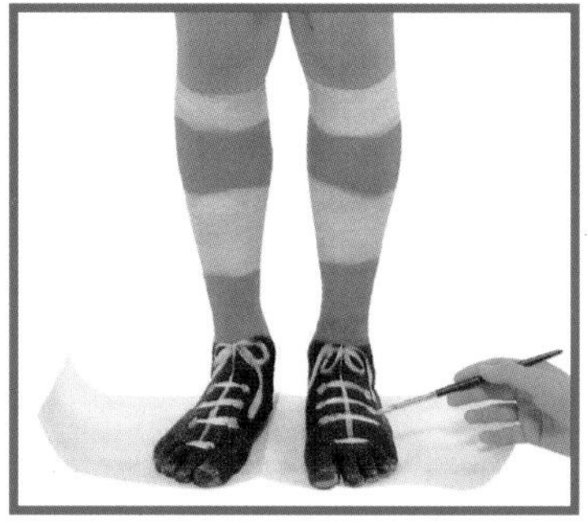

5 Stand as still as you can while the black paint dries. When it is dry, paint on white boot laces with a medium or thick brush. To make the laces show up, apply the white face paint thickly.

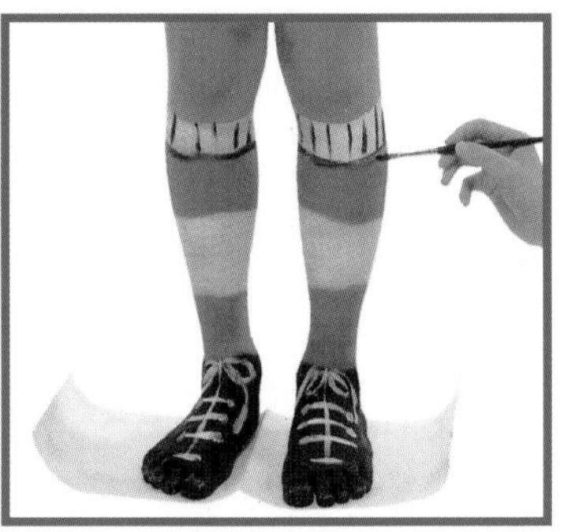

6 Paint short black lines on to the top band with a medium brush. Then paint a black line around the leg for the sock turnovers. The paint must be dry before the football hero can hit the pitch and score the winning goal.

Digital Soccer

Get your friends together and paint each others hands in soccer strip. To play Digital Soccer, divide into two teams and move the ball around a tabletop pitch. Use your fingers to kick the ball into goal. Do headers by bouncing the ball off the back of your hands.

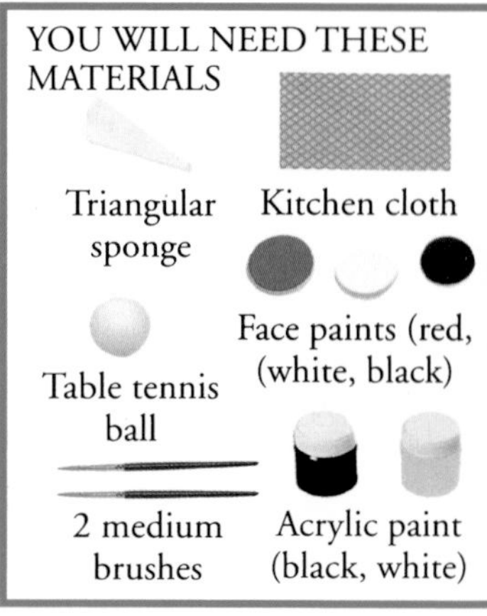

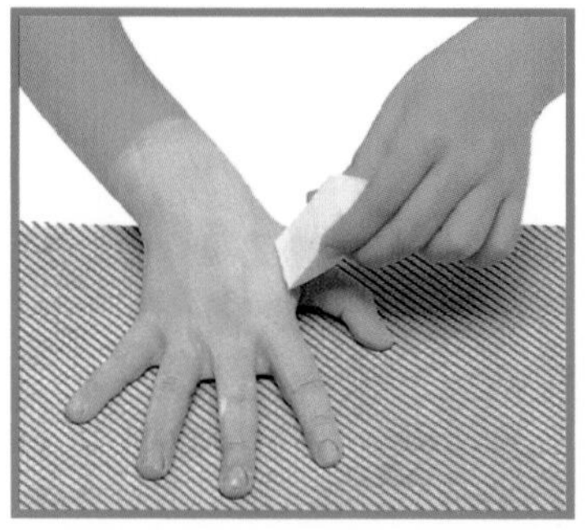

1 Lay the kitchen cloth on your work surface. Apply a base coat of white face paint to one or both hands with a triangular sponge. Leave to dry.

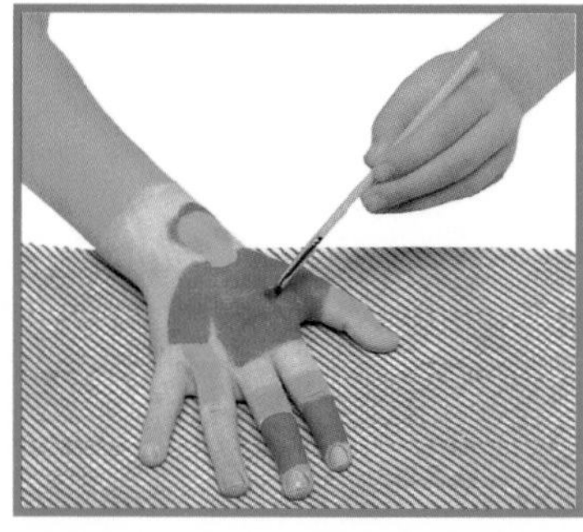

2 Paint the red socks and shirt with the medium brush. Paint the face, arms and knees in a skin tone colour. Leave to dry for a few minutes.

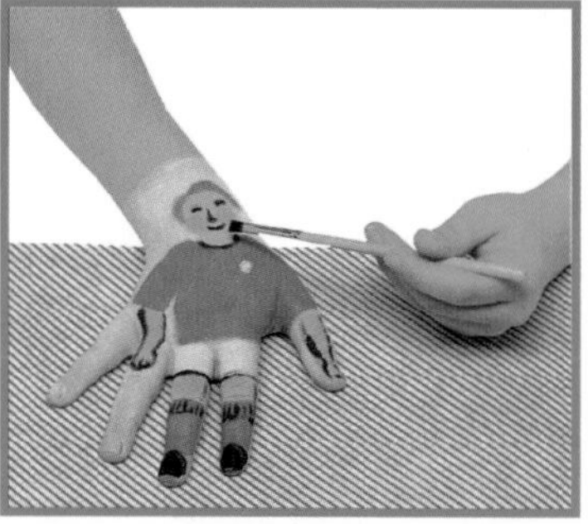

3 Paint a black outline around the footballer. Now you can paint in his black boots and facial features.

4 Paint a table tennis ball with black acrylic paint. When the paint has dried, carefully add the white markings you find on a football. World Cup Digital Soccer, here we come!

To make the pitch, cover a tabletop with newspaper or a large sheet of paper and use a felt-tip pen to mark the lines. Cut one long side end off two small boxes to make the goals. It does not matter what size the boxes are as long as they are exactly the same size. Fix the goals at either end of the pitch using double-sided sticky tape or sticky tack. You are now ready to kick off!

Little Devil

We can use our hands and fingers to make all sorts of shapes and creatures, including this Little Devil. Face paints, a cloak and a trident complete the illusion. The first and fourth fingers form the devil's horns. The two middle fingers curl over to make the hair.

YOU WILL NEED THESE MATERIALS

- Medium brush
- Kitchen cloth 
- Face paints (red, black, white)
- Scissors 
- Triangular sponge
- Black paper
- Nylon netting 
- PVA glue and brush 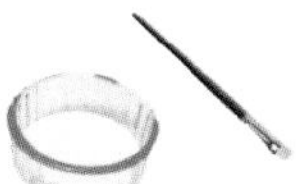
- Gold glitter gel make-up 

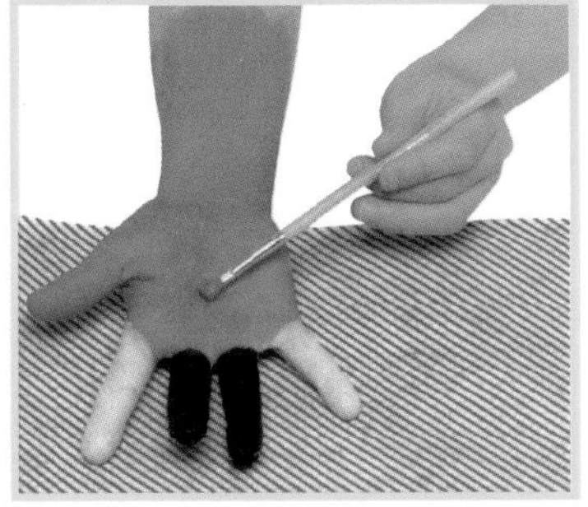

1 Lay down a kitchen cloth. Sponge the palm and back of the hand, wrist and thumb red. Paint the first finger and little finger white and the two middle fingers black with the brush.

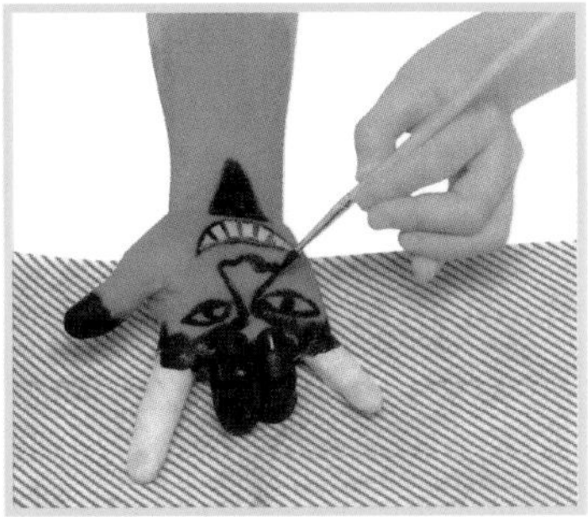

2 When dry, paint the tip of the thumb and the base of the little finger black. Paint Devil's face and beard black using the medium brush. Outline the teeth with black and fill in with white face paint.

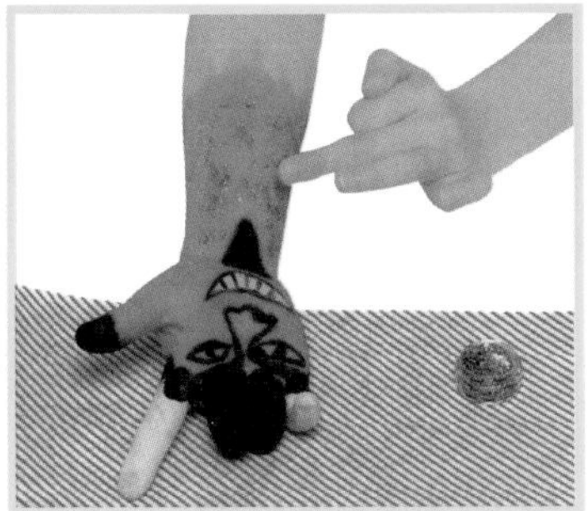

3 Use a finger to gently smear gold glitter gel make-up over the red paint on the wrist. This will make Little Devil's neck glint and shimmer.

To finish, cut a length of red nylon netting and tie it around the wrist. Cut out a trident from black paper and glue it to the front of the cloak.

Alien from Outer Space

Alien lifeforms can come in many different guises. This extra-terrestrial beauty is the famous many-eyed creature from the planet Agog. This alien sees everything. Even when asleep, the extra pair of eyes on its eyelids keep a watchful gaze. Just to be certain it misses nothing, there is a pair of cardboard eyes on straws attached to a headband. Double creepy!

YOU WILL NEED THESE MATERIALS

Hairband or hair elastics

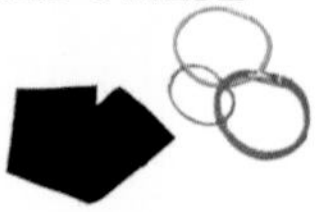

Bowl of water

Absorbent paper towel

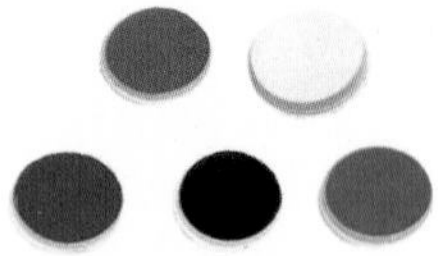

Face paints (green, white, blue, black, red)

Fine and thick brushes

This alien is green, but you could choose to be a red, blue, purple or yellow lifeform. Try to think up an imaginative name for your home planet.

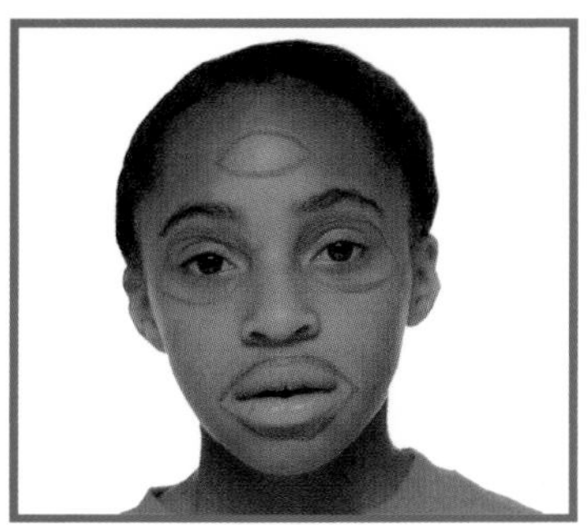

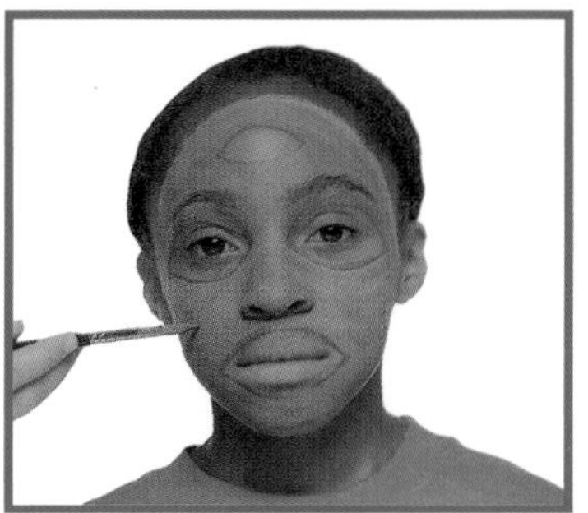

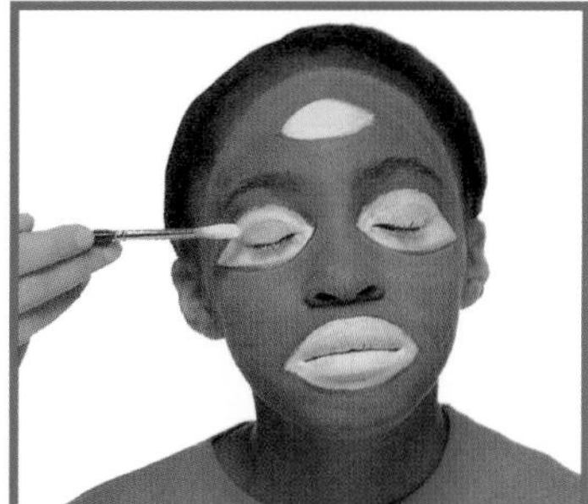

1 Tie the hair back. Use the fine brush to paint the outlines of four oval eye shapes in green face paint. You will need to close your eyes and mouth while the outlines are being painted.

2 Paint the outline of a circle around the face in green face paint with the thick brush. Do two coats, if necessary. Fill in the outline with green. Clean and dry the thick brush thoroughly.

3 When the green face paint is dry, fill in the four eye shapes with white face paint. Do this with the clean thick brush. Apply the paint quite thickly and do two coats, if necessary.

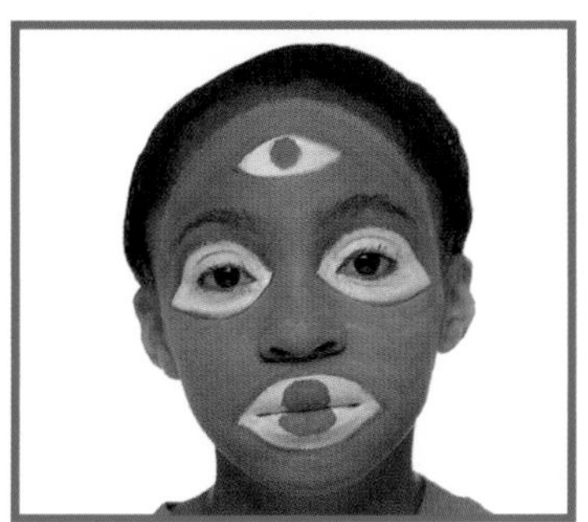

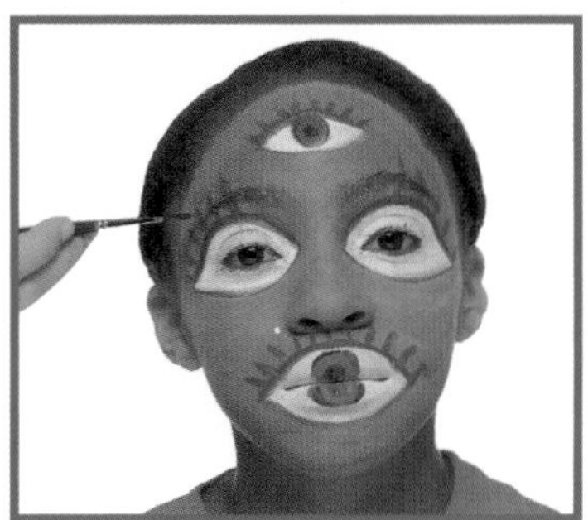

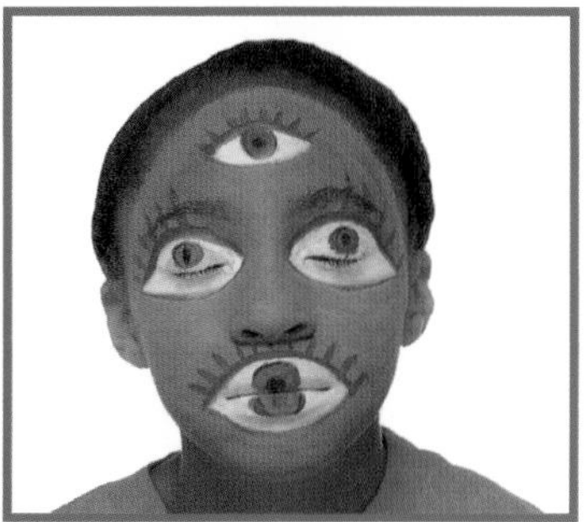

4 Allow the white face paint to dry thoroughly. Then paint blue circles on to the eyes on the lips and forehead. These are the irises of the eyes. Apply two coats if necessary.

5 When the blue face paint is dry, paint a black dot on to the irises to make the pupils. Use the fine brush to paint a red line above the eyes and to make the eyelashes.

6 Close your eyes and stay very still while the irises are painted blue. When the paint is dry, paint on black pupils. Watch out! The many-eyed alien has arrived.

Alien costume

The planet Agog is covered with multi-coloured raffia and so are its inhabitants. Raffia is wound around their heads and used to form a cloak over their shoulders. But do you know what is under the cloak? More pairs of eyes, of course. When you make a pair of eyes to wear on your head, cut out and colour extra pairs and stick them to your T-shirt with double-sided sticky tape. When you open your raffia cloak to reveal the secret eyes, your friends will be agog!

To fasten the cardboard eyes to plastic straws, use sticky tape. To get them to stick on your head, bend the bottom of the straws and push them under a headband. If they wobble about, fix them to the headband with more sticky tape.

Clowning Around

Introduction

So you want to throw things around and catch them again? Create animals out of thin air and rubber? Generally clown around and have fun? Well, you have come to the right place because this is all about juggling and crazy balloon modelling. But be warned – juggling fever is catching and balloon modelling can make your day go with a bang!

Juggling fun

Once you have learned the basics of juggling there is no turning back. You will start with balloon balls and bean bags, then you will want to juggle fruit, plates, cups, sneakers and small pieces of furniture. Before you know it you will be doing Under or Over juggling with the family pet, the Statue of Liberty and an elephant. Nothing is safe – everything can be juggled. Some of the juggling moves are really easy and you will catch on (ha! ha!) in a flash. Other juggling routines will take practice, patience and a bit more practice. If you do not have juggling balls, do not worry – there are instructions for making your own balloon balls and bean bags. But if you just cannot wait to get juggling, you can practise with scarves, fruit (ask permission first) or even socks partially filled with uncooked rice. (Cooked rice is impossible to juggle with!) Do not try juggling priceless pieces of crockery or expensive electronic equipment – just yet!

This is how all new jugglers look – cross-eyed and confused!

Balloon modelling bug

Twist, twist, bend, bend, stretch, twist and pop! No, this is not a new dance, nor a new breakfast cereal. This is the sound of someone with the balloon modelling bug. The good thing about this bug is that it is fun to pass it on! Without so much as a huff or a puff, you will be able to create a world of hairless dogs, featherless birds and flowers that survive without water. You will even be able to build a light-filled, airy house with nothing more than 17 balloons and a balloon pump.

To start, you will make models for yourself, then you will perform feats of balloon magic at parties, fêtes and carnivals. But once the bug has really taken hold you will be balloon modelling while waiting for the bus, during school and under your duvet at night! It is not that you have gone mad, you have simply become a balloonatic!

This is the look of someone who has caught juggling fever and is having a great time!

This is a balloonatic. Her balloon modelling skills have gone totally to her head!

Materials

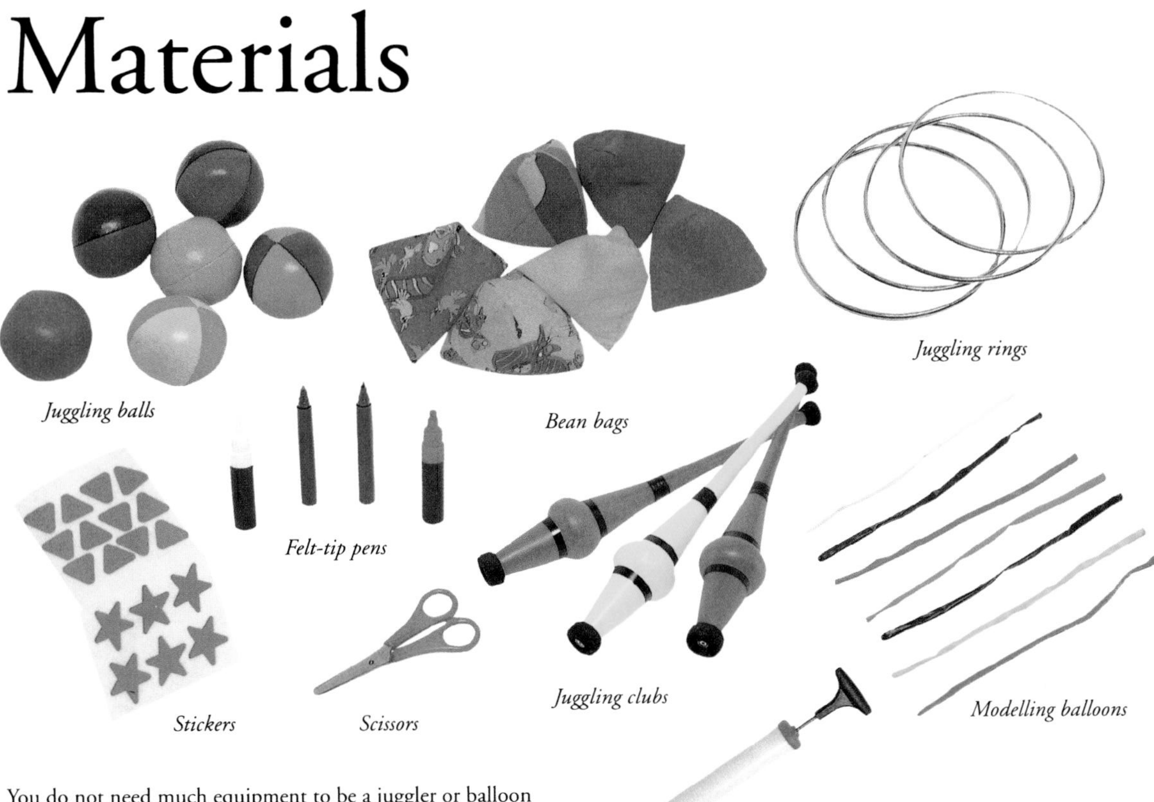

Juggling balls

Bean bags

Juggling rings

Felt-tip pens

Stickers

Scissors

Juggling clubs

Modelling balloons

Balloon pump

You do not need much equipment to be a juggler or balloon modeller. Your greatest assets are your sparkling personality and infectious smile.

Balloon pump There are many types of balloon pumps available, but you must make sure that you get one with a tapered nozzle on the end. These are specially made to inflate modelling balloons. The most effective type of pump is a double-action pump. This pump inflates the balloon when you push the pump in and when you pull it out.
Bean bags These are made from cotton fabric and shaped like pyramids. They are often filled with dried pulses. You can buy them in joke shops and theatrical supply shops, or you can make your own. You will need three or more bean bags.
Felt-tip pens To decorate and draw faces on to your balloon modelling creations you will need indelible felt-tip pens. Indelible means that your drawings will not rub off the smooth surface of the balloon.
Juggling balls These are soft, plastic-covered balls that come in lots of bright colours and patterns. You can buy inexpensive sets of juggling balls in toy shops and joke shops, or make your own using round, party balloons and uncooked rice.
Juggling clubs These can be bought in sets or separately, and they come in various sizes. They are quite expensive. In place of clubs, try your juggling moves with plastic skittles. You can even decorate the skittles to look just like the real thing.
Juggling rings When you become very confident at juggling, you could buy a set of juggling rings. They are made of metal and come in various sizes.
Modelling balloons These are long, thin balloons that come in a variety of colours. You can buy them in bags of 100 in toy and joke shops, and also in specialist theatrical suppliers. All the balloons used in these projects are the '260' type. Modelling balloons can lose some of their quality over time, and are best kept in a cool, dark place.
Scissors You will need a pair of scissors to cut balloons to make balloon balls, to make bean bags and to do one of the tricks.
Stickers You can use stickers to decorate balloon models and juggling equipment. Buy sheets of plain coloured or fancy stickers from toy shops and stationery shops.

Basic Techniques

Inflating modelling balloons and tying knots

Modelling balloons are easier to inflate and less likely to burst if they are warm. You can warm them by stretching them a few times and by keeping them out of the refrigerator. Do not leave balloons in sunlight – this will speed up the process of disintegration.

Bang! Some balloons are (pop! burst!) weaker than others. On average, about one in every 25 to 30 balloons bursts during inflating, so do not (bang!) worry – it is not your fault. Immediately discard the burst balloon and any small pieces that have fallen on the floor by putting them in the dustbin or out of reach of young children and pets.

The only trick to tying a knot in a modelling balloon is patience. If you take it slowly and keep a tight grip on the balloon, the balloon will be tied in knots, not you!

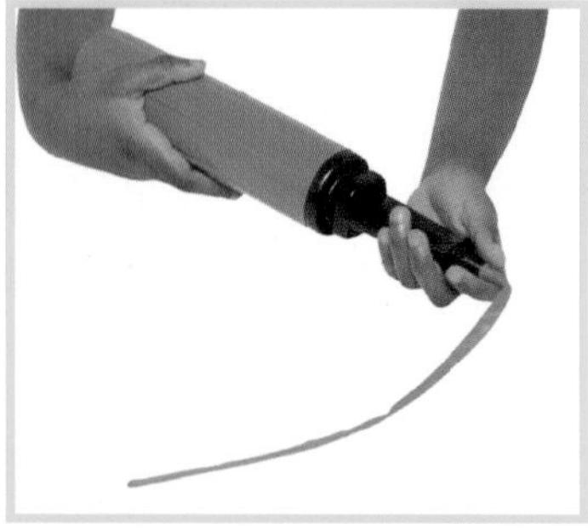

1 **Inflating the balloon** – carefully insert the nozzle of the pump into the mouth of the balloon for about 2cm (3/4in). Hold the balloon in place. If you let go of the balloon while it is being inflated, you can easily imagine what happens.

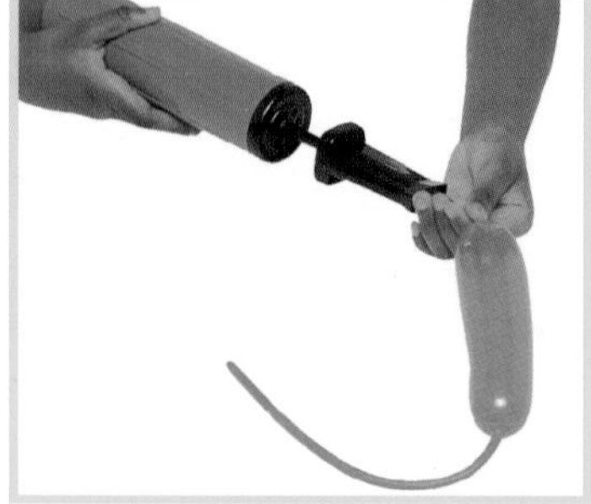

2 Start inflating your balloon, but always leave an uninflated bit at the end. This is important as each time you twist the inflated balloon air will be forced down the balloon. The more twists used to create a model, the longer the uninflated end should be.

3 **Tying a knot** – this is often the cause of much frustration, but really it is not difficult. Hold the end of the mouth of the balloon tightly to keep it sealed. Then stretch the neck of the balloon around two fingers, as shown. Do not pull too tightly – it hurts. Ouch!

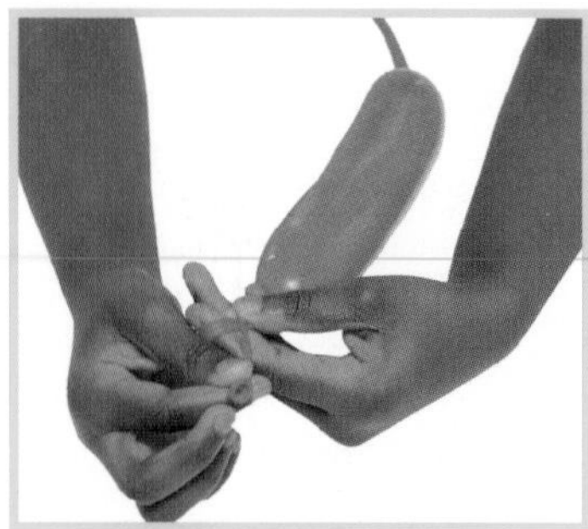

4 Pull on the end of the balloon until it crosses the neck of the balloon and the two fingers. Hold with the thumb.

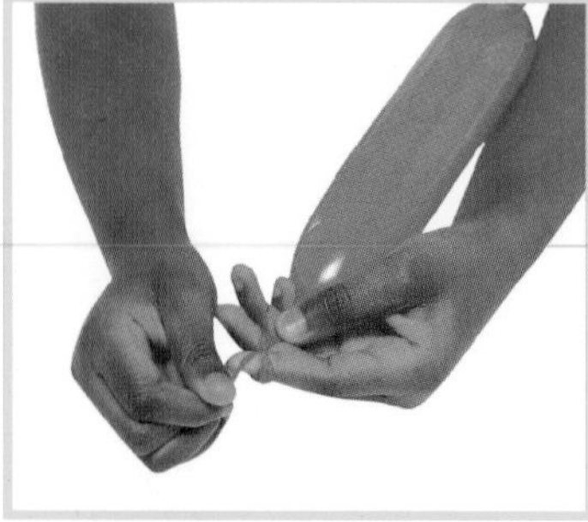

5 Tuck the end of the balloon down between the two fingers and through the circle – in other words, tie a knot!

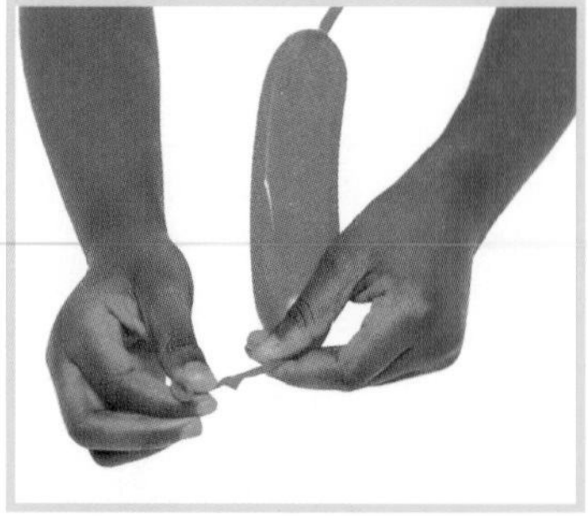

6 Keeping hold of the end, slip your fingers out of the knot and pull it tight. Phew!

Decorating your balloon models

You can make your balloon models more colourful, realistic or comical by drawing on them or decorating them.

The simplest and quickest way to decorate balloons is to use indelible felt-tip pens. As well as using a variety of bright colours, get hold of a white pen if possible. White is really effective when drawing eyes, as it makes them stand out.

Eyes, a nose and mouth are probably the first things you will want to give your animal balloon models. Why not also draw on paws, feathers or fur, or just wild and wonderful patterns? You could give Pampered Pooch, for example, a fancy collar and name tag. If you are making a model for a friend, you could write their name or a message on it. A balloon model elephant that says 'Happy Birthday' on one side would make a very unusual birthday card.

You can also use small stickers to decorate your models. Stickers come in lots of different shapes, textures and colours. There are even sticker packs of eyes, noses, ears and other facial features. Once your sticker is in position, you will not be able to remove it without bursting the balloon.

To apply paint to a balloon model, you first have to mix PVA glue into the paint before you apply it. The PVA glue will make the paint stick to the balloon. Apply the paint gently and use a soft brush.

Juggling safety tips

❖ Do not attempt to juggle with sharp or pointed utensils or heavy objects. Sharp things will cut you, and heavy objects will give you nasty bump on your head or will land slap, bang, ouch on your little toe!

❖ Make sure you have lots of room around you and above you when juggling. Ask an adult to move furniture out of the way so that you do not trip over. Breakable items should be moved to another country for safe keeping!

Just as well this girl was only juggling balloon balls!

Balloon modelling safety tips

Although we set out to have fun with balloons, they can be dangerous, so please follow these few simple precautions. Make sure your friends are also aware of these rules.

❖ Always keep uninflated or burst balloons away from young children and animals to prevent choking accidents.

❖ Never put a whole balloon or a piece of a balloon in your mouth.

❖ Keep balloons away from your eyes, especially when stretching or inflating them.

❖ Always use a balloon pump. Modelling balloons are very difficult to inflate and cause damage to the lungs or ears if you try to inflate them without a pump.

❖ Do not play with balloons in the kitchen – a balloon may land on a hotplate or ignited gas ring – or near open fires or radiators.

❖ Dispose of burst balloons immediately by putting them in a waste bin.

How to Make Balloon Balls

Balloon balls are easy and fun to make. They are also very colourful. To start your juggling career you will need three balloon balls.

1 Cut the stems off two balloons so that you are left with the round part of each balloon. Fill a plastic bag with $1^1/_2$ cups of rice. Seal in the rice by folding the bag around itself.

2 Insert the bag containing the rice into one of the cut balloons. This is a bit fiddly as you have to be careful not to split the bag or the balloon. Do not worry if part of the plastic bag is still visible.

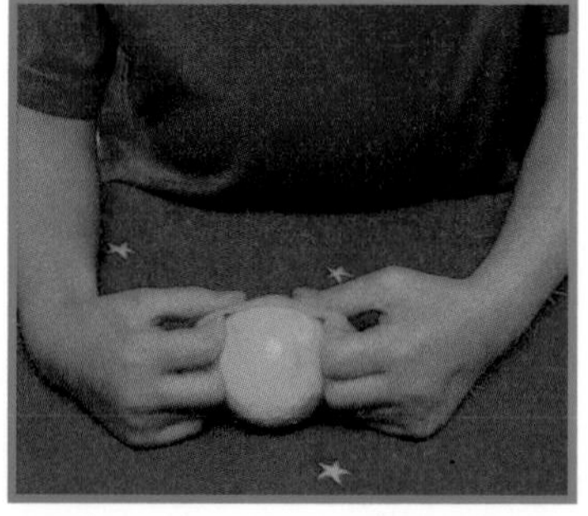

3 Insert the balloon and bag of rice into the second balloon. Make sure the second balloon covers any visible bits of the plastic bag. It does not matter if a part of the first balloon is still visible.

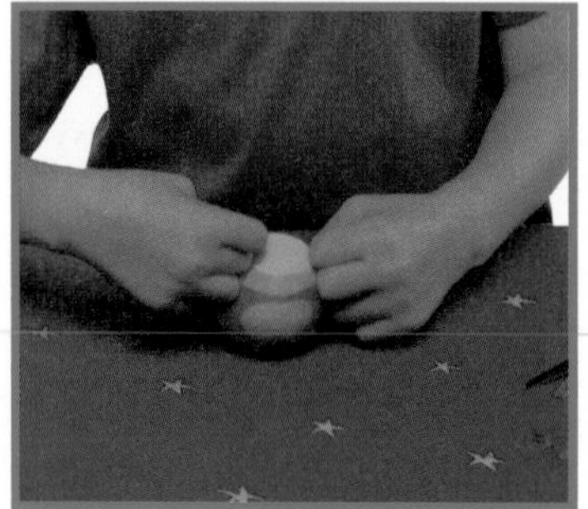

4 Cut the stem off another balloon and cut a few small holes into the round part of the balloon. Stretch this balloon over the balloon ball. Repeat using another cut balloon.

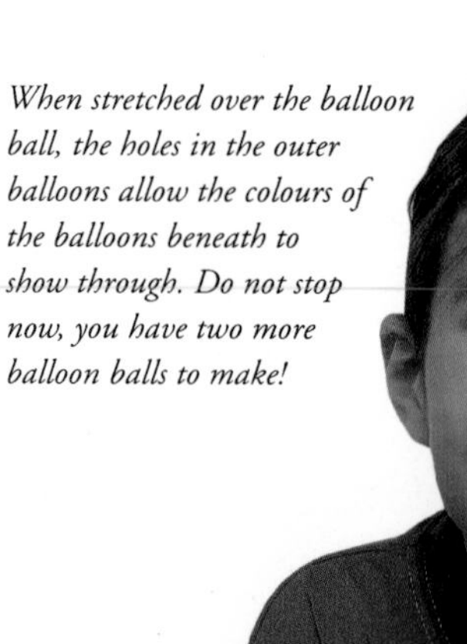

When stretched over the balloon ball, the holes in the outer balloons allow the colours of the balloons beneath to show through. Do not stop now, you have two more balloon balls to make!

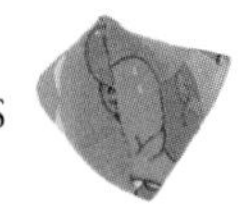

How to Make Bean Bags

Get out your sewing thread and needle, it is time to make a juggler's favourite piece of equipment – bean bags!

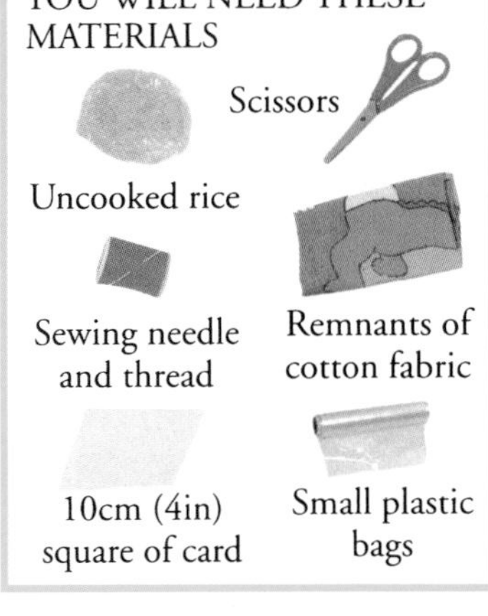

1 Using the square piece of card as a template, cut out two squares of fabric. To make three bean bags you will need six squares of fabric.

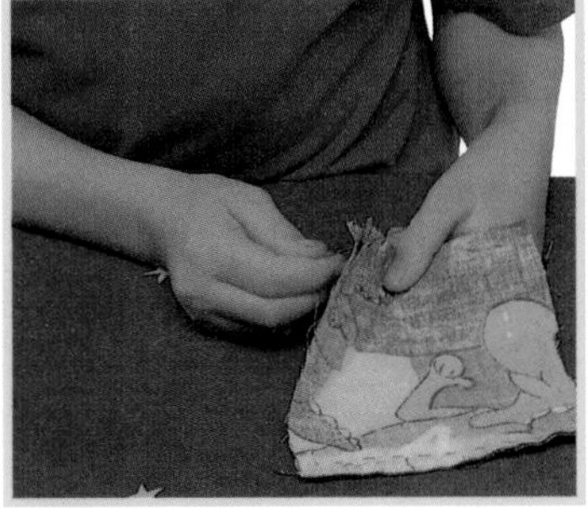

2 Place two squares of fabric right sides facing. Thread the sewing needle and tie a knot at the end of the thread. Sew the squares together along three sides. Turn the fabric bag the right way out.

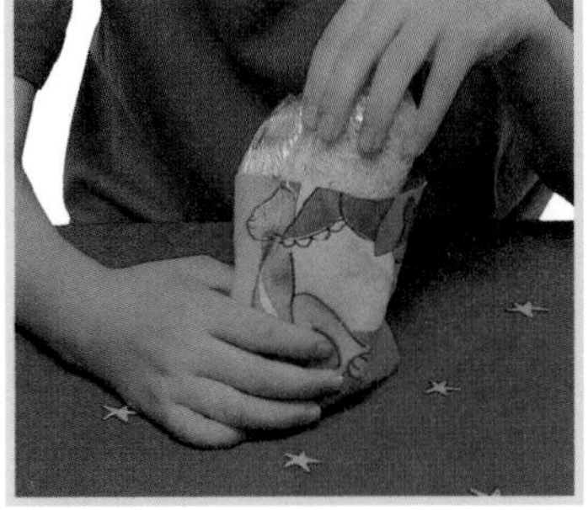

3 Fill the plastic bag with 1 to 2 cups of rice. Seal the plastic bag by wrapping the bag around itself. Place the plastic bag containing the rice inside the fabric bag.

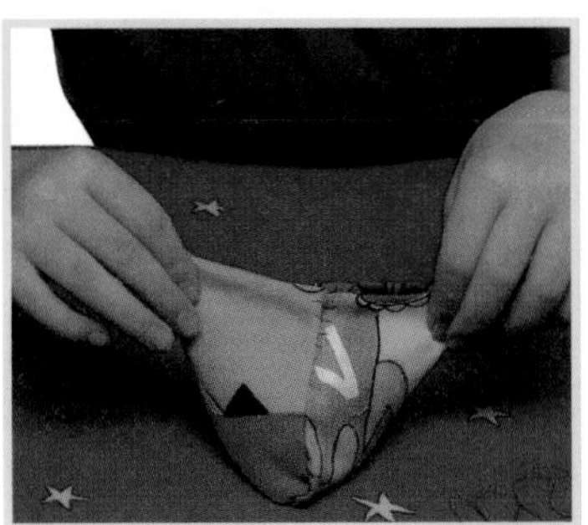

4 Fold over the fabric to make a hem around the opening of the fabric bag. Hold the opening so that the two stitched seams touch, as shown, and sew the edges together to make a pyramid.

You have now made your first bean bag – only two more to go. Try to use differently patterned or coloured fabric for each one. It will make it easier to follow the movement of each bean bag when you start practising.

One-ball Workout

Just like an athlete who has to do warm-up exercises before he or she can take to the track, a juggler also goes through a warm-up workout. These moves will help you to become familiar with the weight and shape of the ball, how it moves through the air and how to anticipate where it will fall. Sounds difficult? Not once you have learned the knack. Do this workout every time before a juggling practice session.

YOU WILL NEED

1 juggling ball, balloon ball or bean bag

Handy hint

This workout can be done using all sorts of objects – sneakers, tennis balls, oranges or even elephants (only small ones, of course!). A good juggler can juggle anything, so now is the time to get in some funny juggling practice.

1 **Clap in time exercise** – this first exercise is really easy. Hold a ball (or small elephant) in your right hand. See, I told you this was easy.

2 Throw the ball in an arc just a little way above your head. While the ball is in the air, clap your hands. Keep your eye on the ball.

3 Catch the ball in your left hand. Now throw the ball from the left hand to the right hand and clap while the ball is in the air.

4 **Under the leg throw** – hold the ball in the right hand and put it under your raised right knee. Throw the ball up, clap and then catch the ball in your left hand. Repeat with the left hand.

5 **Behind the back throw** – hold the ball behind your back in your right hand.Throw the ball up and over your left shoulder. Catch the ball in your left hand. Repeat with the left hand.

6 **Dizzy spin throw** – this exercise tests your balance. Throw the ball up with your right hand. While it is in the air, spin around once. Then catch the ball in your left hand.

7 Repeat the Dizzy Spin Throw, throwing the ball from your left hand to right hand. Spin in the opposite direction. Are you feeling dizzy yet?

The hard workout

Repeat each One-ball Workout exercise five times with each hand. When you can do each exercise without dropping the ball, it is time to move on to the hard workout!

To do the hard workout, repeat the exercises above, but this time throw the ball a little higher and instead of clapping or spinning once, clap three times or spin around twice.

When you can do the hard workout without dropping the ball, do them with your eyes closed. Just joking !

Two-ball Juggle

Do not panic – two-ball juggling is not as hard as it looks. The secret is to keep your eyes on the balls at all times. Forget about your hands, they are always on the end of your arms. The second part of this exercise is called Juggler's Nightmare. Throwing the balls is easy. The hard part is keeping your hands crossed. Experienced jugglers even find this trick difficult.

YOU WILL NEED

Two juggling balls, balloon balls or bean bags

Handy hint

You can make all these exercises harder by clapping or spinning around while the balls are in the air. If you can do Juggler's Nightmare and spin at the same time, it is time you got a job in the circus!

This boy is smiling now, but just you wait till he tries Juggler's Nightmare. When you can do Juggler's Nightmare successfully, challenge your friends to try.

1 Hold a ball in each hand. Throw both balls straight up in the air. Do not throw them too high – just above your head is fine. Catch the balls. Repeat this exercise five times.

2 Stage two of the Two-ball Juggle is to throw the balls so they cross in mid-air and are caught by the opposite hand. Throw one ball a little higher than the other, so they do not collide.

3 For stage three, hold a ball in each hand and throw the balls straight up as in step 1. While the balls are in mid-air, cross over your hands and catch the balls.Try not to go cross-eyed!

4 If you can do this next exercise, you will be juggling three balls within ten minutes. Hold a ball in each hand and relax – this will not hurt a bit!

5 Throw the right-hand ball in an arc above your head in the direction of the left hand. Just as it starts to fall get ready to throw the left-hand ball.

6 Throw the left-hand ball in an arc toward your right hand. Catch the right-hand ball in your left hand, and the left-hand ball in your right hand.

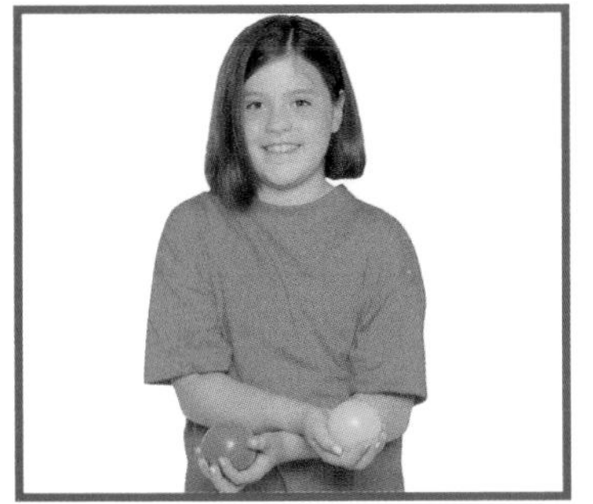

7 **Juggler's Nightmare** – this move is a nasty twist on the one in step 3. Hold a ball in each hand and cross over your arms, as shown.

8 Throw both balls up at the same time so that they cross over and land in the opposite hand. The trick is you have to keep your hands crossed!

9 Catch both balls. Are your hands still crossed? If so, well done. If not, try again. It can take some time to get the hang of Juggler's Nightmare.

Three-ball Frenzy

You had to do it sometime, so grab three juggling balls or bean bags and get ready to perform your first real juggle. You can practise this using scarves if you like. Scarves move more slowly and are easier to catch.

YOU WILL NEED

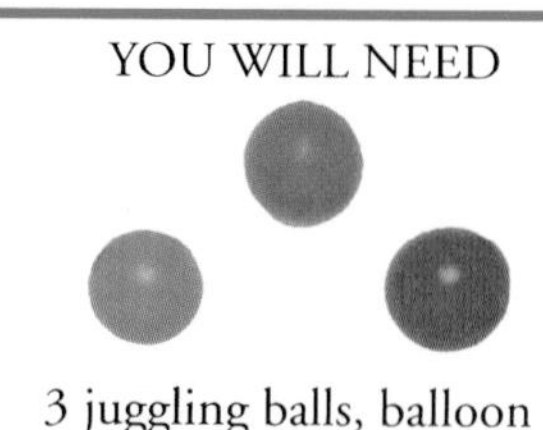

3 juggling balls, balloon balls or bean bags

Handy hint

Remember to throw the balls straight up, not forwards. If you throw them forwards you will soon be walking all over your audience. You will have enough to do juggling and catching three balls without taking a leisurely stroll at the same time!

This boy has just found out something really important. If he counts 'one, one, one, one' when juggling, it helps him to slow down. Counting 'one, two, three, four' makes you speed up and you know what happens then – all the balls end up on the floor!

1 Hold two balls in your right hand. (If you are left-handed, you may want to hold them in your left hand.) Hold one ball in the other hand.

2 Throw the yellow ball in an arc over your head. Keep your eye on the ball and be ready to throw the turquoise ball when the yellow one starts to fall.

3 At this stage the turquoise ball is in mid-air and you have caught the yellow ball. Throw the red ball when the turquoise ball starts to fall.

4 Catch the turquoise ball but keep your eyes on the red ball that is hurtling over your head. Do not look at your hands when they are catching.

5 You can start to breathe again now for you are about to catch the red ball. Well done – you have successfully completed your first three-ball juggle.

6 **Flashy start** –When you are confident doing steps 1 to 5, try this crowd-pleaser. Hold three balls as in step 1.

7 At the same time throw one ball from each hand straight up. As the balls start to fall, throw the remaining ball in an arc over your head. Keep your eyes on the balls, not your hands.

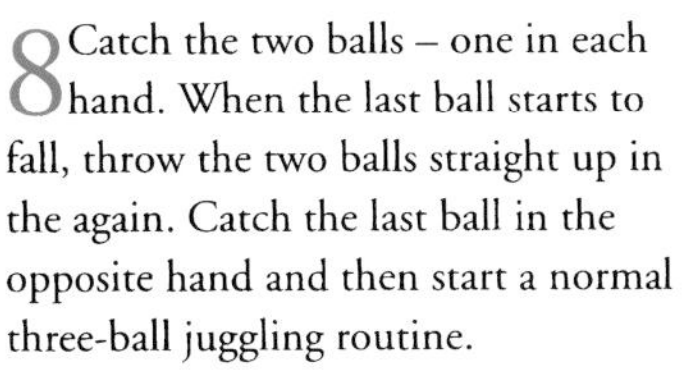

8 Catch the two balls – one in each hand. When the last ball starts to fall, throw the two balls straight up in the again. Catch the last ball in the opposite hand and then start a normal three-ball juggling routine.

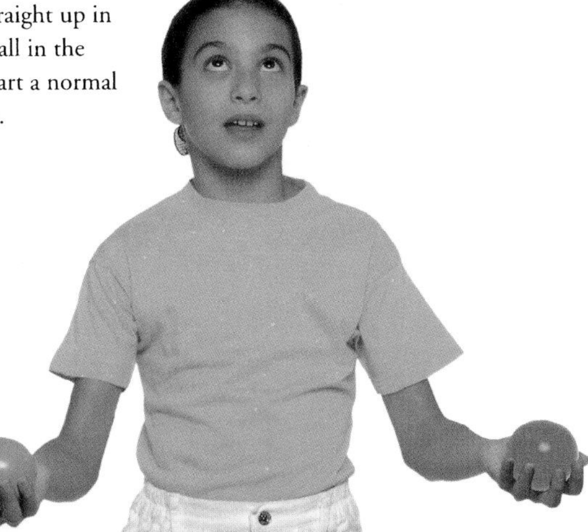

Crazy Juggling

This is a juggling trick for those who really like to perform. You will have to deliver your lines convincingly and look totally embarrassed at the result of your silly trick.

YOU WILL NEED

6 bean bags

1 Tell your audience that you are going to do an impression of the world's worst juggler. Hold three bean bags in each hand. Then wriggle your body and move your hands about as though you are readying yourself to juggle. Keep looking upward.

2 The dramatic movement has arrived – throw all six bean bags in the air. Run about waving your arms in the air trying to catch the bags as they fall. Do not catch any bean bags.

3 As soon as the bean bags land – thud, thud, thud – on the floor, make a desperate face and pretend to be upset. You are, after all, the world's worst juggler!

Monkey Juggling

No, you are not going to juggle monkeys, only bananas. This trick is as easy as falling out of a tree, but to make it funny you have to get in some silly monkey business.

YOU WILL NEED

3 bananas or bean bags

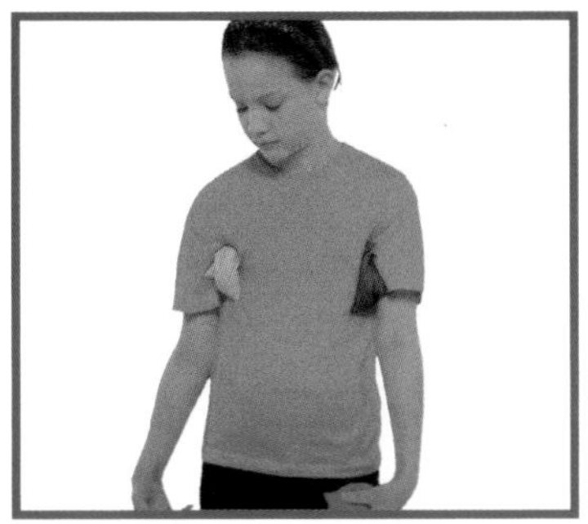

1 Place a beanbag or banana under each arm and hold one in your left hand. Cup your right hand. Release the bean bag tucked under your right arm and catch it smoothly in your right hand while making monkey noises.

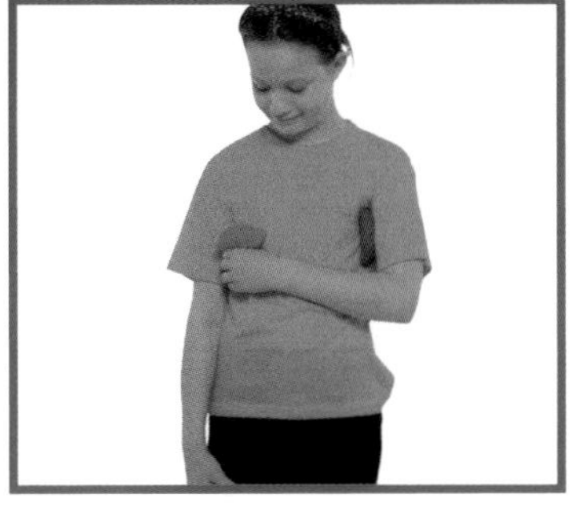

2 While still holding the bean bag in your right hand, tuck the bean bag in your left hand under your right arm. As you bring your left arm down, release the bean bag tucked under your left arm.

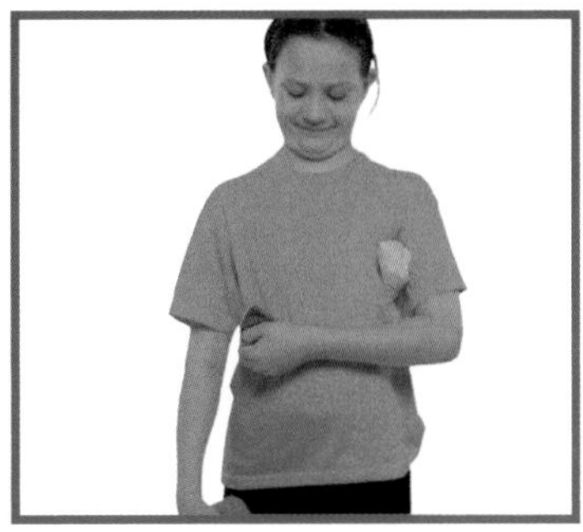

3 Catch the bean bag in your cupped left hand. Tuck the bean bag held in your right hand under your left arm. As you bring your right arm down, release the bean bag tucked under your right arm.

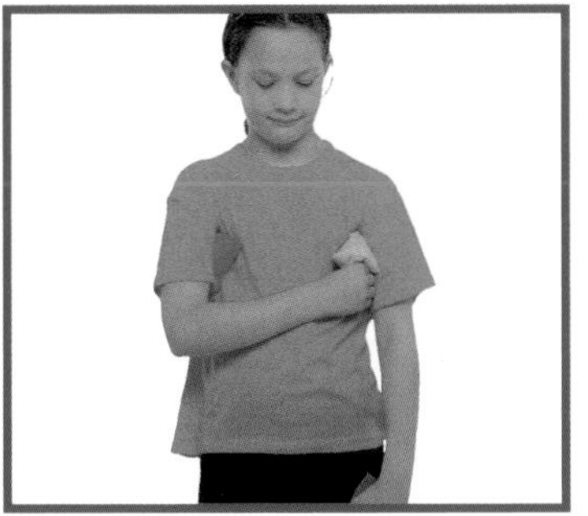

4 Catch the bean bag in your cupped right hand. Now you start the whole routine again. The aim is to practise this so that you become very quick. By the way, did you keep doing the monkey noises or were you just going bananas?

To really get a laugh, start to swing your arms and lope around the stage like a monkey.

Under or Over

This time you are going to juggle three balls under your legs and over your shoulders. Whatever next – juggling under water? The important thing with this trick is to raise your leg, rather than bend down. It certainly makes it easier to balance.

YOU WILL NEED

3 juggling balls, balloon balls or bean bags

Handy hint

If you are left-handed, then hold two balls in your left hand and one in your right. Follow the step-by-step instructions, but use your left hand whenever the right hand is mentioned. Likewise, use your right hand when the left is mentioned in the instructions.

Does this boy have three juggling balls growing out of his ears or is his juggling success just going to his head?

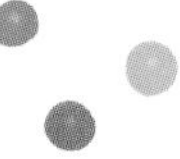

1 **Under the leg juggle** – hold two balls in the right hand and one in the left. Raise your right leg, as shown, and get your balance.

2 Put your right hand under your leg and throw the green ball in an arc toward your left hand. Keep watching the ball.

3 While the green ball is in mid-air, throw the blue ball in your left hand in an arc toward your right hand. Catch the green ball in your left hand.

4 Catch the blue ball in your right hand. Continue juggling normally (see Three-ball Frenzy) except that you will throw the balls from under your leg, not in an arc over your head.

5 **Over the shoulder juggle** – hold two balls in your right hand behind your back. Hold one ball in your left. Look over your shoulder, as shown. Do not stiffen up – try to relax.

6 Throw the yellow ball in your right hand so that it travels upward and then down over your left shoulder. Move your right hand around to the front of your body.

7 When the yellow ball starts to fall, throw the green ball in your left hand in an arc toward your right hand. Catch the yellow ball in your left hand.

8 Catch the green ball in your right hand. Now you can commence to juggle in the normal way, except that you will throw balls over your shoulder.

When you become really good at Under or Over, you can do it with juggling clubs. But mind that you do not hit yourself on the head!

Pampered Pooch

Here we go with your first balloon model. This one should look like a poodle, but do not worry if your first attempt looks more like a bunch of grapes – keep trying!

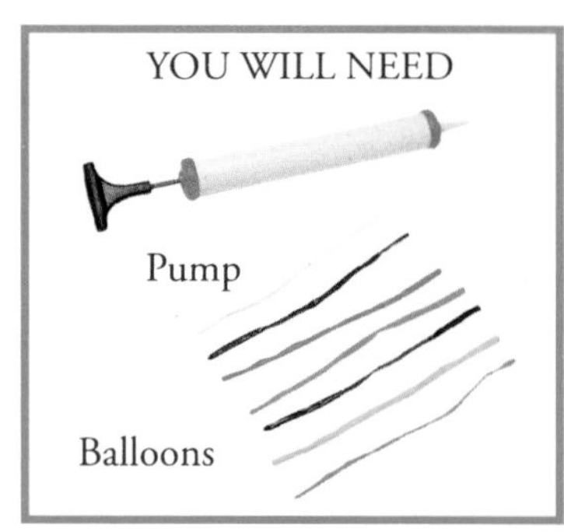

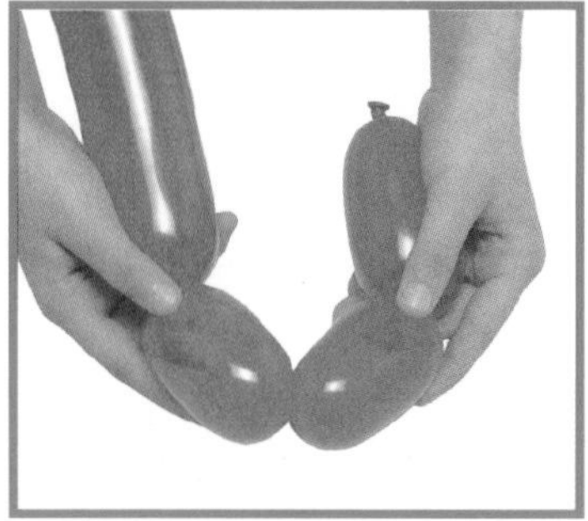

1 Inflate and knot a balloon, leaving 10cm (4in) uninflated at the end. Starting at the knotted end, twist the balloon to make three 8cm (3in) long bubbles. Hold on to the balloon.

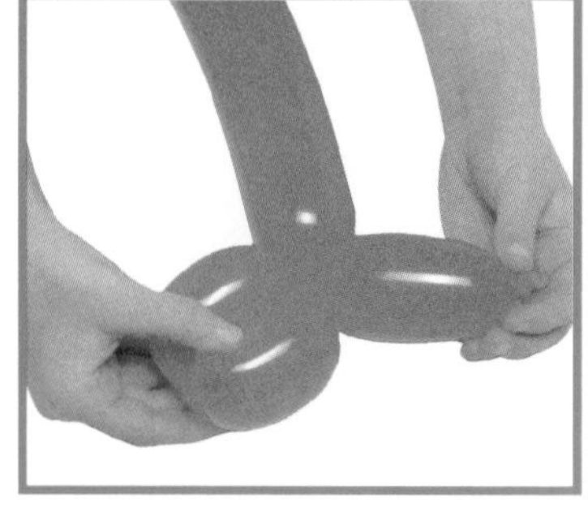

2 To form the ears, twist the second and third bubbles around each other. The bubbles are now locked in place. The first bubble forms Pampered Pooch's head and nose.

3 Make three more bubbles slightly larger than the other bubbles. Twist the second and third bubbles around each other to make the front legs.

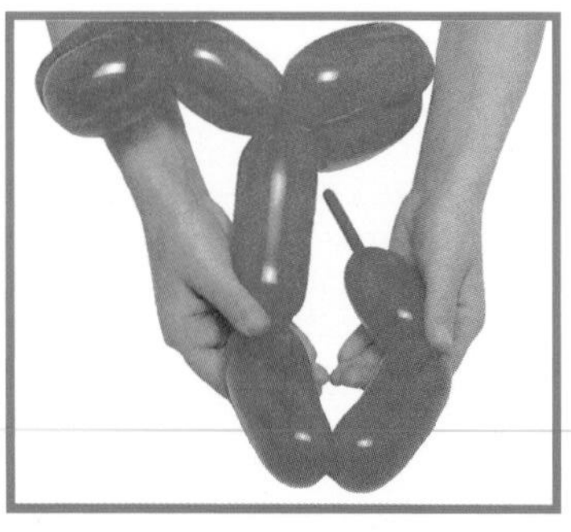

4 Make three bubbles in the other end of the balloon. The first bubble should be 8cm (3in) long, the other two should be slightly larger. Twist together the second and third bubbles to make the hind legs. The bubble nearest the end is pooch's fluffy tail.

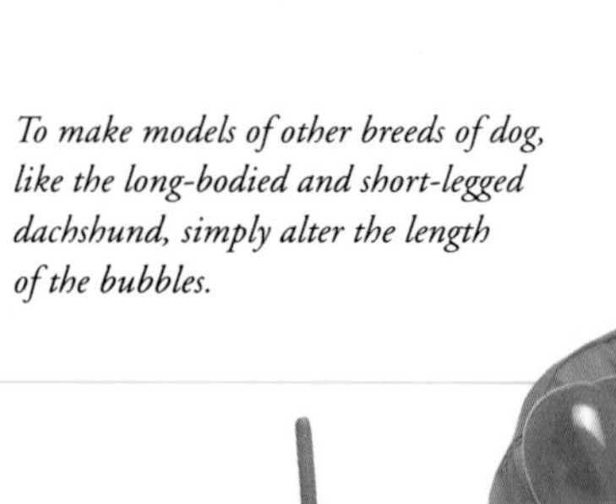

To make models of other breeds of dog, like the long-bodied and short-legged dachshund, simply alter the length of the bubbles.

Parrot on a Perch

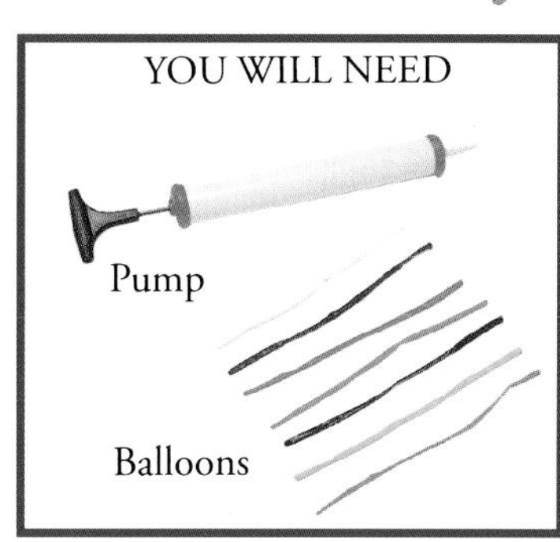

Polly Parrot is a popular bird! When Polly is not on her perch, you can sit her on your head by putting the loop around your chin. No wonder Polly thinks you are crackers!

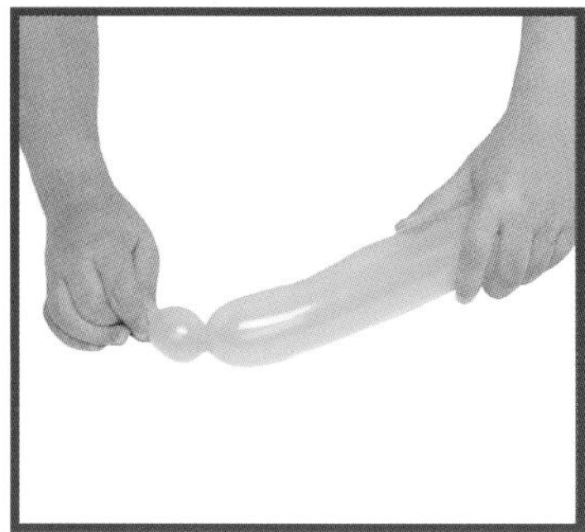

1 Completely inflate a balloon and knot the end. Make a small bubble at the knotted end of the balloon for the parrot's beak.

2 Pull the knot and bubble down beside the rest of the balloon. Twist and lock the knot around the balloon to form another slightly larger bubble. The first bubble is the beak and the second bubble is Polly's head.

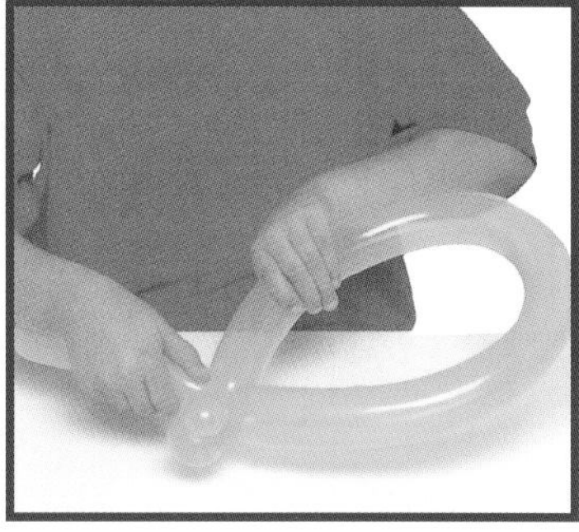

3 You will wonder where the next move is leading, but do not worry, it will soon become obvious. Bend the balloon to form a large loop. Twist the balloon around itself about 18cm (7in) from the end to make the tail.

4 This is the tricky bit, so good luck! Position the tail in the middle of the loop. Pinch and twist the tail and the two sides of the loop together, approximately 8cm (3in) below the head, to make the parrot's body and wings. All you need to do now is arrange Polly on her perch.

This parrot on a perch makes a great decoration. Simply tie one end of a piece of string around the top of the perch and attach the other end to your bedroom wall or ceiling.

Big Elephant

Here is an elephant with a great, long trunk. If you want, you can make the ears bigger and the trunk shorter – it will look just as funny!

YOU WILL NEED

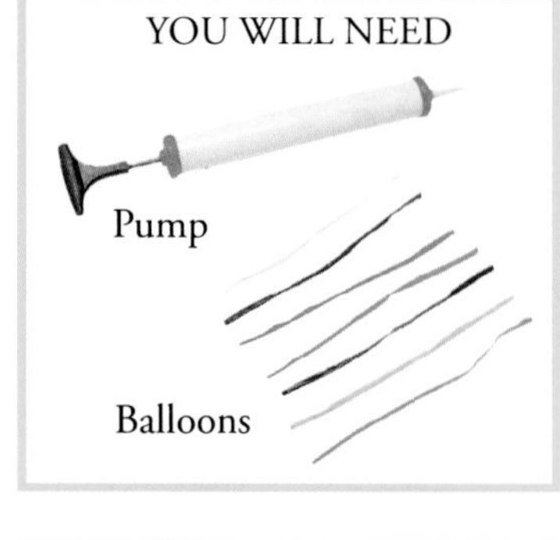

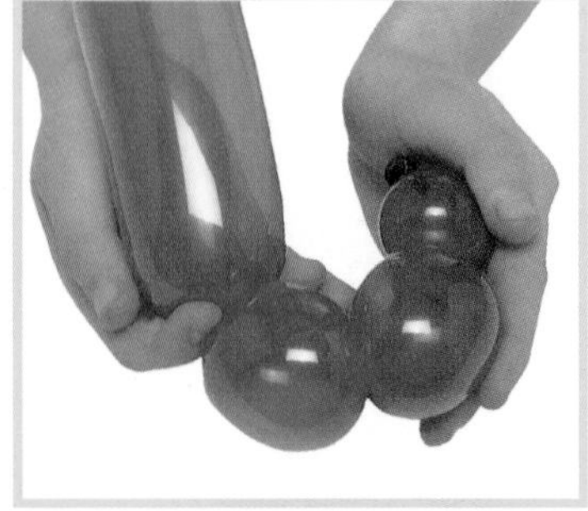

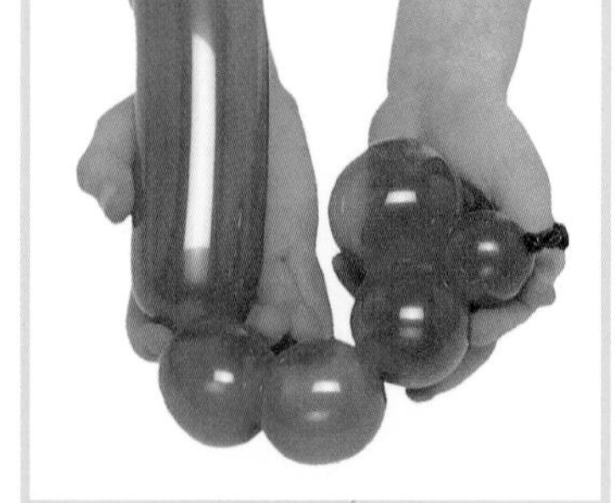

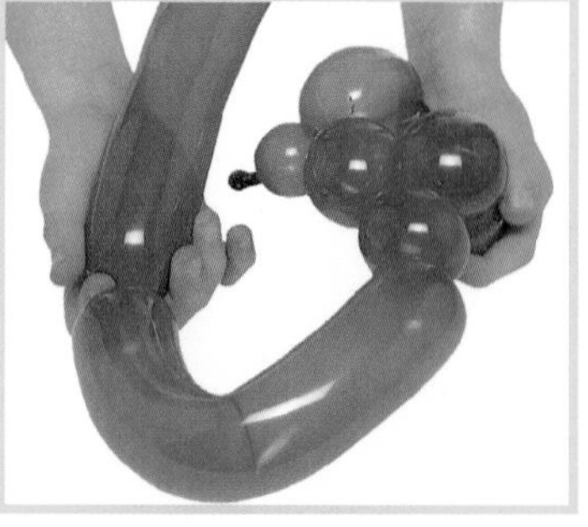

1 To make this balloon model, you start with the tail and work up towards the head. Inflate the balloon, leaving 8cm (3in) uninflated at the end. Knot it. Twist the balloon to make three bubbles, the first 2.5cm (1in) long and the next two 4cm (1½in) long.

2 Twist and lock the two larger bubbles together to form the back legs. The smaller bubble is the elephant's tiny tail. Make three more bubbles, each 4cm (1½in) long, for the body and front legs. Hold on to the bubbles until they are locked into position.

3 Twist and lock the end two bubbles to make the front legs. Make two bubbles – one 2.5cm (1in) long and one 11cm (4½in) long – to make the neck and one ear. Twist the long bubble around the small one.

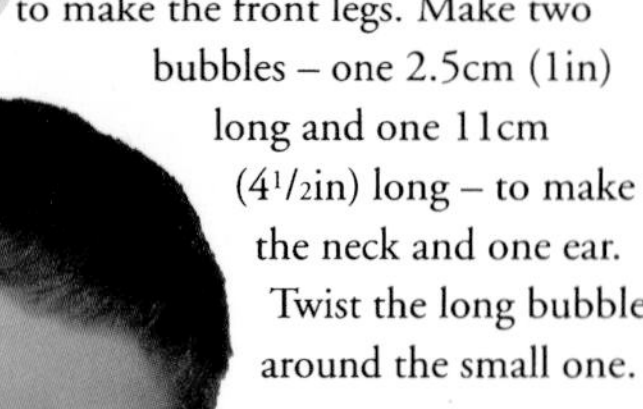

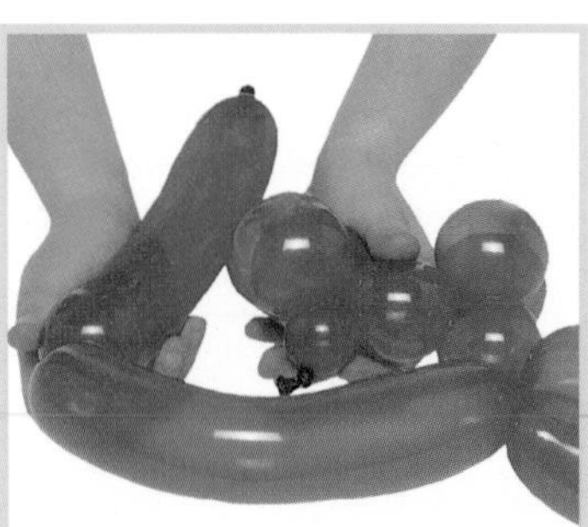

4 Make another 11cm (4½in) bubble. Twist and lock it around the neck bubble. This is the elephant's other ear. Slightly bend the remaining length of balloon to make the enormous, trumpeting trunk.

Tiny Mouse

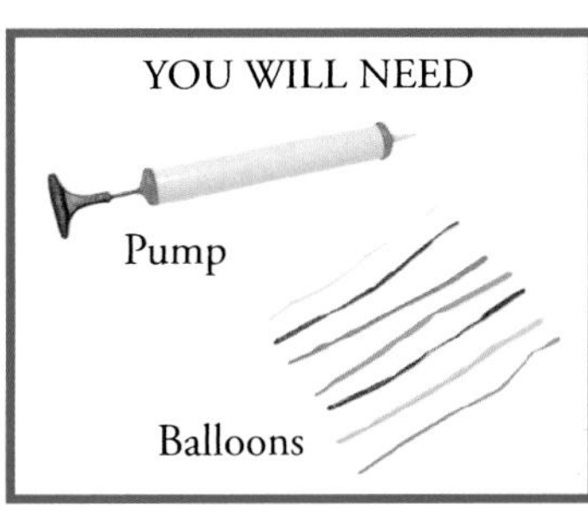

Did you know that elephants are terribly frightened of mice? Funny to think that something so enormous and strong could be scared of something so tiny and cute.

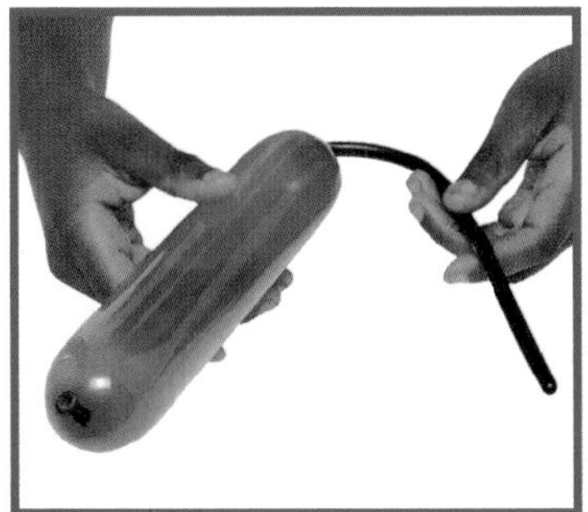

1 To make a tiny mouse, you only need a tiny balloon, so inflate only the first third of the balloon. This will leave the balloon with a long uninflated tail. Tie a knot in the end.

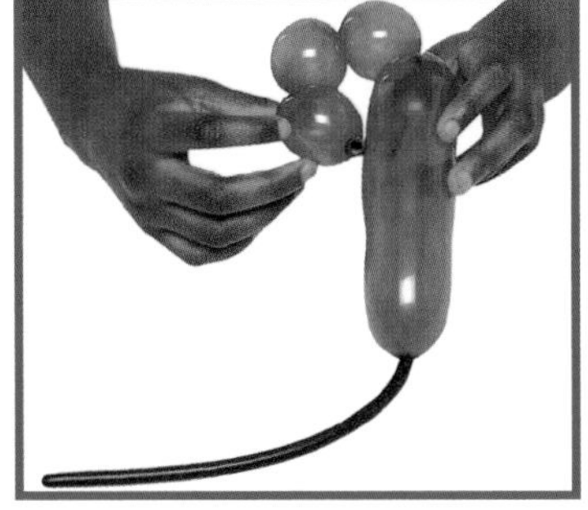

2 To form the head, twist three small bubbles each 4cm (1½in) long. Twist and lock the second and third bubbles together to make the ears. The first bubble forms the head and nose.

3 Twist three small bubbles of the same size to make the neck and front legs. Twist and lock the second and third bubbles as before. See, balloon modelling is easy!

4 Can you guess what comes next? That's right, three more small bubbles! Twist and lock these to form the body and back legs. The rest of the balloon is the mouse's long tail.

Make a family of tiny mice using different coloured balloons.

King of Hearts

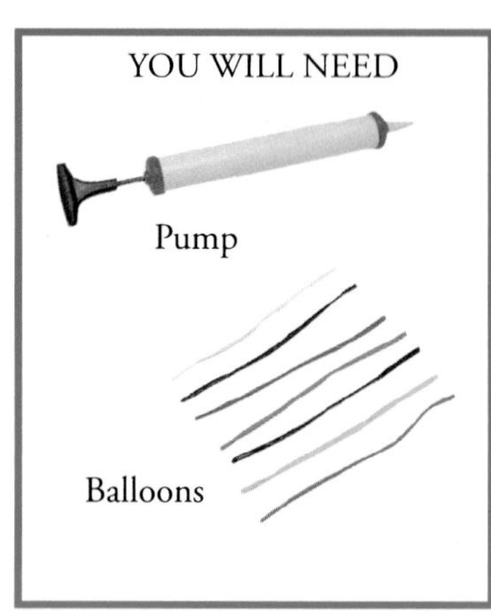

This smart crown will make you look like the King of Hearts. You do not have to add a balloon to the top of your crown, but why not? You could add a heart-shaped or round balloon, or even some bits of ribbon. Go on and make a crown fit for a king – or queen.

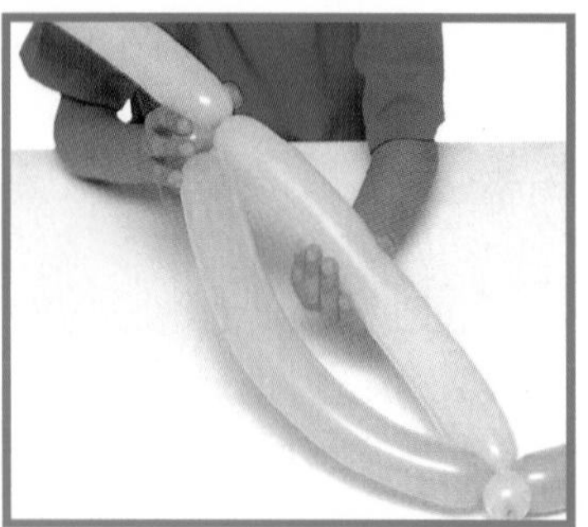

1 Fully inflate two balloons and knot the ends. Twist the balloons together, as shown, to make a headband. The free ends of both balloons should be the same length.

2 Find the mid-point of the free end of each balloon. Twist the two balloons together at the mid-points.

3 Make a small bubble in the end of one free end. Twist it around the headband, halfway along one side.

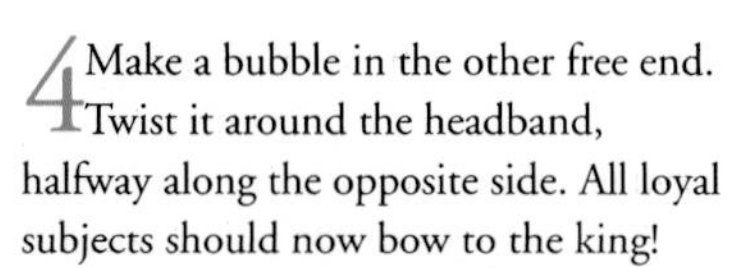

4 Make a bubble in the other free end. Twist it around the headband, halfway along the opposite side. All loyal subjects should now bow to the king!

Why not have a balloon hat-making contest to see which of your friends can create the wackiest hat?

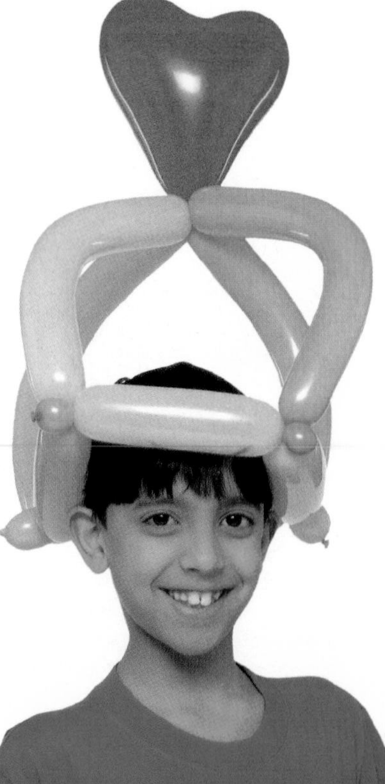

Dashing Sword

This Dashing Sword looks great, but it is not much chop at cutting anything. At least you and your friends will not hurt each other during mock battles! Make a scabbard by joining two balloons together and wearing them around your waist.

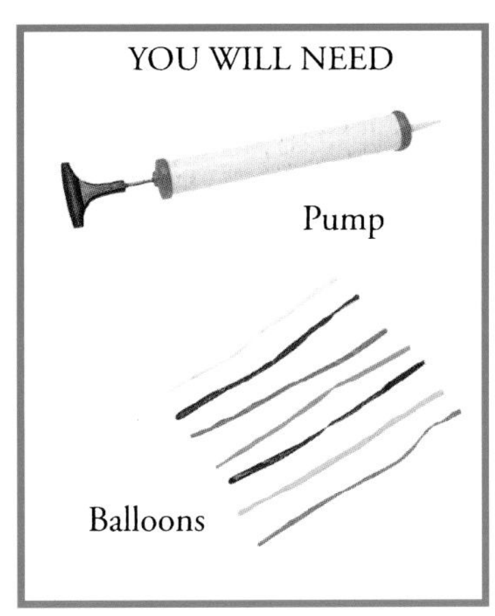

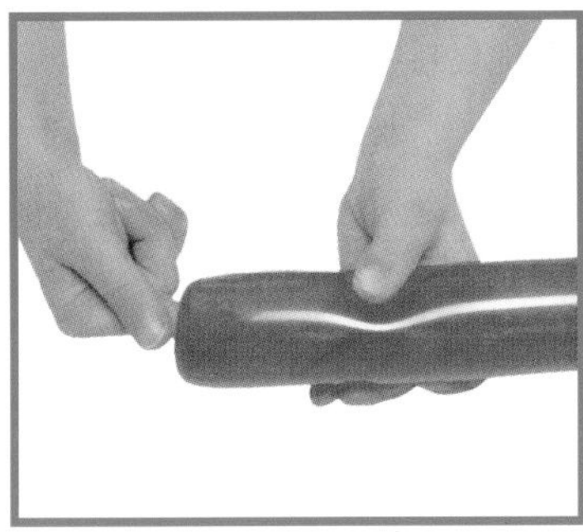

1 Inflate a balloon, leaving 5cm (2in) uninflated at the end. Knot the end. Push the knot inside the balloon about 4cm ($1^1/_2$in) and hold it in position. Use your other hand to squeeze the balloon around the knot. Twist the balloon to hold the knot in place.

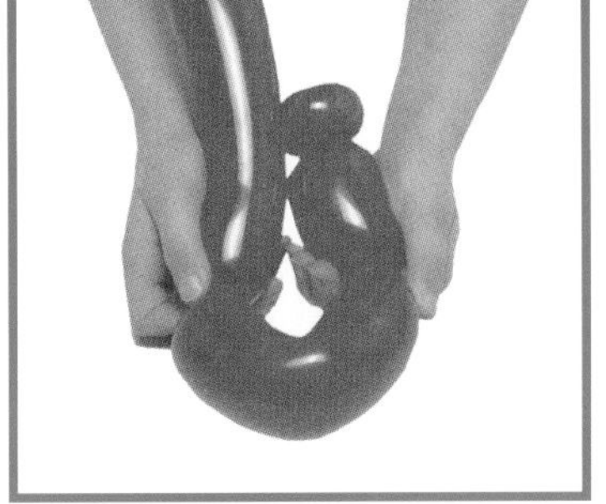

2 Twist the balloon to make two bubbles. The first bubble will form the handle. The second, longer bubble will form one third of the shield that protects the hand. Bend the longer bubble, then twist and lock it around the first bubble.

3 Twist the balloon to make another third of the protective hand shield. Twist and lock it around the handle, as before. If you make the hand shield bubbles too long, your Dashing Sword will be really short!

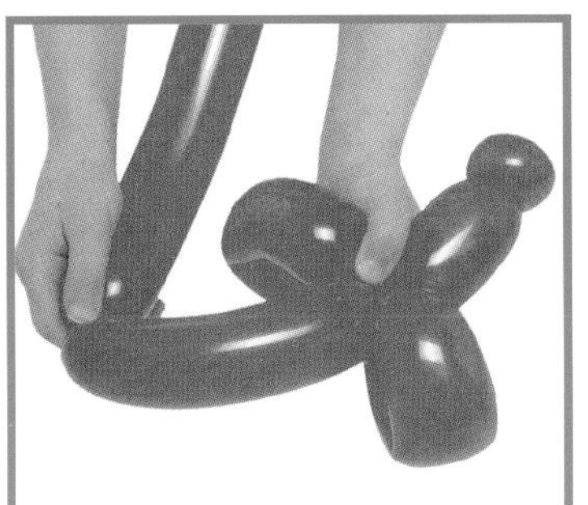

4 Make the final part of the hand shield in the same way.

Balloon swords burst very easily, so make your sword fights really gentle or be ready to make lots of swords.

Crazy Balloon Tricks

Impress and amuse your family and friends with these brilliant balloon stunts. You must never tell anyone the secrets of how to do the tricks!

YOU WILL NEED

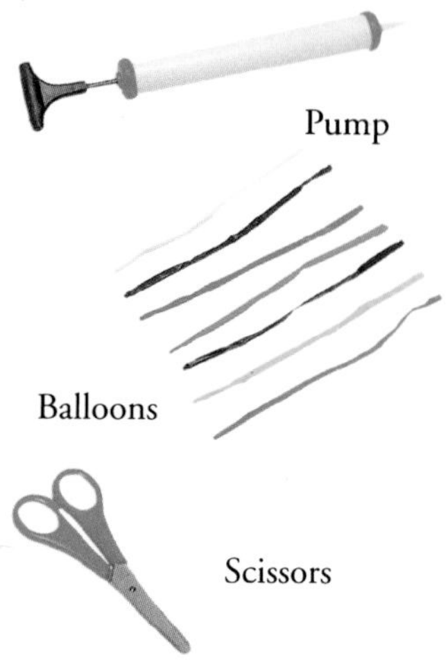

Pump

Balloons

Scissors

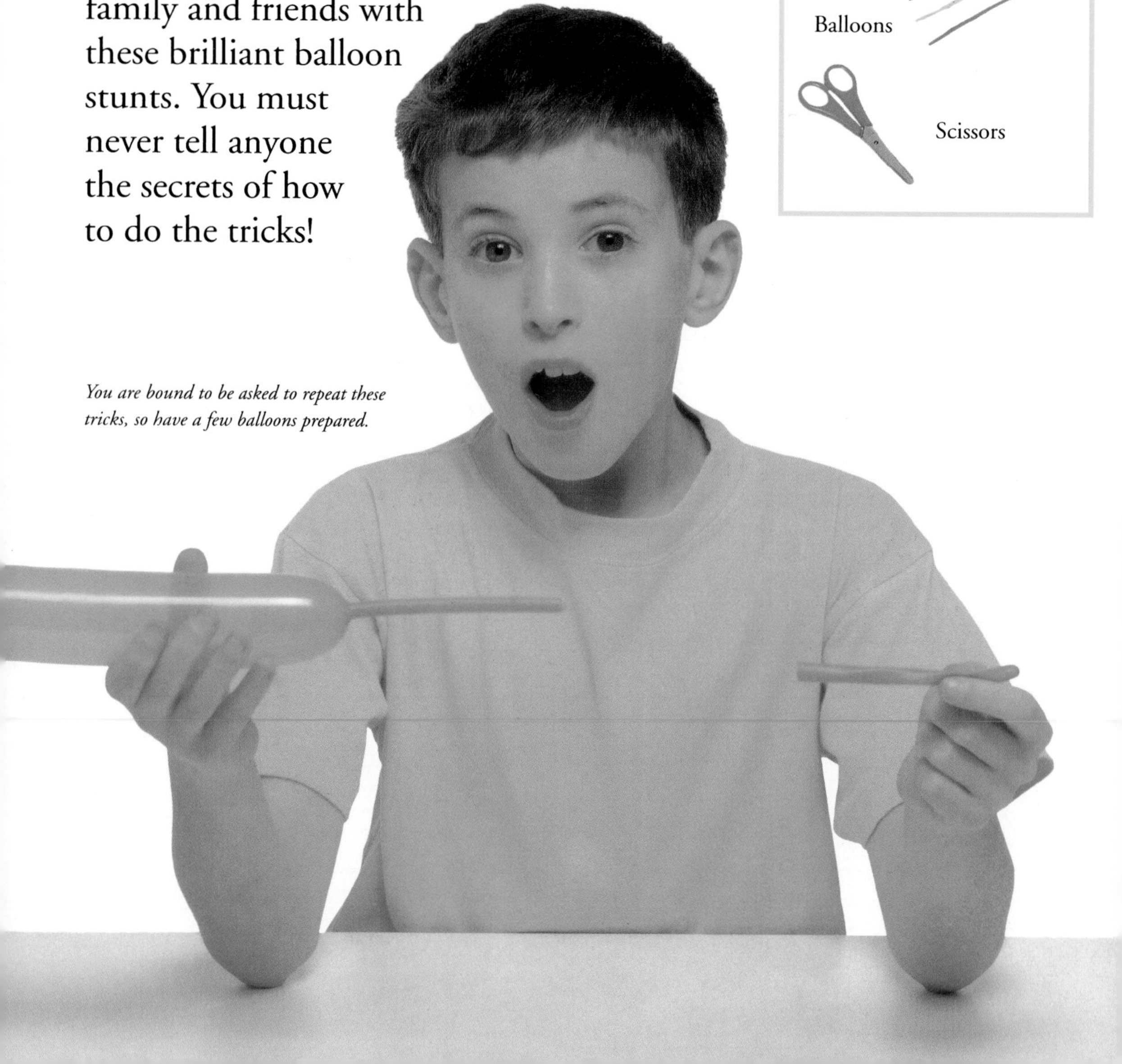

You are bound to be asked to repeat these tricks, so have a few balloons prepared.

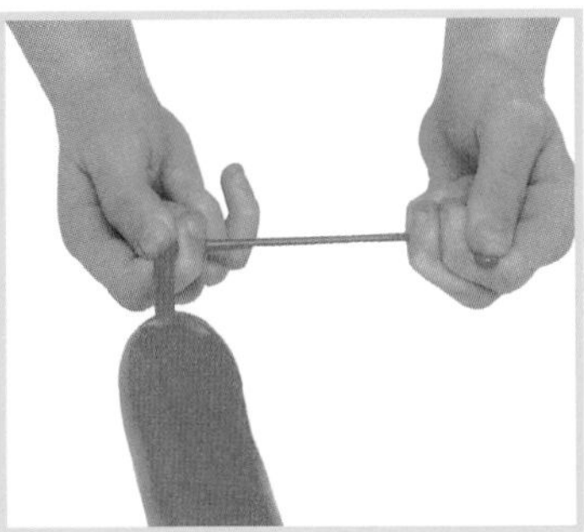

1 **Appearing bubble** – to prepare for this trick, inflate a balloon and leave 18cm (7in) uninflated at the end. Knot the balloon. Grip the uninflated section with both hands, as shown. Now stretch the balloon. Go on, really pull!

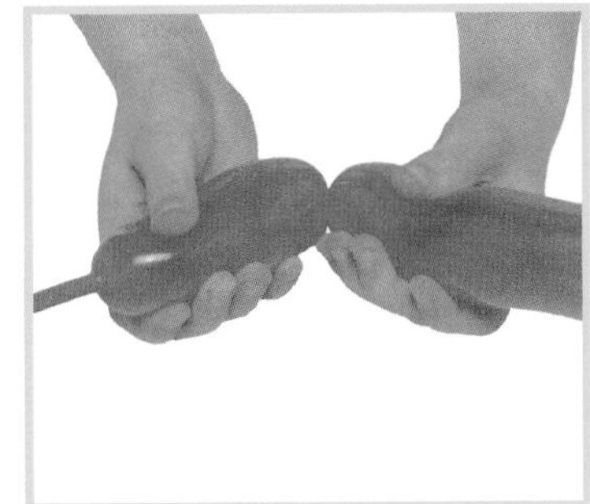

2 To perform the trick, show the audience that it is an ordinary balloon. Twist a bubble 5 to 8cm (2 to 3in) long at the end of the balloon and hold it in your hand. The audience should not see you do this.

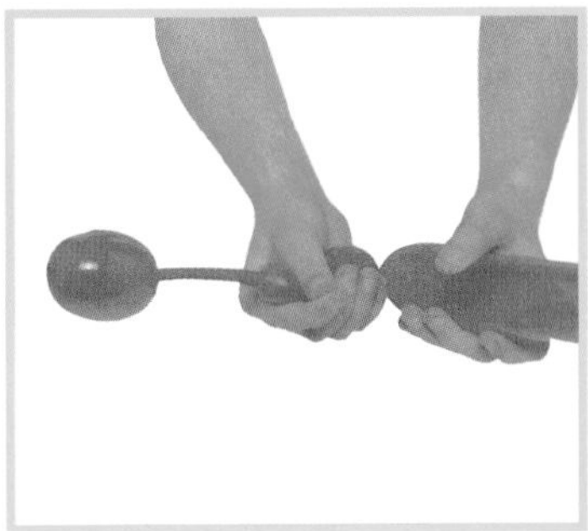

3 Tell the audience that you will make a bubble appear at the end of the balloon. Without the audience seeing, squeeze the bubble really hard. A small bubble should magically appear at the end of the uninflated section.

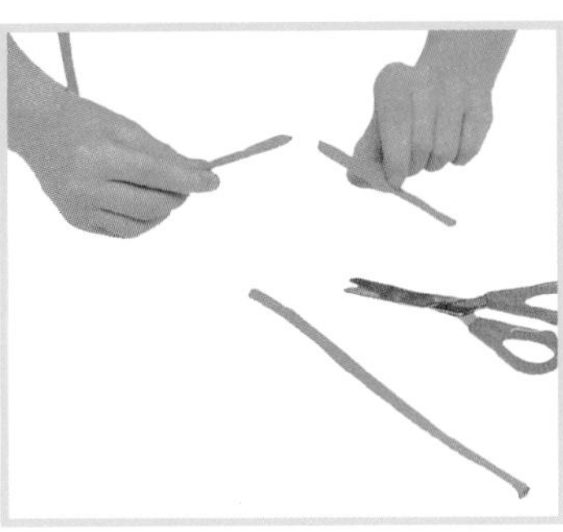

4 **Magic balloon** – to prepare, take two uninflated balloons of the same colour and cut the end off one of them with a pair of scissors. Slip the cut-off end on to the end of the whole balloon.

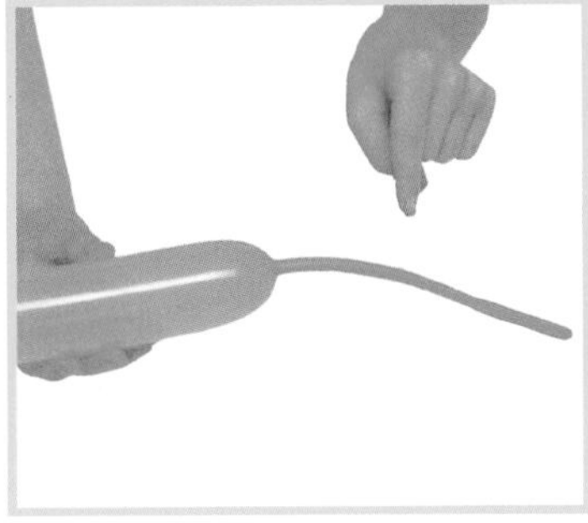

5 Tell your friends you have a magic balloon and offer to show them a trick with it. Inflate the balloon, but leave the end uninflated. There needs to be a space between the real end of the balloon and the false end.

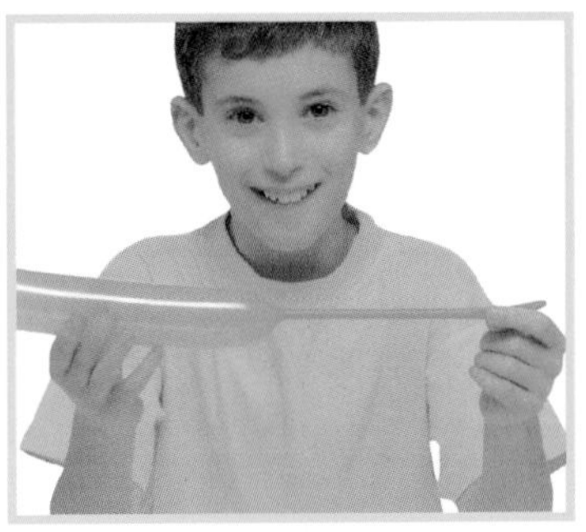

6 Hold the inflated end of the balloon with one hand, and the false end with the other. Say to your friends that the balloon is too long and that you are going to make it shorter. Pull sharply on the false end.

7 Your friends will not understand why the balloon has not deflated.

Practise and prepare

It is important that you practise and prepare these tricks before you perform them in front of an audience. It is also a good idea to work out exactly what you are going to say.

Do not forget that some of the moves in these tricks are not meant to be seen by the audience.

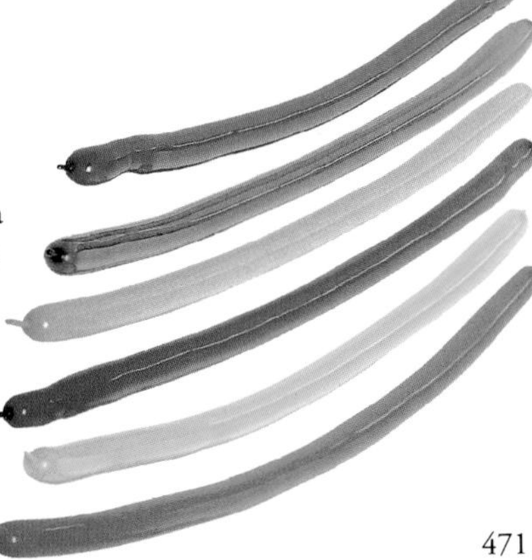

Bunch of Tulips

What a beautiful bunch of tulips! These balloon flowers last longer than real tulips and they do not need watering! You could tie a big, colourful ribbon around the stems to make a lovely present.

YOU WILL NEED

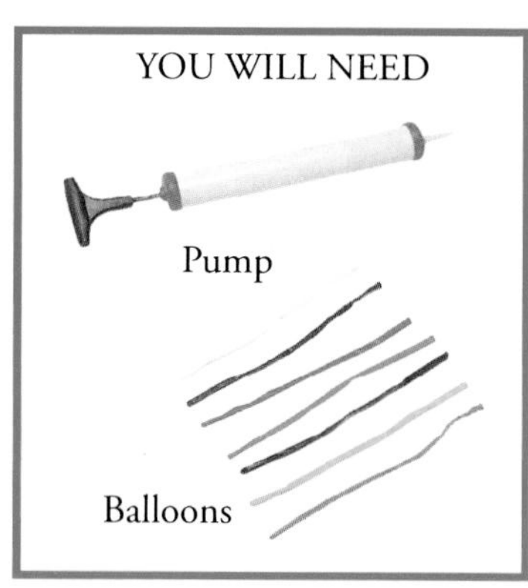

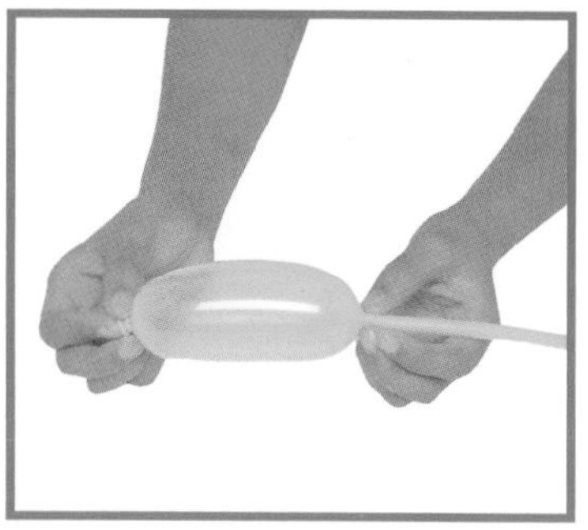

1 Inflate only 8cm (3in) of one balloon, leaving a very long uninflated section. This will be the stem of the tulip. Knot the end. Hold the two ends of the inflated section of the balloon, as shown.

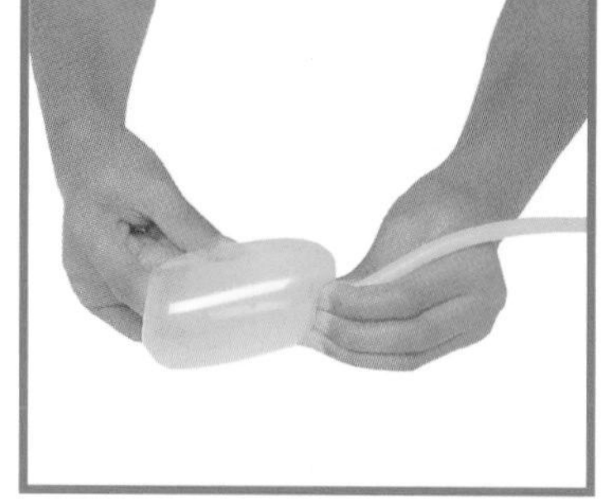

2 Use your finger to push the knot into the balloon until the knot reaches the other end of the inflated section. This will take a little bit of practice, so do not give up after the first attempt.

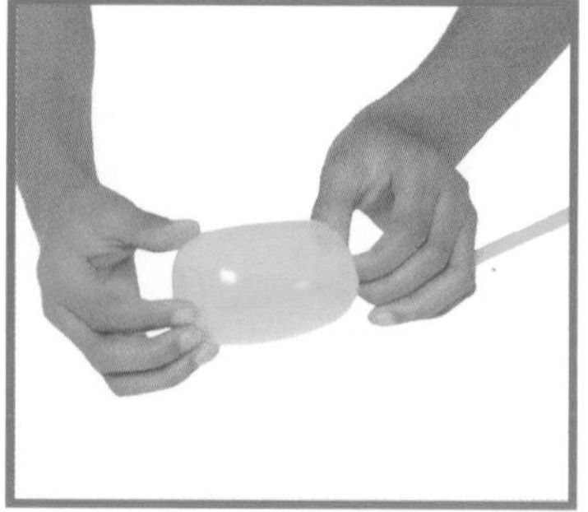

3 Take hold of the knot with the other hand. Remove your finger from inside the balloon. While holding the knot very firmly, twist the balloon several times. This will hold the knot in place.

4 Now that you have made one beautiful tulip, go on to make a whole bunch in different colours.

If you want to be really cunning, you can make the tulips stand up by inserting thin plastic straws inside the balloons before you inflate them.

Sunflowers

Just like real sunflowers, these balloon sunflowers are enormous! But unlike the real ones, they will not turn their colourful heads to face the Sun. Make two or three and use them to decorate your bedroom.

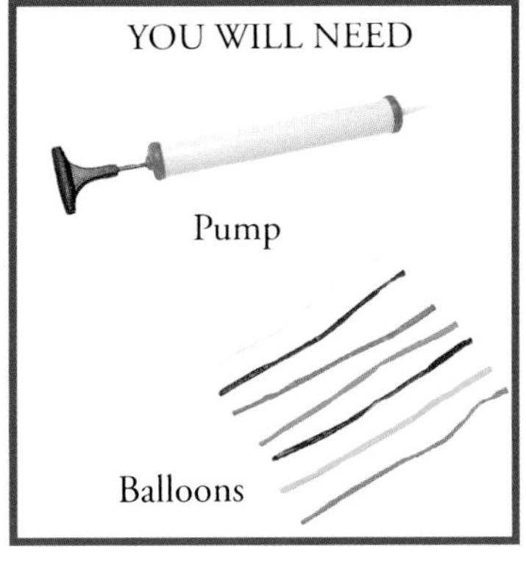

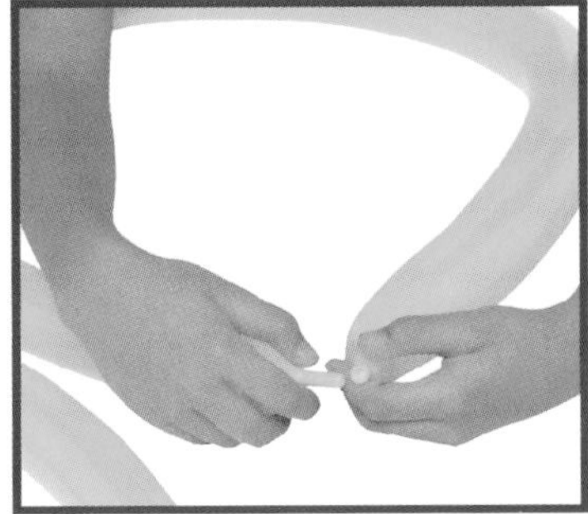

1 Inflate two balloons, leaving only a very short uninflated end in each one. Knot the ends. Tie the knotted end of each balloon to the other end to form two circles.

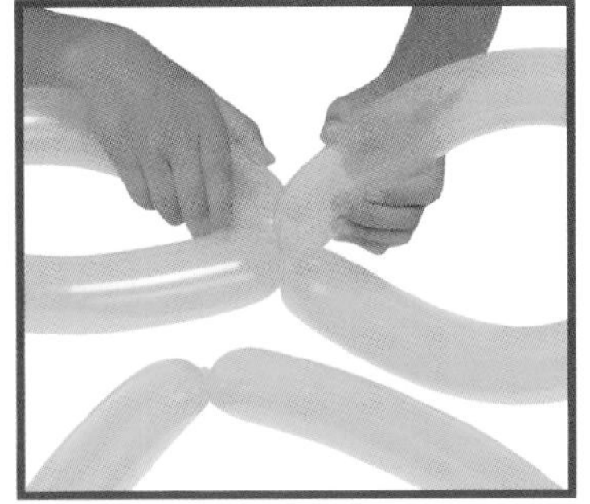

2 Now for a bit of fun and a lot of squeaking. Twist each circle to make a figure 8 shape. Both ends of the figure 8 should be the same size.

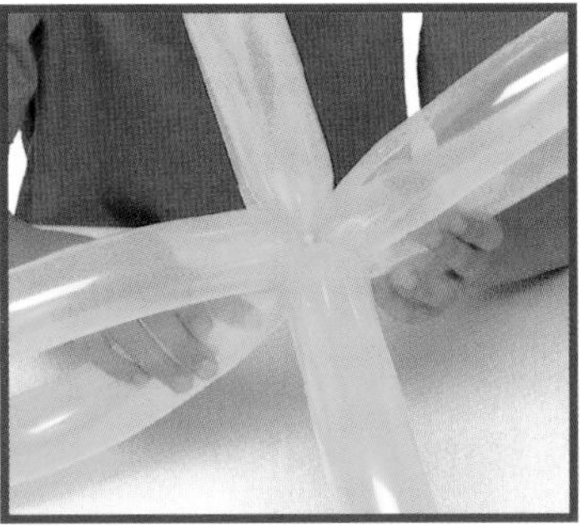

3 Twist the two figures of 8 together to make a cross. These are the gigantic petals of your sunflower. Let us hope there are no gigantic bees or caterpillars about.

4 Inflate another balloon, once again leaving only a small uninflated end. Twist a loop in the centre of the balloon. Twist another loop next to the first one. These are the leaves and stem.

To finish, insert the end of the stem balloon through the centre of the petals. Twist the stem to lock it in place.

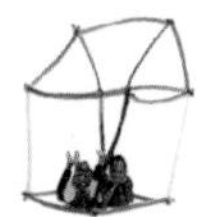

Building a Balloon House

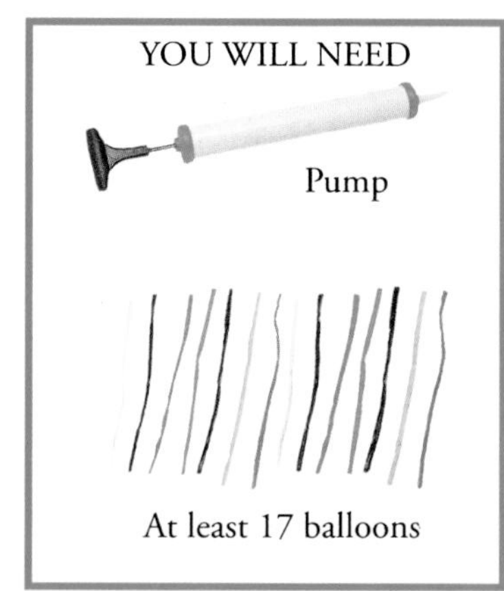

This house is a great favourite and it is really fun to build. Use your imagination to add extra rooms or to make balloon doors, windows, trees, lamp-posts and furniture. Make it as big as you like, but remember that your house will not be very warm in winter and you will get soaked when it rains!

YOU WILL NEED

Pump

At least 17 balloons

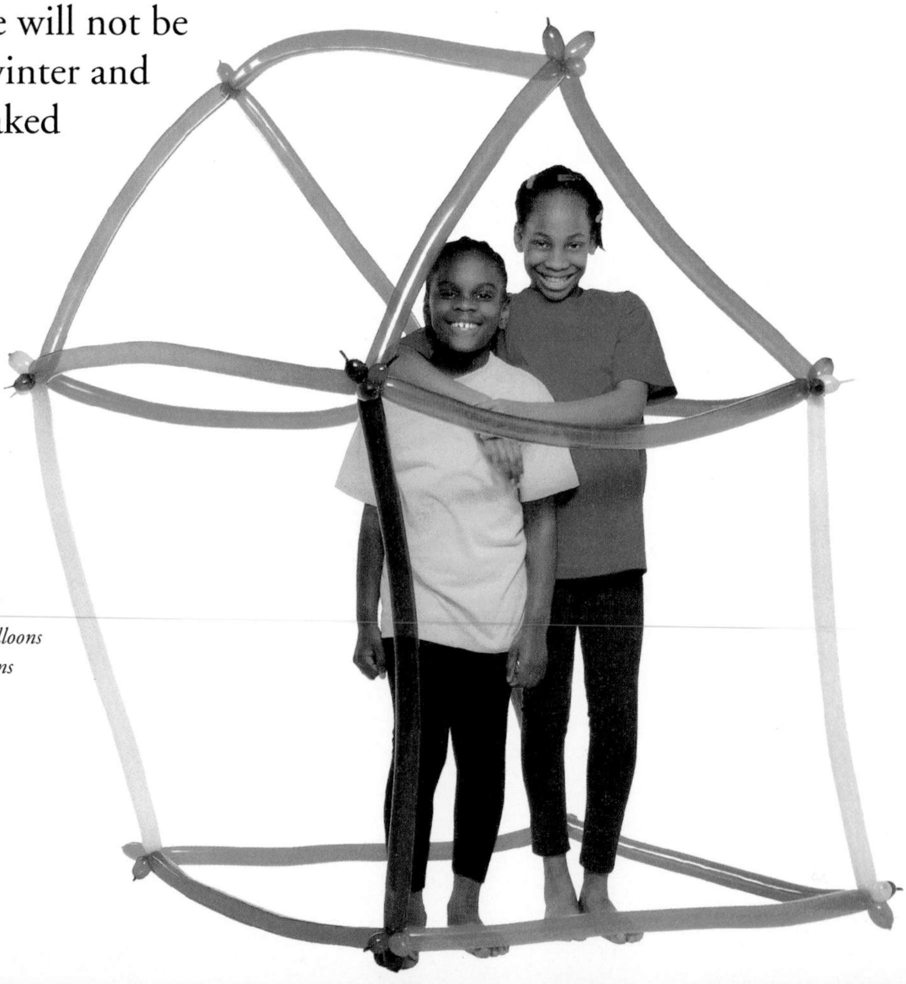

This balloon house is multi-coloured, but you could make your house using red balloons for the walls and black balloons for the roof.

1 Inflate 17 balloons and knot the ends. Seventeen balloons is enough to build this one-room house, but for grander designs you will need more balloons. Twist the ends of four balloons together to make a square. Make another square in the same way.

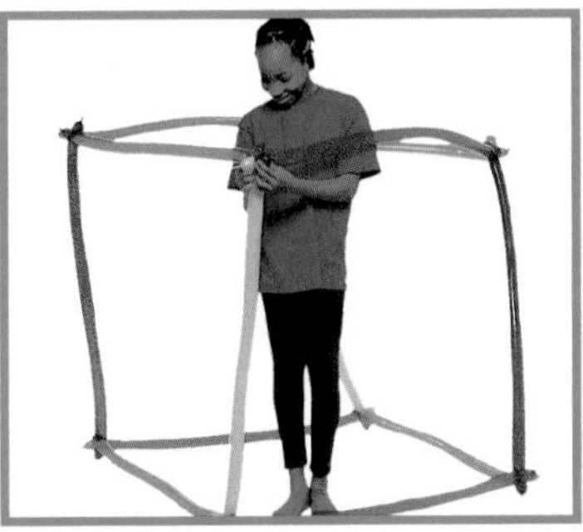

2 Use four more balloons to link the two squares together and make a cube. Twist the ends of the balloons to lock them in position. Is it time for a tea-break yet?

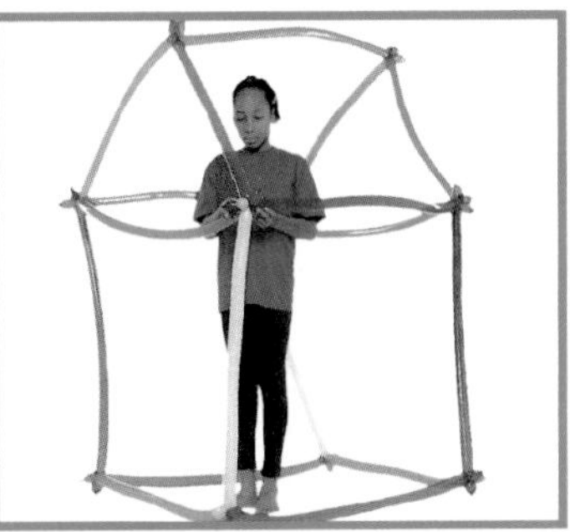

3 Attach a balloon to each top corner of the cube. Twist the end of two balloons together to make a triangle. Do the same with the other two balloons. To finish the roof, link the triangles with a balloon.

4 Well done! You have built a home you can truly call your own. Now is the time to work out ways of adding extra rooms or making your house a little more private.

Once you have built your first house, go on to create other types of houses. This one is called the Wonky Tepee model!

Pop! goes your dream house

Before you start constructing your house make sure that the floor beneath it is smooth and free of splinters or sharp edges. Sadly, your dream house will collapse if the balloons are punctured. It might be a good idea to cover the building site with an old sheet before you start inflating the balloons.

Sneaky, Cheeky Tricks

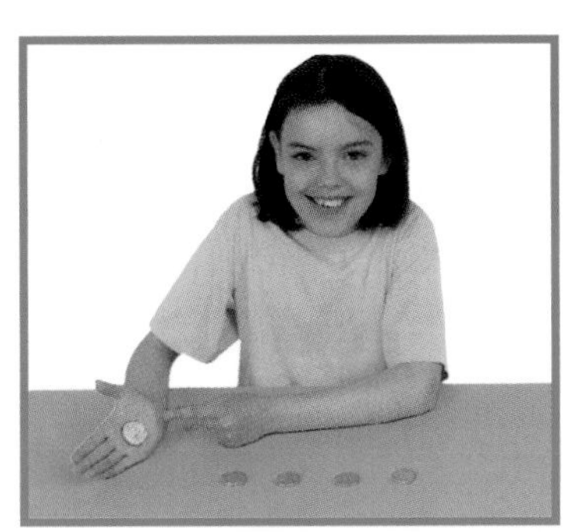

Introduction

To stun and amaze an audience with your cunning tricks, you need to know the three Ps. No, not three garden peas, but the three magic Ps – preparation, presentation and performance. You can forget all about that abracadabra mumbo-jumbo, just remember the three Ps.

Preparation

To avoid getting halfway through a wickedly good trick and realizing that you are missing a vital piece of equipment, you must be prepared. You must have everything you will need at your fingertips. The only way that you can be properly prepared is to make a list of the items that are required for each trick. As you gather them together, tick them off the list. Simple idea, but it works. Have you made your list yet? No, then get to it!

Presentation

This is all about how you dress and act in front of your audience. Presentation is very important if you want your tricks to be a great success. To find out more about presentation read Trickster style.

Performance

You have decided to put on a show. Congratulations! First thing you must do is work out which tricks you will do and the order you will do them in. There are no rules for this, but remember that a short show full of knock-out tricks is better than a long show with only a few good tricks.

This trick is in the bag (or should that be envelope?) because this girl has everything prepared.

The best way to give your show atmosphere is to use music. Try to match the speed and mood of the music to the pace and style of your act. If you are doing lots of quick tricks, use fast music. If your show is spooky and full of shocking surprises, find a piece of really creepy music.

If you do not use music then you will have to write a script and rehearse the words you are going to say. You may want to introduce each trick or tell a little story about where you learned a certain trick. But whatever you say, it is a good idea to have prepared it. It also never hurts to have a couple of good jokes up your sleeve. These can be used to entertain your audience while you get your next trick ready.

Trickster style

Even if you can do some of the hardest tricks in the world, your show might flop if your presentation style is dead boring. To be a big hit with an audience you need to be an entertainer, you have to have style and you have to have pizzazz. Problem is, you cannot buy pizzazz in a supermarket, but you can learn the tricks of great presentation.

Make a big show of displaying empty hands or objects to your audience. It will distract them from seeing what you are really up to!

This boy has trickster style. He is smiling, wearing his favourite hat and looks ready to take a big bow.

A final tip for you is this – let the audience know you have finished a trick by taking a small bow. Save the big bow until the end. As soon as they see you bow, the audience will clap and call out for more.

Entertaining style

This one is easy to explain. If you have a smile on your face and look as though you are enjoying what you are doing, the audience will also enjoy themselves. Try to look confident and relaxed. When you talk to your audience, speak clearly and loudly. No one will hear your great jokes if you mumble and mutter.

Professional style

If the audience ask you to repeat a trick or to tell them how it was done, refuse politely. If you tell all your secrets, you will have to learn a whole new routine, and a trick is never as good second time around.

Dress style

Almost any sort of costume is fine. A colourful waistcoat and a pair of jeans can look smart and professional. If you want to work out your own wacky costume, go ahead. If you feel good, you will look good.

Stage style

To be a show-stopping performer, you must know the secrets of the trade. The first is, always enter from the side or from the back of the stage. Then walk to the middle, smile at your audience and wait for the applause.

The second thing to do is introduce yourself to the audience. You can use your own name or invent a colourful stage-name.

Number three is always to face your audience. This will mean that your props, or equipment, will have to be within easy reach. Your audience have not come to watch you rummage upside-down in a box.

The fourth trade secret is this – if you make a mistake or a trick does not work, try to laugh it off. You can even pretend that the mistake was meant to happen. Then you can do the trick again, but this time do it correctly.

Sometimes it helps to look as surprised as your audience.

Materials

These are some of the main materials and items of equipment you will need.

Carbon copy paper When placed between two sheets of paper, inky side down, it will copy whatever is written on the top sheet of paper.

Coloured and white paper and card For many of the projects, you can recycle pieces of paper and use card from cut-up cereal boxes. Large sheets of card can be bought in stationery shops and craft shops.

Marker pen A marker pen is a type of felt-tip pen that draws quite thick lines. If you do not have a marker pen, use an ordinary felt-tip pen instead.

Paperclips A good collection of paperclips is vital for any promising trickster.

PVA glue This is a strong glue that can be used to stick together paper, wood or even fabric. It can bought in stationery shops and is sometimes called craft glue or white glue. You will need a brush or glue spreader to apply the glue.

Recycled boxes For the projects in this book, you will need two empty boxes – a large one and a small one. A cereal box and a small tea or chocolate box would be ideal.

Rubber bands These are almost as important to the budding trickster as paperclips. You can buy bags of assorted rubber bands in stationery shops.

Ruler Accurate measuring is required for some projects so you will need a ruler divided into centimetres (cm) or inches (in).

Safety scissors Safety scissors are smaller than cutting scissors. Their edges are rounded and the blades are not as sharp as normal scissors.

Sticky-back plastic This plastic material comes in many colours and designs. It is usually bought in rolls. To make it adhere to a surface, you simply peel off the protective backing and press the sticky-back plastic on to the object.

String It does not matter if you use plain or coloured string as long as you have lots of it.

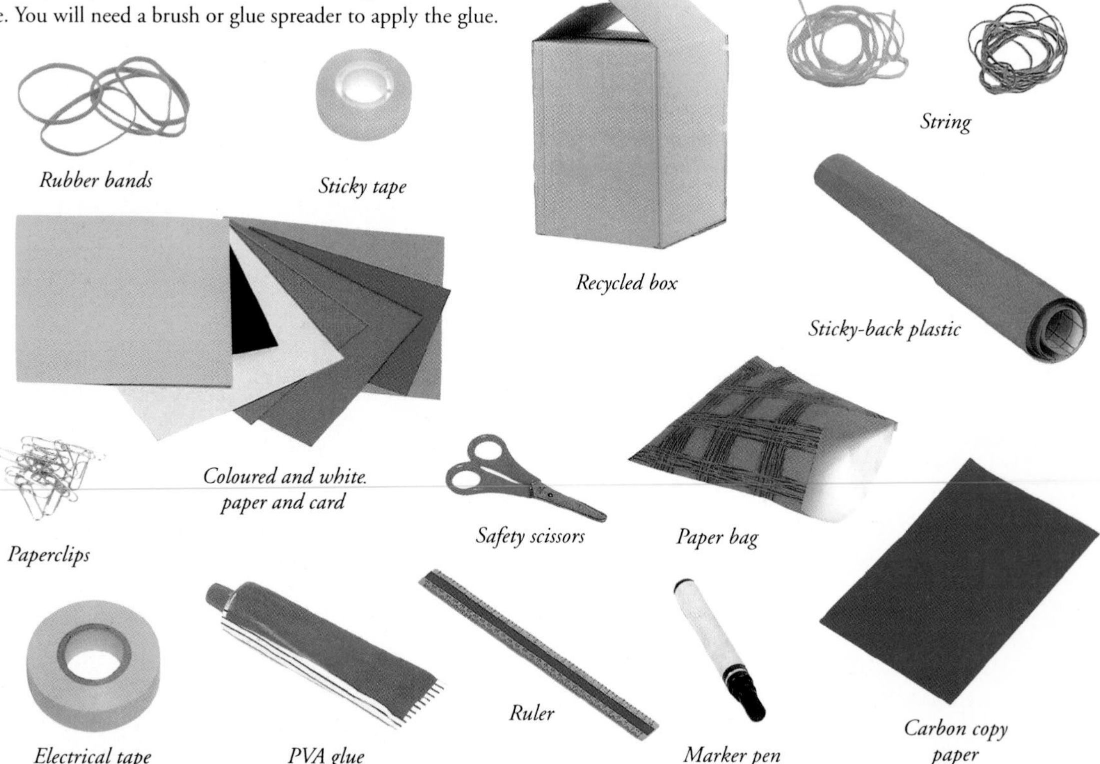

Rubber bands

Sticky tape

Recycled box

String

Sticky-back plastic

Coloured and white paper and card

Paperclips

Safety scissors

Paper bag

Electrical tape

PVA glue

Ruler

Marker pen

Carbon copy paper

Equipment

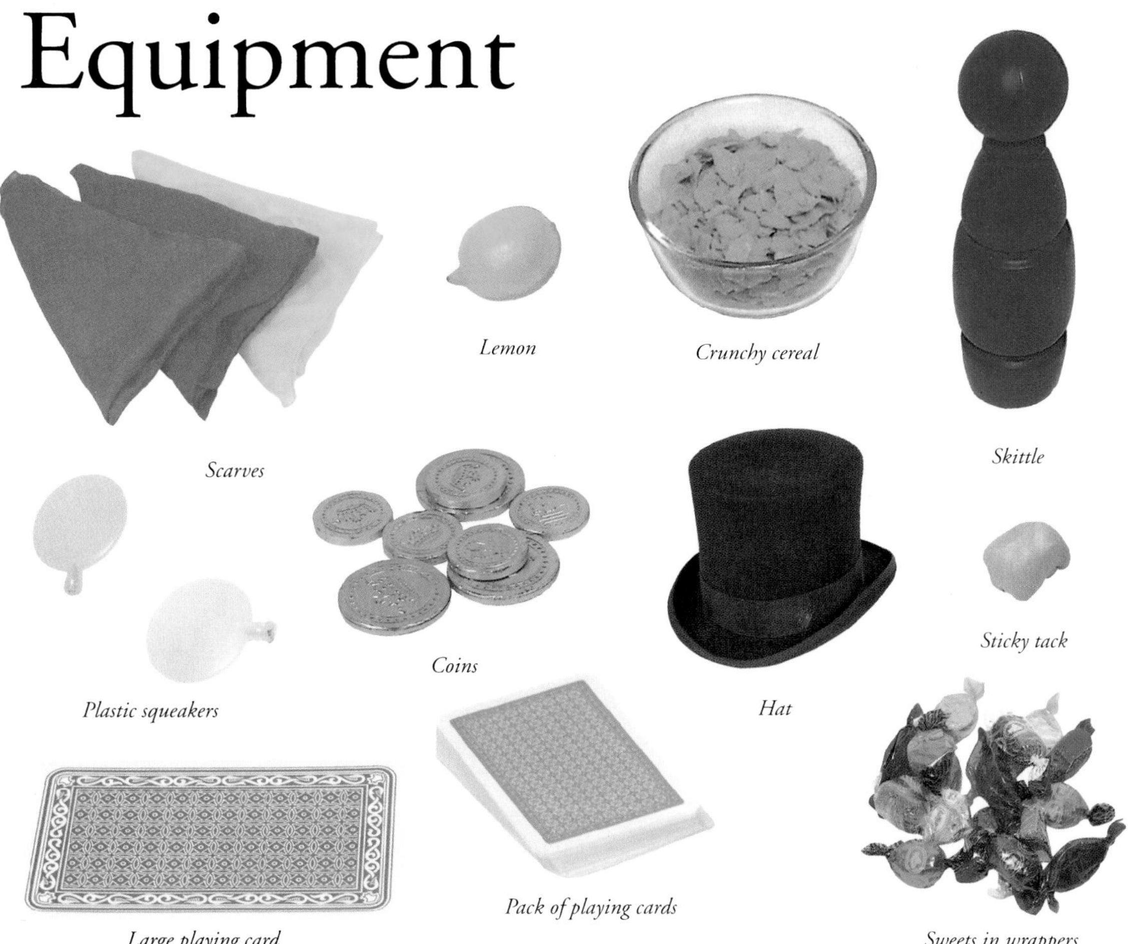

Lemon *Crunchy cereal* *Scarves* *Skittle* *Coins* *Plastic squeakers* *Hat* *Sticky tack* *Large playing card* *Pack of playing cards* *Sweets in wrappers*

Coins You can use real or plastic toy money when practising or performing tricks. You will need five coins.
Crunchy cereal Use a breakfast cereal made of large, crunchy flakes. Ask permission before raiding the kitchen!
Hat Part of a trickster's style is the hat – your audience will love it! It can be a dashing top hat, a favourite baseball cap or even a crazy sunhat.
Large playing card This is about four times the size of a normal playing card. You can buy it in joke shops and toy shops.
Lemon You can use a real or plastic lemon to do the Magic Box trick.
Plastic squeakers These are round, plastic discs that squeak when squeezed. You can buy them in joke shops and toy shops. They are not expensive.
Playing cards A pack of playing cards consists of 52 cards plus two jokers. There are four suits – hearts, diamonds, clubs and spades – numbered from ace to king. There are two black suits and two red suits. To do all the tricks you will need two packs of cards. Playing cards are inexpensive and can be bought in toy shops and stationery shops.
Scarves You can use large or small silky scarves or handkerchieves. Brightly coloured or patterned ones are best.
Skittle This is used when playing indoor or garden bowls. It is made of plastic.
Sticky tack This reusable material is used to fix posters on to walls. You can buy it in packs in stationery shops.
Sweets in wrappers You will need quite a few sweets wrapped in foil or cellophane. Do not start eating them before you have completed the trick!

Missing Money

This trick is every trickster's favorite. Why? Because it cannot go wrong. All you need are five coins and some tape attached to the palm of your hand. Keep the palm of your hand hidden throughout the trick, otherwise the audience will figure out your secret.

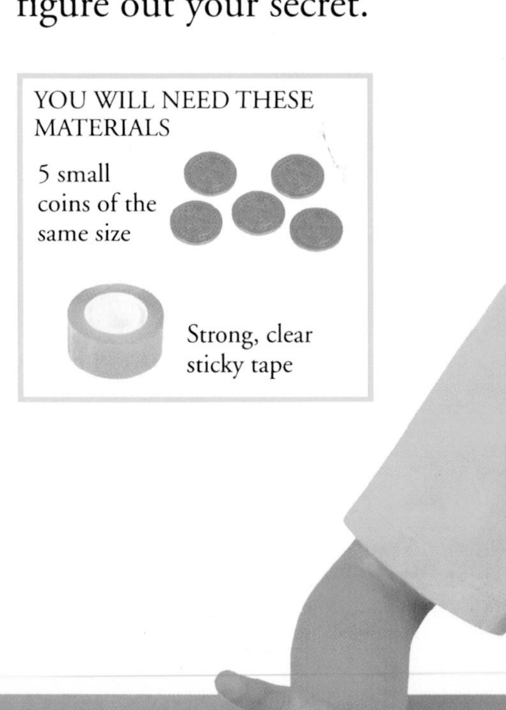

YOU WILL NEED THESE MATERIALS

5 small coins of the same size

Strong, clear sticky tape

Handy hint

In place of a loop of sticky tape you can use a small piece of double-sided tape. Use small coins rather than large ones – large coins are harder to conceal and too heavy to adhere to the tape. You can use plastic coins if you like.

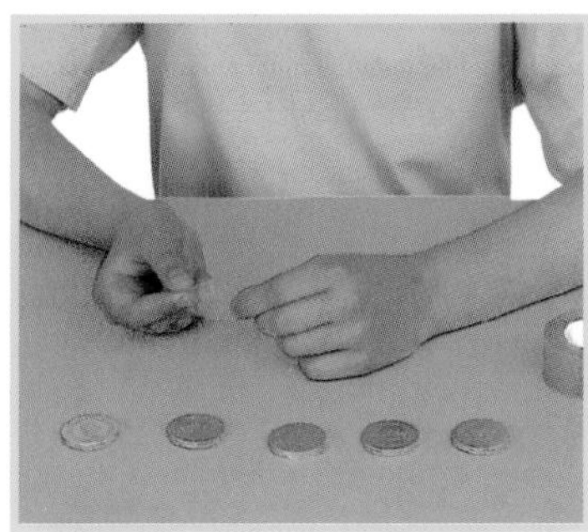

1 Cut a small piece of sticky tape about 5cm (2in) long. Overlap the ends, sticky side out, to make a loop. Place the five coins in front of you on the table.

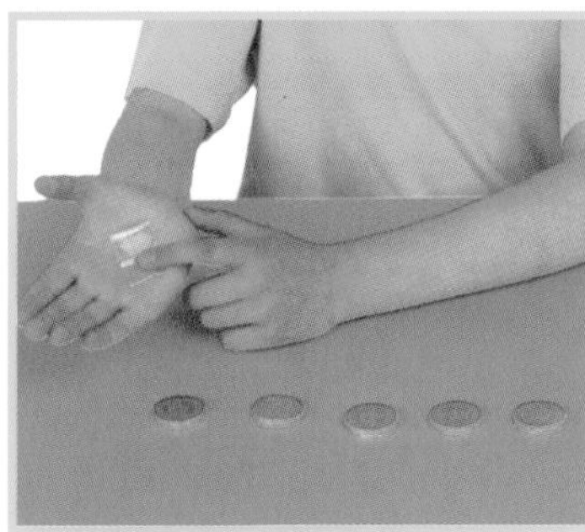

2 Firmly press the loop of tape on to the palm of your hand. Do not let anyone see you doing this. This little bit of tricky sneakiness is just between you and me.

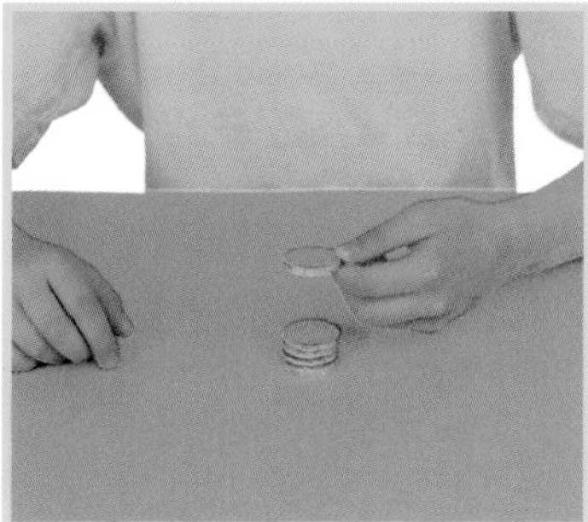

3 Make a big show of counting the five coins one-by-one as you stack them neatly one on top of the other. Ask your audience to count along with you.

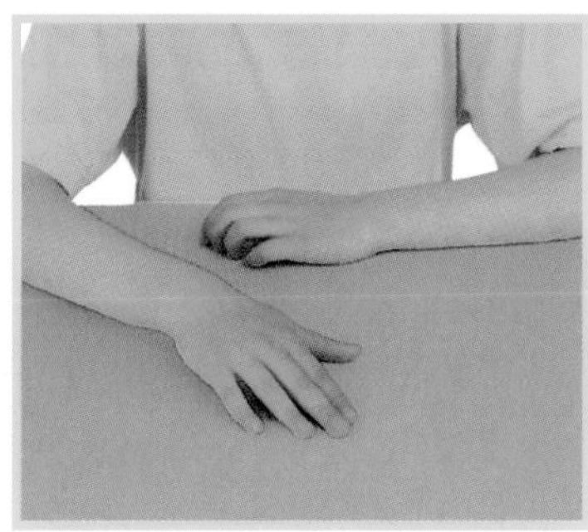

4 Press the hand with the sticky loop on to the pile of coins. Say your chosen magic words and then withdraw your hand. The top coin will be stuck to the loop.

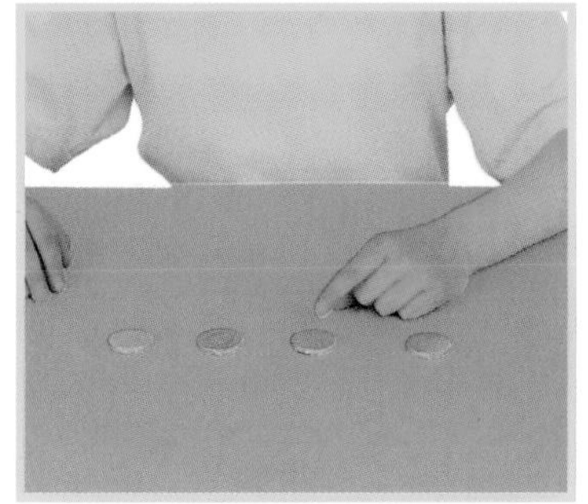

5 Keep the palm concealing the coin flat on the table. With the other hand, spread out the pile of coins and count them out loud. Yikes! There are now only four coins.

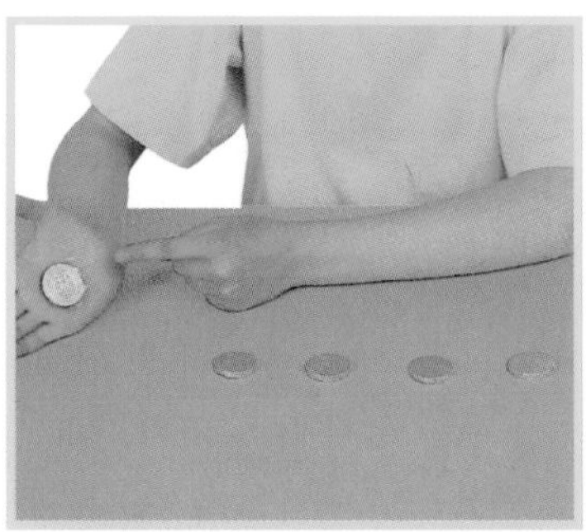

6 The fifth coin, of course, is still stuck to your hand.

It is a secret!

In this trick, the missing coin remains missing. You do not reveal where you have concealed the fifth coin. Remove the coin and sticky tape from your hand discreetly while you are returning the other coins to your pocket or to your magic box.

Tricky Tubes

This is another classic trick that is used by tricksters everywhere. It involves moving a handkerchief from one 'magic' tube to another tube to give the impression that both tubes are empty. In the finale of this trick you stun the audience by producing a handkerchief from the empty tubes.

YOU WILL NEED THESE MATERIALS

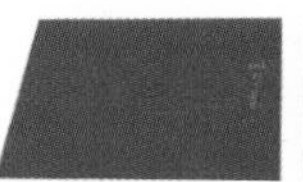

2 pieces of different coloured card 30cm x 30cm (12in x 12in)

Rubber band

Small handkerchief

9 paperclips

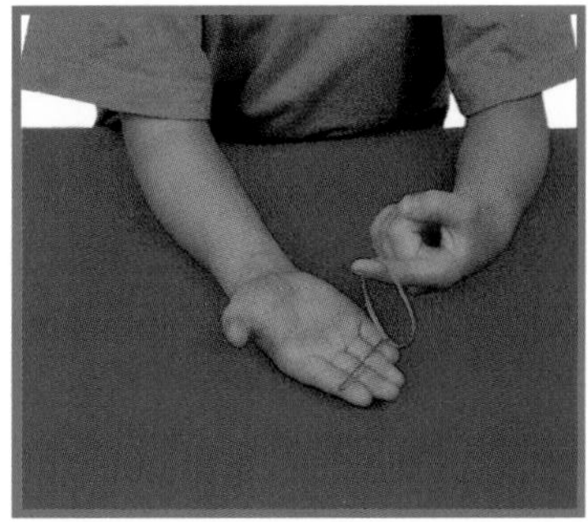

1 Steps 1, 2 and 3 show what you have to do to prepare for this trick. Roll the pieces of card to make tubes. One tube must be narrower so that it will fit inside the larger tube. Secure the tubes with eight paperclips.

2 The device that makes this trick work is a paperclip. Unfold the paperclip to make hooks at either end, as shown. Attach a rubber band to one hook. Roll up the handkerchief and thread it into the rubber band.

3 Hook the other end of the paperclip on to the top of the narrow tube. The rubber band and the handkerchief will be on the inside of the tube. Make sure that the handkerchief is totally hidden from view.

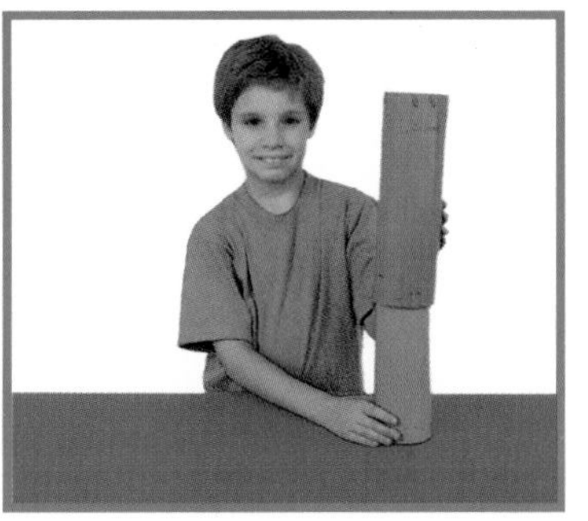

4 Now it is time to get this show on the road! Hold up the large tube so that the audience can see that it is completely empty. This should not be difficult as it really is empty!

5 Pick up the narrow tube and slide it slowly down through the large tube. As you do this the paperclip holding the handkerchief will hook itself on to the large tube.

6 Pull the narrow tube out from the bottom of the large tube. Then, with a flourish, hold up the narrow tube to show your audience that it is empty.

7 Place the narrow tube on the table. Slide the large tube over the narrow tube. The handkerchief will fall inside the narrow tube. Then say to your audience, 'From two empty tubes I will magically produce a handkerchief.' Pull the handkerchief from inside the narrow tube. All you have to do now is wait for the applause and take a bow!

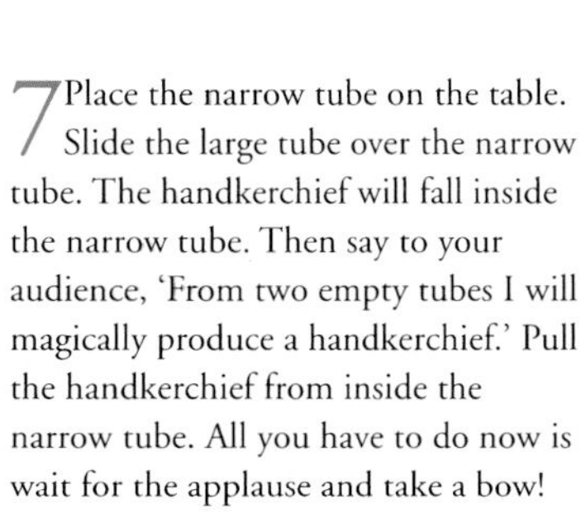

Magic Trick Box

The Magic Trick Box can produce objects out of thin air. One minute the box is empty, the next it's not. Only you know about the secret box that can hold a lemon, a pack of cards or even an elephant. If you plan to pull an elephant out of the box, perhaps this trick should be called the Magic Trunk!

Practice makes perfect

To get this trick right takes lots of practice. You should be so familiar with it that the audience are not even aware that you turn the box around in step 8. One wrong move and the lemon (or the elephant) will come tumbling out for all the world to see! To make this trick really impressive, ask someone in the audience to lend you their watch, wallet or sunglasses. Their mouth will drop when they see their object disappear and then reappear.

YOU WILL NEED THESE MATERIALS

1 small recycled box

1 large recycled box

Sticky tape

Ruler

Scissors

Marker pen

PVA glue

Lemon

Sticky-back plastic

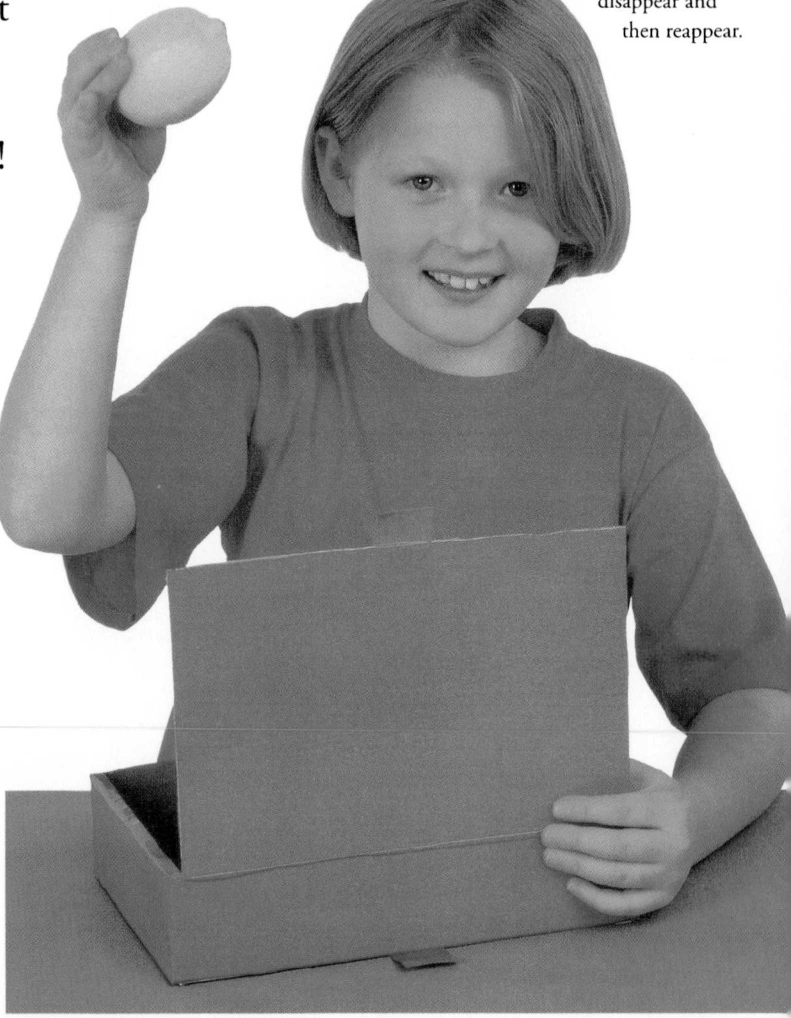

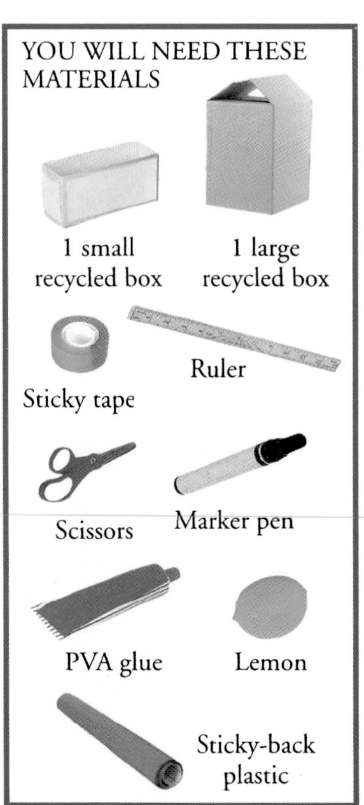

1 To make the Magic Trick Box, tape the ends of the boxes closed. Cut the top off the small box. With your pen and ruler, draw a line along one long and two short edges of the large box.

2 Cut along these lines carefully to make a hinged lid on the large box. By the way, don't forget to empty the boxes before you start this project. Oops, oh well!

3 Do the same to the other side of the large box but this time the hinged lid is on the opposite edge. You must get this right or the Magic Trick Box will not be very magical or tricky.

4 Tape or glue the small box securely to the inside of one of the hinged lids. The opened top of the small box must face in the direction where the lid is hinged.

5 Cover the box with sticky-back plastic. Cut two strips of plastic to make tabs. Fix tabs to the outside edge of the lids, fold in half and fix to the inside edge. Put the lemon in the small box.

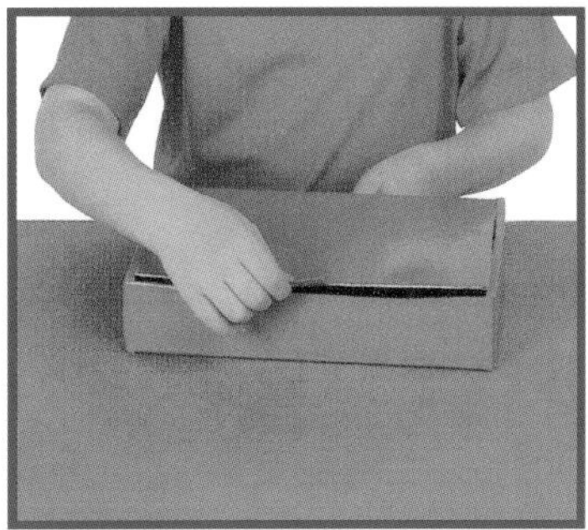

6 Now it is trickster time! Place the box on the table. The lid containing the small box is on the bottom with the tab nearest you. Hold on to both tabs because you are about to open the box.

7 Raise the box and pull on the tabs to open both lids. Say to your audience, "This box is empty – but not for long." Lay the box on the table.

8 The lid containing the lemon should be on the bottom. Turn the box around, hold the tab and lift the lid. Hold up the lemon to the audience.

The Big Picture

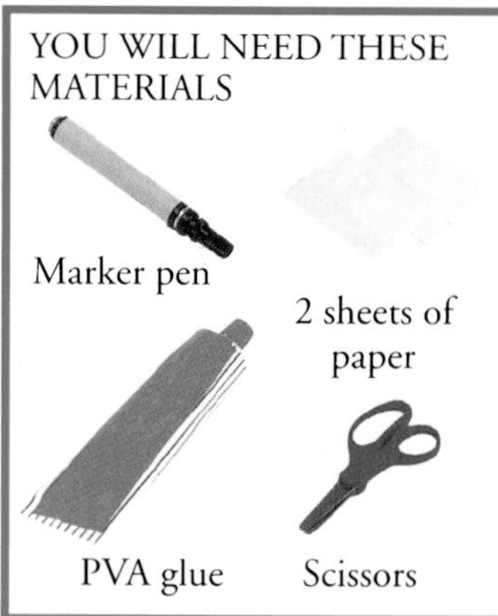

So that you can say hello or farewell to your audience in a trickster way, this special trick has been prepared for you. It is a very simple illusion where a small picture suddenly becomes a big picture. Carefully follow the instructions for folding the paper, or you will be saying hello or goodbye to yourself.

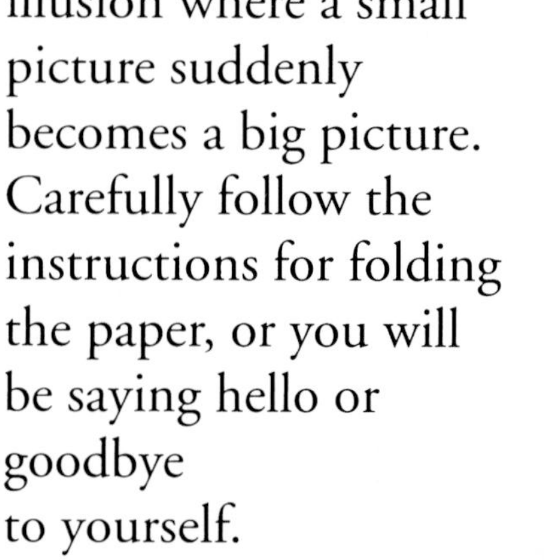

This is how the trick starts. You show the small picture, then, with a quick flick of your wrist, it suddenly becomes the Big Picture!

1 To prepare for this trick, place a sheet of paper with a long side nearest you. Draw a large picture of someone waving on the paper. Keep the drawing simple, you will have to repeat it later.

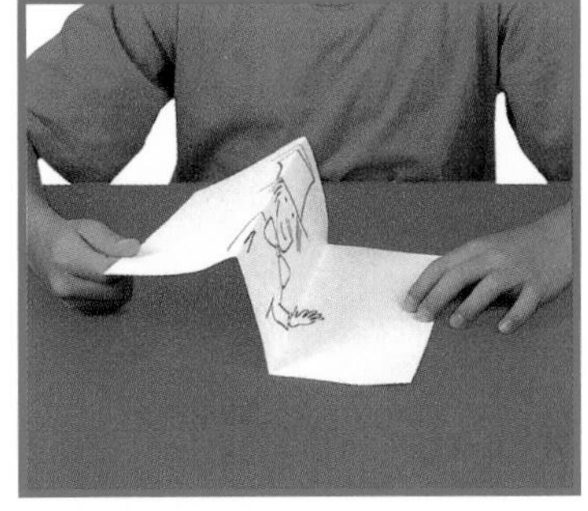

2 Turn the paper so that the picture is upside-down. Fold the paper concertina-style making the right hand flap larger than the other two. The right hand flap is on the bottom, as shown.

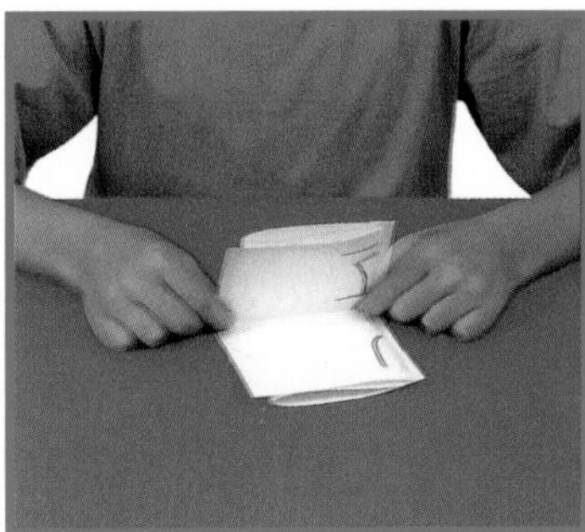

3 Fold the paper away from you, so that the top flap is a little smaller than the bottom flap. I know this sounds complicated, but it is easy. I could not do it if it was too hard.

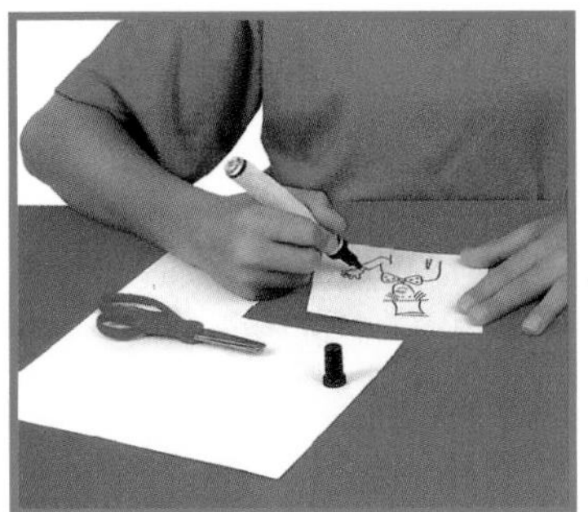

4 Take the other sheet of paper and cut out a rectangle that is exactly the same size as the bottom flap of the folded paper. On to this rectangle, draw the picture that is on the folded paper.

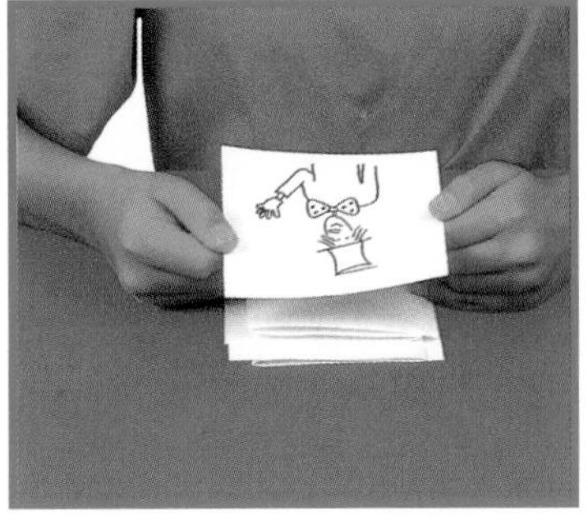

5 Glue this picture on to the front of the large flap. The bottom of the picture will be nearest the fold. (See, I told you this is easy!) Apply the glue carefully so that it does not spread on to the other flaps. You are ready to present the Big Picture.

6 Hold the paper, as shown, with the fold at the bottom and the small drawing facing the audience. To stop the paper unfolding, support the flap with a little finger. Tell the audience that you are going to give them a cheery welcome or a sad farewell wave.

7 Quickly pull sideways so that the folded paper unfolds and the big picture is revealed.

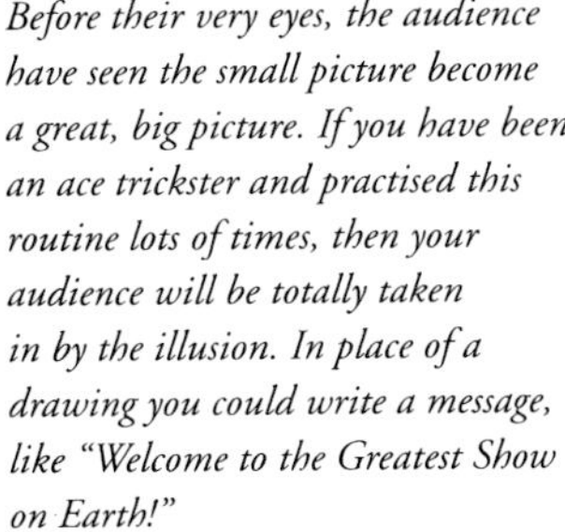

Before their very eyes, the audience have seen the small picture become a great, big picture. If you have been an ace trickster and practised this routine lots of times, then your audience will be totally taken in by the illusion. In place of a drawing you could write a message, like "Welcome to the Greatest Show on Earth!"

The Big Card Trick

You may have seen this trick performed many times, but now you will be able to do it yourself. You can choose any number or suit you want for the large playing card, but a card of the same number and suit must be at the top of your pack of playing cards. The two cards fixed to the large card must be numerically smaller than the big card.

YOU WILL NEED THESE MATERIALS

Pack of playing cards and 1 large envelope

Sticky tack

Large playing card

Handy hint

You can make your own large playing card with stiff white card and a black marker pen. It does not matter which suit or number you choose to draw, as long as it is the same as the top card on your pack of cards.

1 To prepare for this trick, use a small piece of sticky tack to fix a two and a four of any suit on to the back of the large ten of clubs card. Place them in the envelope. Also check that the ten of clubs is the top card on your pack of playing cards. Now let the show begin.

2 Invite someone from the audience to join you on stage and cut the pack of cards. No, not with a pair of scissors. To cut the cards, all your guest has to do is take a pile of cards off the top of the pack and lay them beside the remaining cards.

3 Place the bottom half of the pack on top of the other cards. Place it so that it is at right angles to the cut cards. This will show you where the pack was cut and where you will find the ten of clubs. Tell your guest that they will shortly see their secret card.

4 Remove the upper stack of cards from the pile and turn over the next card. Without looking at the card, show it to your guest. Tell them that they must remember what their secret card is. You know that it is the ten of clubs!

5 Ask your guest to shuffle the cards as much as they like. When they are shuffled, you can put them into the envelope. This envelope contains the large ten of clubs card plus the two other smaller cards.

6 Tell your guest that you are going to find their secret card. Put your hand into the envelope and pull out the two card. Ask if this is the secret card. They will say no. You then ask, 'Is it bigger than this?'

7 Repeat the routine as in step 6, but this time pull out the four card. It is now your big moment to astound and amuse everyone. Put your hand into the envelope again and pull out the large ten of clubs card. Show it to your guest and say, 'Is this big enough?' You have shown your guest that you knew that their chosen card was the ten of clubs all the time.

Double Envelope Trick

To make sure that 'Top Secret' documents sent by post are not read by the wrong person, use the Double Envelope Trick. This sneaky envelope has a hidden compartment that only you and your friend will know about. If anyone else opens it, the envelope will appear empty. To fool snoops, put a false message into the envelope.

YOU WILL NEED THESE MATERIALS

Two large identical envelopes

Scissors

Paper glue

1 Cut the front, including the flap, from one of the large envelopes. Trim a little off the edges of the cut section of envelope.

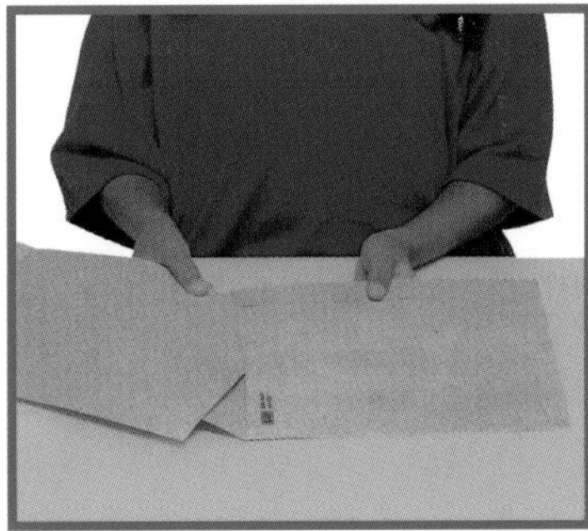

2 Slide the cut section of envelope inside the other envelope. The flaps on both envelopes should line up. So far, so good!

3 Place the secret message into the envelope, sliding it into the opening between the two flaps. Have you ever seen anything so sneaky?

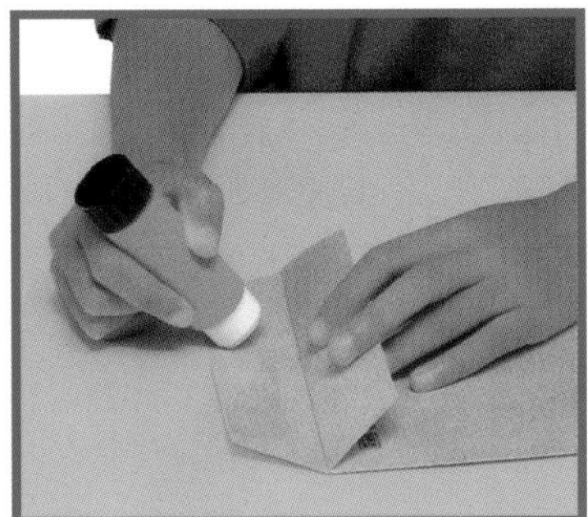

4 Paste the two flaps together with paper glue. This will seal the hidden compartment that contains the message.

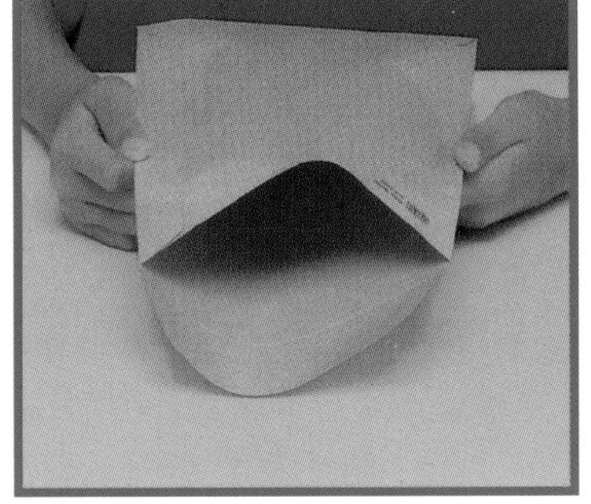

5 If the envelope falls into the wrong hands and it is opened, the envelope will either be empty or contain a false message. The snoopy sneak will be very disappointed or totally confused!

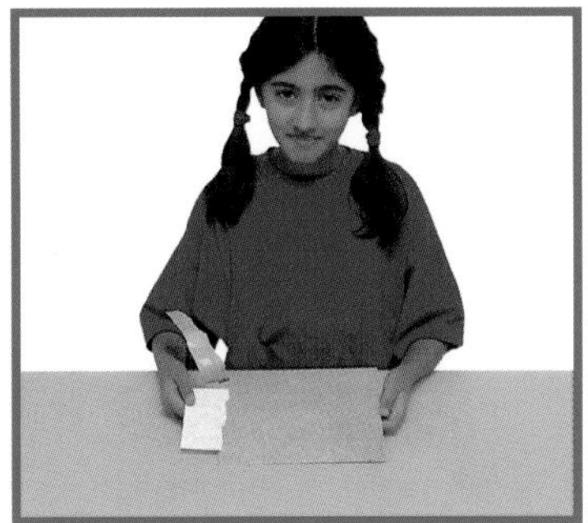

6 You and your friend know exactly what to do with the Secret Envelope. Simply lift up the glued flap and rip it off. Slide a hand inside the now opened hidden compartment and pull out the 'Top Secret' message.

7 The envelope must have contained some surprising news judging by the look on this girl's face.

There are only two snags to the successful use of the Double Envelope Trick. Firstly, it does not work with bulky items like books or gifts. And secondly, you and your friend have to be discreet when preparing and opening the envelope. Never open the envelope where there are prying eyes or your secret will be out of the bag – or should that be out of the envelope!

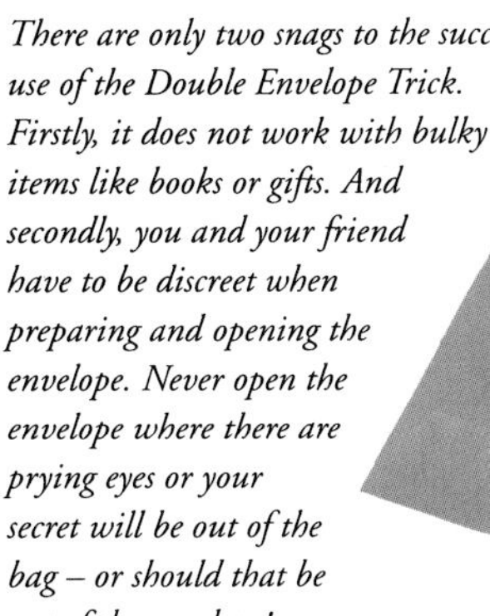

See the Unseen

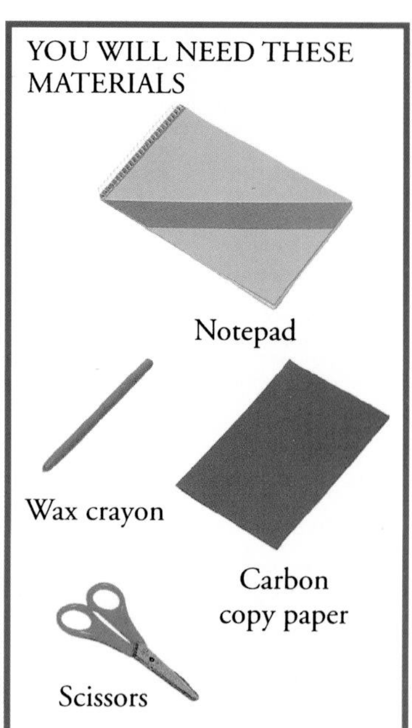

Here are two techniques for seeing the unseen – reading messages that you were never intended to read. For the first method you have to get hold of the notepad quickly.

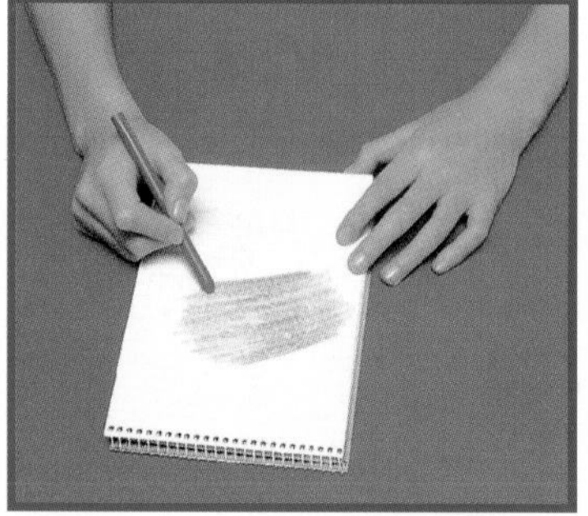

1 **Method 1** – Get the notepad on which the torn-out message was written. Rub the crayon gently over the top sheet. The impressions made by the written message will remain unshaded.

2 **Method 2** –To intercept a message, trim a sheet of carbon copy paper so that it is smaller than the notepad. Turn over two pages of the notepad and insert the copy paper inky side down.

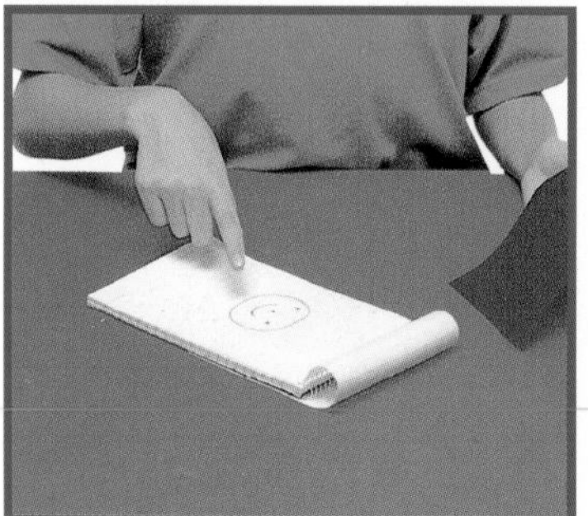

3 Once the message has been written and the person is out of sight, turn the top pages of the notepad over and remove the copy paper. On the page below will be a copy of the message. Take care doing this and never attempt to intercept truly personal messages.

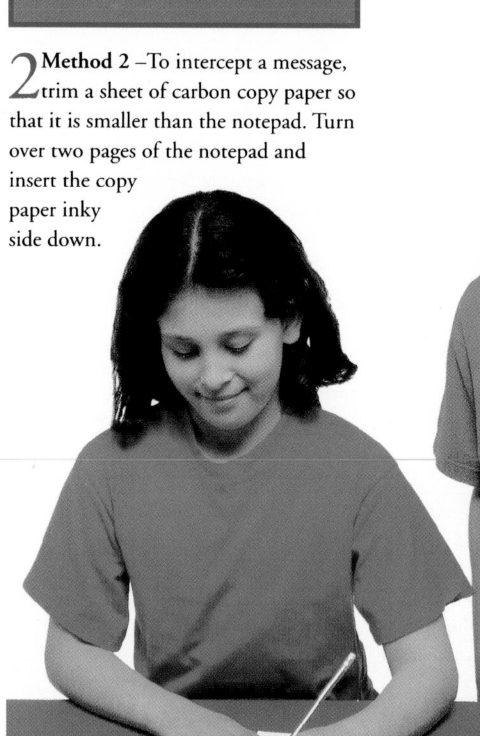

Noisy Alarms

Crunch, crackle, pop, squeak! What are those noises? They are the sounds of your bedroom security devices going into action. Your intruder has got a noisy surprise!

YOU WILL NEED THESE MATERIALS

Crunchy cereal

2 plastic squeakers

1 **Noisy warning 1** – This may sound a little odd, but crunchy cereal makes a great night-time alarm. All you have to do is leave a pile of cereal just outside your bedroom door.

2 When the unwitting intruder steps on the cereal, you will hear the crunch, crackle and pop! The intruder will realize that their sneaky game is up and will run away.

Handy hint

You will have to keep changing the positions of your alarms or they will prove ineffective against intruders.

3 **Noisy warning 2** – In case the intruder misses the crunchy cereal alarm, place one plastic squeaker under a rug near the door and another under the cushion of a chair. (Even intruders have to sit down sometime!) Now all you have to do is wait.

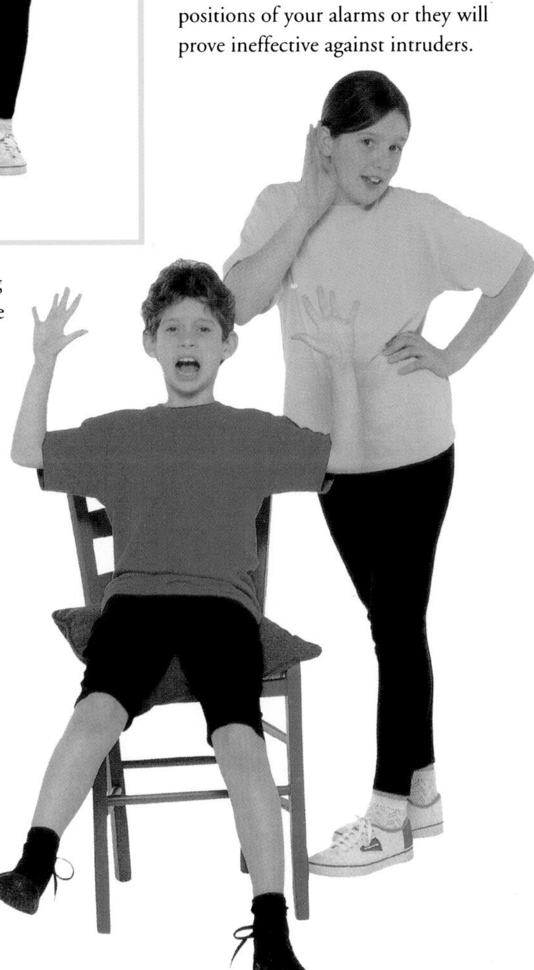

When you hear the squeakers 'squeak' you will know that you have not caught a mouse, but a sneaky rat!

Trick Wallet

Handy hint

If you are going to use your Trick Wallet as part of your act, the wallet should be quite large. This will make it easier for the audience to see what is and what is not happening. When using the wallet for secret messages, make sure it will fit easily into a pocket.

Open one flap of this wallet and it is empty. Open it the other way and – wow! – there is the secret document. Make two identical Trick Wallets so that you and a friend can switch wallets (and secret information) without being detected. When using the wallet to play a trick on someone, distract his or her attention so that they do not notice you turning the wallet over.

YOU WILL NEED THESE MATERIALS

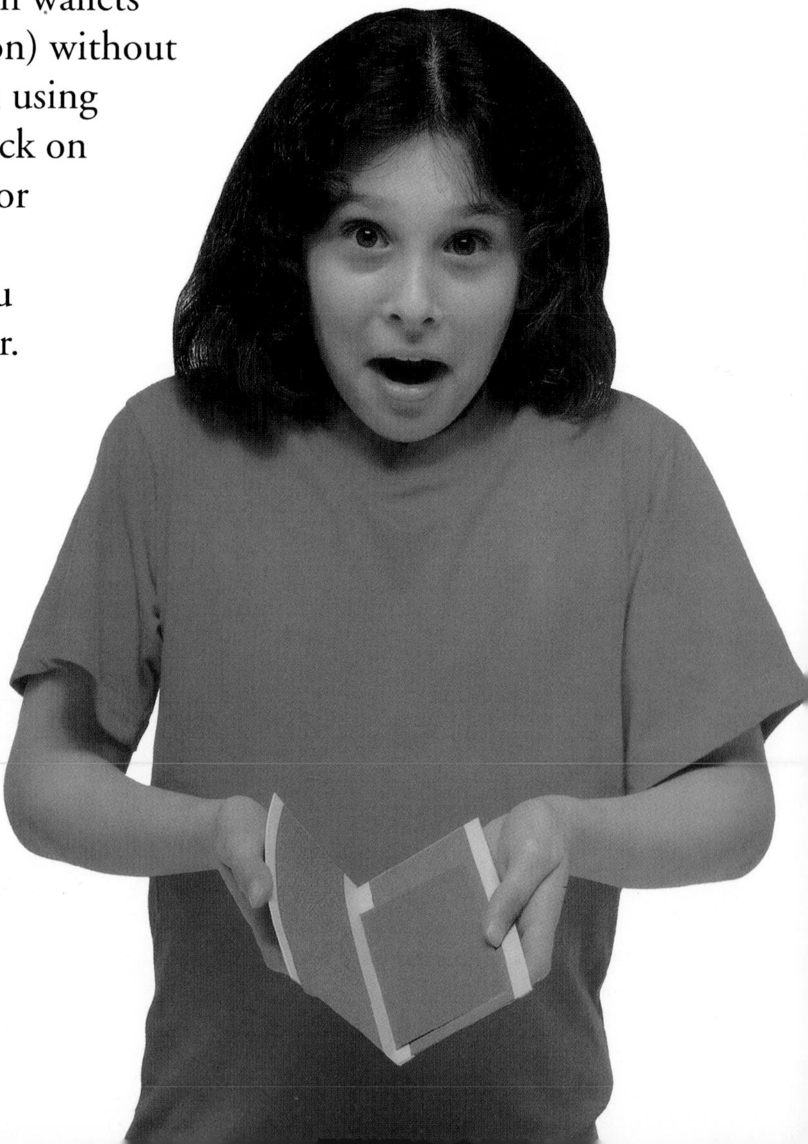

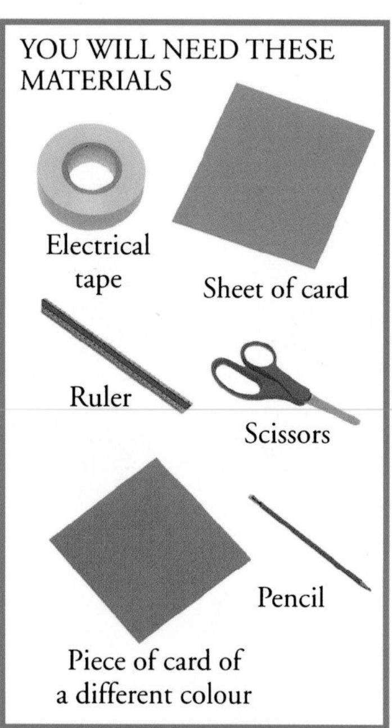

1 Measure and draw three rectangles, each 20cm x 8cm (8in x 3in) on to the sheet of card. Cut out the rectangles. You can make a big wallet by cutting out three larger rectangles.

2 Lay the rectangles side by side and join the edges with electrical tape, as shown. The tape should act like a hinge, allowing each piece of card to fold over easily.

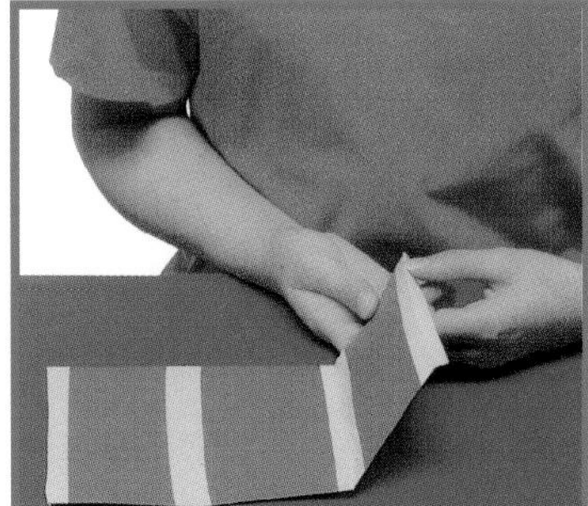

3 Tape the joins on the back of the card and fix electrical tape along the remaining two short sides. Position the tape so that it can be folded over to the back to give a neat finish.

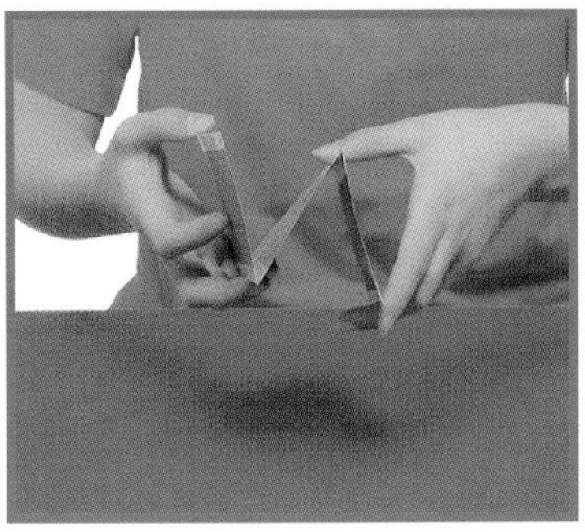

4 Concertina-fold the wallet, as shown. Lay the wallet on to the table and gently press it flat.

5 To test the Trick Wallet, place a small rectangle of the other coloured card between two of the flaps. Close the flaps. Turn the wallet over and open the flap. If the flap is empty you are doing the right thing. Close this flap.

6 Turn the wallet over again and open the flap. If all has gone to plan, the flap will contain the piece of card.

Magic trick wallet

To make the wallet work in a trick show routine, you have to be discreet when turning the wallet over so that your audience does not catch on to the trick. The only way to achieve this sleight of hand is to distract them by making a funny face or telling a joke. A good magician always has (among other things!) a couple of good jokes up his or her sleeve.

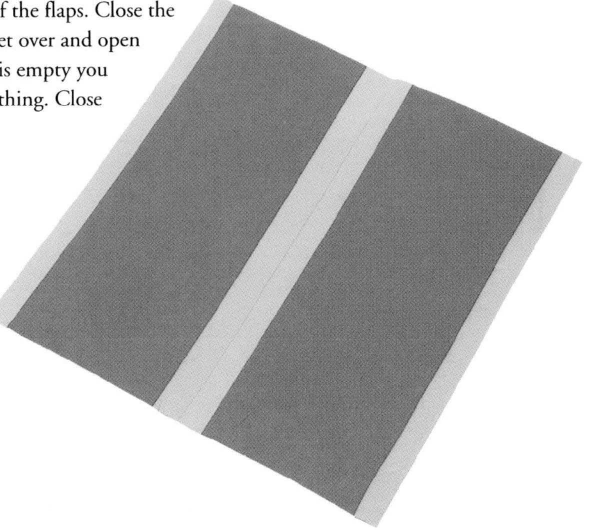

Sweet Disguise

Everyone has heard about sending messages in bottles, but only you will know how to pass on vitally important messages inside sweet wrappers. There is only one problem with Sweet Disguise – resisting the urge to eat the sweets. If you eat the special sweet and discard the wrapper, your message will remain a secret forever.

Handy hint

It is not a good idea to conceal your message inside the wrappers of sticky sweets – your message will be forever stuck to the sweet. The best type of sweets to use are chocolates. Yum, yum!

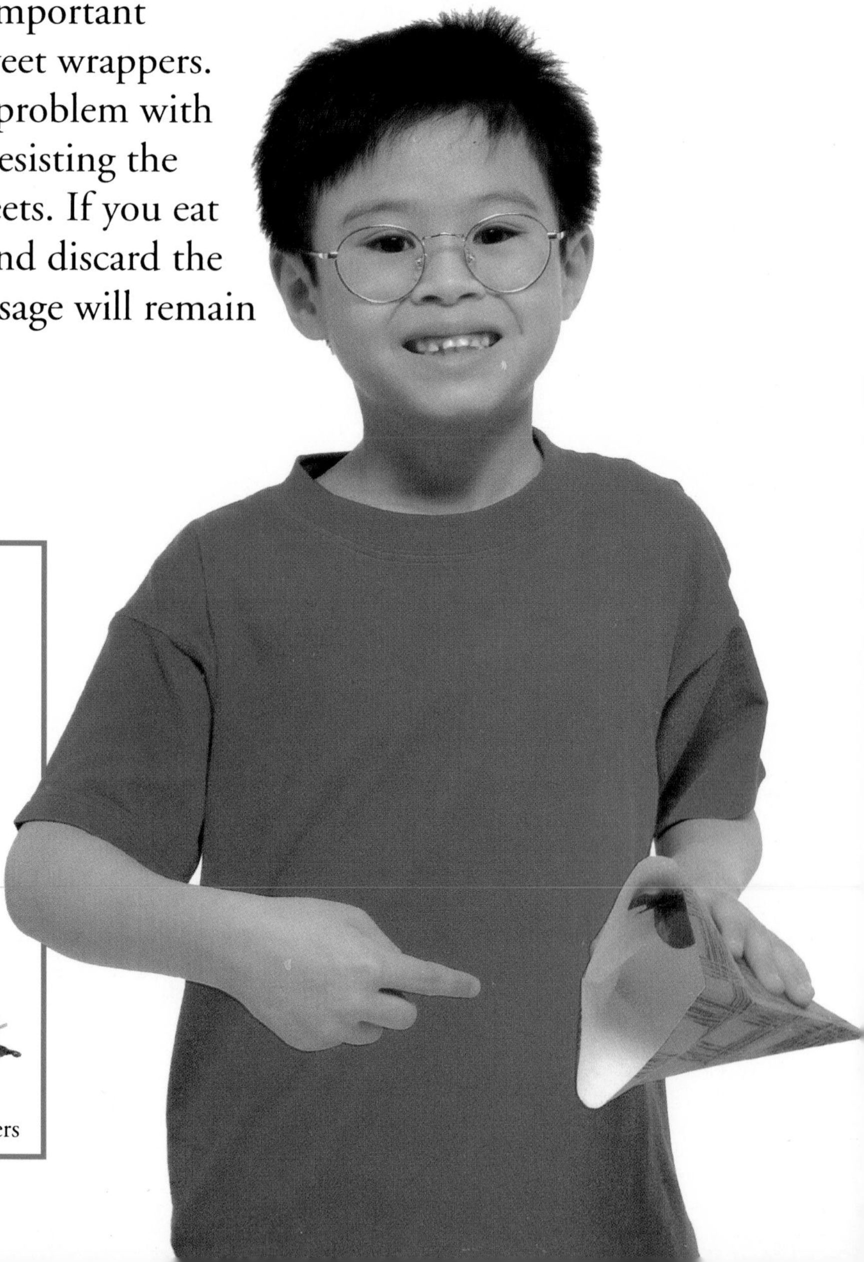

YOU WILL NEED THESE MATERIALS

Pencil or pen

Sheet of paper

Scissors

Sticky tape

Paper bag

Sweets in wrappers

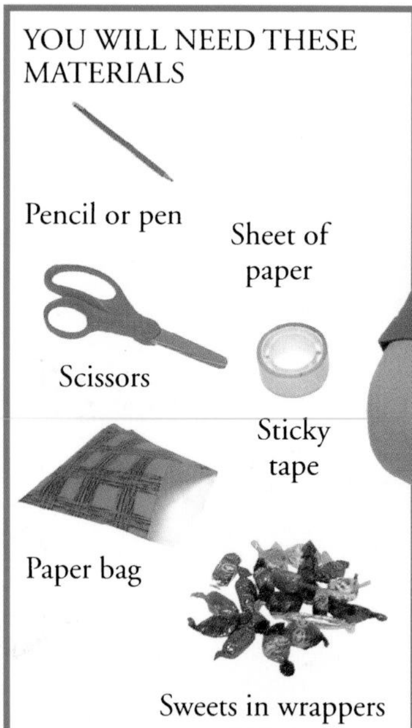

1 Cut out a piece of paper no larger than the wrapper on the sweet. Use this to write your secret message on.

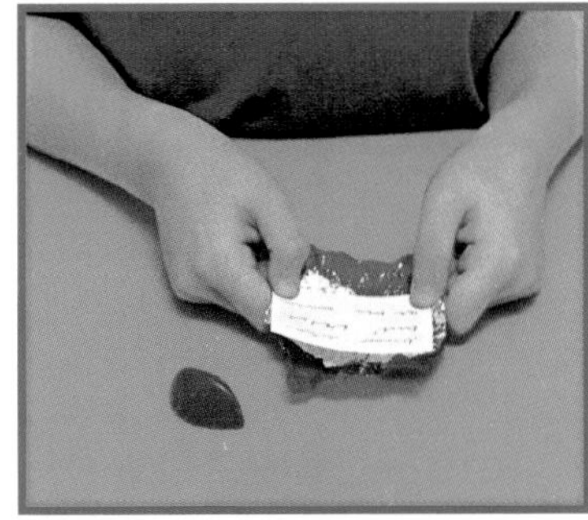

2 Unwrap one of the sweets and lay your message on the inside of the wrapper. Do not eat the sweet – yet!

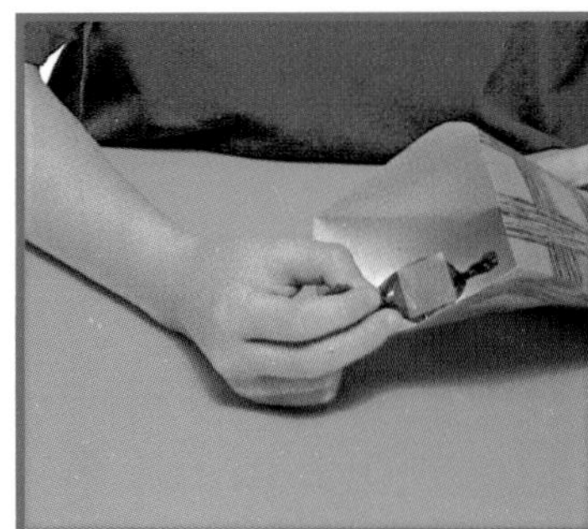

3 Place the sweet on top of the message and the wrapping paper. Rewrap the sweet.

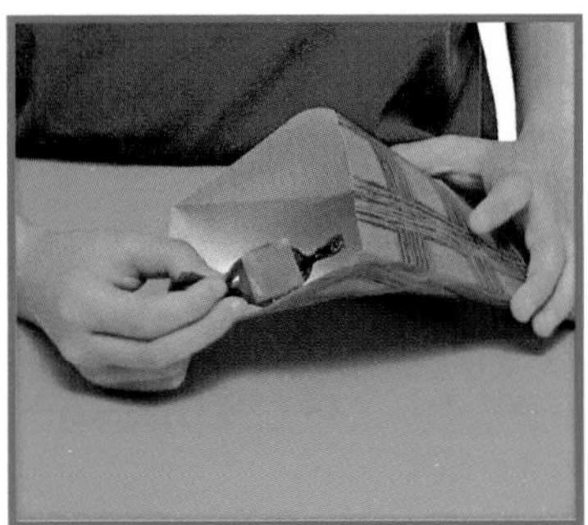

4 Make a loop from a short length of sticky tape. The sticky surface should be on the outside of the loop. Stick the loop to the sweet and then press the sweet to the inside of the paper bag. Fix it about halfway down the bag.

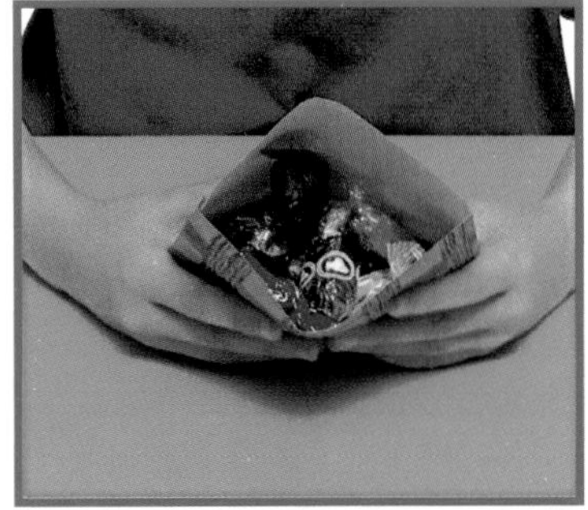

5 Carefully put the rest of the sweets in the bag, making sure that you do not dislodge the special sweet. Your secret message is now safe. No one will suspect that you are carrying vital information inside a bag of sweets.

6 When you are ready to pass on the secret message to your best friend, all you have to do is empty the bag. You can even ask your other friends if they would like a sweet. Not only are you clever, you are also very generous!

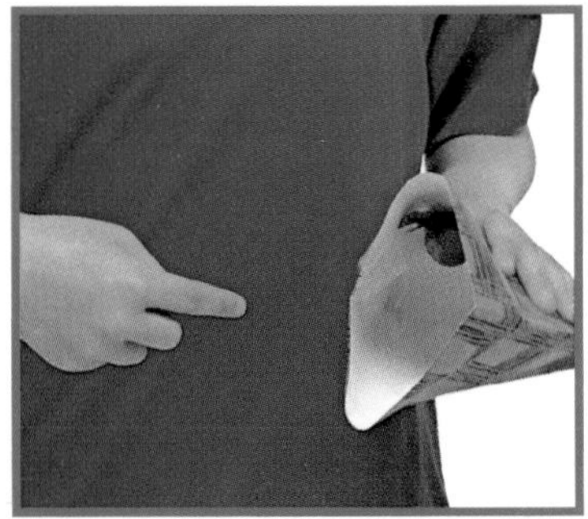

7 See, your secret message is safe! It is still stuck to the inside of the bag. Offer your best friend this sweet. He or she can eat it, while reading your note.

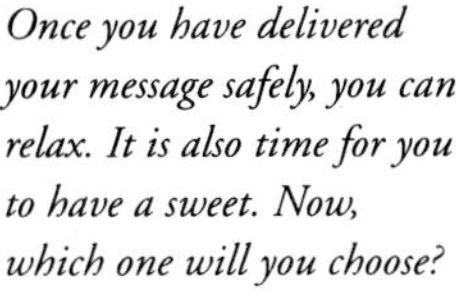

Once you have delivered your message safely, you can relax. It is also time for you to have a sweet. Now, which one will you choose?

Joke in the Post

YOU WILL NEED THESE MATERIALS

1 small envelope

Sticky tape

Sheet of paper or thin card

2 small rubber bands

3 paperclips

Marker pen

Want to send someone a shocking surprise? All it takes is paper, paperclips and sticky tape. Joke in the Post is so easy to assemble that you could make one for each of your friends. But will they still be your friends after you have played this joke on them?

1 Fold the sheet of paper or thin card into equal thirds. Press the folds flat with your hands and then open out the paper again.

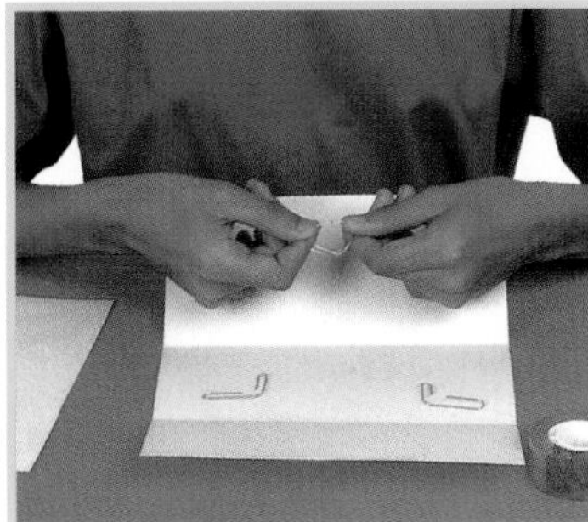

2 Open out two paperclips to make L-shapes, as shown. Bend and shape another paperclip to form a circle. Do this carefully – the ends are sharp.

3 Tape the L-shape paperclips to the paper and loop rubber bands around the ends, as shown. Thread the rubber bands on to the wire circle.

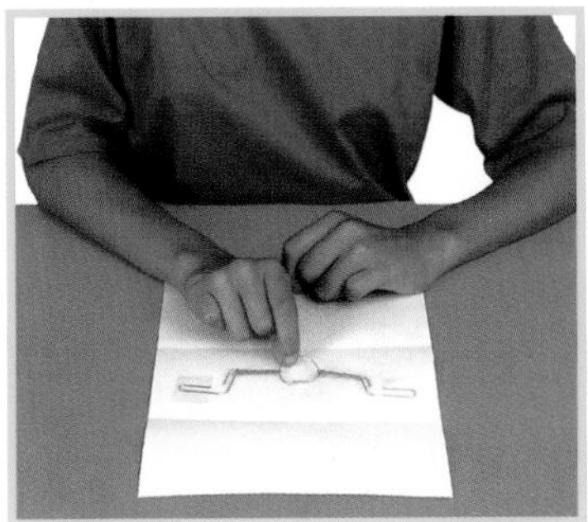

4 Slowly wind the wire circle around and around. The rubber bands will twist and tighten. Whatever you do, do not let go!

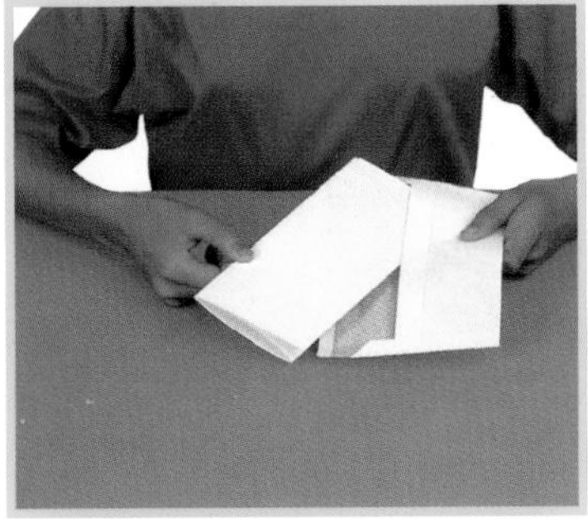

5 Re-fold the paper without letting go of the wire circle. Carefully insert the folded paper into the envelope and seal it.

6 Address the envelope using the marker pen. Post or deliver the envelope to your friend.

7 When your friend opens the letter the rubber bands will unwind causing the wire circle to spin and clatter against the paper. This is bound to make your friend jump in fright.

Handy Signals

Getting messages to friends can be tricky when you are involved in a hush-hush surveillance operation or you are working in the library. So instead of shouting messages, use hand signals. On the next page are examples of just a handful (ha, ha!) of hand signals and their meanings. Use them alone to convey a simple message or link them together for more complicated instructions. When you have mastered these signals, go on to invent your own.

YOU WILL NEED

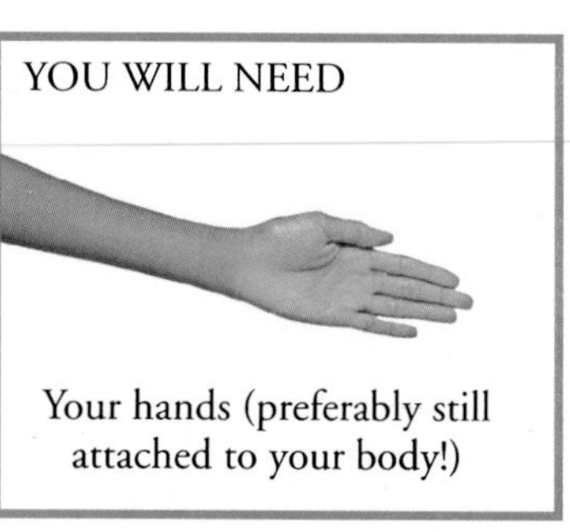

Your hands (preferably still attached to your body!)

1 **Quiet!** – Press a finger to your lips when you want someone to stop talking. Move the finger over to your ear to say 'listen.'

2 **Yes and no** – Resting your chin on a hand with the thumb pointing up means 'yes.' To say 'no', point the thumb down.

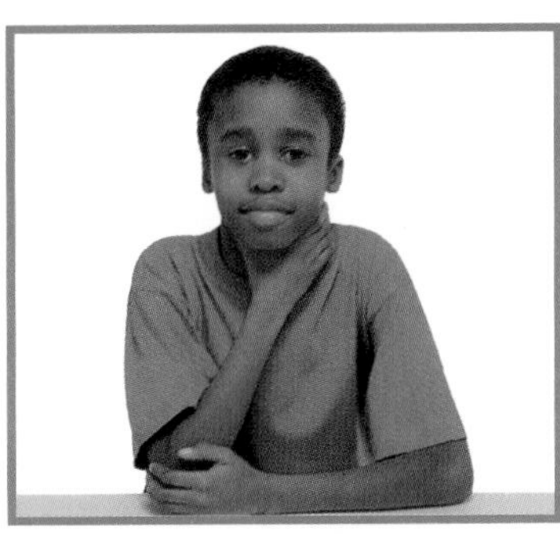

3 **Danger warning** – Place a hand loosely around your throat to warn friends that the situation is dangerous and to take care.

4 **Come here** – Running a hand through your hair from the front to the back means 'come here.'

5 **Go away** – Hiding your face behind one hand means 'go away'. Use two hands to say 'go away quickly.'

6 **Look** – Placing a finger next to the right eye means 'look right.' A finger next to the left eye means 'look left.' Fingers next to both eyes means look straight ahead.

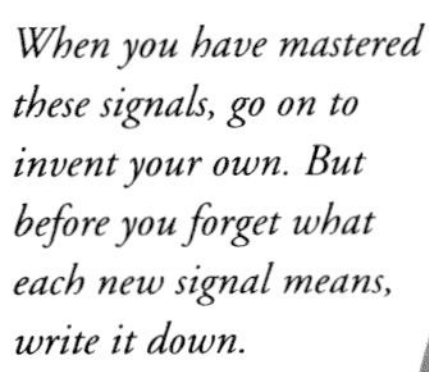

When you have mastered these signals, go on to invent your own. But before you forget what each new signal means, write it down.

Final Challenge

YOU WILL NEED THESE MATERIALS

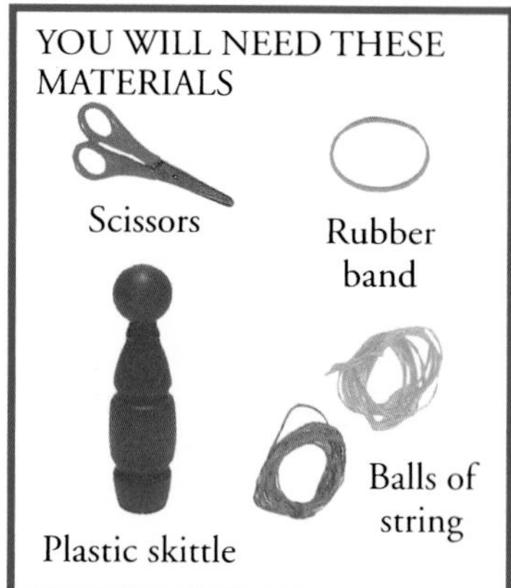

Your mission is to rescue the skittle from the circle using only string and a rubber band. You and your accomplice cannot enter the circle, nor touch the skittle. The only bit of floor the skittle can touch is the area on which it is standing. Good luck!

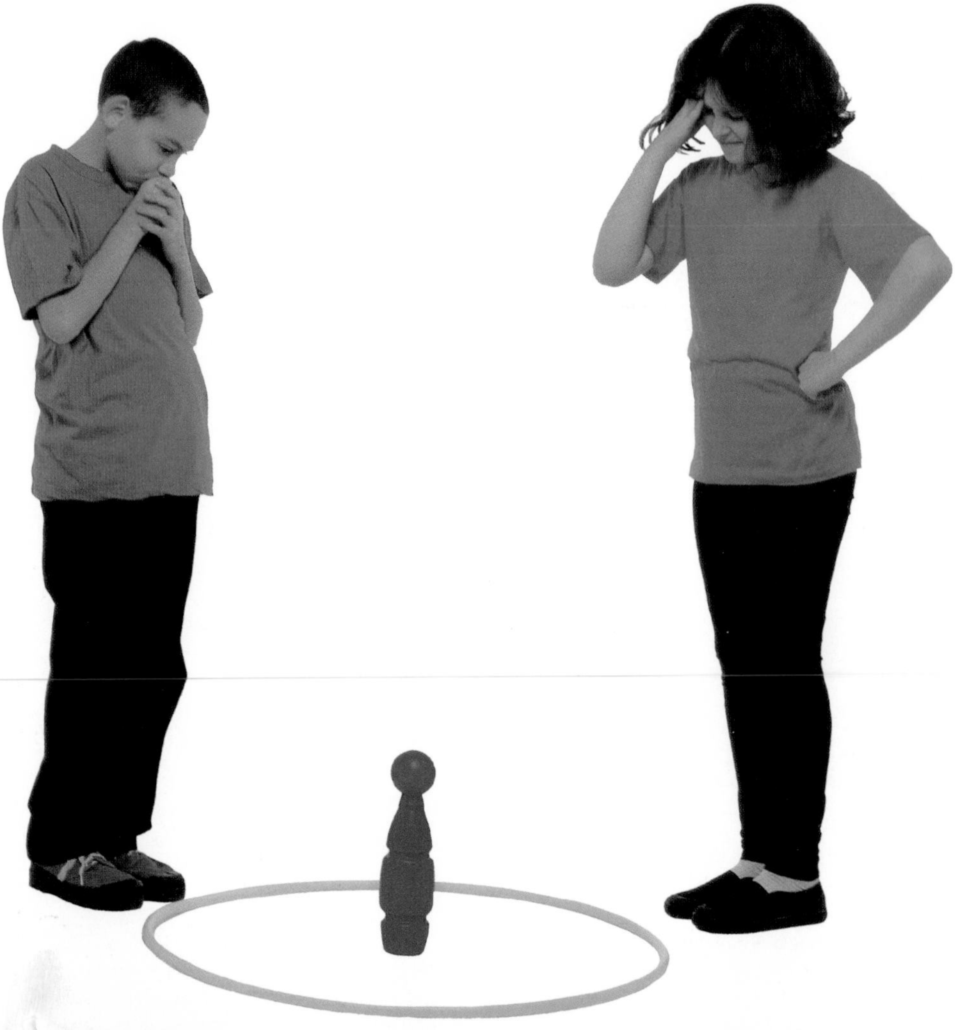

The Final Challenge is not easy, but that makes it all the more challenging. Now it is time to put your thinking caps on – there is a poor damsel skittle in distress that needs to be rescued.

1 Draw a circle $1^1/_2$m (48in) in diameter using the chalk. (A hoop is used here for clarity). Place the skittle in the middle of the circle. Cut four lengths of string 2m (2yd) long.

2 Thread lengths of string through the rubber band. The rubber band should be midway along each string. Hold the ends of the strings, as shown.

3 Gently pull on the strings to stretch the rubber band so that it will fit easily over the top of the skittle. Lower the rubber band over the neck of the skittle.

4 Allow the rubber band to tighten around the skittle by relaxing your pull on the strings. Carefully raise the skittle out of the circle. Do not pull on the strings as this will loosen the rubber band's grip on the skittle.

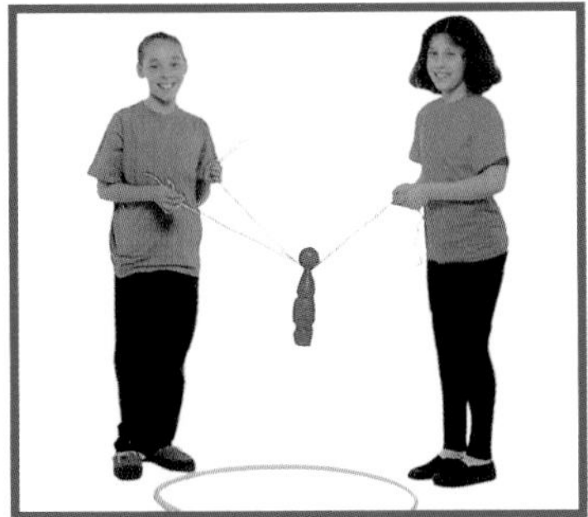

5 Congratulations, you have done it! Now see if your friends can do it.

This is a great game to play at a party. To make it more difficult for your friends, you can set a time limit in which the challenge must be completed.

Index

A

Alien from outer space, 444, 445
 outfit, 445
Alpine garden, 245
Apple dunking, 192, 193
Apron, 9
Arrow bracelet, 354, 355
Arty party wall, 186, 187

B

Back-flip card, 220, 221
Badges
 "I am four", 178, 179
 Wax-resist, 102, 103
Baking modelling material
 Snappy crocodile, 276, 277
Balloon balls, 452
Balloon house, 474, 475
Balloon modelling, 450, 451
 decorating, 451
 hints, 471, 475
 inflating, 450
 materials, 449
 projects, 464-475
 safety, 451
 tying knots, 450

Balloon snowstorm, 124, 125
Banana, frozen lollies, 72, 73
Banded bunches, 369
Basic techniques
 balloon modelling, 450, 451
 cutting circles, 11
 face and body painting, 420, 421
 flattening and cutting up boxes, 10
 friendship bracelets, 330, 331
 hairstyles, 358
 mask-making, 388, 389
 modelling, 266
 painting a mask, 397
 painting plastic, 11
 painting round objects, 11
 painting straight lines, 11
 removing labels, 10
 tracing a template, 12
 T-shirt painting, 298
 varnishing, 11
Basketballer, 314
Basket tiger, 392, 393
Bass, deep box, 150, 151
Battery light show, 126, 127
Beaded plaits, 378, 379
Beading
 friendship bracelets and necklaces,
 332, 334-338, 340, 343,
 348, 349, 352-355
 hairstyles, 378, 379
 hairband, 361
 safety, 378
Beadwork, 29
Beaky bird, 408, 409
Bean bags, 453
Beansprouts
 Chinese-style, 255
Be-bop bunches, 370
Big card trick, 490, 491
Big elephant, 466
Big picture, 488, 489
Binoculars, 42, 43
Birdwatchers, 42, 43
Birthday present, 322, 323
Biscuits, cut-out cookies, 74, 75
Blottography, 90, 91
Body painting

 see Face and body painting
Bouncy bunches, 368
Bound plaits, 381
Boxes
 Deep box bass, 150, 151
 Butterfly blottography, 90, 91
 Jewellery, 30, 31
 Magic, 486, 487
Boxes and bands bracelet, 352, 353
Bubble-printed notebook, 96, 97
Bug collector, 306, 307
Bugle blow, 166, 167
Building a balloon house, 474, 475
Bulbs, 233
Bunch of tulips, 472
Butterfly
 blottography box, 90, 91
 mobile, 26, 27
Bush spirit mask, 406, 407

C

Cake-cream cones, 76, 77
Cakes
 funny faces fairy cakes, 196, 197
 marzipan dinosaur cake, 194, 195
Canal boat, 22, 23
Card, giant sunflower, 20, 21
Cascading strawberries, 241
Castanets, clashing, 146, 147
Caxixi rattle, 158, 159
Cheese dip with dunks, 58, 59
Chemicals, experiments with,
 114, 115
Chemistry, kitchen, 138, 139
Chicken, colourful kebabs, 68, 69
Chimes, flowerpot, 168, 169
Chocolate-pot plant, 252, 253

Christmas
crackers, 86, 87
tree hat, 180, 181
Circle, cutting out, 11
Clearing up, 19
Clowning around, 446-475
Coco the clown, 404, 405
outfit, 405
Coconut
head, 242, 243
shy, 190, 191
Coiled plate, 278
Coin tricks
Coin fold, 212, 213
Coin through hand, 222, 223
Cutting coins, 214, 215
Missing money, 482, 483
Money from nowhere, 208, 209
Cookies, cut-out, 74, 75
Cooking, 50, 51
Cooking equipment, 54, 55
Cork rattlesnake, 34, 35
Corms, 233
Crazy balloon tricks, 470, 471
Crazy glasses, 400
Crazy juggling, 460
Crazy spiral, 316-317
Creatures of the night, 118, 119
Crimping crazy, 382, 383
Cuttings, 233
Cymbals, saucepan lid, 160, 161

D

Daisy frame, 269
Dashing sword, 469
Découpage
pencil-pot, 40, 41
surfaces for, 41
Desert bowl, 244, 245
Digital soccer, 442
Dirty napkin trick, 206, 207
Disco dazzler, 310, 311
Disco diva, 434, 435
Doll's house, 38, 39
Double envelope trick, 492, 493
Dressing-up
Face and body painting, 416-445
Magical masks, 386-415
T-shirt Fun, 294-325
Drum
dustbin, 148, 149
Japanese, 170, 171
Drying modelling material
Grinning cat, 286, 287
Snake pot, 279
Sun and star pot, 272, 273
Treasure chest, 284, 285

E

Easter rabbit, 396, 397
Egg bugs and toadstools, 56, 57
Electricity, experiments with, 114

F

Fabric painting
see T-shirt Fun
Fabulous hairstyles, 356-385
accessories, 360
basic techniques, 358
beading, 378-380
bunches, 368-370
crimping, 382, 383
curling, 371, 384, 385
hair care, 358, 362, 370, 382
hints, 364, 366, 381, 384

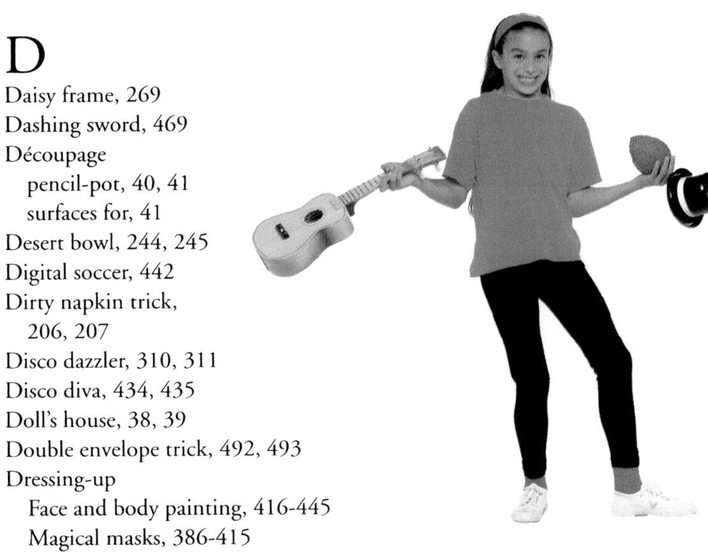

materials, 359
plaits, 372-381
ponytails, 362-367, 377
Face and body painting, 416-445
basic techniques, 420, 421
body painting projects, 430-433, 438-443
face painting projects, 422-429, 434-437, 444, 445
hints, 422, 433, 436, 439
materials, 419, 435
projects, 422-445
safety, 421
Fairy cakes, funny faces, 196, 197
Fake tattoo, 438
Family of pigs, 282, 283
Feather head-dress, 28, 29
Felt-tipped pens, 9
Final challenge, 504, 505
Finger-painted flowers, 98, 99
Fish cakes, swimming, 64, 65
Fish focals, 401
Fishing
Gone fishing, 188, 189
Magnetic fishing game, 46, 47
Flick-painted starscape, 106, 107
Flowering tree, 432, 433
Flowerpot and saucer, 32, 33
Flowerpot chimes, 168, 169

Flowers, finger-painted, 98, 99
Flowery glass, 104, 105
Football hero, 440, 441
Friendship bracelets, 326-355
basic techniques, 330, 331
hints, 331, 332, 335, 340, 342, 343, 346, 348, 350, 352
materials, 329
projects, 332-355
Funky bracelet, 338

G

Gardening equipment, 236, 237
Gardening glossary, 235
Geraniums, jolly, 246, 247
Gift wrap, star and moon stencilled, 84, 85
Glass, flowery, 104, 105
Glitzy hairband, 361
Glitzy stars, 309
Green scientists, 116
Grinning cat, 286, 287
Growing things, 230-261
glossary, 235
materials, 232-237
plant care, 234
projects, 238-261
Guitar, shoebox, 156, 157

H

Hair accessories
Fabulous hairstyles, 360
Glitzy hairband, 361
Hair wrap, 339
Hippy headband, 333
materials for, 359
Stripy beaded hair clip, 346, 347
Hair wrap, 339
Hairband, glitzy, 361
Halloween witch, 426, 427
Ham and sweetcorn roll-ups, 66, 67
Handy signals, 502, 503
Head-dress, feather, 28, 29
Heart and star rings, 288
Heart throb bracelet, 289
Heat, experiments with, 114
High ponytail, 363
Hippy headband, 333
Hungry cat, 324, 325
Hungry wolf, unlucky lamb, 402, 403

I

Ice, experiments with, 114
Iceberg, the great puzzle 136, 137

J

Jam-jar salads, sprouting seeds, 246, 247
Japanese drum, 170, 171
Jelly pond, 78, 79
Jewellery
Jewels galore, 439
friendship bracelets, 332-355
Heart and star rings, 288
Heart throb bracelet, 289
peanut and macaroni, 36, 37
popcorn, 37
Jewellery box, 30, 31
Jewels galore, 439
Joke in the post, 500, 501
Juggler's nightmare, 456, 457
Juggling, 448
balloon balls, 452
bean bags, 453
hints, 454, 456, 458, 462
materials, 449
projects, 454-463
safety, 451
Jungle bracelet, 334, 335

K

Kazoo, singing, 152, 153
Keeping clean, 19
King of hearts, 468
Kitchen
cleanliness and safety in, 52
chemistry, 138, 139
Knotty dotty necklace, 348, 349

L

Laboratories, 116
Lazy summer afternoons, 260, 261
Lemon balm plant, 253
Little devil, 443
Lizard, cork, 35

M

Magic box, 201
Magic secrets, 203
Magic show, a, 198-229
glossary, 204, 205
materials, 204, 205
Magic tricks, 206-229
Magic trick box, 486, 487
Magic trick wallet, 497
Magic wands, 210, 211
Magic words, 204, 205
Magical masks, 386-415

attaching straps and ties, 389
cutting eye and mouth holes, 388, 389
equipment, 391
fitting a mask, 388
hints, 394, 398, 404, 410, 414
materials, 390
painting, 397
projects, 392-415
safety, 389
Magician's hat, 202
Magnetic fishing, 46, 47
Making music, 142-171
instruments
percussion, 144
stringed, 144
wind, 144
projects, 146-171
Making things, 16-47
cleaning up, 19
collecting, 18
materials, 18, 19
projects, 20-47
Maracas, snakey, 162, 163
Marbled pencil box, 108, 109
Marvellous mobiles, 130, 131
Marzipan dinosaur cake, 194, 195
Masks
see Magical masks
Materials, 8, 9
recycling, 10, 18
Middle house mouse, 216, 217
Mirrors, mysterious, 120, 121
Missing money, 482, 483
Mobile
butterfly, 26, 27
marvellous, 130, 131
moving air, 130, 131
Modelling fun, 262-293
basic techniques, 266
equipment, 265
hints, 268, 279, 284
materials, 264, 265, 267
projects, 268-293
safety, 264, 283
salt dough, 267
Money from nowhere, 208, 209
Monkey juggling, 461
Monster sock puppet, 44, 45
Muddy puppy, 320, 321
Music, 144, 145
Musical families, 145
Mussels, 26
Mustard and cress, crazy-shaped, 248, 249
Mysterious mirrors, 120, 121

N

Nasturtiums, 260, 261
Noisy alarms, 495
Notebook
bubble-printed, 96, 97
Noughts and crosses
bracelet, 344, 345
t-shirt, 300, 301

O

Octopus, 430
One-ball workout, 454, 455
Optical illusion, 305

P

Paint pots, 9
Paintbrushes, 9
Painted flowerpot and saucer, 32, 33
Painted stones caterpillar, 88, 89
Painting
face and body, 416-445
fun, 80-109
mask, 397
mixing colours, 82
plastic, 11
round objects, 11
straight lines, 11
t-shirts, 294-323
Painting fun, 80-109
colour mixing, 82
projects, 84-109
techniques, 80, 86, 88, 90, 92, 94, 96, 100
types of paint, 79
Paints, 8
Palm trees, 184, 185

Pampered pooch, 464
Pancakes, ham and sweetcorn
roll-ups, 66, 67
Paper, 9
Paper chains, 176, 177
Paperweight cat, 287
Papier-mâché, 408
Spanish giant, 414, 415
Parrot on a perch, 465
Parties, 174, 175
Party fun, 172-197
materials, 175
projects, 176-197
safety, 182
Pasta shapes with lentil sauce, 60, 61
Peanut and macaroni jewellery,
36, 37
Pencil-pot découpage, 40, 41
Percussion instruments, 144
Perfect ponytail, 362
Pests, garden, 234
Picture frames
Daisy frame, 269
Spotty dog-bone, 94, 95
Wiggly snake frame, 268, 269
Piggyback plant, 251
Pirate Peta, 425
Pizzas, funny face, 62, 63
Place-mat, stencilled cork, 24, 25
Plaiting
see Fabulous hairstyles,
Friendship bracelets
Plaits and bows, 380
Plantlets, 233
Plastic, painting, 11
Plastic modelling material
Space rocket, 270, 271
Tyrannosaurus rex, 290, 291
Wonder boy, 290, 291
Pockets of fun, 312, 313
Pony princess, 364, 365
Popcorn
Crazy popcorn, 70, 71
jewellery, 37
Postman's wand, 218, 219
Potato stamping, 307
Pot marigolds, 260, 261
Pretty plaited flips, 374, 375
Prowling leopard, 436, 437
outfit, 437
Puppets
sock, 44, 45
wooden-spoon, 100, 101
Purple hanky, red hanky, 224
PVA glue, 8

Q

Queen chess piece, 292, 293

R

Racy ribbons, 376
Rattlesnake, cork, 34, 35
Recycling, 10, 18
boxes, 10
Removing labels, 10
Ribbon roll, 377
Ringing up trick, 226, 227
Round objects, painting, 11
Ruler, 9

S

Safety, 13,
in the kitchen, 52, 53,
making models, 264, 283,
making t-shirts, 296,
using beads, 378,
making masks, 389, 395,
using face paints, 421,
juggling, 451
Salt dough
Coiled plate, 278
Daisy frame, 269
Family of pigs, 282, 283
Heart and star rings, 288
Heart throb bracelet, 289
how to make, 267
Spotty clock, 274, 275
Wiggly snake frame, 268, 269
Science equipment, 116, 117
Science record book, 115
Scientific experiments, 118-141
Scissors, 9
Sea life fantasy, 302, 303
Sea world, 422, 423
outfit, 423
See the unseen, 494
Seeds, 233
sprouting, 254, 255
Sewing, 44, 312, 313, 322, 323,
361, 453
tips, 313
Shadows, 118, 119
Shark sock puppet, 45
Simple plait, 372
Sink or swim, 134, 135
Skeleton, 315
Snake pot, 279
Snappy crocodile, 276, 277
Sneaky, cheeky tricks, 476-505
equipment, 481
hints, 482, 486, 490, 495,
496, 498
materials, 480
preparation, 478
presentation, 478,
479
projects, 482-505

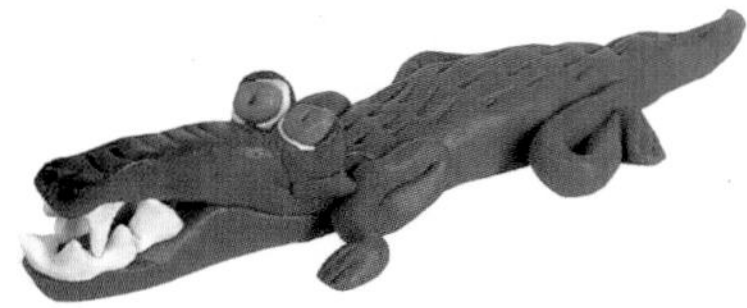

Sock puppet, monster, 44, 45
Space
  rocket, 270, 271
  trekker, 318, 319
Spanish giant, mask, 414, 415
Spider plants, creepy-crawly, 250, 251
Spotty
  clock, 274, 275
  crocodile, 412, 413
  dog-bone picture frame, 94, 95
  puppy, 428, 429
Sprouting seeds, jam-jar salads, 254, 255
Stag, 431
Star and moon stencilled gift wrap, 84, 85
Starscape, flick-painted, 106, 107
Static electricity, 124, 125
Stencils, 13-15, 297
  muddy puppy, 320, 321
Stencilled cork place-mat, 24, 25
Stencilling, 24
Sticky tape, 9
Straight lines, painting, 11
Strawberries, juicy, 240, 241
Stringed instruments, 144
Stripes and beads bracelet, 342, 343
Stripes galore bracelet, 340, 341
Stripy beaded hair clip, 346, 347
Stunning science, 110-141
  equipment, 116, 117
  kinds of, 112, 113
  materials, 116, 117
  preparation, 114
  projects, 118-141
  techniques, 107, 109
Succulent plants, 244, 245
Sun and star pot, 272, 273
Sundial, 122, 123
Sunflowers, 473
Sunflower race, 238, 239
Sunglasses strap, 350, 351
Sunny sunflower, 304
Super robot, 424
Sweet disguise, 498, 499
Swirly spots, 308

T

T-shirt fun, 294-325
  choosing colours, 311, 317
  hints, 302, 312, 316
  materials and tools, 297
  painting tips, 298, 323
  preparation, 298
  projects, 299-325
  safety, 296
  stencils and templates, 299
T-shirt painting, 92, 93, 294-325
Talking house, 410, 411
Tambourine flower, 154, 155
Tasty treats, 48-79
  equipment, 54, 55
  glossary, 54
  preparation, 51-53
  projects, 56-79
  safety, 50, 51
Tattoo, 438
Teeny bopper, 371
Telephone, tumbler, 128, 129
Tell the time by the sun, 122, 123
Templates
  project, 14, 15
  t-shirt, 299
  tracing, 12
The big card trick, 490, 491
The big picture, 488, 489
Three-ball frenzy, 458, 459
Time-bomb escape, 228, 229
Tiny mouse, 467
Topsy turvy ponytail, 366, 367
Transformation mask, 402, 403
Treasure chest, 182, 183, 284, 285
Trick wallet, 496, 497
Tricks
  Crazy balloon, 470, 471
  see Sneaky, cheeky tricks
  see A magic show
Tricky tubes, 484, 485
Triple twist, 373
Tubers, 233
Twisty bracelet, 332

Two-ball juggle, 456, 457
Tyrannosaurus rex, 290, 291

U

Umbrella plants, upside down, 258, 259
Under or over, 462, 463
Underwater Fountain, 137

V

Varnishing, 11
Vegetable-print T-shirt, 92, 93
Vegetable-top forest, 256, 257
Vegetables
  cheese dip with dunks, 58, 59
  preparing, 53
Venetian mask, 394, 395
Vinegar volcano, 140, 141

W

Water
  displacement, 134, 135
  experiments with, 114
  holding upside down, 132, 133
  underwater fountain, 137
Wax-resist badges, 102, 103
Weed jungle, 257
Weeds, 234
Weighing and measuring, 51
Wicked witch, 398, 399
Wiggly snake frame, 268, 269
Wind instruments, 144
Wonder boy, 280, 281
Wonder waves, 384, 385
Wooden-spoon puppets, 100, 101
Woven bracelet, 336, 337
  belt, 337

X

X-ray wand, 226, 227
Xylophone, bottle, 164, 165

Acknowledgements

The publishers would like to thank the following children for appearing in this book, and of course their parents: Nana Addae, Richard Addae, Mohammed Adil Ali Ahmed, Josie and Lawrence Ainscombe, Clive Allen, Deborah Amoah, Charlie Anderson, Lauren Andrews, Rosie Anness, Michael Apeagyei, Tania Steve Aristizabal, Joshua Ashford, Emily Askew, Rula Awad, Nadia el-Ayadi, Joshua Ayshford, Nichola Barnard, Venetia Barrett, Jason Bear, Michael Bewley, Gurjit Kaur Bilkhu, Vikramjit Singh Bilkhu, Maria Bloodworth, Leah Bone, Catherine Brown, Chris Brown, Christopher Brown, Cerys Brunsdon, William Carabine, Daniel Carlow, Kristina Chase, Chan Chuvinh, Ngan Chuvinh, Alexander Clare, Rebecca Clee, Emma Cotton, Charlie Coulson, Brooke Crane, Charley Crittenden, Lawrence Defraitus, Dean Denning, Vicky Dummigan, Kimberley Durrance, Holly Everett, Alaba Fashina, Benjamin Ferguson, Terri Ferguson, Aimee Fermor, Kirsty and Rebecca Fraser, Fiona Fulton, Nicola Game, George Georgiev, Alice Granville, Lana Green, Liam and Lorenzo Green, Sophia Groome, Alexandra and Oliver Hall, Reece Harle, Laura Harris-Stewart, Jonathan Headon, Dominic Henry, Edward and Thomas Hogarth, Lauren Celeste Hooper, Mitzi Johanna Hooper, Sasha Howarth, Briony Irwin, Kayode Irwin, Gerald Ishiekwene, Saadia Jacobs, Stella-Rae James, Isha Janneh, Jade Jeffries, Aribibia Johnson, Rean Johnson, Reece Johnson, Carl Keating, Karina Kelly, Sarah Kenna, Camille Kenny-Ryder, Lee Knight, Nicola Kreinczes, Kevin Lake,Victoria Lebedeva, Barry Lee, Kirsty Lee, Isaac John Lewis, Nicholas Lie, Sophie, Alex and Otis Lindblom-Smith, Chloe Lipton, Scott Longstaff, Ephram Lovemore, Claire McCarthy, Erin McCarthy, Jock Maitland, Gabriella and Izabella Malewska, Ilaira and Joshua Mallalieu, Elouisa Markham, Alexander Martin-Simons, Laura Masters, Hou Mau, Trevor Meechan, Mickey Melaku, Imran Miah, Yew-Hong Mo, Kerry Morgan, Jessica and Alice Moxley, Aiden Mulcahy, Fiona Mulcahy, Tania Murphy, Moriam Mustapha, Lucy Nightingale, Ify Obi, Adenike Odeleye, Wura Odurinde, Laurence Ody, Folake Ogundeyin, Abayomi Ojo, Fola Oladimeji, Ola Olawe, Lucy Oliver, Michael Oloyede, Yemisi Omolewa, Tope Oni, Alexander and Dominic Paneth, Kim Peterson, Mai-Anh Peterson, Patrice Picard, Alice Purton, Josephina Quayson, Pedro Henrique Queiroz, Brandon Rayment, Alexandra Richards, Leigh Richards, Jamie Rosso, Nida Sayeed, Alex Simons, Charlie Simpson,Aaron Singh, Antonino Sipiano, Justine Spiers, Marlon Stewart, Tom Swaine Jameson, Catherine Tolstoy, Maria Tsang, Nicola and Sarah Twiner, Frankie David Viner, Sophie Louise Viner, Nhat Han Vong, Rupert and Roxy Walton, Devika Webb, George Wheeler, Claudius Wilson, Andreas Wiseman. Kate Yudt, Tanyel Yusef.

Contributors: Petra Boase, Stephanie Donaldson, Nick Huckleberry Beak, Sarah Maxwell, Hugh Nightingale, Steve and Jane Parker, Michael Purton, Thomasina Smith, Jacki Wadeson, Sally Walton. Gratitude also to Hampden Gurney School, Walnut Tree Walk Primary School and St John the Baptist C. of E. School.

The authors would like to thank the following for their assistance in providing materials and advice – Boots; Dylon Consumer Advice; Head Gardener, Knightsbridge; Lady Jayne; Mason Pearson, Kent; Molton Brown; Tesco. Special thanks to Justin of Air Circus;'Smiley Face' from Theatre Crew, Tunbridge Wells; and the Bristol Juggling Convention.